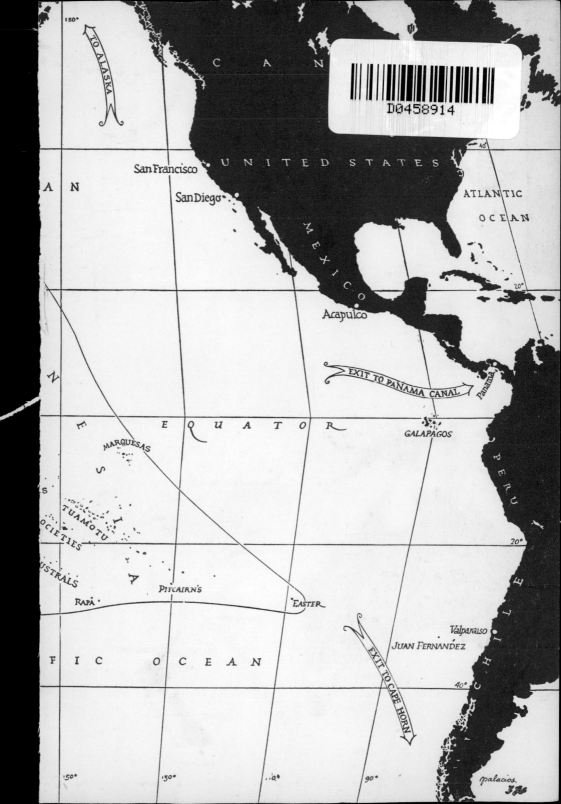

ANATOMY OF PARADISE

ANATOMY *of* PARADISE

HAWAII AND THE ISLANDS OF THE SOUTH SEAS

J. C. FURNAS

... a rustic world, sunshiny, lewd and cruel ...
Stevenson, *Pan's Pipes*

Issued in cooperation with the
AMERICAN INSTITUTE OF PACIFIC RELATIONS

WILLIAM SLOANE ASSOCIATES, INC.
Publishers   *New York*

PUBLISHED SIMULTANEOUSLY IN CANADA BY
GEORGE T. MCLEOD, LTD.

Manufactured in the United States of America

This Is Helen's

Acknowledgment

Individually to acknowledge the obligingness of all the people spotted from Boston to Melbourne who gave material help on this book would mean a list of names about the size of the subscribers' directory of the New Jersey Telephone Company. All are warmly, if anonymously, thanked.

Formally I should acknowledge courtesies from the U. S. Department of State, the U. S. Commercial Company, the U. S. Navy, the U. S. Army Air Force, the Royal New Zealand Air Force; from the American Geographical Society, Pan-American World Airways, the Union Steamship Company of New Zealand, the Matson Navigation Company. For reading facilities and other help I am greatly indebted to the New York Public Library, the Princeton University Library, the Library of Congress, the Bishop Museum, the Honolulu Public Library, the Archives of Hawaii, the Carnegie Library of Suva, the Mitchell Library, the Auckland Public Library.

None of the above organizations and institutions has any responsibility whatever for anything in the book. This project was self-bailing throughout.

The credit for the photograph of Dr. Wilhelm Solf in the illustrated section is Tattersall, Apia.

Contents

Contents

The Institute of Pacific Relations is an unofficial and non-partisan body founded in 1925 to facilitate the scientific study of the peoples of the Pacific area. It is composed of National Councils in eleven countries besides the United States.

The Institute as such and the National Councils of which it is composed are precluded from expressing an opinion on any aspect of national or international affairs. Opinions expressed in this study are, therefore, those of the author.

I

YOUR ATTENTION IS CALLED...

THIS IS ANOTHER BOOK ABOUT "THE SOUTH SEAS." SINCE
the number of books on the subject has probably reached five
figures, an apology is indicated. Fortunately, it is easy to make.
Few books on this area have been general reporting rather than
rhapsody or scientific description. The reporter can include
both fact and fancy—the fancies are symptomatic of much that
handicaps the South Seas, and Americans need to be well
aware of all the facts.[1] Finally, material like this, so much of it
little known to the general public, offers irresistible temptation
to a writer. For our present and past relations with these islands
involve happenings that would make the angels simultaneously
laugh out loud, weep in angry compassion, and stamp their feet
in vexation with the stupidity of all parties concerned.

You may never have been nearer the South Seas than the
screen of the neighborhood movie, and that is very far away indeed, but chances are high that your son or nephew has re-

[1]This book will not cover, except sometimes incidentally, certain South
Sea matters that have been overworked or that retain small current
significance, such as: the "Bounty" story; the "mysteries" of Easter
Island statues and stone ruins in the Carolines; leprosy; military operations of World War II. These omissions do not necessarily mean that
these subjects were neglected in legwork; for instance, I have visited
leper colonies and seen something of the next-to-final phase of the
Pacific war.

cently been there. His presence on a South Sea Island in uniform meant and means that, for good or ill, the United States has become the political and military arbiter of this geographical entity, loosely but workably bounded by a line from Hawaii to the Marianas, to New Zealand, to Easter Island.

In population and resources the South Seas are a negligible part of the great Pacific world. Yet, as the connective tissue of the greatest of oceans, these chains and clumps of islands are crucial strategically. That is why so many Americans, Australians, New Zealanders, Japanese, Fijians, Solomon Islanders, and heaven and hell now know who else, died capturing or recapturing them. The huge, raw, American bases in New Caledonia, Fiji, the New Hebrides, the Solomons, the Society Islands, have been abandoned or handed back to friendly powers-in-charge. But the United States has held on in Micronesia, and the potential American presence will remain all over the Pacific as long as our power exceeds that of our Pacific neighbors and as long as we are vulnerable from the west—a factor greatly increased in importance since Hiroshima. In these days the arm of neither France nor Britain is long or strong enough to guarantee whatever decisions are made as to the future status of the Pacific. Though nearer the scene, the British Dominions have too slim resources and population.[2] The United Nations is acting most gingerly regarding its potential function in the Islands, doing little more than recognize faits accomplis. This or that island may fly the tricolor, the Southern Cross or the Union Jack, but the destiny of this stretch of salt water is determined by the world force implied in the words Pearl Harbor, Guadalcanal, Tokio Bay.

[2] This is admitted by those able to speak without an eye to votes. Said that temperish but valuable palladium of South Seas whites, the Australian Pacific Islands Monthly, (September, 1946): "The white communities of the South Pacific have no hope of survival unless the United States assumes guardianship of the South Pacific. Without American help what could Australia do against the overwhelming masses of Asia? About as much as Australia did in 1942, when the Japanese avalanche was rolling southward. This is no reflection upon Australian courage or military prowess. The point is that in comparison with the human masses in Asia and in North America, Australia simply doesn't count."

So the South Seas are Uncle Sam's baby. Power over an area implies responsibility for it, and responsibility makes understanding highly advisable.

Understanding has been made difficult for us because we have associated with the South Seas some of the most appealing—and most absurd—fairy tales that ever one man told another. If we are to carry out our responsibilities in a fashion not too repugnant to our sense of fair play and political craftsmanship, we must clear away the spun sugar from an actuality that is at once beautiful, small, and immeasurably significant. As an American citizen you are personally and directly answerable for the best interests of 80,000 brown Islanders in Micronesia, and indirectly so for those of a couple of million more assorted Islanders in the rest of the South Seas.

During and after the recent war, inexperienced and insufficiently briefed Navy officers were sent to govern Pacific islands. They usually showed good will but lacked a sense of reality: a sociologist who saw it all from the inside wrote: "Americans regard natives through the focus of the Hollywood movie projector . . ."[3]

Back of that baffled officer on Koror or Manua stand you, who, whether you know it or not, hired him to do what he is supposed to be doing. Unless Americans comprehend better what problems there are like, even a good man will often find the merits of his work ignored by an ill-informed public or worse, misrepresented by busybodies of both good and ill will.

It is also advisable to try to correct the misapprehensions brought home by GIs. The boys were justly annoyed when Waikiki Beach, palm groves and coral islands turned out to be decidedly not as advertised, and they resented impressions back home that Pacific duty consisted of being shacked up with Dorothy Lamour in a terrestrial paradise full of ukuleles. Actually, few soldiers or sailors saw much of Pacific natives. Those who did usually liked them cordially. But the average GI, lacking opportunity for close contact, called them all "Gooks"—

[3]John C. Useem, "Social Reconstruction in Micronesia"; *Far Eastern Survey*, January 30, 1946.

except the Guamanians, whom he liked on sight—and disapproved of them out loud. As a postwar citizen passing on his government's policies in the South Seas, he is too likely to spread the impression that this region, consisting principally of unhomelike pestholes teeming with subhuman Gooks, is hardly worth bothering about. The remedy is to know much more than the GI knew at the time about the actual who, where, when, and why of the South Seas.

Such knowledge may bring disillusion to stay-at-homes. Yet this is no effort to debunk the South Seas in the brash manner of the 'twenties. No matter how much rock-happiness they induced in lonely men in garrison, these islands have a beauty impossible to debunk. The charm of many of their inhabitants, the human validity of all, are beyond reach of carping.

Our current relations out there are anomalous, perplexing, and inevitable. No single book could tell the whole, present or past. But here is what can be made out by one observer. Under the circumstances little of it can be useless.

A particular usefulness, in fact, lies in the principles to be derived from acquaintance with the Islands. This area has been a most important laboratory for anthropology[4] or rather, in this connection, for the ethnological branch of anthropology. The ethnologist's day is now dawning very brightly indeed. Within our time, if he show himself sufficiently flexible and eclectic, he may well take over from the economist as the intellectual bellwether—or, with bad luck, Judas goat—of the world.

That is as much hope as prediction. For, unless the ethnologist supersedes the economist in a humanizing shift away from impersonal formulae in basic human thinking, western man will get tragically little out of the forces now available for social decency. We are likely, of course, to forestall the necessity for this shift by blowing our world to hell with atomic

_____

[4] "Anthropologist" includes measurers of crania and students of primitive tongues as well as the individual here meant—the student of technical and social man working through description and analysis of "cultures."

energy or disintegrating it with bacterial warfare and atomic byproducts; but, until those threats materialize or dissipate, we must act on the assumption that our world will go on. And the ethnologist's approach is the best one to hand.

What that approach is must wait for description until the reader has digested a regional sample of the kind of data from which ethnology works. This is no textbook, nor is the writer in any sense qualified as an ethnologist. But much of what follows has been the raw material of ethnology, or offers horrible examples of what comes through misconceptions that ethnology can correct, or describes situations for which ethnology, with its ancillary sciences, alone promises help. Weighing such material in his own right, the layman can express, as an outsider, an unscientific conclusion, a human attitude, based on the possibility of using ethnology as a social tool.

This nonprofessional moral is that it is impractical as well as hideous to deal with human persons impersonally; that to patronize, sentimentalize about, or try to make a social digit of, any man in any cultural framework is the unforgivable sin against a nontheological Holy Ghost. So stated, it sounds formidable: all it actually means is that the South Seas opposite number of Joe Doakes is as much of a person as Joe, though marvelously unlike him. To handle him on any other assumption makes him an emotional cripple likely to do himself great damage, and to guarantee aching consciences for those responsible for him.

The past and present troubles of the South Seas are an excellent working model of what happens when such ideas are absent. The East Indies, India, Palestine, are now the most conspicuous of the dismal dozens of other examples that could be adduced. All differ remarkably from the South Seas; their clinical histories are all special cases, probably even more complicated. But all are what they are today because of the same general order of strains, some of strictly internal origin, many arising out of contact with westerners ignorant of, or imperfectly affected by, the above sentiments. It is always advisable to approach a complex matter by first taking a good look at a simpler one of similar import.

In the process be warned of many things: misplaced humor, color prejudice, impatience with bungling and, particularly, undue self-reproach. Consider what would have happened if the Polynesians, say, had been in a technological position to move in on western man.

*　　　*　　　*

During early visits from white men South Sea Islanders were often unable to understand why they were so favored. Captain Finch, U.S.S. "Vincennes," reported in 1829 an ingenious theory developed by the Marquesans, whose islands had recently been much frequented by whalers. Observing the greediness with which white seamen approached local women, the wondering natives concluded that this white race must consist of men only and that, in order to enjoy heterosexual relations, whites had to travel all the way to the Marquesas. In their minds no other circumstances could explain the frantic value that these strangers set on women and the persistence with which they kept coming back.

Other theories were produced when the first whites were missionaries. The Rev. James Chalmers, courageous pioneer in New Guinea, wrote a friend:

> The natives thought at first that we had been compelled to leave our native land because of hunger . . . "Have you coconuts in your country?" "No." "Have you yams?" "No." "Have you breadfruit?" "No." "Have you sago?" "No." "Have you plenty of hoop iron and tomahawks?" "Yes, in great abundance." "We understand now why you have come. You have nothing to eat in Beritani, but you have plenty of tomahawks and hoop iron with which you can buy food."[5]

[5]Richard Lovett, *James Chalmers: His Autobiography and Letters*: 210–11. Cheap iron hatchets (usually called tomahawks in the trade, in analogy to such trade items in North America) and iron barrel hoops broken into pieces convenient for working into adzes were often among the most popular early trade goods with South Sea peoples, who lacked metals. This theory would not have occurred so readily to a Polynesian, who did not have the Melanesian's traditional aptitude for ideas involving foreign supply of crucial items.

The deduction is intelligent and not inaccurate. Britain actually was and is still in the position of lacking sufficient home-raised food and importing provisions from overseas in exchange for, among other things, manufactured hardware. Further data, of course, corrected mistakes. When missionaries arrived with wives, the Marquesans saw that after all whites did have women, of a sort; and Islanders taken to Europe met beef, potatoes and bakers' goods and acquired the impression that white men's foods were great luxuries. To this day canned corned beef, canned salmon, ship's biscuit and sugar seem gastronomic delights to the Islander. He eats sugar, in fact, with an avidity which our culture would label infantile—the ration for Fijian labor in the local gold mines is half a pound per man per day.

But all problems implicit in white intrusion were not so easily resolved. For the last century, in fact, the South Seas have known nothing but problems, and they will probably continue to do so. For example: the native was puzzled to find that, whereas all his people usually believed in and did the same things, some whites called missionaries behaved differently from, and hated and slandered, other whites called seamen and traders. Presently, looking around, he found whites insisting that, in some incomprehensible fashion, they had unimpeachable rights of permanent possession to much of his people's better lands. Whites tried to bully him into working for them on these hijacked lands and, when that was not successful, hired or kidnapped outsiders to produce quantities of things sent away on ships—coconut oil, cotton, rock, sugar, pearl shell—far more of each than anybody anywhere could conceivably use. These non-white alien laborers brought additional new ways of doing, which multiplied confusion. Presently came a third breed of white, the doctor or official, inclined to scold both the missionary and the seaman-trader, sometimes trying to check population- and culture-decay, but often doing more harm than good. And then came the romantic traveler, baffling the native by admiring and often paying for performances of the old dances that the missionary had discouraged as shameful . . .

The native did his best to digest all this. He often succeeded in mortising the white man's religion and ethics into his own with results that satisfy him, however they might distress the Y.M.C.A. The recent war, however, brought another tidal wave of emotional and physical displacement. Early Japanese victories damaged white prestige, and later white victories did not necessarily repair all the damage. Bulldozers scraped whole islands raw and whole populations were moved to strange places by both Japanese and whites. Native troops did significantly well at white-style warfare, sometimes better than the whites in bushfighting. Money in return for labor flooded many islands with curious economic consequences.

World War II was a devastating lesson in the paradox that whites, who had suppressed native warfare as uncivilized, would fight like demons among themselves at a relative cost in lives and goods of which no Islander had ever dreamed. Confusion was back on the throne.

Whites are now trying to put things back together, but the native has grounds for wondering if such help is anything to welcome. Here and there he says out loud that he wants more responsibility in whatever reconstruction is achieved. The speed with which he has bounced back from his recent trauma speaks well for his stability. But more responsibility—that is a moot question.

This sort of thing—and hundreds of other aspects of a very complicated world—are what we shall consider.

So far, whether his intentions were good, bad or merely selfish, the white man in the South Seas has been little better than a nuisance in net effect. It was a great pity, if you care to look at it that way, that he ever came bothering the Islands to begin with. To heighten the futility of the affair, he got pathetically little economic good out of his intrusiveness. There is only one thing to be said for the story of how the whites arrived and what happened next and next and next down to our own time: The facts make it clear that matters could have gone no other way.

II

THE INGREDIENTS

1

Misnamed Ocean

I heard the pulse of the besieging sea
Throb far away all night. I heard the wind
Fly crying and convulse tumultuous palms . . .
—Robert Louis Stevenson

THE NECESSARY LESSON IN GEOGRAPHY NEED NOT BE dull. The Pacific Ocean is physically the greatest thing on earth. Astronomers used to wonder if the whole bulk of the moon might not have been torn out to leave its great depths and distances. Up toward Alaska, down toward the Antarctic, it can be as gray and bitter as the North Atlantic. But in the region that concerns us, it shows deep silky blues and greens. The tepid salt water stretches apparently boundlessly all through the South Seas, rich with vegetable and animal life that make coral development possible. It builds land here and tears it away there. It feeds birds that carry the seeds to plant new green life on new islands. Other stretches of ocean are beautiful, but no other is so lavish, and none gives the sun such extensive opportunity to beguile the human eye with color in motion.

Like human beauty, however, this is based on details distasteful to the queasy-minded. A poet finding lyric inspiration in the very words "coral reef" must disregard the fact that coral reef exposed by the tide smells like a distant decayed lobster and looks like a pocked ruin of dishonestly compounded concrete. Its sharp projections slashing white men's soft feet have killed many with septicemia; bits of it lying waterworn on the beach precisely resemble battered old bones; the strange fish in its pools are often savagely poisonous.

It is notorious as well that, in calling this the Pacific Ocean, Magellan was greatly misled by a fine-weather westward passage. Even in the mild South Seas storms can be formidable. This ocean is a lady with a tigerish taste for tempting human beings to settle on atolls and then unleashing hurricanes that annihilate everything—people, houses, trees, even the coral lumps of the exterior beach. A few generations or centuries later she may repeat the performance with equal relish. Contemplating the inhabitants of his first atoll in 1769, Bougainville wrote:

> "I admire their courage if they live without uneasiness on these strips of sand which a tempest can bury under water in the winking of an eye."—*Voyage autour du monde* . . . II, 11.

While bowling westward, Magellan's crew was starving because the island-rich Pacific flightily refused them any landfall promising food. It is no accident that so many famous small-boat voyages made by castaways occurred in this ocean, often in the idyllic South Seas themselves. Distance and chance are cruel hereabouts, requiring high sagacity and endurance in emergencies. The Pacific was made not for men, but for far-ranging whales and seabirds.

A good map gives most of the significant details. Others can be tucked into the text as we go along. But even the best maps omit some important things, or give false impressions on points that cartography was never meant to cope with.

The term "South Seas" itself needs comment, for instance. As used here, it means a lopsidedly diamond-shaped region with the Samoa group near its center of balance. Its vague boundaries are far from the coasts of all continents, sub-continents, and most islands unmistakably attached to a continent, including only those islands primarily dominated by the circumambient presence of the Pacific herself.[1] This area happens

[1] For comparison, see Stevenson, *In the South Seas*, 168; Keesing, *The South Seas in the Modern World*, 3.

to include the climates, flora and peoples associated in the popular mind with "the South Seas." Palms, cannibals, missionaries, coral reefs, grass skirts, bare-bosomed girls, gin-rascally traders, volcanoes, pearls and sharks, are all there somewhere, or were there once. Many of them also do or did exist in the Philippines, the East Indies and New Guinea; but these fascinating places are left out because their scale is too large, they are too close to Asia, or their polity is too formal,[2] to answer the South Seas tradition. New Zealand is included, not because she has coral reefs or palms—being too far south—but because her aborigines were good Polynesians, the traditional denizens of the South Seas. Barring New Zealand and a few scraps of land slightly too far south, such as Rapa and Easter Island, the whole South Seas, as the term is used here, lies tidily between Cancer and Capricorn.

The phrase "South Seas" has a history. It originated in a noted misconception. The isthmus of Panama so twists that Balboa first saw the Pacific south of him, whereas two-fifths of it actually lay to the north. From then on "the South Sea" meant the Pacific to most men mentioning it. Even after it was known up to latitude 40 N., British privateers and buccaneers raiding western South America or cruising after the Manila galleon spoke of "our voyage to the South Sea." (Such immortality of outmoded names is familiar: New Yorkers call the Hudson the North River—a label unknown on any recent map.) Then, with the rise of romancing about glamorous Pacific Isles, "South Seas" contracted and grew sticky connotations. "Pacific" was then used to describe Balboa's discovery, while the earlier phrase suffered apotheosis. "Going out to the Pacific" means one thing to the hearer, "going out to the South Seas" quite another. One is geography and one poetry, or at least a stab at it.

Local names also trip up the new arrival in the Pacific, where

[2]Skipping New Guinea cuts the subcontinental Melanesian away from his Island cousin, which is bad. But there are some limits to what even the boldest writer can hope to cover intelligently. New Guinea is referred to in this book only when it offers indispensable illustration.

islands, individually and by groups, have as many aliases as confidence men. Early discoverers, considering native names meaningless and unwieldy, gave their finds more familiar titles of convenience or prestige. It is confusing that the Friendly Islands means Tonga, the Navigator Isles Samoa, the Sandwich Islands Hawaii; that Kusaie (Carolines) was once Strong's Island and Chain Island (Tuamotu) is Anaa. Duplication is bewildering: Melanesia has a Sandwich Island; and the name of Lord Howe, whom late eighteenth century British captains revered, appears four times on Pacific charts. During their Johnny-come-lately enterprise in the Pacific, the Germans rechristened parts of Melanesia Neu-Pommern, Neu-Mecklenburg and so forth. Generally the earlier the discovery, the worse the confusion. Until the middle of the last century European names predominated on maps and logs; after that, for no assignable reason, native names began to crowd out the alien ones. Some still stick, however, such as those of the Gilberts and the New Hebrides.

The westerners followed no system in giving names. Pitcairn's Island was called after the midshipman who first sighted it; the Society Islands after the Royal Society, sponsors of Cook's first voyage; the Marquesas after the wife of the noble patron of Mendaña's voyages; and Savage Island (Niue) after the observed nature of the inhabitants. It is a pity that some of the better efforts disappeared. La Nouvelle Cythère is excellent for Tahiti, as Bougainville saw it through an erotic mist, and New Zealand would be much better off as Ao-Tea-Roa, the Long White Cloud, a bit of Polynesian poetry inspired by the sight of her snowcapped ranges from far out at sea.

Spelling is another vicious hazard. In the early days missions had not yet standardized the transliteration of South Sea tongues, and it takes some ingenuity to make out that what a conscientious sailorman spelled Bonaby is Ponape (Carolines) and Whytootackee Aitutaki (Cooks). A missionary records fifteen early ways of spelling Fiji, viz.: Beetee, Fegee, Fejee, Feegee, Feejee, Feeje, Fidgee, Fidge, Fidschi, Fiji, Feigee,

Viti, Viji and Vitee[3]—quite as bad as the countless ways of transliterating Russian.

The island-peppered appearance of the map is also deceptive. Even from a plane the human eye seldom gets any such effect in the South Seas. Islands apparently cheek by jowl actually lie far out of eyeshot of one another. Nor do maps show their great variety. The only sound generalization about South Sea islands is that all, without exception, are surrounded by salt water. And the human variety is as great as the topographical, including not only Tahitian houris but the sulky cannibals of the New Hebrides; not only airy and healthy Hawaii but the disease-ridden Solomons; not only the brown Polynesians of legend, but big and little dark peoples of obscure origin, with recent sprinklings of both Caucasoids and Mongoloids. A marine battling malaria and jungle-rot on Bougainville was just as much "in the South Seas" as if he had been sporting with Rarahu in the shade by Loti's pool. Much of New Caledonia and Fiji look not at all like the movies, but a great deal like Texas or Wyoming.

South Sea Islands can be classified, but application on the spot can be difficult. Weston Martyr's bilious approach is a good beginning:

> South Sea Islands are all the same, except that some are high and some low. The low islands are coral atolls, very pretty to look at—from a distance. They can always be counted on to provide bad water, bad food, bad mosquitoes, bad smells, dangerous navigation, boredom, and coconuts. On the high islands there is better water, more to eat, and more disease.
> —*The Wandering Years*, 103.

Generally, all the islands are somehow volcanic. Though fascinating in themselves, the slow processes by which, according to one or another hypothesis, the islands achieved their present shape are of small concern to the traveler, but the distinction between *atoll* and *high island* is fundamental. An atoll is a ring of coral built up hardly above sealevel by coral polyps, enclosing a wholly or partly imprisoned shallow salt lagoon—a

[3]Thomas Williams, *Fiji and the Fijians*, i.

sort of calcareous dimple awash inside and out. Its soil is poorish to poor, but it can support certain vegetation, particularly pandanus and coco palms. The whole ring may be dry land, or sporadic islets may rise from the water in a sort of necklace with a submerged reef for a string. Surf smashes away at the seabeach, while the lagoonbeach gets only unaggressive ripples.

The "uplifted coral" variation is a picturesque affair in some cases, but in others, as in Tongatabu (Tonga), desperately dull. Here the coral platform and wall of the atoll have been heaved above sealevel, sometimes making a saucered plateau. Breakers gnaw at its edges, undercutting the seaward cliff until, in smaller versions, such an island looks like an old-time green Pullman hassock resting on a mirror. The smallest of them become stemmed and capped like a mushroom and eventually break off. Tropical rains may wear gullies inland and leave knolls in the coral limestone, very sharply "dissected" as geologists say. Any marine who fought on Bloody Nose Ridge on Peleliu (Palaus) can tell you what good defensive country these limestone knobs are in a stubborn enemy's hands. A further rise of the sea—or sinking of the land—may flood the gullies, making dark, calm creeks among lush islets.

High islands are the exposed summits of submerged volcanoes or conglomerations of volcanoes, often becoming fantastically craggy at the top as crater walls break down and lighter ash and cinders wash away from the solid basalt cores. The fairy tale beauty of Tahiti, Bora Bora (Societies) and Rarotonga (Cooks) came about in that fashion. It is very hard to believe in the reality of the Tahitian peak called the Diadème, which looks for all the world like a somewhat disorganized crown roast of beef. The windward side of such an island, benefiting from cloud condensation on the peaks, is usually well-watered, the leeward side correspondingly dry. People can do well on such islands, their lives usually concentrated on beaches, protected by surrounding coral reef from the great ocean rollers. In the larger islands of Melanesia, however, there developed hill populations too, differing in various ways from the beach dwellers.

Since coral polyps like their water good and salt, the mouth of a fresh-water stream usually means a gap in the reef opposite, and hence a middling-to-good small harbor for shallow-draft vessels. Honolulu, Papeete (Tahiti), Apia (Samoa) are examples. But all high islands are not so hospitable. Reefless, steep-to Pitcairn's has practically nothing to recommend it from the seaman's point of view, which is why the mutineers of the "Bounty" chose it for their hideaway. Since volcanoes and water behave much the same way the world over, this type of island, with promontories like prostrate camels and sharp-spined, elaborately buttressed mountains in the background, can be seen almost anywhere where plutonic forces have been at work near the sea—in the West Indies, the Aleutians, the Mediterranean. Atolls, however, develop only in waters warm enough for coral.

High in the South Seas can mean very high. The Big Island (Hawaii proper) rises 32,000 feet from the ocean floor, its upper 14,000 feet majestically above water in a saddled summit. But, in illustration of South Seas exceptions, Hawaii is not characteristic. The special volcanic habits of Mauna Kea and Mauna Loa, sister culminations of the great peak, make for colossal oozings of lava, not conebuilding in the grand manner. As a result Hawaii is a great flattish hump, most unlike Rarotonga. The presence of the world's greatest active volcanic craters on Hawaii is also noncharacteristic. That smoking mountain on the backdrop, favorite *cliché* of the movie- or stage-designer, is rather rare in the South Seas. Smoking peaks, some rising straight from the sea like hell-blackened boils, do persist in the northern Marianas, the New Hebrides, New Zealand, the Solomons, Tonga and Samoa. But the principal Pacific points of volcanic activity lie outside our area, in the Dutch East Indies, the Philippines, Japan, Alaska, and on the western coast of South and Central America. The typical South Seas volcano is content to lie quiescent while rain and wind carve its profile.

People who have never been out that way usually picture a South Sea Island as a cozy little scrap of land about as extensive as the average golf course. True, many are not much larger. One of the most enticing is Aguigan, lying off Tinian (Marianas)—a tiny, terraced jewel designed in symmetrical setbacks of weathered crag, green as a bed of moss and accessible at only one chancy point on its western end; elsewhere the surf leaps with sinister enthusiasm at every inch of cliff. But it would take several days to walk round the 100-mile perimeter of Guam even if the roads were better. Both Hawaii and Viti Levu (Fiji) are rather larger than Connecticut as well as notably more habitable, while the Solomons and New Hebrides add up to really considerable accumulations of dry land. New Caledonia would stretch from New York to beyond Washington, D. C.

Even atolls can be built on a generous scale. The dog-legged length of Kwajalein (Marshalls) lagoon is close to eighty miles; Truk (Carolines) lagoon contains 1500 square miles of reef-guarded and island-studded water, deep enough to have been suspected all through the war of being a principal Japanese naval base. Until planes appeared many a South Sea Island had never been seen in entirety by the human eye. Some may never be so seen.

The plane does much to enhance the reputation of the South Seas for beauty. Unimaginative mariners first viewing Tahiti or Nukahiva (Marquesas) from the crosstrees would descend and write ecstatic descriptions that sounded as if they had just met Aphrodite in person. If they had seen a typical atoll from 8,000 feet, they would have been babbling still. It lies there like something painted in the moving sea, clean-cut as an apple paring, weltering in surrounding color as if it were bleeding pigment into the water, water that is royal blue in the offing, abruptly darker all round the island, and then shrill green just off the beach. The interior lagoon is splotched with copper sulphate and squash-yellow and moth-wing purple where coral lies wide and close to the surface. Surf and vegetation on the narrow land contribute a lathery white and a greenish-brown. Conventional accounts of color in natural objects, such as rock scenery in the western States, are usually rhetorical lies confirmed only by cheap inks on picture post cards. Here the rhapsodizer is in no danger of overplaying, for a Pacific atoll from the air is the quintessence of innocent and gracious gaudiness. Naturally there would be pearls and bright fish in such a lagoon, dancing, singing, and beauty ashore. The conclusion is inevitable, though by no means necessarily sound.

Planes do disservice, however, in dulling the impact of Pacific distances. Johnston Island does not seem so hell-and-gone when you drop down on it four hours from Hawaii. To get the point one should have made the trip three generations ago the other way, in a schooner against the trades for seven hundred weary miles of empty water. The plane passenger has no acquaintance with the personality of the Pacific when he knows her only as moiré silk floorcloth flecked with soapsuds some indeterminate thousands of feet below. It is rather like trying to consummate a marriage by television.

For westerners climate is the special attraction of the South Seas, and means semi-nakedness, tropical fruits, indolence. The Maori in New Zealand and the Hawaiian are the only Islanders who ever see snow, and the Hawaiian can touch it only if he climbs the upper slopes of Maui and the Big Island. Within that limit, temperatures here and there range from reasonably cool nights to Turkish bath conditions. The sun brutally predominates. Its glare on a coral sand beach is as cruel as that on a snowfield, suggesting dark glasses or the native's ingenious equivalent of a slitted shade woven of palm leaf. The famous trade winds, though not as consistent as poets insist, keep tepid rivers of air running over most of the islands most of the year, as pleasant a thing as nature ever devised. And sun and temperature encourage vegetation which is as picturesque as it is useful.

Barring New Zealand, New Caledonia, and some other odd bits, palms of some species do, or would, grow on all but the most barren rocks in the South Seas. But these simple saurians of the vegetable world do not predominate on high islands, which tend to develop dense scrub given to thorns, or heavy hardwood forest turning, as you near the equator, into lofty, lightless, dripping jungle, full of writhing vines and huge pale-trunked trees with bony root-buttresses flanging out yards wide. What with lichen-splotched trunks and weird habits of growth, two out of three island trees look to western eyes as if they were diseased. It is easy to understand why South Sea peoples were shy of such forests, peopling them with the ghosts of the maleficent dead and the less benevolent of their minor gods. Too great an accumulation of such growth is definitely depressing as you coast along its broody monotony, particularly in Melanesia. The best description was written about New Ireland by a man who had never seen the Pacific:

> ... two long islands of a greasy green, a rheumatic green ... a narrow strip of sand only a few yards wide, beyond which nothing was visible but certain slopes, all covered, from the summit to the sea, with landslides of dark verdure . . . strange, rather gruesome, islands.—Alphonse Daudet, *Port-Tarascon*, translated by Henry James, 117.

Coco palms prefer the beach or low land behind it, liking "to have their feet in salt water," though they can stand height up to a thousand feet. Where the promontories break down to low foreshore and beach, the brittle flailing of the coco's limber arms and the clean, sandy shade among the ringed trunks are a palpable emotional relief—light, space and air again. In the rising distance inland tradewind clouds are massed on the mountains, blocking off the sun, throwing surly shadows over valleys and ridges. Even sunlight often fails to keep South Seas heights from looking sinister; in fact, the higher the sun and the more intense its light, the gloomier the mountains are. Only the level light of early morning or early evening brings out the composition of the peaks and the dainty detail of their wooded skylines. Photography cannot convey these qualities. Accuracy of spirit was often greater in the steel engravings that illustrated our grandfathers' books.

This chapter was revised in a room whence you can see a humped, furry-green volcanic hill, coco palms and, deep and far beyond them, the blue opaque surface of the great ocean that floats the Islands. I shall probably never see any of them again, though not for lack of wishing. I should like very much to land again on Tupae in a greasy copra-surfboat and walk across to the lagoon beach and see the young palms writhing in the trade wind as foreground for the faraway, preposterous, profile of Bora Bora, a towering splotch of dilute India ink.

It may be just as well that return is unlikely. Nobody in his senses, but a Chinese and a scattering of born-to-the-life natives, would live on Tupae. But in other islands it would be conceivable and, the longer you travel among them, the more conceivable it seems. Wrote a lawyer, of all people:

. . . it is a noticeable feature that Europeans who have made a lengthy stay rarely retire from the group, it is thought from choice as well as from force of circumstance. The islands are said to take hold of a man softly and so that he does not care.
—Robert Mackenzie Watson, *History of Samoa*, 13.

2

Misunderstood People

The man of nature, the *Naturmensch*, does not exist.
—Bronislaw Malinowski, "Culture,"
Encyclopaedia of Social Sciences

"NATIVES"

THE ORIGINAL INHABITANT OF THE SOUTH SEAS—OR his present descendant—is necessarily a "Native," a term used by the English-speaking world when condescending to simpler cultures. Originally it was innocent enough, meaning merely "born on the spot." The Islander too sometimes has such a word; "Maori," the term applied to themselves by the Polynesians of New Zealand means much the same thing. But white arrogance perverted "Native." Even the French, reputedly politer to subject peoples, use *indigène* in the Islands more as a patronizing noun than as an adjective. The proof of the poison lies in the fact that the Islander often heartily dislikes hearing the word "Native" applied to himself. Thus in Tonga, the most self-consciously proud of Polynesian islandgroups, brown skinned medical assistants must be called, not "native medical practitioners," as elsewhere in the Pacific, but "Tongan medical practitioners."

"Native" is difficult to define but profitable to mull over. Chinese and Japanese are seldom thus labeled.[1] Since they are

[1]The exception occurs in New Caledonia, where Mongoloid laborers from Indo-China are sometimes lumped with the island's original Melanesians as *indigènes* for social purposes.

quite as alien to whites as any of the darker peoples, this may show an uneasy sense of respect for their Asiatic home-cultures. Or perhaps a warm climate is essential to the word. No book-writing amateur ever called Ojibways or Siberians "Natives," but the tourist in Mexico readily applies the word to the residents of Taxco. I have heard the same tourist in the West Indies call the local negroes Natives in spite of their obviously recent origin in Africa.

Nobody of European stock is ever seriously a "Native." The English-speaker may have small use for Italians or Serbs, who may strike him as excitable, dirty and of dubious morality. But behind them he feels longstanding accomplishment in terms that might be consonant with his terms. Color as such cannot be significant: many a Scot or Spaniard is as swarthy as many a Polynesian, yet neither is a "Native" at home.[2]

Positively, the meaning of "Native" can be approximated. It means: Darker. Productive of quaint handicrafts. Given to diving after coins thrown from a ship's rail. Greedy for beads, red calico, silk hats and alcoholic drinks. Suspect of cannibalism. Addicted to drumbeating and lewd dancing. More or less naked. Sporadically treacherous. Probably polygynous and simultaneously promiscuous. Picturesque. Comic when trying to speak English or otherwise ape white ways. Or, to define by example: a "Native" is what Robinson Crusoe feared had made that footprint. When he turned up, Friday was a "Native" right enough; so was Melville's Queequeg; so was Tondeleyo, who made "mammy palaver" temporarily part of the American language. The "Natives" are badly spoiled . . . the "Natives" are dying out . . . the "Native" dances are wonderful, but you have to get away from towns to see the real

[2]On the other hand, I have occasionally heard a British voice, usually newly arrived, call South Sea Islanders "niggers." Americans in the Islands are seldom guilty of such bad taste, but cannot plume themselves on it. The American's special situation at home, a national disgrace, makes him sensitively careful about misapplying so explosive a word. During the recent war in New Zealand an occasional drunken GI got into trouble by trying to shove Maoris off the sidewalk as "niggers." It is necessary to explain to New Zealanders that such men were probably from the South and knew no better.

thing . . . he "went Native" . . . the "Native" women aren't so much, but the "Native" babies are the cutest little things you ever saw. . . .

There is in all this an eagerness to regard one's fellow-men as handsomely or grotesquely feral creatures for exhibition in zoos. The concept of the white man's burden combines here with the essential snobbishness and parochialness of the average tourist. It is not pretty.[3]

Nor can the word be left at that. In reaction against the colonial or globe-trotting snob, the sentimentalist has reversed the onus and vested the poor devil of a "Native" with an aura of pure moonshine. To him anything "Native" is by definition morally, aesthetically or technically superior to anything non-"Native," however that would be defined. He shakes his head sadly at the privy that whites force the Native to build, not because it spoils the view or usually defeats its sanitary purpose, but because it is non-"Native" not to defecate on the beach or in the bush. He often insists in print that, by sheer loving-kindness, he succeeded in making fast friends with the Natives and lived among them for months as one of themselves. Never mind if experienced and sympathetic scientists deny that such a psychological and physical feat is possible[4]—the Nativophile says he has done it and for the rest of his life preens himself on the accomplishment.

Reading the resulting books infects the tourist with this attitude. Some of the consequences are grotesque. American railroads advertise Red Indian snake dances, and nice old ladies in Guatemala City tell you, one after another, that experts can actually distinguish the various tribes of Guatemalan Indians by the weave and coloration of their garments—isn't that mar-

[3] "Kanaka" (French version Canaque) is another word which the Islander often dislikes and which the courteous white avoids. It originally meant "man" in Polynesian dialects; it is now used to distinguish natives from whites or other interlopers in Melanesian as well as Polynesian settings. The connotation is contemptuous and toplofty.

[4] "Like most anthropologists, I regard with skepticism the claim of any European writer that he has been accepted by natives as one of themselves."—Raymond Firth, We the Tikopia, 11

velous? That simple fact, as familiar as Scotch tartans, affects them with a rapture ordinarily reserved for the arcana of esoteric mysteries. Something of the same attitude underlies the practice of the Hawaiian white who scatters fifty or sixty Hawaiian words through his talk—only a dozen or so are needed for concepts peculiar to the Islands—and uses them in his tales of ghost armies that his aunt heard marching up Nuuanu Valley. He may also tell the *malahine* that there really is a great deal in old-time Hawaiian medicine, and adduce cases in which resort to a *kahuna* cured an old *hapahaole wahine* of both diabetes and erysipelas. Hawaii is the worst sinner in this respect, but traces of such self-conscious antics occur in the Pacific wherever whites have read "colorful" books about Islands.

These habits would be merely funny if they did not often react damagingly on the Islander. Already prone to misconceive the place of his island in the cosmos, the native leader who finds himself regarded by certain whites as a glory-trailing survivor of the Golden Age can develop—and worse, try to carry out—some very strange notions. He falls in with ideas about "Natives" which his own knowledge of tradition should show him are false. I have heard a famous Maori dance leader tell a tourist audience that the *haka*, the old Maori war dance, was invented to exercise and develop the warrior's muscles— note how every muscle in the body is affected. This was not only nonsense anatomically, as the ensuing dance demonstrated; it was also nonsense historically. This able lady, however, had liked the sound of it when she read or heard it and could not resist the impulse to adopt something alien to Maori thinking, but comfortingly close to Western ways.[5]

The Nativophile is seldom on trickier ground than when admiring "Native" artifacts. Admiration is often justified for a piece of delicately striped Hawaiian *tapa*, an Ellice Islands

[5]"The savage is no scientific hygienist. The Maori was fit because of his mode of life; he did not think out his mode of life in order to be fit. By interpreting Maori social institutions in terms of this hygienic purpose, recent writers have gone sadly astray."—Raymond Firth, *Primitive Economics of the New Zealand Maori*, 37.

mat, a Maori greenstone *mere*, all beautiful objects born of painstaking skill which often wonderfully emphasize the qualities of the material. But, as an eminent ethnologist recently pointed out,[6] it is false to attribute to their makers what we think of as the artistic impulse.[7] The Hawaiian *tapa*-dyer was not exercising personalized creativeness in stamping that pattern or choosing those colors. She was merely repeating traditional patterns and color schemes with timid variations. The same holds good for the finest Island sculpture and wood carving. To neglect this distinction can lead to confounding a Dürer, who was both artist and superb craftsman, with the elderly lady who won first prize with her undeniably beautiful Fox-and-Goose quilt at the county fair. The proof lies in the fact that, once outside his own rigid traditions, the "Native" has atrocious taste. Among the white man's artifacts he almost invariably chooses lurid junk of far lower quality in mass, line, and workmanship than his own productions. Yet a white man does not have to be a professional designer to pick the shoddy from the beautiful in a collection of "Native"-made objects.

The strangest effect of Nativophilia, however, is that it produces fervent pleas that Native cultures be deliberately isolated and encouraged to idiosyncrasy. This merges into the ethnologist's museum-complex to be treated later. But even in amateur form it is smotheringly full of assertions that to give Natives access to pants makes the world less desirable because less diverse. It is hard to acquit Nordhoff of sentimentalism in having written:

> There are certain parts of the world—like our American mountains, deserts, and lonely stretches of coast—which seem planned for the spiritual refreshment of mankind; places from which one carries away a new serenity and the sense of a yearning for beauty satisfied. Ever since the days of Cook the islands of the South Sea have charmed the white man—explorers,

---

[6] Harry L. Shapiro: *Art News*, March, 1946
[7] Leenhardt made the same point: "[the New Caledonian carver] is not a man with full consciousness of his art, who consecrates himself to it with motives of devotion and beauty."—*Gens de la grande terre*, 33.

naturalists, traders, and the rough crews of whaling vessels; the strange beauty of these little lands, insignificant as far as commercial exploitation is concerned, seems worthy of preservation. *And the native, paddling his outlandish canoe or lounging in picturesque attitudes before his house, is indispensable to the scene . . . the native must be preserved if a shadow of the old charm is to linger for the enjoyment of future generations of travelers* [Italics mine].
—*Faery Lands of the South Seas,* 196.

Numerous people considering the South Seas—reporters, doctors, government officials, professional hotel men—have told me that transpacific aviation should make it practical to set up swank tourist hotels on South Sea Islands, to lend atmosphere to which Natives acting quaintly, like Natives, will be essential. Fanning Island, New Caledonia, Tutuila (Samoa), Majuro (Marshalls), have all been mentioned to me in that context, as well as better known places like Bora Bora (Societies) and Kauai (Hawaii). The one comfort is that, in most of these places, it sometimes blows hard enough to push even the swankiest cabaña into the lagoon.

Or Native-preserving may be motivated by a pontifical jealousy for Native welfare.[8] The most curious example still goes on, though somewhat flawed by the recent war, on the small Hawaiian island of Niihau, fifteen miles off Kauai. There, for generations, a group of practically pure-blooded Hawaiians has been kept unspotted from the world by the owners of the island. Originally a Scots family, this group migrated to New Zealand where it prospered. But its sense of family solidarity, centering round a queenly mother, was so strong that it sold its holdings as too small to provide well for all the children, and sought more room elsewhere. In a ship bought for the purpose, stocked with sheep and cattle of the group's own breeding, the Family, as it is called, touched at Hawaii in the 'sixties on the way to British Columbia or, some say, Oregon. Finding North America not to its liking it returned to Hawaii and, for a reputed $10,000 in gold—a generous price at the time—bought

[8]This can make sense—cf. Chapter VII on British policy in the Polynesian islands fringing Melanesia.

Niihau from the Hawaiian Crown. There it built a mansion and started stock ranching, with the Hawaiians working on a semifeudal basis of labor-for-quitrent. Again the Family did well and used other resources besides to establish itself as one of the dominating forces on Kauai, with Niihau kept on as a more or less profitable plaything.

The Niihau Hawaiians were already Christianized and broken to adequate clothing, the only improvements that the Family would have desired. To keep their blood pure, their morals unaffected by white vices and their temperaments docile, these few hundred brown people have ever since been virtually isolated by Family ukase. Only a white superintendent and a couple of Japanese running the Family's sampan between Niihau and Kauai disturbed the atmosphere. Quarantine was enforced with a rigidity that could be comic only to the Martian onlooker. Exceptions were made only in cases that would have meant secession from Hawaii. Thus, school and health inspectors from Kauai County were grudgingly permitted. The superintendent's son could visit his father once a year, provided he applied for special permission each time. When the superintendent, the only man on Niihau allowed to smoke, went to Honolulu on unavoidable business some ten years ago, he saw trolley-cars for the first time. Phonographs and radios were forbidden, and a telephone to the mainland was never installed. An Hawaiian leaving the island for anything but grave illness requiring hospitalization could not return if the Family disapproved his going. Church services and schools, though only up to fourth grade, were conducted in Hawaiian alone. A signal fire on a headland was the only way to communicate with the Family in emergencies. But the head of the Family went over to the kingdom once a year for a stay of several months, was welcomed with feudal pomp and rode in state in a surrey to the rambling old house.

Hawaii has always been full of tales about how the Family resisted U.S. Army attempts to survey the island and complained bitterly about warplanes on manoeuvres frightening the sheep. Only a few intimate friends of the Family were ever taken across the strait. Curious outsiders always found that permission to visit Niihau was the one thing in Hawaii that could not be arranged if you knew the right people. The one man known to have managed it without extreme subterfuge and luck was the pilot of a Japanese fighterplane who made a forced landing on Niihau during the attack on Pearl Harbor. With the aid of one of the Japanese working there he terrorized the island for a short while but eventually, under circumstances which are already the matrix of juicy local legend, was erased by a large Hawaiian couple whom he had been bullying. The virginity of Niihau was avenged, if not restored.[9]

This arbitrary anomaly under the American flag, however benevolently intended, is the *reductio ad absurdum* of the native-quarantined-for-his-own-good. A variant of it, though, the attitude that the world is, and should be, "so full of a number of things" can affect even presumably sage social scientists. Contemplating the Maori's situation in Invercargill, New Zealand, where the "Native" has evidently succeeded brilliantly in fusing socially, economically and politically into the white man's society, the sociologist Duff winds up by mournfully regretting that any such adjustment took place. Though these Maori are unquestionably happier thus than their fellow-"Natives" with less complete adjustment, it somehow offends him to see the old ways so thoroughly wiped out.

A mere restating turns the trick. Mankind needs a spiritual sanitarium; therefore certain Polynesians must adopt careers as therapeutic lay-figures, taking not what their culture needs from among the white man's ways, but doing what will solace the troubled white man's spirits. Or, to put it in another way, the world is more stimulating and attractive if the Persians do things differently from Western peoples; therefore Persia must be discouraged from selling oil to the United States and buying back soap, Persians being quainter when dirty.

These approaches and attitudes toward the complex of ideas

---

[9] The best sources on Niihau are Nordhoff, *Northern California* . . . ; Bird, *Six Months* . . . ; Clark, *Remember Pearl Harbor*; and my own piece in *Coronet*, January, 1937.

and emotions involved in the word "Native" have been gone
into here to avoid confusion later on. Certainly an adult mind
cannot regard the world as a freak show in which the fat lady
must be contrasted with the living skeleton. And with that the
capital N can be dropped. Since no better word is available,
native will be used throughout the following. Understand it
henceforth as meaning "Descendant of the ethnic stocks found
in possession by the white discoverers of any given island."

*   *   *

THIS WAS THE SOUTH SEA ISLANDER

> Savagery has been, for the reading public of the
> last three centuries, a reservoir of unexpected pos-
> sibilities in human nature; and the savage has had
> to adorn this or that hypothesis by becoming cruel
> or noble, licentious or chaste, cannibalistic or hu-
> mane, according to what suited the observer or the
> theory.
> —Bronislaw Malinowski, *The Sexual Life of Sav-
> ages*, 537

I remember a ship news photographer scouting for subjects
on a liner making port at San Francisco from the Islands. On
the forward well deck he caught sight of our Fijian passenger
—well muscled, cocoa-brown, wearing a tweed jacket and wrap-
around skirt with a scalloped hem, his head like a frizzy black
basketball, bare feet apparently twenty inches long and on his
face the standard Fijian expression of dignity mixed with
geniality. The photographer's astonishment was so intense that
for several seconds he made no motion toward his camera.

"What," he demanded of the nearest bystander, "is that
barefoot boy with cheek of tan?"

This reaction to a first look at the most picturesque of South

Sea Islanders was a good one. A full answer to his question would acquaint the reader with much that is significant about Islanders, for the Fijian is the nearest thing to a least common denominator of the Island peoples. Still, it would omit or insufficiently illustrate many a crucial detail; so we must discuss many other Islanders and hope to avoid both confusion and inaccuracy. For one reason or another, all are peoples well worth acquaintance.

Of course, there is not now and never was any such thing as a typical "South Sea Islander." Differences among these peoples' appearances and ways of doing are as numerous as resemblances, although they all originally had some features in common.

All South Seas peoples—barring occasional albinos—were darker than the average among whites discovering them. All lacked draft animals, none knew the wheel or the propelling-oar. All lacked any supply of metals, though some knew of metal and occasionally secured a fantastically valued bit of iron or copper from floating wreckage. Unfamiliar with the nature of the stuff, however, they might try to plant a few of the white man's iron trade spikes to grow more of the precious things. All lived principally on vegetable foods and derived most of their scanty animal proteins from fish rather than from the scarcer hog, dog or rat. All wore fewer clothes than was customary among whites. None had developed writing, relying on memory for record.[10] All somehow recognized private property, but none knew of sole freehold in land. And in practically all cases the basis of government was the prestige of rank and traditional ways rather than formally ascertained consent of the governed.

Contrasts were so striking, however, that the South Seas were early split in three on a basis partly geographical, partly racial. The result naturally did not make scientific sense but has persisted for convenience: Polynesia (Greek for Many Is-

[10]Engraved plaques from Easter Island led some students to believe that a form of writing had developed there. Recent inquiry makes it unlikely. Cf. Peter H. Buck, *Vikings of the Sunrise*, 236.

lands); Micronesia (Little Islands); Melanesia (Black Islands). Many Islands would just as well have fitted the whole area—in fact, "Polynesia" was so used a hundred years ago. Guam (Marianas) and Babelthuap (Palaus) in the Little Islands are much larger than Rarotonga (Cooks) or Tongatabu (Tonga) in the Many Islands. Scattered along the fringes of the Black Islands are groups of probably Polynesian lighter-colored peoples. Also, even in the inaccurate sense in which the word is applied to negroes, the Melanesian is seldom black; rather, dark with a purplish tinge.

And the boundaries of these divisions merge dismayingly. It is more tidiness than ethnic clarity that draws the line between the Micronesian Gilberts and the Polynesian Elliccs. The eastern part of Melanesian Fiji is demonstrably shot through with Polynesian infusion from Tonga, while the Melanesian Loyalties off New Caledonia show marked traces of Polynesian immigration. These divisions, like other abstractions, are useful tools only when used most broadly. You cannot even say that Melanesia consistently differs from the others in possessing malaria—the disease is lacking in Melanesian New Caledonia[11] and Fiji as well as in Polynesia and Micronesia. Merely take it that Polynesia means the eastern half of the sprawling diamond of the South Seas; Micronesia the northeastern quadrant; Melanesia the southwestern quadrant, where islands are bigger and the climate more depressingly tropical. A check list of island groups thus categorized by a recognized authority is appended.[12]

[11]Amateur speculators developed the theory that the universal presence of the scrubby, gnarly niaouli tree (a cousin of the Australian eucalypti) kept New Caledonia malaria-free. But this is poor ecology—Fiji lacks niaouli and malaria too.

[12]Felix M. Keesing, Native Peoples of the Pacific World, lists as follows; I have supplied the more common aliases:

Polynesians inhabited:
  Hawaii (Sandwich Islands)
  Samoa (Navigator Isles)
  New Zealand
  Tonga (Friendly Islands)

Societies (Tahiti, Raiatea, etc.
  Includes both Society and
  Georgian groups of Cook.)
Ellices
Wallis and Horne

Such cataloguing, however, perniciously encourages a blur-ring of perceptions. There was and still is plenty of distinction between the New Zealand Maori and his distant (in both senses) Polynesian cousins in Hawaii. Ever since Prince Lee Boo's time the outgoing, politic, smiling inhabitants of the Palaus have been temperamentally different from their Micro-nesian neighbors in Yap, only a few hundred miles away. In Melanesia cultural splinterism makes the area a miniature universe in itself, practically as fantastic as its larger prototype.

It is hard for a western man to appreciate the isolation of any of these island peoples. When whites found him, the Is-lander's geographical knowledge seldom ranged over a radius of more than a few hundred miles from his village beach, practically never beyond the immediate group. (The exception would be the triangular intercourse in war, diplomacy and trade among Tonga, Fiji and Samoa.) Only dimly did legends of long-ago voyages tell him that there might be other and different lands far away. There he lived, ringed by the horizon-wall, his culture gradually developing by internal momentum into something more and more sharply differentiated from that of others. The Samoan had even forgotten that he orig-inally came from somewhere else. But this isolation was not altogether a matter of salt water. Even on large Melanesian islands each miniature tribe might be sharply different from the people in the next bay—sharply and most intriguingly dif-ferent.

Much as the ethnologist deplores such an attitude, con-noisseurs of the topsy-turvy have wandered entranced through Melanesia. One tiny culture had grown so nonaggressive that

Tuamotu (Paumotus, Low or
    Dangerous Archipelago)
Marquesas
Easter Island (Rapa-nui)
Micronesians inhabited:
    Gilberts (Kingsmills included)
    Marshalls
    Carolines (Palau included)
    Marianas (Ladrones)

Melanesians inhabited:
New Hebrides
New Caledonia (Loyalties in-
    cluded)
Solomons
Bismarcks (New Ireland, New
    Britain, etc.)
Fiji

the necessary executive functions of chiefs were considered a degrading bore. In another women were leaders and providers while men were creative-minded and gossippy aesthetes. A third had no notion that sexual intercourse directly caused pregnancy—a man returning from a year's absence would be delighted to find his wife nursing a new baby—or that eating and nourishment are associated. Another group knew the facts of life but considered that, if a wife had intercourse with her husband within a day of entertaining a lover, the resulting child would be the husband's anyway. On Ugi (Solomons) it was customary to kill one's own children young and purchase children nearer adulthood from neighboring tribes, which gave the advantages of a family without the trouble of rearing. The men of Dobu, off eastern New Guinea, were so hyper-suspicious that they escorted their wives when they went to defecate in the bush—a matter in which Islanders are usually prudish—to make sure that the trip was not a pretext for adultery. And they had so little notion of honest dealing that they attributed performance of a contract in good faith to the efficacy of magic spells worked on Party B by Party A . . .

Yet these are not deliberate travesties of human behavior created by a sardonic minded angel. Instead they are human behavior, demonstrations of how flexible human potentialities are. Much as the Islanders varied, they were merely exhibiting, as we do also, the astounding variety of institutions, emotions and deviations that human beings always manifest. Further, these examples show once and for all that a society can exist with considerable satisfaction to its members when some of its key assumptions signally fail to make objective sense— which should cheer us about our own culture. Some of what follows may dismay those unaccustomed to looking squarely at nonwhite ways of doing; but remember Sumner's testy dictum that anybody likely to be shocked by reading about any folkways, of whatever sort, had better not read about folkways at all.

To repeat for emphasis: These were human beings. When you pricked them, they did bleed. Their talent for living often

impressed hard-headed as well as romantic observers. The ways
that they developed in isolation usually worked harmoniously
and well under their peculiar circumstances. Either conde-
scension toward or hysterical idealization of them is pointless
bad taste.

Yet none of them had the objectivity that you and I need in
order to consider them intelligently. Before the whites came,
they were as committed to their own ways as Puritan Salem;
probably even more so, for they lacked Salem's obscure fer-
ments. Vestiges of this self-centered parochialism are still
among them. Years ago American Samoa was having trouble
with coconuts, its economic mainstay. The U.S. Navy brought
a coconut expert down from Honolulu; he found what was
wrong, and explained cause and cure to a great meeting of
local chiefs. A high talking-chief responded for several quarters
of an hour in the prolix, stately tradition of Samoan eloquence,
devoted to conventionalities, reserving significance for the last
sentence. He thanked the Navy, the Territory of Hawaii, the
Government in Washington, the President and the good Lord
for their kindness in sending this great and wise man to help
them, promised that the event would be recorded to all eternity
in song and dance among the Samoans, and so forth and so on
and so forth . . . He said that no Samoan would dream of
doubting the great and wise man's ideas of coconut culture.
"But," he finished, "in Samoa we don't handle coconuts that
way."

Every culture likes its own way best. The Islander, with so
little opportunity to know that other people's notions could
differ from his, was particularly set in his ways.

*   *   *

. . . neither noble savages nor inhuman brutes, but men.
—Tawney, preface to Raymond Firth, *Primitive Economics of
the New Zealand Maori*, xvii

What the Islanders were like before whites came pestering
them is not easy to make out. Evidence from early explorers is

fragmentary, and usually from untrained observers. Evidence from early missionaries is distorted by pious sensibilities and the need for lively propaganda to attract funds from home congregations. Later evidence, though useful, is flawed by the fact that many details altered subtly or grossly from the very beginning of white contact. Evidence from present day natives is warped by their understandable tendency to romanticize their ancestors in reaction to white arrogance. Besides, Americanizing trends in Hawaii, Anglicizing trends in Fiji, Frenchifying trends in Tahiti, necessarily produced confusing results. Everywhere the white's physical, social and emotional poisons —poisons only to the native, like a blood transfusion from an incompatible donor—affected the native variously, depending on whether missionary, whaler or official had the upper hand. So it will be well to remember that from here on there is at least one glaring exception to every statement made.

Physically, except for more or less skin pigmentation, Islanders have varied about as much as mankind in general. Some Melanesians run short and most have mashed-in faces and heavy brows, but others are taller, with aquiline profiles. Frizzy hair and smallish eyes give them notions of personal beauty at variance with ours—Malinowski's friends in the Trobriands regretfully let him know that they found whites' large eyes, prominent noses, and lank hair, most unattractive. The GI was baffled enough by his first Polynesian beauties, but it was nothing to his feeling when, shovelled ashore in Melanesia, he was shown a local woman, dark, stringy, pendulous-breasted, as a "real South Sea Islander."

Micronesians varied from the shortish, stocky, red-brown Palau to the long-vanished Chamorro type that the Spaniards found on Guam, tall, heavily muscled and richly dark of skin. In general the Micronesian looks more clearly Mongoloid than do the others.

Polynesians, the South Sea Islanders of cheap legend, are quite light enough to tan. A Samoan who customarily wears a shirt shows a V of sunburn at the throat when he strips. Lightness of color was attractive in Polynesia, so aristocratic or vainer women kept out of the sun as much as possible. The modern Hawaiian still cannot understand why white men and women at Waikiki insist on burning themselves as black as possible. The contrast between the commoner and the noble-women of Tahiti (Societies)—the latter were periodically bleached in the shade of Tetiaroa islet—was so marked that one of Wallis' midshipmen mistook them for members of a different race.

Both Polynesian and Micronesian probably have much "white" blood, presumably sharing Caucasoid strains still present in India. While moving spasmodically eastward along the Asiatic and Pacific islands, they picked up local admixtures that darkened skins, thickened lips and sometimes slanted eyes.[13]

Nor is the Melanesian a "nigger." It shouldn't matter anyway, but for the record, his relationship to the African is probably almost as remote as ours. His build is also deceptive. Though not usually big or bulky, he has marvelous wind and is sturdy enough to have been the laboring mainstay of South Sea plantations for four generations.

The Polynesian is husky in any terms, tending to a big-footed, ham-handed, heavy-muscled, fast-reflexed type that makes an ideal football player. The Polynesian handshake feels as if produced by a combination vice and boxing glove; I have seen a six-foot Polynesian of middle age solve an entanglement of the bumpers of two cars by lifting the rear of one car unassisted, apparently thinking nothing of it. In apparent paradox, however, the Polynesian younger man has always looked a trifle womanish. "The young men at a little distance," wrote Mrs. Wallis of Stewart Island, "resembled very pretty girls, and so at first we thought them." When filming Moana in Samoa, Flaherty had to revise his projected story because no native, old or young, had a face strong enough for the original plot. Gauguin noted this androgynism, as did La Farge:

[13] ". . . the Polynesian race originated from a tri-racial mixture of some sort of white or Caucasoid stock with Melanesian-Negroid and Mongoloid elements."—Hooton, Apes, Men and Morons, 144.

". . . the girl form passes into the young man's . . . without a break." The impression may arise partly from body hairlessness—whites are the world's hairiest people—the melting Polynesian eye, and the great grace with which all Polynesians, men included, handle themselves.

Throughout the Islands aristocrats usually run larger than the local average; this difference in size helped early visitors form their theory that chief and commoner were of different breeds. Chiefs could be gigantic. A towering, fat, but powerful arii[14] (or alii or a'ii or ariki, depending on the particular Polynesian dialect) might weigh 400 pounds. His sister ran similarly to tallow, well over six feet, weighing in the same division, with arms like tapered watermelons and breasts like basketballs. Fat was honorific beauty. Lucatt, the early Tahitian merchant, felt distressed when a slender high chieftainess was prepared for marriage by being sent to Tetiaroa to gorge for months and return deliciously hog-fat. James Jarvis described the early Hawaiian chieftainesses:

". . . their flesh hung in deep folds about them; their walk was a majestic stagger; but their carriage was lofty and betokened an innate pride of birth and rank."
—*History of the Hawaiian Islands*, 46

One such giantess broke the cabin sofa in Kotzebue's ship merely by sitting down on it; she wore seaman's boots and her ankle was eighteen inches round. But this was not fat without strength. A Tahitian great lady picked up the ailing Wallis bodily and "lifted him like an infant over such wet and dirty places as they came to in their way." Another Tahitian high chieftainess personally stole the ship's anvil from the Spanish "Aguila" in 1772. So, when you read of a white man enjoying the favors of an Island "queen," his bedfellow was probably not at all the slim brown enchantress you have in mind. It must have been like having an affair with a lady whale in full blubber.

This upper-class hugeness, probably hereditary because of

[14]This term identifies the top ranks of Polynesian societies.

class inbreeding, is sometimes attributed to special diet for upper-class children assisted by incessant massage, at which Islanders are very skilful. It still survives here and there. When two Tongan princes recently announced their intention of each marrying a Tongan noble girl, a local white man declared, after hasty calculation, that the double marriage would add up to just under half a short ton. Fat is still attractive in Polynesia: Beaglehole reports of Vavau (Tonga):

"The average village man's idea of a woman who is beautiful emphasizes . . . that she should be fat in every part of her body . . . a woman . . . whose buttocks and feet are small is looked upon with small favor by the idealists."—*Pangai*, 85

Polynesian women have not lived up to Hollywood in other respects. A flat, broad, nose was often considered a mark of beauty, so mothers solicitously mashed children's noses to suit. Heavy tattooing, ritually important and sometimes piquant, gave in extreme forms a somewhat long-underwearish effect. Shapeliness of breasts seldom survived motherhood in Samoa because children were allowed to hang on the breast while suckling, a stretching process that might go so far that the mother could throw the breast over her shoulder and let the child nurse from behind. Today even the smaller specimens of Polynesian womanhood show that their ancestresses must have been on the heavy-set side, with thick ankles and ill-defined waists.

Variations in average good looks seem to have been marked for, though Hawaii was never noted for pretty girls, those of Samoa, the Marquesas and Tonga were severally advanced as superlative. The writer's own impression is that today the average is higher in Micronesia than anywhere else.

How to account for the legend of South Seas beauty is not too puzzling. A French Navy officer disappointed in the sirens of Tahiti in the 'seventies put his finger on it:

"Poets have sung the Tahitian girl—whom they never met. Navigators celebrated her. After a long voyage, that is excusable."—Henri Rivière, *Souvenirs de la Nouvelle-Calédonie*, 50

This tradition was founded by very dubious witnesses, seafaring men with their judgment warped by six months or a year of seeing no women at all. Or, if they had touched at Patagonia or Tasmania on the way out, the last women they saw would have been those acknowledged to have been the most spectral hags on earth. Bear in mind also that seamen are notorious liars when recounting adventures, and that the eighteenth century's ideas of beauty were not ours, at least below the neck. Hardbitten Benjamin Morrell, sealing- and sandalwood-skipper, drew the bow very long indeed when celebrating "Young William's Group" (probably somewhere in the middle Carolines):

> "The chief's wife then gave me a little garland of wild flowers; and as if this had been a preconcerted signal, two lovely females, naked as they were born, darted from a neighboring thicket, each with a similar token of affection, which they offered me with the most bewitching grace conceivable. Heaven forgive me, if my wicked heart did violence to any one precept of the decalogue! These girls were about sixteen or seventeen, with eyes like the gazelle's, teeth like ivory, and the most delicately formed features I have ever met with. In stature they were about five feet, with small hands, feet and head, long black hair, and then those eyes, sparkling like jet beads swimming in liquid enamel! They had small plump cheeks, with a chin to match, the lips of just the proper thickness for affection's kiss. Their necks were small, and I believe that I could have spanned either of their naked waists with both my hands. Their limbs were beautifully proportioned and so were their busts. Imagination must complete their bewitching portraits; I will only add that the shade of their skin was a light copper color."—Narrative of Four Voyages, 12.

Such a spate of adjectives, applied even to Micronesian girls, who often are very delicately made, cries out for checking by visual evidence from early times. Little worthy of the name exists. Photography was not available. The artists whom explorers usually took along to record peoples and places did well by topography, but their drawings of natives are always too much influenced by examples then fashionable among European drawing-masters. Whatever the Tahitian model may have been like, she cannot have so closely resembled a Romney portrait of Lady Hamilton. The modern full-blood Samoan, Hawaiian, or Tongan, girl is a beauty no oftener than one expects among whites. Apparent exceptions almost certainly have a touch of white or Chinese. Grace of movement, beauty of eye, great charm of manner are often there. But in both Polynesian and Melanesian women features run coarse, tending toward the masculine, the complementary androgynous touch that Gauguin noted. Moerenhout tried to attribute to arduous labor the fact that the part-white women of Pitcairn's were "un peu hommasse"; but the same is true of those in islands where neither sex toils unduly.

Older men in Polynesia and Micronesia, however, make good on the brilliant good looks popularly associated with the South Seas. A Samoan chief with broad, plump, shoulders, cropped gray head, crisp mustache and an air of genial and self-respecting dignity is as fine looking a human being as exists. The effect is of a very distinguished European tinted light brown; his juniors of equal rank, pushing middle age, present a most diverting variety of recognizable white types. I have occupied myself during the prolonged speeches of a Samoan kava ceremony by identifying famous faces in the chiefs sitting at their posts in the circle: Roscoe Turner, James F. Byrnes, Gifford Pinchot, J. A. Krug, Admiral Byrd, the late Senator Penrose. In a gathering of Fijians I have met both Dante and Professor Einstein, the latter bewilderingly to the life.

In many ways the Fijian is the most satisfactory Islander to look at. He must certainly have been so in the old days. His wife, not bad-looking when young as looks go in the Islands, then wore only a fringe of dried vegetation, long or short according to age. He wore somewhat less, but for ceremonies decked himself out in garlands and necklaces of whale teeth sawed into clawlike segments. Extravagant heads of hair were the pride of both their hearts. A high chief with a skilled hair-

dresser would have a coiffure three feet in diameter singed off
so neatly that it looked like a coverless medicine-ball. Dyes of
various colors—originating in the bleaching effect of lime used
to discourage lice—turned the whole mass strawberry blond,
or henna red, or black and white in streaks and stripes. Mission influence repressed the wilder of these coiffures and the
fantastic beards attached; but today you can still see a Fijian
bicycling down the road with his flaring red thatch in gratifying contrast to his rich brown skin.[15]

*   *   *

The simple and natural life of the islander beguiles me; I am
at home with him; all the rites of savagedom find a responsive
echo in my heart; it is as though I remembered something
long forgotten; it is like a dream dimly remembered and at last
realized; it must be that the untamed spirit of some savage
ancestor quickens my blood.—Stoddard, *Summer Cruising in
the South Seas.*

Nobody is sure how the Melanesians got to their muggy,
lovely, jungle-heavy islands that lie like a crescent of shaggy
outworks to protect the long coasts of Australia. To rehearse
scientific speculation on the subject would be tedious. But
things are clearer with the Micronesians and Polynesians on
the spattering of smaller islands farther out.

Our elders formed romantic speculations about these settlements. Accidental resemblances in a few words and details of
custom prompted some to identify the brown Islanders with
the lost tribes of Israel, those peripatetic hardy perennials.
Misguided geology led others to assume a huge Pacific continent that gradually sank, leaving the Islanders surviving on
isolated peaks. Moonshining with a theosophical tinge made
them vestigial remnants of a former world-wide culture. But
by now responsible opinion is well agreed that they got out
there much as our ancestors got from Europe to America—by

[15]The military authorities ordered close clips for the heads of Fijian
soldiers, which produced a temporary fashion of disapproving the old-
time huge-headedness. By now, I am gratified to remark, heads of hair
are coming back in Fiji.

sea. So far as known the details are quite as intriguing as any lost continent of Mu.

Perhaps 2,000 years ago their progenitors left the fringe of large islands along southeastern Asia and, perhaps pushed from behind by Melanesians or Indonesians, struck out for more peaceful dwelling places. They took to sea in gigantic canoes, with freeboard built up by adz-dubbed plank bored along the edges and lashed together with coconut fibre (sinnet). Some carried traditional South Sea outriggers against capsizing; the more spectacular were two-hulled, with deckhouses on the connecting spars amidships. They had sails of matting and paddles worked by crews of as many as a hundred men; specialists bailed, trimmed the sails, coxed, and so forth. In skilled hands such craft were thoroughly seaworthy[16] and these men were stunning seamen, else they could never have populated the islands. Since any vessel that combines speed with seaworthiness is beautiful, they must have made a splendid sight when under way. The early explorers left exhilarating descriptions of deep-sea war canoes on parade, the leader dancing on deck and calling time, twenty paddles a side slashing the water with the precision of a Rockette chorus, the crew's throbbing song punctuated by the regular whack of recovered paddle blades on the gunwale.

The mere map of the Pacific honors both craft and men. Raiatea (Societies), Savaii (Samoa), Rarotonga (Cooks) are suggested secondary swarming points whence, as centuries passed, fresh expeditions colonized still more distant scraps of land. It is 2,700 miles, broken by only a few hard-to-find atolls, from Raiatea to Hawaii; 2,500 from Raiatea to New Zealand; 2,600 from Samoa to Hawaii. From the presence in Polynesia of the sweet potato (kumara in Maori) ethnology argues that the Polynesians also made the west coast of South America, botanical home of that plant. Last year, however, a Danish party succeeded in reaching the Tuamotu from Peru on an old

[16]In 1935 de Bisschop, a French amateur sailor, built such a vessel in Honolulu and, with a crew of one, took her under sail alone to France via the Cape of Good Hope. Cf. Eric de Bisschop, *Kaimiloa*.

Peruvian-style balsawood raft under sail, which suggests that the contact may have gone the other way. In any case, contact between Polynesia and America was slight.

These Polynesian navigators had neither compass nor sextant, and their assignment was much more difficult than that of the similarly ill-equipped Vikings who made North America with easy stages at Iceland and Greenland. Knowledge of how and why they launched on these thousands of miles of naked water comes from surmise skilfully applied to old charts, genealogies, and customs. It is known that they were provisioned with coconuts for both drink and food and, where tabu permitted, with green stuff that would last a while, coconut-fed chickens, prepared breadfruit and taro. They could catch fish and seabirds en route. Such resources, eked out by rain water on occasion, will take determined men a long way; in 1861 a native of Rakahanga survived eight weeks in a small double canoe blown off its course, finally coming ashore in the Ellices 1,500 miles away.

They steered by the stars, which they knew uncannily well, by the steady trade winds and the trend of the swells. Migrating birds gave them hints of faraway islands; the golden plover, a poetic-sounding fowl with a poetic function, played such a role. The long-tailed cuckoo probably showed the way to New Zealand. For shorter-range bearings the canoes might carry land-homing birds to be released experimentally like Noah's dove. These seamen could pick up the scent of land far out at sea; they watched for cloud masses forming over invisible high islands and for the confused waters that develop to right and left as the swells check and bend against an undiscovered shore. The picture of what was practical is so ingeniously brilliant that it is a pity some Polynesianophiles occasionally belittle the old navigators' achievements by ascribing to them psychic powers.[17]

[17]Harold Gatty, The Raft Book, written by the famous flier who is an expert on Pacific navigation, standard equipment on life rafts during the recent war, leaves no room for skepticism about Polynesian navigation.

As to why the Polynesians went colonizing, the causes were probably overpopulation of islands already settled, squabbles between chiefs with the weaker party migrating, a warrior's general sense of adventure. Americans should not need explanation for the explorer-pioneer's impulses. Like our pioneers, they took along the germs of livelihood—roots, seeds, food animals—to make the new home like the old one. The practical omnipresence in the Islands of coconut, breadfruit, taro, sugar cane, sweet potato, yam, ti, banana, kava, paper mulberry (for bark cloth, i.e. tapa or siapo), means they were intentionally imported. The same holds good for fowls, hogs, dogs and rats for meat supply.

The sea seemed to bring out the best in the brown Islanders. In their ships they probably reached the acme of their skill in construction. Even the semi-Melanesian Fijian, a timid deep-water sailor when whites first saw him, made splendid deep-sea canoes for which the Polynesians of nearby Tonga eagerly bartered women and military service. They had room for up to 200 men and could knock off close to twenty knots under a triangular matting-sail as big as the main-topsail of a full-rigged ship; or so seamen who saw them swore. English navigators came home from the Marianas with eye-popping tales of asymmetrical sailing canoes that would make similar speed; Woodes Rogers took one home with him to England to demonstrate. The Solomon Islander's stately war canoe, its soaring black prow studded with inlaid pearl shell, was just as beautiful as the Maori's equivalent, which had the loveliest of cunningly spiraled fretwork in stem-covering and lofty stern-piece. The largest of these, hewn with stone tools out of a log so big that only one added strake of freeboard was needed, ran 110 feet without the ornamental bow- and stern-pieces.

This patience and skill were also expressed elsewhere. The Fijian was engineer enough to build a thirteen-span wooden bridge over the Rewa River; he also dug a canal to shorten the trip from Bau to the Rewa mouth. Everywhere the islands developed elaborate irrigation systems for wet taro, and to this day the stranger marvels at the relics of the old-time New

Caledonian's terracing of whole mountainsides in projects half a mile long and hundreds of feet high. The Samoan house, a great oval basket upside down on posts, light and sturdy enough to be moved bodily on occasion, is often thatched with leaves that make it look crude and shaggy outside; but look aloft inside and the eye never wearies of the fascinating structural beauty of its ribbing and bracing, not a nail in the job, all lashed together with intricate patterns of varicolored sinnet. There is equal fascination in the smashing black-red-and-white designs on the rafters of the Maori's meeting house and in the grave harmonies, apparently as simple as tittattoe, of the *tukutuku* panels on the walls.

But such architecture was not necessarily functional. The windowless Hawaiian grasshouse, with a door so low that the tenant crawled in, was damp, insect-ridden, and stuffy. Even the Samoan house had grave drawbacks. It did not keep out insects, a real health hazard in filariasis-ridden Samoa; it was not hurricane-proof; its pebble floor, though dry enough, caught bits of food impossible to clean out; it precluded privacy among its dwellers. The New Caledonian was probably worst off, in a beehive-shaped affair with only a low curtained door and a smudge burning all night to discourage mosquitoes. In any case, it was all flimsy stuff. There are no ruins of South Sea chiefs' mansions. Only temples, tombs and foundations were made of things that did not need renewing every few years.[18] So a South Seas village, in Cook's time or our own, has a flavor of permanent camping out, a charming Hooverville-by-the-Sea.

Island diet was foreshadowed in the things that the migrating Polynesian took with him. On the poorest atolls he ate little but fish—he always had to be a crack fisherman—pandanus, and coconut for drink when green, for food when ripe. On high or uplifted islands, where humus made richer soil, he did a great deal with *taro*, the starchy root of a plant akin

[18]This will stand until scientists finally make up their minds what was the purpose of the accumulations of stone-capped pillars on Guam and Tinian and the why of the cyclopean masonry in the Carolines.

to Jack-in-the-pulpit. Old Hawaii figured that a forty by forty
foot *taro* patch would feed a man for a year. Baked or boiled,
it is fair eating for a hungry man; fancied up it is very good.
Cooked, pounded, and fermented, it is familiar to tourists in
Hawaii as *poi*, which those who like it like very much indeed.
Modern nutritionists find it rich in high-quality food values—
Hawaii exports it in cans to California as baby food.

Breadfruit was seasonally generous too. An acre of these
beautiful, middle-sized trees with deeply cut leaves would feed
a dozen persons eight or ten months of the year. This was the
item that convinced explorers they had found the earthly paradise. Enormous balls of practically ready-made food apparently
growing without cultivation startled the descendants of white
men who had always toilsomely dug their daily bread out of
cold and stubborn dirt. "Where all partake the earth without
dispute," sang Lord Byron, "and bread itself is gathered as a
fruit." The talented noble lord had been tripped up, like
many after him, by the misnomer applied by discoverers. When
cooked—it is never eaten raw—the stuff is not at all like bread,
rather like a huge, waxy piece of roast chestnut with a slight
raisinish flavor. Most whites like it much better than *taro*. The
Melanesian relied heavily on sago, the pith of a palm-like tree.
Most Islands got more starch—it was all high in carbohydrates
—out of yams, sweet potatoes and various varieties of bananas.
Greens might appear as bits of seaweed, very tasty with their
reek of salt and iodine, or as *taro*-tops, which are marvelous
when cooked with cream pressed from ripe coconut.

Pig, dog or chicken was eaten in quantity only at feasts,
great occasions when everybody gorged for days and the village
was denuded of supplies, perhaps after collecting resources for
the doings for three or four years. On many islands the commoner went for months without meat, for hogs and dogs ate
the same things as people and were expensive luxuries, appear-
ing frequently only before chiefs. Great feasts were stagger-
ingly colossal and so were the appetites of the eaters. A spread
for "King" Cakobau of Fiji a hundred years ago took 200
people a whole morning merely to arrange; it included seventy

large turtles, a wall of kava-root seven feet high and thirty-five feet long, and a breastwork of 35,000 yams.

Some Melanesians had vessels in which to boil their provisions, for they were fair potters, working without the wheel, merely building up the clay by guess. But they also often used the South Seas earth oven, and Polynesia had nothing else.[19] It was efficient enough. A deep hole was paved with large, heated stones and the items to be cooked were wrapped in leaves and put in. Then water was poured over them and all was covered with stones, earth and leaves to steam until done, much the same as in a clambake.

The consequences on pork, fish fresh from the ocean, bananas, taro and suchlike could obviously be mouth-watering. But qualifications intrude here, too. You must think of most of the above as eaten cold or lukewarm, for the South Seas peoples do not share our notion that hot food is particularly tasty. Even when trying courteously to supply western-style food, the Islander cannot quite realize that a stone-cold fried egg is not as good as a hot one. Use of sea water as a dip—the Islands usually lacked salt—also cooled things off. And the pork was often preferred in a condition that you and I would find distastefully half-raw. It also sounds distressing that much fish was eaten raw. But actually, though it can be insanitary, raw fish, marinated Island-style in lime juice, eaten with coconut cream and salt-water, is a great delicacy. The Islander carried it even farther and ate small fish as caught, alive and wiggling. That does not sound appetizing. But reflect that South Sea Islanders can seldom learn to eat cheese, any more than you could ever stomach the New Caledonian's menu recorded by Lemire: roast flying fox (a huge fruit-eating bat), big white grubs dug out of a rotting tree stump, and uncleaned pigeon guts stewed with rice.

Except for relative lack of high-class amino acids, the Island

[19]Lack of suitable clay in Polynesia is usually given as the reason for this technological handicap. But the Maori did not develop pottery on reaching New Zealand, which has good pottery clay; and I have myself seen rough but practical experimental pottery made of clay found in Tahiti by whites looking round for ideas.

diet was good, far better than what many an Islander prefers to eat today. But in other aspects of physical welfare, however, he was not originally as well off as romance would have it—in sanitation, for instance. Hogs and dogs had the run of the place, eating what they could pick up, of which there was usually a good deal. The village was neat, its gravel plaza meticulously weeded, the grass kept short, house-terraces swept daily, mats stacked and laid up neatly within, but by western standards this picture of serene tidiness was not actually clean. The Maori were one of the few Island peoples to develop efficient latrines, though in their colder climate they needed them less. Elsewhere defecation took place in the bush or on the beach below high-water mark. Presumably, vigorous tides carries faeces away, but even now, with whites legally requiring over-water latrines, that smell from the beach is not all seaweed. Fiji provided a fine example of neatness combined with poor sanitation on the key islet of Bau where all filth was deposited on top of the high central hill, whence frequent rains sluiced it down all over the living area. Spitting and hand-wrung nose-blowing went on everywhere as freely as on the porch of an Arkansas general store—daintier people might spit under a lifted pebble or the corner of a mat. Clothing never knew the disinfectant effect of soap, which the Islands did not have. Besides, tapa cloth, made by pounding wet strips of paper-like inner barks together, disintegrated after very little washing. Some Melanesians had a generalized and lively horror of washing of any sort, but as a rule the South Sea person was bathed once or twice a day, in fresh water by preference. Again, however, soap was lacking, and the bath was followed by anointing with coconut oil, often rancid and sometimes perfumed as an antidote with sandalwood or flower petals.

Such matters were probably worst in New Zealand where the Maori, traditionally committed to oiling the skin but lacking coconut oil, used fish- and whale-oils in a state of high redolence. The Micronesians of Kusaie (Carolines) valued fishy odors and used fish oil to perfume coconut oil as a cosmetic. And most Islanders had verminous heads. Even the gods were so troubled; Rehua, a Maori deity, provided food for unexpected human guests with birds that fed on the vermin harboring in his long hair. Between friends or lovers, reciprocal louse-gathering, the lice eaten as found, was a useful and sociable custom. To judge from their eagerness for fine-tooth combs in trade, the Tahitians thought pediculosis a minor evil, and the Fijians first used tobacco as a delousing fumigation. But the New Hebrideans valued lice as tasty bits and were outraged when the early Spanish explorers, thinking it a favor, shaved their frowsy heads for them.

Whence, then, the universal impression in books that the Islander was charmingly clean? It began with eighteenth-century navigators who, relatively, were correct in so testifying. Two centuries ago white standards of cleanliness were low at best: the vermin and stenches of the great towns of Europe would have sickened the average Polynesian. We have learned the rudiments of decency too recently and too imperfectly to afford Pharisaism. Nor did such standards as there were appeal to seamen who, in that day, were mostly too shy of water even to learn to swim as a safety measure. Fo'c'sle Jack, pursuing a Maori girl reeking with fish oil, probably smelled even worse than she did. But it took even early seamen aback when the Easter Islanders were seen first to drink out of a spring and then, following rigid local usage, jump in and wash all over in the same water that the next comer would swallow.

Still the Islander probably had less need for sanitation than Western man. No cleanliness would have suppressed the mosquitoes that often infected him with filariasis—the parasitical disease of the blood and lymph systems of which elephantiasis is the extreme form. And yaws, though fly-borne, has nothing directly to do with filth. His other diseases were boils and ulcers and fungous skin ailments that often covered him with scurfy scales but would probably not have been checked by Lifebuoy baths. Until the white man brought the germs, he had no contact with sputum-transmitted tuberculosis or excrement-transmitted typhoid. Nor was his sense of smell defective. He merely did not have our ideas of what smells intolerably.

One of his skin diseases was sometimes said, unreliably, to be caused by overindulgence in kava ('ava in some islands, yaqona in Fiji) the important and ceremonial South Sea drink. It is made from the root of a pepper shrub and traditionally chewed so the chewer's saliva converts part of its starch into sugar.[20] Then it is spit into a bowl, mixed with water, strained elaborately with hibiscus fibre and served in a coconut shell cup. This milky-chalky infusion was the social core of many Island societies, notably Fiji and Samoa.[21] The intricate detail of serving, with hand clapping, calling of special ceremonial names, preparation only by significant persons, dramatized the whole system of Samoan prestige. A slip in reciting a chief's kava-name or the wrong order in presenting the cup could cause bloody wars. For the white guest these ceremonies would probably still be dull even if he understood all the speeches and legendary references, but the chiefs follow the procedure like an audience at an absorbing play. The drink is dull too, tepid, remotely spicy, mildly tingling on the tongue, surely the least positive of all human indulgences except chewing gum. I have seen kava kept going in a dishpan for the crew below decks on an inter-island vessel in Fiji; in that container its color was dismally appropriate.

Old South Sea hands maintain that too much kava leaves the head clear but temporarily paralyzes the legs. They get mildly fond of it. Suva, capital of Fiji, has a kava-saloon where local businessmen drop in at midmorning on the theory that the stuff is cooling. I have never had enough to feel either cooled or paralyzed, and do not know how many gallons are required for such effects.

Old, large or undried roots are variously said to produce the

[20]Fiji originally grated kava-root; later chewing was taken over from Tongan example. Now, with white ideas of sanitation seeping in, grating or pounding have pretty well replaced chewing.

[21]The relative importance of kava varied from group to group. Hawaii and Tahiti had it, but not very conspicuously. The Maori did without it, though a cousin-plant was indigenous in New Zealand. New Caledonia ignored the presence of the proper plant in the bush. (Maurice Leenhardt, Gens de la grande terre, 88.)

strongest brew. Personally I prefer the theory of Ratu George Cakobau of Fiji that, since *kava* is usually drunk sitting cross-legged, an attitude to which white joints are not accustomed, the paralyzing effect would be arrived at with or without *kava* after several hours. It seems to be an efficient diuretic and, I have it on good authority, is effective as a bush medicine remedy for gonorrhea. German drug firms used to import it in small quantities. The Indian in Fiji drinks it to some extent, but raises it principally for sale to the Fijian himself. Experiments made by GIs in mixing it with gin are said to have produced high exhilaration. *Manuia!*

*   *   *

"Ah, those M'tezo! Incurable heathen! He had given them up long ago . . . They filed their teeth, ate their superfluous female relations, swapped wives every new moon, and never wore a stitch of clothes . . . How they attached themselves to his heart, those black fellows! Such healthy animals! . . . And the Bumbulis, the Kubangos, the Mugwambas! And the Bulanga . . . Really, the Bulanga were the worst of the lot. Not fit to be talked about. And yet, somehow or other, one could not help liking them . . ."

—Norman Douglas, *South Wind*, 44

Nobody has explained why the Islander did not develop fermented drinks. He used fermentation to process both *taro* and breadfruit, so he knew of it, and even the Tasmanian, least developed of human beings, had a kind of eucalyptus beer. Island *ti*-root and sugar cane, both with high sugar content, are admirable raw materials for alcohol, as the whites enthusiastically discovered in no time. But even the Micronesian's murderous palm toddy, a spontaneous fermentation of palm sap, may have been the white man's idea.

The Islander had an impressive range of vices, however, if "vice" consists of indulgence in noxious but enjoyable behavior. Looking into the personal lives of the people of the Palaus, a sociologist told me, completely cured him of notions about innocent savages. Such notions, always tendentious nonsense, need correcting but should not be over-corrected. The reader might compare the following with what he knows of the vices of his own culture.

Tobacco was lacking when whites arrived. But betel nut chewing had spread into Micronesia and Melanesia from southeastern Asia and the blood-red spittle produced is still all over those regions. Betel is the nut of an insubstantially slender palm, and is chewed with lime and the leaf of a pepper-plant. Chewing it turns the lips a lurid raw-meat red and the teeth brownish-black, but it probably does the chewer little more harm than chewing of tobacco, which is no pretty habit either.[22]

Many Polynesians were desperate gamblers. Like the notorious Jim Smiley, they would bet anything on anything. The missionary's insistence on suppressing native games grew out of the native's inability to play without betting; a modern missionary has mourned to me over the fact that his Tahitian charges stay interested in healthy athletic contests only a few months if gambling on them is not allowed. In the old days competition in foot racing, boxing, wrestling, surfriding, canoe racing, swimming, target practice with spear, bow or sling, produced wagers of ornaments, weapons, food supplies, and, more seriously, canoes, wives and one's personal freedom. Western psychiatry tends to regard feverish gambling as a presumptive symptom of serious maladjustment. With due qualification, that is worth thinking of as a possible sign of unsuspected strains in the presumably well-adjusted Island world. Other details also imply that all was not altogether well in the Islander's much-admired character.

Little is known about homosexuality in the prewhite days except that it was widespread and not greatly frowned on. The Polynesian's worst enemy never accused him of lacking virility; but virility did not rule out "queerness." The Hawaiian chiefs

[22]Though the seamen he encountered early were probably mostly to-bacco-chewers, the Islander did not take to the habit as a rule. I am told, however, that the upcountry Fijian occasionally mixes tobacco with betel.

kept boys for purposes that horrified the missions; so did Tahitian chiefs, sending them for cosmetic bleaching along with the women. Youths in New Caledonia were much given to mutual sodomy. There was transvestism here and there. Boas, the great anthropologist, was of the opinion that homosexuality is a normal development among domesticated animals, such as cattle, sheep and men; the subject can be let go at that.

Cannibalism is the vice—if vice it be—oftenest associated with the South Seas. Polynesianophiles deny indignantly that it existed in Hawaii or Tahiti and imply that it was missing all over Polynesia; whereas, though dead in the islands just named by the time whites arrived, it was extremely lively in New Zealand and the Marquesas, known in the Tuamotu, sporadic in Tonga and Samoa. In fairness, however, Melanesia was the focus of man-eating and, for our purposes, Fiji does for a sample. In the nineteenth century Fiji was notorious as the Cannibal Islands *par excellence*; in several senses Fiji is middle ground between Polynesia and Melanesia; and in technical progress it probably excelled any other island group. Cannibalism in so advanced a setting is a striking example of the strange things that people insist on doing. It is specially striking in the Fijian, who is one of the toughest and most intelligent of Islanders and certainly the most likeable as well.

Whatever caused this taste for man-meat, it was not lack of animal protein in the diet. It is impossible in any case to correlate this factor with intensity of cannibalism in the Islands. Apologetic Fijians encouraged whites to surmise that the purpose was to restrict population; or that they killed and ate strangers to prevent epidemics, or to keep the race genetically pure. Sympathetic scientists supplement these implausible ideas by pointing out the magico-emotional factors involved: it was rousing revenge to cook and eat one's fallen enemy and might endow the eater with the *mana* of the dead foe,[23] motives that can appear wherever cannibalism does. Nevertheless, the Fijian seems also to have cannibalized for gastronomic reasons. He *liked* man-meat, and so would you probably, if you

[23]For *mana*, see p. 79.

had been reared to it. So did his distant cousins in New Caledonia, who had a song for opening the annual war season: "This is the time when men are fat," advising warriors to kill only plump enemies with shiny skins.[24]

Ordinarily, however, only the aristocratic Fijian male feasted on *bokolo* (man-meat). Great men recorded the hundreds they had eaten. The chief might reserve for himself the corpse of a specially hated enemy and take several days over it, starting with heart, liver or tongue; or he might smoke the liver and hands and hang them in his house to be nibbled at gloatingly whenever he fell to brooding again over the ancient wrong thus avenged. Whatever their rank, women never were allowed *bokolo*; many South Sea *tabus* tended to deny great delicacies even to women of high rank. What cut was favored varied widely. Lockerby thought boiled intestines most popular, but others said that, like the Marquesans and New Caledonian priests, Fijians particularly relished broiled or boiled hands. Whites or negroes would do for eating, though they were considered badly tainted with tobacco and salt. Sometimes captured boys were castrated to fatten up like shoats against a great future feast. Oven-steaming or boiling was the usual method of cookery but raw man might not be disdained, as when Endicott found a Fijian buck eating a victim's brains out of his shattered skull as if they had been coconut meat.

The thing sounds more gastronomic as it develops. After battle, slain enemies were sent to friendly villages as Lord Covert of Shooting-on-the-Rise might send a basket of game to friends in town. If the bodies grew a little high in transit, nobody minded. The Fijian liked fish and turtle fresh, but he took *bokolo* well-tainted without qualms. White witnesses saw corpses brought in for feasts so putrescent that they could not be picked up without falling apart and had to be made into puddings; the graves of the new-buried were watched for weeks lest neighboring villagers sneak over and exhume grandpa. As cannibalism goes, these details are not notably

[24]For further backing, cf. C. G. Seligmann, *The Melanesians of British New Guinea*, 542; 548 *et seq.*

lurid: The Marquesan too might eat an enemy raw, if bagged too late in the day for cooking; in Dobu the female vulva, in New Guinea the penis split and broiled, were delicacies.

What whites call an orgy—meaning hysterical singing and dancing culminating in erotic excesses—often went with the Fijian cannibal feast. But man-eating never quite degenerated into the straightforward gluttony of a barbecue. The meat was somehow *tabu*, unsafe to handle, so there were special cannibal-forks, sole recorded use of the fork in the South Seas. Still, when the chief felt an urge for *bokolo*, he was as regardless as a Roman emperor ordering oysters from Britain. His retainers might kidnap women fishing off the reef at the next village for, though a woman could not eat *bokolo*, she could be *bokolo* and often was. Failing that, he ate his own people, starting with commoners who were in his black books. He was no more temperate about the revenge-aspect, for he might have prisoners trussed up and cooked alive. At least one pre-white chief cut the forearm from a living prisoner and cooked and ate it while the still-living victim looked on. Nice fellow as the Fijian now is, and apparently always was in quieter moments, he unquestionably leaned toward imaginative torture. A victorious war canoe would sail home with enemy children hung by the heels gradually braining themselves against the mast as the ship rolled. A recalcitrant prisoner would have his hands pinioned and a sheaf of dry coconut frond tied to his shoulders, and then, with the dry leaves set on fire, he would be turned loose to run like a screaming torch wherever his agony dictated.

Cannibalism sometimes sounds comic to people reared on jokes about boiled missionary; to others it is shocking.[25] In its own time and place it was neither, being merely a pressure-releasing institution as intimately bound up with the community as saloons were with the old-time Sierra mining camps. *Bokolo* meant hurray-for-our-side, it meant Thanksgiving turkey, it meant an occasion combining New Year's Eve with

[25]Stevenson said all that can be said to cushion the shock of cannibalism: *In the South Seas*, 107–9.

a burlesque show. And, as mentioned before, it had punitive functions too. When the Marquesans, lacking fresh enemies, sent the butcher's gang looking for "long pig" in their own valley, bad actors were usually knocked on the head first.

Non-cannibal Polynesia used human sacrifice in the same way.[26] The bodies were not burned but left to rot, or sometimes buried after the ceremony, in the high place before the god. If the ceremony required more killings than there were overt bad actors, however, the more lowly innocent were chosen. This helps grimly to show how closely-knit and monolithic Island societies were. Not in war, but in prosperous peace, an unlucky individual could be called on any time to be wantonly killed for the good of the community. The Fijian chief's new canoe was launched over rollers consisting of living men to be crushed to death by its weight. The principal posts of his new house were set in pits deep and wide enough to contain a man in addition. Earth was filled in over timber and living creature alike. The commoner never dreamed of objecting, but merely crawled down into his cylindrical grave and docilely embraced the post.

So it went in the Islands. The curve of the roof one lived under, the post at which one sat for a ceremony, the charm one said before going fishing, the social rank to which one was entitled, were no less cut and dried than the requirement that, if chief and wizard willed it so, their men might come for you without warning or trial, smash the back of your skull, wreath you with flowers and lay you, stiff and naked, face down and buttocks up, where you would do the most good.

While vices are in question it would be pleasant, but untrue, to record that Polynesians eschewed torture for animals as well as for their enemies. Hawaiians killed clean in battle or took prisoners for slaves; but, when collecting dogs for a feast, they let them lie moaning for days with muzzles tied up and forelegs broken and tied over their backs. When Polynesians acquired

---

[26]Some theorists consider that human sacrifice indicates that cannibalism was previously practiced. Thus, the Tahitians gouged out the eye, a recognized cannibal dainty, of the human sacrifice and offered it to the high chief.

horses, their insistence on riding them when badly galled and their neglect to water them sickened, and still does sicken, outsiders. Hawaiian women flocked to see cattle slaughtered as a good show. Melanesia was no better. The Trobrianders singed hogs alive as lingeringly as possible in order to enjoy their screams. South Sea missionaries have accomplished little, and I can find no indication that they ever tried very hard, to encourage humanity toward animals among their converts. You cannot sit in a Samoan village fifteen minutes without hearing the yelps of a dog being stoned for fun by an amusement-seeking child whose elders pay no attention. But here again reproachful whites must step warily. The S.P.C.A. is quite a recent innovation, and even an amateur casuist can find in our culture cruel traditions, bastardy laws, for instance, that leave us little pride in our humanity.

Whether war was a South Seas vice depends on what you think of war in general and of war as an emotionally rewarding game in particular. Game it was, students agree; serious, dangerous, destructive, but primarily social sport.[27] Distinction in war increased the *mana* of the individual aristocrat. Often a boy could not be acknowledged as a man until he had brought home a personally-collected head. He had a wide choice of enemies on whom to demonstrate his and his people's prowess, for as a rule, feuds in one or another degree of exacerbation existed among all Island political units. Before whites came, there was no such thing as a group of islands under one political head, and petty wars between subdivisions were chronic, vivid, and highly stimulating to the adrenal glands.

This *particularismus* was most extreme in Melanesia. Language was one reason. A Polynesian from Tahiti could talk with all his immediate neighbors, and even understand something of cognate Samoan, Maori or Hawaiian. But in most of the

[27]". . . when the competition becomes so intense that the game becomes lethal . . . we have what may be properly called warfare . . . Killing the opponents was only incidental, and was only considered proper if it was done in an accepted way. The difference between a game and a war is primarily technological."—Chapple and Coon, *Principles of Anthropology*, 616.

Black Islands a village in Bay A could not make out ten words of the gibberish spoken in Bay B, though it might be only a few hours' walk distant. New Ireland boasted nine different groups of languages, each split into widely differing dialects peculiar to small groups of hamlets. But even hamlets with the same dialect were sporadically at war, or at least never at anything resembling peace. The Melanesian had no notion that a powerful chief might consolidate and keep order in territories more extensive than he could see from his hut door. A single sizable island would be a political world to itself, full of jangling nations:

> "For a parallel to the political *morcellement* of Melanesia, we may look through the world in vain. Every petty tribal unit . . . was at perpetual war with its neighbors. Every stranger was an enemy, whom it was a virtue to slay."—Amherst and Thomson, *Solomon Islands*, xxiii

And slaying that stranger kept the game going, because his people were in honor bound to see that a member of the slaying tribe, no matter whether personally guilty or not, was duly slain in compensation. That called for reverse retaliation, and so *ad infinitum*, in true Hatfield-McCoy style. The story was not dissimilar in Polynesia, though the units might be larger, a chief of high descent and great *mana* sometimes controlling a whole island. Even so, either might have as many difficulties as an early king of mediaeval France in keeping vassal chiefs from warring on him or among themselves.[28]

As fighting, these Island wars were not too dreadful. There

---

[28] The exceptions to this universal bellicosity are hardly numerous enough to record. The Moriori of the Chatham Islands off New Zealand, descendants of the refugees from the last and most vigorous Polynesian migration into New Zealand, had renounced war and no longer manufactured or used lethal weapons; they settled disputes by ordeal of battle with long staffs, ceasing when blood was drawn.—Alexander Shand, *The Moriori*, 32. The Melanesians of the Laughlan Islands off New Guinea were in similar case, with only a few old spears covered with smoke hanging in their huts as reminders that their ancestors too had been fighters.—H. H. Romilly, *The Western Pacific and New Guinea*, 131.

would be an ambush or a rush on a village or a brief stand-up fight, one side breaking after a few men were killed. A few enemy corpses would be hauled away and eaten, if it were cannibal country; elsewhere heads would be taken as trophies. Much energy was expended in frenzied prebattle ceremonies and in resounding boasts afterwards. In cases where enemy forces confronted one another openly, Homeric-style challenges and single combats might precede the brief mêlée.

But chiefs were relatively safe, not only because they had to be unusually expert in fence and dodge, but also because to kill one was dangerous. The enemy who did so was a marked man for life, a dead chief being a keen disgrace to his people. Tahitian sea battles between fleets of war canoes, however, seem to have been fairly desperate. Probably even more lives were snuffed out when, after a Tahitian force had chased the enemy warriors from the field, they sought out the bush hide-outs of the foe's women, old people and children and massacred them until the sport palled. For though a game, this was not necessarily a sporting game. Even the Maori, reputedly chivalrous, liked a good juicy massacre on occasion. Destruction of the enemy's coco and taro plantations was part of the procedure. Fortifications bulked large in Fijian, Tongan and Maori wars, and Rapa, far south of Tahiti, was as striking a nest of fortified hilltops as the country round Auckland. In attacking such places investiture or treachery were much more popular than storming.

South Seas weapons helped keep matters relatively bloodless. Thrown or slung stones, spears with stone, wooden or bone points, clubs, wooden or stone daggers, can eventually pile killings one on another to the point of massacre, but require more effort than firearms. Melanesia alone used the bow in war; to the Polynesian it was a mere sporting toy.[29] Nowhere did the South Seas use it for seriously massed firepower, in the style of the mediaeval English.

[29]Caillot makes the Polynesians of the Gambiers an exception. (*Histoire de la Polynésie orientale*, 407.) Tonga had acquired the war-bow from Melanesians in Fiji. William Mariner, *Tonga, passim*.

There was some body armor. The Gilbert Islanders, whose lances, bills, and swords edged with razor-sharp shark's teeth, were certainly the dirtiest weapons in the Pacific, had heavy and effective paddings of coconut fibre; the Hawaiian version of this turned small shot when Cook fired at a mat-girded warrior at Kealakekua Bay. But the Hawaiian chief also made himself militarily absurd by going into battle wearing a singularly Greek-appearing helmet made of nothing stouter than red and yellow feathers. Weapons had often become clumsy relics; Sir Peter Buck (Te Rangi Hiroa) tells of an old Maori chief at an exhibition of Fijian war dancing with clubs, who spat on the ground and said that anybody taking such a weapon and such a style of fence into a Maori mêlée would have found himself dead, cooked, and eaten, before he knew where he was.

But the Islander was not usually inept with the arms he had. His handiness with a thrown stone cracked many an early seaman's skull. Reliable witnesses swear that Melanesians were accurate with slung stones up to 200 yards, and their recorded accuracy with spears is highly respectable. The Maori, toughest of South Sea warriors, were devils at close quarters with short clubs, particularly the beaver-tailed or fiddle-shaped mere, with which they reputedly could take off the top of an enemy's skull as dexterously as an Englishman opens his breakfast egg. But the Islander's only weapon with the diabolical quality in which whites have specialized was the Melanesian spear- or arrow-head of human bone, poisoned by steeping in vegetable juices, septic mud or, they say, the insides of a festering corpse, all with incantations to match. Whether spell or treatment were more important, numerous seamen, missionaries and bluejackets died of lockjaw after being struck by such a New Hebridean arrow.[30] Nor, though South Seas war was relatively harmless by civilized standards, should it be concluded that the players were not savage about their game; in Tahiti:

[30]H. H. Romilly, *The Western Pacific and New Guinea*, 92, et seq., is skeptical about the poisoning. So is Codrington, *The Melanesians*, 307–12. Most of the evidence comes from an era before general acceptance of the germ theory of disease.

"When a man had slain his enemy, in order fully to satiate his revenge and intimidate his foes, he sometimes beat the body flat, and then cut a hole with a stone battle-ax through the back and stomach and passed his own head through the aperture . . . with the head and arms of the slain hanging down before, and the legs behind him, he marched to renew the conflict."—William Ellis, *Polynesian Researches*, I, 310.

Stripped to a G string, face daubed black or red, drunk with the mass-excitement of pending battle and the hysteria of pre-battle dancing, the South Seas fighting man was nobody that the average European without a gun would care to meet.

Sometimes, besides, he fought for keeps. Being taking prisoner usually meant slavery—not a harsh slavery, as such things go, for often he could marry a free enemy-woman and have free children. But in cannibal islands he would spend his captivity wondering when a shortage of more recent captives would get him eaten; and at best slavery meant separation from relatives, landlessness, namelessness, all social horrors to the Islander. The Maori would send water to the thirsting garrison of an invested fort to keep premature surrender from spoiling the fun. But elsewhere, if warring chiefs were thoroughly exasperated, a defeated community or faction might have to choose between annihilation and forced migration by agreement.

"After battle the vanquished were hunted like game. . . . A chance for life on the open sea was preferable to almost certain death on shore."—Peter H. Buck, *Vikings of the Sunrise*, 212.

* * *

"Here is neither toil nor care. Man stretcheth forth his hand and eateth without parsimony or anticipated cost."—John Ledyard, *A Journal of Captain Cook's Last Voyage*, 119.

Books usually imply that the South Sea Islander was a hospitable gentleman of leisure with nothing more pressing to do than fish and dance for his own amusement. I remember a witty white man attributing the current high birth rate in the

South Seas to the fact that procreation is one of the few important human activities usually accomplished lying down.

As it happens, however, the Islander was not exactly lazy. The things he accomplished make that plain: That Maori canoe was hollowed out of a log 110 feet long and a good eight feet in diameter with only fire and easily-dulled stone tools to fell and dub it out with. The log itself had to be manhandled to a stream big enough to float it to the seashore. Tongan chiefs' mausoleums were built, and still stand, in three or four terraces as big as a tennis court, each faced with coral flags the size of a card table. Or consider the statues of Easter Island, freestanding busts on a scale suggesting a primitive Gutzon Borglum, again wrought with stone tools, sweat and patience. Lazy men could not leave behind them so many monuments of a character that would make an Irish railroad gang go on strike.

The Land of the Doasyoulikes, where the little roast pigs ran round crying Eat me! may exist somewhere, but not between the tropics in the Pacific. Taro, yams, kumaras (sweet potatoes) had to be planted with no better tool than a heavy pole with a stilt-style step toward the pointed end. Breadfruit also had to be planted, and required some care. Coconuts had to be husked on a stake set in the ground, which takes strength as well as skill, or climbed after if wanted for drinking—how long would it take you to get up an eighty-foot trunk swaying in the trade wind? In some places women, in others men, did the heavy gardening, but whichever it was, the other sex might look after fishing, canoemaking, housebuilding and a dozen other activities necessary even in paradise. True, the climate made pointless extra labor for clothing, fuel and insulating construction. Certain foods did grow spontaneously. But there was much work, with the canoe and human back as sole carriers.

White observers erred about native laziness primarily because the native did his jobs in unfamiliar rhythms. He worked hard to finish a specific task, then laid off several days until the next job came round on the calendar. During those days he looked very lazy indeed. He also did what was necessary in the

early morning and the late afternoon and took his ease during
the heat of the day, which was sensible, but affronted the energetic white man bustling past his hut at high noon. The chief
was foreman of the community, depended on for initiative and
supervision, so the commoner lacked individualistic enterprise;
but when the big man spoke, the little man jumped and stayed
on the job until authority was satisfied. Accustomed to working in gangs, he was uncomfortable toiling alone and would
organize working parties to swap chores around, making a
social occasion of something that the observing white man
thought should be soberly endured. He was often inefficient,
due to the waste motion implicit in superstitions and *tabus,*
but he expended a very considerable number of foot-pounds
in the course of any given year on things other than dancing
and visiting. And sometimes he had the psychological drive of
the chief's example, for work was an honorific activity in many
islands, and chiefs could pride themselves on their skill in
canoebuilding as much as in arms. The final touch to the misconception was added by white contact with natives already
disorganized and discouraged by western influences. Says
Firth:

> "Most or all of the observers who had commented on the shift-
> lessness or incapacity for steady industry on the part of the
> Maori have seen him after he has come under the persistent
> influence of our European culture . . . the old native set of
> values had been replaced, the objects of economic interest
> were different, much of the old communal organization had
> been broken down, the authority of the chiefs and more par-
> ticularly of the priests had been lessened, the stringent rules
> of *tapu* had been lifted."—Raymond Firth, *Primitive Eco-
> nomics of the New Zealand Maori,* 183.[31]

Granted that the Maori, due to climate perhaps, were the
"workingest" of all Islanders, that criticism of white conclusions holds good to some degree everywhere.

In personal skills the Islander put most western men to

[31]*Tapu* is the Maori cognate of the more familiar *tabu;* the Hawaiian
cognate is *kapu.* For discussion of *tabu* in general, see pp. 80–81.

shame; he had to be as versatile as the American pioneer, because division of labor had hardly begun in his environment. There might be experts in some things, but the average commoner needed to be able to build a practical hut and canoe, have an uncanny knowledge of the ways of fish and birds, handle plants like a nurseryman, make and repair stone and wooden tools and weapons, all in the day's work. Thus he was far more at home in his world than we, who cannot make as well as drive an automobile, and can only call the serviceman, over the telephone, which we could not repair, when something goes wrong with the oil burner.

His techniques, however, were not always well-advised. Knowing little of fertilization and crop rotation, he usually stuck to "slash-and-burn" agriculture—clearing and burning a patch, exhausting it, then clearing and burning another. While the rich wood ash lasted, plants grew well. But fire destroyed humus, and the subsequent growth in the abandoned area was sometimes grass or low scrub that would let nothing else grow to reconstitute the soil in fallow. As Island populations increase, this can be a chronic headache for the white administrator. It appears that "civilized" man is not the only person who may wreck his environment by exploiting it.

The Islander's lack of clothes has been exaggerated almost as much as his laziness. In a climate far cooler than his northern cousins ever knew, the Maori bundled up in "flax"-kilts and cloaks which, though hardly stifling, kept off wind and rain quite well. Tahitian and Marquesan women wore sizable kilts of tapa and a sort of mantle over shoulders and breasts; if Polynesian topsides had not been usually somewhat covered, there would have been no point in the custom of respectfully stripping to the waist in presence of a chief. But there are no rules here. The Gilbertese girl wore only a short fringe on a string round the bulge of the hips. That was enough, for in many of the Gilberts it was death for a man to touch such a garment, even when the owner was not wearing it. And down in Melanesia the tendency to wear little became a tendency to wear just about nothing at all.

In some Black Islands either men or women went literally stark, or with only a narrow belt concealing nothing strategic. In deference to Mrs. Grundy it might be *tabu* to look at the genitals of the other sex, and both men and women were taught postures calculated to minimize exposure. In worse case were the New Hebridean women whose sword-shaped genitals-shielding leaf was hung from a waist belt and pulled through from the front but not attached in back, so the poor dears could never take a free stride for fear of their modesty coming adrift. In contrast Erromangan women wore ground-sweeping skirts on special occasions. But the Melanesian average was no more than a short, bulky, grass skirt for women; for men, limb, neck and perhaps nose ornaments, and a "pubic leaf" or penis-wrapper which, like the mediaeval codpiece, rather emphasized than concealed the location and dimensions of the chief end of man. This arrangement produced the standard Island joke among Frenchmen: that one pair of gloves would fully clothe ten New Caledonian warriors. The original idea, it is surmised, was to protect a sensitive organ from scratches as the owner pushed through saw-edged grass or thorny scrub. Its historical function was to scandalize missionaries. But it was no good for fund-raising propaganda, since it could not be described, still less illustrated, in literature to be distributed in Sunday Schools.

*   *   *

". . . the most delightful feature [of the hospitality of the natives of Raiatea (Societies) c. 1910] . . . was that it was due to no training, to no complex social ideas, but that it was the untutored and spontaneous outpouring of their hearts."
—Jack London, *The Cruise of the Snark*, 210

One function of a book like this is to correct misconceptions —as to laziness, nakedness or whatnot—with as good temper as possible. Island hospitality particularly needs such attention.

The romantic tradition is that the Islander, approached with good will, was a smiling cross between the Good Samaritan and the host of Liberty Hall. His treatment of guest-strangers is often made to sound almost weak-minded. Nothing could be worse misconceived. Far from being weak-minded, the brown Islander was hospitable to excess when it suited his book, but when it did not, he could be as standoffish as a fine lady or as dangerous as an ogre seeking babies for breakfast. No hypocrisy is implied. He probably felt hospitable on most occasions when he was acting so. A human being with good practical reasons for being generous or benevolent usually experiences the corresponding emotions. As for the Melanesian, he was seldom hospitable at all in any such sense as his cousins to north and east. Significantly, Melanesia had few beach-combers. The ship-jumping sailor, the runaway convict from Australia, and later the lotus-hungry romantic, usually avoided this area.[32] You didn't fool with the Black Islands. Their idea of a proper farewell for a ship's boat with which they had been trading was a sudden shower of arrows from the cover of the beach-fringing bush.

The milder Islander's motives for hospitality were several and, from his point of view, sound. To be discourteous or refuse a favor might lead to retaliation by black magic; the rudely-treated stranger might be endowed with nobody knew what supernatural powers. The Islander also felt that practically all human intercourse must somehow involve gift exchange—a matter to be elaborated presently. The main motive however was, paradoxically, the feeling that a stranger is by definition an enemy who may be rightfully plundered and killed. All this sounds very crass; but it does not mean that the patterns of Island hospitality were not pleasant for both host and guest. The psychology from which human institutions develop has about as much to do with the amenities of the eventual institution as the obscenities of birth have to do with the attractiveness of the beautiful young lady resulting twenty years later. Nobody but the obsessive or the cynic keeps Freud's

[32]Cf. Thomson, *The Fijians*, 234. The author of *Isles of Illusion*, an autobiographical work well worth reading for the clinical feel of Melanesia as well as for the author's neuroticism, is one of the few cases of a man's trying to eat lotus in the New Hebrides. He had little notion how to set about it.

theories of family life constantly in mind when going home to Christmas dinner.

To clarify the stranger-enemy theory: Island societies tended to be a succession of self-maintained equilibria *in vacuo.* A member of a tribe known to exist across the bay might be either a chronic enemy to be killed if caught straying or a tolerated partner in a long-standing economic give-and-take. Either way he had a recognized niche. But the unaccountable stranger— white explorer or missionary or native castaway drifted from another group—had no such niche and was assumed to be mysteriously dangerous. This is said to hold good among pre- literates in many parts of the world.[33] It certainly held good in the Pacific. Malinowski's Kula-voyagers knew that they faced death if they landed anywhere but at islands where they had established relations. Stevenson wrote of the Tuamotu in 1890:

> "Even to this day in certain outlying islands danger lingers; and the civilized Paumotuan dreads to land, and hesitates to accost his backward brother."—*In the South Seas,* 202.

The Fijian had a proverb about the necessity for killing people "with salt water in their eyes," meaning those come ashore from the high seas in distress. No amount of well-meant white- washing by sympathetic historians can conceal the fact that its implications were often carried out.

Death might not always result, however. The castaway could be stripped and enslaved. Or stripping and surveillance might be a temporary precaution lest newcomers prove treach- erous; on departure they were given back the same or equiva- lent equipment. A fast-thinking castaway might succeed in throwing himself on the mercy of a powerful chief or a mem- ber of his immediate family—much like Captain John Smith and Pocahantas. But all those were exceptions to a grim rule which, unpleasant as it sounds, made sense in the pre-white Pacific where long-range pleasure parties hardly existed. An

[33]Cf. Bronislaw Malinowski, *Argonauts of the Pacific,* 222, 345; Chapple and Coon, *Principles of Anthropology,* 343.

unexpected canoeload of outlanders pretty certainly portended raid or conquest. In any case such strangers came from an outlandish place with magic formulae alien and hostile to the visited tribe. Also it was known that the advent of strangers might mean sweeping epidemics and, to the Islander, sickness usually spelled sorcery, domestic or foreign. The Savage Islanders ascribed to the danger of epidemics their rigid practice of killing not only strangers, but even their own people who had been away from the home-island. Romilly found the same rationalization in the Solomons. Not that these explanations should be taken as gospel, for the reason the native gives to account for a custom is acknowledged frequently to be erroneous when the custom has outlived the situation that created it. The native often talks like the subject of posthypnotic suggestion who, asked why he performs the suggested act, gives a plausible but obviously false reason.[34]

Thus, for various reasons, the outsider approaching the serene, palm-shaded beach of a South Seas village was, other things being equal, in very hot water indeed. Even when able to protect himself and full of friendly intentions, he had to be constantly on guard against thievery—a matter that caused infinite trouble to white explorers.

Exceptions usually meant that things were not equal. The stranger or party of strangers might possess obviously formidable mana,[35] that is, be too dangerous to attack. They might offer economic advantages which would vanish if they were killed or driven away. When killing thus became impractical or ill-timed, the Islander was in a troublesome quandary. To obviate the necessity for precautionary murder he developed ingenious social dodges. For instance, he fused the stranger into the community (which considered itself a group or groups of interrelated people) by adopting him as blood brother and supplying him with ceremonial tokens of this adoption, such as food, shelter, women and ritual gifts. It was a clear case of

[34]Cf. Chapple and Coon, Principles of Anthropology, footnote, 357; Raymond Firth, Primitive Economics of the New Zealand Maori, 62.
[35]For explanation of mana, cf. p. 79.

kiss-him-or-kill-him. We retain vestiges of such feelings in vaguely hostile reactions toward "foreigners" in the lump, and in such customs as giving distinguished visitors "the keys of the city."

In Polynesia the process of disinfecting a stranger often required him to be singled out by a native of equal social standing who exchanged names with him. *Taio* (vaguely "friend") was the Tahitian word for this adoptive brother. Then, on a scale reflecting the presumed importance of the visitor, dances and games took place, feasts were prepared, women supplied. Alien Islanders acquainted with similar ideas at home understood what was going on and took it at its own value. The smiling faces, the presents of food and clothing, the nods and becks of pretty girls trotted up for selection, were just part of the initiation, like riding the goat. But the uninformed white intruder often missed the point, and wrote home that these people were miraculously generous and most appreciative of the charms of his seaworn person. The Islander also knew that such a reception might cloak later treachery, and kept his eyes open. The white would be self-righteously outraged when he woke to find a presumed tribal brother standing over him with a club. Cook called Tonga the Friendly Islands because of the particular cordiality of his welcome there; he died unaware that the hospitable Tongans had been prevented from highjacking his ships only by disagreement among the chiefs as to the best time and tactics.

For a practical illustration, take early white contacts with Tahiti. The English navigator, Samuel Wallis, brought the first whites and the first ship that Tahiti is known to have seen. While his ship's boats were sounding for an anchorage, the natives put out in canoes with tentatively hostile gestures that were brushed away. After the ship anchored within the reef, they attacked in force with showers of stones and spears answered, of course, with cannon- and musket-fire that quickly routed them. This was enough of a trial of strength. Obviously this formidable vessel and these outlandish people had marvelous possessions and tremendous *mana*, and would be better friends than enemies. The tone changed in a twinkling and the Englishmen were received ashore with a dramatic hospitality that made Tahiti a proverb. When Bougainville arrived in another Tahiti harbor a few months later, news of Wallis had spread so impressively that no hostilities were attempted. His apparently spontaneous reception produced memorable passages in his account of his voyage and memorable results in white thinking about the South Seas:[36]

> "All came crying tayo . . . The canoes were filled with women whose pleasing faces need concede nothing to the majority of Europeans and, for beauty of body, could rival any. Most of these nymphs were naked, for the men and old women with them removed the loincloths in which they usually wrapped themselves. At first they made from their canoes little teasing gestures . . . The men, simpler, or else freer, made matters clearer; they urged us each to choose a girl, follow her to shore, and their unequivocal gestures showed the fashion in which we were to make their acquaintance."—Voyage autour du monde, II, 29.

Other attitudes, however, appeared when the odds were different. The ship's cook sneaked ashore alone with a girl, only to have his clothes stripped off the moment he landed; the treatment he got was so terrifying that, though later turned loose with his girl to enjoy himself, he was too nervous to consummate his desires.

When the ship sailed the natives' farewell could be highly dramatic, with colossal weeping and gashing of head and bosom with shark's teeth—a demonstration of grief such as whites would hardly expect on the Day of Judgment. That too was flattering, except that Polynesians were, and still are, marvelously ready with tears and wailing. I have seen two-thirds of the native crowd down at the wharf for the departure of an interisland boat from Vavau (Tonga) bathed in sociable tears. The Islander—and no doubt it is good mental hygiene—values

[36]Cf. VI. Fayaway's Children. Where standard translations of French texts quoted were available in English, the writer uses them. Where they do not, he apologetically does his own translating.

emotion for its own sake and wallows in the opportunity for a good cry.

Historians as well as romantics maintain that white brutality usually started trouble between whites and Islanders. There is dismal truth here. Crews and skippers too were often callous scum, and in too many instances behaved in ways well calculated to provoke resistance followed by brief and bloody massacre.[37] But there is more to be said than that. Superstitions of which whites could not possibly know might enter the picture. For instance, a vessel calling early at the Bay of Islands in New Zealand got on well with the local Maori. They were fascinated by the skipper's watch, which they took to be a private demon. Just before sailing the skipper had the bad luck to drop the watch overboard, a fact of which the Maori were aware. When within a few weeks they were decimated by a savage epidemic, it was locally attributed to the presence of the ticking demon out there under the waters of the Bay. So, on the Island principle that revenge on any white was revenge on all whites, the crew of the next ship to call was massacred without provocation. Trying to account for the fact that the New Caledonians were polite to Cook, their first discoverer, but savage toward his successors, Leenhardt concluded that the natives thought Cook and his crew were their ancestral spirits visible in the flesh, belonging to the community. Cook stayed within the bailiwick of one village and got along well, but whites coming later tried to wander afield and were attacked to keep them from carrying the advantages of their divinity and great possessions to enemy villages.

Consider the complications of Island tabu[38] and reflect on the many probable occasions when, with all possible good will, some hapless sailorman violated local sensibilities and was killed for his ignorance. His mates would see no reason for not retaliating. Then add the principle of kiss-him-or-kill-him. Even so hearty a believer in the theory of the white man's guilt as Corney grants that the Tahitian attacks on Wallis were of

[37]Cf. IV, The Interlopers, for some unpleasant details.
[38]Again, see pp. 80–81 for discussion of tabu.

native initiative. J. C. Beaglehole adduces pages of evidence to prove whites invariably guilty, but he often achieves the contrary effect:

For instance when de Quiros reached the Polynesian island that he called Gente Hermosa,[39] the natives came out singing in numerous canoes, seized on a line over the bow of the ship's launch and tried to tow her ashore, even grappling for her anchor. They would not let go until they found that the cold bright sticks with which the whites threatened them cut their hands when grasped at. This sounds, not like hospitality as Beaglehole thinks, but like preparation for seizing and plundering strangers. When Tasman first touched New Zealand, Maori canoes rammed a boat that put off from the ship and clubbed several of her crew to death; there was no hint of provocation. Even Beaglehole admits that this looks bad. In this respect Melanesia and Micronesia seem both to have been worse than Polynesia. Says Romilly of the Melanesians: "They sometimes may attempt a stranger's life out of pure curiosity."[40]

Apologists stubbornly maintain that such apparently unprovoked attacks were in retaliation for previous white brutality—that because Navigator A massacred the people of Tarafu[41] in 1723, their great-grandchildren attacked Navigator B in 1784. This is plausible but inapplicable to any of the previous examples or to others at islands where, so far as is known, no white vessel had put in before. The apologist retorts that early Spanish ships must have landed there without getting back to report, which is sheer gratuitous assumption. Any reasonable jury acquainted with the kiss-or-kill theory of strangers would have to conclude that, when shooting started in the early days, at least a portion of whatever blame is pertinent might often attach to the innocent native. It might even conclude that blame is pointless. It is a miracle that more slaughter did not

[39]B. G. Corney (Tahiti, I, 222) thinks this was Swain's Island, off Samoa.
[40]Also cf. S. W. Reed, The Making of Modern New Guinea, 78.
[41]Tarafu is an imaginary island created for convenience in generalization. It seems to have a predominantly Polynesian flavor.

occur oftener when violent whites who wanted provisions and women and did not much care how they got them met natives who considered strangers fair game as far as safety permitted.

All this distresses westerners reared in the Christian tradition of hospitality for its own generous sake—a tradition not so well-honored among us as theory envisions, however. But the westerner can never know when his own taken-for-granted values shock the Islander:

For a small thing, white men's neglect to shave their armpits struck the Tahitian as disgusting. For a very large one, the western attitude toward distribution of goods struck him as appallingly inhumane. Within very wide limits, no matter how incompetent or sluggish he might be, a Polynesian never lacked minimum food and shelter so long as a relative of his, and that theoretically included the whole community, had a piece of taro and a roof. This was not communism, as early observers thought, but a wide application of the principle of mutual back-scratching among blood relatives. The Tongans were startled and amused when Mariner and his mates finally worked up courage to ask how they were supposed to eat when not specifically invited to partake:

> [The chief] "inquired how food was obtained in England; and when he heard that every man purchased the necessary supplies for himself and his family, and that his friends . . . only partook by invitation . . . he laughed at what he called the ill nature and selfishness of the white people; and told Mr. Mariner . . . that he had nothing to do when he felt himself hungry but to go into any house where eating was going forward, sit himself down without invitation, and partake with the company . . . After this, when any stranger came into their houses to eat with them, they would say jocosely 'No! we shall treat you after the manner of the Papalagis; go home and eat what you have got and we shall eat what we have got!' "—William Mariner, Tonga, I, 70–1.

The Samoan was aghast when, as the white man's charity was explained to him, it came out that whites permitted the existence of a class called "the poor." The situation of "the poor"

could not be made real to him because he could not conceive
of denying subsistence to any member of the community:

> " 'How is it?' he will always say. 'No food! Has he no friends?
> No house to live in! Where did he grow? Are there no houses
> belonging to his friends? Have the people there no love for
> each other?' "—George Turner, Nineteen Years in Polynesia,
> 264–5.

*   *   *

> . . . until one has dismissed from one's mind the notion of
> government such as Europeans conceived it, one must always
> misunderstand the South Seas. Memoirs of Arii Tamai, 7.

Note that these arrangements are always in terms of friends
or relatives, which is why adoption into the community was
necessary. Within any political unit Island sense of kinship was
practically limitless. That is the key to most island societies.
They were organized by ancestry, the given individual's pedi-
gree being his greatest social, political and economic asset,
roughly determining his place and arranging mutual support
between him and all his actual or presumed relatives. The result is best described as aristocratic collectivism. Private property existed in women (with qualifications), tools, housing,
food, sometimes in land and useful trees. But private rights
were always subject to overriding by the community, rather
like our willingness to see government confiscate anything
needed in war or disaster. In some degree the principal chief
and underchiefs were trustees holding all land for the tribe or
village; the chief's identification with community interests was
so complete that he often spoke of it all as "my land." So, to
the confusion of the early white, might anybody else in the
tribe. Society and the individual were so confounded that a
Maori recounting tribal history would say: "I captured such
and such a fort" in referring to an action fought ten generations before he was born.

Upper-class hegemony, exercised by the ablest man of the

highest ranking family strain,[42] by no means always the eldest
son of the deceased predecessor, sometimes gave way in
Micronesia to a council of heads of families. In Melanesia such
prerogatives varied from something like despotism to honorary
feebleness. Among Maori and Samoans the system was nothing like as dictatorial as among Tahitians, Marquesans and,
notably, Hawaiians. The former usually discussed problems in
councils of higher-ranking chiefs with decisions arrived at in
Quaker meeting style. Anybody who observed due deference
could speak; in the less dictatorial islands this applied even to
commoners. Then the top chief gave the community decision,
accurately stated and seldom questioned, much like a president
consulting his cabinet.

Though it may disappoint the liberal sentimentalist, there
was no such thing as a vote to determine popular sentiment.
But there is little reason to doubt that, since the great chief's
prestige would make most agree with him and since the chief
depended to some extent on his people's good opinion of his
judgment, majority sentiment, if it could have been ascertained, was probably reflected. The chief assigned community
work, saw that it was accomplished, handled relations with
neighboring peoples, often commanded in war, and was in
general father-foreman-pilot of the community. Even when,
if he proved incompetent, his administrative functions were
delegated to a highborn deputy, he might retain the magical
mana[43] that was the supernatural prop of the tribe and would
still lead ceremonies intended to foster it.

Social distinctions were often sharp to the point of brutality.
The slave was nobody. The expert (tohunga, kahuna or what
not in Polynesian) in tool-making, canoe- or housebuilding,
magic or tattooing, usually inherited his craft or knowledge
from wellborn forefathers and had high social standing. The

[42]In somewhat metaphysical terms, Maurice Leenhardt (Gens de la
grande terre, 149–51; 198–9) has a fascinating discussion of the way in
which Island societies were controlled by the emotions appropriate to
the family rather than to politics as we know them.

[43]Again for discussion of mana, see p. 79.

black magician rated below the beneficent physician and well below the priest, who might also be a high chief.[44]

In more tyrannical islands the chief could ride a very high horse indeed. Cook saw a Tongan commoner killed with one blow of a club for stepping too close to a great man. A Marquesan chief told Captain Fanning that any of his people who hindered the ship's watering-party were to be killed out of hand. The chief's sons had the run of nonnoble women, a right frequently exercised. Since letting consequent children live would pollute the lordly strain, they were usually killed at birth. When the captain of the "Aguila" found some Tahitians skulking in the chains obviously bent on pilfering, he asked the chiefs on board whether he or they should punish? Requested to do it himself, he had the offenders flogged, not severely in terms of the time, but no eighteenth-century naval flogging was a joke. Two lady chiefs protested that the punishment was too mild: one turned to kicking the culprits—remember her probable size and strength—and the other had to be restrained from attacking them with a club.

No matter how valiantly he fought in war, no Polynesian or Micronesian could rise from the ranks; he stayed in the niche into which he was born. In Hawaii he prostrated himself when a chief passed; in Fiji he cowered and tama-d, that is, uttered a special charm to show respect; in Tahiti he stripped to the waist. An early Fijian chief punished retainers who had broken a prized glass demijohn by making them eat the broken bits; this chief was a notoriously bad lot, but nobody questioned his right to enforce such an order. When H.M.S. "Havannah" demonstrated her big guns for "King" Cakobau of Fiji and he wearied of firing at a rock on shore, he suggested using as target a canoeload of his own people in the offing.

Even religion respected social rank. Hawaiian chiefs all belonged to a special religious lodge. The Maori cult of Io, a Supreme Being in whom students see analogies to the western God, was so well kept from the commonalty that it did not

[44]Some specialists could rate very low, however; e.g., barbers in Tonga. Cf. William Mariner, Tonga, II, 96.

even know Io existed. A chief outrageously abusive of power might be overthrown and killed, usually by a conspiracy headed by an ambitious understudy; or his people and their new head might merely go away to settle elsewhere. But that happened too seldom to check his power in the up-to-boiling-point stages. The most fantastic token of his prestige was the upper-class language, common in Polynesia, a special vocabulary to neglect which was deadly insult; it was most inadvisable to use the common word for canoe or tree in addressing a chief.

This socio-political structure—which worked about as well as a big farm operated by a strong-minded old father and his sons' families—was bolstered by mana and tabu, two Island institutions the Island names of which have become scientific terms for similar notions found around the world. Libraries have been written about them, so a brief description cannot be altogether accurate.[45]

Best quotes Williams' Maori Dictionary defining mana as: "authority, control, influence, prestige, power, psychic force, effectual, authoritative, having influence or power, to be effectual." That will do for a starter, but it underemphasizes the supernatural angle. Mana was "what it takes," with some aspects of the Latin virtus. It was an attribute accorded by the gods to man or tribe; it was the personal force, applied through spells, that enabled the wizard to blast a tree, smash a stone or kill a man at long range. With it came victory, health, wealth, and prestige. The chief had more of it than others, which is why he was chief. His ancestors had passed it on to him, sometimes by an actual ceremony, as when Elijah endowed Elisha with his cloak. This mana of the chief's, partaking of, but not necessarily coextensive with, that of the tribe, was what procured him obedience. Obviously it was a great cohesive force. Chief, tribe or wizard could lose mana by defeat in war or by anything else that led to loss of prestige, or indicated that the favor of the gods had receded or departed from his doings.

Violation of tabu was supposed always to be the primary

[45]An excellent and compact authoritative discussion is: Linton and Wingert, Art in the South Seas, 12–13.

cause of any *mana*-decreasing event. So here goes for *tabu*, and a thorny subject too: In a sense this was Island legislation—an array of don'ts, largely traditional, sometimes temporarily imposed, intended to keep the community on good terms with the supernatural and so running smoothly. The temporary type could make practical objective sense, as when a chief effected a closed season by *tabu* on overexploited fish or fruits. But the bulk of these restrictions, never written down, traditionally known to all, were valuable only because they fostered a sense of orderly relation with the universe. Such was the denial of pork to Hawaiian women; of canoes to Marquesan women; the *tabu* on touching the head of a Maori chief, or standing higher than an Hawaiian chief, or taking cooked food in a war canoe. Any ethnological text has hundreds of examples that, for all their social importance in their own context, are arbitrary to the point of whimsicality. Many were rationalized by reference to superstitions, but that probably occurred only when outsiders questioned things; left to himself, the *tabu* observer had little occasion or impulse to ask why.

For violations penalties were supposed to be automatic, illness or accident visiting the violator or a close relative or, in serious cases, the whole community. For breaking a *tabu* damaged *mana*, and *mana* alone kept people safe and prosperous. Crops would fail, storms wreck houses, enemies raid the village, if breach of *tabu* went unexpiated. The violator was a reeking source of ill fortune to all round him, so it is not strange that, if detected, he might be indignantly knocked on the head, which put a highly realistic sanction on observance. There was also the breaker's devout belief that the consequences would be illness or death, which often caused him to fall ill and die of sheer credulity. Most people knew most *tabus*, but there was always a chance of one hidden by the chief or wizard who imposed it, so the cautious Tongan daily performed *moemoe*, a magical act of blanket penance for unconscious offenses.

Anybody who went to Sunday School should be able to supply numerous Biblical parallels. Students trace some consistent patterns in the details, one built round a conviction that women pollute things, another, particularly in Polynesia, making *tabu* mean "holy" rather than "forbidden," hence "crucial" and "dangerous" to profane persons—consider the history of the Ark of the Covenant. Because he infected with *tabu*-ness whatever his foot was set on the Tahitian chief always went abroad on the shoulders of a retainer; "King George only rides on a horse," said Pomare II; "I ride on a man." In fact, the thing was rather like an electrical charge, most risky to come in contact with unless one were spiritually insulated.

Like a legal code, any set of *tabus* left gaps to our way of thinking. Tonga applied no sanctions to feud killings, nor to rape, unless the lady were married or greatly one's social superior. But then the Islander considered it strange that whites applied no rules to who eats what, when and with whom. Our food *tabus*, of which we have many, are merely matters of unenforced public sentiment often disguised as matters of institutionalized good taste. The soft-minded sometimes insist that all Island *tabus* worked out to the sanitary or social good of the community, a thing obviously absurd. What specific benefit came of making Marquesan girls swim when a canoe would have been handier? But now and again such a benefit occurred accidentally, as in the related case of Island sorcery:

Like others of his craft, the Island wizard planning to witch a man to death preferred to start with something intimately connected with him—hair, spittle, excrement, a finger-nail paring, or a bit of food he had nibbled. So the Islander was trained from childhood to keep such things away from others; he never knew when a wizard would want raw material to kill him with. He excreted either privately or where water would wash away traces; he burned or hid leftover food. Hawaiian chiefs had special retainers carrying spittoons into which their spittle was collected for safe disposition. The net effect was, aesthetically if ineffectively, close to what would have been done with wastes if they had understood modern sanitation.

Beyond such happy accidents, the use of Island magic lay in

peace of mind. Western man, having had some success in controlling his environment, goes on the theory that there is mechanical cause and effect in everything and that, if he knew still more along lines already plotted, he could eradicate disease and, in general, make the sun and moon stand still at command. The Islander, with much less scientific knowledge, confronted by illness, earthquakes, accidents, the hazards of war and agriculture, of business and love, was better at home in the universe if he considered all such things affected, and often controlled, by supernatural powers which a man who had enough mana could himself control.

Kahunas, expert in magic white or black, probably believed in their own powers themselves. They worked the weather and, if floods came, attributed them to counterspells cast by enemy wizards; wars might be fought for such reasons. They detected criminals by one or another ritual ordeal; the most picturesque was that of the New Caledonian sorcerer who would sit urinating drop by drop while running through the names of possible suspects—the name coinciding with the last drop was the guilty man's. That was only one way in which a wizard with a grudge could affect social measures, only one of the reasons why he was a power in the land. Usually hand and glove with the chief, he cast the community omens, thereby affecting policy. He advised when to plant and when to reap; he selected human sacrifices. Priesthood and wizardhood, often related, were usually family affairs, a given genealogical line passing requisite lore and mana on from the present expert to the bright boy in the next generation. Some islands even had schools of divinity and magic with specialized curricula. In New Zealand the equivalent of the aspirant's doctorate dissertation was to kill a man by remote control—sometimes a slave, sometimes a relative selected by the professor, sometimes the professor himself, if he were old and tired and particularly admired his pupil.

So the Land of the Doasyoulikes had rigid discipline, grim sanctions and high personal responsibility for misdoing. Whether this added up to law as we understand it is an issue for metaphysicians. There certainly were no notions of equality before the law. Penalties—or rather expiations—for *tabu* breaking varied according to the social standing and prosperity of the breaker. Customary Island procedures still baffle white judges. For instance, pigs paid over by a Samoan delinquent to his village are eaten joyously by the very chiefs who set the number to be paid. Early in the German period in Samoa, one of the three highest Samoan chiefs came to the governor complaining that native magistrates installed in his country were guilty of the audacity of fining *his* close relatives—that, he said bitterly, was not *fa'a Samoa*.

The Island chief was usually wealthy, or at least commanded valuable goods and services. He had several wives as a rule, partly because he needed numerous hands to increase his wealth by making *tapa* or fine mats, and partly to cultivate the lands reserved for him out of community holdings or held in his family line. He needed such resources because he was particularly obligated to generosity, since he was responsible for seeing that ceremonial feasts and gifts to friendly neighbors were impressive enough to uphold tribal *mana*. If worsted in ceremonial exchange of presents, the tribe could never hold up its head again. This takes us into gift exchange and so into Island economics.

*   *   *

". . . the spirit of Polynesian hospitality. Give and receive, receive and give, not for the material benefit, but for the sake of one's honor."—PETER H. BUCK, *Vikings of the Sunrise*, 195.

It is already clear that early observers erred in calling Island economics communistic in either a classic or a Marxist sense. In classic communism gift exchange would have been absurd since, where everybody has equal title to everything, a gift is meaningless. Yet gift exchange was as fundamental to Island life as breathing. Malinowski authoritatively emphasizes its importance:

"Whether we have to deal with the widespread fallacy of the primitive Golden Age characterized mainly by the absence of

any distinction between mine and thine; or whether we take
the more sophisticated view, which postulates stages of individual search for food, or of isolated household catering . . .
in none of these can we find even a hint of the real state of
affairs in the Trobriands; namely, that *the whole tribal life is
permeated by a constant give and take;* that every ceremony,
every legal and customary act is done to the accompaniment
of material gift and counter gift; that wealth, given and taken,
is one of the main instruments of social organization, of the
power of the chief, of the bonds of kinship, and of relationships in law."   —Argonauts of the Western Pacific, 167.

For the rest, take Keesing:

"By native custom, a person who is given a 'gift' is expected to
return in due course something of equivalent value to the
giver. Instead of using a bank, the native remembers his debits
and credits in terms of such reciprocal giving. Natives frequently pass over such 'gifts' to the newcomer in ceremonious
fashion, usually not asking for anything in return. It is from
this custom that the tradition has grown up of the 'generosity'
of the South Sea Islanders."—Native Peoples of the Pacific
World, 66.

The principle was so prevalent that, as Mariner noted with
astonishment, even periodical tribute to chiefs was considered
a gift. No tax officer saw that the amounts were proper; fear
of getting into the chief's bad books took care of that. The
Tongan house carpenter expert, working hard for somebody
else's comfort, got no pay as we think of it. Instead he and his
gang were well fed during the job and expected a substantial
mass of gifts when it was well advanced. If the amount were not
adequate to his dignity, he left the house unfinished and never
came back. Since all such experts had a trade-union-style traditional compact never to touch another man's work, the nig-
gardly client was left with two thirds of a house and worse, a
great loss of mana, until he could make his peace.

In New Ireland an adulterous lady traditionally receives a
specified sum of shell money—never mind the matter of Island

money for the moment—from the Tertium Quid and hands it to her husband. The adultery does not grieve him, but lack of the appropriate return money-gift would.

What to us is inter-community trade the Islands thought of as gift giving. Seacoast Maori had fish that inland Maori wanted, inland Maori had birds potted in grease that seacoast Maori wanted. So, at logical seasons, the Seacoasts made the Inlands a handsome present of fish and expected in return an equally handsome mess of birds. It was not barter at all. There was no bargaining, no specification of so many fish equal a bird —all was left to the sense of fitness on both sides. We ourselves retain bits of such a system on a personal basis. Mrs. Jones takes Mrs. Smith a pie out of today's baking, so Mrs. Smith feels in honor bound to reciprocate with a jar of strawberry jam when she puts up a batch.

The difficulty of intelligent dealing with unknown peoples is shown in the early white man's complaint that Islanders never said thanks, accepting invaluable bits of hoop iron without a word. As Harrisson points out, the Melanesian does not say thanks because no gift makes him feel thankful. On the contrary, to receive a valuable present reduces his prestige until he can return something of equal, or if possible, greater, value. All his holdings of hogs and ancient mats may not suffice. To refuse a gift dangerously insults the giver, to accept is to carry a nagging social debt until it is made good. So his feelings are rather like those of a man who has had the Queen of Spades slipped him in a game of Hearts.

Polynesia never developed much intertribal trade and had nothing resembling money. On Tikopia, a relatively untouched Polynesian island, Firth found the natives throwing away money given them by ship's crews as useless. But some Melanesian peoples were warm traders well on the way to money— that is, using prestige-bearing things as permanent media of exchange without primary regard to their practical uses. Here and there extratribal trade was important, as when a seaside tribe preferring to cook in fresh water would swap salt water for fresh with an inland tribe with opposite tastes; sometimes a people making pottery or shellwork would swap with another for pigs or sago.

But—here is the Island touch, though still recognizable among us—the prime motive of accumulating goods was not their usefulness, but the prestige attaching to great possessions. The Trobrianders had competitive displays of the year's yam crop; the fact that the crop was nourishing was secondary to its prestige-value. They never minded in the slightest when an oversupply rotted and had to be thrown away; in fact they used spells to cut down appetite so they would have more food to show off. Money, also accumulated for prestige, appeared as specially-worked shells, dogs' or human teeth, useless but potentially exchangeable against things in general. The mint might consist of a certain tribe that paid for imports by collecting and laboriously working certain shells into accepted shape. Magic spells, pigs for feasts, even white man's money when it appeared, all had fixed exchange value against such currencies.

The most famous and certainly the queerest Island currency is Micronesian—the great stone "money" discs of Yap, imported by immense effort from the Palaus to be propped up outside the village clubhouse in ostentatious display of wealth. Many of them are too big to be moved except by the joint efforts of many people. These could be treated like gold reserves. Once a particularly huge disc was lost overboard in transit and, though it was somewhere at the bottom of the sea, the village that had planned to import it still used it as an asset that could be pledged as security.

Again this sounds like parody, but worse follows. Some Melanesian peoples had arrangements that look like simple versions of instalment buying. Others, exploiting deferred payments, developed a trick remarkably like check-kiting. After studying the famous *Kula*-ring of ceremonious exchange, Malinowski concluded that, whereas the actual function of the process was a salutary swapping of useful goods, the participants had no idea of accomplishing any such thing. Their motive was the enhancement of prestige by periodically coming into possession of certain highly valued ornamental tokens that gradually worked round the circle of islands concerned.

Value set on the useless was as conspicuous in Melanesia as in New York. The Samoan reckoned wealth in fine mats, which at least could be worn, but Melanesia's valuable mats might be ragged, ancient things, hung in smoke for generations until they dripped soot. The New Hebridean knocked out the upper teeth of pigs so the lower-jaw tusks could grow painfully through the upper lip, recurving into successive circles as long as the unhappy animal lived—the more rings, the more prestige a tooth carried. Some cultivated specially valued breeds of hogs that produced frequent hermaphrodites. For, expanding the Polynesian idea that gift exchange was necessary to mana, the Melanesian based his whole system on ostentatious display and exchange. He had nothing of the miser, but much of the plutocrat, in him. He wanted heaps of taro, numbers of hogs, piles of well-sooted mats because, by giving feasts with them or presenting them to others, he demonstrated his success as a man. He sometimes believed that the quality of his quarters and women in the next world depended on his economic standing in this one—a notion worthy of the Mormons. He had no truck at all with The-rank-is-but-the-guinea's-stamp,-A-man's-a-man-for-a'-that—a point of view peculiar largely to western man in fairly recent times.

Ethnologists know even stranger examples of social climbing by display of wealth, but even this sounds unpleasantly like a Westchester country club in 1928. A propos, in some Melanesian societies, the men's clubhouse—where bachelors and often husbands slept and gossipped—evolved into a sort of Masonic lodge, in which higher ranks were obtained by gifts to superiors. Here wealth directly entered politics, for the lodge was congruent with the male population. Social standing among men did not exist outside it. It ran along with, rather than determined, rank by birth, which also existed. That is, those of lower birth did not have the same facilities as aristocrats for seeking higher rank by ostentatious giving, though if a commoner had a windfall, there might be exceptions.

I have often been struck by the confessed inability of experts to claim understanding of Island life. The higher you go, the farther away from the amateur, the enthusiast and the romanticist, the more doubt your man expresses as to his "understanding" natives. One with excellent ethnological training and fourteen years of sympathetic experience with one Island people told me that he did not yet have the hang of their attitudes and probably never would have. A brilliant native leader, asked how many whites understood his people, gave me two names, after some thought, one confidently of a dead man, one hesitantly of a man still alive.

For examples of what baffles experts, take the Island principle that a white man owes gifts to a native who has accepted his assistance. The skipper of an early *bêche-de-mer* ship in Fiji doctored a native whose hand had been blown off by the explosion of his own trade musket. Discharged as cured, the native claimed that the skipper owed him another musket in compensation for permitting treatment. Refused the musket, he burned the skipper's drying shed in revenge. The Maori used similarly to demand *utu* (compensation of an eye-for-an-eye nature but not necessarily punitive) from missionaries for taking medicines as prescribed. Dr. Lambert seems to have been quite brusque with a New Guinea native who, only a few years ago, demanded twenty-five sticks of trade tobacco for having let the doctor treat his injured hand. Somewhere in these mystifying goings on, which the plaintiff obviously thought perfectly just, is another queer ramification of gift exchange mingled with the revenge principle. But I doubt if any white man could ever trace the exact connection or if any native could ever convey them to him.[46]

Even the late Elsdon Best, who certainly knew more about the Maori than any other white, confessed himself unable to fathom the Maori custom of *muru*, which had vague counter-

---

[46]I am sure there is over-simplification in Roberts' explanation (*Population Problems of the Pacific*, 134): "for the custom with the sick was to let them slide, and if a stranger saved the life of a sick person, then it must be for some advantage to himself, argued the native."

parts elsewhere in the islands. To the outsider it looked this way: ". . . a man smitten by sudden calamity was politely plundered of all he possessed . . . the principle under which the wounded shark is torn to pieces by his fellows."[47] To the insider it was somehow a means whereby relatives of an aggrieved person or community exacted compensation for injury —utu again. In a clear case, a Maori man caught philandering would be swooped down on by his wife's relatives, stripped of all his movable property, food included, perhaps have his house burned. The motivation of getting their relative's own back is here fairly plain, though of course those food supplies and that house were also needed by the lady thus avenged.

But the plundered transgressor would also have felt offended if there had been no muru raid—it signified that he was important enough in the community to have his misconduct worth taking notice of. From here on things get complicated. A man incapacitated by a serious accident would be muru-d because his carelessness had deprived the community of his services. The relatives of a dead man might be muru-d because they had no business letting a useful member of the community die. During a fire the neighbors flocked round and rescued valuables, not for the owner, but to confiscate them in muru for allowing this threat to common safety: ". . . in many cases," says Best helplessly, "one cannot possibly apply the term evildoer to the sufferer."[48] Yet to the Maori it was unquestionably quite fair. The best one can say for this overextension of a highly social principle is that it kept anybody from gathering great stores of the things that made up Maori wealth. A conspicuously prosperous man would be frequently muru-d on such slim pretexts as that he was remotely related to somebody miles away who had broken a leg last week.

After all, it was in New Zealand that Samuel Butler got the hint for Erewhon, the place where criminals were considered invalids and invalids were considered criminals.

[47]William P. Reeves, New Zealand, 62.
[48]Best, The Maori, I, 360.

"... the ancient society of Tahiti had plenty of vices, and was a sort of Paris in its refinements of wickedness; but these had not prevented the islanders from leading as happy lives as had ever been known among men."—*Memoirs of Arii Tamai,* 137–8.

Even the Islander's erotic life, his best-known and presumably simplest aspect, is not easy to explore. The details will not shock us as they did our grandfathers. They are not necessarily as charming as romance has made them, but it is important to make it clear that these people were neither high-minded free lovers nor rabbits. Much significance which probably was not there at all has been read into this aspect of Island behavior. The Islander was nowhere promiscuous. No known society ever was completely so.[49] All Island peoples somehow or other recognized that adultery injures the spouse, whether importantly or not, and sternly prohibited intercourse with some categories of actual or presumed relatives. Though most generously permitted premarital affairs, these too were subject to *tabus* based somehow on incest. The early white observer, unaware of such complications and given wide privileges himself, made unholy errors in describing what he thought he saw. Firth's description of the Polynesians of Tikopia is clarifying:

"Though sex intercourse between young people is common, . . . morals are not easy—a differentiation which many white people who have acquaintance with natives do not perceive. Proposals are frequent, but by no means all are accepted. There is a great deal of personal choice exercised, and as a result a considerable amount of unrequited desire, which finds expression in anger and recrimination, or a more purposeful outlet in slanderous songs, or even in suicide. The crudity and violence of passion in this little community gives the lie to the popular notion of the idyllic love life of the unsophisticated savage."
—*We the Tikopia,* 513.

Take that with you the next time you go to a South Seas movie.

Virginity was obviously rare. Many Island peoples consid-

[49]Cf. Bronislaw Malinowski, "Culture," *Encyclopaedia of Social Sciences.*

ered sexual intercourse necessary to a girl's physical development. In the outer Tuamotu, it appears, a shy girl may still be
raped into compliance for her own good by a group of boys,
which puts a semimoral aspect on the thing. And there was
much of the attitude of which Don Luis de Barreda wrote to
the Duchess of Medinia Sidonia: "[The Tahitians] think
meanly of being virgins and resent being twitted with it."[50]

Yet sometimes virginity was highly important. The Samoan
taupo—sacerdotal virgin of the village, delegated to perform
social honors for her people—was obliged to remain intact
until her marriage, which usually carried political import. Her
steadfastness was proved in public defloration performed sometimes by hand, sometimes with a stick; the blood-spotted tapa
bearing proof of trauma was shown around or flown as a flag
over the village, presumably in token that that was some record
for that vicinity. The Maori had a somewhat less striking version of the taupo. In Tikopia young chiefs demanded virginity
of the girls they chose. If such a highborn Don Juan found that
he had been forestalled, he might order the girl to start swimming and never come back, and she meekly obeyed. His de-
flowering of a virgin was matter for boasting—he wore a
smudge of the resulting blood on his forehead next morning
in token of triumph. There were even unpleasant shadows of
the notion that virginity was a marketable commodity, and it
took little contact with whites to set Tongan mothers bringing
virgin daughters on board white ships to trade for first honors.
The price was a broad-ax at first; competition soon brought it
down to an old razor, a pair of scissors or a large nail.

Nobody has yet satisfactorily accounted for the apparent fact
that pregnancies seldom resulted from Island young folks'
carnalities. The Islands' impression is that, if a girl does not
favor the same boy too consistently but spreads her affections
round sociably, risk of pregnancy is low; Dr. Mcad's Samoans
took pregnancy as proof that the girl had been too constant.
For lack of better, Malinowski and Pitt-Rivers take this theory

[50] B. G. Corney, *Tahiti*, II, 471.

seriously. But Firth found that Tikopian young people practice *coitus interruptus* to avoid premarital pregnancy, though
feeling obligated to neglect it after marriage. Pregnancy was
the signal for marriage, as in many Island societies; the girl
usually wanted marriage, the boy did not, so intercourse might
become a contest of seductive strength. Thus in a manner of
speaking the Islands institutionalized the shotgun wedding.

In these contexts, however, "marriage" is a misleading term.
In Micronesia rules were stiffer than elsewhere, female adultery
justifying the husband in killing the culprit, and premarital
promiscuity being frowned on. But in Melanesia and Polynesia
there was little tendency to regard married fidelity as a theoretical good for most members of the community.[51] Presumably marriage ended the period of premarital "experiment,"
to use the white theorist's owlish term—Judge Ben B.
Lindsay might have invented this system. After marriage—
usually a sort of common-law consent celebrated by both families with prestige-enhancing gift exchange—there was nothing
to prevent an uxorious Islander from confining his attentions
to his wife or wives. In many cases female jealousy might
achieve that result, as the philandering husband gradually
found a quiet life worth self-control. But divorce was usually
very easy indeed, a mere mutual agreement to terminate the
relationship.[52] And, low as observance of the Seventh Com-
mandment may be among whites, it was probably lower still in
the Isles of the Blest. With utter realism Melanesian women
in Dobu recommended keeping one's husband venereally exhausted in precaution against temptations to stray.

Double standards crop up in the Islands: Wife-lending was
a common politeness toward guests even in monogynous societies, but the line between that and the wife's pleasing herself
was definite. An Islander might prostitute his wife for trade

[51]The Maori may have been something of an exception. Cf. Raymond
Firth, *Primitive Economics of the New Zealand Maori*, 106.

[52]Tonga, Mariner insists, was noted for intra-marital devotion and,
though divorce was simple, in his time two-thirds of married women
were faithful. He considers this in sharp contrast with such gayer islands
as Hawaii and Tahiti.—*Tonga*, II, 170.

goods, but she was seldom permitted to enter business on her own initiative. Said Moerenhout of the Tahitians of his day:

"What [husbands] required was that their wives should not spontaneously dispose of themselves of their own accord."
—Voyage aux iles, II, 64.

In Hawaii and Tahiti, a man wanting to sleep with another man's wife had to ask leave of her husband, but refusal was considered mean or even insulting. The discarded wife of a Samoan chief could not remarry, for that injured her former spouse's dignity, so she usually attached herself to the village guesthouse for the accommodation of visitors.

There were other checks to infidelity, besides a jealous wife's taking a stick to an erring husband or an outraged husband's beating an erring wife into unconsciousness or death—in which matters the community took no formal interest. In Dobu an injured husband might climb a coco palm and throw himself down as a suicide; that solved his problems and obligated his relatives to take physical or economic revenge on his wife's relatives. A Polynesian commoner caught in flagrante delictu with an aristocratic lady was probably a gone goose, not on moral grounds but because he might pollute the lofty strain with commoner blood.

Here is an old human problem. No set of rules about who-sleeps-with-whom can ever match the vagaries of human desire; so explicit or implicit double standards, breaches of accepted custom, emotionally damaging strains and most unpleasant feelings inevitably result. The Islands had not solved the sex problem; in some ways they had complicated it even more clumsily than western man.

The Micronesian men's clubhouse, for instance, usually contained unmarried girls bought or kidnapped from neighboring villages to solace bachelors and, if required, married men. Thus to use a girl from one's own village was shameful, but no onus attached to playing such a role away from home. When Hawaiian women were slow to conceive, they joined in erotic dance-games got up to fertilize the barren—only married people took part, say apologists, as if that helped from the western point of view. As chance in the game developed the appropriate mood in any pair, whether spouses or not, they went into the darkness to settle matters. Hawaii was specially imaginative in the matter of incest *tabus*, which were relaxed for high chiefs—brothers married sisters, and sons inherited their fathers' wives. The Hawaiian *punalua*, a relationship giving a husband presumptive rights over all his wife's sisters and she-cousins, with converse rights for the other sex, was made famous by Morgan, the early anthropologist, who considered it a definite stage in progress toward monogamy. Traces of a similar institution appear elsewhere. For some obscure biological reason the Marquesas had more men than women, so polyandry made practical sense; but the Marquesans rationalized it as necessary because Husband One was usually a chief and barred from work, Two was of high enough birth to make work shameful,[53] and, without Three and Four, who would support the household?

And, as previously indicated, rape was not serious in the Islands. It automatically followed capture in war. Even mission influence could not alter this attitude. As recently as the 'eighties the native-made but mission-bolstered legal code of Raiatea (Societies) carried the following scale of fines: murder $155; smuggling liquor $50; rape $10.

It is risky to say that the Islands could not take erotics as seriously as whites. In apparent contradiction, much of their speech, ceremonial life, and amusements centered almost obsessively around sex. Intercourse and all associated with it were either juicy jokes or lustily engrossing games, as in the talk of barracks, lumber camp and forecastle. Many a stately-sounding Maori place-name would be unprintable in translation—even more so than the French *voyageurs'* surviving designation for the Grand Teton mountains in Wyoming. The Hawaiians gave pet names to all parts of the body of the well born, genitals included—one queen's were called "the frisky one."

[53]This is one of the numerous exceptions to the previous statement that work could be honorific for chiefs.

But there is significance in Fortune's grave explanation of the Dobuan custom of barring adolescent boys from their parents' house to prevent possible incest with their sisters, which enabled them to have premarital affairs with girls outside the houses:

"There is not necessarily love in it as we understand love. The youths sleep with the girls in the first place because it is the custom to deny them houseroom at home."—*Sorcerers of Dobu*, 29.

That is the strangest reason for carnality adduced since the lady in *Sylvia Scarlett* went bad because she was afraid to sleep alone. Many an escape-seeking white man in the Islands has been forced pathetically to record his reluctant discovery that, jolly a bedfellow as she was, his little brown girl never quite got the idea of how he felt about her and wanted her to feel about him.[54] Only that still-to-be-born science, a supracultural psychiatry, can determine whether this love without overtones is emotionally superior or inferior to our hard-breathing sort of thing.

In any case, Tahiti put on the capsheaf. The data are slim and masked by either missionary squeamishness or apologetic omissions; but what the old accounts boil down to is fascinating and disquieting: The Arioi of Tahiti were a religious lodge dedicated to travel from village to village to sing, dance and encourage orgies; an itinerant brothel de luxe with aesthetic and religious overtones. Members renounced parenthood, being sworn to kill all children born as a moral duty.[55] They toiled not, neither did they spin, and membership was a high honor. The highest born of both sexes were admitted. Neophytes went through elaborate novitiates and were tattooed by stages betokening the attaining of successively higher

[54]Cf. Alec Waugh, *Hot Countries*, 139–40 for a comically backhanded statement of this difficulty.
[55]Apologists maintain that abortion and infanticide were necessary because pregnancy and care of children interfered with the lady Arioi's duties as entertainer—in both senses. Cf. Peter H. Buck, *Vikings of the Sunrise*, 85.

grades. The assertiveness and prestige of this highly organized cult and the flagrant antisocialness of its principles are tough nuts for the functional anthropologist to crack.

Privacy in intercourse, though mildly valued, was not easy when the whole household—husband, wife or wives, children, other people's children, aunts, uncles, cousins and visiting relatives—slept in a single-roomed hut, often with a night light to keep off evil spirits. But these things are different among a people all of whose lives are lived with little more privacy than in an army barracks. When Bougainville's men got ashore in Tahiti, each household offered a girl; if the white stranger evinced willingness, the hut immediately filled with sightseers eager to observe the newcomer's technique. The narrator of the voyage was not at all sure that the boys refused to fall in with local expectation of open covenants openly arrived at. Cook's men found curious a Tahitian performance for their pleasure:

> "A young man, near six feet high, performed the rites of Venus with a little girl about eleven or twelve years of age before several of our people, and a great number of the natives, without the least sense of its being improper or indecent, but as appeared, in perfect conformity with the custom of the place. Among the spectators were several women of superior rank, particularly Oberea, who may be said to have assisted at the ceremony, for they gave instructions to the girl how to perform her part, which, young as she was, she did not seem to stand much in need of." —Three Voyages, I, 56.

Many western men would attend such a show, but few would expect great ladies to take such interest in front of their guests.[56]

The mixture of venery with gift exchange naturally confused the white sailor. The ghosted account of Cook's second voyage tried to qualify the white's first impression of Polynesian round-heeledness, only to make still more errors. Tahitian society, it concluded, exhibited a bottom class of prostitutes,

[56]This may well have been an Arioi show. Cf. J. A. Moerenhout, Voyage aux iles du grand océan, II, 131.

but also higher classes of women who were approachable depending on rank and whether they were unmarried. Actually, the Islands had no prostitution proper when the whites arrived. Their set of values could not spawn that dingy institution. True, the commoner-girl who favored Jack ashore from the "Dolphin" or "Endeavour" expected something nice—perhaps a piece of red cloth or a comb[57]—not as payment, but as a gift expressing his share of the relation. True also, she was more easily swayed in favor of a sailor who let her know in advance that something so valuable was what he had in mind. But her motives for obliging him would be inquisitiveness about white men, a feeling that to accommodate one would increase her prestige and, principally, social duty.

Under white influence the Islands did develop genuine prostitution and it was not pretty. But these girls were not making a living by fixing up sailors or anybody else and, as Cook noted, were not socially outcast for so doing. Even in those parts of Melanesia where erotic morality was pretty stiff and social onus attached to what looked like prostitution, it was in a fashion alien to our ideas. In some parts of the Solomons compulsory prostitution was the penalty for a woman's breaking exogamy tabus, the chief sharing her earnings; but as soon as she accumulated enough valuable goods to become a good match she was married off, the entire community, including her new husband, being obligated by custom never to refer to her unfortunate past. That sounds either most humane, or like a happy realism determining that, since the lady's transgression put her outside the pale of propriety, the chief and she might as well make a good thing of it.

Another point that Cook missed was the social distinction in this department of guest-cherishing. His writing that "the fa-

[57]In this respect the Trobrianders' attitude, says Malinowski, . . . "implies that sexual intercourse, even where there is mutual attachment, is a service rendered by the female to the male. As such it has to be repaid in accordance with the rule of . . . give and take which pervades tribal life, . . . Above all, it would be erroneous to draw any parallel with forms of prostitution in higher cultures."—*Sexual Life of Savages*, 319; 321.

vours of . . . women of the better sort are as difficult to be obtained here as in any country whatsoever"[58] is misleading. At her husband's or father's request many an Island chieftainess threw herself at an explorer-captain with an ardor that astounded him at the time and would certainly not have been imitated by a royal duchess at home. A Tahitian chieftainess proved willing to accommodate one of Cook's officers in consideration of the sheets off his bunk. For, in the Islands, ship's officers were great chiefs entitled to women of equivalent rank; whereas the high-class lady, aware that she was reserved for her peers, had nothing to do with foremast hands or even petty officers. Thus what happened could look like lower-class prostitution without actually being any such thing. The ugliest aspect of prostitution—a woman flouting a principal moral tenet of her culture for economic gain—was not present at all.

The social position of Island women has already been suggested while other matters were discussed. It was generally lower than that of men, but with significant inconsistencies. In Polynesia the most highly born might share rule with the highest chiefs. In Samoa, for instance, the first high chief known to have temporarily combined all the necessary "names" for nominal hegemony over the group was a woman. Women of lower ranks had important and arduous work, though a less active voice in affairs. But sanctions and restrictions were the rule. Missionaries united in bewailing the degrading, beast-of-burden status of Melanesian women, and with good cause. The wives of a dead Fijian chief were in honor bound to let themselves be strangled to accompany him to the other world.[59] If rescued by missionary pleading, or more often by a ransom in trade goods, they bitterly upbraided their rescuers. Though Polynesians were often slack about

[58]*Three Voyages* I, 421.
[59]Thomas Williams (*Fiji and the Fijians*, 165–8) has a long description of a Fijian wife-strangling that, in spite of his prejudices, gives an immediate feeling of the real emotional values of the situation. In some of the New Hebrides, e.g. Aneityum, women were similarly strangled as escorts for a dead child who had been specially loved. (George Turner, *Nineteen Years in Polynesia*, 372.)

THE INGREDIENTS 99

exercising the right to kill an unfaithful wife, Micronesians and Fijians were not. One such chief, having killed his wife for unspecified reasons, was assailed by a missionary with graphic descriptions of the tortures of hell:

> "After a pause, he inquired: 'Is my wife in hell?' I feared she was. He seemed gratified ..."—Thomas Williams, *Fiji and the Fijians*, 504.

Williams also tells of a runaway wife, seeking shelter in a near-by village and pursued by her husband's emissary bearing a whale's tooth, the ceremonious gift necessary for opening negotiations about sending her back for discipline. The inhabitants of the village of refuge, reflecting that she would probably be killed on reaching home, thriftily decided to kill and eat her themselves.

It is difficult not to overstate such matters in either direction. Even harsh Melanesia showed loopholes and exceptions, where rules against philandering were often honored in the breech, even as among us. Frigidity was probably less frequent in these women than with us. Malinowski found the Trobriand women great devotees of Priapus and contemptuous of white men's techniques. The Island woman could break loose on great occasions, when a plethora of food and drumming and dancing gave the signal. Then, jiggling in rhythm with the whole overstimulated community, she could watch her chance and dive into the bush with the nearest man she had her eye on. This was risky but very often done. However—and this emphasizes the great hold of convention on these people in particular—even in erotic frenzy her impromptu partner could not come from one of the social divisions to which she was sexually *tabu*.

According to her lights she was a good mother, carefully observing prenatal and postnatal *tabus*, nursing her child long, seeing that it was properly fed into the smooth machine of village life.[60] In some islands, such as Fiji, the *tabu* system gave

[60]Margaret Mead, *Coming of Age in Samoa*, is the classic on Polynesian child-rearing, possibly somewhat prettified.

her an admirably eugenic three years between pregnancies, her husband solacing himself with unmarried girls or other people's wives. She had at command various devices for terminating unwanted pregnancies, some mechanical and probably dangerous, some concocted from old wives' herbs, the effectiveness of which is disputed.[61] Both parents would be very fond of children as such. Playing with toddlers was an adult Islander's idea of the world's finest pastime, and fathers readily took over child watching when necessary. The gift of one's child to another was joyfully received, or even asked for before birth. Violent tempers sometimes endangered the child's limbs or life but, from our point of view, the Islanders generally spoiled their children, and very good it probably was for their small psyches—if, that is, they survived to be reared. For infanticide was general, taken as much for granted as a western couple's right to contraception.

Child killing certainly helped to keep down population on islands with limited resources. Island women occasionally told missionaries that they disposed of newborn babies to save the trouble of rearing them or because suckling spoiled the breasts. Whatever the reason they could have been more humane about it, for burying alive was common. In some islands children could be killed only the first day; elsewhere, notably on Hawaii, parents could do so with impunity at any age. As an additional population check, infant mortality was undoubtedly very high, sanitary conditions being what they were. The Maori, for instance, isolated a parturient woman in a flimsily constructed shack, with perhaps only a few branches set up as windbreak, where she gave birth on the ground, no matter what the weather, and then stayed there with the baby for three days.

It is again plain, as in their treatment of animals, that Islanders had small sense of suffering in themselves or others. Their cripples were objects of ridicule or contempt, even of

[61]Cf. R. F. Fortune, Sorcerers of Dobu, 239–40; S. M. Lambert, A Yankee Doctor in Paradise, 47.

blame for not being "good" men, else calamity would not have overtaken them. Useless old people might be killed by their own families and duly wailed over afterward. Williams swore that the Tahitians used to throw old people into pits and let them starve or suffocate. It was better all round when the old gentleman would decide his time had come and, by some miracle of mind over matter, die on schedule of no assignable cause. If he failed to bring it off, his family might smother or bury him alive out of a feeling that it was unbecoming to live on after determining to die. Such things set western teeth on edge, but our intelligence can never be sure that we are justified in our elaborate efforts to keep the old alive as long as possible, instead of deciding for them whether their lives are worth living. Here the Islander, connoisseur of the more obvious advantages of living, may have been as sensible as he was callous.

In any case, the Island physician could have done little for the old. Island medicine had no geriatrics. The physician was primarily a wizard, bound to the principle that malevolent magic sometimes involving spirits caused all serious ailments and nonviolent deaths. His patient was equally convinced. He was something of a surgeon with a sharp-edged flake of obsidian, a shark's tooth or a razor-edged splint of bamboo, and he was an adept, if often damagingly violent, masseur. But his mana exercised in counter-spells was his mainstay and his cures were numerous. How much that means is for the science of psychosomatics to determine. His reliance on specifics, mostly vegetable, and his neglect of asepsis put him about on a par with most western physicians before the germ theory of disease. He had at least one idea that laymen will applaud: when putting his patient on a diet, he had to observe it himself if it was to be effective. But he was in no sense a scientist and had no faculty of research. Some modern physicians profess to be impressed by the Island doctor, but it is difficult not to suspect them of overgenerosity toward picturesque colleagues. Plenty of things in Island life are admirable—beauty of setting, comradely effort, love of children, high skills, splen-

did dignity, beautiful manners. But why let admiration slop
over into the fatuous?

*   *   *

On the whole, in that category of human endeavor called
"the arts and sciences," the Island world was spotty but respectable. Its talent for engineering and its lovely, patient
miracles of handicraft have been touched upon. Its instrumental music was stirring but limited, confined largely to per-
cussion with feeble aid from such things as three-stopped
nose-flutes, wooden jew's-harps, a one-stringed fiddle with the
open mouth of the player for sounding box, perhaps rude
Pan's pipes. Its singing was magnificent. Its dancing, if often
indecorous, was also stunning. When the Maori got to pounding the earth with their great horny feet in the *haka* (war
dance), the ground shook and people miles away could hear
the beat of foot and voice defying the foe. When Fijians
staged a great *meke* (dancing festival), the precision of their
synchronization and the happy aptness of their symbols impressed even salt-rimed sea captains as superlatively fine. Some
islands had a sort of theatre, with comic pieces about the
guests, and legends acted out in song and pantomime. We
shall never know just what they were like until the ghost of
James Cook comes back to tell us.

To judge from his language, the Polynesian at least had fair
literary equipment. He lacked abstract words but knew a wide
variety of expressions for subtle aspects of natural objects: one
term for "the color of the underside of a wave as it approaches
the beach"; another for "the moment when the moon rises
before the sun has set." Obviously this was a great vehicle for
poetry and much was written, or rather composed and handed
down via the miraculous Island memory. Missionaries, and
then ethnologists, recorded many poems. Those qualified to
study them in the original claim high merits for them. But it
is a grave question whether most special students of Polynesian
are competent judges of literary values. As literature their
translations, on an average, though no doubt faithful to sense,

are dismally dull, relieved only by occasional obscenity, and cast doubt on the translators' skill in letters. The same holds good of prose legends. Even Sir George Grey's classic collection of Maori myths is no great pleasure to read, scholar though the translator was. Padraic Colum, who made a long and earnest effort to get some quality into Hawaiian myths, finally concluded that these "long and monotonous stories told in the old days"[62] must have derived their value as entertainment, not from intrinsic values, but from the extravagant skill in gesture and intonation of the native story-teller. And the average little book of South Sea legends is either kittenishly handled by its maiden-lady author, or as bald and confused as the Indian legends that infuriated Mark Twain in Life on the Mississippi. Here is a sample from a New Zealand source:

> "According to tradition, the name Tikitere is derived from a particularly sad, yet romantic episode in the history of a 'hapu' or sub-tribe of the Arawa people who lived in this district. A lovely maiden of high rank named Huritini was given by her people to be one of the many wives of a renowned warrior, also of rangatira rank, as a reward for his great efforts in battle against neighbouring tribes. Huritini conceived the idea that Rangiteaorere, her chieftain husband, was treating her with contempt and failing to pay due honour to her rank. In Maori eyes this was an insult and a reproach to her people as well as to herself, and one night she put an end to her unhappiness by jumping into one of the boiling pools, now called Huritini in her memory. When her act was discovered it was exclaimed 'Taku tiki e tere nei.' Literally translated, 'Alas, our beloved tiki (first daughter) has floated away forever.' Thus through the passage of time the commemoration of this sad incident has clung to the locality, but has been abbreviated to 'Tiki-tere.' "

Nevertheless Stevenson, a master of language who had a reasonable acquaintance with one Polynesian tongue, thought highly of Samoan poetry and legendary material. The outsider can only take the beauties of Island literature on the word of ex-

[62]Padraic Colum, At the Gateways of the Day, xix.

perts and regard with a very bilious eye the white enthusiast who, without knowing any Island idiom well, yet tries to tell him how marvelous the old chants and narratives were.[63]

There can be no skepticism about the fact that, when it was worth their while, most of these people could be great virtuosos in dignity and courtesy. Generations ago Dana's stranded Hawaiians on San Pedro beach were "the most interesting, intelligent and kindhearted people I ever fell in with."[64] Of Polynesians the Earl of Pembroke, himself attested a great gentleman by the College of Heralds, said "nearly every one from the highest to the lowest is a gentleman or a lady."[65] The great Dr. Johnson swore that, when the pair had a light behind them, he could not distinguish Omai, the Tahitian commoner whom Lieutenant Furneaux brought home with him, from a peer of the realm—which, considering what a snob the Great Cham was, is most impressive. The people these men spoke of are long since dead, but their descendants show the same qualities to a convincing degree.

But the Islands were not the Land of the Doasyoulikes. That misconception arose because the Island peoples did so

[63]If samples of poetry-translation are needed, here are two from authentic early sources:

Above is Te-ao-uri,
Below is Te-ao-tea,
All encompassed by the birds
As they look toward the east!
Grandson of Piho (splash and
    shout) of the seaweed girdle,
Gird on thy girdle of seaweed,
Porapora of the silent paddle,
Paddling is thy diversion.
Teuira Henry, *Ancient Tahiti*,
123.

A dwelling remote is the island
Tiapa,
A land whence appears well Maupiti,
Unequalled among thousands of
    lands.
Easy is the access to Tuanai;
Elevated is the rock Tauraurau,
The eating place of Ouboure;
Where the point of land meets
    the coral reef.
Cease to weep, great Ipo,
Here is beautiful Maupiti,
O the waters of Atimo,
Ane also at Maupiti.
William Ellis, *Polynesian Researches*, I, 202.

[64]R. H. Dana, *Two Years before the Mast*, 137.
[65]Earl of Pembroke, *South Sea Bubbles*, 281.

many things that western culture prohibited. Another crucial misunderstanding needs clearing up: The Islands had no tradition of social criticism, no scope for the impulse to shatter the world and remold it nearer to the heart's desire. All, like Fortune's Dobuan, took "all established custom as the order according to which the universe was created."[66] It sounds, and was, stagnant compared to our tradition of challenging, tinkering with, mistrusting and yet relying on, the established order. But there were compensations in lack of emotional wear and tear. The Islander had few agonies of decision. It was practically never necessary for him to consider, "Does doing this now and in this manner make as much sense as perhaps doing it differently at another time, or perhaps not doing it at all, or doing something else that gets at the same end differently? And am I sure that I desire that end anyway?" That is probably the crucial difference between the white man and the pre-white Islander. No wonder the damage was immense when the white man appeared offering astounding new choices.

And the Islander had other advantages. The man who fitted into his small niche in his small world possessed great security. He would never go hungry. If the chief's son raped his wife, or tabud his pigs for his own lordly use, it was at worst a temporary annoyance, sometimes a kind of honor. He was deathly afraid of the dark, of ghosts, of wizards, instead of the poorhouse, but they were probably little on his mind by daylight. The chances of his being killed in battle or drowned in an upset off the reef or taken by a shark were not high enough for a healthy man living outdoors to brood over. His all-important prestige did not obsess him in most of the Islands, though, if he had an emotional weak spot, that was certainly it. And though his life sounds dull to us, it was not so for him.

Nobody had ever infected him with the idea that life could be dull, or anything else than just living as other people lived. Besides, he had an enviable ability to take things big on occasion. When he feasted, he gorged for days. When he went on a tear, such as in observances of the death of an Hawaiian

[66] R. F. Fortune, *Sorcerers of Dobu*, 15.

high chief, he combined Saturnalia with the sack of a mediaeval city. When he felt sad he sluiced tears while the feeling
lasted, and then pretty well forgot about it. When he cursed,
he instructed the object of his ire to perform a variety of *tabu*
infringements specially connected with sacrilege and the canni-
balizing of relatives: a sample from Tonga:

> "Dig up your grandfather by moonlight and make soup of his
> bones; bake his skin to cracknel; devour your mother; dig up
> your aunt and cut her to pieces; feed on the earth of your own
> grave; strike your god; chew the heart of your grandfather;
> swallow the eyes of your uncle; eat the grisly bones of your
> children; suck the brains of your grandmother; dress yourself
> up in the skin of your father and tie it on with the entrails of
> your mother . . ."   —William Mariner, Tonga, I, 238–9.

The least that such a curse proves is that Islanders did not lack
imagination and energy.

To varying degrees the present Islanders still have much in
common with these ancestors. They were anything but our
kind, and people who try to tell you that they were just like
ourselves, only more natural, are abysmal asses deceiving either
themselves or you. Nevertheless they sum up as something
quite pleasant to contemplate, if the spectacle of humans vegetating does not ruffle your western-nurtured habits of mind. A
great many people liked and still like them. Whether you do
or not is not important. Like them or not, you have them on
your hands; and the obligation to do right by them has nothing to do with personal tastes.

III

LAND OF MAKEBELIEVE
COME TRUE

Hawaii and the Hawaiians have today a dangerous
number of sentimental friends.
—Ernest Beaglehole, *Some Modern Hawaiians*

GEOGRAPHY MADE HAWAII THE LIKELIEST PLACE IN the South Seas for American encroachers, military or private, pious and otherwise. To cover Hawaii in some detail will make American readers more at home in other parts of the area though, in some ways, Hawaii is not too good a sample. Its people were neither the most prepossessing, the most vigorous, nor the most self-respecting, of South Seas natives. Whites usually found them personally likeable, however—gay, malleable and gullible. And they did manage, poor devils, to experience most of the untoward consequences that white intrusion forced on the South Seas. Their history is a sort of elementary survey-course in the whole subject.[1]

Never mind identifying the first white discoverer of Hawaii. Misty tales of early white castaways, bits of broken sword found on the Big Island, Spanish charts showing islands in the latitude of Hawaii, are insignificant. Spanish vessels on their prescribed course westward from Acapulco to Manila may well have glimpsed Hawaii at some time during the two centuries of their practical monopoly on transpacific navigation. The

[1] To be precise, blackbirding and unsuccessful warfare against the whites were the only two standard items with which the Hawaiian Islands were not favored.

peaks of the Big Island are visible very far at sea and, rigidly as Spanish skippers followed sailing orders, weather or navigational error could easily have thrown them far enough north for such a landfall. If one were made, however, the cautious Spaniards kept mum about it and it had little effect on either Spaniards or Hawaiians. Hawaii was unknown to the western world when Captain James Cook anchored his two ships off Waimea on Kauai in 1778 and was duly offered a young chieftainess to sleep with. The curtain had gone up again on the always chancy drama of an Island people meeting their first whites. The several accounts of this voyage combine with testimony available in native accounts collected later by missionaries.[2]

The natives of Kauai were clearly as astounded by this visit as Cedar Rapids would be if a party of Martians in a space-ship landed on the roof of the Quaker Oats plant. In fact, the impression must have been even deeper. Cedar Rapids is vaguely aware that there may be Martians and space-ships, but the people of Kauai had no previous data to prepare them for these huge floating structures teeming with beings who might be men or gods, had holes in their skins into which they thrust their hands, and talked gibberish among themselves with every air of understanding one another.

Yet the native reaction was sensible. Reconnoitring canoes reported these floating islands rich in marvelous things, including iron. A reputable chief ashore, who claimed that the despoiling of strangers was his specialty, tried to exercise that function at once and was shot and killed in the attempt. Others, made more cautious, boarded with a show of friendliness and began snatching up every reasonably portable object in sight, particularly if it were of metal. Cook's men, already used to Polynesian light-fingeredness, tried to be open-minded about it, pointing out that a mixed lot of Europeans unexpectedly exposed to gold and diamonds—of which metal and cloth were Polynesian equivalents—would probably also turn sneak thieves. This attitude was commendable, though it showed

[2]Cook called his discovery the Sandwich Islands in compliment to the Earl of Sandwich, his patron at the Admiralty.

small knowledge of Polynesian concepts of property. As such thievery went, these new Polynesians behaved no worse than most, and were quite polite, even asking permission to spit on the deck. Friendly relations were quickly set up and the ships soon had wood, water, vegetables and women.

Obsessed with cannibalism, Cook's men looked out sharply for it here. They need not have troubled for, whatever they had once done, the Hawaiians no longer ate men. Language difficulties—most of the whites spoke Tahitian, cognate with Hawaiian but not identical—may account for the official report that an Hawaiian assured some sailors that strangers venturing ashore would certainly be eaten. It is harder to discount the item among the presents brought on board which a ship's surgeon swore was a baked human arm. Yet the weight of evidence the other way is so heavy that this learned verdict must be ignored.

Pleased with so handy a supply depot between the South Pacific and the theoretical far end of the Northwest Passage, the ships also visited Niihau, the small dry island west of Kauai.[3] In both places Cook tried to keep venereal cases away from women. The attempt failed, for when he anchored 361 days later at Kealakekua Bay on the Big Island, 300 miles away, V-D was already there ahead of him, the first item out of Pandora's box of troubles for Hawaii.[4]

The following year Cook's ships refreshed at the Big Island after an arduous northern voyage. Identifying Cook as the high god Lono, who had sailed away from Hawaii in the dim past promising to return some day, the chiefs and people were

[3] Cf. II, The Ingredients; "Natives."
[4] It also gives an index of the vigor of Hawaiian eroticism. Kauai is sixty-five miles of boisterous open water against the trade wind from Oahu; that in turn is a long and difficult voyage, still against the wind, from the Big Island; Kauai's isolation was great enough for it to be culturally distinct from the rest of the Islands, with some sounds differently pronounced and local vegetables unrepresented elsewhere (William Ellis, Narrative of a Tour Through Hawaii, 29–30). Communication between Kauai and its windward neighbors cannot have been too frequent, yet this plague spread with a speed that can only mean great goings on every time a canoe made a windward trip.

moved to lavish veneration, provisions and women on the visitors. They let Cook set up an astronomical observatory in a temple-area, no doubt mistaking instruments and observations for matters of supernal magic, and cautiously swallowed their bewildered resentment when the god's followers proved ignorant of how, in Hawaiian terms, guests should behave. These awesome strangers violated *tabus* right and left with impunity. As more whites came and did the same, the damaging lesson began to sink in—Pandora's second contribution.

The average Hawaiian commoner was well accustomed to seeing the hogs and *taro* that he had worked to raise snapped up by his chiefs, and probably saw little wrong in the fact that it was the same chiefs who got most of the iron, red baize, and other trade goods that Lono & Company produced in return. But the ships' appetite for supplies was insatiable, and the chiefs themselves can hardly have been displeased when Lono departed, shaking out the white wings of his floating islands and leaving behind the raw material for many a turgid legend.

Unhappily one of the floating islands sprung a mast in a storm and both ships returned for emergency repairs. This time the natives were glum and Cook tactless. After several small jarring incidents, a ship's boat was stolen. Cook resorted to a well-tried expedient; he blocked the bay with guard boats and kidnaped a chief as hostage against the return of the missing property.[5] At other Polynesian islands, when something important was stolen or natives were hiding deserters, the kidnaped chief would shed buckets of tears, so would his people ashore, and in a short time, the men or the pilfered items were restored. This time, however, while Cook was ashore ensnaring his chief with blarney, the crew of a guard boat shot and killed another chief who was trying to run the blockade. Things came to a scuffle in which Cook was killed, probably by an

[5] George Gilbert, one of Cook's lieutenants, vouched for the efficacy of this proceeding elsewhere; it was, he wrote, "certainly the best method that could possibly be taken in these cases to prevent bloodshed." —Walter Besant, *Captain Cook*, 130.

iron trade dagger forged by his own smith. As musket fire and grapeshot retaliated, numerous natives followed him to the other world. An eventual truce enabled his officers to secure Cook's remains—a few bones and a few pounds of flesh—and to learn that the boat, broken up for its nails, was already unreturnable. The mutilation of Cook's body was evidence, not of cannibalism, as was suspected, but of the honors customarily done the remains of a great chief. The ships then sailed to continue surveying the North Pacific, leaving Hawaii assured that, whatever else white men might be, gods they were not. The Hawaiians seem to have borne little resentment—Polynesia seldom applied to the conduct of great chiefs anything that we should consider nice moral criteria.

Polynesianophiles, of course, call Cook an insensitive villain who got what he deserved. Others blame Hawaiian fickleness and treachery. The curious missionary position was that his death was the penalty for cynically letting himself be worshiped instead of denouncing paganism and trying to convert the Hawaiians. Pompous companions of his former voyages claimed it would not have happened if they had been there to coach him. Actually, his death was probably just a case of the pitcher going to the well once too often, as when a renowned mountaineer finally misjudges a snowbridge over a bottomless crevasse. In view of how arbitrarily powerful the eighteenth-century man-of-war captain was, it is a marvel that Cook got on so well so long with so many kinds of strange brown folk of whose language he knew only a smattering, and whose customs and sensibilities were a closed book to him. Both the monuments that commemorate him in Hawaii are well deserved. He certainly did not deserve the ignominious error of a learned Japanese whose pre-Pearl Harbor book on Micronesia mentions the great English navigator, Thomas Cook.

The Hawaii and Hawaiians that played backdrop and chorus in this drama differed considerably from the modern islands and their people. There were no vast fields of sugar cane and pineapple—no pineapples, in fact, since whites had not yet brought the plant from the West Indies. The variety of plants, including sugar cane and animals acclimatized by early Polynesian immigrants, was nothing like so wide as the range of exotics to be introduced by western man—guava, orange, lemon, coffee, mango, eucalyptus, algaroba, prickly pear, numerous grasses, mongoose, mynah, Norway rat, horse, cow, sheep, goat, bee, mosquito, flea, cockroach, scorpion, and toad. Most of these have gone wild and some now dominate whole landscapes.[6] The same process is starting today on Guadalcanal, where zinnias, sown for ornament around officers' quarters, are going weedily wild down the adjacent slopes. On the leeward sides of the Islands irrigation has created shady greenery where previously nature kept things arid—notably in Honolulu, the glare and dust of which greatly irked the wives of early missionaries. But the climate, rather cooler, and all the better for it than in much of the South Seas, is still the same. Hawaii, said a local wit, has the climate that Southern California advertises.

Though indubitably Polynesians, the natives had detailed originalities, many of which vanished or went underground under white attrition. They tattooed only sparingly and often kept hogs for pets. Specially ingratiating swine might remain members of the family when full-grown, sometimes sleeping with the children under the same *tapa*. Anybody who has ever known pigs socially should have a sneaking sympathy with this.[7] They had unique games, one consisting of distance sliding, belly-bump, on long narrow sleds down specially prepared slopes of slippery glass. Chieftainesses played it and it would have been worth a voyage round the world to see a rotund Hawaiian "princess" hurtling downhill on so insubstantial a vehicle. If the old legends are true, even goddesses played; Pele, goddess of fire and volcanoes, vengefully pursued a famous chief-slider all over the Islands when he bested her in a challenge match.

Hawaiian dances, now largely relegated to side show wrig-

[6]Sea gulls, introduced to become harbor scavengers, were unsuccessful, nobody knows why.
[7]Tahiti even had a special heaven for pigs' departed souls. William Ellis, *Polynesian Researches*, I, 77.

gling or faint imitation by young Honolulu matrons, are said by experts to have been highly significant and beautiful. The spectator of contemporary efforts by the archeologically-minded to revive the more dignified *hulas* can sometimes see that high aesthetic quality may have been shown.[8] In any case, they were socially important and not at all spontaneous; we can erase the mental picture of the carefree native tearing off a *hula* out of sheer *joie de vivre*.

"The ancient Hawaiians did not personally and informally in-dulge in the dance for their own amusement . . . left it to be done for them by a body of trained and paid performers . . . the dance was an affair of premeditation, an organized effort, guarded by the traditions of a somber religion . . . these chil-dren of nature, as we are wont to call them, in this regard were less free and spontaneous than the more advanced race to which we are proud to belong."—R. W. Emerson, *Unwritten Literature of Hawaii*, 13.

Hawaiians were good shipwrights, making great dugouts from the huge logs that occasionally drifted from the Pacific northwest to Hawaiian beaches, tapping their own mountain forests for big trees only when such flotsam was unavailable. Their artificial fishponds and irrigated *taro* terraces were excel-

[8]As frequent guest of King Kalakaua, Stevenson probably had adequate opportunity to see authentic hulas under genuine auspices. He called them "surely the most dull of man's inventions, and the spectator yawns under its length as at a college lecture or a parliamentary de-bate." The context shows great liking for native dances in the Gilberts, so this is no case of inability to appreciate. (*In the South Seas*, 301.) Seventy years earlier, however, young Otto von Kotzebue wrote admir-ingly that the pre-missionary hula gave "an impression of pure nature" which, though obviously romantic nonsense, was intended to be highly complimentary. (*A Voyage of Discovery*, I, 337.) Over the last genera-tion ballyhoo, from both show business and reverent devotees of the Hawaiian past, has totally obviated any chance of intelligent balance on the subject. How the recent hula would impress the uninstructed white mind in any but the tent show version is well shown in a letter home from a nice young lady visiting Honolulu in 1917: ". . . the hula-hula, the old court dance . . . visitors desire to see it, but . . . it is neither graceful nor pretty." (M. L. Crawford, *Seven Weeks in Ha-waii*, 48.)

lent engineering,[9] but their handicrafts, except their *tapa*, were inferior, it is generally agreed, to those of other Polynesians. So, as hinted previously, was their level of female beauty. Said Cook, who knew Tahiti and Tonga well for contrast:

". . . neither remarkable for a beautiful shape nor for striking features . . . if any of them can claim a share of beauty, it was most conspicuous among the young men."—*Three Voyages*, II, 246–7.

But:

". . . no women I ever met with were less reserved. Indeed it appeared to me that they visited us with no other view than to make a surrender of their persons."—*Three Voyages*, II, 398.

They were also strangely unconcerned about the whites' destructive powers. When the ships bombarded the shore to avenge Cook's death, with huts flaming and puzzled natives dying in puzzled heaps:

". . . the women of the island, who were on board, never offered to leave us, nor discovered the smallest apprehensions, either for themselves or for their friends ashore . . . some of them, who were on deck when the town was in flames, seemed to admire the sight and frequently cried out that it was *maitai*, or very fine."—*Three Voyages*, II, 398.

These were probably commoner-women, with inferior sense of stake in the general welfare. For Hawaii was notable, even

[9]". . . along the whole narrow bottom [of an Hawaiian stream-gorge] and climbing often in terraces the steep hillsides, you will see the little taro patches, skilfully laid so as to catch the water directly from the main stream, or from canals taking water out above. Such a taro patch oftenest contains a sixteenth, less frequently an eighth, of an acre. It consists of soil painfully brought down from above, and secured by means of substantial stone walls, plastered with mud and covered with grass, strong enough to resist the force of the torrent. Each little patch or flat is so laid that a part of the stream shall flow over it without carrying away the soil; indeed, it is expected to leave some sediment. And as you look up such a valley you see terrace after terrace of taro rising before you, the patches often fifty or sixty feet above the brawling stream, but each receiving its proper proportion of water."—Charles Nordhoff, *Northern California, Oregon and the Sandwich Islands*, 77.

in Polynesia, for social stratification and upper-class despotism in an organization so close to European feudal precedents that it was called a "satire on . . . the courts of Europe."[10] Each large island was partitioned among ranking chiefs who allotted land in fief to lesser vassals. They in turn developed under-vassals who let land to commoners as tenants-at-will to culti-vate and harvest, paying indeterminate dues in kind. Protection from hostile raids was set against labor on demand, an arrange-ment that seems to have worked out no better for the common man's security here than in the confusions of eleventh-century France. One principal difference was that the commoner was not formally bound to military service though, if he knew what was good for him, he joined his lord's war parties promptly. Nor was he bound to the land serf-fashion, though he seldom renounced a weak or overtyrannical lord to take up with another, since that exiled him from his closer relatives, who bulked so large in the Polynesian's emotions and econ-omy. Nor were fiefs hereditary, so the death of an over-chief meant a destructive scramble to redistribute power and pres-tige; nor was there a nominal or actual overlord of the whole group of islands.

Theoretically the chief was solicitous of his people's wel-fare because his military strength and supplies depended on their affection and prosperity. Malinowski saw fit to admire this aspect of ancient Hawaiian polity, but David Malo, a principal native source for pre-white Hawaii, did not:

> ". . . only a small portion of the kings and chiefs ruled with kindness; the large majority simply lorded it over the people."
> —Hawaiian Antiquities, 87.

The whole arrangement was dangerously arbitrary. The com-moner possessed few rights to curb irresponsible exactions on his food supply, his time or his life.[11] Cook certainly got the im-

[10] J. J. Jarves, Kiana, 72.
[11] Queen Liliuokalani's autobiography tries to maintain in the teeth of evidence that her unspoiled ancestors never exploited their vassals. Some of it is worth quoting because it sounds so much like a white southerner explaining how the old South was good to its negroes:

pression that things could be ruthless: while he lay off Waimea, a chief's double canoe coming out to see the new wonder ran down and sank several commoners' canoes that happened to be in the way. The *tabu* against standing higher than a chief was so rigid that, if a chief went below on board, all commoners on deck instantly dived overside; and the list of possible *tabu* breaches calling for summary death in connection with chiefs' persons reads like an eighteenth-century penal code in Europe. This vigorous, ruthless chieftainship was well illustrated in missionary times in the person of Kuakini (John Adams), governor of Hawaii:

"... with an iron will, fearing neither man nor monarch, prone to call out a thousand men to build a causeway, or a dam for enclosing fish, or to cut sandalwood in the mountains or to build a large church-edifice . . . he would occasionally make a tour of the whole island, sending messengers before to command the natives to build him large houses at all places where he would spend a night . . . to prepare large quantities of fish, fowl, eggs, poi, potatoes etc. against his arrival. When he swept around the island, his attendants would number two- or threescore of men, women and children, all to be fed by the people where he lodged . . . he would sometimes encamp for a month, consuming almost all the eatables within a radius of two or three miles."—Titus Coan, *Life in Hawaii*, 227–8.

Yet a solicitous chief could, and often did, do well by his people and, much as the system encouraged exaction and war, it worked without the island-wide famines that sometimes occurred in Tonga and the Marquesas. The fecundity of taro plus possibly superior Hawaiian industriousness kept the population teeming in spite of infanticide and frequent battles. Cook estimated 400,000 Hawaiians in 1778. Subsequent students revise

"... it has been at times asserted by foreigners that the abundance of the chief was procured by the poverty of his followers . . . Nothing could be more incorrect . . . The chief, whose retainers were in any poverty or want would have felt, not only their sufferings but, further, his own disgrace . . . My father was surrounded by hundreds of his own people, all of whom looked to him, and never in vain, for sustenance." *Hawaii's Story by Hawaii's Queen*, 3.

that downward, but seldom below 300,000. The Hawaiian Islands did not again support so many people until 1924. Nor must it be assumed—this mistake was common among missionaries—that the Hawaiian commoner was miserable. He sometimes, taking advantage of discontent, had the privilege of going to war against a tyrant behind a rebel chief, and most of the time he seems to have managed to be a jolly and good-natured sort. Since he knew of no possibility of running a society in any other way, he probably took the disadvantages and advantages of the Hawaiian system as natural, world-without-end elements in his environment, like the dangers of fishing and the refreshment of coconut water.

There the Islands lay on New Year's, 1778—Niihau, Kauai, Oahu, Molokai, Lanai, Kahoolawe, Maui, Hawaii—the trades sluicing rain on the windward slopes, Pele sporting with her cronies in the incandescent surf of Halemaumau crater, the naked brown babies playing on the black sand beaches and learning to swim almost spontaneously. Sacrifices—some hog, some human—were rotting together in the temples, the kahunas were setting bones, applying simples and occasionally praying a man to death; periodically the drums boomed for some feast or other. Possessed like all Polynesian cultures of some strikingly genial aspects, spontaneous, adventitious, organic, with a bold and leisured beauty that did not preclude blood on the temple stones, it had developed by processes still imperfectly understood and was following its own tendencies along lines determined by vegetable materials, stone implements, lush vegetation.

January brought the white man. After that there was no longer much validity in the chief's splendid cloak of yellow feathers or in the bones of his ancestors in the caves that pit the cliffs of Kealakekua Bay.

*   *   *

"Some Hawaiians, however, seemed to doubt the propriety of foreigners coming in to reside permanently among them. They said they had heard that in several countries where foreigners had intermingled with the original natives, the latter had soon disappeared."—William Ellis, *Narrative of a Tour Through Hawaii*, 235.

After Cook the Islands, richer by syphilis, gonorrhea and some odd hardware, were left alone for seven years. Some attribute this to a reputation for unbridled savagery consequent on the killing of so world-famous a man. The point is dubious, the reputation ill-deserved. The Hawaiians were among the most supine of South Sea peoples in the face of white infiltration. After a few experiences of what *haole*[12] cannon and muskets could do, they renounced violent resistance; their most signal anti-white military exploit was the forcible suppression without fighting of a handful of filibustering Russians on Kauai. They used white weapons largely against their own people, without much effort to see what powder and shot would do to pants-wearing interlopers. Such conduct would have made a Maori or a Marquesan blush.

The China trade brought the first important return of the *haole*. As early as 1785 British and American fur traders, *en route* from the Northwest coast with sea-otter pelts to trade in China, started putting in for provisions at Lahaina and Honolulu, which last port thus began to develop from prewhite obscurity. China proved to want not only furs but also sandalwood for an incense base and fancy cabinetwork; and sandalwood grew wild on Hawaiian mountains. Thus it paid as supplement to a China-bound cargo in exchange for the tea, silks, porcelains and ginger that brought such stunning prices in Boston and London. For their sandalwood the Hawaiian chiefs got rum, guns, shirts, beads, mirrors, hardware, clocks, beaver hats, textiles, even ships. The commoners got little or nothing; they merely cut the trees and transported them to the shore for the chief's account. High-pressure salesmanship soon extended heavy credits to the chiefs payable in sandalwood by the *picul*, the Canton price running from a dollar and a half to

[12]*Haole* originally meant outsider in Hawaiian and applied to negroes and orientals as well as whites. Since the first outsiders were almost exclusively white, it came gradually to mean white alone.

twelve dollars a *picul*, according to quality.[13] To amass the payments, commoners were sent into the hills day after day, while crops suffered and the unwonted monotony and arduousness of such labor depressed the nation's spirits. Kamehameha I made some efforts to conserve the sandalwood supply in Hawaii, characteristically by way of a monopoly in his own favor. But his death took off the lid and the tree was practically exterminated, though as late as 1864 it was still found at the rate of three tons a year. Until sugar developed, it was the Islands' most considerable export.

The culminating foolishness was the purchase, by Kamehameha II (Liholiho) of "Cleopatra's Barge," former private yacht of Benjamin Crowninshield of Salem, Mass., probably the most luxurious vessel afloat at the time, for some $50,000 worth of sandalwood. No matter how faithfully the commoners chopped and hauled, the chiefs stayed deep in arrears. In 1826 Commodore Thomas ap Catesby Jones, U.S.N.—who flits in and out of Pacific history without ever quite living up to his memorable Welsh name—came to Honolulu in the U.S.S. "Peacock" to put the screws on chiefs who had owed American traders too much too long, a total at the moment of 14,000 *piculs*. His deal included a promise from the king and chiefs to tax each male Hawaiian one *picul* of sandalwood or four Spanish dollars, the proceeds to be applied on the debts. To sweeten his drudgery, a man could also cut half a *picul* on his own account. Boki, native governing chief of Oahu, became a legend in 1828 by trying to cover his debts with a two-ship expedition after sandalwood in the New Hebrides. The smaller vessel eventually got home in very bad shape without any cargo. The larger, carrying Boki, was never reliably heard of again. Her disappearance was presumed to be connected with native carelessness about smoking near gunpowder.

Sandalwooding left its mark. The hunt for it destroyed a good deal of timberland, as the natives lazily burned the forest

[13]The *picul* was the weight a man could carry on his back handily. At Manila in the early nineteenth century it was approximately 140 pounds. (William Endicott, *Wrecked Among Cannibals*, 25.)

to detect stands of it by the smell. But far more destructive was the fact that the trade attracted whites, whose very presence was subversive. Besides, they brought for trade the tools of western war and the men who could handle them. Kamehameha, an energetic high chief in the Big Island, apparently realized ahead of his rivals what firearms might mean in native warfare and built up, by piracy and trading, the first Western-style arsenal in the Islands. In 1804 he commanded 600 muskets, fourteen small cannon, forty swivel guns and some twenty small sailing craft more or less armed, as well as white retainers to operate them and train Hawaiians in their use. When he invaded Oahu in the crucial phase of an imperialistic war of conquest, seven renegade whites marched with him as gunners and advisors. The most conspicuous were John Young and Isaac Davis, British seamen who had been spared in a native attack on an unscrupulous American trader and her tender. Both married into high native society and ranked as chiefs themselves; a granddaughter of Young's became queen of Hawaii and social protégée of Queen Victoria. Several other such ambitious beachcombers founded *hapa-haole* (half-white) families still highly regarded in the Islands; one was an American assigned by Kamehameha I to shoot and salt wild cattle for trade to ships.

Kamehameha's rivals also had tame white men and guns, but not in comparable numbers. So he succeeded bloodily in his ambition to consolidate the whole group. Only Kauai managed to hold out, though even there Kaumualii, its "king," had to make a gesture of homage. Some local historians call this Kamehameha I "the Napoleon of the Pacific"; which, considering the relative scale, is about as if Tom Prendergast were labelled "the Bismarck of the Americas." Many scholars profess great veneration for his memory as a national hero of Hawaii. I confess that I can see little difference between him and half a dozen other megalomanic chiefs who rose to hegemony in the South Seas in consequence of white infiltration. His wars were waged strictly for power and prestige, Hawaiians in general receiving only incidental benefits. Hobbs maintains, quite plausibly, that his monolithic imperialism, which obviated the necessity for chiefs to do well by their people, broke down whatever reality there had been in chieftain paternalism.

Yet Kamehameha was a brilliant opportunist, as able a Polynesian as the white man ever saw. Vancouver, who plied him with self-righteous good advice in the 1790's, reported him as shrewd, covetous, composed and by no means unlikeable. His portraits exude character, almost humor.[14] He consented to an abortive British offer to send him teachers of the white man's religion, no doubt thinking its magic essential to the manufacture of broadcloth and ordnance, and made a vague request for a British protectorate over the Islands that was to plague diplomats for the next two generations. After that, the story is, he flew British colors until, during the war of 1812, Americans pointed out that the United States might take it amiss as unneutral; so, impartially mixing the Union Jack with American stripes, he concocted a flag that remained the Hawaiian colors until the kingdom was extinguished in 1893.

His warehouses were full of a pack rat's collection of costly junk from Europe and America. His own dress was of nankeen, broadcloth and cambric. But he was capable of selectivity among white notions. When he sent a ship of his own with sandalwood to China and she returned at a loss attributed to high port dues, he had port dues explained to him and quickly instituted them—high ones too. When Captain Cleveland landed the Islands' first horses in 1803 as a present for him, he saw them through their paces and granted they were a good way to get to places in a hurry; but concluded that in a place like Hawaii, their feed would be more than they were worth. His subjects disagreed; from then on Hawaii was horse-mad. The same strength and dexterity that made them great surfriders made them splendid, if brutal, horsemen and -women. Long before the missionaries arrived to be shocked, the Hawaiian wahine (female) was riding astride like a she-centaur.[15]

[14]The heroic statue of him in Honolulu is strictly an imaginary portrait, an idealization of the generalized Hawaiian chieftain.

[15]Amateur gynecologists have suggested that this intemperate hard riding when in an interesting condition had something to do with the

As ships multiplied—whalers first made Honolulu in 1819—Pandora's box spilled calamities wholesale. Not even Kamehameha the Great could have succeeded, if it had occurred to him to try, in teaching his people enough new things quickly enough to stave off the virtual destruction of their culture. Every year more whites stayed ashore, poisoning the place with alien habits, virtues and vices.

Hawaiians drank rum greedily, having no more notion than the Red Indian that possessing a bottle did not necessarily mean getting drunk. An escaped convict from New South Wales is usually credited with bringing distilling to Hawaii, using an iron pot for the retort, a gun-barrel for the worm and a mash of *ti*-root, which is high in sugars. The product, hot as fire, was *okolehao*, the literal meaning of which is still less decorous than the usually given "iron bottom."[16] Native women, Kotzebue reported in 1816, drank as hard as the men; he was startled when John Young excused himself from attending a royal *hula* because his Hawaiian wife was too drunk to be left safely alone. The best Kotzebue could say for the result was that these inebriated Hawaiians were "most cheerful and affectionate,"[17] not murderously quarrelsome like seamen. Children learned to smoke as soon as they could walk. As fresh infection came ashore with each ship, venereal diseases burrowed deeper into the population. Western epidemic diseases apparently struck first in 1804, with something horribly devastating that may have been cholera. Vancouver was even sure that, in the thirteen years between his first sight of the Islands as a lieutenant of Cook's and his return in 1791, the

---

calamitous post-white decline of the Hawaiian birthrate. Riding astride for women was one of the Hawaiian ideas that the respectable white community took over in the mid-century. In a voluminous divided skirt the Hawaiian-born lady was straddling her steed two generations ahead of her mainland cousin.

[16]Usually shortened to *oke* nowadays. Properly aged, it is about as good as good Bourbon. This is hard for the casual visitor to Hawaii to test. A sound piece of Island advice runs: "Don't drink any *oke* you can buy." The best of it ten years ago was moonshined during prohibition and carefully kept and aged by solicitous Island families.

[17]Otto von Kotzebue, A Voyage of Discovery, II, 192.

girls' attractiveness had gone off. But then, George Vancouver
was thirteen years older.

Even more ominously, traditional ways were losing prestige.
Castoff seamen's frocks and secondhand broadcloth coats were
garments of choice, along with tattered shirts, never washed,
for the natives had not been accustomed to launder tapa
garments. In such clothes in such a climate they sweated like
pigs. This started well before missionaries arrived to teach them
that white men's clothes were more righteous than brown
men's half-nakedness. The chieftainess who, in the old days,
would have rolled up in tapa for a big ceremony now substi-
tuted white man's textiles, the more costly the better. One
such lady was wound in seventy-two yards of fine cashmere,
half orange, half red, so that her arms stuck out horizontally
and her attendants carried half the bolt as a hundred-foot train
behind her. Even the local grass house deteriorated as the goats
and cattle that white men introduced ate off grasses formerly reserved for thatch. The old games were neglected in favor of
cards, which gave a better gambler's run for time consumed;
Kotzebue found much of the population of Honolulu stretched
on the ground playing whist day and night.

The missionaries, still to arrive, are often accused of breaking up the old Hawaii. Much they certainly did in that direction and would have liked to do still more. But the breakup was
well on its way before they appeared to accelerate it. True, some
of the old life probably continued, relatively unflawed, on
Kauai, Niihau, Molokai and in the back country of the Big
Island. But Kamehameha's conquests had taken the starch out
of the old régimes and, Louis XIV-style, concentrated all significance on him and his court, where white influences came
most heavily to bear. When the old man died in 1819, full of
years, conquest and fame of a sort, the ruin of his race was
virtually, if not actually, complete.

*   *   *

How sad it is to think of the millions who have gone to their graves in this beautiful island and never knew there was a hell.
—MARK TWAIN, *Roughing It.*

The old gentleman's successor, a son named Liholiho whom history styles Kamehameha II, was conventionally huge and reputed able to drink a bottle of rum at a draft. He did not last long.

His achievement of being the first Hawaiian king to see the outside world was the death of him. With his principal wife, who was also his half sister, and a small retinue, he went voyaging halfway round the world to London to see King George and other educational objects. On the way the party were badly swindled but, once government became aware of their presence, were shown a good time with splendid presents and visits to the theatre. Their hotel bill, which emphasizes cider and oysters more than spirits, indicates that they even managed to stay sober much of the time. Before a royal audience could be arranged, however, Liholiho and his consort died of measles. The queen went first. There in cold and dirty London her attendants laid her out Island-style, barefooted, bare to the waist, a flower *lei* on the cold, dark head—though they were not Island flowers—and carried her to the dying king to show him that his lady's dignity had been reverently attended to.[18]

Short though his reign was, however, Liholiho left his mark wide and deep on Hawaii. He officially shattered the pre-white island culture by jettisoning the *tabu* system and the worship of the old gods, the main interlacing fibres of its structure. Causes seem to have been partly the past forty years of white attrition, partly vague rumors of Tahiti's idol-burning under missionary influence, partly a movement among powerful

[18]Boki, the chief who later made that fatal sandalwooding voyage, kept his suzerain's engagement with George IV and, during the conversation, asked if it were wise for Hawaii to encourage the missionaries who had recently appeared there. The King, probably as immoral a creature as England afforded at the time, replied: "Yes, they are a people to make others good. I always have some of them by me."—*Voyage of the Blonde,* 67.

chieftainesses to rid Hawaiians of *tabu* restrictions. During much of the period when the decision was made, Liholiho seems to have been drunk and perhaps unusually suggestible.

The women's part in this is nothing remarkable in Polynesia. Hawaiian chieftainesses, though never paramount, sat high in council, acted as regents for young heirs and received such honors as prostration from commoners and the death penalty for inferiors who crossed their shadows. But *tabus* did not apply equally, so rifts in the old order leading to new regulations would probably mean gain for women; they had already been clandestinely eating *tabu* foods with white men when their own men were not present. This explanation may be more rational than what actually occurred. Social revolutions seldom spring from clearly assignable causes. But there was a flavor of women's rights about the proceedings as Kaahumanu, one of old Kamehameha's widows, took a leading part in persuading her stepson to the awesome step of breaking *tabus*.

The culminating occasion was a feast, at which the king ate in public with his women, a thing as repugnant to old Hawaii as swine's flesh was to the Sepoys of the Mutiny. Apparently terrified, yet exhilarated, by the royal boldness, his retainers took up the cry of "The *tabu* is broken" and proceeded to destroy all handy idols, the symbols of the old ways, with their lofty crests, gaping teeth and candid genitals. The court and the adjacent villages seem to have been ripe for such action, but not all Hawaiians were. *Tabu* flouting cost Liholiho a short, sharp war with a minority of hard-shell vassals who renounced him as a blasphemous overlord; part of their insurgency probably came from an ambition to pull down the upstart Kamehameha dynasty, only two generations in the saddle and no more august than several other noble strains. Liholiho's forces, headed by a redoubtable old war chief, were victorious. The rebels' loyalty to their insulted gods was greater than that of their gods to them.

No dramatist could invent better action-symbols of the effect of white infiltration on South Seas cultures. Racine would have written five stately acts about it. Yet, as hinted before, there is a special element here. Nowhere else in the South Seas did the framework of tradition collapse under a self-administered kick before missionaries arrived. In Tahiti, for instance, no natives reached the idol-burning point until after fifty years of white influence, including almost twenty years of missionary effort. Such an impression is difficult to state intelligibly, but there remains a suspicion that somehow Hawaiian culture had more sap than pith.

On their arrival in Hawaii, only a few months after the tabu war, the missionaries saw no mystery in this spontaneous iconoclasm. The hand of the Lord had obviously overthrown Dagon in prelude to the saints' assault on Satan's Polynesian stronghold. To anybody asking why the Lord had not similarly favored hard-pressed English missionaries in Tahiti instead of letting them agonize for so many years, the answer would have come pat: He moves in a mysterious way. They broke into holy cheers when they heard the news. In jealous hindsight, a Catholic mission historian later pointed out that it may not have been anything to cheer about: ". . . we doubt that agnosticism, religious indifference and an unwillingness to bear any restraint are dispositions of the soul favorable to the reception of the truths and commands of the religion of Christ."[19]

At any rate, whether with good omens or bad, here the Yankee mission was in 1820, staring at the Big Island over the bulwarks of the brig "Thaddeus" of Boston. Among other presents the missionaries brought with them for King Liholiho a fancy and specially inscribed Bible from the American Bible Society, which apparently was unaware that His Majesty could not read English, or indeed any other language.

This missionary expedition had been some while in preparation under the American Board of Commissioners for Foreign Missions (ABCFM), a non-denominational but predominantly Congregationalist and Presbyterian body with headquarters in Boston. Talent had been recruited among young and zealous parsons and laymen, wives of due godliness had

[19]Father Reginald Yzendoorn, History of the Catholic Mission, 21

been found for those lacking the helpmeets that the Board considered necessary, and liaison provided in the persons of several Hawaiian youths who had drifted to New England and been educated for the purpose in a special school at Cornwall, Conn. This sensible measure, assuring the mission of sympathetic interpreters and teachers of the language, brings up one of the standard missionary legends, that of Henry Obookiah (or Opukaia):

Kamehameha the Great had determined to send one of his sons for a Yankee education under the wing of a Captain Brintnall of New Haven. A couple of wellborn boys of the prince's own age were told off to go as companions. The prince never sailed, but the companions did. Brintnall is said to have paid them little attention on reaching home. Presently one of them was found on the steps of Yale College weeping bitterly because he and his people were ignorant and nobody was doing anything about it. Kindly and learned Christians took him up, along with his crony, Thomas Hopu. The interesting presence of the pair is supposed to have greatly stimulated the idea of a mission to Hawaii, the founding of the Cornwall school—which was to include a Tahitian, a Marquesan, a Malay and several American Indians—and recruiting for the mission. Hopu survived to sail on the "Thaddeus," presumably briefed for maximum usefulness in English, Christianity and sanitation. Obookiah died of civilization and is now buried in the hilly old Cornwall graveyard, probably still wondering at the snow that clogs the dark conifers in this strange country.

King Liholiho's behavior was hardly that of a man who was wax in the Lord's hands, and certainly did not bear out the theory that his *tabu* breaking had been of heavenly inspiration. Negotiations for permission for the mission to land and promulgate the Gospel were disquietingly slow. The king's explicit objections are said to have been that he liked a number of wives and these militant whites might try to persuade him against that comfortable custom; and that the British, whom he considered Hawaii's sponsors in the white world, would dislike his according privileges to white *kahunas* from another country. The Rev. Hiram Bingham, arch-zealot of the mission but no fool, also surmised that, having shed all his old moral and religious hampering restrictions, the king was in no hurry to risk having to assume another set. John Young is said to have put in a good word for the missionaries. The upshot was grudging permission for the newcomers to operate on a year's probation on the Big Island and Oahu. Presently they were permitted to erect dwellings according to their own taste, the first relaxation of a ruling imposed on all *haoles* by Kamehameha I. The camel's nose was now inside the tent.

Liholiho required that the mission's doctor stay handy on the Big Island, his principal seat. Here appears a great tactical advantage for the white; his system of medicine was new to the natives and sometimes more effective than that of the *kahunas*. The white man's bedside manner contrasted favorably with the *kahuna's* stern absorption in herbs, spells and massage, and white therapy speedily gained a high reputation, easily exploitable for diplomatic and religious purposes.[20]

The decision to bring wives and families along was another piece of tactical luck. The theory was that examples of the Christian-western-white household would move the heathen to imitation. This is dubious, for Yankee industry and rigidity can hardly have seemed attractive in the happy-go-lucky atmosphere of the Nuuanu Valley. But though the mission did not know it, the presence of women on the scene had always been a known South Seas token of amicable intent. When anti-mission *haoles* tried to persuade Liholiho that these interlopers were harbingers of foreign conquest, he asked why, if conquest were their object, had they brought women and children? And among the child-loving natives the children were a great mollifying influence in their own right.

The wives' skill with the needle was a third asset. Gigantic chieftainesses early descended on them with demands for gowns made *haole*-style. They had little notion of the amount of work

[20]In recent parallel, American military forces in the Solomons found that a fine avenue to friendly relations with the natives consisted in encouraging their women to come for treatment to military doctors.

involved in cutting out and stitching, nor in view of their peremptory natures, would they have cared much if they had. But to propitiate these demanding barbarians would be a great stroke in the Lord's service, so Mrs. Bingham, Mrs. Chamberlain, Mrs. Holman and the rest toiled day and night turning bolts of cambric into garments that must have presented engineering difficulties like those of making a circus tent.[21] They demurred only at sewing on Sunday, a *tabu*-like idea that the chieftainesses understood. The ladies also made ruffled shirts by the dozen for exigent chiefs, and even turned tailor, constructing broadcloth suits for them with their husbands' Sunday clothes as patterns.

That was wearing in itself, but the ladies often had other reasons to wish themselves back home in Connecticut or upper York State though, dutifully, they seldom complained. It was dismaying when a cordial chieftainess, returning from her morning swim, would drop in stark naked to chat—bare, brown and bulging. To the credit of the natives I find only one case in which an Hawaiian offered amatory violence to a mission

[21] "Out of this welter of stitches came the *holoku*, the traditional post-white dress of Hawaiian women, which many whites adopted and often wore until a generation ago. Legend says that the original pattern was the long-sleeved, high-necked, yoked Yankee nightgown. Since the models that the chieftainesses saw first must have been the mission ladies' daytime gowns, legend is probably wrong. According to a likelier legend, the short train which the *holoku* developed came from the up-in-front-and-down-behind effect produced by putting a sackish garment over the tremendous bellies of these chieftainess-customers—they were delighted with it, it appears. (*Hawaii with Sidney A. Clark*, 114.) To modern eyes the *holoku* looks graceless; but the latter nineteenth century, clear up to Charmian London's time for that matter, thought it becoming. Nordhoff's attitude is typical: "It is a little startling at first to see women walking about in what, to our perverted tastes, look like calico or black stuff nightgowns; but this dress grows on you as you become accustomed to it; it lends itself readily to bright ornamentation; it is eminently fit for the climate; and a stately Hawaiian dame, marching through the street in black *holoku* . . . with a long necklace or *lei*, of bright scarlet or brilliant yellow flowers, bare and untrammeled feet, and flowing hair, ornamented often by a low-crowned felt hat, compares very favorably with a high-heeled, wasp-waisted, absurdly-bonneted, fashionable white lady."—*Northern California, Oregon and the Sandwich Islands*, 31.

lady—this was a "vile heathen priest"[22] who seems to have been smitten by Mrs. Thurston. The lady was rescued well in time and, for all one knows, the heathen's motives may have been mostly curiosity.

As always happens, the mission children picked up the language much faster than their elders. That was calamitous, for Hawaiians disputing or merely joking would say things to each other that westerners would hardly chalk on fences even if they had the ingenuity to think of them. Hence an early decision, on advice of expert veterans from the London Missionary Society in Tahiti, to segregate mission children from the natives. A generation ago the stricter Hawaiian whites retained an impression that it was a little low to learn to talk native. Early insulation was so successful that, when sent to school in the States at thirteen, young Sereno Bishop was shocked and startled by his schoolmates' dirty talk.

Children were thus sent home for education until the mission founded Oahu College, now a high-ranking preparatory school. Segregation was undemocratic and possibly un-Christian, but only thus could the little Judds and Thurstons be saved from learning the facts of life and some of its more intriguing fictions in liquid Polynesian. The principle cut both ways too, for, though the mission taught English to chiefs to facilitate their dealings with whites, it long refused that privilege to commoners so as to keep them from corruption from sailormen whom the Rev. Mr. Bingham called "an ungodly class of profane abusers of our noble English."

These messengers of God's word had little concern in any case with the equalitarianism that we consider democratic. They felt like this on first viewing their converts-to-be:

"Some of our number with gushing tears turned away from the spectacle. Others with firmer nerve continued their gaze but were ready to exclaim, "Can these be human beings? How dark and comfortless their state of mind and heart! How imminent the danger to the immortal soul, shrouded in this deep pagan gloom! Can such beings be civilized? Can they be

[22]Hiram Bingham, A Residence, 125.

Christianized? Can we throw ourselves upon these rude shores, and take up our abode, for life, among such a people, for the purpose of training them for heaven?"—Hiram Bingham, A Residence, 81.[23]

Further neglecting the scriptural injunction to be no respecters of persons, standard missionary tactics called for converting chiefs first. The chiefs' example would lead to mass conversion among followers, and sometimes to wider influence for the mission. Besides, having on the whole wider acquaintance with white ways, chiefs were more inclined to listen, and took it for granted that they should sit at the first table when the bread of righteousness was served. In asking the mission for spelling books, in fact, Liholiho stipulated that learning be withheld from commoners lest school distract them from their task of cutting sandalwood to pay his debts.

Sermons in the Yankees' halting Hawaiian were never so well and so respectfully attended as when the local chief sat by the preacher enjoining silence and attention. When starting their career on windward Oahu, the Rev. and Mrs. Emerson were blissfully astonished to see the first service in their new grass-roofed chapel attended by teeming hundreds, crowding the place to bursting and frantically trying to jam inside when it was obviously a physical impossibility. An elderly native lady with one leg had hopped nearly four miles to be present. The Emersons' awed impression that a thirst for the waters of life had infected the whole population was rudely changed, however, when a skeptical veteran colleague found that the local chief had announced to all his people that every man, woman and child had better be inside that chapel that Sunday or very definitely else.

Liholiho was eager to learn reading, that handy white man's secret, but by and large he seems to have been little better than bored with what the mission conveyed to him of what it considered Christianity to be. He suffered grace before meat if

---

[23]That passage is notable, not only for its compassionate contempt for the native but also as evidence of the standing tendency of missionaries to take their emotional and physical hardships big in print.

missionaries were present; but when reproached for lukewarm-
ness, he cynically offered to strike a bargain, promising eventual
reformation in return for five years more of pleasing his lustful
soul. On another occasion he refused to attend a mission service
on the unimpeachable grounds that he was too drunk; he was
recalcitrant about banning *hulas* on Sunday; and went to his
death, to say the least, well short of being a professed Christian.

Slightly lesser chiefs, however, listened better. Old Kaumualii, "king" of Kauai, who alone had managed to hold out
even halfway against Kamehameha I, favored missions—partly
because the mission brought him back his son George, a Cornwall School boy, partly because he was jealous of the mission's
having gone first to the Kamehameha dynasty on Hawaii. His
Christianity was edifyingly strenuous. One story has him reading the Hawaiian Bible held out of water with his left hand
while swimming streams; another, continuing his prayers with
Socratic meekness even after his principal wife, who disliked
new ways, threw a calabash at his head. There was Kalanimoku, Liholiho's victorious general, who stole a march on his
countrymen by experimentally getting baptized in 1819, along
with Boki, his younger brother, by the chaplain of a visiting
French man-of-war. While returning from England with the
bodies of Liholiho and wife, Boki broad-mindedly made it
double by accepting another baptism from the Protestant chaplain of H.M.S. "Blonde." There was Kapiolani, a very high
chieftainess, who pluckily testified to her conversion by going
to Kilauea crater and defiantly eating Pele's *tabu ohelo*-berries
—an invaluable public demonstration of the impotence of the
old gods.

But the turning point came when Kaahumanu knuckled
down to Jesus. Heading the movement to break *tabu* was only
one of this formidable chieftainess' distinctions. She had begun
as an important heiress taken by Kamehameha when only
thirteen and, though he took more wives later, was so highly
valued that a specific *tabu* stipulated death for any other man
having intercourse with her. One unlucky young chief paid
the penalty.

Her temper seems to have been as tempestuous as her history. In her preconversion phase, a missionary chronicler loaded her with these epithets: ". . . haughty, filthy, lewd, tyrannical, cruel, wrathful, murderous." At Kamehameha's death she became principal regent for Liholiho and, on Liholiho's death, headed the regency for his small son, so distinguishing herself as ruler that the post of female vice-king (*kuhina nui*) was written into the first formal Hawaiian constitution. With another of Kamehameha's former wives she was co-admiral of a fleet of canoes that helped greatly in subduing the *tabu* rebels in 1819. When Liholiho got possession—some say by treachery—of the person of old Kaumualii, Kaahumanu was told off to marry him, to tie the royal dynasty of Kauai firmly to the Kamehamehas. To make doubly sure, she simultaneously married one of the old man's sons.

To convert her would be like getting Cardinal Richelieu on your side. At first she scoffed insultingly, receiving mission visits lying on her vast belly as she played cards with her suite, greeting mission ladies with a disdainfully crooked little finger. But the solicitude with which missionaries tended her during a serious illness softened her gigantic heart. Then the mission unwittingly played an ace by showing her a little book printed in her own language—first fruit of the printing press fetched along as a mighty weapon for the Lord. Reducing Hawaiian to Roman characters had been a thorny and tedious task, even though previous work of the sort in Tahiti had shown the way.[24] Now all that toil proved its worth. Kaahumanu dropped cards for letters and, being intelligent, was soon reading fluently. To her credit, she was the first powerful chief to insist that the mission start teaching commoners to read as soon as the chiefs had learned.

When eventually baptized, she backed the mission in its every measure; was in fact often out ahead of her preceptors in

[24]One of the worst troubles came from the confusion in Hawaiian pronounciation between K and T. Choosing to spell Kauai thus instead of Tauai, for instance, was arbitrary; and the Hawaiian *kapu* (tabu) now used throughout the Islands for Keep Off signs could just as well have been *tapu*.

schemes to foist Christian morality on her people. In her view, the only penal code that Hawaii needed was the Ten Commandments literally enforced. She used to dandle female missionaries on her colossal lap, like a great dog expressing at once affection and superior strength. "She is tall, stately and dignified," wrote Mrs. Judd of this star convert, "often overbearing in her manner, but with a countenance beaming with love whenever she addresses her teachers."[25] Hawaiians took enthusiastically to wheels and Kaahumanu, who as a heathen queen had been carried in litters, paid her post-1820 calls in a light-blue handcart with upholstered cushions, sitting backward where the tail gate should have been, her calves and feet dangling in the dust kicked up by the retainers who pulled the contraption.

She died clutching the first complete copy of the New Testament in Hawaiian, her last words as edifying as a tract, at least in the missionary version. The early paganism, the late piety, and the masterful qualities above all, make hers a strange and pathetic career, if a woman with the body of a porpoise and the temperament of a buck sergeant can be pathetic.

With this strategic conversion, the camel had his whole neck inside the tent. But there would be many struggles and heartburnings before, seventy years later, he could climactically stand up and walk off with poles and canvas. The interim situation was well summed up for the Rev. Mr. Bingham: Traveling on Kauai with some "untutored natives," he took occasion to point out some of the beauties of that loveliest of the Hawaiian Islands, went on to bring God into the matter and finally asked them who it was that created this beautiful world and men too.

The untutored natives said they did not know. Mr. Bingham said that he knew his God had created both the world and himself, and what did they think of that? The untutored natives said that they did not know whether this haole god had anything to do with them—it was the haole god he was talking about?

[25] Laura F. Judd, *Honolulu*, 4-5.

"Yes," said good Mr. Bingham. "And is he not yours also?"
"No," said the untutored natives. "Our gods are dead."[26]

*   *   *

"What!" cried the convert. "Are you going to respect a taboo at a time like this? And you were always so opposed to taboos when you were alive!"
"To other people's," said the missionary. "Never to my own."
—Robert Louis Stevenson, *Something In It.*

Within eight years of arriving, the Rev. Mr. Bingham, proud of his record of having once prayed for an hour and a half hand running, was preaching in a pole-and-thatch tabernacle in Honolulu to congregations of 2,000 natives. On the Big Island in the 'thirties the Rev. Titus Coan's congregations were so huge that, in order for all to get under one shed, the natives packed in as tight as they could stand, men on one side, women on the other; then, at a signal, all sat down simultaneously. Within sixty years over 70,000 Hawaiians had been baptized. It had been well worth while to persist in spite of Kaahumanu's snubs.

This great success, still alive in Hawaiian congregations throughout the Islands and in Hawaiian-backed missions in Micronesia, was unmistakably the fruit of devotion and zeal. Though missionary hardships in Hawaii were never as severe as those encountered later in Melanesia, they were not negligible. No sneers can impugn the steadfastness of those who endured them. The mere trip from an outlying island to attend the annual Conference in Honolulu would have daunted many. The Hawaiian-manned schooner would be packed to the rails with seasick natives, pigs, children and dogs; the rough Island channels often combined with contrary winds to make the voyage last ten or twelve days. When you woke in the morning you often found the helm lashed, all hands asleep, sails slatting, and nothing to prevent disaster in a sudden squall. The Rev. Mr. Coan's self-admiring tales of hard riding over lava fields and fording streams in spate via a life line of devoted

[26]Hiram Bingham, A Residence, 143.

natives up to their chins in roaring water are not only true but a tribute to his rugged virtues. One of his predecessors on the Big Island, the Rev. Mr. Goodrich, often made his circuits barefoot—and Hawaiian trails are stony—for lack of boots that had failed to turn up in the last load of supplies from Boston.

All these men could have made small but easy livings with high prestige as pastors at home. Real self-sacrifice was involved in their staying in Hawaii to save heathen souls. (The emotional tensions that made them insist on doing so are another matter, but this is no textbook of psychiatry.) Their wives stuck with them, got seasick on the schooners, cooked in chamber pots borrowed from sea captains for lack of more appropriate utensils, held up gracefully or grimly against vermin and short supplies of flour and sugar, taught school, held sewing classes and prayer meetings in the teeth of staggering discouragements, kept house with inquisitive natives milling underfoot day and night. Considering their frailer physical endowment and the handicap of frequent childbearing, these women undoubtedly deserve equal credit with their husbands.

White prestige in the Islands had always been high; as the stubborn missionaries won over a few high-ranking chiefs, their prestige rose level with that of ships' captains, and even beyond. The commoner was flattered, perhaps stirred, when the white *kahuna* finally got round to telling him that any native, of whatever social stratum, had a soul of which Christ was solicitous. Nothing in his pre-white culture had ever led him to consider himself important to anybody.

Preaching was hampered by the Hawaiian vocabulary, which had no equivalents for the indispensable Christian metaphors of solicitous father and erring children; those emotional situations were lacking among Polynesians in any western sense. Foreign words and tedious interpretation had to fill such gaps. But other innovations came more easily. The New England Sabbath, forbidding cooking, working, dancing, playing, an obvious equivalent of the old-time *la tabu* (*tabu* day), was readily accepted.[27]

[27]Says Beaglehole, an authority on social Hawaii: ". . . a religion based on ten *tapus* was easily understandable by a mind nurtured in a way of

By thus supplying genuine social and emotional needs, the missionary effort justified the money and labor that it demanded of converts. Other aspects were less admirable. The missionaries unshamedly used quite worldly considerations in recommending Christianity to the native, as the Rev. Mr. Ellis recorded:

> "They immediately endeavoured to give a different turn to the conversation by saying: 'What a fine country yours must be compared to this! What large bales of cloth come from thence, while the clothing of Hawaii is small in quantity and very bad. The soil there must be very prolific, and property easily obtained . . .' I informed them that the difference was not so great between the countries as between the peoples. That, many ages back, the ancestors of the present inhabitants of England and America possessed fewer comforts than the Sandwich Islanders now enjoy; . . . but since they had become enlightened and industrious, and had embraced Christianity, they had been wise and rich; and many, there was reason to hope, had after death gone to a state of happiness in another world; . . . They said perhaps it was so; perhaps industry and instruction would make them happier and better, and, if the chiefs wished it, by and by they would attend to both."—*Narrative of a Tour Through Hawaii*, 64–5.

As mission influence grew in political weight, expediency began to play a large part in native thirst after righteousness. Said Jarves:

> "By fraud, by even giving up much-loved sins, and by ready knowledge of the Scriptures, many managed to become church members, because by it their importance was increased, and their chances of political preferment bettered."—*History of the Sandwich Islands*, 149.

---

life where the multitudinous observation of *tapus* gave one secular and religious satisfaction . . . the native was used to gods that were all-powerful and all-dreadful, sometimes benign, sometimes ruthless. He, best of all, could appreciate the severity of proselytizing Protestantism, as a sign and symbol of its power and prestige."—*Some Modern Hawaiians*, 18.

So in many Stateside communities it is still advisable for the life insurance salesman or Chamber of Commerce politician to turn up regularly in a well-considered church.

Nor were missionaries above using calamities *in terrorem.* The Rev. Mr. Coan makes much in his memoirs, and surely did so in his sermons, of a native village in the Big Island that remained stiff-necked under exhortation, and was duly wiped out by a lava flow from Mauna Loa. This demonstration of divine displeasure failed to soften the villagers, who merely rebuilt nearby; so the smallpox epidemic of 1853 attacked them alone in the whole district of Puna. Mr. Coan then struck while the iron was hot:

> "I visited this scene of sorrow and desolation, gathered the stricken remnant of the sufferers, spoke words of condolence, and encouraged them to come with their sins and sorrows to the Saviour. They seemed subdued, welcomed their pastor, and were, I trust, 'saved as by fire.' "—*Life in Hawaii,* 81.

You and I may think it an unmitigated shame that whites brought smallpox to the South Seas. The missionary knew that in this also God had His own good purposes.

But he was never clear where Christianity left off and the strictly secular tenor of white men's ways began. The New Testament does not mention bonnets, frame houses, and industrious habits as essential to salvation. Yet from the beginning, the ABCFM mission went on the principle that western customs must go hand-in-hand with the Gospel. In view of St. Paul on matrimony, Christian marriage was firmly insisted upon. In a few months of 1828 the Rev. Mr..Richards married over 600 couples at Lahaina; instead of "I do," the grooms, whose English came from seamen, often responded "Aye, aye." In addition to these blessings on unavoidable carnality, a strange mixture of exhortations appeared: leave off adultery; cover the body; go tee-total; swallow the Scripture kiver-to-kiver. Since the three Rs, needlework and singing classes were fundamental in Yankee education of the period, the Hawaiians were put through them all. Many were astoundingly quick at arithmetic. Mrs. Coan somehow acquired a bull fiddle from a ship and, though she had never before touched such an instrument, succeeded in teaching native converts to play it.

Though mats, calabashes and tapa were not exactly found inimical to Christianity, it was easily conveyed that somehow pots, pans, and carpets were superior. The natives already thought so, as their trade purchases showed. In 1828 Mrs. Judd recorded with approval that Liliha, Boki's headstrong consort, owned a crimson sofa, a center table, a mahogany secretary and enough colored silks to clothe her forty "maids of honor."[28] Presently Mrs. Judd was teaching Kinau, kuhina nui after Kaahumanu, how to make bread, cakes and pies. Poi and fish were surely healthier diet, but then nobody had any such ideas in nutrition, and how could you be Christian and not eat pie? By 1836 Kekauluohi, a high chieftainess, was giving a "Christian tea party" for chiefs and missionaries at which numerous white man's comestibles appeared in recognizable form, and tunes were played on a barrel organ which the captain of a French man-of-war had presented to the hostess. Consider the lilies of the field . . . without staff or scrip . . . where moth and rust do corrupt . . . Kekauluohi listening beamingly to the treadling tunes of her barrel organ was not a tenth as ridiculous as her preceptors.[29]

So the Gospel, of a sort, rained on the chief and dripped on the commoner until, somehow or other, it moistened most of the population. But the process was not smooth. Other kinds of white ways offered too much hindrance. Sandalwooders, whalers, and men-of-war brought thousands of white men with

[28] Civilized objects were not always used correctly: when the chieftainesses of Honolulu gave a haole style dinner for Captain Finch, U.S.N., the mission ladies checking the table arrangements were taken aback by the sight of a large white chamber pot set at each place. (J. J. Jarves, Scenes and Scenery, 66.) Number, size and beauty of chamber pots remained an important matter among Hawaiians for generations.

[29] Naturally the mission did not carry the principle of stimulating the acquisition of this world's goods to damaging excess. Excessive personal ornament among commoners was frowned on, since the money to buy gay textiles and gewgaws would very likely be earned not so much by industry as by carnally entertaining sailors.

a rival complex of customs, profanity, rum, cards, tobacco, prostitution, and late hours, a school of behavior to which the native took all too kindly. The Rev. Mr. Cheever called Lahaina, prominent Hawaiian whaling-haven, "one of the breathing holes of hell."[30] No doubt it looked so to him, and moral morbidity was probably present in quantity. Yet the old accounts sound as if this were not exactly the same as contemporary big-seaport vice in London, New York or San Francisco. One feels that the Hawaiian *wahine*, however much she slept and drank with Jack ashore, however freely her husband or brother pimped for her, managed to be less shattered about it than her opposite number among the slack-jawed slatterns of the Barbary Coast. The stews of Lahaina probably looked, smelled, and acted better than those of Limehouse or the Five Points. According to the natives' original moral standards, voluntary sexual intercourse with strangers was nothing to fret oneself about, and much of that attitude probably survived. In the early 'sixties, it was estimated that two out of three professional prostitutes in the Islands were at least nominally married. No doubt they had a good time on the whole.

To missionaries, however, that would be farfetched, so they crusaded against vice in familiar Yankee style as soon as they could command support from zealously Christianized chiefs, usually women. The mission decried tobacco so loudly that natives had the impression that "Thou shalt not smoke" was one of the Ten Commandments. Known drinkers, lechers, gamesters, were either denied baptism, with its social advantages, or excommunicated if their conduct was too flagrant after baptism. The crew of U.S.S. "Dolphin" were not the only seamen rioting and threatening violence to missionaries when they found that, for fear of a pious chieftainess' strong arm, no girl in town would accommodate them. Convicts working out sentences for adultery built the first road on Maui, and the chiefs' constables, searching huts for sinners, made life in the ports quite exciting.

Temperance societies imitating those in the States prospered,

[30]Henry T. Cheever, *Life in the Sandwich Islands*, 65.

for the natives were, and still are, fond of meetings and parades. In 1843 Mrs. Judd was delighted with a 1,400-strong procession of the Honolulu children's "cold-water army" carrying banners inscribed "Down with Rum!" All chiefs took the pledge in 1842. So, when the missionaries tendered a dinner of thanks to Admiral Thomas in 1843 for having restored native sovereignty (meaning missionary ascendancy), the affair was strictly cold-water. One officer guest mentioned that lack of stronger drink had given him stomach cramps. The not too unsympathetic Mrs. Judd was tempted to get him a glass of wine from the medicine chest. But "there sat our sovereign and chiefs, and I would not set wine before them for a kingdom."[31] In 1832 Kamehameha III still dared drink wine in Mr. Bingham's presence at dinner on U.S.S. "Potomac"; but at the return dinner he gave for the ship's officers, he apologized for lack of wine in a whisper: "The missionaries don't like it."[32]

Spasmodic and sporadic results came from these crusades against ungodly doings.[33] But some chiefs helped scoffing whites to sabotage the war on sin. Nahienaena, sister of Kamehameha II, found a mission education insufficient armor against the flesh and the devil; she died young, but had enjoyed herself immensely in the meantime. Kamehameha III himself, piously reared under Kaahumanu's converted eye, went magnificently off the rails when the old lady died and, from then on, suffered memorable fits of backsliding. Boki misbehaved sadly at intervals, even setting up a saloon called the Blonde Hotel (probably in memory of Lord Byron's ship, not of a

[31]Laura F. Judd, *Honolulu*, 125.
[32]J. N. Reynolds, *Voyage of the . . . "Potomac,"* 413.
[33]Mr. Coan's description of Hilo under efficient prohibition in 1849: "Whale ships are now in, and our streets are all alive with sailors . . . No man staggers, no man fights, none are noisy and boisterous. We have nothing here to inflame the blood, nothing to madden the brain. Our verdant landscapes, our peaceful streets, our pure cold water, and the absence of those inebriating vials of wrath which consume all good, induce wise commanders to visit this port, in order to refresh and give liberty to their crews."—Letter to the American Seamen's Friend Society, quoted in Henry T. Cheever, *The Island World of the Pacific*, 335.

lady) and starting a system of licensed prostitution in Honolulu. And Kuakini, governor of the Big Island and a sort of subking in his own right, backslid in later life, was more than suspected of bootlegging rum to those able to pay two dollars a bottle, and, when the mission told converts to stop growing tobacco, pronounced: "*Listen* to your teachers. But *do* as I tell you. I tell you to plant tobacco."[34] Though he had an excellent previous record as vice hunter, Kuakini was excommunicated for such capers, a courageous step on the mission's part.

The old games, inextricably involved with gambling, were prohibited. So, for obvious reasons, were *hulas*. So was flower wearing, which seemed extreme even to the Rev. Mr. Cheever; still, wearing a certain flower in a certain way is a recognized Polynesian signal that the wearer needs a bedfellow. Obviously the mission had bitten off more than it could chew. In prewhite days *tabu* breaking had meant death, exile or mysterious illness; breaking a missionary-inspired *tabu* meant merely hard labor and imprisonment or a fine. So it is not surprising that, of 522 Hawaiian offenses booked in the late 'thirties, adultery accounted for 246, seduction and lewdness for ninety-nine; of 427 police cases involving natives in Honolulu in 1846, the charges were adultery or fornication in 253, evenly divided between men and women.[35] It disheartened the mission considerably when pressure from godless whites secured elementary legal rights for sinners, curbing the constables' former freedom to force their way in at any time if a certain hut were suspected of harboring sin.

Even the Hawaiian youths educated at Cornwall were disappointing. Young George Kaumualii was useful for a while as a foot in the door on Kauai, but wound up as unsuccessful rebel against the Kamehamehas, with bullets whistling round Mr. Bingham's scandalized ears. Another went to the California gold fields in 1850. None turned out really well. Every

[34]Titus Coan, *Life in Hawaii*, 228.
[35]Quoting these figures, Jarves duly points out that they probably represent a small proportion of the actual transgressions occurring.

year more Hawaiian youngsters went to sea on *haole* ships—
3,000 were said to be thus away at one time—to come back
exuding vices. Recognizing this menace, the missions began
to entertain whaling captains and to inveigle their crews into
seamen's chapels. Now and again a captain actually promised
to read the Bible to the hands and renounce Sunday whaling,
much to the detriment of his owners and his own "lay" in the
voyage.[36] The missionaries cross-examined returning Kanaka
hands as to whether such pledges were kept.

Even converts who managed to stay on the books were not
too satisfactory. They might understand that a practicing
Christian could not do so-and-so, but seldom acquired much
idea of what the mission took to be the higher spiritual values
of the Gospel. There were exceptions to this. Stevenson, who
was nicely discriminating in Christian values, maintained that
Hawaiian native teachers whom he met in the South Seas were
often Christian in a higher sense than most white communicants. But, from any but a Pharasaical point of view, Mrs.
Judd's admiring picture of her prize Hawaiian convert is not
edifying. She quotes a portrait of a dead native wife written by
the sorrowing *haole* widower who, it appears, had made a
pass at the girl, been rebuffed, and then married her:

> "Nothing could persuade her into evil . . . Her unqualified
> exemption from all bad habits, so prevalent among her people,
> was truly remarkable. She never used tobacco, nor gave her
> consent to its use in her house. In fact, she persuaded me from

[36]Though whaler and mission were usually at loggerheads for obvious
reasons, relations were sometimes friendly and useful. Captain Allen of
the *Maro*, who first exploited the Japan ground in 1820, was a good
Quaker and a good friend of the missions. (Hiram Bingham, *A Residence*, 134.) Time and again badly needed supplies of flour, paper, ink
and prunes came to Hawaii in the holds of whalers owned by pious men
on whom the ABCFM had put pressure. Whaling captains often consented to take home to Yankeeland the missionaries' children sent
home for the schooling that they could not yet get in the vineyard
where their fathers labored. There were "temperance ships" too, renouncing the daily issue of free rum; some of these, though willing to
economize on board, hypocritically carried trade rum for bargaining
with the natives.

its use, as she did from other idle and vicious habits, which a single and careless man is apt to contract. She never went into the streets to see people pass; never romped or went to festivals, other than religious ones, or school celebrations. She detested gewgaws and finery and would never consent to my getting her more than decency required . . . She looked back with peculiar horror on the degradation of her ancestors . . . She could never excuse anyone for licentiousness or wickedness of any kind on the plea of ignorance; her reason being a simple and forcible one, viz.: there was not a Hawaiian but had had the same advantages of education with herself, and that she always knew better."—*Honolulu*, 162–3.

This quite unfamiliar version of the tale of the white man who marries the South Seas maiden would make a good plot for W. Somerset Maugham.

* * *

Honolulu . . . has long been familiar with demonstrations of puerile excitement and folly.—Hiram Bingham, *A Residence*, 350.

How the missionaries, presumably engrossed in saving souls and specifically instructed not to intervene in native politics, came to preponderant power is still to be told. The facts are damning. The Honolulu water front early knew Mr. Bingham as "King Hiram." Within a generation of the first landing of missionaries, five of his colleagues had resigned to enter native government. Thenceforth the bullying man-of-war captain, intriguing foreign consul, or corner-cutting trader, found himself dealing, not with confused Polynesians, but with persistent and self-righteous Yankees zealously guarding what they took to be the natives' best interests. These white policy makers and watchdogs—Judd, the mission physician, Richards, former preacher at Lahaina—naturally did not renounce the company or influence of their former colleagues or curb their instincts toward pious authoritarianism. The implications would be equally clear if five members of the Soviet legation in London were successively to resign, swear allegiance to the throne and be installed in the government.

Yet this was no conspiracy; some such development was inevitable as Hawaiian chiefs learned to regard missionaries as vehicles of prestige and good things. The Hawaiian had no notion of salutary cleavage between church and state. He was not even aware that a distinction existed. In his society religious and political sanctions merged at the top in the hands of chiefs who were part priests, and priests who, as sources of omens, were part political advisors. So when Christianity appeared, the missionary being white, knowing white ways and becoming opposite number of the former *kahuna*, the chiefs naturally turned to him for steering.

The Rev. Mr. Richards' first moves on taking office in 1838 were to lecture the chiefs on political economy—much he probably knew about it himself—and draw up a fundamental code of law in the western style, so that erring whites could be called to account in the manner to which they were accustomed in police courts at home. The first clause of his code is explicitly Mosaic: ". . . no law shall be enacted which is at variance with the word of the Lord Jehovah." That was a triumph; but Mr. Richards was not too brilliant a success as king's minister. Dr. Judd did better in his task of bringing order out of the inchoate Hawaiian nation's fiscal confusion. Port dues, customs duties, and purchases on credit brought in cash and goods on a basis strange to Polynesia, the chiefs of which had always used resources on hand as needed, and demanded more from commoners at will. In this sort of matter whites could give genuine help, as when Commodore Wilkes, finding lack of small change a nuisance in the Islands, had Spanish dollars cut into quarters and eighths.

On the whole Brookes is probably right in the verdict: "Certainly none of these [missionary] officials was a big-caliber man";[37] nor well trained for his job, it might have been added. True, missionaries occasionally tried to recruit expert lay talent from the mainland before consenting to handle law or finance themselves. Yet their reluctance to dabble in government was not perfervid. They assumed, probably correctly, that God's

[37]J. I. Brookes, *International Rivalry*, 181.

emissaries would advise native rulers more scrupulously than the white merchants, skippers and beachcombers who would otherwise be called on. Beyond that was something deeper and, however well rationalized, more powerful. In that day Yankees had yet to lose their traditional leaning toward government by the righteous through the ministers of congregations. An hierocracy founded and governed Massachusetts Bay and Hartford and, though subversive new notions had crippled hierocracy in the States, pious Yankees transplanted to Hawaii found it easy to acquiesce when events threatened to invest them with political power. It was tempting, this unsought opportunity to become judge in Israel. The Rev. Mr. Bingham made no bones about it:

"The state, deriving all its power from God, both rulers and subjects being bound to do God's will, and its chief magistrate being emphatically God's minister, ought to be, and in an important sense *is, a religious institution.*"—*A Residence*, 278.

To Thomas Jefferson such words from an American would have been close to treason; to John Endicott self-evident truths. In Honolulu no objection was likely from people whose opinion King Hiram respected. Besides, the thing was practical. The more the chiefs came under the thumb of mission-connected advisers, the easier it was to get laws written and enforced against sin. In Kaahumanu's regency, formal appointments were not needed. That stern nestler in Abraham's bosom did little without making sure that her actions pleased her preceptors' God. After her death, the regency for young Kamehameha III was most respectful of missionaries. As the young king entered on active rule, events pushed him into making parsons his official aides.

The bitterness with which the water fronts assailed this development went far to assure missionaries that, in advising native government, they were doing right. They had long felt, with justification, that the frontier-like growth of secular influence in Honolulu, Lahaina and Hilo was ominous in both quantity and quality, bad for missions and natives alike.

"Honolulu was a hard-looking old camp in those days," wrote the reminiscing Rev. Sereno Bishop.[38] As early as 1823 the flat, dry, ugly, jerry-built settlement had four "mercantile houses," three Yankee, one run by New Yorkers, selling piece goods, hardware, crockery, hats, shoes, ship's chandlery and rum to any customer able to pay in sandalwood or Spanish dollars. By 1827 two dollar-a-day "hotels," two billiard parlors and a dozen bars were operating. Whalers began to use Honolulu as a port of deposit, landing oil for reshipment to the States and going back for more, instead of wasting time in the long voyage round the Horn. There was also a small but growing trade in hides, wool and tallow which whites on Kauai and the Big Island produced by shooting wild cattle and sheep and flaying and boiling them down.[39] Other small items were edible fungus gathered for the China trade and *pulu*, the down of large ferns, which made good pillow stuffing. In 1820, just after the missionaries landed, a United States commercial agent was installed at Honolulu to see that American interests got fair play. Every year more whites settled down to exploit Hawaii in any fashion suggested by ingenuity and hope. Some of these interlopers, such as the Spaniard Marin, the Frenchman Rives and numbers of English and Americans, were years ahead of the mission.

Consuls, merchants and barkeepers seldom saw eye to eye with Jehovah on what was good for the Islands. Bradley says that, since they thought of themselves as exploiting transients, they were regrettably "indifferent to local problems and to the welfare of the population."[40] They wanted whalers well supplied, not only with spars and canvas but with rum and girls; they sold the rum, and could sell the girls finery in exchange for their earnings; they wanted the chiefs to spend freely on drink and luxuries at sucker prices. The mission did its best

[38]Sereno E. Bishop, *Reminiscences*, 35.

[39]These animals were descendants of the stock put ashore in the very early days by Vancouver and others. Kamehameha I tabud cattle for ten years in order to ensure their propagating well.

[40]H. W. Bradley, *The American Frontier in Hawaii*, 82.

against such profitable activity, getting prostitution prohibited, warning natives that they were being swindled. The profit-minded also wanted to buy land for warehouse- and groggery-sites and later for plantation experiments, preferring to pay as little as the inexperienced native owner-chief would take.

The chiefs sometimes sold, but only according to their traditional lights which assumed that, as in grants to native vassals, the holder could be ejected at will. That infuriated white purchasers fancying themselves in full title. In such disputes the mission often backed the chief, maintaining that Hawaiian feudal custom was good law in Hawaii and Stateside land laws were not. No wonder that, often with consular backing, the water front loudly protested against "missionary meddling."

The history of this head-on clash of God and Mammon bristles with special pleading, rationalization, irresponsible accusation, downright lies and unedifying finagling on both sides. That the missionaries meddled is unquestionably a true bill, whether or not their doing so was justified. In 1825 the Rev. Mr. Ellis roundly denied—never did minister of the Gospel lie more gallantly—that the mission ever had or ever would mix in Island government. Dibble, an early missionary-historian, grudgingly admitted the fact. A generation later the Rev. Mr. Cheever was ebulliently indiscreet:

> "As to the charge of meddling with government, we think it would have been much better for the nation had it been truer, and had missionaries much earlier been concerned in the councils and laws of the kingdom . . . We hold it to be as much the duty of ministers nowadays to instruct kings and governors in the law of God . . . as it was the duty of the Jewish prophets of old . . . and in this sense, we take it, the missionaries at the Sandwich Islands have meddled . . ."
> —The Island World of the Pacific, 212–13.

In the first decades, before the water fronts grew too strong, the mission could keep the chiefs in hand and defy criticism. It also sought to perpetuate its influence by educating the rising generation of chiefs in a special school, the pupils of which, in the 'thirties, included practically everybody who should henceforth sit on the throne of Hawaii. But the mission was not well-advised to try to enlist commercial enterprise on Jehovah's side. In 1833 there came to Honolulu a group of young Yankees with Boston capital—the rumor that they were financed by the ABCFM is probably not true—to establish a mercantile business on "purely Christian principles" as "a pattern card of mercantile morality."[41] Guiding spirit of this Ladd & Company was one J. A. Brinsmade, a former theological student who taught a missionary Bible class in Honolulu. He handled much of the mission's business affairs and probably used mission influence in getting a needed royal land concession on Kauai to start the first important sugar plantation in the Islands. Much to the displeasure of dispossessed small local chiefs, an annual $300 to the crown secured the company a large tract devoted to sugar, coffee, and bananas worked by Hawaiian labor.

While this project was still in the betwixt and between stage, Brinsmade and Richards, the pregnant lecturer on political economy, grew grandiose. The complaisant government accorded Ladd & Company vague grants to "all unoccupied and unimproved land" in the Islands as basis for a scheme to persuade European capital and immigration to "develop as promptly as possible the civilization and resources of the Sandwich Islands." The mission was heartily behind it all, apparently believing that, if economic power were in the hands of the godly Ladd & Company, guided by the godly Richards, Mammon would become a great ally of the Lord. Off to Europe went Brinsmade to float this new South Sea Bubble. He actually did get a grandiloquent contract with a Belgian group, but when the push came, no cash was forthcoming. All Ladd & Company ever realized was a series of lawsuits. The Lord got nothing but increased enmity from Honolulu mercantile interests, indignant at seeing missionary influence over government used to promote a semimonopoly of the Islands' economic future.

In the same period foreign governments turned aggressive, threatening the mission through the government that the mis-

[41]Manley Hopkins, *Hawaii*, 281.

sionaries tutored. France was first. Allegedly at the suggestion of Rives, the stowaway swindler, the newly founded Société de Picpus despatched a couple of French Catholic missionary priests to Hawaii. In that day the word "Popery" was still a live and snorting bogey and the reaction of King Hiram and his retainers was violent. Jarves recorded that:

> "One of the oldest and most intelligent ladies on the mission said to me that she had rather reside among the cannibals and licentious savages of the Marquesas than in a community of Roman Catholics; she actually thought herself safer among the former than the latter. Another was afraid to send her children to the United States, for fear they would become Papists . . ."—*Scenes and Scenery*, 202.

The missionaries tried later to maintain that they were not responsible for what happened to those missionary priests. This is disingenuous. Kaahumanu, then all-powerful, was obviously infected by her preceptors' feeling that Catholics were the Devil's own. The missionaries' records show that some of their number preached against Catholics in public and advised chiefs against them in private; and that they put into the chiefs' heads the handiest objection, that Catholics were idolaters, as the images in their chapels proved. Wrote the Rev. Lowell Smith:

> "During my morning discourse, . . . I alluded to the sentiments and practices of Roman Catholics . . . stated that a Roman Catholic priest had just come to this place and that it was my *manao* [thought] that it would be *pono* [good, right] for him to return in the same vessel in which he came."—Mary D. Frear, *Lowell and Abigail*, 109.

Reynolds recorded with what reluctance King Hiram translated for Kamehameha III Commodore Downes' lecture on tolerating people of conflicting faiths. In 1831, the General Meeting of the mission made it clear that, though the Lord had doubts about the ethics of persecuting Papists, he had none about the advisability of deporting Catholic wolves in sheep's clothing. When Kaahumanu took the high hand with

Catholics, King Hiram protested perfunctorily, but there was no mistaking his satisfaction when she expelled idolmongers regardless. Though they wriggled and lied in a most undignified fashion, the reverend fathers were finally got on board a vessel that landed them, in very bad temper, at San Pedro, California, the nearest spot under Catholic influence.[42]

There was trouble about that with the French government. There was worse in the late 'thirties when, Catholic infiltrators having reappeared, the native government not only tried to deport Catholic priests, but also imprisoned and mistreated Catholic converts. This was probably legal, since Hawaii as yet had no freedom-of-worship clause in a bill of rights, but it was most indiscreet. At the time the French were feeling their oats in the Pacific and using mishaps to French missionaries as pretexts for serious intervention in several island groups. Perhaps tardily realizing as much, the mission helped to rescue the jailed converts and persuaded Kamehameha III to decree religious toleration for Catholics in June, 1839.

Discretion came too late. "L'Artémise," sixty guns, as formidable a vessel as Honolulu had yet seen, was already on her vengeful way, fit again after knocking a hole in her bottom on a similar errand at Tahiti. Though toleration had been official for three weeks when she arrived, Captain La Place was not to be mollified by words on paper. He landed men, celebrated a mass ashore under guard, and demanded a $20,000 cash guaranty that Catholics would be persecuted no more.

In that time and place the sum was enormous. La Place had no instructions about taking over Hawaii, but he was known to be jealous for his country of growing American influence there, and obviously desired occasions for encroachment. The mission went hat in hand to local merchants to raise the wind for the government. The water front had been pleased to see the Catholics appear, considering them a likely spoke in King

[42]The missionaries were suave enough to lend the priests some Hawaiian texts to study the language from. "This," says Manley Hopkins with a cultivated grin, "was very liberal; but there is a great charm in having one's book read, even by our adversaries." (Hawaii, 221.)

Hiram's wheel; in fact, three water front Americans, including the U.S. commercial agent, had had their children baptized Catholics as an anti-Bingham gesture. But when the chips were down, the prospect of the French taking over bodily was also alarming. So the money was raised and "L'Artémise" departed with her loot on board.[43] The image-worshiping, Bible-suppressing, Pope-dominated enemies of righteousness remained. By approaching the natives on a more equalitarian basis than the ABCFM believed in, they acquired quite a respectable number of converts.

Ten years later there was another French demonstration. Not only were Catholics again being mistreated, claimed Admiral de Tromelin, but high duties on liquors were ruining the Hawaiian market for French brandy. Both he and the mission knew that those duties were supposed to make hard liquor inaccessible to the bulk of the natives; but the mission found itself in the curious position of quoting figures to prove in rebuttal that local consumption of brandy was increasing. They revenged themselves by well-aimed sarcasm at French bad taste in coupling one kind of water of life with another. Still, sarcasm and statistics alike were feeble against the grinning broadsides of "La Poursuivante" and "Le Gassendi"—this last the first warsteamer that Honolulu had seen. When the chiefs proved argumentative, de Tromelin seized and looted the fort of Honolulu. Within a few years French pressure on the Islands, still harping on Catholics and brandy, was so strong that the king made an abortive effort to hand the Islands to the United States as preferable to France. By then, as it happened, international diplomatic exchanges had pretty well removed the practical possibility of the French doing to Hawaii what they had earlier done to Tahiti and the Marquesas. But chancelleries could not disguise the black eye that mission prestige had again suffered. Having tied their worldly fortunes to the Hawaiian government, the missionaries had to share the repercussions of that government's weakness.

[43] To their credit, the French returned the money seven years later, still packed in the same cases.

They had fared better when the English grew violent in 1843. This trouble stemmed from a land tangle closely affecting the pocketbook of the mission-scorning British consul.[44] He and his side made things sound so inflammatory that H.M.S. "Carysfort," under Captain Lord George Paulet, "a pleasant-looking young man with a fresh complexion, blue eyes and chestnut hair curling all over his head,"[45] was ordered from Valparaiso to remedy matters. Paulet seems to have been formally courteous to missionaries, but went far out of his way to insult rival consuls and American merchants, and outraged the mission in practical effect by harsh demands on the native government. On missionary advice, Kamehameha III plaintively surrendered his sovereignty, the theory being that Paulet only needed enough rope to hang himself. Paulet landed men, ran up British colors and enlisted natives in a militia sworn into Queen Victoria's service. Among his administrative changes was the abrogation of laws against fornication except when committed in public streets, which definitely identified him as a limb of Satan. At Hilo the mission was strong enough quietly to undo everything the moment the "Carysfort" sailed away again. But Honolulu had months of British bayonet rule and at least some of the water front rejoiced at seeing the psalm singers' noses out of joint. Herman Melville, clerking in Honolulu at the time, was hotly to assure the world in print that the British had been justified throughout.

Neither Jehovah nor Whitehall agreed with him. Unwilling

[44] This was an English seaman-trader with previous Hawaiian experience, named Richard Charlton, of whom Hopkins, his countryman, said: "he seems to have the faculty of acting in the most injudicious manner conceivable upon every occasion." (*Hawaii*, 241.) Moerenhout, however (*Voyage auxíles* II, 499), says he heard nothing but good of Charlton's work in Hawaii as controlling influencer of English seamen ashore. In any case, he must have been a man of imagination. When sailing from England to assume his post, he shipped with him as potentially profitable merchandise a mixed cargo of donkeys and jew's-harps. No doubt some of the donkeys were ancestors of those innocent and shaggy beasts now prevalent on the west coast of the Big Island, known locally as "Kona nightingales."

[45] Titus Coan, *Life in Hawaii*, 106.

for ports so important to American whalers to be in British hands, Washington protested sharply. John Bull was already nervous about Uncle Sam *in re* Texas and Oregon. But, before instructions could reach the Pacific from England, Rear-Admiral Thomas, Paulet's senior, arrived at Honolulu in H.M.S. "Dublin" and formally repudiated his lordship's doings. The king was reinstated in a ceremony still commemorated by the name of Thomas Square in Honolulu. In demure triumph the flag hoisted in place of the Union Jack bore the missionary symbol of dove and olive branch and "The Lord reigns, let the earth rejoice," wrote the Rev. Lowell Smith, missionary.

Score a round for heaven. Two years later, however, the mission itself dealt its influence a heavy blow. The land tenure problem was still troublesome, not only to entrepreneurs but also to pious Yankees disturbed by the Hawaiian commoner's small share in real property. A dozen of the highest chiefs held the bulk of Hawaiian land; the total of holders, large and small, was barely 600. The mission associated thrift, sobriety, and industry, virtues still scarce among their converts, with the small farms that God-fearing folk held in fee simple in New England. So they persuaded king and chiefs to abolish feudal suzerainty in favor of freehold, a move that, their Catholic rivals agreed for once, would do great things for the average Kanaka. It took years to sort out conflicting and tenuous rights, but in the end the government proper held 1,500,000 acres, the king personally owned around 1,000,000 acres, the high chiefs divided another 1,500,000, and the commoners' share was some 30,000 acres. Though small in area, this consisted almost wholly of the most fertile lands in the kingdom, whereas the bulk of the large holdings was arid or mountainous waste, the best of it useless without elaborate irrigation.

Commoners were to have title to lands that they had been cultivating as tenants. It sounded fair and progressive and was certainly generous of the chiefs. But untoward consequences are still conspicuous in the Islands. Many commoners neglected to complete their titles by registration; others, blarneyed by whites with cash glittering in hand, sold for a song, squandered the proceeds, and found themselves thenceforth landless, less secure than when the chiefs had exploited, but also protected, them. Though Hawaiian legislatures took care of the interests of chiefs who failed to comply with necessary registration formalities, commoners of similar carelessness had little recourse. Thus many an Hawaiian was ripped loose from the land and started on the proletarian career still prevalent among his descendants. The vast noble or royal estates, on the other hand, became parts of the great sugar and pineapple plantations that now dominate the Islands' economy. A great deal of the land in these great developments is held on long lease from the government or the estates of chiefs' descendants, many of whose daughters married white men and so managed to keep their lands together. Yet the mission had meant so well! Damage to the objects of their solicitude came from inability to see that what was a good idea in the neighborhood of Mt. Greylock might not necessarily be so in the neighborhood of Haleakala. Again as in the case of Ladd & Company, it was demonstrated that parsons were poor social and economic engineers.

The crowning error was in allowing *haoles* to buy land on the same freehold basis as natives. That set merchants and planters inevitably on the upbeat. Within a short while enterprising whites were experimenting with wheat, sugar, potatoes, rice, coffee, cotton, silk and well-organized ranching. Some of these trials paid—wheat and potatoes boomed when pioneer California became a handy and greedy market. Gold-rushed San Francisco even sent dirty shirts for laundering to Honolulu. In witness of mainlanders' new closeness to the Islands, Californians planned filibustering expeditions of small calibre to relieve the Kamehameha dynasty of the cares of sovereignty. From the mid-century on, the economic pulse of the Islands unmistakably quickens and, in spite of severe ups and downs, beat more and more strongly up to the depression of the 1930's. It is clear, at least chronologically, that the Great *Mahele*, as Hawaiians called the new land program, set off the whole process.

Simultaneously missionary hegemony tended to weaken. Dr. Judd, ablest missionary-politician, was ousted as scapegoat of the 1853 smallpox epidemic, which killed 3,000. In 1850 there had appeared stiff evangelistic competition from the Mormons, failures at first, then doing extremely well under the leadership of George Q. Cannon. Much of this success was due to tact in telling the Hawaiians that Polynesians were descendants of the lost tribes of Israel whose adventures the Book of Mormon celebrates in so prolix a style. No words could magnify the devotion involved in Cannon's feat of translating Joe Smith's great work into Hawaiian. By now Catholics, Mormons, Adventists, and Episcopalians together outnumber the Hawaiian Church that the Yankee mission founded.

Anglicanism appeared under august auspices. Kamehameha III who, sot and vacillator though he was, had been an ally of the mission most of the time, died in 1855; his successor, Kamehameha IV, was somewhat Anglophile himself[46] and married Emma Rooke, *hapa-haole* granddaughter of John Young, who was zealously so. Their accession meant growing English influence, marked by an invasion by a Church of England mission complete with a real, live bishop. With Queen Emma ecstatically clutching a prayer book, the missionary monopoly on royal piety was broken. The same period saw gradual abandonment of the old policy of teaching only Hawaiian in Island schools, with its implication of discouraging contact between natives and invading whites.

Nevertheless King Hiram's successors—the old gentleman went home to retire in the early 'forties—had a sublime confidence. When the ABCFM decided in the 'fifties that the Hawaiian church was old and strong enough for support gradually to be withdrawn, the missionaries on the spot welcomed the decision as an accolade. Happily they constituted themselves pastors of self-supporting Hawaiian congregations, or-

[46]The king was also plainly anti-American. The reason was, says an old and probably true story, that when he and his brother were traveling with Dr. Judd in the States as young princes, they were mistaken for negroes on a railroad train and insulted. Cf. J. I. Brookes, *International Relations*, 215.

dained numbers of native pastors and considered themselves rewarded as good and faithful servants. They or their predecessors had been sent to win Hawaii to Christ, and lo, they had done it.

Perhaps they had. At least they had made Hawaiians one of the world's most literate peoples, albeit in an obscure dialect; trained them to wear clothes; to sing; and to go through the motions of Congregationalism. Some Yankee missionary churches still stand, brown-skinned natives still worship in them, other such natives have gone forth on funds raised by such congregations to preach the same Gospel successfully in Micronesia. But, though they won their war with heathenism, the missionaries lost their war with sin. The Rev. Mr. Palmer, modern clerical commentator on Hawaii, does not hesitate to say that the way the ABCFM pushed the Hawaiian mission out of the nest was "premature and it resulted disastrously."[47]

The principal mark that the mission left on the Islands, in fact, is economic. It engineered the Great *Mahele* which its sons and countrymen exploited. Some sons continued the good fight; King Hiram's boy, for instance, was the heart and soul of the Micronesian mission. But many more, heirs to Yankee shrewdness as well as Yankee self-righteousness, followed the ward politician's maxim of "if you can't lick 'em, jine 'em," and whored after strange gods among the money changers. They entered mercantile houses, intermarried with Mammon's minions, leased land, experimented with imports and crops, and prospered exceedingly. The ill-informed are wrong in accusing the missionaries of stealing the natives' land. But it is true that the core of the efforts to exploit Island resources, which pushed the native aside, consisted of the progeny of missionaries. Castle & Cooke, Alexander & Baldwin, peerless in Hawaiian finance and industry, are all missionary names.[48] So

[47] *The Human Side of Hawaii*, 43.
[48] Of the "Big Five"—the mercantile agencies that control most of Hawaiian business—only two were not American in origin. Theo. H. Davies & Company was founded by an Englishman; American Factors was originally German as Hackfeld & Company and was taken over as alien property during World War I, bought in by predominating Big

were Thurston and Dole, key names in the proannexation revolution of 1893. Other names from mission rolls still stud any modern list of men in Island politics and business.

*   *   *

". . . that curious pinhead kingdom of the Pacific."—W. R. Bliss, *Paradise of the Pacific*, 7.

As the world spun fast down the ringing grooves of change in the 'sixties, Hawaii was not exempt. Just before the Civil War coal oil began to threaten whaling, chief stay of the Hawaiian economy. Then C.S.S. "Shenandoah" burned Yankee whalers all over the Pacific; a few years later Arctic ice crushed most of the remains of the right whale fleet, never to base on Honolulu again. After that the Islands had to look inward for a living.

They found it in sugar. Artificial demand mushrooming during the Civil War expanded Hawaiian cane production, and the aftermath taught Island sugar planters two valuable lessons: It paid constantly to seek out improved varieties of cane to plant as well as better methods of harvest and manufacture. And really juicy profits depended on getting under, over, or around the tariff barrier between the Islands and their markets on the West Coast. All through the reigns of Kamehameha V and Kamehameha VI, sugar interests kept putting pressure on

Five interests. In 1874 Nordhoff described the process, familiar in most colonial histories, whereby the agency-firms came into firm control of Hawaiian sugar raising: "If a sugar planter has his land and machinery heavily mortgaged at ten or twelve per cent; if then he sends the product to an agent in Honolulu, who charges him five per cent more . . . if besides all this the planter buys his supplies on credit and is charged one per cent a month on these, compounded every three months until it is paid, and pays almost as much freight on his sugar from the plantation to Honolulu as from there to its final market—it is highly probably that he will, in the course of time, fail . . . a good deal of money has been made, but not by the planters . . . so many planters are in need of money, which they borrow in Honolulu, with the understanding that they will submit their product to the management of agents there." Charles Nordhoff, *Northern California, Oregon and the Sandwich Islands*, 58–61.

the throne and on American consuls. In 1876 under Kalakaua, the desired deal was consummated, a reciprocity treaty admitting Hawaiian sugar to the States tariff free, in return for a guarantee that naval base privileges at Pearl Harbor, on which the U.S. Navy had long had its eye, would not go to any other power. That presaged completion of what whalers had started— the absorption of Hawaii by Uncle Sam; and it ensured what would change the face of Hawaii—primacy of sugar in the Island economy. Insects had smothered cotton, coffee was a disappointment, rice could not compete as an export, beef would not pay shipping costs to the mainland, silk, wheat, potatoes, sisal, rubber, had variously petered out. But, if you had the enterprise to fertilize and irrigate intelligently, sugar fairly spurted out of the Islands' lowlands.

The fact that sugar was a hand-labor crop produced the next change:

Island population-decline was already acute, and nobody knew where expanding sugar would get more hands to cut more cane. Disease and possibly emotional disintegration[49] had so depressed the birth rate and increased the death rate that in the 'seventies only 56,000 souls inhabited the Islands. The missionaries deplored this gradual massacre, but perhaps here too God was working mysteriously. The invaluable Cheever wrote in 1850:

". . . none need be sorry for the occasion that has called forth . . . so convincing a success, which will be none the less real and true though, in the mysterious providence of God, the whole native race expire just as it is Christianized."—*The Island World of the Pacific*, 214.

He sounds like the mediaeval saint who ran a ferry across the Rhine and used forcibly to baptize passengers in midstream, after which he drowned them overside to make sure they went to heaven before they could defile their newly cleansed souls. Others were not so philosophical about depopulation. Never

[49]Cf. V, *Their Gods Are Dead* for further discussion.

mind the next world; in this one kings wanted subjects to pay taxes and planters wanted labor. Immigration was the only answer.

That was all the clearer because what natives were left did not distinguish themselves as toilers. The prewhite Hawaiian had led a pretty industrious life, but strictly in his own way, which was not geared to white ideas of efficiency. From sugar's point of view, the place had always been practically uninhabited since the 'forties, when Ladd & Company's manager complained of "the complete worthlessness" of Hawaiian labor. The Hawaiians, wrote Crawford, "preferred to stand by while this new civilization rushed along, not because of indolence, but because they had not made the necessary cultural adjustment. Not to be in the main current of progress did not greatly worry them, and does not now."[50] There had been exceptions; both the Mormons on Oahu, and some sugar planters on Maui and the Big Island apparently succeeded in getting reasonable industry out of Hawaiians. But their secret, whatever it was, did not spread. The Hawaiian did splendidly in jobs that he liked, such as seaman or cowpuncher, which offered small emergencies in quantity, or a chance to ride horses. But he did not care for long hours of slogging with a cane knife through a choking, sun-baked thicket of cane. That job has never appealed to anybody able to avoid it. So there was more than dwindling population behind the movement to bring outsiders to the Islands.

Steered by white advisors still, though men directly from the mission were scarcer among them, successive royal governments imported labor on mass contract, with sanctions derived from Yankee apprenticeship and maritime laws which would strike us as harsh and arbitrary, though they were nothing out of the way then. Islanders from the Gilberts, Tahiti, and Samoa proved as unsatisfactory as their Hawaiian cousins. So government ships under white command raided Melanesia for black-birded labor. None too scrupulous methods persuaded Tannese, Erromangans, Mallicolans to toil in Hawaii for a pit-

[50] *Paradox in Hawaii*, 29-30.

tance[51]—an unsavory example of one breed of South Sea Islander exploiting another. In the 'sixties somewhat more ethical enterprise imported Chinese and Japanese, the Chinese predominating for a generation, the great flow of Japanese waiting until the late 'eighties. The Islands were gradually flooded with Orientals, plus odds and ends of group-imported Scandinavians, Russians, Portuguese from Madeira and the Azores.

Thus culminated the process that began when whites brought exotic trees and shrubs to crowd indigenous vegetation off the landscape. In the end lands were practically all under white control, tilled by small yellow strangers cultivating and harvesting sugar cane, which prewhite Hawaiians had considered merely a vegetable confection with leaves useful for thatch. The Hawaiian did not resent it as much as some others would have done. He, and more notably she, mingled readily with Portygee, Chinaman and Jap—when the Jap was feeling sociable—and founded a progressively hybridizing race noted for both sturdiness and ethnic variety. Modern white Hawaii takes pride in the relative lack of race prejudice in the Islands. The sentiment is admirable but in white mouths, impertinent; all the *haole* did was to shovel different races successively together and pay no more attention.

Though the rise of sugar is the prevalent fact, the Islands showed interesting strains between the decline of missionary influence and annexation. For instance, the English bugaboo frightened hypersuspicious Americans in Honolulu. As annexation to the United States grew more imminent, the nervous Yankee contended more and more vehemently that if Uncle Sam did not, England would. There was just enough historical fact behind this to alarm such fleeting visitors as Mark Twain.

The Islands had always prided themselves, a bit snobbishly, on being a special concern of Beritani—as near as Polynesians could get to pronouncing Britain. Vancouver had been mentor of Kamehameha the Great. Liholiho, seeking British patronage, had come home feet foremost but in charge of a peer of

[51]Cf. IV, 6, *Unsavory Characters.*

the realm. Admiral Thomas had "restored the life of the nation." Queen Emma had not only imported the Church of England but also been entertained by Queen Victoria as a royal, if dusky, cousin. A principal street in Honolulu is named Beritania.

Modern Honolulu still has a haunting resemblance to an English colonial capital; look closely and it disappears like a blur in vision, but relax and there it is again. Something about the way business is done, the reticences of the powers that be, the tone of commercial architecture, the "Ltd." on firm names . . . The most popular visitor to the Islands during this transition was the royal Duke of Edinburgh as commander of H.M.S. "Galatea," who enjoyed himself hugely ashore and, reputedly, left behind him several *hapa-haole* youngsters. Lord Charles Beresford, then a young officer of his, nearly caused an international incident by stealing the official sign from outside the American consulate and nailing it up over a disreputable Chinese shop.

Yet most of this muttering about British influence was mere shadow play. Several times the United States had made it clear that European adventures in Hawaii would be taken as seriously as French adventures in Mexico. However strategic in the Pacific, Hawaii was not worth Britain's while to the extent of marked strain with the United States; and the States were entrenched in the Islands more solidly than even clever men in Honolulu always realized.

True, the white colony had always been mixed. Mexican cowboys taught Hawaiians cowpunching, hence the Hawaiian deep-seated saddle and word for cowhand, *paniola*, a kenning for Español; the Island way of loading cattle aboard ship by swimming them through the surf is said to have originated along the Gulf of California. A well-received ranching family on Maui belonged originally to the Polish gentry, come by way of New Zealand, where an immediate ancestor was a hero of the Maori wars. Back in 1824 Kalanimoku had a Prussian armorer-blacksmith; both the leader of the Royal Hawaiian Band, established in 1872, and the founder of Hackfeld &

Company, a principal Island mercantile agency, were Germans. A Frenchman held key portfolios in the cabinets of the 'sixties. The British, if you counted Scotchmen, were a principal minority. But all non-Americans banded together had no genuine hope of displacing the Yankees.

The natives, however, had better, if slim, chances. For fifty years they resisted with increasing energy. Signs of articulate Hawaii-for-the-Hawaiians feeling appeared in the 'forties while the missionaries were still in the saddle and the native government was subserviently celebrating the Fourth of July. As missionary influence waned, nativist feeling coagulated around the royal-noble-hapa-haole-rancher-Americanophobe pole of the Hawaiian solution. The other pole attracted the sugar-mercantile-agency-missionary-American interests. In terms of power, this second complex of interests represented the haves and was customarily labeled the "missionary" interest. Though both camps showed anomalies and queer shifts of small splinter-groups, that was the rough line-up thirty years after the Great Mahele opened the way to white greediness for land.

This nativism was real. For all superficial Christianization, old ways and beliefs persisted as a submerged stratum of behavior, parallel with or subtly undermining haole ways. Tabu sites along inland trails were likely to receive furtive offerings of tapa, fruit, or leaves left by cautious wayfarers doing what their grandfathers had always done at the same spots. The kahunas' magical powers, particularly in medicine and praying-to-death, were little discussed but considerably respected, even among Sunday-pious communicants.[52] When Kamehameha V's queen died, natives revived the old fantastically protracted and orgiastic mourning period. Such survivals are familiar elsewhere, as among negroes in the West Indies and the Black Belt. So there is no cause for wonder in the fact that Princess Ruth, educated in the missionary school for chiefs, quelled an

[52]Haole residents of the Islands were not immune. I have heard of a Deep South-born parson of a certain Island church still enough impressed by tales of the menuhene (Hawaiian "little people") to go hunting some troublesome specimens in the parsonage basement with a specially constructed net.

eruption of Mauna Loa in the 'seventies by traveling—very modernly via steamboat—to the Big Island to perform rites to propitiate Pele. Surviving photographs of this bull-voiced chieftainess make it conceivable that her face could stop a lava flow dead in its tracks.

Western-style governmental devices offered another vent for nativist feeling. In one form or another, representative assemblies persisted through various changes in constitutions. Though property qualifications kept many natives from voting, the bulk of the electorate was usually Hawaiian and, under the later kings, legislative debate was ominously concerned with efforts to avoid white-type governmental exactions. Direct cash taxes, however small, were difficult for natives to pay; they were often levied on horses and dogs, in which natives excessively delighted; and one legislative session so hotly deliberated whether to repeal taxes on bitches that it went into history as the Female Dog Legislature. Though the grievances aired were often childish, feeling behind them was serious; and Polynesian long-windedness and legislators' hopes of re-election contributed to a formidable body of native sentiment, often organized in the form of secret or benevolent societies. In support, along came little newspapers printed in Hawaiian edited by opportunistic whites or *hapa-haoles* to appeal to the nativist. And there was a steadily stronger seepage into cabinets of white or half-breed men insisting that Hawaii was a sovereign state and could be master in her own house; a palpable fiction, but pleasant hearing.

The high tide of nativism coincided with the reign of Kalakaua, Hawaii's Merry Monarch. He was no Kamehameha —the last of them died in King William C. Lunalilo, a popular hard drinker and victim of tuberculosis—but his blood had ranked very high in prewhite Hawaii. His accession was contested by Queen Emma, widowed consort of Kamehameha IV. American influence rallied behind Kalakaua and, with considerable suspicion of dirty work, elected him. The resulting riot roughed up the legislature and damaged the government building; American and British marines from warships in the harbor calmed the mob and seated Kalakaua firmly on the throne. In due return, he took a large hand in negotiating the Hawaii-United States reciprocity treaty that first put sugar firmly on its feet in the Islands.

Later he was to disappoint the respectable. His life and times are worth lingering over for reasons serious and otherwise. He was a large, convivial, and dignified alumnus of the mission school for children of chiefs, rather resembling Joe Louis with a mustache and sideburns. Most of his predecessors had been fast men with a bottle, sometimes with unhappy consequences; Kamehameha IV, for instance, killed his secretary while drunk. But Kalakaua could not only outdrink anybody; he could walk away with what he drank. Stevenson wrote home:

". . . a very fine, intelligent fellow, but . . . what a crop for the drink! He carries it, too, like a mountain with a sparrow on its shoulders. We calculated five bottles of champagne in three hours and a half (afternoon) and the sovereign quite presentable, although perceptibly more dignified at the end."— *Letters*, III, 99.[53]

This mid-Pacific King of Yvetot traveled widely, first to Washington for the reciprocity treaty, later round the world. His white suite found him a troublesome charge. In San Francisco a spread-eagle oration of welcome predicting Hawaiian hegemony over all Polynesia infected him with an idea that was later greatly to embarrass all rational Hawaii. His reception in Japan moved him to propose, without consulting his advisors, a marriage between an imperial prince of Japan and Kaiulani, the pretty young heir presumptive to the Hawaiian throne. By the time he reached Siam he was deep in a feeling that white men's goods and ways did not give them a monopoly

[53]Mrs. Isobel Strong Field maintains that the king's extraordinary capacity was due to his always taking *poi* mixed with milk before a drinking bout, which insulated his stomach-coat against too quick absorption of alcohol. (*This Life I've Loved*, 165.) He may have done so, but no such insulation would be proof against so much in so short a period. The bulky majesty of Hawaii undoubtedly had a head like a Russian lumberjack.

on power and splendor. In Italy he allowed himself to be hijacked by an Italian adventurer named Moreno, a former hanger-on of his, who had been entrusted with seeing that several *hapa-haole* youths got a good military education in that country; the only thing that rescued the king from Moreno's clutches was his discovery that Moreno had been representing the boys as royal bastards.

He returned very proud of having been the first king to circumnavigate the globe, and thenceforth was given to absurdly grandiose gestures and unqualified commitment to nativist doings. He was not the first Hawaiian king to fail to make any sense out of the white theory that a king could reign but not rule; but, having been greatly attracted by the claims to divine descent of the Japanese imperial house, he was the first and last to make efforts to have himself deified. He bought a $20,000 battery of Austrian field guns and had himself a lavish European-style coronation at which, like Napoleon, he crowned himself and his spouse with jeweled crowns costing $10,000 apiece. His predecessors had built a stately royal palace and government building, and a large hotel for tourists and visiting bigwigs. Under Kalakaua appeared horsecars, a small opera house—performances in which were infrequent—containing a huge box surmounted by a royal cipher, and a telephone system installed ahead of most mainland cities. Once a dirt-streeted frontier village dominated by the great coral-built missionary church as a French Canadian village is dwarfed by its parish church, Honolulu was now a capital with architecture and gadgets to prove it.[54]

But his most fantastic caper was his "Primacy of the Pacific" policy in which he was encouraged by Walter Murray Gibson,

[54]Nordhoff swore that, in the mid-'seventies, Honolulu looked like nothing so much as a New England country town: "The white frame houses with green blinds, the picket-fences whitewashed until they shine, the stone walls, the small barns, the scanty pastures, the little white frame churches . . . you have only to eliminate the palms, the bananas, and other tropical vegetation . . . the incorrigible Puritans who founded this bit of civilization . . . sought from the beginning to make New England men and women of these Hawaiians."—(*Southern California, Oregon and the Sandwich Islands*, 22–33.)

a renegade Mormon who dominated his cabinets in the mideighties.[55] At the time Tonga, Samoa, the Gilberts and Carolines had not yet been formally taken over by white powers. So Kalakaua, master of an annual personal revenue round $35,000 and a subject population about as large as that of present-day McKeesport, Penna., proposed to make Hawaii suzerain of Oceania. He began with Samoa, then and later a hot bone of contention between Germany, Britain and the States. The rivals, particularly Germany, were not amused when the *hapahaole* editor of a Honolulu nativist paper appeared in Samoa as envoy extraordinary indeed from His Hawaiian Majesty to negotiate confederation of the two island groups. His presence was presently re-enforced by the arrival of H.H.M.S. "Kaimiloa," a small copra-steamer crudely converted into a popgun man-of-war at an alleged cost of $50,000, manned by a few whites and a great many unruly boys from Hawaii's reform school. The embassy stirred up all three native factions in Samoan politics, signed a treaty with one of them, and highly irritated the chancelleries of the world. After six months, having drunk everything in sight and exhausted their funds, the wavery and headachy complement of the "Kaimiloa" weighed anchor, a half-Samoan sailing master having been borrowed to make sure the ship would make port.

Kalakaua's yearning to assert Polynesian values appeared in darker ways. Greatly attached to Masonry—the craft had long flourished in Hawaii—he founded the *Hale Naua*, a native fraternal order admitting both sexes, patterned somewhat on Masonry and named after the ancient chiefs' secret society. It took much of its ritual from the days of *kahunas* and blood sacrifice; it also had a weird "scientific" aspect, aiming to reestablish heathen cosmogony, medicine and ethics. Many accused Kalakaua of reviving old religious ceremonies, rebuilding an ancient *heiau* (temple) and dedicating it with the sacrifice of a hog instead of a man. One enemy quoted him directly:

> "I have seen the Christian nations and observed that they are turning away from Jehovah. He represents a waning cause.

[55] Cf. IV, 6, *Unsavory Characters* for full account.

Shall we Hawaiians take up the worship of a god whom foreigners are discarding? The old gods of Hawaii are good enough for us."—Rev. S. E. Bishop in *Hawaiian Gazette*, Feb. 11, 1893; quoted in W. F. Blackman, *The Making of Hawaii*, 88.

He certainly sponsored the old *hulas* on a scale and with a lack of decorum that struck the godly with blank horror. Gossip even said he revived that old aristocratic group-game which, as one modern source chastely puts it, was like Post Office only more serious.[56]

The gossips are practically all dead now, and distinguishing fact from fiction in Honolulu is more difficult than anywhere else in the world. Plainly, however, Kalakaua reached back on deliberate principle into the existent substrata of prewhite values in order to reassert the Polynesians' right to live in Polynesia as seemed good to them; the same thing that has been done to great applause by the Irish, for instance. In spite of the king's telltale megalomanic traits—the order he founded was called the Star of Oceania, thus taking in the whole of the Pacific islands—it is possible to ask what was wrong with this objective except impracticality?

You are not to picture a pompous, drunken, cult-ridden caricature. Practically everybody who met Kalakaua, whether

[56]Emerson probably best surmounted the difficulties of describing Hawaiian erotic games without crossing the hawse of the postal authorities: "The *ula kilu* was so called from being used in a sport which was much patronized by the *alii* class of the ancient régime . . . forfeits were pledged, the payment of which was met by a performance of a dance . . . which not unfrequently called for liberties and concessions that could not be permitted on the spot, or in public, but must wait the opportunity for seclusion . . . kings and queens were not above participating in the pleasures of this sport . . . King nor queen could plead exemption from the forfeits incurred, nor deny to another the full exercise of privileges acquired under the rules . . . The payment of these extreme forfeits was delayed until a convenient season, or might be commuted—on grounds of policy, or at the request of a loser, if a king or queen—by an equivalent of land or other valuable possession. Still, no fault could be found if the winner insisted on strict payment of the forfeit. The game of *kilu* was often got up as a compliment, a supreme expression of hospitality, to distinguished visitors of rank, thus more than making good the polite phrase of the Spanish don 'all that I have is yours.' "—*Unwritten Literature of Hawaii*, 235-6.

friendly to his schemes or not, found him urbane, outgoing, and perceptive in his own way. A true Polynesian gambler, he loved poker, that most universally appealing of white inventions. Legends of his poker parties at his Waikiki beachhouse persist—how he won a pot from Claus Spreckels, the California sugar magnate who was muscling into the Islands with royal approval, by saying "I have five kings," laying down four from his hand and pointing to himself as the fifth. His admirers considered that he remained kingly even when, at a party, he borrowed a guitar from the orchestra and sang a contemporary comic song:

> Hokey, pokey, winky, wum—
> How d'ye want your 'taters done?
> Boiled or with their jackets on?
> Sang the King of the Sandwich Islands!
> —Isobel S. Field, *This Life I've Loved,* 175

For all that his realm could not afford them, his court functions seem to have tastefully mingled ceremony, luxurious eating and drinking, and great gaiety in the ballroom. Up to his death in the Palace Hotel in San Francisco in 1891, this was The First Gentleman of the Pacific.

But expense was expense. Raising cash to promote Polynesian prestige and his own pleasure led Kalakaua far from political discretion. His advisors or intimates were partly glib adventurers like Gibson and Moreno, partly local whites, some honest, some not, with an occasional financial adventurer like Spreckels. Too few of these hangers-on could see much wrong with malodorous money-making schemes which obligingly appeared when the treasury was low, such as a proposition from the Louisiana Lottery which, ejected from the States, was willing to pay high for peace, quiet, and a mailing address. An even less savory tale involved an enterprising Chinese bidder for a government opium monopoly who was somehow bilked of a huge sum which he swore he had personally handed to the king as a solicited bribe. There were all-too-plausible stories about how the king used the royal frank to smuggle in quantities of liquor for a local dealer who, in turn, supplied royal canvassers with free election-gin.

Such facts and rumors convinced the sugar-missionary-respectable element that Kalakaua was really getting out of hand. In an armed uprising in 1887 they forced on the king a new constitution making his cabinet directly responsible to the legislature and imposing other restrictions. The adventurers immediately left office. Two years later an armed revolt in the interests of an increased royal prerogative was led by a fiercely mustached youth named Wilcox, one of those whom Moreno had taken to Italy to learn the art of war. Quelled by the loss of six respectable lives, the ringleaders claimed on trial that they had had royal sponsorship; a native jury acquitted them on the convenient juridical principle that "the king can do no wrong." The "missionaries" were not likely to forget such goings on. Kalakaua probably died just about in time.

He is embarrassing for those who prefer to see in him a Polynesian statesman. There are and always were Polynesian statesmen, but this was not one. He had been round the world and seen the white man's power; his inability to grasp the discrepancy between his schemes and his strength verges on the pathological. Yet it is understandable that many looked back on his reign as Hawaii's Golden Age. No labor problems, because government let sugar bring in Orientals ad lib.; no floods of tourists to infest Waikiki; no apprehensions about what Washington would do next in the way of sending carpetbaggers to Honolulu. Plenty of young officers to dance with at balls on or for American, British, French, or Russian warships; plenty of game Island horses to ride; long visits with hospitable relatives and friends on plantations and ranches; and the never-to-be-recaptured thrill of steamer day, when a whole month's bag of letters and newspapers gave the stimulating illusion of being in touch with the great world. Though "missionaries" fought "the royal crowd" and vice versa, they mostly spoke to one another; in fact, many of them were closely related. When the invitations came from the Palace, both factions went dressed fit to kill, the "missionaries" to pay their respects with the dignity due their positions, the "royal crowd" to have a marvelous time. The Chinese, who got out of the cane fields as soon as possible, proved competent shopkeepers and servants.[57] Most of the Hawaiians lived in odd corners on fish and *poi*, a healthy diet, and were said to be perfectly happy. One hopes it pleased them to see how thoroughly the *haoles* were enjoying themselves in the Kanakas' lovely islands.

None of it belonged on a group of volcano summits protruding from the Pacific Ocean. The whites' colonially lavish manners and Kalakaua's miniature pomp—the slightly threadbare uniforms and royal relics are piously preserved in Honolulu museums—were intrusions. "King" itself was no Polynesian concept; crown and medals were imposed from outside, just like codified law, court trials, budgets, cabinets, standing corps of guards and all the rest of the anomalous paraphernalia by means of which Hawaiian royalty blundered and stumbled its way to extinction. In his own time and place, *Ka Moi*, the highest chief, hog-fat, bone-lazy and tree-tall, whose shadow it was death to cross, had been anything but ridiculous. It is easy condescendingly to describe Kalakaua's picturesque little court as comic opera. Actually it was the dissonant and troubling, if definitely minor, type of tragedy that sets one's teeth on edge.

* * *

"Do nothing unrighteous, but as regards the [Hawaiian] problem, take the Islands first and solve the problem afterwards."
—Alfred Thayer Mahan to Theodore Roosevelt, quoted in Puleston, *Mahan*, 182.

So Kalakaua died and was gathered to his fathers, who were probably all feasting in hell as chiefs should, and Liliuokalani, his sister, succeeded. Adept like Kalakaua in the Hawaiian school of hymn-inspired music, she is still remembered as composer of *Aloha Oe*. In her own day she was, according to the

[57]Blackman quotes figures showing that the Chinese in 1889 had 57% of wholesale spirit licenses; 62% of retail merchandise licenses; 84.7% of victualling licenses; 20.6% of butcher licenses. (*The Making of Hawaii*, 197.)

point of view, patriot, martyr, Jezebel, stubborn fool or sadly misguided woman.

This bulky, proud person, mildly reminiscent of Kaahumanu, depicted her ancestors as the kingmakers who put and kept the upstart, Kamehameha the Great, on the throne of *Hawaii Nei*. She had collaborated with her brother in nativism more cordially than mere loyalty implied, and retained his kind of advisors as far as the new constitution permitted, perhaps sometimes farther.

To start her off in hot water, the lottery- and opium-schemes stayed disquietingly alive. Going her brother one better the queen, supported by nativists, presently drafted and planned to promulgate by fiat a new constitution disfranchising whites and making her ministers responsible directly to her. At least that was the public impression, probably not inaccurate, of what she had in mind. Here was Hawaii-for-the-Hawaiians with a vengeance. The reaction of respectable nervous systems still mindful of 1889 was necessarily violent. There was excited talk of revolution long before rebellion actually occurred.

The queen had already done enough to make her seat on the throne most precarious, and reaped the reward in gossip about her private life. In 1891 the death of her husband, a long, weedy, former merchant-seaman named John Dominis, robbed her of a restraining influence. Yet the monarchy had survived previous storms and might have survived this, if events in the States had not made it imperative for sugar to pull the throne down. The McKinley tariff of 1890 had wiped out the competitive advantage of Hawaiian over other foreign sugars in the American market, on which the Island sugar industry was inextricably dependent. There was talk of shifting to the Australian and New Zealand markets but, though a fair amount of sugar had been going that way, no realist considered this a hopeful expedient. The most powerful forces in the Islands had either to get the new tariff revised in favor of Hawaii, a most improbable scheme that would spell bankruptcy if delayed too long, or somehow get Hawaii inside the States' tariff barrier. That meant annexation.

The idea was nothing new. In the 'fifties, Kamehameha III, trying to stave off French pressure and apprehensive of California filibusters, had negotiated a treaty of annexation with the United States which his death immediately afterward abrogated; its chances of ratification were slim anyway, since it granted Hawaii immediate statehood. From then on American consuls and ministers in Hawaii steadily peppered the State Department with reports about the advisability of taking over Hawaii to keep some other power from doing so, or for strategic reasons, or just because the idea appeared to be in the cards. ". . . annexationist opinions," Brookes wrote drily, "were a curious mixture of the concepts of republicanism ('manifest destiny'), and the American tariff policy."[58] In the 'sixties regular steamer service between Hawaii and the Coast had tied things closer; after reciprocity, mainland capital had been attracted into the Islands' sugar-sustained prosperity. Annexation had never been consummated, however, because reciprocity enabled Honolulu to reap the benefits of attachment to the States without the inconvenience of having to stop doing things in Honolulu's own peculiar way.

In 1893 the American Minister to Hawaii was a raggedly bearded Down East Republican named John L. Stevens. Former newspaper-partner of James G. Blaine (Harrison's first Secretary of State) he was, like his great friend, a warm manifest-destineer. As crisis built up in Honolulu, drilling going on, Committees of Safety forming, Stevens went half out of his mind with opportunistic excitement. Though the complete story can never be known, he was indubitably close to this respectable insurgency—"we [the revolutionists] knew the United States Minister was in sympathy with us," wrote Sanford B. Dole demurely.[59] When the insurgents struck, nobody was less surprised than Stevens, or more eager to see the monarchy overthrown as prelude to annexation. Nor, as Cleveland's message to Congress stated later, was he "inconveniently scrupulous as to the means employed to that end."[60]

His own despatches witness that the presence at Honolulu

[58]*International Rivalry*, 213.
[59]*Memoirs of the Hawaiian Revolution*, 74.
[60]Presidential message, Dec. 18, 1893.

of U.S.S. "Boston," one of the crack White Squadron cruisers that formed the nucleus of the New Navy, was a deterrent to rebellion. At the moment of the outbreak the "Boston," with Stevens on board, was taking a pointless little cruise to the Big Island, a coincidence that he never succeeded in explaining. Then, as soon as the "missionaries" had openly revolted, here were Stevens and the "Boston" back again, landing marines ostensibly to protect Americans and their property but also to "assist in the preservation of public order" as Captain Wiltse's orders to the leathernecks ran. Liliuokalani witnessed their march up the street and concluded that the U.S. Navy was finishing what the "missionaries" had begun. The marines set up their posts, not round American-owned residences and warehouses, but in places well calculated to overawe the queen's supporters. Stevens countenanced running up the American flag on the pretext of forestalling precautionary action by the British or Japanese. There was no counterdemonstration, though the rebels as yet were ill-organized. Hastily they formed a provisional government and despatched to Washington a delegation to negotiate annexation. The head of the new government was Judge Sanford Ballard Dole, a missionary's son of integrity and ability who, with his long white beard and noble eyes and forehead, was probably the handsomest *haole* in the Islands.

The whole thing sounds like Theodore Roosevelt in his "I took Panama" mood. In Washington a hastily drafted treaty of annexation went to the Senate for ratification. But, neat as their timing had been so far, the PGs—new nickname for the "missionaries," abbreviating Provisional Government—now slipped a cog. Cleveland had defeated Harrison in the 1892 elections; Inauguration Day, 1893, came along before the Senate had acted on Hawaii. Cleveland, a doggedly honest man given to decisive gestures according to his lights, sniffed cautiously at the treaty, withdrew it and sent a personal representative to Hawaii to check up. His position seems to have been that, though annexation might well be a good thing for strategic reasons, he preferred to arrive at that end with some decency.

The frustrated PGs naturally accused him of political spite; or referred this action to the machinations of an English-born Honolulu merchant, Theo. H. Davies, a power in sugar and imports whose firm is still one of the Big Five of Hawaii. He was guardian of Kaiulani, the heiress-presumptive to Liliuokalani, child of a Scotsman and an Hawaiian high chieftainess —a young woman charming enough to have received a nice little poem about herself from Robert Louis Stevenson. Davies' loyalty to his ward's interests and distaste for American rule apparently moved him more than the profits that annexation promised his sugar interests. When the revolution struck, he and Kaiulani, in England at the time, hastened to Washington in a theatrical but well-aimed effort to turn sentiment in favor of the Hawaiian royal house. They met the Clevelands, and the princess' charm may well have had some effect on the president-elect. Certainly Davies' appeal issued in Kaiulani's name when she landed in New York would have been effective with a far uglier context:

> "*To the American people:* Unbidden I stand upon your shores today, where I thought so soon to receive a royal welcome . . . I hear that Commissioners from my own land have been for many days asking this great nation to take away my little vineyard . . . they would leave me without a home or a name or a nation. Seventy years ago America sent over Christian men and women to give religion and civilization to Hawaii . . . we learned to love and trust America. Today three of the sons of those missionaries are at your capital, asking you to undo their fathers' work . . . Today I, a poor, weak girl . . . am strong in the strength of seventy million people, who in this free land will hear my cry, and will refuse to let their flag cover dishonour to mine."—Mary H. Krout, *Hawaii and a Revolution*, 174–5.

The presidential emissary carrying plenary powers to Hawaii, James H. Blount, former Chairman of the House Foreign Relations Committee, was to become one of the best-hated men in Island history, a distinction greatly to his credit. Stevens greeted Blount as his ship docked, to say that the Provisional

Government had prepared him a nice house, servants, and carriage for which he need pay no more than was convenient. Blount declined the offer; he also declined the competing royal carriage sent to fetch him under care of the queen's chamberlain. His first official act was to haul down the American flag and substitute the Hawaiian; the "Boston" sulkily failed to salute the substitute. All the way he courteously resisted PG blandishments, insisted on asking questions of the PGs' opponents. The PGs, recalling that Blount had been a Confederate colonel, began to mutter that no unreconstructed rebel could be fair to Hawaii, which had stoutly supported the Union in the Civil War. He had already opposed reciprocity in the 1883 session of Congress. Eventually he reported to Cleveland that the thing had been a put-up job and the United States had sadly overreached itself when its armed forces were permitted apparently to countenance the rebellion.[61]

[61]Needless to say, this was not the interpretation of these happenings favored in Hawaii. In the "missionary" version, Blount was a prejudiced imbecile, Stevens never overstepped his authority in the slightest, the presence of the marines had nothing to do with the success of the rebellion. This point of view is well expressed, if anybody wants to look it up, in The Hawaiian Question, Charles L. Carter; The Real Hawaii, Lucien Young, who was a lieutenant on the "Boston" at the time; American Expansion in Hawaii, Sylvester K. Stevens; Memories of the Hawaiian Revolution, Sanford B. Dole; Hawaii and a Revolution, Mary H. Krout. The author's position here is based on not only his own best judgment after examining the recorded facts, but on the opinions of such eminent scholars in American history as the Beards and Nevins. As usual, when a case is glaring, the best evidence of culpability comes from the culprits: Carter admits that Stevens had offered the marines for the use of the cabinet against Liliuokalani, when it looked as if they themselves would head the rebellion; and that a popular referendum would probably have given a slight majority in favor of the queen and against the "missionaries," "owing to a dangerous element of low whites who had the right to vote and who in recent years had acquired great influence over the Hawaiians." Stevens admits that Wiltse's orders to the marines exceeded the tenor of the Minister's request for their presence ashore; that it was to shelter the PG government that he consented to have the American flag raised over the government building; and that the departure of the "Boston" for the Big Island was in some sort the signal for the PG revolt (Picturesque Hawaii, passim).

Cleveland put his sentiments into acid writing:

"The control of both sides of a bargain . . . is called by a familiar and unpleasant name when found in private transactions . . . I mistake the American people if they favor the odious doctrine that there is no such thing as international morality . . . and that even by indirection a strong power may with impunity despoil a weaker one of its territory."—Robert McElroy, *Grover Cleveland,* 65.

and then let the treaty rot. Still furious nine years later, the great Captain Mahan considered this glaring evidence that Cleveland had been unfit to govern. In Honolulu, when Blount sailed back to the mainland, the Royal Hawaiian Band played him, Georgian and former Confederate, off with *Marching Through Georgia.* The PGs insisted it was just a natural mistake on the part of dear old Henri Berger, German-reared bandmaster.

Treaty or not, they were still in power and working hard to consolidate, by means of 1,200 militia, rigid control of the press, and fine and imprisonment for anybody heard speaking against them. In a few weeks they were *de facto* and to spare. Presently came a new American Minister, Albert S. Willis, to put Humpty Dumpty back together again, a thankless task.

Willis was instructed to obtain from Liliuokalani general amnesty for the rebels in return for American countenance in regaining her throne. The lady was in no mood for conditions touching her resumption of sovereignty. Once back on the throne, she told him, she would see all the rebel ringleaders executed as traitors; with relish she mentioned beheading. The most Willis could get her to concede at first was exile and confiscation of property, which would have cut a heavy swathe through the Honolulu business district.[62] In time she gave in and promised amnesty with grim reluctance.

[62]The queen's autobiography tried hard to make all this a combination of verbal misunderstanding with misrepresentation. It makes much of the contention that beheading was not an Hawaiian custom. Yet, according to Sheldon Dibble (*History of the Sandwich Islands,* 103), beheading was used as penalty for *tabu* infringements in Liholiho's

Willis's troubles should then have been over; but astute and cool parties in the PG government knew their strength and his weaknesses. When he suggested that they step down, they replied at polite length in a masterpiece of argument that boils down to: No, why should we? When he bluffed by getting American warships in the harbor to make ostentatious preparations for a landing in the queen's behalf, the PGs refused to scare; they knew that he would never dare ask American forces to open fire on American born or derived kinsmen in order to restore a dark-skinned native to any throne anywhere. Mainland newspaper reports overfavorable to the PGs had been especially poor preparation for any such move. Of correspondents on the spot, two were patently irresponsible women with little sense of the obligations of their job. The rebels gave Mary H. Krout the use of the royal throneroom as an office. Kate Field submitted all her despatches to the rebel cabinet for approval; her biographer points out happily that most of them passed without alteration. There is also reason to believe that some American naval officers, overfriendly to the PGs, let the rebels know they had little actually to fear.

Between a vengeful-minded woman and a smugly arbitrary faction sitting on a *fait accompli*, Willis could do nothing. That is precisely what he did. While the mainland was distracted with the panic of 1893 and the subsequent depression, the PGs went blandly on setting up a republic in Hawaii, with Dole as president. The queen stayed under surveillance in her private house in Honolulu. Little Kaiulani presently died in Scotland, where the climate is especially unkind to Polynesians.

Two years later a miniature nativist revolt killed one fine young fellow among the PGs and implicated the queen. She was convicted of conspiracy, but her sentence was remitted. In 1896, there was a diplomatic stir when the British opened

---

time. The whole idea of treason in any western sense would, of course, have been alien to pre-white Hawaii. The conquered rebel chief was either knocked in the head as a sacrifice or sent home unharmed to lick his wounds in Coventry.

negotiations with the PGs about leasing Necker Island for a cable station, the matter being dropped when Washington protested.

The moment William McKinley was nominated as Republican candidate for president in 1896, the PG Secretary of State was closeted with him at the behest of Henry Cabot Lodge, ardent expansionist. When McKinley beat Bryan, Hawaii assumed that annexation was settled. A new treaty went before the Senate in 1897. But it took the Spanish War, during which Hawaii was a fine staging base for operations in the Philippines, to settle the matter by way of a joint resolution of both houses. The American flag run up at the annexation ceremony was the same one that tactless Mr. Blount had had hauled down five years before. And sugar stocks boomed gloriously on the Honolulu stock exchange.

Liliuokalani, who had once publicly acknowledged the validity of the PG government, again raised her voice in protest against annexation. Few listened. The one impressive note of dissent came from a retired politician named Cleveland, writing to Richard Olney:

"Hawaii is ours. As I look back upon the first steps in this miserable business, and as I contemplate the means used to complete the outrage, I am ashamed of the whole affair."
—Robert McElroy, Grover Cleveland, 73.

The constitution that the PGs had set up had had striking features besides its basic provision that annexation to the United States was part of the fundamental law of the land. Some sections of its bill of rights would have curled Mr. Jefferson's hair almost as tightly as the Rev. Mr. Bingham's ideas on the relations of church and state:

"Article 2: All men are free to worship God according to the dictates of their own consciences; but this privilege shall not be so construed as to justify acts of licentiousness or practices inconsistent with the peace or safety of the Republic.
"Article 3: All men may freely speak, write and publish their sentiments on all subjects; and no law shall be enacted to restrain the liberty of speech or of the press; but all persons shall

be responsible for the abuse of such rights. Provided, however, that the Legislature may enact any such laws as may be necessary to restrain and prevent the publication or public utterance of indecent or seditious language."

At least annexation abrogated this extraordinary document. But it would be another fifty years before Hawaii caught up with the prevalent sentiments of the mainland on formal human rights.

Liliuokalani lived on, comfortably embittered. In 1910 the Territorial courts finally ruled out her claim to income from crown lands confiscated by the Republic. But, before her death, World War I persuaded her to display the flag of the government that succeeded the usurpers, and even to appear on the same platform as Judge Dole at a Red Cross rally.

* * *

"Honolulu . . . a civilization which, if not very distinguished, is certainly very elaborate."—W. Somerset Maugham, *The Trembling of a Leaf*, 208.

With annexation the pertinence of the case history of Hawaii might have ended. But as it has turned out, modern Hawaii is worth accounting for in its own right.

The Islands were annexed as a small but solid going concern dominated by vigorous men accustomed to self-righteous power. The United States Constitution had never envisaged integrating highly organized communities into the Union as either States or Territories; as in the previous case of Mormon Utah, there were embarrassments on both sides when the thing was tried. In fixing the status of Hawaii Congress was considerate; to quell Hawaiian uneasiness about "carpetbaggers," for instance, it was provided that the Territorial governor, though appointed from Washington, should have resided in the Territory for at least five years. And President McKinley was tactful; President Dole of the superseded Republic of Hawaii became Governor without even moving out of his office.

That looked promising. But the PGs were too parochial for

friction not to arise. The suspicion, sometimes expressed before annexation, that faraway Washington might not have Island interests sufficiently at heart soon proved well founded. The PGs suggested confidently that Congress should exempt Hawaii from the provisions of the Chinese Exclusion Act; else how could the plantations maintain their labor supply? In Honolulu it was obvious that a right-minded government would consent, whatever California might think about it; so Honolulu was grieved when Congress failed to agree. Further disappointment came when the strains of the early twentieth century cut off fresh Japanese labor from the cane fields.

Still annexation also gave the manpower-hungry planters new cards because the poor man's empire that the States acquired from Spain offered several likely sources of labor within United States jurisdiction. Porto Ricans were tried first. Though sturdy, they proved unruly. Filipinos were far better; thousands of them were brought in on short-term contracts and sugar was easy in its mind again. Well into the nineteen-thirties it was largely the Little Brown Brother who cut the cane that sweetened the coffee of that portion of the American public using Hawaiian sugar.

There was another early shock when the first Territorial legislature contained a nativist and "antimissionary" majority for "Home Rule." The forces that had made even PGs admit in 1893 that a plebiscite would vote for retaining the throne and independence were still strong. But the PGs' heirs quietly infiltrated local politics with discreet use of power, and no such scandal occurred again. The Islands rather quickly reverted to Big Five-controlled economic development.

The new Territory acquired two new industries—pineapple and tourists, both comfortable sources of mainland funds with which to pay for mainland supplies. This reliance on other climes for the necessities of life had begun long ago when missionaries sent home for flour and calico instead of using taro and tapa, and suppressed schemes to distill in the Islands the rum that sailors on liberty bought so greedily. By now the Islands that once fed 300,000 Hawaiians pretty well import six-tenths of what they eat—beef is the only item in which they are nearly self-supporting—and practically all their apparel, building material, furniture and production goods. The same factor-corporations that control the plantations are importing agents and own shipping-lines, thus taking the underwriter's, carrier's and salesman's cut coming and going.

Before Pearl Harbor the armed forces fretted over how awkward it would be if Hawaii were cut off by enemy action or dearth of shipping from mainland ports, and tried to get at least more green stuff raised on the premises. Such efforts came to little until 1941. Honolulu has the impression that some of the ruling influences preferred not to see alterations in the pattern that tied the Islands so firmly to well-controlled procedures. So these tropical paradises import practically all their oranges, some fish, and most of the curios they sell; and practically everything produced goes eastward in bags or cans. Even the girls in the stiffly regulated pre-Pearl Harbor Honolulu brothels were imports from the coast on six-month tours of duty, with the police prohibiting local talent from such employment.[63] In practically suppressing both commercial fishing and controlled brothels, the recent war made inconsistent changes in this situation. But it is not likely that, as ties between the Islands and the mainland grow daily closer, the fundamentals of the picture will ever change.

James D. Dole, a relative outsider, though a distant cousin and admirer of Sanford B., first showed Hawaii, not that pineapple would grow there—that had long been known—but that the mainland would pay well for it in cans. This crop did not compete with sugar, preferring higher and drier lands, so Dole's company went as far as it liked and was not taken over by the Big Five until the great depression gave the easy opportunity. The other two large Island pineapplegrowers are mainland canning corporations that get along quite harmoniously with Island interests. Pineapple has been good for the Islands. It put otherwise useless land to work, increased gross

[63]The idea was not original. Mediaeval Avignon tried it. (Sumner, *Folkways*, 530.)

income for ships serving Hawaii, gave the Islands much free publicity in the skilful and glamorous advertising that sold canned pineapple to the mainland public; it even improved the appearance of the place. Cane is a frowsy, sprawly crop, rather like gigantic crab grass, which looks worse the nearer you get; whereas nothing can be handsomer, close up or far away, than the sweeping precise rows of gray-green pineapple plants against the red soil of an upland plantation on Lanai or Oahu.

The tourist industry began earlier but developed more slowly. Back in the Kamehamehas' time the government built an expensive hotel in mid-Honolulu for visiting firemen and the occasional pleasure traveler of the day; the cost made a small scandal that ruined a couple of political reputations. In 1892 a visiting Frenchman noted that the attractions of the volcano and a bland winter climate were building up a small but steady tourist business. But it took an outsider, the late Alexander Hume Ford, to turn it into something with cumulative momentum. This energetic mainlander, journalist and precocious playwright of *The Little Confederate*, struck the Islands looking for dramatic material in 1910 and stayed to make a career of promoting them. Witnessing his amateur efforts in the midst of apathy, Jack London wrote of the Islanders: "They are poor boosters."[64] Twenty years later, so well did Ford's work bear fruit, nobody in his right mind could have said such a thing.

Surfriding, a sport then practically dead among natives, practiced only occasionally at Lahaina, was what particularly caught Ford's eupeptic eye. He had practically to revive the art singlehanded. But in a short time he had the hang of it, was teaching it to others, and begging from the estate of Queen Emma the site of the now famous Outrigger Club on Waikiki Beach, international headquarters of surfriding on both boards and canoes. Whether intentionally or not, Ford had here a natural for advertising art. The surfrider was the best piece of visual promotion since His Master's Voice. That bronzed Kanaka standing precariously godlike on the forward rush of

[64]In Charmian London, *Our Hawaii*, 7.

a Waikiki comber has been worth millions to the Islands ever since.[65]

Promotion also had climate, palms, active volcanoes, *hula-dancers* and tropical fruits to work with. As better steamers came on the run, as veterans of the Spanish-American war and articulate visitors like the Londons told the mainland how lovely the Islands are, a truth that neither cynicism nor over-selling can mar, things began to move. In due season Waikiki, that cluttered strip of sand which disappoints so many, was endowed with the kind of fame that attaches to the Folies Bergères, the Pyramids, the Cheshire Cheese, the Jungfrau and Old Faithful. The place had come a long way from being a mere seaside suburb where Hawaiian royalty relaxed in seclusion. With neon lights, souvenir joints, sit up lunches and cottage colonies, Kalakaua Avenue may not look as much like Coney Island as hand-wringing *kamaainas*[66] say it does, but the spiritual resemblance is strong.

In the 'twenties the tourist business was far enough along for an overenterprising California press-agent to convince the powers in the land that big time publicity was worth spending money on. In this period grandiose steamers were built for the California–Hawaii run, since doing noble service as transports in the recent war, and the Royal Hawaiian Hotel, that pink pavilion of princely delights, was built smack in the middle of Waikiki. Tourist revenue helped force more and better roads and interisland plane service. When the Japanese struck Pearl Harbor from the north, they flew over one of the world's best organized places-to-go. The only thing for which the Hawaiian Tourist Bureau cannot provide in normal times is an eruption of Kilauea to order.

Yet perhaps ungratefully, perhaps with good taste, the modern *haole* is not always pleased with the tourist. He sus-

[65] Ford also organized the Pan-Pacific Institute to make Honolulu the intellectual and informational center of the Pacific littoral, an objective which, though by no means wholly achieved, was intelligent.
[66] "Old-timer" in modern Hawaiian jargon; original meaning "child of the land."

pects that his cash-dripping visitor, whether Hollywood star or vacationing schoolmarm, is unreliable, slightly ridiculous, and probably vulgar. The upper levels of established *haole* society send their sons to conservative mainland colleges, have been long accustomed to ample incomes suavely spent, and are still marked with missionary respectability and Anglophile snobbishness. They pay the bills for press-agentry through subsidiary corporations, but they themselves could never have created such ballyhoo about their patrimony. Nor do they fancy the prospect that, if the tourist business is still to pay, Hawaii will have to furnish more and better second-class accommodations and cater to two-week flying trippers demanding more than Waikiki affords. The outer Islands, hitherto little touched by tourists, are fated to resort development. That will show the vacationing visitor a great many beautiful things, but it will also occasion gnashing of teeth among the better people.

Another kind of outsider, the plantation worker, presented one of the Islands' more curious problems by refusing to stay an outsider. As soon as the children of successive waves of such immigrants were processed by the universal free education that is a credit to Hawaii, they would have nothing to do with plantation jobs. As annexation made further recruiting more difficult, sugar growers launched on schemes to make the hands' life more attractive. A plantation had always been a little world in itself, lodging and rudimentary social services thrown in with the meagre wages, so there was a tradition to work with. By the mid-thirties most of the slatternly old shacks were gone. The characteristic, though not universal, picture was a neat company village with fresh paint, some plumbing, free athletic facilities, free movies, free medical services, free baby clinics. Even the company store, that handiest instrument of extortion, sold at competitive prices and often permitted outsiders to set up shop next door on company land.

To management's bewilderment, however, this guarded lavishness—and lavish it looked by comparison—often got the plantations denounced for subversive paternalism. Nor did it stop the drift away from cane labor. The field hand, of whatever origin, had imbibed too much of the American idea. He did not want secluded paternalism for his children; he wanted them to do something that seemed to him and them better than swinging a cane knife. True, he was healthier, better paid and fed than he would have been on similar work in Colorado or Louisiana. But he didn't like it and when, at the instance of either his own leaders or mainland organizers, he tried to form a union through which to express discontent, there was always bigger trouble with the boss, and sometimes the National Guard, than he could cope with. For years his only recourse was to get off the plantation in his own person or that of his children. So the Chinese, Portuguese, Koreans and Japanese who once provided the sweat for sugar now do most of the Islands' storekeeping, gas pumping, taxi driving, clothes pressing, table waiting, as well as schoolgoing.

Of the thousand effects of World War II on Hawaii, all tending somehow to knit the Islands more closely to the mainland, none was more important than the capitulation of Island management to the organization of Island labor. The Wagner Act began the process. But it was the armed forces' need of steadily working hands and centralization of labor responsibility that completed it. Both sugar and pineapple are now thoroughly organized by the C.I.O., in the shape of the International Longshoremen's and Warehousemen's Union. The A.F. of L. is much stronger than it was in scattering trades. To the mainlander that may not sound very striking, but to anybody who knows the Islands at all it is as epoch-marking as if Andrew Mellon had suggested the *Internationale* as the national anthem.

One conspicuous result is the elimination of plantation "paternalism." The Hawaiian Pineapple Company led the way in 1946, putting company housing in the hands of a body of outside trustees who collect rents and otherwise act as landlords, setting up a cooperative doctoring program on an actuarial basis, generally dropping the old tradition of see-what-the-boss-does-for-you. The sugar companies followed suit in

1947 as one sequel of a prolonged strike notable for the fact that, though both sides wanted such "perquisites" eliminated, neither could resist the temptation to use them as a bargaining point. Why the unions want paternalism extinguished is clear enough. But the employers' willingness to see it go is obscure, since for years it was the backbone of their personnel policies. Actually, this shift in attitude is a fruit of U.S. social policies since 1933. Every year more and more headaches piled up as various Washington agencies insisted on differing estimates of the cash value of "perquisites." Every time a new union contract was to be negotiated, wrangling over the same issue added confusion to a situation already aggravated enough. Gradually the employers had come round to feeling that the whole tangled business was more trouble than it was worth. A mainlander could have told them that twenty years ago. But in the Islands lessons sink in with semi-Bourbon slowness.

The Island employer and the lower *échelons* of Island union leaders are, and will be for a generation, well below even the mainland level of labor relations. But eventually—here is a rash prediction—the Islands' tradition of centralization and situation-freezing will probably win out, and the holding company-factors will find unionization an asset from the point of view of management. As many a mainland employer already knows, it simplifies matters to deal with a monolithic union. That amounts to a sort of informal N.R.A. Hawaiian union leaders now have in mind a campaign of gradual attrition to break up the firm control of the "Big Five" over the Islands' production of export crops. But they may find in the long run that they have instead introduced the very mechanism that will enable the Big Five to stay snug in the citadel while conceding the outworks.

The unions will probably have to insist on a certain amount of "featherbedding," for instance, always a defensive tactic. As war made labor scarce in the Islands, the plantations had frantically to mechanize their operations. They succeeded so well with harvesting machinery that it is no longer true that the field hand with the cane knife is absolutely indispensable.

Tons of cane gathered per man-hour increased amazingly, demand for unskilled labor slacked off for keeps, need for semi-skilled or skilled labor skyrocketed, and total numbers on agricultural pay rolls dipped sharply. There is no good reason why they should ever increase again. A further dip is likelier. With Hawaii as isolated as she is, precluding much migration to outside labor markets, this permanent diminution in the plantations' demand for help is a serious thing in a community now half a million strong. Post-war dislocations have postponed this effect. But as matters tend to seek their level, Hawaiian labor, which was being coaxed into the fields ten years ago, will find itself in a less favorable bargaining position. That is just one of the elements that make the aforesaid private N.R.A. likely in the Islands.

Much of that parallels similar developments on the mainland, and so ties in with the likelihood that Hawaii will soon become the forty-ninth state.

To have taken Hawaii into the sisterhood of the Union before the recent war would have meant admitting a privately owned principality thirty years behind the times in economic organization. Though the matter had been perennially broached ever since 1900, the Big Five passively resisted statehood, preferring the insulation of Territorial status. But they changed their minds hastily when New Deal controls classed Hawaiian sugar in a status inferior to mainland-grown sugar— just what happened when the McKinley tariff made annexation imperative.

Such discrimination would certainly never have occurred if, instead of a mere nonvoting Territorial delegate in Congress, Hawaii had had a couple of senators and a couple of representatives swapping votes in the cloakrooms. The cry that, even as a Territory, Hawaii was an integral part of the Union and no stepchild, developed into an intensive campaign to insure the future with statehood. A local plebiscite taken shortly before the war showed two-to-one in favor. That was not entirely due to Big Five publicity campaigns either, for a good many people in the Islands had always felt that, if the powers that were didn't want statehood, it must be a good thing. Now there seems to be a corresponding feeling among some of the same people that, if the Big Five want it so badly, it must be a bad thing. But by and large, Island sentiment, whether among management of Island business, Island labor or Islanders in general, is united behind the project, which may well come to pass before this book reaches the bookstores. Necessary legislation passed the lower house in the Congress of 1947.

World War II robbed uneasy mainland legislators of the one plausible reason why Hawaii should not become a state—the presence there of too many Japanese of dubious loyalty. The point was not ill-taken. The largest single ethnic group in the Islands, the Japanese stuck by themselves more rigidly than other groups, insisted on special, privately supported schools teaching their children Japanese and heaven only knew what else, and even set up a Young Men's Buddhist Association with close connections in Japan. Honolulu, as well as Congress, was chronically nervous about so many apparently confirmed outlanders having so many children who would automatically become U.S. citizens with votes. Shrill statesmen objected to the possibility of U.S. senators named Yamamoto. . . .

The war-record of Hawaii's Japanese changed all that. The F.B.I. has officially announced that no act of sabotage by a local-born Japanese was detected during the entire proceedings. Older Japanese, many precluded by law from citizenship, distinguished themselves in civilian war activities. The younger men in uniform hung up a record for gallantry in action equal to that of any men who ever fought under the Stars and Stripes. By miraculous inspiration the War Department neglected the grudging precedent of World War I, when Japanese were used only as garrison troops in the Islands. Two combat units of Hawaiian Japanese were activated and sent to Italy, where they dived into German fighting, in one of the most grueling theatres of war, with a pluck and skill that made them immortal. Other local Japanese, assigned to intelligence and hide-out hunting in the Pacific theatre, were equally loyal and brilliant in less dramatic circumstances. Japanese names grimly predominate in Hawaiian lists of war dead. True, these boys were on a spot and knew it. They were watched most suspiciously until they proved themselves. But neither fear nor time-serving could account for the dash and integration of their performance, and it grew steadily clearer that the Hawaii-born Japanese U.S. citizen was unexpectedly close to being as good an American as anybody else. When Hawaii does become a state, it will be more than anything else the doing of the tough, stocky, indefatigable Nisei who fought in the rubbly hell of Cassino.

That is an unmistakable compliment to the degree to which Hawaii has avoided racial strains. It was never true, though the *haole* still piously tells the outsider so, that racial friction has never existed in the Islands. The Chinese, who used to be played up before the war as everything admirable that the Japanese were not, are now targets of considerable backbiting. It is said they made too much money out of the war, their syndicates (*hui*) are buying into or undermining *haole* business, they will bear a lot of watching . . . all in a vein uncomfortably cognate with the situation of the Chinese in Tahiti or, if you like, that of the Jew in Berlin twenty years ago. And there are few signs that the marked social cleavage between the *haole* and everybody else that always characterized the Islands, and was bridged only by the best-accepted and usually chief-descended Hawaiians is yet starting to break down. But on the whole a mutual tolerance admirably promoted by Hawaii's public schools and encouraged by the local tradition of intermarriage between ethnic groups has kept trouble to a gratifying minimum, certainly less than most mainland communities would have shown under the same circumstances.

Hawaiians, Portuguese, Chinese, Porto Ricans, Koreans, even Japanese to an increasing extent, mix gloriously, though not always by formal marriage, into a conglomeration of stocks that, anthropologists predict, will result in a new, vigorous and quick-on-the-uptake type of average resident of the Hawaiian Islands. The partnership notices in Honolulu newspapers customarily read like these samples:

Jimmie's Light Lunch, lunchwagon business, located at Heeia, Kaneohe, Oahu; partners, James C. Crawford, Dorothy Pactol, Bernice Kauhana, Mary Wong Chong . . .

International Construction Company, general contracting business, located at 939 Hauoli Street, Honolulu; partners, Harry H. Y. Kim, Hilario C. Hoomanawanui, Francis I. Sato, Kershaw A. Weston . . .

All that is far enough from the hushed, cool business palaces in which the Big Five ponder the problem of keeping the economic keys of the Islands decently in *haole* hands. But the insulation between the two categories of people is wearing steadily thinner, and the hybrid Islander is the clue to whatever the future of the Islands may be.

Anthropologists consider that the Hawaiian strain in these people will not be lost, but rather will contribute markedly to their physical endowment and cultural patterns. One hopes they are right. There is some dignity in that sort of survival. The Polynesian came of at least a three-way ethnic mixture. Even from the point of view of the hysterical race purist, there is no tenable reason why he should not be thrown back into the stockpot as an ingredient in a new formula. Many of his comrades in this experiment could use the broad shoulders and heavy musculature of the Hawaiian as well as the smiling nonchalance and the hedonistic values that will form part of the background of successive generations of steadily hybridizing children. Thus the Hawaiian may not die out, but be born again. Certainly there is no dignity in the alternative—artificial survival of the Hawaiian as a half-pauperized, specially privileged member of a minority, in the Islands he once dominated.

As of now, the native's balance sheet is necessarily depressing. The number of fullblood Hawaiians has shrunk below a twentieth of the population. Of *haole* contributions to living, the Hawaiian has made important use of clothes—he likes gay garments—church and fraternal organizations, alcohol—which is bad for him—tobacco, and education. That is, he is as literate as the rest of the Island's admirably literate local-born people. Intensive, large-scale agriculture has pretty well passed him by, of which he is probably glad. So far no effort to homestead him back on the land has worked too well. He is forbidden to alienate title to such holdings, so he usually leases his modest allotment of fertile soil to a big plantation which does most of the work more efficiently than he could alone, harvests and sells the crop and pays the owner a share that, combined with odd fishing and perhaps a small taro patch, keeps him alive, cheerful and relaxed. It amounts to what Crawford called "merely absentee landlordism on a small scale."[67] Yet the dominating haoles, inclined to keep Hawaiians for pets, are patronizingly eager to give them opportunities. As early as 1924 Adams found that 36% of Hawaiian and part-Hawaiian men were in "preferred occupations" compared to 26% for Chinese and Japanese.

Many Hawaiians are by no means unwilling to trade on the haole's sentimental patronage. The missionaries contributed to this when they taught their converts white man's music. The original native music, though by no means simple as performed, was so primitive in organization that the missionary erroneously concluded that the native knew nothing of music at all. Since Christianity implied mass worship and that implied hymns, the mission early translated Yankee hymns into Hawaiian and taught the appropriate tunes to brands about to be snatched from the burning. Whether converts or not, Hawaiians took to haole-style singing with the enthusiasm of a Chautauqua audience and developed their own music on the haole diatonic scale. Sailors' songs contributed; an unmistakably Spanish influence came by way of the Mexican vaqueros brought in for cattle ranching. But you need be no trained musician to perceive that the singing of the Hawaiian chorus that serenades your ship as you land in Honolulu is just a new and most intriguing version of the way they attack In the Sweet Bye-and-bye in an Iowa country church. The influence is

[67]Paradox in Hawaii, 174.

still there, though less identifiable, in the stunning choir of Kawaiahao church. In less formal contexts, the "Hawaiian" music that the mainland first met in *Aloha Oe* has very little to do with the sounds that entertained the grandfather of Kamehameha the Great and a great, great deal to do with Moody and Sankey. "Hawaiian" instruments are also exotics. They say the Portuguese brought the guitar, which became the steel guitar when a nail was run up the vibrating strings. A miniature guitar became the *ukulele*.[68]

It need astound nobody previously acquainted with what "natives" do with white man's things that this world-welcomed style of popular music should stem from the nasal carolings of bleak Yankee housewives filtered through instruments brought by crossbred and underprivileged Iberians. In Hawaiian music folk- or tin-pan-alley tunes from the mainland are often taken over, coming out, still hauntingly recognizable, as in the close affinity of *The Cockeyed Mayor of Keaunakakai* with *Casey Jones.*

This music could have been pure gain for the Hawaiian in fractional recompense for all the *haoles* robbed him of. Actually it is often the means to further degeneration, since it helps to produce the class of professional Hawaiians which is now the single most distressing aspect of the remains of Kamehameha's people. Hawaiian music from Hawaiian musicians is the keystone of Island tourist ballyhoo, the universally recognized signature of the whole grass-skirt-bottom-wriggling-beach-at-Waikiki complex. Still, more than musicians is needed. Languorous isles completely equipped with trade winds, palms, and private baths must˙have several varieties of picturesque natives to match. For those eligible the assignment is no empty honor. Fat Kanaka women had always sold *leis*[69] on the streets of Honolulu, but now it is a solid business, said normally to take in $200,000 a year, with a trade associa-

[68]The word is Hawaiian for *flea*, literally "jumping louse," presumably in token of the player's briskly shifting left-hand fingers.

[69]Flower-wreaths used in complimentary greeting and as general ornaments; the word also applies to wreaths of shells and feathers.

tion to control prices. At prices charged in wartime Honolulu and after, it must have been a million. And the "beach-boy," looking startlingly child-of-nature, was hired by Waikiki hotels to teach guests to surfride, massage them in the old Hawaiian way, and, when not otherwise engaged, clown enthusiastically on the sand.

Such a person is an embarrassing object. His success and that of professional Hawaiians in general, hula-dancers and hula-teachers, musicians, singers, guides, was so marked that even haole residents of Honolulu—this is true most notably among mainland born white-collar immigrants—came to swallow the implications of tourist ballyhoo almost as readily as the tourists themselves. Their womenfolk actually take hula lessons, and are ever after prone to kick off their shoes after dining with a few friends and go to slithering on the living room rug. The contemporary hula, luau[70], and Hawaiian make them pine for the old days before Captain Cook landed. They might as well dine in Mexico City on chicken enchiladas, learn to sing La Cucaracha and feel themselves in tune with the pre-Cortez days when priests tore out steaming human hearts in the war-gods' temple.

Professional Hawaiianism occasionally combines with Kalakaua-like nativism to produce something even more troubling. I remember a middle-aged Hawaiian who made a career of building and living in a prewhite style house, reverting to poi eaten strictly from a calabash, wearing the malo and admitting tourists to see a real live Hawaiian living as in the old days. The interior was stuck full of inscribed visiting cards of industrialists, admirals, film stars, chief stewards off ships, and others who the proprietor had been given to understand were important. He had a smooth, fluid patter competently describing in excellent English every detail of the establishment, the pseudopoetic phrase "in the olden times" pat at the end of every other sentence: ". . . everything just the way it was in the olden times. Everything was an art then and I am an

[70]Native-style feast, including poi and roast pig, at a price, hula girls extra.

artist the way they were in the olden times . . . I have read books and done research and I give lectures about the way things were in the olden times . . ." The last time I saw the place, he had ready to hang up at the roadside a wooden sign lettered "Nature's Kingdom" in pink painted shells. Yet the man's craftmanship was superb; better, to judge from old accounts, than much of his people's prewhite work; and he was unquestionably clinging, primarily from emotional causes, only secondarily for a livelihood, to the cultural heritage that the *haole* shattered.

As Adams' figures showed, however, many a native has a constructive and useful place in the modern Islands. He is often a policeman, skilled craftsman or seaman; as previously noted, he makes an admirable cowhand in the important Hawaiian beef industry, if handled on a semifeudal basis. In spite of vestigial remnants of incongruent ways of doing and of artificialities in his environment, his future looks far better than it did when, in the 'eighties, interloping populations first outnumbered him. The adjustment was unnecessarily brutal, but the worst of it is over now, and he is certain to survive as significant flavoring in a sturdy new race. This last may be a judgment on the missionaries. The thing that has made this kind of survival certain has been the Hawaiian's easygoing and enthusiastic eroticism, which the missions did their very special best to eradicate.

There is what happened to Hawaii, an account necessarily telescoped. Many residents of the Islands will not like it. But then few of them ever have liked anything objective written about themselves, as responsible writers have found to their sorrow ever since the mid-century. Some used shrinkingly to apologize to their Island friends in advance. Hawaii is too small, too self-conscious, and too vulnerable to afford objectivity about itself. There was a tale, which I hope is true and is certainly true in spirit, of a Honolulu *haole* encountering a newspaperman on the day of Pearl Harbor and barking at him indignantly: "I suppose the mainland papers will exaggerate this!"

The intention here, however, was not to concentrate on special angles of Hawaii. Remember this is a laboratory sample. Acquaintance with Kamehameha helps in understanding Pomare of Tahiti, Cakobau of Fiji, George Tubou of Tonga; Kalakaua's nativism helps explain the processes that still seethe in Samoa . . . No two South Seas peoples are alike. But pressures on them were often identical and many of the consequences were sadly similar.

IV

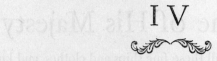

THE INTERLOPERS

1

In the Name of His Majesty

Having all these fine ships and clothes, and knowing all about engines and glass and the like, whatever makes you white people come out here, where
we have so little to give you?
—Fijian chief to Stonehewer Cooper,
The Islands of the Pacific, 106

WHITES ON PACIFIC ISLANDS SOMETIMES MOODILY
ask themselves what on earth they are doing there anyway—
not always an easy question to answer. History offers little
coherent help except to hint that the western world intruded
originally because of faulty geography and persisted because
of some false, some sound, assumptions sparked by ill-directed
greed.

Magellan, first to sail these waters, was sound enough; he
was demonstrating that East Indian spices could be secured
by sailing through the American barrier. But his only discovery
in the South Seas proper was the Marianas,[1] so pointless at the
time that a century and a half elapsed before Spain did anything about them. Mendaña, sent out from Peru in 1567,
sought rich kingdoms on the Inca-Aztec pattern and found only
the Solomons. They did not fit specifications, though their
name commemorates their discoverer's baseless assertion that

[1] This was the final name of the group comprising Guam, Rota, Tinian,
Saipan and the long tail of volcanic islets north toward Japan. Impressed
by the rig of the natives' splendid sailing canoes, Magellan first called
them the Islands of Lateen Sails; after experiencing the expert light-
fingeredness of the natives of Guam, he changed it to the Islands of
Thieves (Ladrones).

they were the former site of King Solomon's mines. Miners brought along, just in case, had said they thought gold might be found there—and three hundred and fifty years later were proved correct.

Navigation was still so primitive that, though the explorer could tell roughly how far north or south he was (latitude), east and west (longitude) were still a mere mathematical trap. So, though the Solomons group is hundreds of miles long and well over a hundred wide, Mendaña could not find it again when he tried to found a colony there thirty-eight years later. Instead, in the first appearance of whites in Polynesia, he stumbled on the Marquesas and then on the Santa Cruz group, where he grandiloquently and elaborately set up his colony. It disintegrated under quarrels and disease almost as soon as founded. One of Mendaña's associates, de Quiros, tried again in 1605 from Callao, found the New Hebrides, which he mistook for a continent, and made another abortive settlement. Luis de Torres, in charge of one of his ships, first navigated the hazardous passage between Australia and New Guinea called Torres Strait. These far-sailing Dons intrigue romantic-minded students, but that was the sum of their accomplishments.

Thenceforth Spanish exploring energy flagged. Though the west coast of South America was an excellent take-off area for Pacific discovery, Spain used her arrogantly claimed new ocean only as a highway. Yearly a great galleon sailed from Manila for Mexico, using Guam as seamark, working north to pick up favoring winds for California, then south to Acapulco. There her silks and spices from the Asiatic trade of Manila procured Mexican silver for the eternally silver-hungry East; her return trip was made in low north latitudes below Hawaii. On these routes Spanish skippers discovered, but made little stir about, several Micronesian islands. Making a stir would have been difficult if they had wished to; their reports disappeared into the royal archives, for jealous Spain wanted outsiders to know as little as possible of the Pacific.

There was good reason. Outward- or homeward-bound, the

Manila galleon made a rich prize. Periodically English raiders braved Cape Horn and scurvy to try to intercept her. During a hundred and fifty years several actually succeeded in this hunt for a square-rigged needle in an oceanic haystack. Their tales were good reading but their discoveries scanty—they had no time for exploration—and their presence was significant only to the annoyed Spaniards. They did contribute to the task of investigating the Pacific, however, through excessive loss of human life. Anson sailed from England with five ships in 1740; he made Tinian (Marianas) for badly needed supplies with only his flagship left and barely enough survivors of all five to work her. He took the galleon right enough; but he also demonstrated that, even under brilliant command, cruising this ocean from European bases was hardly practical unless navigation and marine hygiene greatly improved. The odds were appalling: a scholar's compilation of French voyages South Sea-wards up to Bougainville's time shows 168 ships sailing, only 117 returning.

It could be done, given luck as well as skill. In 1615 Schouten and Le Maire, a pair of brash Dutchmen, grew restive under the Dutch East India Company monopoly which forbade potential competitors in the spice trade to enter the Pacific by either the Straits of Magellan or the Cape of Good Hope—the only known ways. They set out to find a third, and did, at least technically: Le Maire's name sticks to the strait that led them round Cape Horn, Schouten's to a group of islands once conspicuous in war news. The Company, skeptical of their technical excuse, jailed them when they made the Indies, but en route they had become mildly immortal by discovering something that was probably Tonga and contributing to the delineation of New Guinea.

The king Dutchman among Pacific navigators, Tasman, whose name remains in Tasmania and the Tasman Sea, was a Company man based on the Indies, which simplified problems immensely. His complications, and his fame, came from looking for something that was not there. Geography then taught that the known world was badly out of balance, the

masses of Asia-Europe and North America being countered
only by Africa and slender South America. Yet the world
was obviously stable; hence there had to be a still undiscovered
Great South Continent in Atlantic or Pacific. De Quiros had
already been looking for it; for hundreds of years exploring
captains were ordered to find what science insisted on adum-
brating, all being successively disappointed. But their searching
did a great deal to tape out the greatest of oceans. Thus, in
1642-3, Tasman found not only Tasmania and New Zealand;
he also went home north-about and was the first white man to
lay eyes on Fiji.

He came near leaving his and his ship's bones in Fiji, which
still has a nasty name among sailors for sneaky reefs, fickle
winds, and treacherous currents. When captains of steamers
and motor vessels feel that way in waters now fairly well
charted, the reader should try to imagine what navigating them
was like without charts, in vessels fundamentally at the mercy
of wind, wave, and current. By modern standards Tasman was
a sketchy navigator; science had not yet developed the complicated, accurate gadgets and tables that lighten the task. But he
—and his predecessors and successors among first-class Pacific
discoverers—must have had most sagacious instincts and diabolical skill in seamanship. Small as they were by modern
standards, their ships drew so much water and loomed so high
that they were death-traps in any but expert hands, when picking their way through unknown island groups. The few sentences in an old book that tell how Tasman shot the reef in
Fiji when there was no other chance of safety are the more
stirring for their brevity. One lookout peering from the bow,
another at the masthead, the skipper himself often going aloft
when things were thick, two hands heaving the lead with
interminable apprehension, the crew twitching at their stations as the leadsmen called shoaler and shoaler figures, the
whole ship whispering through the water and seeming herself
to shrink from the not-so-distant sound of invisible breakers
—that sort of thing, routine for days on end, makes it clear
how plucky and competent such captains as Tasman were.

The great period of Pacific navigation began in the middle of the eighteenth century and was galvanized by rivalry between France and England. The Spanish were asleep, waking only momentarily after Wallis, Cook, and Bougainville, in a feckless effort to settle Tahiti. The Dutch were realistically confining their energies to exploiting the already known-to-be-rich East Indies. But Britain and France were at semi-permanent odds in America and India, and the attrition of their friction soon shredded away Spain's claim to the whole South Sea. Small and large considerations like the China trade, the strategic advantages of the Falkland Islands, the possibilities of trade with the western coast of South America, drew jealous attention to the desirability of shortening routes to the Pacific. The legend of the Great South Continent, which would be a lordly prize, was supplemented by equally hoary hopes of a short cut into the great ocean, a Northwest or perhaps Northeast Passage that would ease by thousands of miles and months of high hardship the known ways of getting from Bordeaux or Bristol to Canton or Callao. An old-time Spanish sailor named Juan de Fuca had found something quite like this strategic strait generations before. In the seafaring thought of the time this idea was as pivotal as that of a canal through Central America was in the nineteenth century, affecting international policy for generations before the job was actually carried out.

So emphasis shifted from raiding to exploration. Commodore Byron, a former lieutenant of Anson, was sent in 1764 to forestall the French in the Falklands and to smell out possibilities in the Pacific. When he succeeded in getting home again without proving much, one of his officers, Samuel Wallis, was sent out again to prove more. The French were close behind: the Sieur de Bougainville, a gallant young veteran of the French wars in Canada, set out on an assignment similar to Wallis'. By extraordinary coincidence both made previously unknown Tahiti within less than a year of one another. With British luck, Wallis was first. Bougainville also saw much of the New Hebrides and rediscovered the long lost Solomons so far from where Mendaña had thought they were that he was not at all sure of the identification; his name lives in Bougainville Island of evil memory and in a lovely flowering vine. Captain Carteret, in command of Wallis' consort, was early separated from him and came home with other independent discoveries of some importance.

These voyages so encouraged British interest that Wallis was hardly home before James Cook, already noted for a skilful survey of Newfoundland waters, was sent to follow up. King of seagoing discoverers, this country boy had gone to sea through the hawsehole, learning sailoring in the tricky English coastwise coal trade, and was the essence of self-made man. Tall, big-nosed, grave, magnificently reliable, he had the mind of an engineer, the temperament of a born commander, and the painstakingness of a laboratory researcher. The wealthy young English scientist, Joseph Banks—his name remains on both a peninsula in New Zealand and a group of Melanesian islands —sponsored Cook's appointment to the new Pacific expedition and emphasized faith in his man by going along. The scientific occasion for the voyage was to advance techniques of navigation by observing at Tahiti a transit of the planet Venus across the sun; Point Venus, near Papeete, is not named, as one might think, for the principal obsession of the natives. Another motive may have been to see what a very well-thought-out expedition could accomplish toward making the Pacific a chartable reality.

Thus the chosen vessel was no warship but a slow, sturdy, capacious, utterly seaworthy, shallow-draft collier, the very sort of craft in which Cook had learned his trade. She carried several kinds of chronometers for cross-checking in the search for sounder methods of determining longitude; her officers made incessant observations and calculations for comparison. Researching the problem of keeping seamen healthy on long voyages, Cook's ships always carried experimental provisions aimed at preventing scurvy—sauerkraut, dehydrated vegetables, and something called "portable soup." Routine in airing, fumigating, clothes drying, messing, was as rigid as that of a modern hospital.

Nobody knew about vitamins then. Scurvy was as often considered a matter of sea air or dampness as of diet; but the Admiralty wanted everything tried out, as lime juice had been tried shortly before on the West Indies station. By thus taking all possible precautions—and by shipping fresh provisions wherever possible en route—Cook made three prolonged and valuable voyages without losing as many men as probably would have died ashore in the insanitary stews of England. He showed for all time that forethought, discipline, equipment, and seamanship could make a voyage from England to the Antarctic to Bering's Strait almost as practical as his old run from Newcastle to London.

In fresh discoveries he did little better than some rivals: New Caledonia, the Cook group, and Hawaii alone fall to his exclusive credit. But his three voyages made New Zealand and Australia realities instead of vaguely glimpsed terrae incognitae, laid the Great South Continent to rest along with St. Brandon's Isle, and surveyed the Societies, Tonga, the New Hebrides, the Marquesas, the coasts of Northwest America and Siberia. He was as much at home poking into the Antarctic ice as, in his better-known phase, watching brown-skinned ballets perform in Tonga. Sailing with and trained under him were half a dozen young officers who later added brilliantly to his unfinished work—Vancouver and Bligh were Cook's men. His reputation grew so high that both American and French armed vessels in the Revolutionary War had orders not to molest, but rather to aid, his ships if encountered. That confused brawl on Kealakekua beach killed a man who probably knew his business better than Columbus and Eric the Red put together.

This does not derogate his successors, rival or friendly. The French were on New Zealand, finding the Maori tough, almost as soon as Cook. The Frenchman la Pérouse was the first white to investigate Samoa and Maui (Hawaii); it was just hard luck that smashed his ships on a Melanesian reef; the explanatory bits were not found for forty years. His countryman d'Entrecasteaux, sent to look for him, made great contributions. In the next generation French surveyors, such as Duperrey and Dumont-d'Urville, did more than Englishmen to fill in details of the Pacific. East Indiamen and Australian convict-ships routed to China by unknown waters often came home with news of new islands. As routine, ships headed Pacific-wards on whatever errand, were ordered to look about them within reason. Highly valuable results came of Edwards' unlucky voyage to find, arrest, and fetch home the mutineers of the "Bounty" and from Bligh's second voyage to take bread-fruit to the West Indies—uneventfully successful this time.

This is in sharp contrast with Spain's ordering her captains to stick to sterile known courses between the Philippines and Mexico. Even the Russians, not a traditional seagoing people but seeking to bolster their colonial venture in Alaska, were active in a neglected chapter of Pacific history. Krusenstern and Kotzebue were expert island-finders. For a while their backers bade fair to make California and Hawaii subject to St. Petersburg. But Russia proved a flash in the pan; of these voyages nothing lasted but Russian names on a few out-of-the-way scraps of land: like Lisiansky Island in the chain northwest of Hawaii, and Suvarov Island (mispronounced Suwarrow through Germanized transliteration) in the Manihikis.

The political map of the Pacific dispels forever the notion that finders-keepers means anything internationally. If it did, Spain would have a South Seas empire consisting of the Marquesas, Solomons, New Hebrides, Marianas and Carolines; the Dutch would rule Samoa, Tonga, Fiji, and New Zealand. The French would have no foothold in the Pacific at all. Seeking mineral wealth, the Spaniards were never close to the gold of Fiji and New Zealand. Seeking empire, the French acquired only a chain of South Pacific bases of which they never made aggressive use. Looking principally for profit and the glory of God, with small thought of sovereignty, the United States did rather better than the French. Always drawing back from responsibility in the Islands, the British got more and richer holdings than anybody else. For there was much more to Island history than merely sending in a boat's crew to run up a flag and utter solemn words in the name of his Most Christian or Imperial or Britannic Majesty. The chain of the humdrum and the brilliantly accidental in Bligh's career is typical: Wallis found breadfruit in Tahiti; West Indies planters wanted it for cheap slave-food; for this prosaic assignment Bligh picked the wrong man as master on his ship; so, turned loose in a small boat, he was forced to sail slap through Fiji in what amounted to an important rediscovery of a major group.

Other discoverers' objectives failed to match the net of their discoveries. Cook's third voyage, which found Hawaii, was officially "to determine the position and extent of the west side of North America; its distance from Asia; and the practicability of a northern passage to Europe." Vancouver was on the same mission. Kotzebue's idyllic experiences in the Marshalls were mere distractions from the interests of Russian enterprise in Siberia. These men noted down Tahiti, Tongatabu and Hawaii primarily because their presence made a voyage to Puget Sound or Kamschatka healthier by supplying fresh pork and greens. Their advantages as refreshing points explain why the early navigators often took out sheep and cattle as presents for Island chiefs. Time and again the exactions of European vessels depleted provisions to the danger point in thickly-populated Islands; herds of semiwild cattle and sheep on the unused uplands would not only solve that problem but give seamen a better diet. Pleasant as it was to visit the Islands, the European's basic purpose was to connect more efficiently with China in order to make profits out of tea and silk. So mankind discovered a multiple paradise by trying to make money. There must be a more fitting way, but that is how it happened.

2

The Glory That Was Grease

HERE WAS A WHOLE OUTSIZE OCEAN WELL EXPLORED by 1800: query, what to do with it? The first responses affected only its margins. Loss of the American colonies deprived Britain of a place to send inconvenient people; Australia was made a substitute. Thenceforth malefactors not quite deserving hanging were sent to Port Jackson—"Botany Bay" in long-lived error, now called Sydney. That founded the port destined to be the prime commercial depot of the South Seas, easily outstripping San Francisco, Honolulu, Papeete, Suva, Auckland, Valparaiso. The reason is obvious and geographical. More islands lie within a reasonable radius of Sydney. A belt of empty water, wider than the Atlantic, separates the Americas from the Islands. Theoretically, if one judges strictly by miles and bearings, the whole South Seas should have come under suzerainty of Australia, the continental mass handicst to Polynesia and Melanesia. That nothing of the sort happened is probably due to national variations in economic temperament. For the people who first showed how to use the South Seas for more than a means of communication were the least likely of all candidates. True, the Australian convict settlement sometimes drew on the Islands for provisions, and Russians went to Hawaii for salt, kukui-oil[1] and vegetables. But Americans went farther and fared very much better.

This was no official governmental effort. The new United States had taken no hand in exploring the Pacific because no such nation had existed when the job developed. Not until sixty years after the Declaration of Independence was Commodore Wilkes sent to do such surveying work as, in one sense or another, naval officers in national ships from England, France, Russia, and Spain had been doing for centuries. But the eighteenth century still had time to run when news of South Pacific seals and whales brought Americans spontaneously round the Horn to inaugurate the now intimate American involvement in the South Seas.

The consequences were widespread: Until a generation ago the partly American-descended people of Lord Howe Island,[2] 7,000 miles from the Golden Gate, celebrated the Fourth of July and, for that matter, still eat pumpkin pie and fried chicken. In the 'seventies a British yachtsman was annoyed to find the natives of Ponape (Carolines) talking English full of such Americanisms as "I guess" and "fixing" things. The cause was simple: of fifty-six whalers calling there in nine months a few years earlier, forty-nine had been American. A Russian exploring squadron fogbound near a presumably unknown island in the South Pacific in 1820 were startled when the fog lifted to disclose an American sealer already perfectly at home. Such enterprise was not in uniform, carried no commission, preferred to be inconspicuous; but it accomplished much penetration and influence in the South Seas without the

[1] Kukui (this is the Hawaiian name) is a small tree common in the Islands producing what whites call candlenuts. Their oil is rich and volatile enough for the Polynesian device of stringing them on a coconut-leaf rib and using the string as a candle. Just now Fiji is trying to build up a small industry processing kukui-oil for sale in world markets as a drying oil.

[2] This is the Lord Howe in the Tasman Sea between Sydney and Norfolk Island. Cf. my "Utopia Limited," Saturday Evening Post, Aug. 13, 1936.

bother of burying lead plates or erecting crosses. Individual profit can be a mighty force.

In this connection "American" should narrow down to "Yankee." Much fine seamanship came to the Pacific out of New York, Philadelphia and Baltimore. But the New Englander left his mark so deep on the South Seas that, from Fiji to the Marquesas, Americans were earliest known as "Boston men." Yankee John Ledyard, one of Cook's last crew, was volunteer propagandist for American entrance into the Northwest-to-China fur trade. Winters on the American West Coast took Yankees to Hawaii to recruit and so arose the first Island commercial enterprise, the vandalistic and hard-nosed sandalwood trade. Characteristic details appear elsewhere.[3] The point here is that before 1800 Yankee seamen were being left ashore to cut sandalwood on Kauai, and that this parasitic timber taught that money could be made directly out of the Islands.

In a short few years American vessels, sometimes based on Sydney, were braving the reefs and cannibals of Fiji to trade for the stuff, bringing the first whites voluntarily to go ashore there. Many came to grief; wrecks and massacres stud the story, but profits were immense and worth risk. Lockerby figured that a schooner sandalwooding[4] out of Sydney could make £4,400 profit (say $22,000) in six months on an investment of £3,350. Presently sharp Yankees noticed that Fijian shallows were rich with bêche-de-mer,[5] the unprepossessing sea-slug other-

[3] Cf. III, Land of Makebelieve Come True; V, Their Gods Are Dead.
[4] The Spanish out of Manila were mildly active in sandalwood round the close of the eighteenth century. Manila and Batavia were the centers where sandalwood from the Southwest Pacific was sold and transshipped to China. (Derrick, History of Fiji, 39.)
[5] "The bêche-de-mer is generally taken in three or four feet of water; after which they are taken to the shore, where they are split at one end with a knife . . . Through this opening the entrails are forced out by pressure . . . The article is then washed and afterward boiled to a certain degree . . . then buried in the ground for four hours; then boiled again for a short time, after which they are dried, either by the fire or the sun. Those cured by the sun are worth the most; but where one picul (133⅓ lb.) can be cured that way, I can cure thirty picul by fire.

wise called *trepang*, for which Chinese paid high to Manila and East Indies traders. So sandalwooders persuaded Fijian tribes to claw *bêche-de-mer* off their reefs, and processed it on shore under palm-leaf shelters. Such more intimate contact meant even more violence and damage to the natives, of course; but again it was profitable.

In the same decade came the superlative burst of Yankee enterprise in sealing and whaling. It was only 1791 when the "Beaver" of Nantucket poked her boxy bows round Cape Horn to pioneer American whaling in the Pacific. Six more Yankee whalers made the same voyage that year. Successive explorations of new waters gradually taught New Bedford, Nantucket, and Sag Harbor that the Pacific was a stunning whaling-ground—right whales in the far north, sperm on the Japan ground, the Line, the offshore ground, the waters approaching the Antarctic. The British were in first. Their "Amelia" was whaling down under in 1787; Bligh found seamen from the wrecked British whaler "Matilda" on Tahiti in 1792. Dutch and Germans were soon trying their luck; in the early nineteenth century sea-minded France heavily subsidized Pacific whalers. But within a generation Pacific whaling was a Yankee quasi-monopoly, much as Hollywood was to be in the world of movies. Significantly, many officers on British and French whalers were expert Yankees tempted to sail under alien flags by higher earnings.

The sealer entered the Island regions of the Pacific because sea otter was hunted on the Northwest Coast; smart Yankees could no longer maintain the supply even by illicit deals with the Spanish in California; and the Chinese would buy seal if nothing better offered. The sealer was usually a Yankee too, often from Stonington, Conn. The "Betsy," of Stonington,

---

... The Chinese consider *bêche-de-mer* a very great luxury, believing that it wonderfully strengthens the system and renews the exhausted vigor of the immoderate voluptuary."—Morrell, *Narrative of Four Voyages*, 401. This gives current prices at Canton ranging from $90 a picul for top quality to $4 for bottom. Derrick (*History of Fiji*, 67) derives *bêche-de-mer* from the Portuguese *bicho-do-mar*—sea-slug.

was sealing at Mas Afuera, off Chile, in 1797; the "Union," Yankee sealer operating out of Sydney, went a sandalwooding voyage to Fiji in 1800; the gap of 7,000 miles between the two places indicates the scope of these doings. Nobody knows where all sealers did go. They were a secretive lot, leaving few accounts of their tough and bloody business as they took Yankee keels among the Islands and left behind much Yankee influence in the way of deserters, diseases, and ways of doing. Whalers could afford to swap information about likely locations for their quarry, since three or four whales at a time was all that any ship could cope with and it was no skin off Captain Starbuck's nose if Captain Coffin's boats were also fast to a couple of fish. But sealing was wholesale massacre ashore, often on small islands, and a newly discovered rookery was like a mine of precious metal, too easily exhausted to tell rivals about. Such finds were so ruthlessly exploited that within a generation the trade was unprofitable in most of the Pacific.

It does not follow, however, that whalers and sealers under American colors meant purely American influences. These crews were the sweepings of all ports—English, Irish, Chilean, Portuguese, Scandinavian, negro, and so through the whole Tower of Babel. The deserters or stranded sailors who early gave beachcombing a bad name, came from everywhere. Charlie Savage, who terrorized Fiji for years, going forth to war in a spearproofed sedan chair, was a Swede; in one of Pomare's wars in Tahiti two Swedes fought against a Scotchman, an Irishman, and an English Jew.

If either whaler or sealer was to stay at sea long enough to justify the tremendous voyage to the Pacific, the crew had to have occasional "refreshment"—sometimes the word is "recruiting"—ashore. Fruit and green stuff staved off scurvy, getting drunk and sleeping with girls staved off mutiny, fresh supplies of pork or beef to salt, water, firewood, potatoes, yams, enabled the old hooker to carry on till her hold was full of oil in cask. So whalers exchanged information as to which islands were best for such purposes much as tramps exchange word of where handouts are easy: Hawaii, the high islands of the Carolines, Tahiti, the Marquesas, the Bay of Islands, and the extreme south in New Zealand, were conspicuous. Regularizing and making profits from such needs, clever whites—again often Yankees—set up shore stations, raising potatoes, cattle and hogs, running grogshops and brothels, advertising in Yankee whaling circles that fresh provisions and boarding facilities were available at such and such a place the other side of the world. Such previously uninhabited but attractive islands as Lord Howe and the Bonins were thus settled, as well as large islands like Aneityum (New Hebrides). The multitude of whales round New Zealand created land based whaling, using fast boats and headland lookouts in the old Nantucket style. Scholars trace the enterprising and well assimilated, largely half-white, Maori of Invercargill to such white shore whalers and their Maori girls.

Discretion was needed in choosing recruiting spots. If, for instance, Captain Coffin had wife and family along, as he often did, he would prefer a place with the protection of a resident missionary when leaving them ashore for respite from seafaring while he sailed after more whales. Why wives might be left ashore is indicated in Benjamin Morrell's account of the occasion when he was trying to get his schooner "Antarctic" clawed off from a menacing array of breakers in the Carolines:

> "The breakers were running twenty feet high and there was no land in sight from the masthead . . . At the very crisis of our fate, my wife came on deck and asked me if I would have my hat."—Narrative of Four Voyages, 378–9.

The hazard of runaway hands was also important. During the Australian gold rush Sydney was shunned because a whaler putting in there was likely to see her crew desert for the diggings in a body. As Lahaina and the Bay of Islands developed into whalers' hells, conservative skippers avoided them, perhaps partly from moral scruples, certainly in precaution against desertion, venereal disease, and mayhem. Others intentionally sought them, since deserters could be replaced by signing on previous deserters already broke and "on the beach," and the amount of the delinquents' forfeited pay was often greater than advances on earnings when shipping new hands. Or natives eager to see the world, who usually made good seamen, could easily be signed; few Pacific whalers lacked a sprinkling of Polynesians, who often rose to the dignity of harpooners.

Native chiefs might tempt men to skip ship, using native girls to persuade them to take to the hills and hide until the ship sailed. If the captain made trouble, the chief ostensibly hunted for the fugitive, while actually warning him to stay deep in the bush. His motive was not so much hospitality as the desire to acquire a white man adept in the mysteries of gunpowder and ironworking, which were great military and economic assets in Island eyes. Sometimes a forecastle hand with his wits about him did well by himself thus: Churchill of the "Bounty" was chief in a Tahitian district until a jealous comrade shot him. In the 'forties Wilkes found well-fed beachcombers on several islands in the Gilberts, treated with respect and long married to young women of standing; they usually wanted to go home, but had little to complain of. In the early days many Fijian chiefs had such tame white men, regarding them as mannerless but useful; to have one was part of a chief's prestige. Many of these white men in the service of chiefs were brutes, some stupid, some cunning. Some were convicts escaped from Australia.

In such cases life was certainly better than if the renegades had stayed in the noisome forecastle of the "Huldah" whaler or on sadistic Norfolk Island. But luck was not always good. A sailor of Morrell's named Shaw escaped a sudden massacre in the Carolines because the chief wanted a blacksmith. But Shaw knew nothing of forging, which annoyed his patron, in whose culture most men could do most things. Deprived of his clothes and shoes, skin fried off him in the blistering sun, feet cut to pieces on coral, living on cast-off fish offal, constantly in hot water because he could not produce satisfactory iron knives, he barely managed to hang on until Morrell returned to rescue him and take a bloody revenge.

As small settlements grew up at whalers' haven, other whites, frequently enterprising ships' officers with good Yankee commercial instincts, stayed ashore and set up trading stores to service ships and chiefs wanting white men's goods—stores with counters, shelves, and a system of bookkeeping. As they prospered, they might go in for tall hats and broadcloth suits on Sunday, and rear families on the spot by white wives or native girls, whom they frequently married.

These port towns were often on sites that had been unimportant to the native. Canoes did not require great depth of water, holding ground for anchors, or reasonable likelihood of offshore breezes to waft a ship out as well as the tradewind to fetch her in. The Hawaiian used Waikiki beach, but had little use for the cramped port a few miles away that whites found the handiest harbor in the group. The Samoans' chief settlements on Upolu ignored the break in the reef that constitutes Apia harbor; on Tutuila, Leone Bay was better for natives than deep and sheltered Pago Pago. Missionaries contributed to the growth of these new towns at the expense of prewhite settlements; they wanted to be near shipping for supplies. So hardly a principal town in the South Seas today stands on the site of the old chief village. Already new ways were unpreventably turning the Islands upside down.

Whales, seals, and the cutting of slow-growing sandalwood meant a kind of mining, a rapid exploitation of easily exhausted resources. Such mining had the moral advantage of not evicting the native from his communal lands. But he would not be so fortunate when the interloping white, pondering further cash profit, took the next logical step.

Missions paved the way by persuading native converts to contribute arrowroot and coconut oil to the support of the church.[6] This successful example moved the trader to compete for oil with Misi. The coco palm, which Mark Twain said looked like a feather duster struck by lightning, promised to

[6]Cf. IV, 5, Fishers of Men.

enable the western world to make steady profit from the soil of the Islands themselves.[7]

At first the industry was catch-as-catch-can: The native picked up nuts as they ripened and fell, opened them with the cutlass (or machete or bush-knife or whatever you prefer) that he had acquired from the trader, let the halves dry a while, scooped out the firm, white, sweetish meat, chopped it up in a large wooden trough and set it to render in the hot sun. Then he poured the oil into sections of large bamboo and exchanged it with the trader, or with the trading schooner that called periodically at his island, for cloth, rum or nails; or took it to Misi for the greater glory of God. You can still see the native making his own supply of coconut oil by this method today.

But the white world was getting cleaner and demanding more soap than waste animal fats could supply; and these wasteful doings—for sun-rendering by no means extracts all the oil—looked disgraceful to conscientious businessmen. In the mid-century efficient-minded Germans replaced this small, sloppy sort of thing with western ideas.

This introduces the great German firm of J. C. Godeffroy & Son, the economic enterprise that the Pacific still remembers with most respect. The Godeffroys had been French Huguenots who moved to Hamburg after the Revocation of the Edict of Nantes—a migration also responsible for New Rochelle, N. Y., and the silk trade of London's Spitalfields. Six generations later they were shipowners and merchants, involved in the China trade, transport of immigrants to Australia and odd enterprises on the west coast of South America, particularly in nitrates. Their manager at Valparaiso grew interested in Tahiti, which bought foodstuffs in Chile. A new branch in Papeete did so well that the firm went on into Samoa, which was just then coming into notice, its port of Apia succeeding to the peripatetic title of "Hell of the Pacific." Samoa, centrally

[7]Masterman (*Origins of International Rivalry in Samoa*, 57 et seq.) dates the economic importance of coconut oil from the 'forties, when it was first used in England as ingredient of soap and candles. The missions were shipping it much earlier than that, however, in small quantities.

located, relatively fertile, relatively unexploited, was to become Godeffroys' Pacific headquarters.

There they borrowed an idea from the East Indies and made copra instead of locally extracted oil. Copra—coconut meat dried so it will keep long periods—became the cornerstone of Island economics. It could be sent to Europe where all the oil was pressed out with complicated, expensive machinery and the residue sold for cattle-cake. The native learned readily to dry copra either in the sun, which makes a superior product, or in smoke.[8] Process and product so imbedded themselves in Island life that I have heard missionaries call copra the ruin of the South Seas native—it is too simple for him to earn his small cash needs by a few days' work with knife and drying-rack. The slightly spicy, definitely rancid, odor of the result has long been as characteristic of the South Seas as the smell of burning coconut husk, and the copra bug, a persistent little creature inseparable from copra, is ubiquitous in port towns and Island schooners.

Godeffroys led this procession. Their ships and trading stations reached directly or by affiliated firms into Tonga, Hawaii, and Fiji, up into Micronesia, over into Melanesia from the Samoan base. Their competitors, operating out of Tahiti, Auckland, Sydney, San Francisco, often relied on the more respectable type of beachcomber as storekeeper. He was not too reliable or enterprising; whereas Godeffroys, more foresighted, staffed their stores with smart, sober, hard, young fellows brought out from Europe or recruited in the larger Pacific towns, by no means all Germans. Their instructions were realistic: Learn the native language. Don't get into quarrels with local whites. Have no truck with missionaries, except as humanity requires, for Misi and the trader are born enemies. Get a native woman of your own, but no nonsense about marrying her. And get in that copra.

But even harsh young storekeepers could not rationalize supply. Natives persisted in giving copra to Misi; or in poorer islands showed reluctance to trade in their staple food; or,

[8]The modern plantation often uses a complicated hot-air drier.

annoyed when the trader refused to over-extend credit, boy-cotted him. So Theodor Weber, Godeffroys' overweening com-manding officer in the Pacific, determined to put the firm into copra production on its own. Taking advantage of the Sa-moans' need for arms in their chronic feuds, he bought large areas of Samoan land, careless of whether such sales were good in Samoan custom, and started to plant coconuts.[9] When the Samoan proved an unreliable laborer, Chinese coolies and Melanesian "boys" were imported to weed the plantations and gather and process the nuts. As cash gradually replaced barter, the firm flooded the Islands with Chilean and Bolivian "iron dollars"—large, handsome coins into which the issuing govern-ments had neglected to put much silver, which Godeffroys procured at heavy discount in South America and passed for full face value on the native. That was all right as long as the coins stayed in the Islands. But missions protested bitterly when they found that iron dollars in the collection basket meant a devastating discount in Sydney or London.

Fraudulent currency, fraudulent land-purchase, concubinage were all necessary details of Weber's schemes. He had further plans for German immigration to the Samoan uplands, im-plicitly involving dispossession of the Samoan. These develop-ments were no less brilliant for their only flaw: they disre-garded the original inhabitant of Upolu or any other island where plantations would pay.

The Godeffroy firm was bankrupted by the French blockade of Hamburg during the Franco-Prussian War, but Weber's ideas went on under successor firms. Competing whites flocked into coco plantations from New Guinea to Tahiti, a trend culminating in the majestic appearance on the Pacific scene of Lever Brothers, British kings of soap, whose coco plantings in the Solomons and elsewhere were most impressive until com-petition from African oils and governmental distrust of Uni-levers' large ideas discouraged the firm's management.

In the mid-century the word "plantation" grew magical in

[9]Godeffroys had their own arsenal for making trade rifles at Liège. (Cooper, The Islands of the Pacific, 233.)

other contexts. The rowdy white colony at Levuka in Fiji, skimping along on desultory trading, developed the notion that cotton, for which demand was apparently unlimited, would do well in Fijian soil. Experimentally grown Fijian samples made a sensation in Manchester. Then the American Civil War blockaded the principal world source of cotton and the fever was on, by no means only in Fiji. In spite of cannibal natives a doughty American named Hart cleared and established booming plantations in the Marquesas; a group of Englishmen bought some 10,000 acres on Tahiti and imported thousands of Chinese to grow cotton, sugar, and coffee on them. But Fiji was far ahead as Australian settlers and capital poured in, wanting land. They got it—at native expense.

American production did not return to normal for some years after Appomattox, so the boom lasted up to a decade, particularly in Fiji, for the long-staple cotton of which France paid over four shillings a pound in 1869. But the Franco-Prussian war ruined that, just as it ruined Godeffroys, and the return of the American South to cotton prevented later revival. Now little remains of the whole development but wild cotton here and there, nobody taking much notice of its fluffy white balls, and the descendants of the Chinese or Melanesian labor imported to chop and pick the crop when, as usual, the local native proved to dislike such steady toil in the mid-day sun. Still, the immigration of substantial people during the cotton boom did start to make Fiji respectable—not an achievement to be belittled.

Sugar has much the same South Seas history; it was experimented with before the Civil War, boomed when American sugar was blockaded, discouraged when the South returned to production. But this crop managed to stay alive, sketchily in Tahiti, sturdily in Fiji, brilliantly in Hawaii.[10] In Hawaii Oriental labor was necessary for sugar, in Fiji Indian labor, in the post-1919 Japanese plantation in the Marianas Okinawan labor. It all meant more capital in the Islands, more outsiders looking about them for opportunity—types different from the

[10]Cf. III, *Land of Makebelieve Come True.*

beachcombers who had formerly hired out to sandalwooders as sluggish go-betweens at four pounds a month.

So experiments in other kinds of plantations multiplied. In its time coffee has looked very good in Hawaii, New Caledonia, Tahiti; but blight and Brazil depressed it, though the only coffee in the world better than Hawaii's is New Caledonia's. Pineapple has done magnificently under American mass production methods in Hawaii; nowhere else, though it has been played with in Fiji. Citrus is still alive in the Cooks, though severely handicapped by governmental bungling. Here and there exports of bananas bring in some cash for the native; cocoa is probably a fixture in Western Samoa, because the local variety is unusually rich in cocoa butter, a high demand by-product. Trochus shell, pearl shell, vanilla, are small-quantity items that stay alive, particularly in the French Establishments. And on many islands, on lands too poor or dry to tempt the planter, cattle are run for local meat supply—New Caledonian beef, canned for French army rations, is known to the rank and file as *singe* (monkey). The reader tempted to suggest that all this sounds like rather small change is quite right.

More workmanlike kinds of mining have affected the Islands only sporadically. French exploitation of nickel and chrome in New Caledonia, though lackadaisical, has been the backbone of the island's economy. Guano on lonely bits of island is pretty well worked out; so is the phosphate of French-owned Makatea (Societies). There is any amount of phosphate left on Ocean Island and Nauru, but that affects nobody but the semigovernmental corporations doing the work, the natives of those islands who are paid royalties in return for having their patrimonies torn apart,[11] and the outside laborers—from the

[11] Ocean Island is so messed up by this time that Britain has moved its Micronesian inhabitants to the island of Rabe in Fiji. Rabe was once a Lever Brothers' plantation; under governmental auspices, the Ocean Islanders' accumulated royalty money was used to buy it, with much of the copra-handling equipment intact. Some Gilbert Islanders were also in on the deal. When I paid a brief visit to Rabe in 1946, there were great difficulties in adjustment—the colonists' ideas of housebuilding, for instance, were by no means suited to the climate of Fiji—but there seemed little doubt that the government had got round to doing what it could to help.

usual sources—are paid low cash wages and regularly sent home at the expiration of their contracts.

Just as in Samoa under Weber, these white men's projects seldom offer the native much participating future. There is a fundamental difference between the white man (and his Oriental imitators) and the South Seas native as to what land is for. The native considers how best to adapt himself to the land's superficial potentialities, as the Maori did in New Zealand; the white considers how best to adapt the land to his existing elaborate techniques.

The plantation-cum-mining economy here described, however, is not conspicuous in the modern South Seas. Except in the southern Marianas, Hawaii and some parts of Fiji, exploitation never got far. For all the whites' exploratory hopes, most of the Islands are economic misfits in the world of great enterprises—too far, too small, too recalcitrant about work. This fact is somewhat masked now by luxuriantly high prices for Island products, as the postwar world snatches for fats, fertilizers and miscellaneous raw materials. For several years this high price level will probably hold, but eventually the Islands will probably see the coach turn into a pumpkin again. Palm and soy oils have put copra in an unfavorable spot in world economy. Both dietician and economist would agree that the world has too much sugar. Old-line mercantile and shipping firms in the Islands—local names to conjure with, such as Burns-Philp, Hedstrom, Ballande—are stabilized on a basis satisfactory to the shareholders but none amounts to a major phenomenon in terms of the outside world. Their market is composed largely of natives whose normal cash income hardly averages over fifty dollars per capita in good years, much of which goes into church collections rather than directly across the merchant's counter.

So there are ghost towns in the South Seas, and bush and beach, not smelter and plantation, are what usually meet the outsider's eye on any given island. Superficially, Tarafu is much the same as when H.M. Armed Vessel "Towser" first coasted along its reef. By and large all the hurly-burly, the sanguine schemes, the schoonerloads of blackbirded labor, the dispossession of the native and the squinting shrewdness of the pajama-clad trader, have shaken down to little, as the world goes—just a hand-truck trundling copra along the sleepy waterfront of Levuka. Said the wife of an American consul, pondering the cost when the Apia hurricane wrecked six foreign warships in 1889:

"Samoa was never worth it; . . . the whole archipelago might be taken just as it is and set down in Lake Ontario and not become a serious menace to navigation."—Churchill, *Samoa 'Uma,* 13.

But two qualifications to her statement are necessary. To shift Samoa in any such way would annoy some 80,000 Samoans who like their present climate; and, sound though she was, Mrs. Churchill was a civilian insensitive to the powder-and-shot aspect of why those ships were wrecked. Entrepreneurs may change their minds every generation about the economic importance of the Pacific Islands. But admirals, characteristically, have never altered their estimate of their strategic importance. It took the recent war to show that, though often wrong in detail, the admirals were always essentially right.

3

The Good Frigate Grab-bag

ONE OF THE MOST CURIOUS SIGHTS IN THE SOUTH SEAS is the German warship "Adler" lying on her side a long pistol shot from shore, high out of water on the reef in Apia harbor. Fifty-eight years ago she was "tossed up there like a school-boy's cap upon a shelf . . . a thing to dream of."[1] She is broken in three, her rust is sulky brown-red and somehow enough organic matter has accumulated on the afterportion for green things to grow there. One of her consorts lies under the submarine bulge of the reef, sucked in below after she struck. The other ships that died with her—still another German, three Americans—are long since salvaged or broken up. All were there on account of strategic rivalry.

It is an old story: Three nations were squabbling over the Samoan islands and each had men-of-war in Apia harbor. Though storm warnings were unmistakable and the harbor is a known deathtrap in a heavy northerly blow, no naval commander concerned dared put out to seek sea room lest a rival steal a march on him ashore. The wind picked up, great seas charged in through the break in the reef; it was already too late for these weak-engined craft. Americans and Germans tried steaming to their anchors, but one by one the lift and

[1]Stevenson, A Footnote to History, 284.

weight of the wind-driven seas was too much for them. The sole Britisher called on the engine room for more steam than his ship's builders had ever dreamed of, slipped his cable, and stood out to sea. It took minutes to gain inches. Twice she collided with disabled rivals. The crew of U.S.S. "Trenton," seeing that H.M.S. "Calliope" had a sporting chance where they had none, lined the rail and cheered her as she crept and pitched past in the teeth of the wind and battering water like a well-handled surfboat. Mrs. Churchill was right: you could have bought all Samoa for the cost in lives and machinery. But navies and governments do not keep books that way. Here follow the general ideas and some of the specific events behind this strange catastrophe. The American hand in the game will be disproportionately emphasized, but one's own family history is often especially interesting:

It had long been routine, as previously noted, for naval commanders to poke round in the Pacific. But not until 1825 did the British, French and U.S. navies find it necessary regularly to assign warships to the great ocean. Cruising there was good training for officers and men, but that was not the primary purpose. The presence of numerous missionaries, traders, whalers, sealers, blacklegs and opportunists implied hundreds of small complications for the periodically-appearing man-of-war to prevent or straighten out. Thus, the first U.S. warship in the Pacific was Captain Porter's "Essex," rounding the Horn in 1814 to clean up British whalers which, under letters of marque, were rapidly exterminating their American rivals. The second was Captain Biddle's "Ontario," visiting Coquimbo in 1816 to cool off Chilean customs officers with whom Captain Fanning,[2] pioneer sealer, had got embroiled. The U.S. commercial agent in Honolulu sketched a sample situation in a letter to the commodore of the new U.S. Pacific squadron in 1826, begging him to get vessels under his command to Hawaii a little oftener.

"The waters of [Honolulu] harbor have at one time floated more than three millions of American property, and this

[2]Fanning, Voyages and Discoveries, 294.

amount is almost at the mercy of a race of savages and law-
less outcasts that infest these islands. . . ."—Paullin, *Diplomatic Negotiations of American Naval Officers*, 235.

Survey work in areas imperfectly charted, aiding vessels in distress, "showing the flag," acting as self-appointed umpire in
native crises and, with salutary frequency, punishing native
violent attempts to get their own back from the white man—
the commander of a warship on such missions had, and liked
to use, wide latitude in his actions.

The commodore of a western squadron on the Pacific station
needed ships powerful enough to stand on equal footing with
those from other nations, not so much for potential international combat as because native chiefs were quick to gauge
relative strength. The prestige of a given nation ashore often
depended on the number of guns carried by the last frigate
calling under that flag. So some of the most glamorous vessels
in the Old Navy—"Constitution," "Constellation," "United
States"—showed their colors in these waters.

Now such Pacific squadrons began early to feel the need of
reliable sources of supplies and instructions nearer than their
home bases halfway round the world. The usual makeshift was
a friendly foreign port; thus Paulet's "Carysfort"[3] based at
Valparaiso; as late as 1898 Dewey based at Hongkong. Far
better was a properly located island with right of entry dependent, not on the whim of a native chief or twopenny local
government, but on established sovereignty with exclusive
privileges good against men-of-war of competing nations.
Hence Britain developed Hongkong and Auckland, and the
States the several deepwater harbors of California and Oregon.
But such bases merely on the margin of areas to be cruised
feel inadequate to admirals. Once acquired, San Francisco and
Puget Sound obviously need protection from farther out—say
in the Aleutians and Hawaii. Then, as offshore bases, Alaska
and Hawaii need sub-subsidiary bases still farther out as screening points, listening posts and minor depots for spars and naval
stores. An admiral thinks of these things like the farmer in the

[3]Cf. III, *Land of Makebelieve Come True*.

story attributed to Lincoln who said: "I ain't greedy about land—I only want what jines mine." Give strategic logic its head and a navy conscientious about screening continents, guarding shipping routes and "showing the flag" requires a round-the-world chain of bases from shore to shore of all oceans.

The reasoning is often circular as well as global. The historian Weinberg compares it to suicide by swallowing one's tail.[4] Dulles saw it clearly in the Philippine question:

> "With Dewey in Manila [the naval expansionists] had urged the annexation of Hawaii in order to secure a basis of support for his fleet; now that we had taken [Hawaii] they declared that we had to have the Philippines to protect Hawaii."— *Americans in the Pacific*, 235.[5]

Another angle was less publicly discussed. Minor naval bases scattered round the globe would pay off nicely in case of war, enabling raiders to get in among enemy shipping much more quickly than if they had to enter the Pacific from, say, Atlantic bases. American naval strength in Hawaii could cut all routes between Canada and the Antipodes; so could French naval strength in New Caledonia. In World War I the Germans demonstrated the theory in their early use of von Spee's isolated China squadron, and numerous raiders basing in Micronesia. The oftener ships crossed the Pacific, the farther the margins of the great ocean developed economically, the more such considerations appealed to brass hats and, sometimes, statesmen.

Engineering stimulated it all. American-developed transcontinental railroads terminating at San Francisco and Panama made the States look narrowly at the waters beyond. Chronic schemes for an Isthmian canal had the same result, as much

---

[4] *Manifest Destiny*, 70.
[5] Comparably, whereas in 1895 Lodge maintained that the States needed Hawaii to protect the Panama Canal that she would eventually build ("Our Blundering Foreign Policy," *Forum*, March, 1893), in 1898 McKinley maintained that the States now had to build the canal to protect Hawaii (Millis, *The Martial Spirit*, 389).

in British and French as in American minds, emphasized in 1869 by the opening of the Suez Canal. The advent of coal-fired steamers greatly whetted appetites for Pacific islands: A sailing vessel could cross an ocean or keep the sea for years, as whalers often did, without needing more than occasional water, firewood, cordage and provisions. But a steamer's coal bunkers lacked capacity for such feats of endurance. Since coal was locally available round the Pacific littoral only in Australia and New Zealand,[6] a steam navy in the Pacific implied permanent collier-supplied fueling depots at both mainland bases and island steppingstones. When Commodore Perry so high-handedly ran up the flag on the Ryukyus and Bonins in the 'fifties, he had transpacific liners as much on his mind as naval cruisers; he even detached a vessel to look into the availability and quality of Formosan coal. In 1890, Mahan, chief rationalizer of American big-navy feeling, thundered:

> "It should be an inviolable resolution of our national policy that no foreign state should henceforth acquire a coaling station within three thousand miles of San Francisco."—"The United States Looking Outward," *Atlantic Monthly*, December, 1890.

For those unable to read maps, he pointed out that this took in the Galapagos and the coasts of Central America as well as Hawaii. In cold fact it also covered the Line Islands, the Aleutians and the Marquesas—a mammoth bite of ocean for a presumably self-contained power. Then, as international law intruded on the Pacific—the old-timers' idea, zealously demonstrated, had been "no law west of Cape Horn"—naval need for the shelter of one's own flag sharpened, for belligerent vessels could no longer base permanently on ports of nations declaring themselves neutral. Thus Dewey would have had to capture Manila or some other Spanish port, even if there had been no Spanish squadron to destroy. The only legal alternative was to return all the way to California and operate as a pointless coast defense screen.

[6]Only theoretically in Japan, China, Formosa, Alaska at the time.

Considerations based on coal apply equally to petroleum products as fuel for ship and, up to now anyway, for aircraft. Oil-wells too exist only at the periphery of the Pacific. Tankers must wallow long distances from the East Indies, California, Sakhalin or Mexico to where patrol- or combat-craft can make the most of fuel. Refueling of ships at sea proved practical during the recent war but is unhandy at best; the time factor too makes well-spotted island bases far preferable. So the advent of transpacific aviation in the 'thirties produced an undignified scramble for island steppingstones to and from the Antipodes and the Far East.

Lack of anchorage off lonely mid-Pacific atolls had long meant international neglect, where guano was lacking. But safe anchorage means less to a seaplane able to sit down on the lagoon or a landplane seeking an atoll air strip, so the isolated Pacific islet occasionally experienced a dramatic renascence. Bits of land that had escaped attention since discovery by a sealer in James Monroe's time suddenly found themselves descended on by parties representing nations armed with hazy old claims, painful politeness and a great disinclination to arbitrate. Johnston, Wake, Clipperton Islands were the meaningless names in stickfuls of type on front pages. Some details of what nation has what rights on certain of the Line Islands— Fanning and Christmas, for instance—are not settled yet.

One party from the U.S. Department of the Interior sailed under secret orders and set up radio stations, manned by Hawaiians, on Jarvis, Baker and Howland Islands before any rival —meaning Britain—knew what went on. But on Canton Island they found a British radio party who had got wind of their purpose over Stateside radio. From six in the morning until noon matters were chilly between the two groups; then, sensibly concluding that all were only agents, and the affair should be settled not with chunks of coral on Canton but by negotiation between capitals, British and Americans settled down sociably to discuss the supply of beer that the firstcomers had in their kerosene refrigerator. For a while discussions in their respective capitals were less amicable. But it all ended in agreement that Canton should go under British-American condominium. Few Americans are aware that, on this gigantic circle of coral sand, Uncle Sam has been in governmental partnership with perfidious Albion a dozen years. It works well enough; except airfield personnel there is nothing much to govern but fish and birds.

The chain-of-air-bases principle so conspicuous in the recent war parallels the chain-of-naval-bases theory after which navies hankered even before steam. Some air bases were very queer affairs indeed. Johnston Island is incredible—a kite-shaped scrap of unmistakably man-reconstructed dry land absolutely nowhere, a mere heap of dredged and bulldozed and filled coral, its imprisoned inhabitants as abjectly dependent as a ship at sea on outside sources for food and water. A comic map of the place in the A.T.C. terminal shows a plane-pilot approaching, leaning out to gape at the spot he is supposed to sit down on and saying: "Are they kidding?"

Though long regarded in practice, the chain theory was not formulated until comparatively recent times.[7] During the nineteenth century the Royal Navy nevertheless came close actually to realizing a round-the-globe chain, the Pacific links being Sydney, Auckland, Hongkong, Fiji, Esquimalt. The gap in the eastern half of the ocean is significant as showing that the Foreign and Colonial Offices were by no means hand in glove with the Admiralty, else Rapa (Australs), Bora Bora (Societies) and Hawaii might have been added to complete the web. Since the Admiralty was operating largely by inarticulate instinct, however, it was possible for the Empire as a whole to sabotage the Royal Navy's strategy for generations without either party's being altogether clear what was happening. Those convinced that Britain has been congenitally land- and power-greedy should have a long look at the story of how she acquired the cream of the Pacific Islands. Much of the time lords and

[7]Say the Sprouts (*The Rise of American Naval Power*, 205): Mahan became the world's greatest naval theorist largely through "organizing into a coherent system or philosophy the strategic principles which the British Admiralty had been following more or less blindly for over two hundred years."

gentlemen in London offices were busier courteously declining to have anything to do with acquiring islands than scheming to plant the Union Jack in new places.[8] Ambitious naval officers and colonials found it highly exasperating.

Britain wanted Australia and took elaborate precautions against intrusion. But she did not want New Zealand. Thirty years of missionary involvement, trouble ashore with rowdy whites, disgracefully unregulated trade, enthusiastic propaganda by Wakefield's New Zealand Company, and irritation with France's patent ambition to colonize the place dragged past before the Treaty of Waitangi acknowledged that Queen Victoria would find New Zealand less nuisance inside than outside the Empire. Britain did not want Hawaii enough to get tough about it, as has been seen. She did not want Samoa, as will presently be shown. She did not want Tahiti and crisply told Queen Pomare so. She did not want Fiji: the tale of political encroachment there is fantastically typical of how these things developed.

It began back in the 'forties, the period when they said you needed no chart to find Fiji, you need only follow the increasing number of empty gin bottles floating in the sea. Growing American interests there had necessitated installing a U.S. consular agent, and the incumbent, one Williams, like other such officials since, was deep in local business schemes. As a patriot, he overcelebrated a Fourth of July at his seat on a small island; during the party a cannon was fired off, burst, and set fire to the house. As it burned Fijians present took advantage of an immemorial custom—probably a local version of the Maoris' *muru* previously described—and looted the place. Williams, presently finding himself sober, houseless, and annoyed, presented Cakobau, "king" of Fiji, a bill for $5,001.38 damages.

[8] ". . . while Britain might have annexed almost every coast outside Europe except the Atlantic coast of the United States, she limited herself to calling ports for her shipping on the ocean road to the Indies, and to such colonial developments in unoccupied regions as were forced on her by her own adventurers, whom she tried in vain to check." —MacKinder, *Democratic Ideals and Reality*, 134.

Now Cakobau, though the most conspicuous high chief in Fiji, lord of Bau and terror of Viti Levu, was not "king" of Fiji or anywhere else in any intelligible sense. Though frequently misapplied by whites out of ignorance or design, the word was always an anomaly in the South Seas. Fiji had no notion of any political entity resembling royalty. A ruthless and successful enough high chief could exact homage and tribute from all Fiji, but that his ascendancy established a dynasty or a presumptive and permanent authority was a thoroughly alien idea. At the time, Cakobau's power over rival powerful high chiefs, mere *force majeure* at best, was tenuous, because the Tongans were filibustering strongly into Fiji from the east. Cakobau had also recently weakened his general influence by turning Christian. Still, Williams' predecessor had once flattered him by calling him "Tui Viti"—as near as the language permitted to "King of Fiji"—and Williams, at odds with Cakobau anyway, chose to regard him as a responsible sovereign obliged to make good his subjects' depredations.

Neither Cakobau nor any other Fijian had any such sum, nor would he have paid it over if he had. Things dragged on. As various Americans suffered damage in native squabbles, Williams added their claims to his. When U.S.S. "John Adams" appeared in 1855, her commander browbeat Cakobau into signing an acknowledgment of owing Americans a total of $43,531. Three years later Cakobau had still to pay a penny. This time U.S.S. "Vandalia" got the claim acknowledged at $45,000, interest included. On paper Mr. Williams' belongings and houses—he lost another by fire set by marauding natives —still looked like an excellent investment.

But Cakobau had an ace up his sleeve. Fearful of the increasingly aggressive Tongans, mortally convinced that, unless the debt were somehow settled, the States would move in on him as France had moved in on Tahiti, he began to listen attentively to the opportunistic British consul—a lively and veteran South Seas hand named Pritchard, son of the stormy petrel of Tahiti,[9] who was an enthusiast about the future of

[9] Cf. IV, 5, *Fishers of Men.*

cotton in Fiji. Between them they agreed that, if Britain would settle with the Americans and guarantee Cakobau status as first gentleman of Fiji, she could have a protectorate over the Islands—which would scare away the Tongans—and have also 200,000 acres of land to develop. Pritchard dropped everything and hurried to London to secure ratification. Then, having delivered a glowing sales talk to his superiors at home, he returned to assume something the same mayor-of-the-palace power under Cakobau that his father had enjoyed under Queen Pomare.

Shortly before two high-ranking Royal Navy officers had told their government that Fiji was strategically well worth having as a coaling station to hook up with Isthmian canal schemes. Government was dubious, however—partly, Pritchard claimed, because his background was London Missionary Society while Fiji was the bailiwick of the Wesleyans, who were jealous of him. A Colonel Smythe of the Royal Artillery, accompanied by a wife who did charming water colors of Fijian scenery, and a German botanist named Seemann who wrote a fine book about the place, was sent to investigate. The Colonel looked, questioned, and disliked the idea. He took a very dim view of the local whites, unquestionably a scaly lot; he studied the map and concluded that Rapa, still no man's land, was better situated for a coaling station; he saw little reason to believe that Fiji would ever come to much economically; and he could find no evidence that Cakobau was a king or could hand over any 200,000 acres. Seemann, who saw infinite agricultural possibilities, and Pritchard, who yearned to be an Empire builder, were outraged. But Smythe reported home an elaborate No, and in 1863 H.M.S. "Miranda" appeared with a polite message doing Cakobau to wit that Queen Victoria wished him very well indeed—on his own.

Australia also was outraged. Though exploitation of their own subcontinent was only begun, Australians were already subimperial-minded. The cotton boom was taking many of them to Fiji, and the various Australian colonies, not even federated yet, wrung their hands when the Empire rejected so tempting an offer. Captain Robert Towns, the Queensland plantation builder, even offered personally to pay Williams if that would help consummate a protectorate. Geographically, true, Australia is the logical guardian of Fiji. But for all that, Cakobau was right back where he had started, except for the loss of mana involved in having offered homage to another and seeing it refused. Fortunately, a 1000% increase in the white population of his sphere of influence was keeping the Tongans at bay, and the same Federal blockade that boomed cotton was keeping the U.S. Navy too busy to bother about Fiji. Williams could only turn his claims over to a speculative land company in which he was interested, to be revived when chance suited.

In the 'seventies the white colony in Fiji was large and crafty-minded enough to try government nearer modern lines than Cakobau's indecisive personal rule. They made the old gentleman a constitutional monarch with a crown, a flag carrying the Dove of Peace as well as numerous heathen symbols, a bicameral parliament and no votes for natives. He was old; he probably felt the lack of dignity in his position and disliked the cabals, riots and grandiloquently-named vigilance committees that the whites kept stirring up among themselves. So again he offered his islands to Britain on condition that the American claims be paid and his chiefs' privileges reserved. This time, because Britain had grown more Pacific-minded, it worked. The Queen would graciously accept, but only unconditionally. Cakobau agreed that conditions between chiefs were unworthy. The debt was covered by a deal with Australian capital, and Cakobau received a pension of £1,500 a year. At the ceremony of cession he gave the Queen's representative his favorite war club to forward to his new sovereign, saying, with good South Seas courtesy, that it was the only thing he owned that she might value. Bound in silver, it is now the ceremonial mace of the Fijian legislative council. Within a year began the flood of Indian indentured labor to work on sugar-plantations. . . .[10] There you have all the essential elements that extinguished native autonomy in the Pacific:

[10]Cf. V, Their Gods Are Dead.

busybody missionaries, overeager naval captains, grand strategy, hopeful planters and aggressive consuls.

Australians were equally eager to control New Guinea, the New Hebrides, New Caledonia and the Solomons. John G. Paton, durable pioneer missionary in the New Hebrides, made his every visit to Sydney another occasion for urging the rescue of such islands from the pernicious complementary threats of popery and French rule. But London was still bored. New Caledonia, an island apparently created to be a dependency of Australia, went by default in the 'fifties to French opportunism. The Crimean war was in progress and the French rightly judged that, as valued allies, they could take liberties with the Lion that might be inadvisable later. The question of the New Hebrides dragged on, settled in 1887—if you call it settlement—by agreement on a French-British condominium, famous in the Pacific as "the Pandemonium," that has tended gradually to extirpate Australian influence in the group. While London dallied about New Guinea, Germans pushed in from the north. When Queensland, just across the Torres Strait, took the bit in her colonial teeth and ran up flags in well-chosen spots, she was forced to back out by British, not German, protest. In the end Germany got half of Western New Guinea, Australia the other half. At one time or another Britain could have had everything in the Pacific for the asking, barring perhaps Hawaii and Samoa. What she did get was fat, as islands go, but there was little consistent purpose behind the getting. The critical factor seems often to have been the Islander's firm belief that, if some western guardian were necessary, Beritani was the best choice.

The French were contrastingly consistent and logical; perhaps in consequence of such clarity of mind, they came off second. Through Restoration, July Monarchy, Second Empire, French aggressiveness meant colony- and sea-mindedness. In the 'forties France often had more floating firepower in the Pacific than Britain and the States combined. When the row with Britain about Tahiti was amicably settled,[11] French feel-

[11]Cf. IV, 5, *Fishers of Men.*

ing toward Guizot's pusillanimity over a mountainous island about the size of an American county was so strong that some think it seriously contributed to Louis Philippe's downfall. True, France's adventures in the Pacific were minor compared to those in Africa, Indo-China and Mexico, but they are worth study as clean examples of explicit action.

French warships on survey missions led off as soon as the Napoleonic wars were over. Missionaries followed up.[12] As will be seen, no reasonable person, French or not, denies that French Catholic missions were candidly regarded as a tool of Empire. Whenever local disturbances gave a pretext, vessels of the French Pacific squadron would appear, expostulate, aggravate and, when risks looked worth it, take over. The technique failed in Hawaii, probably because both Britain and the States were too openly annoyed; in New Zealand because British subjects were entrenched there ahead of their government; in Tonga because the British Wesleyans' hold on the natives combined too well with native toughness. But the French understood the Hitlerish strategy of striking for maxima while consolidating minima. With Britain conveniently careless and the States paying little heed, France dominated the middle of the South Pacific by 1860, holding a constellation of mutually-supporting potential bases including the Marquesas, Gambiers, Tuamotu, Australs and Tahiti, New Caledonia and Wallis Island.

Economically and socially most of these proved little, but they must have appeared most gratifying on the big map at the Ministry of Marine. When the gigantic French filibuster in Mexico was launched in the 'sixties, it looked as if France would acquire Acapulco and Vera Cruz in addition to longstanding footholds in the Caribbean area at Martinique and Cayenne—meaning potential control of both entrances of the projected canal as well as the southeastern entrance to the Pacific. And only the gap represented by the Cooks, Samoa and Tonga spoiled the pattern of a chain of bases slap across the

[12]Cf. IV, 5, *Fishers of Men*.

Pacific. But events left this implicit project behind. The Civil War ended the wrong way and Mexico was lost. The western part of the Societies were acquired in the 'eighties with grudging British consent; but once again droopiness at home frustrated naval purposes. The bases that should have been built at Noumea and Bora Bora remained mere dreams, and civil administration of such islands replaced naval.

As it grew plainer around the turn of the century that France was most unlikely to fight any traditional Pacific power, a great futility descended on the components of her Pacific empire. The Marquesas quietly rotted away—even a scheme to send convicts there came to nothing. The Gambiers practically disappeared from human cognizance, as did Rapa, once, though briefly, a coaling station for ships from Australia to Panama. Tahiti subsided into a Polynesian-flavored Montparnasse. When New Caledonia's usefulness as a convict colony ended in the 'nineties, the place slid into semiparalysis imposed by the colonial *fonctionnaire*, financed by somewhat desultory mining of its magnificent mineral resources and supported by indentured labor from Java and Indo-China. Now the French have most reason of all whites to look about them on their Pacific isles and ask what the devil they are doing in that galley. But, as usual, their taste was flawless. They came out of the game with a bag of islands averaging the highest of any nation's possessions in beauty and versatility of terrain.

The Germans, zealous latecomers, operated, also as usual, without any taste at all. Godeffroys, a private project long predating the German Empire, soon acquired a semigovernmental flavor. Their Pacific viceroy, the aforesaid Weber, was also the pathologically active German consul in Samoa. Their successors —the best known was the "Long Handle Firm," short for *Zweigniederlassung der Deutschen Handels- und Plantagen-Gesellschaft der Südseeinseln*—became almost as much viceregal governments as the British East India Company had been.

For a while things were under wraps because Bismarck was scornful of empire, saying in 1868:

"For Germany to possess colonies would be like a poverty-stricken Polish nobleman acquiring a silken sable coat when he needed shirts."—Masterman, *The Origins of International Rivalry in Samoa*, 78.

But colony-mindedness built up just the same. German cruisers early began poking round for treaties of amity and coaling stations in Tonga, close under the British wing, and in Raiatea, close under the French. In 1878 the government barely managed to defeat in the Reichstag legislation for Reich financing of German trade in the Islands. When, in the mid-eighties, Bismarck reversed himself, the New Germany was boldly committed to naval power and colonies to match. Which came first, whether either was necessary, raised no difficulties. The psychology was well explained by Theodore Roosevelt, Jr. in commenting on American expansion in the Pacific:

". . . colonies were a badge of importance as far as a nation was concerned . . . like the letters after a man's name in Who's Who. They gave to a country owning them a standing among nations, and were a guarantee that the nation had come of age."—*Colonial Policies of the United States*, 74.

Africa and China, likely places for carving out empire, were principal objectives; but the Islands also were to be favored. Germany was out for colonies in the mood of a *nouveau riche* buying a library by the yard.

She took over the dying plantations of the Marquesas; she tinkered with cotton-planting in the Spanish-owned Marianas; she encouraged German missions, both Catholic and Protestant, in Micronesia. She descended on New Guinea and what was soon to be known as the Bismarck Archipelago (New Ireland, New Britain and so forth) with Samoa-style plantations worked by imported Melanesians. She moved into the Marshalls which, though nothing like as worth having as the Bismarcks, added another item to the list. Jaluit atoll became a miniature commercial capital, again with government and business inextricably mingled. She set up trading shop in the Palaus and tried to establish sovereignty over Yap (Carolines);

but Spain protested querulously, called in the Pope as arbiter, and managed to remain in possession, though forced to promise full commercial privileges to Germany.[13] Germany was briskly active in the Gilberts until, with well-founded suspicion, the British set up a protectorate there. One way or another, by 1900 Germany was mistress of a miniature Pacific empire, including a rich quarter of New Guinea, all the lush big islands north of it, the western third of the Solomons, the important two-thirds of Samoa, and all Micronesia except American-owned Guam and the British-held Gilberts.

Indiscriminate opportunism was the means. During a generation, as in the three-cornered squabbling over Samoa, the German elbow had usually been sharpest and the German tongue the shrillest. The way was not smooth in Samoa because Britain was growingly suspicious, and the States were having a premonitory attack of imperialism of their own; the Samoans themselves were sulky and had to be shot up at intervals by all parties. But Britain, never overcommitted, was willing to deal when, at the turn of the century, the powers again tried to settle the squabble. Africa, where Germany was openly cheering on the embattled Boers, and the Solomons, where British interests were growing, seemed to Britain more important than the lovely islands of Upolu and Savaii. So Western Samoa went to Germany at long last; Eastern Samoa, including the fine small harbor of Pago Pago, went to the States, whose strategic interest there dated back to Grant's time; and Britain accepted most of the Solomons and odd concessions in Africa. In 1899 Germany had exploited Spanish discouragement after the Spanish-American War by buying all Spain's rights in Micronesia, which completely surrounded the States' newly acquired Guam.[14] She got little out of these

[13]At the time Spain was having a feckless fit of ambition in her loosely-held Micronesian islands, particularly trying to introduce white ideas into the Carolines. All that resulted was a vigorous revolt of the natives, which Spanish soldiers never succeeded in suppressing altogether. This was also the period when Chile asserted a claim, which nobody bothered much about, to Easter Island and its satellite Sala-y-Gomez.
[14]Cf. IV, 4, Destiny's Helpers.

acquisitions except local prestige. But, when the Japanese occupied Micronesia in 1914 as nominal ally of the Entente, the
picture snapped sharply into focus. Micronesia was the perfect
screen for an ambitious empire in the Northwest Pacific. Germany had not planned to build so snug a nest for the Japanese
cuckoo, but that is precisely what she accomplished.

Beyond that the principal feature of German rule in the
Pacific was Dr. Wilhelm Solf, perennial governor of German
Samoa—a granite-faced, monocle-eyed, rigidly hefty satrap of
empire whom the Islands still remember as a most considerable man. Aware that British rule in Fiji was reputed fair and
firm, he prefixed to his Samoan assignment a long visit to Fiji
and applied what he learned about "indirect rule" without
servile imitation but with clever improvisation, especially regarding the proud, factious, sea-lawyer types prevalent among
Samoan chiefs. Old-timers in Apia still look back on his regime
as a sort of grim Golden Age when, however arbitrary government was, everybody knew just where he stood, or at least
could rapidly find out by stepping out of line. Solf did not fool,
and knew just how to use the big stick that consisted of the
German China Squadron.

The plantations got their blackbirded labor, but their previous impression, heritage from the days of Weber, that they
were to run Samoa was rudely dispelled. Pan-German planters
and traders on Savaii, cooled off with infuriating skill, were unable to do more about it than write scurrilous letters home to
produce questions in the Reichstag. Solf was present at one
such inquiry, says an old story: part of the charge was that he
had gone native and lolled about with flowers in his hair. He
stood up, took off his hat, and made one devastating gesture
toward the crown of his head, which was bald as a baby's
bottom.

His notions of relations between white and native included
much typically, but by no means exclusively, German nonsense about superior races and white destiny to rule. But he did
his best to honor German commitments to local politicians,
and to give the Samoans face-saving nominal participation in

government. He also had a shrewd but harsh understanding of native respect for force; when unrealistic ambition in a brilliant Savaii talking-chief named Lauati culminated in armed defiance of the government, he easily maintained his *mana* by showing nothing but easygoing contempt and simultaneously whistling up warships. In the end, without actual shooting, he got Lauati and company exiled for life on Saipan (Marianas), where they were given land and encouraged to set up Samoan life and customs to their hearts' content; local convicts were told off to build Samoa-type houses for them. Solf did not even lose perspective when "the Beach"[15] tried to make him trouble from the habit acquired in the old days of three-nation intrigue: H. J. Moors, the enterprising American,[16] was one of the most active. Much of Solf's rule was a pernicious example in western eyes, but it worked as nothing had worked in Samoa before. When New Zealand took over in 1914, she was handicapped not only by lack of experience, Samoan subtlety, and local businessmen's sulkiness, but also by invidious memories of the great Dr. Solf, who had left to be Reich colonial minister just before the outbreak of World War I and had already acquired a grudgingly awarded halo.

The wreck of the "Adler" is not the only relic of Germany in Samoa. The larger boardinghouse in Apia was built for bachelor quarters for German officials; German additions to Stevenson's beloved house at Vailima make it even more of a Subpriorsford than ever. Half the private subscribers to the local telephone have German names and, as this is written, one of the highest Samoan chiefs is trying to get government permission for part-Samoan relatives in Germany to come to Apia. A German-Samoan half-caste has been notably active in recent scheming for Samoan autonomy, and Samoan children playing soldier in remote villages are heard to shout: "Achtung! Ein, zwei, drei,

---

[15]"The Beach" is South Sea talk for the complex of interests, proverbs, and gossip emanating from the commercial element of an island. The people involved are either whites or part-whites or natives trying to live in white man's terms.

[16]Cf. VI, 1, *Hurry, Hurry, Hurry* . . .

vier . . ." A photograph of Dr. Solf, monocle and all, hangs in the government offices along with the string of post-1914 New Zealand administrators. He will long be remembered thereabouts.

In taking over Samoa New Zealand dealt herself into a game in which there was much prestige to lose and little credit to be gained. But she badly wanted to play anyway for, in parallel with Australia, she precociously developed imperial notions. A century ago the great Sir George Grey, scholarly and able governor, and the great Bishop Selwyn, scholarly and able Anglican missionary,[17] determined that the struggling new colony needed hegemony over a British-controlled Pacific empire consisting of all islands not yet tied down—meaning, at the time, practically everything but French holdings. Nothing came of it but great eloquence from knight and bishop. In another generation, however, Sir Julius Vogel, hyperkinetic premier of New Zealand, revived those ideas with particular emphasis on Samoa, where, as usual, things were boiling rapidly.

Thenceforth, whenever Samoa was in the news, diplomats would receive suggestions that New Zealand would be glad to take the place off the world's hands. At the turn of the century the ambitious little dominion got Britain to turn over to her the less strategic Cook group, where she developed a reputation, so far as the world paid any attention, for handling the natives kindly. She was also credited with civilized attitudes toward the Maori, her own home Polynesians. So, when the Southern Cross went up over German Samoa in 1914, it eventually made sense to the world's conscience that New Zealand should have the League of Nations Class C mandate, amounting to virtual sovereignty. Conscience was not necessarily concerned anyway, else Micronesia might never have been turned over to the Japanese. In both cases a stubborn conqueror, with no idea whatever of abandoning the territory conquered, was made to look like a legal guardian. That is unmistakable in the parallel case of Australia's demand for at least Class C mandates

[17]Cf. IV, 5, *Fishers of Men*.

over former German holdings in New Guinea and the Western Solomons.

The somewhat hysterical history of Western Samoa as a ward of New Zealand belongs in a later chapter.[18] Here, with the treaties of 1919, the process of dividing up the Pacific Islands ends with a stability that, essentially, survived even World War II.[19] The only subsequent change of significance was the inheritance by the United States of Micronesia, most of which has seen four ruler-nations within fifty years. This also marked the culmination of a most devious and curious process—the gradual involvement of the United States in the Pacific:

[18] Cf. V, *Their Gods Are Dead.*

[19] Specialists in Latin-American history may consider that this book scamps the influence of South America on the Islands. So far as the writer knows, it was interesting but tenuous: there was little of note except the early Spanish explorations from Peruvian bases; the Chilean title to Easter Island; the role played by South American ports in the whaling trade and the basing of men-of-war; the Mexican influence on the cattle industry of Hawaii; the coincidence that both the Picpus missionaries and the Godeffroy firm went into the Islands by way of Valparaiso; the prevalence of South American coinage in many of the Islands; the Peruvian slavers; and the probable fact that the neat little ponies of the Cook Islands spring from stock imported from Chile in the early days.

4

Destiny's Helpers

Today's tender conscience is likely to blush at the tale of how Uncle Sam got involved. The impulse is commendable, but a conscience with better perspective would not suffer so much. In comparison with French and German capers, even with some British doings, the American record looks pretty fair. Said Weinberg:

> "American history is an excellent laboratory for the study of expansionist ideology, but not because its expansionism calls for sharper moral criticism . . . It is perhaps the most cheerful record of such perilous ambitions."—*Manifest Destiny*, 8.[1]

Nor, though often unscrupulous, were American jugglings in the Islands necessarily bad for the world in the long run. This devious intrusion of American power was an eventual guarantee that Japan, aggressive as early as 1890, could somehow be checked in her drive for East Asia and its fringing and screening islands. As Americans we assume that the political and emotional flexibilities of our culture are good things; and conversely, that Japanese political and emotional rigidities are

[1] Or, for the opinion of a scholarly non-American, take Scholefield, a New Zealander: "The advent of the United States as a Pacific power was to a large extent accidental, the corollary of national duties rather than the expansion of national ambitions."—*The Pacific, Its Past and Future*, 183.

poisonous to what we consider the human spirit to be. Like all such assumptions, though vulnerable to analysis, these are valid in operation.

Whitewashing, of course, can be carried too far. There were unmistakable traces of aggression, profit seeking, busybodiness, and megalomania in the background of Manila—and Tokio—Bay. Only because it was unaware of that background could the American public still be startled in 1898 when Uncle Sam, who had presumably been fighting to rescue Cuba from Spanish tyranny, suddenly found himself knee-deep in islands four-fifths of the way to China.

Until war with Spain made what to do about Hawaii and the Philippines a major issue overnight, Americans had seldom been greatly or consistently concerned with whether the States needed or had the right to expand far into the Pacific. Even now, with a staggering Pacific war so recent and our Pacific responsibilities heavy, it seldom occurs to the average man to wonder why and how it all happened. By Pearl Harbor time we had been out there for enough years to make it seem natural, and had long approached such issues as that of independence for the Philippines, which alone reminded us of our Pacific commitments, as if they concerned only exporters and domestic manufacturers of sugar, fats and cordage.[2] Only specialists thought farther, sometimes concluding that, if any such adventure were to have been embarked on, we should have fared better by going farther earlier.

But that leaves out the naval officers and diplomats who—usually without their employers, the American people, being aware of it—had already sketched quite a framework for American interest in the great ocean. Porter started it in 1814, when chasing whalers in the "Essex," by building a fortified base on

---

[2] What Bywater wrote in 1921 is still essentially true: "When the United States relieved Spain of the Philippines, she gave hostages to fortune in a sense which the American people have never fully realized. But for the acquisition of these islands, they need never have maintained a powerful fleet in the Pacific or have gone to the expense of constructing great naval bases on the Western Coast."—Sea-Power in the Pacific, 254.

Nukahiva (Marquesas) and, with due flag raising, taking possession of its site. He called the new port Madisonville and its small but well protected harbor Massachusetts Bay. The natives, Porter averred, were "all much pleased at being Mellikees."[3]

Little came of this gesture except some colorful chapters in his journal and, when he saw fit to interfere in local feuds, some dead Marquesans. His superiors had probably not contemplated his enlarging the boundaries of the United States, or his taking sides in a chronic war among touchy but charming medium-brown cannibals. Yet, when he reached home after losing the "Essex" to the British in the famous fight at Valparaiso, he was not censured for exceeding instructions. And though Madisonville was allowed to decay as if it had never been built, the U.S. Navy had a Pacific squadron operating out of South American ports within twelve years.

These ships, or others sent on special missions, got as far afield as Quallah Battoo in the East Indies, Canton, Korea and Japan, and inflicted various degrees of violence on Asiatics who took too little account of a gaudily striped flag. In the Island area, Commodore Thomas ap Catesby Jones, U.S.S. "Peacock," negotiated an early treaty of amity with the Hawaiian monarchy and, exerting the versatile functions demanded of cruising naval commanders, refereed a dispute between traders and missionaries. He also strongly advised keeping the royal revenues in an ironbound box. In 1842 this same Jones took too eagerly a rumor that Mexico had sold California to England, and imaginatively seized Monterey, capital of Upper California, withdrawing only when events failed to live up to his bellicose expectations. In the same period the elaborate Wilkes surveying expedition was systematically covering most of the Pacific, incidentally trying nominally to annex Spanish Wake Island, and shooting up and burning Fijian villages that had got too gay with American skippers. Ten years later the Perry expedition to open up Japan planted the Stars and Stripes on both the Bonins and Okinawa, in island groups that cost many thou-

[3] *Journal of a Cruize*, II, 82.

sands of American lives in World War II. Again, none of these improvisations had permanent territorial results. But they had begun to make a significant pattern. A student of his career labeled Perry "the first American imperialist."[4]

Official dreams of an American naval base in Hawaii date back to 1841. As the 'fifties became the 'sixties, consuls and cabinets occasionally helped the Navy play the game that it had begun almost absent-mindedly. With the Isthmian Canal in mind, the States acquired a perpetual option on the Gulf of Fonseca, between Nicaragua and Honduras, for a potential naval base. In 1854 Uncle Sam sat down on the Galapagos Islands, covering the southern approach to the canal, pulling out nervously when the British and French protested. Consul and Navy cooperated, as has been already seen, in harassing Fiji. To the disgust of the French, already in the saddle in nearby Tahiti, another U.S. consul blarneyed the chiefs of Raiatea into handing that island over to the States in 1858. A reformed medical missionary who had become a State Department agent in China, cooked up with American commercial adventurers an abortive scheme to bring Formosa under the American flag.[5] In 1867 Alaska was bought for reasons little appreciated at the time Midway Island was officially nailed down as American for use as a coaling station.[6] And Samoa bulked large in certain naval and diplomatic eyes long before the average American had ever heard of the place.

In the interests of schemes for American-flag steamer service

[4]William S. Rossiter, North American Review, 1906, Vol. 182.

[5]This Dr. Peter Parker pioneered medical missions in China; a useful diplomatic go-between and interpreter, he was appointed U.S. commissioner in due season. Says Dennett (Americans in Eastern Asia, 288): "Much reading of international law since the eye doctor became a diplomat had made Dr. Parker a little mad." His allies in the Formosa scheme were Gideon Nye, Jr. and a Peruvian named Robinet who ran a camphor trading outfit on Formosa. They failed to interest Washington. But Formosan coal had already been an object of interest to the P & O steamship line.

[6]Readers of The Wrecker will remember how the crew of the "Currency Lass" were so tragically deceived by printed information that Pacific Mail steamers were actually coaling at Midway.

between Australasia and the west coast, U.S.S. "Narragansett," Commander Meade, surveyed Pago Pago harbor on Tutuila, the best haven in Samoa and one of the finest in the Pacific, with a coaling depot in mind. The alleged occasion was German encroachment to the same end; the actual, imagination-tickling reason appeared in the instructions given Meade through his commanding officer by the American minister to Hawaii:

> "In view of the Future domination of the United States in the N. & S. Pacific Oceans; it is very important that the Navigator Islands [Samoa] should be under American control—ruling through the native authorities."—Ryden, *Foreign Policy of the United States*, 60.

Meade returned with not only a survey, but also a treaty, with "the great chief of the bay of Pago Pago"—a designation that would have made the highest Samoan chiefs smile derisively—and the achievement of having organized the chiefs of Tutuila into a league with a flag that he had designed himself.[7]

Congress ignored the treaty, with its vague promise of "protection" for Samoa in return for exclusive coaling rights at Pago Pago. But not long after the State Department, still under pressure from shipping interests, saw fit to send to Samoa as special commissioner a strange amateur diplomat, an alleged crony of U. S. Grant named Col. A. B. Steinberger. Landing from his own yacht, which he seems to have furnished from somebody's private funds, Steinberger ignored his limited instructions to observe and report, and was presently busy setting up a white-style constitution in turbulent Samoa, arrogating to himself the position of guide, philosopher and friend to the Samoan people, for whom he seems to have had a genuine liking. Considerations of space forbid full description of his fantastic career. Washington failed to back him in ambitions to consolidate himself as premier and mayor of the palace to a

[7]The flag sounds like rather an heraldic hash: varicolored stripes symbolized the large and small islands of the Samoan group; two crescent moons were arranged to approximate the letter S for Samoa.

stable Samoan kingdom, though the States were unwise enough to lend him trappings that made his ambitions look very plausible indeed in Apia. His adventure came to an inglorious end, the hero was deported from Samoa by a British man-of-war, when it came out through an illegal search that Steinberger had sold his soul to the Long Handle Firm and was pledged, in consideration of mercantile commissions and royalties on copra, to use his influence as an American diplomat to further German interests. But the "Steinberger constitution" is still lively in Samoan minds as they toy with ideas of autonomy, and the remaining impression that Tutuila and its beautiful harbor were somehow specially destined for American use developed into sovereign fact thirty years later.

Fragmentary as it all sounds—and was—resolutely to have followed up all such gestures would have studded the Pacific with very well-placed American flags: The Galapagos, the Gulf of Fonseca, San Diego, San Francisco, Puget Sound, Dutch Harbor, Wake, the Bonins, Okinawa, Formosa, Fiji, Samoa, Raiatea, the Marquesas, Hawaii, constitute a formidable net with Hawaii as the spider in the middle enclosing the crucial northern half of the Pacific, outdoing French schemes to cover approaches to the as-yet-unbuilt Isthmian Canal. It sews up the great-circle shipping routes from California to the Far East, and from California to New Zealand and Australia. Out of the whole series of wishful gestures, however, only Perry's got much publicity at home. In fact if God had not sent Samoa so bad a storm in 1889, and if Cleveland had not made a stench about Hawaii in 1893, few Americans would ever have been at all aware of these prefaces to Manila Bay and Pearl Harbor.

Little of this was deliberate strategy, which in one way makes it more impressive. Much of it was the seagoing aspect of Manifest Destiny, which did not die after the Mexican War, but merely retired somewhat from the public eye for an all-star revival in the 'nineties. Mildly or militantly Pacific-minded Secretaries of State had appeared in Webster, Seward, Blaine. Yet somehow the U.S. Navy was usually out ahead of large-ideaed civilians. It often acted as more than just the devoted agent of Destiny. On many occasions commodores and commanders seemed, in a sort of somnambulistic fashion, to be helping to direct its brooding gaze to spots that would pay off in naval terms. To describe the Navy's role in Manifest Destiny in the Pacific, in fact, compels borrowing from the Declaration of Independence: these United States, Navy men often apparently felt, were and ought to be a Pacific power but they never bothered to clarify whether *ought to be* or *were* came first.

Yet the Navy is not to be specially reproached for its century of encroachment of which its civilian constituents knew so little. Duty-bound to patrol the Pacific, operating in a partial vacuum as armies and navies do in peace and would like to do in war, often in suspicious contact with aggressive naval rivals, its officers naturally proceeded in the groove of strategic instinct without troubling over what Bloomington, Ill., might think about it. It can even be argued that, by occasionally overreaching itself within reason, a navy maintains a resilient tone while, at any time it chooses, civilian government can always repudiate the consequences of naval exuberance, pay damages if necessary, and forget the matter. Thus, in 1844, it must have been very good for morale on board the U.S.S. "Constitution" when Commodore Kearny anchored her practically yardarm to yardarm with Paulet's ships and defied the British seizure of Hawaii by saluting the proscribed Hawaiian flag. That risked war if shooting started and certainly exceeded any instructions that Kearny might have had, but it was useful at the time. In the same port in 1851, when the French "La Serieuse" was bullying Hawaii, the commander of the U.S.S. "Vandalia" agreed to moor her between the Frenchman and the shore to inhibit a threatened bombardment. In 1868 Captain Reynolds of the U.S.S. "Lackawanna" disregarded orders in order to fish in troubled Hawaiian waters, and hysterically recommended to Washington the seizure of the Islands. Such incidents without sequel make it easier to understand the suspicious delays that led to the disaster at Apia.

With the New Navy hesitantly developing toward the end

of the nineteenth century, the whole expansion complex gathered formidable momentum—whether as cause or effect, who can say? Five years before Manila Bay Carl Schurz lashed out at the logic involved, mentioning:

". . . naval officers and others who advocate a large increase of our war fleet to support a vigorous foreign policy, and a vigorous foreign policy to give congenial occupation and to secure further increase to our war fleet."—"Manifest Destiny," *Harper's Monthly*, Oct. 1893.

There is no doubt about his target. It was that elderly U.S. Navy officer, Captain Alfred Thayer Mahan, who next year was openly urging the eagle to join the Navy and see the world:

"In our infancy we bordered upon the Atlantic only; our youth carried our boundary to the Gulf of Mexico; today maturity sees us upon the Pacific. Have we no right or no call to progress farther in any direction? Are there for us none of those essential interests, of those evident dangers, which impose a policy and confer rights? . . . the annexation, even, of Hawaii, would be no mere sporadic effort, irrational because disconnected from adequate motive, but a first fruit and a token that the nation in its evolution has roused itself to the necessity of carrying its life . . . beyond the borders which heretofore have sufficed for its activities."—*The Interest of America in Sea-Power*, 35, 49.

The tone is unmistakably that of the pulpit, and appeared again in the same sort of context a few years later, when Albert J. Beveridge, "the Boy Orator of Fall Creek," was beating his drum for annexation of the Philippines.

The year 1885 apparently initiated the major phase that committed the United States to the Pacific for all time. Much of it smells of enthusiastic conspiracy in high places, specifically among the navy- and imperialist-minded cronies who centered round Mahan, Henry Cabot Lodge and Theodore Roosevelt. Their habits of mind are well seen in John La Farge, artist and friend of Lodge and Henry Adams, meditating in and on Samoa in 1891:

"I am impressed by the force that Americans could have for good, and by the careful calculation on the part of those who know us best, the Germans and English, upon our weakness of action and irresponsibility, and our not knowing our enormous powers. The Pacific should be ours, and it must be."
—*Reminiscences of the South Seas*, 278.

Should and must; chicken and egg confounded, as in Fascist or Marxist propaganda. Yet no small mutual admiration society could have accomplished so sweeping a result if the national temper had not been congruent. It probably accelerated events, but the American people themselves—or an articulate and numerous segment thereof—had to be abreast of the cabal for its schemes to work.

It was Mahan, "the pedantic sailor,"[8] "the advance agent of American Imperialism,"[9] "the amateur historian,"[10] who infected high places with Pacific fever. In 1885, he says, his mind shifted from continentalism to imperialism, a word about which he made no bones, a shift to which he determined the United States should conform.[11] It coincided with his lecturership on naval history at the new Naval War College, and produced his noted masterpiece, *The Influence of Sea Power on History*. Famous overnight as analyzer of British sea power, he then applied the same principles to the situation of the States, demanding bases in the Pacific and West Indies to screen American coasts and American proprietorship of the Isthmian Canal. He was read not widely but in the right places: his admirers included such sea-minded keymen as Admiral Togo, Kaiser Wilhelm II, Lord Charles Beresford—and Lodge and young T. Roosevelt. Mahan was thick as thieves with Harrison's Secretary of the Navy Tracy, who fathered the then astounding proposal that the Navy should at once lay down twenty battleships and sixty fast cruisers. But there is no need to labor the importance of this solemn man's role in

[8]A. Whitney Griswold, *The Far Eastern Policy of the United States*, 9.
[9]Foster Rhea Dulles, *America in the Pacific*, 187.
[10]Charles and Mary Beard, *A Basic History of the United States*, 339.
[11]Cf. Mahan, "Retrospect and Prospect," *World's Work*, Dec., 1901.

forcing American imperialism into bloom. Students of the subject agree that he was crucial.

Spykman, the geopolitician, says that Mahan's task was lightened because, to Americans, Europe and not the Pacific was the breeding zone of "foreign entanglements." The fact is merely negative. The best illustration of the positive element is—of all people—an eminent Doctor of Divinity who was actually out ahead of Mahan. In 1885, when Mahan was just making his shift, the Rev. Josiah Strong, sometime General Secretary of the Evangelical Alliance for the United States, young incumbent pastor of the Central Congregational Church of Cincinnati, was asked to revise *Our Country*, a pamphlet promoting home missions. Expanded with his own turgid ideas, it became a sizable book that sold 146,000 copies in five years —the *per capita* equivalent of 350,000 now, a bestseller indeed. Its content was so blatant an exhortation to take up the white man's burden—a phrase that Kipling had yet to coin— that, when Strong wrote a sequel in 1900, Mahan was only too pleased to supply a laudatory preface. Thus Strong had the same function at wide places in the road, among people who went to church and took parsons seriously, that Mahan had at little dinners of high-placed public men.

Our Country is not worth reading now, but it was once. Its author was anti-Catholic, anti-Mormon, anti-immigrant, antiliquor and antisocialist, a combination of dislikes guaranteeing a wide hearing; he was also rabidly pro-Protestant and pro-Anglo-Saxon, a term then widely supposed to have intelligible ethnic meaning. He reasoned as follows: Anglo-Saxons specialize in the cultivation of civil liberties and "spiritual Christianity." These two ingredients equal "the highest Christian civilization." Therefore:

". . . it is to the English and American people that we must look for the evangelization of the world . . . the Anglo-Saxon, as the great representative of these two ideas, . . . is divinely commissioned to be, in a peculiar sense, his brother's keeper . . . It seems to me that God, with infinite wisdom and skill, is training the Anglo-Saxon race for an hour sure to come . . . this powerful race will move down upon Mexico, down upon Central America and South America, out upon the islands of the sea, over upon Africa and beyond . . . God has two hands. Not only is he preparing in our civilization the die with which to stamp the nations . . . he is preparing mankind to receive our impress."—*Our Country*, 209, 214, 225, 227.

His sequel is in a style even clottier—"we have already crossed the Rubicon that bounded our insularity"—and contains the extraordinary statement that, since foreign capital must be protected and plagues prevented from spreading:

> "The popular notion in this country that there can be no rightful government of a people without their consent, was formed when world conditions were radically different, and peoples could live separate lives."
> —*Expansion under World Conditions*, 257

In view of the wide circulation of these books, such ideas help greatly to understand why so many pious people wanted the Philippines annexed and what lay behind President McKinley's famous statement that God helped him decide what to do with that bothersome archipelago—namely, keep it.[12]

This curious couple—the sailor who preferred to stay ashore and the divine who preferred to jettison Christian charity—are as far as this book need go in accounting for Uncle Sam's presence in the Pacific. The rest has been told authoritatively and expertly many times. How Roosevelt, taking advantage of his chief's absence from work, briefed Commodore Dewey

---

[12]For the record, Strong became a principal founder of the Federal Council of Churches of Christ in America, originator of the Safety First movement, and leading spirit in something called the American Institute for Social Service. He was not the first to tell Americans that it was their duty to do good to backward heathen, whether they were willing or not: the Rev. Henry T. Cheever, author of glowing books about Hawaiian missions in the 'fifties, mentions the intimate relations of Providence, Destiny and the Anglo-Saxon. Commodore Perry, writing home before he ever reached the Pacific, told of his plans to seize Okinawa, which would result in—with a sailorly snuffle—"the amelioration of the condition of the natives." (Rossiter, "The First American Imperialist," *North American Review*, Vol. 182.)

(his personal selection to command the Asiatic Squadron) on attacking Manila long before war with Spain was declared, and put the Navy on a war footing on his own responsibility; how Spanish offers to concede everything made war unnecessary; how, when the Philippines were seized, certain "Americans had suffered so long from an inferiority complex in the presence of older and more patronizing nations that they hugged to their bosoms the opportunity to lord it over a lesser race;"[13] how Hawaii was hastily annexed on the pretext that it was an indispensable staging base for operations in the Philippines, whereas its new "missionary" government was un-neutrally welcoming American troops anyway; how William Jennings Bryan outsmarted himself, a thing not too difficult, by asking Democratic senators to ratify annexation of the Philippines in hopes that that step would prove a lethal club to beat the Republican dog with in the election of 1900 . . . Here we need only be aware that Uncle Sam's Pacific adventuring came from an emotional and political climate already well confirmed when aggressive facts caught up with the overweening talk.

That is unmistakable in the event. Up to a few months before the "Maine" was sunk nobody, not even Mahan the omniscient, had ever included the Philippines in even the most grandiose westward expansion. Nobody knew anything about them. One glance at the globe would have shown that they were, and still are, a military liability. The decision to annex them was sheer improvisation. The tide of glory in possession —never mind of what—was strong, the lofty-minded were bent, as Mr. Dooley said, on doing the Filipinos good if they had to break every bone in their bodies. And practical minds had swiftly convinced themselves that, in American hands, Manila would be another Shanghai or Singapore as focus of Asiatic trade—the lamest of hopes. True, as some maintained, an American base close to the mainland of Asia would help implement the States' longstanding "Open Door" policy in China. But it was also true that any such base should be a

[13] Paxton Hibben, *The Peerless Leader*, 221.

sound one, and Manila Bay is no such thing, as the U.S. Navy's yearning to shift to Leyte Gulf shows fifty years later. Germany strengthened the annexationists by churlish opportunism from the squadron she sent to watch Dewey. Britain welcomed American cousins to the worshipful company of imperialists with the enthusiasm of the fox that lost his tail. It is a complicated affair, with some of the annexationist positions specious, some almost tenable.[14] But the essence of the matter comes out in a letter from Lodge to Roosevelt in June, 1898:

> "Day [assistant Secretary of State] . . . dined with me the other night and Mahan and I talked the Philippines with him for two hours. He said at the end that he thought we could not escape our destiny there."—*Selections from the Correspondence of Theodore Roosevelt and Henry Cabot Lodge*, I, 313.

Improvising is dangerous, as the mutual admiration society at once proved. They were hand in glove with those responsible for settling up the Spanish War; among them a most critical trick was abjectly missed. The original error of acquiring the Philippines was remediable. All that was needed to make them a secure nuisance to other naval powers with interests in Asia was a solid bridge to the American mainland, seven thousand miles away via Hawaii and the Spanish islands in Micronesia. Conversely, to let anybody else hold Micronesia meant that the Philippines were so screened off from support that they were practically useless in American grand strategy in the Pacific. Yet, of all those islands, only Guam and Hawaii were taken over by the States when making peace with a prostrate enemy. With Mahan, Roosevelt[15] & Company asleep at the switch, Germany snapped up all the rest of Spanish Micronesia in a prearranged deal the moment the war-terminating treaty

[14] A. K. Weinberg, *Manifest Destiny*, is a full-dress treatment that is also an intellectual treat.
[15] Emil Witte, the disgruntled German diplomatic official, even claimed that Roosevelt was responsible for the Carolines being omitted from American demands due to the blandishments of his German diplomatic friends. (*Revelations of a German Attaché*, 60.)

was signed. The U.S. Navy, though aware that the deal was cooking, failed to clarify its strategic implications for the American delegates.

Thenceforth American empire in the Pacific was a dead duck at any time that a hostile power strong in the Western Pacific and possessed of the Palaus and Carolines, wished to make it so. In 1914, as already seen, Japan took over Micronesia; in 1941 she wished to make it so. Or, to put it as carefully as possible: even if the Philippines might have been defensible, as General MacArthur said they could be; even if a properly alerted Hawaii had annihilated the Japanese attackers and so crippled the Japanese Navy; even if Guam had been as heavily fortified as the Navy wished and Congress did not—in 1898 it was still lunatic chance-taking not to make Micronesia the solid keystone of the new Pacific bridge. This Mahan was a mover of mountains, naval equivalent of von Clausewitz; this Roosevelt was probably the most intelligent fan the U.S. Navy ever had. But, as sponsors of aggressive Pacific strategy, they showed themselves much less acute than the semi-anonymous commanders of Navy sloops and frigates who had scoured the Pacific in their fathers' time and hopefully staked claim to any islands that felt good to their spontaneous, unformulated instincts.

Yet civilians should be warned again not to load too much onus on the Navy for its share in Pacific expansionism. It was civilians who most helped Mahan in his mission. The U.S. Navy never showed the realistic bad taste of the French Navy in lending warships to missionaries for transport and prestige. And admirals' hopes were steadily braked by intuitive apathy in cabinets as well as in Congress. Thirty-five years after Pearl Harbor was formally betrothed to the States, nobody had yet cleared away the coral ledge that barred it to deep-draft vessels —that waited until Japanese hostility, consequent on Japanese exclusion in 1907, had become unmistakable. Twenty years after the Navy acquired coaling sites at Pago Pago the place boasted only 350 tons of coal and three small barges; it is a very one-horse installation even now.

Besides, brooding over what your grandfather did, the old scoundrel, even though you still live in the house paid for by his sharp practices, is pathological in individuals and probably so in nations. William Graham Sumner fought like a bitter wildcat against the imperialism that swept the country after the Spanish War; but he also wrote this pregnant sentence, wholly applicable to the situation that now confronts the States in the Pacific:

"The whole history of mankind is a series of acts which are open to doubt, dispute and criticism as to their right and justice, but all subsequent history has been forced to take up the consequences of these acts and go on."—Folkways, 66.

5

Fishers of Men

Lead us to some sunny isle
Yonder in the western deep,
Where the skies forever smile
And the blacks forever weep.
—Lady Emily Sheepshanks

ACQUAINTANCE SOLELY WITH HAWAIIAN MISSIONS
omits some things, notably in the field of hazards. The relatively supine Hawaiian accepted missionary tutelage without
much of the nervous violence that hampered missions elsewhere in the South Seas. In the end there appeared practically
everywhere a nominally triumphant Christianity masking a
persistent substratum of heathen doings. But the interval had
often meant arson, insult and—occasionally—murder. Rugged
as mission life in Hawaii might have seemed, its hardships were
less than those of missions on many other islands.

For example Mrs. Judd, wife of the ABCFM doctor, had to
contend only with the psychological hazards of Hawaiian
obscenity and curiosity. In Fiji, however, the wife of an early
Wesleyan missionary complained to the local chief about some
stolen laundry; promising to look into it, he returned the next
day bearing not the expected shirts, but a bundle of fresh-
amputated little fingers taken from the thieves and presented
as ritual soro—apology for her loss, Fijian style. A lady always
wondering when something like that will happen naturally
becomes nervous. Nor were all mission wives as fortunate as
Mrs. Thurston in avoiding rape by an enamored or inquisitive
native. In the 'thirties several Marquesan bucks came very suc-

259

cessfully to grips with missionary wives.[1] Even masculinity was no safeguard against sexual outrage—as witness the experiences of Mr. Harris of the London Missionary Society in those same turbulent and highly stylized Marquesas.

All the long voyage out on the first L.M.S. missionary ship, when the mission flock was planning who should be stationed where, this Harris, a cooper by trade, insisted the Marquesas were his. He infected with his own enthusiasm a younger colleague named Crook; the pair were duly taken to the Marquesas after the main body was established on Tahiti. When they went ashore to spy out the land, Crook returned to the ship, game to settle down to do good among the savages; but the ferocious appearance of his flock-to-be and the dark ways of their extremely un-English lives had shaken Harris. He vacillated for days, unable to muster courage to go permanently ashore with Crook, until the day before the ship sailed. Next morning the crew saw him signalling frantically from the beach and sent in a boat. It appeared that the chief with whom he was to live had gone a journey overnight and, like a hospitable Polynesian, handed his wife over to Harris, who declined the honor. The indignant and alarmed wife got her women-friends together and, while Harris slept, they crept in on him. He woke to find them manually investigating whether he had the equipment and potential neccssary for courtesy if he had so chosen. Any remains of his enthusiasm for the Marquesas vanished in outraged panic; he was "determined to leave a place where the people were so abandoned, and given up to wickedness; a cause," says the official account equivocally, "which should have excited a contrary resolution."[2]

So he fled to the relative safety of Tahiti while Crook valiantly stayed on. How he solved the problem of insistent bedfellows is not recorded, but he did not lack troubles. The "Aspasia" sealer found him also eager to escape a few months

[1] Says Caillot "avec des raffinements inouïs jusque sous les yeux de leurs époux." (*Histoire de la Polynésie Orientale*, 339.) It would be a pity to put that into English.
[2] *Voyage of the Duff*, 141.

later. The natives had stripped him of all Christian clothes; clothed only in a malo[3] for weeks, he was burned as dark as a Marquesan; and, having made an enemy of the Italian right hand man of a local chief, he walked in constant fear of his life. Nevertheless he was plucky enough to try again on Nukahiva, another Marquesan island, where the "Aspasia" set him ashore with misgivings plus a new outfit of clothes, food and equipment. It was no use; Nukahiva was just as rowdy as Ua-Pu. Within another few months Crook too landed off a rescuing whaler at Tahiti, sorrowfully shaking the sand of Marquesan beaches from his feet.

At least he survived. Others had less luck. The first effort to convert Tonga meant death for three of ten missionaries landed. Eromanga (New Hebrides) appears in missionary lore as "The Martyrs' Isle" because within a few years six missionaries, starting with the brilliant and able John Williams, were killed there. As late as 1901 the Rev. James Chalmers, probably the most intelligent missionary ever to work the Pacific, was knocked in the head in a New Guinea men's house. In many such cases, notably that of the Rev. Mr. Baker in Fiji,[4] these martyrs deliberately pushed into places notoriously hostile to whites in regions where the natives did not yet fully comprehend the power of white punitive measures. It was part of their sacred duty to walk, clothed on with faith as with a garment, into lions' dens and fiery furnaces. The ratio of success was high, partly because the missionary's bland confidence in the Lord often moved puzzled natives to leave him unharmed, probably on the principle that such foolhardiness implied possession of very special magic. It is a nice question whether a man walking into deadly danger because he is sure that an omnipotent God is with him displays courage in any customary sense. But a parson doing so certainly shows striking ability to

[3]This is the Hawaiian word for the Polynesian loincloth for men—a strip of tapa wound round the waist through the legs, and tucked in for security.

[4]Jack London's The Whale's Tooth, based on the Baker incident, is an excellent re-creation of the emotional atmosphere involved.

practice what he preaches. The stamina behind it is all the more impressive because, as many medical officers found in the recent war, the malaria, dysentery, and tropical ulcers that often came with the assignment are those diseases best calculated to break morale.

The methods of the Right Reverend George Augustus Selwyn, Bishop of Melanesia, prettily dramatize how to approach cannibal strangers armed with only zeal and Christian love. Selwyn was a wonderfully handsome aristocrat who had been a great athlete and a pious Anglican at school and University. When touring his diocese, which included many of the surliest islands in the South Seas, he never allowed a boat's crew to share the risk of approaching a virgin native settlement. He alone, dressed in flannel under the contemporary impression that this was a proper swimming costume, and wearing his hat, would drop overside and swim ashore to scramble over the reef, wade up the beach, and stop ankle-deep without apparent alarm at the way his communicants-to-be were waving spears and clubs. Somehow, though streaming salt water and half a mile from help, he could display the necessary dignity and confidence as he took off his hat and extracted from it enough of the right presents for the chiefs to start matters off on a friendly basis. Few profane whites in the Pacific would have dared any such dauntless caper.

Selwyn died in bed. His successor, the famous Bishop Patteson, versed in Selwyn's methods, died with his boots on, the right side of his head crushed with a *tapa*-mallet as he lay resting in a village on Nukapu (Santa Cruz Islands). The calibre of these two men is best shown by the fact that their personalities and shipboard sermons made a famous missionary out of George Brown, a tough young runaway seaman.

Patteson was killed, it appeared later, to avenge the recent kidnapping of five local men by a schooner pretending to be a mission vessel.[5] Others of his colleagues were killed for disease-bringing sorcerers. Too often the landing of the Rev. and Mrs.

[5] E. S. Armstrong, *The Melanesian Mission*, 121. Cf. IV, *Their Gods Are Dead* for the background of blackbirding.

Grundy on Tarafu was followed by a decimating epidemic of dysentery or influenza; local chiefs concluded that these white sorcerers brought it on by malicious and wilful magic—it was most suspicious that the missionary couple themselves did not suffer. In some cases the missionaries followed the Rev. Mr. Coan and indiscreetly substantiated the theory by pointing to the epidemic as God's just punishment for natives stiff-necked about the Gospel. Since neither party was acquainted with modern epidemiology and immunology, their explanations of the coincidence were equally superstitious. And the next time the mission ship came round, the most she would find would be a native convert-assistant gibbering with fear and telling how Misi Grundy was riddled with spears and his wife had disappeared—there was Misi Grundy's skull fourth from the right under the eaves of the men's house.

Mission history does not make too much of these native assistants.[6] They seem to have been considered distinctly expendable. But the usual spearhead of the Gospel on a hazardous island was not a white parson—white personnel was valuable and scarce—but a Tahitian, Samoan, Tongan or Hawaiian convert, often with his native wife, skimpily grounded in what Christian doctrine he had been able to absorb, and set ashore to see if his brown skin would protect him long enough to stir up a thirst after righteousness among local people. There was some chance of safety in the prestige of landing from a white man's ship with a boatload of trade goods. But all too often the native crusader would be stripped of his black coat and white shirt and his wife dragged into the scrub for obvious purposes. If he lived, it would be as a semienslaved outcast, without local relatives to appeal to, a very hopeless situation for both him and the Lord. In 1840 Captain Belcher, H.M.S. "Sulphur," found on Aneityum (New Hebrides) some utterly miserable Samoan missionaries:

". . . a mere thatched hovel, in which five unfortunate natives of the Navigators were literally imprisoned, being compelled to close the door immediately one entered or departed, to pre-

[6] Frank Paton, *Lomai of Lenakel*, is an honorable exception.

vent the intrusion of the natives . . . suffering more or less from fever and ague[7] . . . very uneasy and unhappy and painfully anxious to return to their native land . . . the frequent repetition of "Samoa, Samoa" from the sick within the hut sounded like the cry of the condemned."—Voyage "Sulphur," II, 58–9.

Yet the native auxiliary got results often enough to set him high in the missions' scheme of tactics. He was produced in wholesale lots. Within a generation the L.M.S. seminary at Malua on Upolu (Samoa) trained upwards of 2,000 native teachers and preachers. In 1879 the Wesleyans' Tubou Theological School on Tongatabu had a hundred native students. Alumni of both were scattered from the Marshalls to the New Hebrides and from the Marquesas to the Admiralties. The Anglicans persuaded local Melanesian chiefs to let the mission ship take local youths and maidens away to New Zealand, later to Norfolk Island, to be trained in white ways. As soon as they appeared to have the hang of soap, water, chastity, and literacy, they were returned resplendent in white men's clothes and oozing the prestige of knowing many of the white man's mysteries. If they did not backslide on repatriation—and breakage does not seem to have been high—the mission vessel had a foothold ashore on her next trip, and duly exploited it.

Putting the native in the forefront of the battle was not as callous as it sounds, however. He did have special advantages. Anywhere in Polynesia a Polynesian could learn the local language much more quickly than a white; his diplomacy worked better because he felt the significance of a hundred details that would escape a white man. To a lesser extent, this held good in Melanesia too. He could persuade raw material into Christian ways with more subtle adaptations. Though often bigoted and always ignorant, these native auxiliaries were often heroes in the sight of man as well as of God, for instance the ABCFM Hawaiian in the Marquesas who ransomed a captive whaler's mate with his own official whaleboat, the pride of his heart.

[7]Samoa, like other Polynesian groups, has no malaria; these Samoans were meeting it for the first time in the New Hebrides.

The heroism consisted not so much in the price as in the fact that, by paying so high to keep a man from being eaten, he was risking his own neck in a tactless display of disapproval. It is a pleasure to read that President Lincoln sent him a new whale-boat and a suitably engraved watch as thanks from the rescued mate's countrymen. Such a native missionary seldom had illusions about what he was running into. When the Wesleyans sent Fijian auxiliaries to New Britain in 1877, the white authorities expostulated on the grounds that they might not fully understand the dangers involved.

"We are all of one mind," said the party's spokesman. "We know what those islands are. We have given ourselves to this work. If we get killed, well; if we live, well. We have had everything explained to us and know the danger; we are willing to go."[8] Very shortly four of their number were killed and eaten.

The first foray of the Cross into the South Seas happened to be the bloodiest. Spanish Jesuit missionaries accompanied Spanish secular power in effective occupation of the Marianas in 1668—among Spaniards, Gospel and sword were always coupled. The Chamorro chiefs on Guam, Rota, Tinian and Saipan were impressed by white possessions and, like many other Islanders, were inclined to welcome a new religion apparently associated with having such things. But they made awkward conditions: the chiefs would receive instruction only if the commonalty did not. They feared that brotherhood in Christ would blur the rigid caste distinctions of Chamorro culture.[9] The Jesuits refused to be respecters of persons. The chiefs gathered their closer retainers to see what spears, bows and very accurate slinging of fire-hardened stones could do against these leveling interlopers. Their resolution was strength-

[8] C. F. Gordon-Cumming, At Home in Fiji, 322–3.
[9] The same issue appeared in other Micronesian islands. The religious wars on Ponape (Carolines) were due to "the puritanical teaching of the Boston mission which preached the equality of all men before God and disrupted the relationship between subjects and their feudal lords." (Hambruch quoted in Yanaihara, Pacific Islands Under Japanese Mandate, 237.) "Boston mission" is the South Seas name for the ABCFM.

ened by a castaway Chinese on Guam who told them that the
Spaniards had been driven from home as undesirables, and that
the holy water with which the Jesuits baptized Chamorro children was poison—see, since the ceremony, several of these
children had died.[10] This is really notable: two hundred and
seventy-five years ago, when missions first attacked a South Sea
Island, a beachcomber was already there to make them trouble.

In the subsequent fighting ad majorem Dei gloriam a number of Jesuits died. So did the bulk of the population of the
Marianas, an extermination furthered by epidemic diseases
coming ashore with the whites. By 1700 so few natives were
left that government stripped Saipan and Tinian of survivors
and concentrated all on Guam, conveniently under its thumb.[11]
The Chamorros kept on dying off. Though the modern Guamanian is called Chamorro and can still speak fragments of the
prewhite language, is a very nice fellow and an appealing governmental problem, he has very little aboriginal stock in him,
being descended mostly from Filipino immigrants, many of
them transported convicts, with admixtures of Spanish, Mexican, American, English, German and various off-island Micronesian strains.

He is also a devout Catholic so, from one point of view, the
venture was a success. But after that, except for a feeble gesture
toward Tahiti in the 1770's, Spanish missions left the South
Seas severely alone. Only after a lapse of generations did
Protestantism step into the breach. When Catholicism decided
to re-enter the field a generation later, the Protestant outcry
would have led an outsider to believe that the whole area was
owned in fee by Calvin, Wesley & Tudor, Inc.

[10]The impression may have been strengthened by the missionaries' tactic
of selecting very sick children for baptism to save their souls before
death.

[11]Concentrating native populations under the sheltering wings of soldier
and priest seems to have been a standard Spanish colonial technique.
Witness their proceedings in California; also, the 100th question which
the third Spanish expedition to Tahiti was to determine read: "Might
it be easy to concentrate [the natives] into a town?"
—Corney, Tahiti, II, 28.

This harks back again to Captain Cook. His successive voyages set all England agog about new worlds down yonder, and various people reacted in characteristic ways, the godly in a godly fashion. William Cowper included in his long poem *The Task* some pious remarks about Omai;[12] and Selina, dowager Countess of Huntingdon, "that pious though rather eccentric person,"[13] whom the Rev. Augustus Toplady called "the most precious saint of God he ever knew,"[14] became very troubled about so many souls unable to slake their spiritual thirst on the Gospel. Her chaplain, the Rev. Dr. Haweis, was instrumental in directing the attention of her newly founded London Missionary Society to the Islands, reading about which had fascinated him. Founded in 1795, the L.M.S. was non-sectarian but, like the peeress who helped found it, carried a distinct dissenting flavor, with Congregationalism and Presbyterianism discernible. English Baptists were already evangelizing India, the Wesleyans were nibbling away at Africa, but the L.M.S., still a great force in the South Seas, was first to distinguish itself in Polynesia.

The ship "Duff," chartered for the voyage in 1796, carried thither a large batch of L.M.S.-chosen missionaries, only four of whom were ordained ministers, and only one a qualified surgeon. The rest were serious craftsmen and workers, what the period called "mechanics": several carpenters, a harness maker, a tailor, two shoemakers, a whitesmith, a blacksmith and brazier, a butcher, a couple of weavers, a hatter, a bricklayer, a linen draper, a cabinetmaker. Crook, whom we have seen stripped by the Marquesans, had been a gentleman's servant and then a tinworker—surely no South Seas adventurer of any stripe ever had a stranger career. Mr. Nott, the bricklayer, was to become exclusive spiritual and temporal advisor to Pomare II and principal author of the Tahitian code of laws.

This mixture of trades was intentional. The new missionary colony would have many skills at its disposal and the artisans

[12]Cf. II, 3, *This Was the South Sea Islander.*
[13]Russell, *Polynesia*, 87.
[14]*Dictionary of National Biography*, IX, 133.

could teach the natives useful things. But the distribution was ragged; it should have included a printer, a couple of ship-wrights, a ship's captain, a gardener and several farmers. The linen draper, the hatter, and the cabinetmaker are of course patent absurdities. Also the average level of education was low, a fault occasionally admitted by the devout, with the defiant addendum that Christ's apostles, too, had been neither polite nor learned men.

A sound point, but lack of education and knowledge of the world was awkward when the L.M.S. missionaries became virtual political masters of the whole Societies group. The late eighteenth century knew little enough of ethnology, sociology, government, and public health; what bits of knowledge it did have formed no part of the equipment of the "Duff's" passengers. It was also diplomatically regrettable that visiting dignitaries, such as captains of men-of-war, were snobbish about the depressing lack of gentlemen among mission personnel. Captain Belcher disdainfully called them "overzealous, half-educated sectarians."[15] Missionizing did not seem to attract gentlemen of birth, though Selwyn was one of the few exceptions. If the South Seas had had to wait until the peerage got round to relieving its spiritual darkness in person, it would be black as the pit there still.[16] Still, the crudity of these pioneering evangelists can be exaggerated. Moerenhout, notably hostile to missions, said that the chiefs of the L.M.S. delegation on Tahiti in the 'forties were dignified, likeable and sociable; the Earl of Pembroke, an aristocrat who disliked psalm singers, spoke highly of the L.M.S. men he met down in the Islands during the 'seventies.

The "Duff's" first complement was notable for more than ill-informed zeal. Her master, a thorough seaman named James Wilson, had served John Company in India, been captured by

[15]Voyage "Sulphur," 273–4.

[16]Lovett, official historian of the L.M.S. frankly accused it of bad judgment in selecting its first emissaries (History of the London Missionary Society, 46). But even after standards were raised and training instituted, these shortcomings were still conspicuous for generations.

the French and turned over to Hyder Ali's henchmen, in whose sadistic hands he barely survived. Turned devout after retiring from sea, he volunteered to command the mission ship; of the crew he signed, half were church members, the rest piously given. King's ships anchored near the "Duff" while she was fitting out were mystified by this trig vessel that exuded hymn singing day and night and maintained smart discipline without cursing. As she dropped down the Channel in August, 1796, to take in her final stores and join a convoy at Portsmouth, she was hailed by a patrol vessel:

"Whither bound?"

"Tahiti."

"What cargo?"

"Missionaries and provisions!"[17]

Breakage of personnel began at once. The turbulence of the Channel terrified Mrs. Hudden, wife of the butcher; at Portsmouth she and Hudden were put ashore without uncharitable remarks. There too the twelve-year-old boy on board died, leaving youth represented by a baby of two years and another of sixteen weeks. Arrived in the South Seas, the crew was godly enough at first to resist the attractions that plagued Cook with desertions and produced the "Bounty" mutiny. The chronicler of the "Duff" beamed over the spectacle of her seamen repairing the rigging at Ua-Pu (Marquesas) attended aloft by practically naked brown girls sociably holding tar buckets for them. "No ship's company without great restraints from God's grace . . . would have resisted such temptations.[18] But later, at Moorea the fairyland backdrop for proverbial South Seas delights, across the strait from Tahiti, God's grace ran thin. John Micklewright, captain's steward, sloped ashore, took up with a Swedish beachcomber and became a thorn in the mission's flesh. With native connivance William Tucker, seaman, deserted at Matavai Bay. Threats to hold the chief as hostage, Cook-style, brought Tucker back tied up in the bottom of a canoe, swearing like a cat at native "treachery." There are

[17]Richard Lovett, History of the London Missionary Society, 130.
[18]Voyage of the Duff, 137.

different overtones in Samuel Hurst, cabin boy, who skipped ship leaving an incoherent note about how "being of a dwarfish size, he was apprehensive of falling into want in his own country; therefore he preferred settling where nakedness was no hardship . . ."[19]

Not even the missionaries' morals remained stainless. After Polynesia had worked on him a while Mr. Lewis, an ordained minister no less, stated a desire to marry a native girl; refused permission, on the curious grounds that such marriage would be "directly contrary to the Word of God," he did it anyway the wrong side of the blanket and was excommunicated. After three years of futile missionary effort, Mr. Broomhall, former harness maker, grew skeptical and shacked up with a native girl; then he drifted off to India where, under the influence of a high fever and a broken leg, Baptist missionaries prowling the hospital brought him back to his spiritual bearings. Mr. Shelly, former cabinetmaker heeded the call of Mammon and turned sandalwooder and pearler. His associates thought well of him in this phase, but his former comrades in the mission were pleasantly edified when his vessel was cut out and plundered by the enterprising natives of the Tuamotu. (None of these backsliders turned out as lurid as the Rev. Mr. Yate of the Church of England mission in New Zealand, who spent most of his time at the Bay of Islands practicing sodomy with both natives and white sailors.) To the edification of the missionaries, most of such delinquents met misfortune proportionate to their sins: Lewis was murdered in his shack by an unknown hand; despite his reconversion, Broomhall was lost at sea.[20]

Discouragement among the Tahiti contingent was understandable. The natives had not changed much since they had

[19]Voyage of the Duff, 217.
[20]George Veeson (or Vason), former bricklayer, had better luck, in this world at least. Abandoning the Tongan L.M.S. mission to live with a native woman, he got safe home on the "Royal Admiral" in 1801 and lived to become governor of Nottingham jail.—Lockerby, Journal, note, 176.

amused themselves by chorusing jocose obscenities at the Spanish Catholic priests. Violent, unruly, scornful, they paid heed to missionaries only when presents of cloth and iron were forthcoming. After years of frustration, a majority of the mission fled to Australia, leaving only seven to carry on—the particular occasion was the stripping and brutal beating of a mission party by emissaries of young Tu, disgruntled "king" of Tahiti, later known as Pomare. Actually Tu's mana on the island was definitely far less than that of the heads of the Teva clan, a matter that the mission never understood clearly; said a surviving Teva in the 'nineties:

". . . the natives looked on the missionaries as a kind of children or idiots, incapable of understanding the simplest facts of island politics or society, and serving only as the unconscious tools of the Tu family."—*Memoirs Arii Tamai*, 128.

For this mistake, the mission paid dearly. The fortunes of Christianity in Tahiti became inextricably confused with those of Tu. When the Teva forced him to flee from Tahiti to Moorea, the mission was extinguished, following the first deserters to Australia. Only the stubborn Mr. Nott remained with Tu in exile to fan the spark of righteousness in the "king's" soul. It is hard to blame the runaways in view of their situation as described to the governor of New South Wales:

". . . our houses being burnt, our gardens destroyed, and much of our property plundered, we were thrown into such a situation as we could not pursue the object of our mission, nor continue much longer in the islands with any reasonable prospect of safety . . . we have no inducement whatever for the continuance of the mission. Our time is apparently spent in vain . . . No one appears desirous of instruction . . . two vessels lately from Port Jackson gave us no reason to think that the Directors of the Missionary Society trouble themselves much about us."—Lockerby, *Journal*, 121–6.

On their way to Australia they had been wrecked in Fiji and fried on a sandbank for a dismally long time until rescued by a passing sandalwooder.[21] All these tight-lipped little souls could remember of the glories of fighting the Lord's battle among heathen was the natives' indignation when more texts than muskets were given out, the horrors of lascivious dances staged cheek by jowl with prayer meetings, the distractions provided when natives grinningly started dogfights right under the preacher's nose.

In his sulky exile, however, Pomare (Tu) occasionally listened negligently to Mr. Nott. Finally, disgusted with the ill fortune sent by his own gods, he determined to try the white man's God. He was baptized, publicly broke *tabu* by eating turtle without proper decontaminating ceremonies—and survived, much to the astonishment of his followers. Partly from tact, no doubt, as well as revulsion against superstition, they too became Christians. From that moment Pomare's fortunes mended. In the first of the Christian *vs.* heathen wars that usually followed when the Gospel got a foothold in the Islands, he fought his way to hegemony of Tahiti. The conquered Teva asserted that the crucial ingredient in the final battle was a corps of native teachers armed with guns as well as Bibles. The implications of victory were by no means lost on either the natives or the missionaries reared in the history of the Canaan-conquering Jews. The old gods' *mana* never recovered, and Mr. Nott's comrades returned rejoicing from their anomalous position among the drunken militia and old lags of Port Jackson. There is no record that Nott made any remarks about where were you, brave Crillon, but then he was not an educated man.

Neither was Pomare a model convert like Kaahumanu. Though he helped to translate the Scriptures into Tahitian, he was often seen headed for the summerhouse where he worked with a Bible under one arm and a bottle of rum under the other; he unquestionably drank himself to death, and had

[21]The first reinforcement for the Tahiti mission, sent out in consequence of prematurely enthusiastic reports from the "Duff," was captured at sea by a French cruiser and put ashore at Rio de Janeiro to make the best of its way home. The party all made it, but the experience cured most of them of missionarying.

more elaborate vices. But he did build the mission a native-style meetinghouse 712 feet long, with three pulpits and 133 windows, he never overtly apostatized; and he allowed the mission to educate his heirs.

So, after his death in 1819, the mission was the effective government of Tahiti and Moorea in prophetic parallel to the Hawaiian situation a few years later. Every Sunday the Tahitian wenches turned out for church in dresses, bonnets, and bare feet and imposed a daylong boycott on carnal intercourse. Ships' crews were forced to return on board at sunset, and distilling and selling rum to natives were forbidden. A printing press was presently knocking off tapa-bound Tahitian versions of Genesis and St. Mark and, striking while the iron was hot, the mission formed its teeming new congregations into local missionary societies. Why should the Lord depend solely on contributions from the pious in England?

Why, indeed? But ceremonial contributions of coconut oil and arrowroot put the Lord blatantly into business, a tactical mistake in which South Sea missions still persist here and there to the exasperation of traders and planters. The Wesleyan missionary ship, the "John Wesley," was known through Island barrooms as the "Palm-Oil Trader." On such an island as Aitutaki (Cooks), too small to attract traders in 1850, the L.M.S. missionary could have it all his own way, making sure that the native got only decorous dividends from his oil making. Godly visitors found men and boys in white shirts and trousers, women were kept out of sight but doubtless decently clad, and themselves were forbidden to leave the landing beach as a precaution against immorality. "Home of perpetual infancy and innocence!" caroled the Rev. Mr. Lyman of this spiritual quarantine station. "Who would not be content always to live under such limitations?"[22]

The men of Mammon had numerous good reasons to hate missions. They interfered with sexual relations of all degrees of irregularity, opposed drinking, and often warned the native that the trader or land speculator was swindling him. Since at

[22]*Hawaiian Yesterdays*, 250.

first the native usually knew nothing of money, the mission competed with the trader by using trade goods to ingratiate itself with chiefs and to persuade commoners to work as builders and house servants; it rankled that, since it got goods at no expense to itself, the mission could be generous. And it soothed Mammon not at all when the native missionary-society dodge brought heaps of marketable commodities to the white parson's feet but not to the trader's store. In the 'eighties King Tembinok of Abemama (Gilberts), who ran a royal monopoly in copra trading, encountered such competition from a native missionary. He kicked him off the island and would thenceforth never so much as permit a missionary of any color to land.

The first cargo of mission-acquired coconut oil sent from Tahiti realized £1,900, quite a sum in those days, augmented by the duties piously remitted by the crown. Misi encouraged rivalry between individuals and villages as to who should come down most handsomely for the Lord—a device with which natives easily fell in, since it was like the old days of competition in bringing the richest present to the chief. As the native learned money and as specie grew commoner, cash replaced offerings in kind; the communicant loved to parade up the aisle, using his mouth as a purse, to spew shillings one by one while the congregation counted, first breathlessly and then enviously. Mammon savagely resented the fat sacks of silver that went away on the annual mission ship. Fat they were—in Turner's time Samoa's annual contribution to the L.M.S. was round £1,200; in 1869 the Wesleyans got £6,000 out of Tonga. "They are such cheerful givers!" a missionary told me on Tonga last year, turning up his eyes like a duck in thunder. He might well say so—at the moment the church he represented had a building fund of £35,000 mostly accumulated during the dollar boom on Tongatabu during the recent war. In the same period in Samoa Wesleyan contributions from natives ran from 700% to 800% of prewar expectation. The owner of a nicer nose, however, might suspect that this giving may be not so much cheerful as pharisaical.

Samoan scoffers used to maintain that the best time to find a girl to sleep with in Apia was a week or so before the annual missionary contribution. That was the simplest way to procure a respectable show of money for the occasion. For the native church member was, and still is, prone to take church as more of a social than a moral institution; Melville's Tahitian girl assured him a hundred years ago that, though "mickonaree" as to head and heart, she was by no means mickonaree in other parts of the body.

The trader might have been grateful to the mission, however, for stimulating demand for white goods, particularly clothing. The convert was supposed to appear in church garbed as nearly as possible like his preceptors; the native church officer had to have a black suit like Misi's. Sunday shoes were so important that the owner of a pair would wear them down the church aisle, then take them off and drop them out the window to a waiting friend to wear in turn. Since hatless women in God's house were anathema, the trader sold many fantastic bonnets, or even old newspaper to serve as foundation for trimmings.

Mammon was on firmer ground in objecting when missions went into actual trading. They bred cattle and sold milk and beef to ships and white residents; they used native convert labor, working as much for devotion as for livelihood, to grow vegetables for sale to greens-hungry ships; they often acted as agents for ships' stewards, for a stern suggestion from Misi made all the difference when natives were lackadaisical about bringing hogs or yams in sufficient quantity.

The Tahiti L.M.S. mission was as crude as any. It went partners with Pomare II in the pearler "Haweis"; it started sugar plantations on Moorea, only to find that they would not pay unless the molasses were turned into rum; it imported looms and spindles and tried to grow and manufacture cotton. No matter how innocent the intention or how holy the contemplated end, this was about as bad taste as the rich real-estate holdings of New York's Trinity Church.

Nor were individual missionaries above profit. When the

French ejected the Rev. Mr. Pritchard from Tahiti, he claimed to have lost £4,000 in property left behind—not bad for a man presumed to be taking no thought for the morrow. In Fiji his son found a Wesleyan missionary owning the best house in Levuka and employing boats' crews to collect coconut oil on his private account up and down the coasts—an activity in which missionary prestige was very useful. These men were still official members of their missions. At least the Yankee missionaries in Hawaii resigned before going into business.

Many a missionary undeniably did himself very well, and still does, in Island terms. Protestant parsons had no intention of living the life of their flock, as the Founder of their faith might have done, on fish and *poi* in a thatched shack. The first plastered or masonry building on most islands was the house that the mission erected as soon as it could command labor to get some coral burned for lime. Misi's whaleboat for pastoral visits was the smartest craft on the island, bright with fresh paint, comfortably cushioned and awninged, rowed by a uniformed convert crew. Only by such examples of Christian engineering and neatness, said the mission, could the natives learn living like respectable Christians, just as bringing one's wife along was supposed to show the native the joys of Christian connubiality and housewifery. But, in South Sea eyes, great resources go with great chiefs. The first native honor paid Stevenson in Samoa was the title of "the Rich Man." So, inevitably, Misi was likely to become the big man of the community, as much so as the town banker in the big house on the hill over a Pennsylvania mining town, or as the Pope in mediaeval Rome.

Comparable prestige might attach to the native incumbent in places too small for white ministry. On Funafuti (Ellices) in 1897 the local chief's salary was a pound a year, while the local Samoan pastor got ten; since the pastor's wife also owned the only sewing machine on the island, the relative importance of chief and pastor was doubly clear. During the last century the South Seas teemed with smug, haughty, pious, native interlopers tyrannizing with the Bible in one hand and a Draconic code of sumptuary and moral laws in the other. These coffee-colored Pecksniffs were as set on Biblical precedent as any Connecticut parson. Such laws and precedents were no more arbitrary than the home-grown *tabus* they had replaced, but it is questionable if they suited the inhabitants' needs as well. Besides, the native pastors often got things by the wrong end in interpretation.

Confronted by a lady parishioner who wanted a divorce, for instance, the native pastor on Funafuti (Ellices) looked in his Bible and told her it appeared she would have to commit adultery to make it possible; so she did, unaware that she was in exactly the same legal boat as her white sisters in New York State. In the Marshalls a native on a newly evangelized island killed another. The native pastor determined to hold a white-style legal trial for murder instead of leaving the matter to the victim's family to avenge in customary vendetta. When the killer was duly convicted, the pastor told off another parishioner to execute him, which was duly accomplished. But then it occurred to somebody that the executioner too must be tried for having killed a man, and tried he was and convicted and executed in turn, thus making *his* executioner liable. Depopulation was threatening the island when the mission vessel appeared and stopped the endless chain with fuller explanation.

Once part of Tikopia was converted, its native pastor encouraged his flock to sacrifice to the old gods for the safety of their revered missionary bishop known to be at sea during a bad storm. The first chapel built on Rarotonga (Cooks) was ornamented with "many indelicate heathen figures"[23] because its native builders assumed that the style of thing appropriate to heathen worship was equally so here. The newly-converted natives of Anaa (Tuamotu) seized and plundered a ship suspected of pearling without a license, and then trooped in a body to church to give thanks for their loot. In trying to head

[23]John Williams, A Narrative of Missionary Enterprise, I, 130.

off possible misunderstanding, the Rev. Lowell Smith of the ABCFM got into trouble with pickthank whites:

> "My text was Matthew 7, 12. 'All things whatsoever that ye would men should do to you, do ye even so to them, for this is the law and the prophets.' In illustrating the text, I was unfortunate in one case by saying, If A is vile enough to lend his wife to B, it does not follow that B shall do the same to A . . . For this reason some of the unpenitent residents have taken umbrage, . . ."—Mary Frear, *Lowell and Abigail*, 151.

The Rev. Mr. Smith was probably well-advised. Heaven only knows what a Polynesian casuist accustomed to gift exchange might have made out of that text.

Strange things happened when Little Bethel came to grips with the Islander. Even to pets: native pastors often encouraged Christian morals by vice-patrols searching huts for fornicators after dark. On Funafuti (Ellices) the fornicators bethought themselves to install watchdogs, which was so effective that the pastors forbade all dog-owning. Funafuti went dogless the rest of the century. The Trobriand Islanders, you remember, had no notion that men had anything to do with procreation. For them sexual intercourse was merely a pleasant, personal two-player game, so mission talk about the Immaculate Conception and God the Father was meaningless; worse, for when the missionaries insisted that their theory of conception was superior to the Trobrianders', they lost face as obviously rude and ignorant persons. Many Polynesians insisted that the mission should pay them for attending church or sending children to school. On Tanna (New Hebrides), converted villages stood to their promise to fight for the mission's safety, but developed hurt feelings when the missionaries refused to join the war parties, and even refused to lend fowling pieces to their own protectors. But missionaries were not consistent on this point: When natives of Duke of York Island massacred four Fijian Wesleyan teachers, the Rev. George Brown organized and led a punitive expedition of whites that killed numbers of natives and burned several villages; he probably strutted a good deal about being such a muscular Christian. On Tubuai (Australs) natives converted by L.M.S. teachers from Raiatea fought bloodily with natives converted by L.M.S. teachers from Tahiti over whether hymns should be sung standing or sitting, a matter which the L.M.S. had neglected to standardize.

Missions did try to prevent the obvious hazard of competing sects. Wesleyans, L.M.S. and ABCFM early divided the South Seas into formal spheres of influence—the ABCFM got all north of the Equator, and English missions everything south, the Wesleyans taking Tonga, for instance, the L.M.S. the Societies and Samoa. This national division has persisted in politics.

But as generations passed, it was spiritually impossible for the brethren to stick to their agreements. Wesleyanism filtered into Fiji by way of Tongan immigrants, being known in Fiji as the *lotu Tonga* and forming an integral part of the average Tongan's aggressive self-esteem. The Anglicans went to work on the New Hebrides, which the L.M.S. pioneered; Presbyterian interlopers from Scotland and Canada tangled into the picture; and, in the latter half of the century, Seventh Day Adventists and two kinds of Mormons injected themselves into this welter of faiths. The Mormonism now so successful in Hawaii and the Tuamotu, is hardly anything that Parley P. Pratt would recognize, but is active and popular for all that.

The natives had already supplied home-grown confusions. Within ten or fifteen years of the nominal conversion of an island group, there usually appeared a home-grown nativist cult, a hedonistic parody of Christianity dreamed up by a back-country prophet and spreading like smallpox while missionaries wrung their hands and wondered why the devil was so specially busy in their preserves. In New Zealand it was Hauhauism, springboard for one of the bloodiest of the Maori wars, mingling the Bible with old Maori ways. In Hawaii an elderly prophetess appeared claiming to have replaced the Holy Ghost in the Trinity. In Samoa whites called the local prophet Joe Gimlet; sometime forecastle hand on ships out of Sydney, he turned into a Polynesian John the Baptist, predicting the coming of a new Christ who approved of polygamy and dancing. In Fiji one Tuka was really elaborate. The whites had tried to drown him, he said, by throwing him into the sea bound to an anchor, but he had miraculously escaped. He said that for from ten shillings to two pounds in trade, his converts could acquire immortality by drinking from his bottle of miraculous water. He had a sacred bodyguard and a sizable harem of choice young girls whom he guaranteed perpetually renewed virginity. Christ and Jehovah were again conspicuous as white man's reincarnations of the old Fijian gods.

But the cream of the lot was the Mamaia cult in Tahiti, which almost unhorsed the Pomares, mission and all. The prophet of Mamaia was Teau, a deacon of the mission church who developed delusions of grandeur and publicly proclaimed himself Christ. Confined as insane, he escaped to the bush to join adherents, for he had been secretly proselyting for some time. Under mission pressure, the Tahitian chiefs took such strong measures as exile and cruel and unusual punishments. As usual, the blood of the martyrs was the seed of the new church. The net effect of exiling Mamaians to Raiatea was so to infect that island with the new cult that the Rev. John Williams, its missionary-dictator, had to flee to his spiritual appanage of Rarotonga. In no time neighboring Tahaa and Bora Bora had also gone Mamaia, as did Pomare IV, new queen of Tahiti and nominal suzerain of the whole group. The new cult, with overtones of the old Areoi, was undeniably attractive. Communicants read the Bible and prayed frequently, believed profoundly in Christ and—there must have been a Catholic influence somewhere—in John and Paul or the Virgin as patron saints. But Solomon's harem and concubines also attracted favorable attention. Mamaia considered marriage dissoluble at will and felt that it was nobody's business at all what unmarried young people did on moonlit nights. Every believer went to heaven—a place full of beautiful women who never aged and never said No.

Mamaia succumbed first on Tahiti, where missions were best

entrenched. Each of the Leeward Islands[24] retained enough of
a Christian party to keep a savage little war going that worked
out to costly victory for the Christians. Brash Mamaia promises
about the Second Coming and the Last Day failed to materialize, and the cult lost face. Before a critical battle Topoa, ranking chief of Tahaa and a leader of Mamaia, promised that, if
killed, he would revive in three days. Killed he was and revive
he did not. A Mamaia chief's wife, finding her husband missing
after battle, assured the faithful that she had personally seen
him snatched up to heaven like Elijah—a boast hard to recon-
cile with the finding of his dead body, already well decayed,
in the bush. Between such damaging incidents and military
luck on the Christian side, Mamaia presently dwindled and
died.

But it is most important to note that these ecclesiastical cults
were not merely religious comic opera. They usually reflected
local political rivalries, disguising feuds between tribes and
chiefs with religious issues, as German princes used heresy or
orthodoxy as pretexts for political aggrandizement during the
wars of the Reformation. And, for all their ridiculous tenets,
there is no mistaking the seriousness of the emotional background they sprang from. Ethnology sees in them the native's
unstable effort to reassert himself against the steady pressure
of mission and trader. The diagnosis is probably correct; but
I know of no satisfactory explanation for the fact that such
cults usually arose in islands largely under Protestant influence:
whereas the natives of Catholic-dominated islands seldom developed anything but a cowed, childishly dependent acquies-
cence in anything the good fathers saw fit to do.

[24]Group nomenclature in the neighborhood of Tahiti is so badly confused that clarity and succinctness cannot coexist. Early navigators split
the group in two; the eastern part, including Tahiti, being called the
Georgian Islands, and the western part (Raiatea, Bora Bora, Huahine
and so forth), the Society Islands. Gradually "Society Islands" came to
be applied to the whole lot, with "Georgian" forgotten. It was the Georgians, as the particular bailiwick of the Pomare family, that the French
took over, distinguishing the western group as the Leeward Islands
(Îles-sous-le-vent), which remained nominally independent much
longer.

Here may be the necessary time for taking up the major phase of Catholicism in the South Seas. Practically dead since the Spanish victory-fiasco in the Marianas, Rome's interest in the Islands brilliantly revived when Protestantism got firmly based in the area. The agency first in the field was The Congregation of the Sacred Hearts of Jesus and Mary and of the Perpetual Adoration of the Blessed Sacrament of the Altar, usually called the Congregation of Picpus from the street in Paris in which its headquarters were placed. Presently the Marist fathers as well were in the Islands, by Papal stipulation working the western half, while the Picpus covered the bulk of Polynesia.

Why Rome was so apathetic and then so energetic is not clear. But a flavor of French imperialism is easily distinguished. Personnel, funds, political and military support for these activities, were always predominantly French. The French Catholic missionary was harbinger of the French man-of-war in every Pacific group that France now holds, as well as several in which Britain or the States nosed the French out. Mgr. Blanc, bishop of the Catholic missionary diocese based on Wallis Island, not only made pastoral tours on French war vessels but wrote cheerfully that this arrangement "had the advantage of showing the natives the unity of France and the religion they had adopted."[25] A colleague describing Rotuma in 1871 said: "For [the natives] religion is personified in France."[26]

The first Catholic effort, on Hawaii, has already been sketched.[27] For the next decade Rome was cautious, attacking only virgin and strategically located islands. In 1834 the Picpus went ashore on the Gambiers, the knot of high islands at the eastern end of the Tuamotu; in 1837 the Marists set up

---

[25]Blanc, Les Iles Wallis, 90, 130.

[26]There were equally blatant parallels on the heretical side of the fence: When Britain took over Fiji in 1878, the local Wesleyan mission, crowing holily, told the new governor in a lengthy address of welcome and self-gratulation, that "but for the blessing of God upon the mission's labors, there would have been no British Fiji at the present day."

[27]Cf. III, Land of Makebelieve Come True.

shop on Wallis Island,[28] a dainty scrap of a place with a good lagoon anchorage between Fiji and Samoa. But it was soon apparent that, far from having learned in Hawaii to shinny politely on their own side, the Catholics still aimed to concentrate on islands where heresy was already established. Tahiti, Samoa, Fiji, Tonga, Rotuma, New Zealand, were some of the Protestant areas early invaded; in due season New Guinea, New Caledonia, the New Hebrides, the Loyalties, and the Solomons received attention in the wake of Protestant effort.

This challenging aggressiveness was, of course, just what ambitious Frenchmen under the July Monarchy and the Second Empire wanted. Outraged Protestants attributed it to the direct inspiration of the devil, who was known to be intimately connected with Rome. Even a Protestant divine, however, should have been able to see more in it than that; the snorting L.M.S. parson should have recalled that the Roman Church had always taken heresy more seriously than paganism. A heathen as yet unaware of the Gospel might be in less peril of damnation than the heretic; the many former heathen in the Islands infected with soul-destroying perversions of the true religion demanded rescue. The untouched savage converted along the way would be gratifying, but the emergency lay in the necessity for salvaging the viciously imperiled Tahitians, Hawaiians and so forth, already poisoned by English-speaking heretics. Said Père Caret, mighty man of the Picpus:

"Mary the August, whom the Church styles the destroyer of all heresies, will soon know how to annihilate it in Tahiti."— Henri Russier, *La Partage de l'Océanie*, 126.

French commentators have seldom made any bones about this matter; Russier, for instance, explains:

". . . the master preoccupation of French missionaries is less to convert pagans than to tear peoples already converted by

---

[28]The place was not technically virgin, however. Wesleyanism had appeared briefly the year before, by way of an invasion of warlike native Christians from Tonga. The Wallis Islanders, cousins of the Tongans and no weaklings, massacred the lot. (Blanc, *Les Iles Wallis*, 12.)

Protestant missions from heresy and, at the same time, to combat the progress of English or American influences."—*La Partage de l'Océanie,* 234.

Thus, having at least tried to spare the native the perplexities of rivalry between Congregationalists and Wesleyans, Protestant soldiers of God had to see their raw material twisted all out of shape by the differences between the Pope and the rest of the field.

Tahiti, first to be attacked below the Equator, saw the same unedifying scenes as Hawaii: Heretics got Catholic missionaries deported, Catholics resisted with greater stubbornness than frankness, the French man-of-war demanded tolerance for Catholics at point-blank range. This time, however, the result was the deportation of the turbulent Rev. Mr. Pritchard, L.M.S. missionary doubling as British consul, and the establishment of a French protectorate over the windward end of the Societies group. In Fiji—and this was standard tactics— the Protestants reinforced their warnings against popery by showing the chiefs lurid pictures of the tortures of the Inquisition. There then ensued the strange spectacle of French Catholic missionaries appealing to a British man-of-war for protection against Fijian and white-heretical persecution. The commander of H.M.S. "Calliope" excused himself, mentioning that, speaking of pictures, he had himself seen in the house of a Catholic missionary on Tongatabu an equally lurid print depicting a tree "from the branches of which all who did not adhere to the Popish church were represented as falling into hell-fire."[29]

From the beginning religious tolerance had no part in native thinking, and very little in missionary habits of mind. Rarotongan converts to Christ were accustomed to refer to their heathen brethren as "Satanees," a word obviously borrowed from white lips. Heathen villages in Samoa were invariably identified as the property of the devil. So it is not surprising that, on Rotuma and in the Tuamotu, natives committed to popery went to war with natives addicted to heresy,

[29]Thomas Williams, *Fiji and the Fijians,* 366.

and neither priest nor pastor was above blessing the arms of his embattled congregation. Naturally rival chiefs used religious affiliations in the game of prestige and power, most notably in Tonga, where Catholicism was identified with the doughty men of Bea, and Wesleyanism with the conquering George Tubou.

In this no-holds-barred controversy, heresy, as first comer, had the advantage of being more firmly entrenched with native government. Popery had more picturesque ritual, novelty, and could exploit native restlessness under the existing blue laws. By playing this card shrewdly popery might temper discipline to make itself more popular, as on Wallis Island, where even in a tight Catholic monopoly converts were allowed to play athletic games on Sunday afternoon, a thing unthinkable on heretical islands. Because heretical parsons knew well that a convert unduly irked by discipline would get a warm welcome if he shifted allegiance to the "popis," they tended to sing smaller and go more slowly. But on no important island could popery stamp out heresy as planned; it had to content itself with existing side-by-side with it. On Tahiti the L.M.S. had so successfully conditioned the native against Catholicism that, even after French occupation, the island remained prevalently Protestant. Intentional regulations gradually moved out the English missionaries on the ground there, but it was found necessary to send French Protestant pastors to take their places in the social structure of the island.

Catholic missionaries often resisted the temptation to make their careers too mundanely comfortable, as the heretics signally did not. A French naval officer making the acquaintance of the Islands in the late 'sixties wrote wonderingly of the contrast between the Protestant and Catholic ministers on the Loyalties. The Protestants, he remarked:

". . . go right to the point—to their own and their converts' material interests. By good advice and example they led their flocks to fruitful harvests, cleanliness and well being . . . On certain days designated in advance they are ready to receive their dues in kind and in cash. If these dues do not arrive, they do not complain, but deprive the delinquent of the help of their advice. . . . The native houses grouped round the chapel are clean and well kept, the women and children decently clothed in blue cottons, and having an air of happiness and health. As for the pastor in his parsonage with white walls covered with climbing vines, he has his wife for company, his waxed walnut furniture, his "keepsake" on the round table, and tea served with biscuits . . . At the other end of the is- land the French missionary lives in a hut on a little bread, when he knows how to bake it, and fruits that he gets from the trees. His garment is worn, his hat rubbed napless, his beard long and unkempt. His ragged troop of natives, whom he tries to clothe, sing hymns or run the woods dirty, hypocritical and corrupt. Nevertheless the reverend father is not sorrowful. His love for his Church and his hatred for Protestants suffice him." —Henri Rivière, *Souvenirs de la Nouvelle Calédonie*, 83–84.

Such examples of holy laxness and slatternliness were not, however, universal. Those accustomed to consider Catholicism always latitudinarian and to identify harsh blue laws with Puritanism—a point of view common among Americans— need to make the acquaintance of the hierocratic dictatorship that Père Laval of Picpus set up on Mangareva, principal island of the Gambiers.

This Père Laval had some reason to feel that the tall, hand- some and normally mercurial Polynesian people of the Gam- biers needed stern handling. When he and Père Caret landed there out of the Picpus establishment at Valparaiso, they were welcomed and taken to a hut where there were pretty girls eager to be nice. Even as Mr. Harris, the priests refused the honor and found that this was taken as an insult or sign of enmity, as indeed it was in Polynesian terms.[30] With darkness, Laval and Caret crept out of the hut and took to the mountain to wait for daylight, when they hoped to be able to sneak back to their boat. The natives discovered their escape and began to

[30]George Hamilton, surgeon of H.M.S. "Pandora," made the same dis- covery on Moorea in 1791. But he mended matters satisfactorily by sleeping with his *taio's* wife, since his profession did not impose chas- tity. (Basil Thomson [Ed.] Voyage of H.M.S. "Pandora," 109–10.)

beat the bushes for them. The priests took refuge in a cave; the natives fired the bush to smoke them out; it was just by God's grace that they were not smothered where they lay. Having survived, they moved to a smaller island near by where, through lucky cures of ailing chiefs, they obtained and cleverly expanded a foothold. In two years all local idols were burned and the mission was consolidated. For once God had a clear field. The mission dominated the principal chiefs and, since Mangareva was not a well-frequented spot, the fathers were not likely to be challenged for anything they chose to do.

They chose building, among other things. Laval had the monumental complex, so Mangareva was heaped high with a huge cathedral, a number of large churches, convents, and a jail, all on a megalomaniacal scale in Cyclopean masonry for which forced native labor provided the foot-pounds. The lagoon round the Gambiers had good pearl shell and occasional pearls, so the natives were also set to toiling as divers, heaping up more and more of these commodities which the mission sold in Tahiti for funds for the good cause. Estimates of the annual cash intake run over 60,000 francs, a very considerable sum in those days. So much arduous labor discouraged the natives, good Polynesians and never too fond of steady slavery, and led them to neglect their fishing and gardening. Their dwellings degenerated into mere hovels, their clothing into filthy rags, their diet into something well below subsistence. Intent on souls and not the things of this world, the mission paid little heed. Instead, as population declined, Laval organized expeditions to the Tuamotu to kidnap brawny heathens and bring them to Mangareva to fill the dwindling ranks of the godly.[31] Sometimes parties of despairing natives tried to escape in canoes. If caught, they were in very bad trouble; if not, they sometimes made land, sometimes were never heard of again.

The jail was always crowded with offenders against chastity and other Christian virtues. Flogging was a common punish-

[31]Spanish missions in California apparently followed the same procedure in their vigorous period. (Belcher, Sulphur, 119.)

ment. The confessional enabled the mission to detect sin and, as the culprit was marched off to rigorous discipline, passers-by threw filth at him in angry reprehension. A French skipper putting in to trade in 1854 was accused of eating meat on Friday, tied up and thrown into jail; the very hut he had stayed in was fumigated to remove the taint of sin, his bedclothes were publicly burned. Every night all unmarried girls were locked into a convent to prevent carnal congress during darkness. On the eve of every holy day married women too were incarcerated, lest their husbands pollute themselves. Laval perfectly exemplified Mr. Dooley's definition of a fanatic as "a man who does what he thinks God would do if He knew the facts of the case."

None of it could have been accomplished without hearty cooperation from the upper classes of Mangareva, exploiting the native tradition of obedience to arbitrary, bred-in-the-bone authority. It is easily possible to exaggerate the shock to the native. After all, he had never been able to call his soul his own before the white man came, and this was just a matter of a less comfortable set of tabus. But there is no such palliation for Laval. From any civilized western point of view his regime was an unmitigated disgrace.

It went unchecked for thirty years. The Gambiers were part of the French protectorate system in the Pacific with headquarters in Tahiti, but barring some gossip in Papeete, no official attention was paid to what was happening there. Then a French trader named Pignon, accompanied by his wife and an employee, came to Mangareva for a cargo of shell. Laval threw all three in jail on unspecified charges. Presently M. et Mme. Pignon were set free with instructions to go away and never come back, but the employee cooled his heels three months longer without trial on charges of adultery, whether with Mme. Pignon was not stated. Pignon protested, agonizedly—and loudly enough to be heard in Paris. The government of Mangareva was held liable to pay him 160,000 francs damages. But the Picpus order had good friends in Paris. The authorities in Tahiti allowed themselves to be calmed down, and little of the amount was ever paid. The transfer of Laval to another post was the only substantial result.

All this proved little, because the colleague who succeeded him carried on with his methods undisturbed while the Franco-Prussian war effectually distracted Paris from any such small matter as the holy bullying of a few hundred aborigines in the South Pacific. It was 1887 before responsible French authority came to the Gambiers; during all that interval the mission had run roughshod over the disappearing natives. By then Laval was dead.[32] He doubtless died confident that on his entry into Paradise the souls which he had saved from sin in spite of themselves would flock to welcome him.

As various island groups proclaimed white-style legal codes under Protestant persuasion, there appeared strange mixtures of codified liberality and personal restriction. Having searched the scriptures, Tahiti could find no excuse for capital punishment; exile was the heaviest permissible sentence. Raiatea installed trial by jury. But on the same islands confessions of adultery and other legally proscribed sins were obtained by looping a rope round a woman's middle with strong men dragging on either end until she either was cut in two or chose to talk. On conviction she was ineradicably tattooed in the forehead with a South Seas equivalent of the Scarlet Letter—the one instance in which Christianization did not frown on tattooing. Perhaps such use of rope, which recalls the Fijian method of wife-strangling, was the natives' idea; but mission protest could have stopped it. In Tonga a woman found without her blouse even in her own hut was fined two dollars; smoking cost her four in fine and costs; a shirtless man owed the law ten. The Broome Road on Tahiti, still the principal highway of the island, was built by native sinners working out fines at so many fathoms of road per offense, principally sins of the flesh. None of this astonishes anybody previously ac-

[32]Mangareva, Wallis Island, the Isle of Pines (off New Caledonia) still enjoy a South Seas reputation for being priest-ridden. See Sir Harry Luke, *From a South Sea Diary*, 199–204, for a marvelous case in the New Hebrides of a modern French Catholic missionary instigating wholesale murder among his flock out of the best motives.

quainted with missionaries' ideas of law and penology on Hawaii. But here it is a salutary reminder that, whether Catholic or Protestant, early missionary attitudes were often most uncivilized. And the consequences of their intrusion were often depressing, even to themselves.

On the other hand, missionaries cannot be rejected *en bloc* as personally and socially monstrous. Father Damien, the martyr of Molokai, was as much a member of the Congregation of Picpus as Laval. As for Protestants, it is worth while to know more about such a man as the Rev. John Williams of the L.M.S., already identified as the first Christian martyr of Eromanga, whose work under staggering difficulties stamps him a clever, earnest man of heart, hands and bowels. Successive L.M.S. mission ships have been named after him. "John Williams" is not as beautiful a name as some given these vessels, such as "Morning Star," "Southern Cross," "Jubilee," "Dayspring,"[33] but the honor is deserved, and a knowledge of the man's doughty doings must help greatly to bolster the morale of the modern tyro-missionary who boards the latest "John Williams" headed for his maiden station.

Williams was not perfect. He was at least morally responsible for the barbarism of criminal procedure on Raiatea, his particular island; and he was very hard on Mrs. Williams. She accompanied him whenever possible, had children as fast as John could beget them, and they died about as fast as she could deliver them. Nevertheless this ruddy, blocky man was the James Cook of the missionary world. He personally discovered Rarotonga (Cook Islands);[34] became chief pioneer of the gospel in the leeward group of the Societies, the Cooks and Samoa; died in harness trying to open up the New Hebrides for

[33]The first "Morning Star," "Southern Cross," etc. were built from funds contributed by Sunday School children buying ten cent or sixpenny shares.

[34]Or thought he did. The schooner "Cumberland," Goodenough master, brought to Port Jackson in 1814 a cargo of dyewood procured at "Larotonga," sixteen leagues east of Tongatabu, which Sir Everard im Thurn identifies as Rarotonga. Read 160 and it makes sense. Williams' discovery was in 1822. (Im Thurn, *Lockerby Journal*, 209.)

the L.M.S.; and was a sort of ordained Robinson Crusoe to boot.

Moved to range far and wide among the heathen, he badly wanted a ship; but all the L.M.S. had was an occasional chartered vessel to fetch supplies and reinforcements. On Rarotonga Williams had timber and could lay hands on a certain amount of iron—always a popular item in mission trade goods —and knew that with iron and timber ships were built. But he knew nothing of shipbuilding and little of seamanship, so he went at the matter step by step.

To work iron meant a forge; a forge meant a smith's bellows; so he made one on a design of his own, being unable to recall the details of the conventional type. After several changes and failures, it worked nicely. Ordinary mission equipment included hammers and sledges, so an efficient blacksmithy was possible, as soon as Williams had acquired, by trial and error, and taught the native converts, the art of forging. Next was a homemade turning lathe, no less, to make blocks for the running rigging out of ironwood (casuarina). There was no lack of labor. With the white man's metal adzes the natives squared timbers and worked split tree trunks down to planking, a technique already familiar in building up the freeboard of their large canoes. Cordage was rove out of tough and supple hibiscus fibre, sails were pandanus matting quilted for extra strength. The rudder pintles were cobbled together from a piece of broken pickax, a cooper's adz and a large hoe—on the vessel's first appearance in Tahiti "the officers of the vessels lying there . . . hastened on board to see this prodigy, and expressed not a little astonishment at every part of the ship, but especially at the rudder irons"[35]—as well they might.

In three months of such inspired improvisation Williams had a sixty-foot, seventy-ton hull that floated right side up and handled adequately under fore-and-aft rig. She was christened "The Messenger of Peace" and proved by a maiden voyage to Tahiti, where she received more conventional canvas and, to judge from illustrations in Williams' memoirs, was re-sparred

[35]Williams, *Narrative of Missionary Enterprise*, I, 170.

for square rig forward. Then, with a dove and olive branch—the missionary device—floating meekly at her masthead, manned largely by Polynesians, she took the reverend gentleman on an exploratory voyage round the Samoan group as competently as if a King's dockyard had taken a year to build her. Williams, of course, attributed her success principally to the Lord.

Such a man patently made sense of his own sort. He lived an effectively full life and died a hero.[36] It is unfair to reproach him or the better specimens among his colleagues for failure to make sense in terms of a hundred years later. Williams and his ilk implicitly believed that Protestant Christianity was as necessary to the welfare of human souls in this world and the next as insulin is to the diabetic. To take it to those who needed it they would go through hell and high water. Further, in order to set up the emotional climate conducive to Christian virtues which, without adequate Scriptural authority, they took to be chastity, sobriety. industry, reverence and cleanliness, they felt justified in encouraging native covetousness after white man's clothes and gadgets. The missionary should be "highly approving of whatever had a tendency to civilize the natives, to furnish them with useful employment"; the native should be taught that "idleness and irregular and debasing habits of life were as opposed to the principles of Christianity as to their own personal comfort;" and the mission was bound to "increase their wants or to make some of the comforts and decencies of society as desirable as the bare necessities of life."[37]

It sounds fatally more like the Proverbs of Solomon than the precepts of the Gospels. But these missionaries were inescapably as much European petty bourgeois or "mechanics"

[36]As mentioned before, the Melanesian natives of Eromanga in the New Hebrides knocked him in the head when he and a colleague were exploring mission possibilities thereabouts. I like his epitaph in the churchyard of the old mission church on Rarotonga: "Sacred/to the/Memory/of the/Rev. J. Williams/London Miss. Society/who, with his/Friend, Mr. Harris/was massacred by/deluded natives at/Eromanga while/attempting to convey/to them the blessings/of/Salvation. /Nov. 20, 1839."

[37]William Ellis, Polynesian Researches, II, 279.

with an ascetic bent as they were ministers of the Word. They came to the South Seas freighted, not only with the doctrine of salvation through the blood of Jesus Christ our Lord, but also with all the arbitrary moral attitudes of Manchester or Hartford, Conn. Nobody had ever told them, nor could they have understood, that the Gospel did not necessarily have anything to do with the desirability of plastered walls. The Gospel was one feature of white culture as the missionaries knew it at home; another was a concern with saving one's soul; a third was regular hours of work. Unquestioning, the missionary inculcated all three. Only in the last couple of generations has missionary zeal been diluted by the notion that a native can retain native economics or technology and still be a Christian.

Missions would have been better off if they had managed to keep their converts segregated from impious whites, whose versions of how things were done in Boston or Beritani differed confusingly from Misi's. A Maori chief, observing the floating brothels run by whites opposite the mission at the Bay of Islands, asked a missionary why he didn't make Christians of his own people before going to work on the Maori? Christians *tabud* fornication, drink, cheating? What about the resplendent naval captain, whom even Misi treated with respect, with his wine on the cabin table? What about the swindling, pimping trader, the woman-thirsty foremast hand? Misi might explain that such people were not exactly Christians in the full sense, but that was hard for the native to grasp. In his culture, unobserved *tabus* were inconceivable; a neglected *tabu* died, and neglect was rare. In modern jargon, the native was up against the phenomenon of the subculture, the sociological fact that, in a complex modern society, behavior patterns differ in overlapping, interpermeating stratifications. These lapses of continuity in western social anatomy are puzzling enough to the western-trained mind; at first they were utterly impossible for the South Seas native, reared in a monolithic, small scale, isolated culture, lacking written history to let him know that things had not always been as he knew them. In consequence he tended to slip confusedly from one set of white values to another; and so make a queer, but sometimes organically consistent, automatic selection of them to mortise into his own behavior.

Of his old values he usually retained the arbitrariness at least. The first step was exemplified in what happened in New Guinea when a Catholic missionary, trying to undermine *tabu* in a certain village, forcibly dragged native women through the *tabu*-to-women men's house. The men did not dare take vengeance on the missionary but, as soon as his back was turned, they redeemed the community's standing with the gods by killing the four women. Then came assimilation, sometimes grossly, sometimes subtly askew. Sunday on a *lotu*[38] island was observed with a rigidity that would have frightened Cotton Mather. A ship goes aground in a Fijian harbor, certain to break up if not re-floated before the tide changes. The native missionary says "but it's Sunday," and no help is forthcoming. Another Fijian Sunday coincides with the rising of the *palolo*[39] worm, the great annual but evanescent South Seas delicacy; the Wesleyan converts have to go to chapel all day and do without *palolo* that year, while the less Sabbatarian Catholic natives gorge on them. Williams records proudly how some of his natives, adrift in a canoe and starving, refused a good opportunity to fish because it was the Sabbath.

Those things occurred long ago; but even in recent times the *tabu*-mindedness of Islands would shame a Maccabean Jew. In 1934 a Japanese naval party sent to Truk (Carolines) to observe an eclipse reported on the inhabitants with irritation: No smoking, no drinking; when accompanying newspapermen asked for native songs, all the population knew was hymns; and when the officer in charge, eager to complete foundations

[38]*Lotu* was the Polynesian-developed word for the white man's religion in any form.

[39]The rising of *palolo*, the timing of which is a matter of great debate in the South Seas, marks the mating season of the creature. It appears that the organisms that come to the surface, where the natives scoop them in in great quantities, are the sexual portions of the worms themselves, which never leave their holes in the coral far below, where they remain drearily behind. Aldous Huxley might have dreamed it up.

for his instruments in time for the eclipse, asked the natives to help pour concrete on Sunday they refused as open-mouthed as if he had suggested their cutting their throats in the interests of science.

In 1946 I was on Majuro (Marshalls) just after the arrival of the first white missionary to return there. The first question put to her by the chiefs and elders was whether the young men, who had taken mightily to cigarettes during the American occupation, could remain church members if they continued to smoke.

Assimilation of white ways often meant serious social damage. Catholic missions in the Marquesas have long segregated girls not only in the interests of morality, Laval-style, but to check population decline, on the theory that the Marquesan taste for intercourse long before puberty damaged the reproductive organs. The objective is proper, however dubious medically; but the result damages the whole Marquesan pattern of emotional development. On Tikopia custom associated pregnancy only with marriage; so Tikopian lovers usually took precautions, whereas spouses did not, the community counting on infanticide or forced emigration to relieve population pressures. Christianity appeared, rejecting infanticide and insisting that a boy caught with a girl had to marry her, whether pregnant or not, making for earlier marriage and greater fecundity for, once being married, the new husband felt no customary obligation to be careful. When last heard from, the population was growing to dangerous heights. Missions could hardly have been expected to foresee that supernatural sanctions on marital fidelity would thus stimulate the birth rate; but the moral is that, once you tinker with the equilibrium of custom that makes up a society, you never know where repercussions will appear. Wrote Dr. Gordon Brown:

"Of those who intrude themselves into the life of a group other than their own, even with due sympathy and humility, we must say: 'Father, forgive them, they know not what they do.'"
—Quoted in Felix M. Keesing, The South Seas in the Modern World, 87.

That same French naval officer previously quoted on the contrasts between heretic and Popish missionary, later grew meditative about the great Mgr. Bataillon, the Marist missionary bishop who was to Wallis Island what Hiram Bingham was to Hawaii:

". . . a bishop of the twelfth century strayed into our own time . . . this huge old man of sixty-six with a long white beard, the beak of an eagle, pale blue eyes and the asceticism of a hermit, unbending, intrepid and authoritarian, has made the island Catholic from end to end . . . he is master of Wallis. He never allowed English missionaries to get a foothold there. He had no instructions to that effect, but he did not wish it, and that was that . . . He made the people fetch stones on their backs to build a cathedral which, with its two heavy, massive towers, rises toward heaven in the midst of the tiny native huts, a strange monument to another time and another world. Nevertheless the great bishop's old age is troubled and sad. He has so bent these innocents under yoke and rule that they no longer have either their own vices or their own virtues. Of the vices hypocrisy remains, of the virtues gayety, simplicity and cordiality have disappeared . . . Monseigneur Bataillon feels that his work is not good, but for all that he has no wish to mistrust it . . . He remains a great figure among those sowers of religion who harvest only barrenness."—Henri Rivière, Souvenirs de la Nouvelle Calédonie, 60–63.

Though, as this implies, South Seas missions have been a failure from any general point of view, they deserve fragmentary credit in some respects. On dry islands they often improved the native's water supply by building large churches, the corrugated iron roofs of which make excellent sanitary rain-water catchment. From kindness as well as good tactics, they did their ill-trained best to cure the native's ulcers, bellyaches and fevers, a charity that was perilous if an influential patient did not do well, and they have promoted cleanliness among their flocks. They accomplished much in discouraging internecine warfare among natives, partly by direct tactics, partly by backing native chiefs seeking a monopolistic power that could keep the peace which, on balance, was probably a good thing. They often wrought valiantly to protect the native from being swindled or kidnapped. They are primarily responsible for the high literacy—which has not relieved immense ignorance—among South Sea natives, particularly in Polynesia and Micronesia.

These achievements gradually encouraged intelligent people to contend that, however dim a view early observers like Melville and Kotzebue took of them, missions have on the whole been salutary for the native. Said Stevenson, a close and devout observer:

"I had conceived a great prejudice against Missions in the South Seas . . . that prejudice was at first reduced and then annihilated. Those who deblaterate against missions have only . . . to come and see them on the spot. They will see a great deal of good done; . . . At the same time . . . they will see a great deal of harm done. I am very glad to think that the new class of missionaries are by no means so radical as their predecessors . . . I wish I could say how strongly I feel the importance and efficiency of this new view."—Graham Balfour, *Life of Robert Louis Stevenson*, II, 229.

Some administrators in the Islands, particularly American and, in their day, Japanese, have done and do missions the compliment of actively desiring their presence, believing that the church not only gives the native something innocuous to keep him busy, but makes him positively more controllable. Others, particularly British, rely on missions for much native education and supplementary health measures. In his address opening the 1947 South Pacific Conference in Canberra, Dr. Evatt of Australia specified more and better missions as a desideratum for the Islands. These things chime in with Stevenson's approval of the new type of missionary as "less radical"—which, being interpreted, means more tolerant of any but the most startling native ways of doing. That may be said to have begun when the Rev. James Chalmers, renouncing previous mission attitudes about clothes, persuaded government to prohibit clothing above the waist for the natives of New Guinea. Many a modern South Seas missionary has been somewhat trained in ethnology or psychology to help him toward intelligent objectivity in handling his flock.

It sounds admirable. To object to less ignorance and more tolerance in missionaries or anybody else is a strange reaction. Yet for missions to shift their emphasis from soul-saving to social service means to abandon the only emotional basis that justifies their existence at all. Considering the Wesleyans in Tonga, Basil Thomson saw that clearly:

> "Missionaries are by the nature of their calling intolerant. Tolerance in an evangelist is a sign that he is unfit for his mission."
> —*The Diversions of a Prime Minister*, 202.[40]

The missionary can, in some fashion, help cushion the continuing shocks of white ways on natives, teach them reading and writing, dose their ailments and train them in sanitation, guided throughout by objective attitudes borrowed from science. But so far as those aims distract him from his prime function of soul-saving, he is perpetrating a well-meaning swindle on his backers, whether native or western.

There was higher intellectual integrity about his bigoted and ignorant predecessor who thought rival sects snares for the unwary, violations of the Decalogue risks of damnation, and who viewed without alarm the damage to his flock that necessarily resulted from his efforts to force them into godliness. It is reassuring to hear a nice young English girl in the South Seas say that she thinks it a shame to excommunicate from church a native girl who has an illegitimate baby: "The natives just don't think of sin the same way we do, and that's all there is

[40] If the reader tends to gag at this point, I recommend his reading Walter Lippmann, *American Inquisitors*, Chapter II; says Socrates to Thomas Jefferson: "Have you ever stopped to think what it means when a man acquires the scientific spirit? It means that he is ready to let things be what they may, whether or not he wants them to be that way. . . . that he has conquered his desire to have the world justify his prejudices . . . that he has learned to live without the support of any creed, that he can be happy, or at least serene, that he can be good, or at least humane, no matter what conclusion men may come to as to the origin of the world, or its plan, or its destiny . . . It is only when he has ceased to care about the result that he can trust himself wholly to free inquiry."

to it." Only if she feels that way, and a very good way too, she should not be, as she is, wife of a missionary. On another island I have waltzed with the head missionary's wife to the music of a Sunday School orchestra at a party for the church's social organization of young natives in a building erected by one of John Williams' most trusted colleagues. I contemplated the head missionary, also waltzing among his lambs, and felt mortally convinced that, for all his lack of tolerance, his long dead predecessor had done a far better job of preaching Christ and Him crucified to the heathen—which is, after all, what both of them went out there for.

Perhaps in reflection of this inconsistency, one finds zeal and energy most conspicuous in the modern South Seas among the missionaries of religious splinter-groups—Mormons or Adventists—than among those of the L.M.S., the Wesleyans, the Catholics, who pioneered the field. Natural dwindling of momentum has been accentuated by the new trend toward efforts at tolerance. Pleasant as the modern old-line missionary often is, the true spirit of Pentecost must be sought among the scrawny, chinless, half-baked soldiers of newer and livelier faiths who are now struggling to take converts away from their elder rivals. Since religious schism in a village usually means civil discord to match, governments view their activities with distaste. The authorities of several island groups are trying to freeze out the zealots by granting entry permits to missionaries on a quota basis. Thus, if Tarafu today has 20,000 Wesleyans, 5,000 L.M.S., 4,000 Catholics, 2,000 Mormons, and 500 Adventists, among the native population, and one missionary per 1,000 communicants is permitted, the Mormons and Adventists are badly handicapped in any active proselyting. Tonga accomplishes the same result by freezing the number of missionaries per sect at the number in service during one of the war years, when most of the Mormon emissaries, being young fellows earning their spurs in the Church, had gone home to go into uniform. The Tongan State Church is a great thing in local politics and takes a dim view of energetic rivals.

Mormons occupy a special corner of this background. From

the American hive an annual swarm of nondescript young men migrates to the South Seas to missionize for the period required of all aspirants to the complicated hierarchy of the Saints' church. Both the Salt Lake (polygamous in doctrine) and the Independence, Mo. (the contrary) varieties are represented. They are handicapped by Joe Smith's Word of Wisdom forbidding tea, coffee, alcohol, and tobacco, which they sometimes make the tactical error of trying to impose on a native very fond of all those things. But they have plenty of backing and energy and, as one official said sourly, "If they don't get everything they think they have a right to here, they come right round and try to flap the American eagle at me." So a picture of Brigham Young often appears on the wall of the native shack along with King George or General de Gaulle. Their superiors wisely give them good grounding in appropriate native languages before loosing them, and some New Zealanders profess considerable admiration for the Saints' sporadic success in keeping the Maori at work and sober.

No responsible observer can deny that many a modern missionary is a good fellow, as parsons go. I remember a young Catholic priest, sweaty in dungarees, toiling with great good humor to get a chapel rebuilt with assistance from native converts, planning re-education of his flock in land use and in the introduction of new crops—a capable young man without a selfish shred in his body and unmistakably fond of his communicants. He was doing them good—material good. He should have been out under the trees preaching the passion of Our Lord or the efficacy of the Sacraments. Why use a priest as an amateur county agent?

This point is beginning to make its way in the thinking of some responsible officials in the Islands. Native contributions to their white-supervised local churches, now usually autonomous or close to it, are often as high per capita as taxes. They are, in fact, ecclesiastical taxes and, having prestige and public opinion as sanctions, are more readily collected. The native gets a good deal of value back in the shape of schooling and good advice; but that situation may not continue to be taken for granted. The Islands in general need more outside manufactures, medicines, construction equipment, consumers' goods, and more expert assistance in medicine, engineering, and agriculture, than they now get. Both are costly, and export resources with which to pay for them are slender, while Congresses and Parliaments tend to balk at heavier subsidy of Island economies. Money now going to the mission church would certainly buy more such necessaries if the government handled it. One high official told me, "I know nothing that missions do for natives, except perhaps saving their souls, that government could not do better at less cost." Said another more crisply, "If it could be managed gradually over five years, I'd like to see every missionary off the island." Such talk would have been unthinkable a generation ago, when mission funds and mission prestige were indispensable in the Island picture.

Nevertheless, emotional and economic vested interests and the cohesive momentum characteristic of all institutions will probably keep South Sea missions existing for a long time to come. Children's pennies, adults' quarters in perforated envelopes, will continue to drop into green-lined wooden plates in sooty-bricked churches and some of them will pay for the transportation and regular Sabbaticals of parsons and wives down among the Islands. The native will continue to give the Lord more than he can afford—although no doubt, the bargain is worth while in social satisfaction. And the government will continue to wish that it had the dread of hell and the stimulus of ostentation to help it collect its rightful dues.

A queer business altogether, with shockingly little life in it from any Christian point of view. The gigantic churches are being replastered along the north side of Upolu; but it has been a long time since intruding parsons really believed they were saving native souls from eternal perdition. The crumbly gray coral church on Rarotonga which shelters the monument to John Williams already looks a thousand, not an actual hundred, years old.

Recently I stood watching a sunset from a headland over Matavai Bay where the "Duff" landed the first contingent of the Lord's soldiers seriously to assail the spiritual darkness of Polynesia. By now every Tahitian is somehow converted. In token of this brilliant victory of white spiritual values, the population is rotten with syphilis and drunkenness, about as near promiscuous as ever, hopeless and shiftless; unless those who should know are utterly mistaken, not one in a hundred modern Tahitians is close enough to the spiritual hang of Christianity to have any hope of avoiding frying in hell.[41] I kept thinking of the honest and able little missionary I had talked with a few weeks before on another island who, in a moment of candid discouragement, said that the best anybody could do with these people was to make rigid Pharisees out of them—and even that seldom happened. After all, it took two thousand years to produce even the small proportion of western churchgoers who could, in any conceivable sense of the word, be called Christians. No wonder the missionary with some education and energy prefers to do amateur social work, where he can occasionally see some small results.

[41]The terrors of hell seem to play a large part in native pastors' sermons and, though few results are visible in the Islanders' behavior, there is some reason to believe that they have bitten rather deeply into the emotional substructure of some natives. For an account of the devil-and-pitchfork trend of bad dreams in a Polynesian society, as uncovered by a physician interested in psychiatry, see Beaglehole, "Psychic Stress in a Tongan Village," Proceedings of the Sixth Pacific Science Congress, Vol. IV.

6

Unsavory Characters

> . . . if they were not convicts, they ought to have
> been.
>
> —Basil Thomson, *The Fijians*

IN ANY AREA THAT ATTRACTS MISFITS AND RENEGADES, some unsavory characters rise to the top to leave personal marks on the scum. In early times the South Seas probably suffered rascals equal to any, but most of them are indistinct. Little is known of Rives, French toady to Kamehameha II; or of the Yankee skipper who kidnapped the Easter Islanders; or of Charlie Savage, the terrible Swede of Fiji. But, as men-of-war began regularly to police the Islands and report home, as western powers took up investigation of South Sea imbroglios, the second half of the nineteenth century produced details about a number of most peculiar individuals. Here are a few known samples, at least two of whom could be called American:

The most famous, some would say the most romantic, was William Henry ("Bully") Hayes. Hack writers have used him in Robin-Hoodish novels, and the works of Louis Becke, who claimed to have sailed as his supercargo, are full of admiration of the great man. In all fairness he seems actually to have been a smalltime thief and swindler and a nasty type of woman chaser with a touch of homicidal mania and a neurotic mistrust of alcohol. The one good thing recorded of him is that he was kind to animals; though that would sound better if he had not been so savage toward human beings. But he was also glib and charming. A trader whom Hayes offhandedly left stranded on a poverty-stricken atoll in the Marshalls for several years confessed that, angry as he was, the great man could probably jolly him out of it in ten minutes if he wished. Twice Hayes squirmed out of arrest by the captain of a man-of-war— once H.M.S. "Rosario," once U.S.S. "Narragansett." He did not altogether succeed in staying out of jail; but, if he had done time for his every frowsy crime, a millennium would not have been long enough.

This "great, big-bearded, bald-headed man weighing 236 pounds with a soft voice and persuading ways"[1] was nevertheless the single best known "character" in the South Seas. (Out that way the word has a special meaning; when an old-timer admiringly tells you that so-and-so is a "character," prepare yourself for the smart aleck, the antisocial, the egocentric, often the psychopathic.) Some said that Hayes was Cleveland-born and learned seamanship on Lake schooners; others that he was son of a Mississippi bargeman and started his career by absconding with $4,000 of his father's money: there is no explanation of how a bargeman acquired so much. Romantics cherished rumors that he had been an officer in the U.S. Navy and quit the service after a quarrel over a lady with a brother-officer. But then a similar past is attributed to Benjamin ("Bully") Pease who, as occasional partner and frequent adversary, supports Hayes in South Sea yarns. A skilful singer and player of accordion and piano, Hayes is said to have first come to the Pacific as head of a variety troupe touring New Zealand. An ugly little story has him abducting a stage-struck girl of seventeen and seducing her forcibly when she failed to give in to his charm. Then he was master of a collier between Newcastle (Australia) and New Zealand, which enabled him to run guns and ammunition to Maori rebels.

It is all shadowy, and usually shady, patched together by Hayes fans from apocryphal tales and newspaper clippings. In any case the man was hither and yon in the South Seas in the

[1] Frederick Moss, *Through Atolls and Islands*, 84.

'sixties and 'seventies in one or another fast, trim, heavily-armed brig or schooner, putting in wherever law was weak or nonexistent and a dishonest dollar could be turned. His crews were hard-cased mixtures of Filipinos, Chileños, Portuguese and Islanders; and, being a sort of seagoing tomcat, he usually had one or more women on board. The big, fast-talking, cocksure man—I picture him with the very wide-open, shiny eyes that characterize certain psychopathological types—did very well with women. His "wives," white or brown, were often eloped with, sometimes stolen, sometimes bought. One of the best-known in the succession lost her standing by being too sentimental; annoyed by her snivelling over his brutality toward natives, Hayes put her ashore in Honolulu, where she became locally well known as "Stormbird Emma," a seamstress for Kalakaua's court. Stormbird Emma loved snuff, gin and hymns. When old and blind and full of gin, she would weep over the wickedness she had seen with Hayes; and her favorite hymn, which she would ask a neighbor child to sing over and over, was *Count Your Many Blessings*.

A typical and well-authenticated Hayes caper started with his appearance at a small New Zealand port in the "Rona," on board which he had three white poodles, two white "wives," each with a baby, and a cargo of general merchandise acquired heaven knows how. The inhabitants of the isolated town eagerly bought at auction and paid cash, goods to be landed next day. Hayes sailed at daybreak, keeping the cash, neglecting to land the goods. It was as simple as that. When the sheriff of Maui (Hawaii) attached his ship for unpaid bills, Hayes got the law drunk belowside and then sailed defiantly, sending his victim ashore in a small boat. Naturally he never went back to Maui, but the Pacific was full of fresh islands. Many a ship's chandler or other shore creditor knew how adept Bully Hayes was at "paying with the fore-topsail." His economics also included dabbling in the human head trade, sometimes decapitating his own raw material; using force or forged orders to collect other men's oil or copra from isolated trading stations; ship stealing—his best known vessel, the beautiful "Leonora," was said to have been stolen from Bully Pease; and blackbirding.

The blackbirding began, they say, when his ship came to grief on Manahiki and the natives helped him build a small vessel to get away in. In return Hayes offered to transport a number of them to a wedding feast on near-by Rakahanga. Somehow they missed Rakahanga and got to Samoa, where the natives found themselves persuaded to sign on as plantation labor, Hayes receiving so much per head. He did better later taking a batch of Chinese labor to an Australian contractor, Hayes to pay £10 per Chinese as head tax due at Melbourne. Off Melbourne he had the ship pumped half-full of water and flew signals of distress. Rescue craft came out; Hayes urged them to "save the poor Chinamen" while he and the crew hunted for the leak. The moment the Chinese were ashore, he began to pump ship and presently cracked on all sail and disappeared over the horizon, Chinese landed and £3,000 in tax money still in his strongbox.

For him that was a big operation. Nor was labor recruiting his specialty, since it required some reliability. His petty villainies probably never made him a rich man though, of course, legend had him burying $250,000 on Kusaie (Carolines), a favorite haunt of his. As long as it suited his book, they say, he had the "Boston" missionaries on Kusaie convinced that he was a devout Congregationalist. But another tale has him so irritated by the intrusion of the "Morning Star" mission ship at Pingelap (Marshalls) that he forced the mission party to dance themselves to exhaustion to the music of his accordion. Doubtless he could appear pious well enough on occasion. He managed to borrow $50 from the Rev. Mr. Damon of Hawaii, and he talked guilt and repentance very handsomely to the Rev. Mr. Chalmers during a charter voyage in which the "Leonora" took a mission party home from Niue (Savage Island), where their ship had been wrecked. If he had only had proper influences when a boy, said this reeking rascal, he would not have been so wicked. He not only put up with prayers in the cabin before meals, as he had agreed to, he actually curbed his own blasphemy—he usually swore every time he opened his mouth—and ordered the astounded crew to muster aft and listen respectfully at every service the missionaries chose to hold. Chalmers paid him in gold in a small canvas bag; the day after the payment Hayes slugged and killed his mate with that same bag of godly gold.

What became of him is not certain. He was heard of in Manila as imprisoned for helping convicts escape from Guam, getting converted to Catholicism—coming the pious again—which moved the Bishop of Manila to intercede for his release, and going back to the States at public expense as a destitute seaman. Then, one story goes, he promoted himself a small vessel and sailed from San Francisco on his last voyage. Brutalizing his Scandinavian cook—some say it was a Chinese—too expertly, he was defied and went below for his revolver. When his head reappeared up the companionway, the cook cracked it with the iron boom crutch, weighted the unconscious body and pushed it overboard. How he died is not significant. That he lived so long was the scandal. His best epitaph was written by Mrs. Robert Louis Stevenson: " 'Bully Hayes' and 'Bully Pease' . . . of whose names I'm quite sick."[2]

At worst, however, this was a killer at retail. Charles-Marie-Bonaventure du Breil, Marquis de Rays, was a killer at wholesale, operating at the victim's expense and at long range, without the risk of going to the South Seas himself.

He was not a marquis, he was probably not noble at all. Growing up during the July Monarchy and the Second Empire, when France was actively imperialistic, he developed a neurotic degree of colonial mindedness. After adventures in the American West, it appears, he was a trader in Senegal; when further efforts to gain colonial experience in Madagascar or Indo-China were fruitless, he retired to a penurious life in his native Brittany. Somehow he acquired the title of Bolivian consul at Brest. Blue-eyed, ruddy, and stoutish, with a fat but not fierce moustache, rather like a blond version of Grover Cleveland, he inspired confidence both by his presence and his

[2] Cruise of the "Janet Nichol," 92.

ostentatiously devout Catholicism. His politics, of an aristocratic tinge, led him to look sourly at that turbulent child of
the times, the Third Republic.

In studying distant places, the Marquis was attracted by
enthusiastic descriptions of New Ireland as an earthly paradise. France had small claim to New Ireland, but the status of
most of Melanesia was still vague, and the Marquis rather preferred to play a lone hand without government help. He
envisioned an idyllic, pious, fertile colony at a spot which he
renamed Port-Breton, where Frenchmen and others of good
will were to get away from the jangling, anticlerical, antiroyal-
ist atmosphere of the French 'seventies and live industrious,
happy, peaceful, prosperous lives like decent people and good
Catholics.

In 1877 a Paris newspaper carried the first advertisement of
Port-Breton. Within two years the Marquis had a propaganda
organ of his own—*La Nouvelle-France*—subscribers and volun-
teers for emigration to apply at offices in Marseilles and Le
Havre. This imaginative paper carried a standing cut of Port-
Breton with a beautiful cascade in the background, the foreground occupied by jolly French planters fraternizing with
respectful and admiring natives. All this, if you please, before
a single colonist had set foot on the place. But the Marquis
was not clever at the thorny metaphysical problem of distinguishing between what may be and what already is. The worse
things grew later at Port-Breton—and they got very bad indeed
—the more determinedly did he publish pictures of rich fields
of growing corn, flourishing plantations of coconut and banana,
and neat public works, cathedrals, bridges and offices. It was
Martin Chuzzlewit's Eden revived in Melanesia. With the
same gambit that Zephaniah Scadder used to impress Martin,
the Marquis' propaganda occasionally made candid admis-
sions: Hogs did marvellously at Port-Breton, but nobody could
deny that the climate did not suit sheep.

Anybody who thinks Frenchmen congenitally hardheaded
should study Port-Breton. On the platform and in print the
Marquis crooned about tropical breezes, rich lands, crystal

streams, teeming crops, and pious industry under one's own vine and fig-tree, and suckers appeared at the subscription offices in gratifying numbers. It stood to reason that so devout a nobleman would not take so much trouble unless he knew his scheme to be practical. Small *rentiers*, peasants, white-collar workers, liquidated their savings to buy shares in the *Société des Fermiers-Généraux* which was to exploit lands at Port-Breton purchased by stay-at-home investors, and in the *Société des Sucreries et des Distilleries*, which was to make brilliant profits from the sugar cane that, it was implied, already covered large areas of the colony. The devout who could not invest were urged to send in fittings for the churches and clothing for the savages of the colony.

If de Rays had been a simple swindler, he would have collected funds as long as possible and then decamped—as Daudet made him do in *Port-Tarascon*. But, unable to disbelieve his own fantasies, he insisted on actually sending out colonists. He was not too successful in recruiting his own countrymen. The first group of adventurers consisted of forty Germans, only twenty-five Frenchmen, a scattering of Swiss and Belgians; later he did great execution among credulous Italians. The first ship was a 900-ton three-master called the "Chandernagor," bought with subscription funds. Each embarking colonist was given a written promise of food, lodging, five francs a month pocket money and, at the end of five years, five hectares of land and a four-room house of coral, stone or brick. It is difficult not to grin at the great show of businesslike definiteness, but it proved no joke for the poor souls making the passage.

The French authorities refused the ship clearance, and captain and crew quit. De Rays had her towed to Antwerp, the colonists following by rail. The Belgian government also was dubious; he shifted the ship to Flushing. A fresh crew was signed on and she sailed hurriedly at three A.M. to give the Dutch minimum time to think the matter over. The eighty-nine innocents thus smuggled to sea had better luck than they deserved, making Melanesia without mishap; they saw the

Laughlan Islands, off the eastern end of New Guinea, on January 4, 1880. Seventeen settlers with three months' stores landed to colonize there, why is not clear, and the rest went ashore at Port-Breton and took formal possession in the name of the Marquis. Apparently they did not wonder why, in view of representations already made, such a ceremony was necessary.

Perhaps they were distracted by physical troubles, which came quickly and thickly. The water was brackish. The climate was steamy. The place teemed with mosquitoes and soon with malaria. There were no medicines, no sign of buildings. The famous cascade was a disappointing trickle. A few rational persons who tried to get back on board after looking about ashore were warned off at revolver-point, and the ship sailed for Sydney to cable de Rays for more supplies.

The consequences hardly need describing. A Melanesian foreshore is no place for people neither accustomed to nor equipped for the deep tropics. The natives did not attack; soon, in fact, the colonists were bartering their clothes with the natives for food. But all other calamities reported present. To make matters worse, the emigrants were a mixture of misfits and jangling nationalities and, according to the Rev. George Brown who rescued some of them, many were too peevish or discouraged even to help build emergency shelters for their own sick.

The fate of the party on the Laughlans is a good sample: a few fled in a canoe and were rescued at Teste Island with one man dead. Those left behind were taken off by a British brig after four had already died. A canoe party of six from Port-Breton managed to make Buka (Solomons), where natives found them drifting exhausted, tied them up and carried them to their chief. Five were eventually killed and eaten. The sixth, a born-lucky Italian, survived by the chief's favor, but had to turn cannibal to avoid offending his patron. It is not stated whether portions of his comrades were included in his diet. The bulk of the Port-Breton party was rescued by Wesleyan missionaries in such bad shape that twelve died on the rescue voyage. The worst of this very grim joke came when the

"Chandernagor," returning from Sydney to find only ten plucky colonists still on the spot, proved loaded, not with food, but with inedible building materials and industrial materials, a steam crane, incubators, sugar refining machinery, and tools including knives without handles and wheelbarrows without wheels. The remaining ten gave up. For the time being Port-Breton was deserted.

But back in Europe de Rays was solemnly proceeding with plans. The French authorities had grown so querulous that he shifted headquarters to Barcelona, where genius would be less hampered. He founded and sold shares in a shipping line to connect Le Havre with China and Port-Breton. On his coat were decorations from the Bey of Tunis and the Republic of Liberia, which professed to admire his scheme as somehow benefitting the negro race. And he did despatch a supply ship under Liberian registry to Port-Breton, which arrived to find the colony vanished.

Incredible as it sounds, two more emigrant ships eventually went out, carrying administrative and police officers and priests to look after souls and convert heathen. The Marquis thought of everything. Convalescing survivors of the first expedition had been greatly edified to receive complete, detailed instructions as to laying out the colony—one district for noblesse, one for bourgeoisie, a third for workmen; a central barracks for the police; and not only the site, but the heroic dimensions of, the cathedral. Reinforcements fared no better than vanguard, and had the extra handicap of including women. The site was shifted, but malaria and dysentery were everywhere.

The most sensible man in the picture was the captain of the Nouvelle-Bretagne, the last ship to arrive. Finding the colony rotten with disease and gloom, he sailed off to Manila and cabled the Marquis for funds for emergency provisions and medicines. A return cable promised 150,000 francs. Only 27,-000 arrived; whereas the captain had already loaded far more than 27,000 francs' worth of goods. On complaint of an uneasy merchant the Spanish authorities seized the ship for unpaid bills. Desperately conscious of death and starvation at Port-

Breton, the captain slipped his cable with six Spanish men-in-possession on board and paid his bills with the fore-topsail true Hayes-style, if for different motives, releasing the guards in a small boat only when reaching the open sea.

So supplies reached the starving. But a few days later a Spanish gunboat steamed fiercely over the horizon and took ship and captain back to Manila. The Spanish allowed humanitarian motives as exonerating the captain, but he was confined for months during successive trials. So the only hero in the story, except possibly the cannibalistic Italian, did time in jail for his heroism.

Nevertheless the gunboat offered escape to some of the colonists; the rest got away later on the supply ship, which had been rusting at anchor all the while. Some of the Italians settled in New South Wales, where a survivor or two can still be found. The French trickled back to France to make indignant noises about the Marquis de Rays. With his lieutenants, some of whom apparently believed in him, the Marquis was haled into court. And high time.

His defense was partly that he was being persecuted, partly that he had acted from the highest motives throughout. Nevertheless he had spent some 2,000,000 francs (then $400,000) of other people's money and accomplished only the deaths of a ghastly proportion of them; and he had had the bad taste to live well himself, in sharp contrast with conditions at Port-Breton, running through an impressive list of toothsome women and rich wines. He got four years and 3,000 francs fine. A more fitting penalty would have been exile to Port-Breton where, it was reported a while ago, only a huge rusty cogwheel half-buried in the sand of the beach remains of the whole fantasy.

Guileful imagination responded vigorously to South Sea air. It stimulated an adventurer called Walter Murray Gibson into becoming one of the few ever to swindle Brigham Young and get away scot-free.

The most indicative glimpse of Gibson comes via Nathaniel Hawthorne. While the novelist was U.S. consul at Liverpool,

Gibson came asking a guarantee of thirty pounds for a steamer-passage back to the States. It was granted. But instead of taking his gains and disappearing, this gentlemanly applicant stayed for hours, overwhelming the consul with well-told but windy globe-trotting lies about ape men in Ceylon[3] and Sumatran houris. What particularly fascinated Hawthorne, however, was the man's account of his errand in England:

He was born on an American-bound Spanish ship, he said; he had always considered as his parents the American couple who took him ashore in New York and reared him as their own. But he had lately discovered that, the same night on that ship, an aristocratic Englishwoman had given birth to a boy, and—as any devotee of the Victorian drama could readily have foreseen—the babies got swapped. Though lacking any strawberry mark on his left shoulder, Gibson had come to England seeking his rights to an unidentified coronet and, unsuccessful, was returning in disgust to more democratic climes.

A man who would try such a tale with a straight face in a big seaport consulate obviously had special qualities. Throughout his career Gibson never used a plausible lie when an implausible one could be concocted; in his own extravagant way he was an artist. Teacher, traveler, amateur filibuster, inventor, lecturer, author, missionary, politician, vendor of international snake oil, and shyster champion of the dark-skinned underdog, he demands attention for versatility alone.

That story of his birth at sea does well enough to get him on stage. For years after that there is only his somewhat fly-blown word for his history. He drifted South—or maybe West, for he also told yarns about living with Indian tribes—taught school in the Carolinas, married and was early left a widower with two children. He may have visited San Francisco in Gold Rush times and made some sort of killing. He was somehow in Mexico, then in Guatemala tied up with a group of intending revolutionists, in whose behalf he was to command a revo-

[3]It was the Dutch East Indies that harbored these creatures when Gibson reported them later to the American Geographical and Statistical Society.

lutionary navy. Presently he was in New York with resources sufficient to buy the start of it in the shape of an obsolete revenue cutter, the "Flirt."

He took her south with a cargo of ice and nobody knows what as armament, but he never made Guatemala. Ice and vessel melted away; the next seen of the latter she was off Sumatra in the Dutch East Indies. Whatever Central American junta had paid for her, she was now a private yacht and Gibson was "Captain Walter," her wealthy owner sailing for his pleasure, with the incidental purpose of collecting a long overdue inheritance from the estate of a deceased relative in Singapore.

Aware of unrest in their East Indian empire, the Dutch studied the "Flirt's" gun ports and surmised that Gibson might be more than a mere well-heeled gypsy. He was reported talking wildly of touchy matters ashore; then up the coast his mate was arrested in possession of a damning letter from Captain Walter to a disaffected local sultan. It mentioned getting rid of all Dutchmen and hinted that Captain Walter had at beck and call the resources of the United States, with "no want of powder, bullets, muskets, guns, . . . steamers, and warships." The man was playing filibuster in the richest possessions under the Dutch flag. Naturally, he landed behind bars.

The sheer lunacy of the idea was nothing to trouble him. He was always the amateur with too seething an imagination for any sense of proportion. In this emergency his story was that he had meant the letter solely as a cordial gesture; and that the native who composed it for him must have been an agent provocateur, for he himself did not know enough Malay to check the tenor of what he had signed. After several trials and appeals he was lucky to get off with half an hour in the pillory and fifteen years at hard labor. Before starting to serve his sentence he escaped, under circumstances which suggest that the Dutch, perhaps uncertain as to his precise importance and backing, were not unwilling to get him off their hands after clearing up the record.

Smuggled on board an American vessel, he landed in the

States crying for vengeance, prevailing on the State Department to lodge him a claim on the Dutch for $100,000 damages. The Dutch refused to pay serious attention, and the U.S. minister at the Hague vaguely threatened hostile action. But Gibson's case turned up a fatal flaw; when at low ebb in prison, he had written the Dutch governor a letter confessing himself a guilty ass:

"I now desire . . . to throw myself on your Excellency's clemency. I avow . . . that I have allowed my fancy and my vanity to get the better of my judgment . . . I remember to have indulged in bravados that I would become a potentate in the East . . . but I must ever add that this was after a plentiful indulgence in wine. I have been too often led away in life by some highly colored romantic idea . . ."[4]

A copy of this letter had been in the file on Gibson sent to Washington by the Dutch to rebut his claim. But presently there was no such paper to correspond to the docket of the file. It was recalled that Captain Gibson had been given access to this file early in the proceedings. The appropriate conclusion was drawn, and Uncle Sam hastily dropped the case.

Gibson went on a lecture tour describing with equal fervor his own wrongs and the beauties, human and physiographical, of the Malay lands. He also wrote a fictionized account of his adventures called *The Prison of Weltevreden*. Its lush yet kittenish style shows him spending his time in prison learning Malay, converting natives to Christianity, and tossing off mechanical inventions for the Dutch, who gladly availed themselves of his genius. Urbane long-suffering is the keynote, well sustained. And his only crime, he gently makes it clear, was too great sympathy with the natives.[5]

Just before the Civil War he turned up in Salt Lake City where, as a minor celebrity, he met Brigham Young. The pair got on well. Gibson said that Young nursed him affectionately through a serious illness. To his new friend the convalescent

[4] *The Shepherd Saint of Lanai*, 26.
[5] Principal sources on Gibson up to this point are *The Prison of Weltevreden* and *The Shepherd Saint of Lanai*.

unfolded what was henceforth his chronic obsession, a project for a benevolent colony in the South Pacific, sometimes in his beloved Indies, sometimes in Papua which, though he had never been there, sounded like an empty and likely place. Young listened. He had just fought off Federal efforts to align Utah with the rest of the nation and, still apprehensive, seems to have been projecting yet another Zion far from the meddling Stars and Stripes. Now he suggested that this enterprising Gentile study Mormonism; if its doctrines appealed, business might be done.

Gibson studied, professed belief—as he would have professed belief in Voodoo to further his schemes—and was sent to Hawaii to bolster Mormon influence in the Pacific. The nucleus of Saints recently planted on Lanai had been recalled for "the Mormon War"; but a few converted natives remained and the land-grants obtained from local chiefs were still viable. They centered in Palawai Basin, an extinct volcanic crater which lacked only adequate water for its rich soil. The Mormon settlement within this crater was called the City of Joseph.

Gibson squared off the land titles and, to judge from scraps of his diary, fell in love with Lanai, not a prepossessing spot naturally, but for which he foresaw a great future as a springboard for a Pacific-minded schemer:

"The Hawaiian islands take the place of the Malay archipelago in my thoughts . . . They are material for a very little kingdom . . . and surely seem but small material for me after all the hope and grasp of my heart . . . a little kingdom of love and worship . . . I would fill this lovely crater with corn and wine and oil and babies and love and brotherly rejoicing and sisterly kisses and the memory of me forever more . . . there with my brown ragamuffins [i.e., Hawaiian converts] I could bid the Prince of Peace welcome . . . I for want of a better am their Prince and their Father . . . I claim direct revelation as well as Moses and Elisha . . . Lanai shall be famous in Malaysia, in Oceanica . . . Blessed is Lanai among the isles of the sea."—Typescript of portion of Gibson diary, Hawaiian Archives.

Psychiatry has labels for these symptoms, but they rarely appear in so mellifluously benevolent a form. Throughout Gibson thinks of himself as "lover of the weak island races that had no friend," and patronizingly but kindly calls the Hawaiian "an interesting yet feeble younger brother, a subject for an Oceanic empire."[6] In preparation for empire building he learned Hawaiian—a present-day expert highly admires his style in that deceptively simple language—and industriously experimented with cotton, corn, sisal, sheep, cattle, to build up the resources of his arid principality.

His next move was foreshadowed by a curious lack in his diary: it seldom mentions Mormonism. When pinned down by the inquisitive in Honolulu, Gibson never quite admitted himself a Mormon emissary, though there was no secret about the Saints' activity in the Islands and he owed his hold on Lanai to his standing as Young's deputy for the Pacific. Honolulu suspected him anyway. Whereas the Islands were hot for the Union, Gibson sometimes slipped into secessionist-flavored talk; rumor said he was flying the Rebel flag on Lanai. Investigation, however, proved the flag in question to display eight stars for the eight Islands and the mystic inscription CJCLDSIH—initials of "Church of Jesus Christ of the Latter Day Saints in Hawaii." But Hawaii already had a flag; and the filibuster scares of the 'fifties, with one of which Sam Brannan, the Mormon renegade, had been connected, were still lively in Island minds. The thoughtful kept a suspicious eye cocked in Gibson's direction.

Within three years suspicion had something to feed on. Gibson's methods in recruiting immigrants for Lanai were sometimes highhanded. Rebellious aides denounced him in Honolulu as a penurious dictator; disgruntled native converts appealed to Salt Lake City. A Mormon commission of inquiry found plenty of reason to expel Gibson from the Church and did so, summoning him to quit Lanai and turn over the Saints' holdings. A hitch developed. The titles were sound, but they ran not in the name CJCLDSIH, but in that of one Walter

[6] Typescript of portion of Gibson diary, Hawaiian Archives.

Murray Gibson. Brigham Young had been shamelessly led up the garden path. The Church's only recourse was to inscribe the traitor's name high on the roll of Mormon apostates. A reporter covering the Confederate flag incident had already recorded a detail that sounded wistful in retrospect: the favorite hymn of the Lanai Mormons was "When I can read my title clear . . ."

Secure in his island kingdom, Gibson ignored the Saints' outraged bellows—though Honolulu gossip had his steps dogged by Mormon assassins in a melodramatic vein that he 'may well have authored himself—and began to feel his way into Island politics. He began with adhering to the respectable, non-native elements but, piously as he talked, got nowhere. So he turned *haole* leader of nativism, with, it was said, some Catholic support. Avowed friend of dark-skinned peoples, head of an Hawaiian community and expert in the Hawaiian language, he was admirably situated for fishing in the troubled waters surrounding the last Kamehamehas and Kalakaua. Moving to Honolulu, he published little newspapers called successively *Nuhou* (News) and *Elele* (Messenger), which worked to inflame the native sense of grievance. Elected to the Hawaiian legislature, he championed nativist projects. When Kalakaua came to the throne and turned nativist, Gibson was ready for his opportunity.

One of his minor grafts makes curious reading. The legislature granted him $1,500 to write and publish a booklet on *Sanitary Instructions for Hawaiians*, for which task his experience as moral and physical guardian of Lanai was considered to qualify him. Enemies said that $250 would have been high. But they could not complain of lack of sense in the copy. Gibson was an able man; but it was unfortunately true that he also had a shingle off. His booklet pronounced soundly against alcohol, overeating, irregular meals, the sterilizing effect of gonorrhea, love philtres, picking the teeth in public, using highways and paths as latrines, and horseback riding for pregnant women. He favored vegetables to prevent constipation, frequent washing, marital fidelity, and privacy in the home as promoting virtue. His most original point was insistence that Hawaiian women would be more chaste if they wore drawers; he seemed to think that promiscuity came from a germ that insulation would baffle. Casanova once maintained the same thesis from another point of view.

Shortly before the storm broke over Kalakaua in 1887, Gibson acted in a crude farce that further damaged what standing he had among the respectable. He was ensnared by a young widow from the mainland working the book-agent business in Honolulu. He told her that, old as he looked, he could still ride his forty miles a day; he regaled her with his travels; and, she insisted, he proposed marriage, only to jilt her at the instance of his busybody daughter. She had never accepted an engagement ring, the widow said, because she already had enough rings; but cash had been something else.

When the lady sued for breach of promise, the Honolulu press had savage fun. As Gibson's counsel pointed out, there was no shred of written evidence; even the lady's name—Flora Howard St. Clair—was highly improbable; and some of Gibson's enemies were unscrupulous enough to rouse suspicion of a frame-up. But the jury awarded the widow $10,000, being unduly mindful, as a juryman later confessed, of the political significance of the defendant.[7] Gibson had already left the Islands when the case was tried, but it probably served a purpose in making it unlikely that, with so heavy a judgment outstanding against him, he would ever return. The owner of the "Flirt" had again been "led astray in life by some highly colored romantic idea."

The old schemer's star was sinking anyway. In the summer of 1887 the respectable whites who forced Kalakaua to sign the "Bayonet Constitution" did not forget his faithful minister. They marched Gibson down to the water front under escort of something that, though many of its members were powers in the land, looked considerably like a mob. One of them carried a rope and indicated by word and gesture that, if Kipikona, as the Hawaiians called Gibson, ever came back, it would be used

[7] *Pa Gibby's Wooing*—Hawaiian Archives.

with a running noose at the business end. Genteel and long-suffering, just as he had been in the Dutch tyrants' prison, the great man let himself be hustled on board a San Francisco-bound sugar bark and landed in San Francisco, where reporters were impressed by his gentlemanly demeanor.

He died of tuberculosis January 21, 1888. Honolulu had long ridiculed his constant cough. So he never founded that benevolent principality in his beloved Malaysia—or perhaps Papua. The Lanai lands passed into the hands of the Hawaiian Pineapple Company a generation ago. Palawai Basin is now one mass of beautifully-contoured fields of pineapples, proving too late that Kipikona's darling island could be made to bear with the abundance of which he dreamed. But one detail is regrettable. The little knoll that was the site of the City of Joseph, where the chronic but amateur filibuster rhapsodized about the isles of the sea, is now occupied by the company piggery.

The only member of this nosegay of notorieties ever honored by a monument—a half-again-life-size bronze on Ha'apai (Tonga)—was the Rev. Shirley Waldemar Baker, founder of the Free Church of Tonga and, in his day, unquestionably the most exasperating man in the Pacific. Still he was probably the least pathological of the lot. Hayes, de Rays, Gibson, sound close to the line beyond which emotional disability becomes dangerous—somewhat to the subject and considerably to the object. But, barring some mild delusions of persecution, Shirley Baker could have been a useful, if unpleasant, citizen in several situations in life other than that to which he thought God called him. Some still maintain that he actually was a useful citizen as politician-missionary—a role for which, according to old photographs, he dressed marvelously in stout boots, white trousers, black clerical coat and sun helmet.[8]

Yet, though he drew salary from the Wesleyan mission, he was virtually not a missionary at all. That was his mother's idea, not his. While he was still a baby, she uttered a deathbed wish

[8]Principal sources for Baker are: Basil Thomson, *Diversions of a Prime Minister*; and Beatrice Shirley Baker's memoir of her father.

that he would minister to the heathen and, in spite of his several efforts to do something else, the infinite purpose of God brought him to a missionary career in the end. Evidently the Lord took Mrs. Baker's suggestions very seriously.

She was daughter of a Wesleyan parson in Gloucestershire. Her husband was a Church of England clergyman and headmaster of a London grammar school. Early motifs reappear in Baker's life with a patness gratifying to the biographer. In his time he was both Wesleyan and Anglican missionary. As a youngster he wanted to study law, and so eventually he became principal architect of the legal code of Tonga. Then an uncle, an eminent physician, tempted him toward medicine and gave him elementary grounding in the profession; the nephew was later sole medical practitioner in Tonga, reputedly rather skilful. He wrote D. M. after his name, though it is not known what medical faculty granted him that degree; his uncle's teaching and a volunteer year of "walking the hospitals" in Australia while on leave are the only family record of medical education. Not that there was anything out of the way in a missionary's turning amateur physician. But Baker somehow owed it to his knotty, self-admiring, ingenious self to lie about his formal qualifications.

Though he flirted with profane professions and was educated with the Anglican ministry in mind, his dissenting fate caught up with him when, as a young man, he visited another uncle who was Crown Protector of Aborigines in Australia. No Church of England congregation being handy, young Baker attended Wesleyan chapel, evidently with mounting zeal. Presently he wrote his father that he was going to turn Wesleyan and missionary. His father pompously approved. After ordination and marriage—both advisable from the mission point of view—the Rev. Shirley Baker was detailed to Tonga in 1860. The place was never to be the same again.

Wesleyanism was extremely well intrenched there among an aggressive, self-satisfied, intelligent Polynesian people, who Baker early came to believe were descendants of those wearisome lost tribes. Their head was King George Tubou, a large, able chief who had had a lively career as an imperious meddler with his neighbors, the Fijians. The old gentleman was already over sixty and people said later that Baker's influence over him coincided with his descent into dotage. He liked this dynamic new missionary who within a month could preach in the Tongan language and had so practical an attitude toward his work, writing in his journal that "while the mission had been most successful in spiritual matters . . . nothing had been done to raise up the Tongans as a nation."[9] This belittling a spiritual victory, odd as it sounds from a parson, fitted the circumstances. So far as Wesleyanism could save their souls, the Tongans were a finished job; their salvation was threatened only by a Catholic minority. The next step for the well-meaning white man was to organize their security in a world hazardous for small native polities. It seems never to have occurred to Baker that that, however, was no job for the clergy.

Within two years the King had asked Baker to draw up legislation to relieve the commoner of the exactions of the chiefs, and to stabilize cash revenue for them. Baker's recommendations are still fundamental law in Tonga.[10] Within four years he had designed a handsome royal coat of arms and a flag—red, with a red cross on a white first quarter—still flown by the Kingdom of Tonga under its present British protectorate. Baker might have been thinking of himself as much as of the King when composing the royal motto: "God and Tonga are my inheritance." This rapid rise to influence was already causing backbiting among his missionary brethren. Later he drew up a white-style constitution for the kingdom, with a bicameral legislature, compulsory education—Catholics permitted the Douai Bible—and a ministry responsible only to the King. He is usually credited with the grotesque Tongan laws on personal morality that so moved the ungodly to derision. But these seem to have been the work of predecessors, which Baker affirmed without protest. He became editor of

[9]Beatrice Shirley Baker, *Memoirs of* . . . , 6.
[10]Cf. V, *Their Gods Are Dead*, for details of the arrangements and present consequences.

both the English and the Tongan newspapers published by
the mission. By 1869 he was head of the mission. Long since
the King had asked him to become premier, but he refused,
saying he could do more good by advising from outside. Not
until 1880 did he formally enter the government.

So far this might have been merely another extreme case of
a parson's turning mayor of the palace. But "Burley Shaker,"
as hostile whites called him, was egregiously energetic and
doomed to egregious scrapes. The Wesleyans in Tonga were
as sharp as any about squeezing contributions for their general
funds out of native converts; as before noted, the method of
choice was to work up competition, according prestige to
heavy contributors and proportionate shame to others. Baker
encouraged natives to borrow in advance on growing copra in
order to make a fine showing. There were rumblings of disapproval when judgments were executed on defaulters who
could not repay debts thus contracted with traders. Worse,
Baker openly co-operated with the traders, particularly with
the German Long Handle Firm, in midwifing such advances.
The Germans presently held mortgages on the bulk of Tongan
copra, and paid the mission ten per cent above going prices in
consideration of the Lord's help and consequent savings in
overhead. It was a good bargain on both sides, but it unquestionably smelled of money-changing in the Temple and dangerously exasperated The Firm's competitors, who concluded
that the Church and Germany were in unholy alliance.

There was further reason to wonder just how close "Misi
Beika" and the Germans were. Well before Britain had treaty
relations with Tonga, Baker sponsored a German-Tongan
treaty that gave Emperor William exclusive coaling rights in
the fine harbor of Vavau. Then the Tongan government broke
with its traditional business agents in Sydney and gave the
business to Germans known to be close to The Firm. The heir
apparent of Tonga went under Baker's wing to Auckland for
medical treatment and died there; Baker brought the body
back with a flourish on a German man-of-war that had oppor-
tunely offered that courtesy. He even admitted in public that,

next to Britain, he preferred Germany among the great powers.

Much of that may have been an attempt to play Germany against Britain in pursuance of Baker's avowed purpose to "make the Tongans a nation, independent and self-support-ing." But as Britain's Pacific policy sharpened in the 'seventies, Britons found it indecent for an English-derived missionary not to support the Union Jack by precept and, if indicated, action. Sir Arthur Gordon, High Commissioner of the West-ern Pacific, might write, ostensibly in sorrow, that Baker's snuggling up to Germany might be "unfriendly and unbecom-ing, but it could not be styled disloyal."[11] Nevertheless it was unforgivable, and gossip burgeoned back in Australia, in New Zealand where Tonga did much of its business, in the Colonial Office, in Wesleyan headquarters in London, and wherever two or three were gathered together over a gin-bottle. "Old Jikote"—the *jikote*, Thomson explains, is the brash and bus-tling Tongan kingfisher—was in the Germans' pay . . . the Kaiser had decorated him for that treaty . . . he was a Ger-man anyway; nobody but a German would have a middle name like Waldemar . . . he was a quack, an embezzler, a neglecter of mission business while journeying to Auckland so often on errands for the King . . . "A great man here," wrote Steven-son with amused exaggeration after having Baker to lunch at Vailima, "accused of theft, rape, judicial murder, abortion, misappropriation of public moneys . . ."[12]

By 1879 Baker was arraigned before a missionary commission of inquiry with the British vice-consul at Tonga as complain-ing witness. King, native councillors, and missionaries, de-posed in sworn affidavits—never checked by cross-examination —that German treaty, copra loans, distress proceedings, had all been their doing, not Baker's. But it took more than hard swearing to dispel the day-by-day impression that Misi Beika was too much of a power in the land. Embezzlement was never proved; but he alone handled the auditing of accounts, collec-

[11]Baker, *Memoirs of* . . . , 22.
[12]*Letters*, (South Seas Edition), III, 229.

tion of taxes, payment of bills and letting of contracts—certainly a position with opportunities. He probably did not pad his pockets directly. But neither did he muzzle the ox that treadeth out the corn. A great house for him was shipped knockdown from New Zealand at the same time as the wooden royal palace; both are still in use, Baker's a lofty, galleried affair like a Deep South plantation mansion. His buggy was so handsome that, when enemies damaged it, repairs cost over forty pounds. When the impudent British took over his office, they found its locked back room full of fine wines and liquors marked "government property," which proved to have been reserved strictly for the refreshment of Misi Beika.

Whether money stuck to his fingers or not, it was money that led to his fatal gesture of moving Tonga to secede from Wesleyanism. Baker and the King had long disliked seeing so many thousands of pounds in cash leave the Kingdom to support missions elsewhere. They had tried in vain to persuade Wesleyan authorities to grant Tongan Wesleyanism financial autonomy. In 1885, when Baker's enemies in the mission were close to British schemers who wanted Tonga annexed, the self-confident premier cut the Gordian knot. After sending his superiors an ultimatum that could not reach them before the time limit expired, he had the King set up the Free Church of Tonga to replace the Wesleyan-connected organization. The King was titular head, the communicants were all Tongans who thought it worth while to stand in with the government. Some 15,000 of them found a change of religion immediately advisable.

A few thousand others were stiff-necked, however, largely from political motives, and neither King nor premier was the type to stand nonsense. Tongans in general were never averse to physical violence in religio-political controversy, as their turbulent pre-Baker history showed. The Free Church invited the zealously pro-Free Church and pro-King men of Ha'apai and Vavau to come and reason with the recalcitrants, who were strongest on Tongatabu, the seat of government. With fire and sword dissenters were chastened, but a residue of recalcitrance remained. The sequel was exile—voluntary, said Baker, forced, said others—of 200 stubborn Tongan Wesleyans to a small uninhabited island whence they migrated to Fiji, right under the nose of the High Commissioner of the Western Pacific.

The High Commissioner's sharp protests extracted from Baker a promise to repatriate the exiles and allow them religious freedom. Those promises were never honored, which was rash. Burley Shaker was a dogged man and, next year, his discretion was probably affected by personal danger. One evening, while he was driving himself, his son and daughter home in his buggy, one of four recently escaped Tongan prisoners took a shot at him. He had reined up when he saw a man with a gun standing in the road; his son alighted to disarm the attacker. But the man fired as he approached and badly shattered his arm, the shot going on to wound the girl in the hip and frighten the horse into bolting. The girl was thrown out and crippled for life. The effect on the adrenal glands of a man like Baker is understandable. Nobody had been killed but he called the incident "the assassination" and, in a mood of so-they-want-to-play-rough-do-they, went forth to get revenge on his attackers and prove them tools of his ungodly Wesleyan-British enemies.

Six natives had been shot for the crime after secret trial, and more were in jail awaiting their fate when H.M.S. "Rapid" appeared, bearing the High Commissioner. Baker stopped the massacre but still maintained that the attackers had been suborned by Wesleyans—had they not hidden in the grounds of the Wesleyan College?—and that the gun used had been lent by the British vice-consul. Henceforth he put in even more time in Auckland and, when in Tonga, sported an armed bodyguard.

Years came and went more and more highhandedly. In 1889 many Tongans, taking the only way to express dissatisfaction with their best friend's administration, refused to pay taxes, and Tonga was headed for galloping bankruptcy. This crisis, combined with the fact that the Wesleyan exiles were still hanging their harps on the coconut palms of Fiji, stirred Sir John Thurston, a new High Commissioner, to drastic action. Arriving in Tonga on a man-of-war he formally ordered Baker, "as a person dangerous to the peace and safety of the Western Pacific," to leave on the next mail steamer. Even Misi Beika saw that the jig was up. He stormed and snarled and sarcastically sent the government a bill for the board of the royal prince who had lived a year in his Auckland house while at school. But he departed, leaving British officials in possession, with the unenviable task of cleaning up the financial and administrative mess consequent on so long a virtual dictatorship. Ten years later Britain formally assumed a protectorate over the Kingdom of Tonga.[13]

Still, Baker could not be so easily exorcised. From Auckland he continued to edit the Free Church press; his right hand, the Rev. Mr. Watkin, was mainstay of the Free Church on the ground. For years it looked as if Baker would make a career of traveling and writing to set his side of the case before everybody from beach-gossips in Samoa to the U.S. Government in Washington. Then he suddenly shifted ground and secured from the Anglican Bishop of Dunedin an assignment as missionary. Back in the bosom of the Church of England, he was to set up in Tonga the nucleus of a C. of E. mission program in western Polynesia. Dropping the Free Church as if it burned him, Baker bought land on Ha'apai and began to preach and organize Sunday Schools in opposition to his former flock. His first four years, he claimed, converted to Anglicanism some 300 natives on Ha'apai and 500 on Tongatabu—not bad, even after discounting his poor head for exact figures.

He died on the job in 1903; one of his daughters still survives on Ha'apia, site of the blocky bronze statue that his dutiful children paid for. Stevenson remarked that he looked like John Bull in the political cartoons and made a nicely significant distinction about his temperament: "the man, though wholly insincere, is a thousand miles from ill-meaning; and see to what excesses he was forced or led."[14]

[13]Cf. V, *Their Gods Are Dead*, for a summary of modern Tongan polity.
[14]*Letters* (South Seas Edition), IV, 34.

That might be over-charitable. But there is small doubt that, as one aspect of his egocentricity, Baker did have what he conceived to be the good of Tonga at heart. In fact, the disquieting thing about such figures in South Seas history is that, so far as the natives could make out, the Bakers and Gibsons were their best friends among white men. Abler, more honest, better educated men were increasingly present; but they did not come with so convincing a show of desire primarily to help Tonga or Hawaii adjust to the white man's ideas.

Twenty years ago Queen Salote, King George's universally respected granddaughter, tried to amalgamate Free Church and Wesleyans. The result was merely another schism, for numerous stubborn Free Churchers refused the official compromise. In Tonga, once established, things last a long time. You can still see plodding about in the grounds of the palace, which looks like a jigsaw seaside residence of the 'eighties, a lady land tortoise which, legend says, was presented to the Tui Tonga by Captain Cook in 1777. The story is not biologically impossible; these beasts live practically forever. The poor old thing has been run over by trucks and half-roasted in bush fires, but she is still on deck and has long been half-deified, under title of Tui Malila, receiving regular offerings of ceremonial kava, which she drinks with royal decorum. It is a great pity that she cannot be interviewed about Shirley Baker.

V

THEIR GODS ARE DEAD

The virtues and arts of civilization are almost as
disastrous to the uncivilized as its vices.

—Sumner, *Folkways*

A boat from H.M. Armed Transport "Towser" pulled smartly toward Tarafu beach. In the stern sheets sat the Old Man himself in full-dress uniform, and the men were resplendent in clean frocks with new ribbons on their flat straw hats. A second boat in their wake contained a squad of glittering marines. Native canoes that had been out trading with the crew paddled after in inquisitive haste, and the huts back among the coco palms on shore emptied of older men, women and children streaming to the beach to see what the strangers were doing now. Chatteringly but politely they made way as the captain went forward to shake hands with the chief and explain something with many gestures and some help from his Tahitian interpreter, who knew little more than he himself did of the local language.

The chief gathered that he was to be presented with a parti-colored piece of cloth carried reverently in a neat bundle as a gift from "Tingi Jawji," the great chief over this lesser but still great chief of the ship. He nodded and smiled; the captain shook hands again and barked at his men. Trailing a rope, one of them climbed a coco palm in a clutching fashion that, for all his sailor's agility, struck the natives as slow and clumsy.

Once aloft he decapitated the palm, a wasteful thing to do. His mates below tied the bundle of cloth to the rope and hoisted it to the top, then a jerk on a lighter rope cleverly dissolved the bundle and the cloth streamed out in the trade wind, stunningly blue, red and white in converging stripes. Drums snarled, fife and bugle brayed and twittered. The men in the gorgeous red coats—obviously great chiefs from their resplendent garments—stood in line and let off those clumsy thunder-sticks that whites carry, which caused some apprehension. Then all took off their hats and waved them and uttered an excited noise in unison three times, while smoke billowed from the side of the distant ship and a subsequent brief bout of thunder made all the natives look apprehensively at the sky.

Again the captain shook hands with the chief and made another speech of some three minutes which, excepting further mentions of Tingi Jawji, was mostly lost. Before the crowd had well settled down the boats were pulling away, leaving presents piled before the chief. Presently the ship was winged in white, as she had been on arrival the day before, seven native girls who had spent the night on board were shooed overside to swim ashore, and "Towser" was under way, following the ebb through the pass in the fringing reef.

Thus the British crown took possession of Tarafu. It was often done elsewhere with more ceremony, seldom with any better native understanding of what such ceremonies implied. But then native ceremonies were equally baffling to whites.

Whether it were three years or thirty before another ship appeared, Tarafu would never be the same again. Changes were implicit, not only in the impressive presence and occasional rudeness or clumsiness of the whites. Even more catalytic were the items in that heap of presents—big and little iron nails, marvelous for carving tools; lengths of ravishing red cloth; needles; thread; beads; a plumed hat such as the captain wore; a bottle of dark-brown, sweet, and fiery stuff that the chief tried and spat out, but presently re-investigated with a curiosity that was greatly rewarded; and a Bible. Each such item was a germ carrying white man's ways ashore. There would be many more until now you can sit in a high chief's house under an electric light and observe his golf clubs hanging on the wall.

*　　*　　*

"Our friends [in Tahiti] have benefited little from their intercourse with Europeans . . . they are so altered that I believe in future no European will ever know what their ancient customs of receiving strangers were."—William Bligh (1792) quoted in Lee, *Captain Bligh's Second Voyage to the South Seas*, 74, 79.

Traveling the Islands during or in the wake of war was made incessantly amusing by the ingenious uses that natives had found for the débris of war. Here on the lagoon beach of an atoll is a pretty little canoe consisting of a wooden outrigger attached to a belly-tank from a military plane. Just as you think how nice a plaything for some bright-eyed Marshallese child, a grown man launches it and paddles out to a ketch lying at anchor. Behind you are decorative borders of Coca-Cola bottles placed butts up in the sand and neat low fences of the filigreed steel strips used to firm the landing surfaces of airfields. On Goodenough Island, I am told, natives made admirable spears out of light steel rods intended for carrying prism-shaped cases of shells. I have seen native handicraft dyed brown with iodine, red with mercurochrome from military medical stores, yellow with atabrin tablets begged from GIs to whom they were issued as a malaria suppresser. New shapes, new materials woven into older uses, a thing that always occurs when one set of ways of doing impinges on another. This is the material part of what ethnologists solemnly call "acculturation." ·

Natives' use of new things is often unpredictable. To us fencing wire is good for keeping hogs and cattle where they belong; the native sharpens it into flexible, diverging prongs for a fish spear. Recently a United States Commercial Company officer on Koror (Palaus), short of American stocks to drain off piled up native purchasing power, was delighted to find a quantity of Japanese sun helmets in good shape. In the southern islands of the group, he knew, the same article had sold like hot cakes. But when he put them on sale they were a drug on the market. The trouble was that the natives valued them too highly. To their minds the sun helmet, connoting white prestige, was the prerogative of chiefs alone; a commoner had no more use for one than an enlisted man for an admiral's cap with scrambled eggs on the visor. When last seen, those thousands of brand-new sun helmets were still on the shelves.

From ready demand for peroxide of hydrogen in some islands, a pharmacist might deduce a gratifying awareness of antisepsis among the natives; actually they want it not as germicide but as hair bleach. Ghastly cheap perfume has been a popular item in trading stores on other islands; forbidden distilled liquors, natives buy perfumes to drink. So it has gone since the days when chiefs, given uniform frock coats by captains, donned them pants-fashion, legs in the sleeves and skirts girdled round the waist; and Islanders eagerly sought glass bottles, not as receptacles, but to be broken into sharp-edged bits for razors. Gunpowder plundered from an early party of distressed whites in Fiji was seized on for ceremonial blackening of face and hair; one warrior thus embellished leaned over a fire and was snatched indecorously baldheaded by a whoosh of inexplicable flame that left a marvellously bad odor. Such inevitable errors still occur. During the recent war flotsam from torpedoed vessels coming ashore on an island in eastern Fiji included cocoa and face powder destined for a PX. The natives took the face powder for flour and tried to make bread of it; they were sure the cocoa was brown water paint and painted the church with it, only to see it all wash off in the next rain.

Metal, as already seen in Hawaii, was usually an instant success. Its virtues were easily recognizable and its uses close to those among whites. Thus, though a nail was a tool rather than a fastening, iron hammers and hatchets became both tools and weapons. It was quite true that, at first, most Islanders would do anything whatsoever for metal. When the "Glide" came to grief in Fiji, her hold was full of cured *bêche-de-mer*[1] that rotted as water seeped in through the bilged planking. Nothing could be more noisome than such a brew of slimy marine animals and salt water putrefying in close, hot quarters. But the natives got wind of a cask of iron hatchets at the foot of the mainmast and persistently dived again and again into "this loathsome mass" until, retching and half-smothered, each man had his coveted hatchet head. Samoans, however, haughtily professed no interest in metal when the French brought it. Stone tools were *fa'aSamoa*[2] and no Samoan would accord a casual stranger the satisfaction of an admission that anything *fa'aSamoa* was not better than anything *fa'apapalagi*.

Firearms did not impress the Samoan either, at least visibly. For that matter, when d'Entrecasteaux tried to demonstrate the eighteenth century musket to Tongans on live birds as marks, both his best marksmen missed. Finally a scornful native picked up his bow, and transfixed the bird at the first try. Other South Sea peoples missed the point of guns because, though willing to see magic in them, they traced no causal connection between the report of a gun and the sudden death of a creature thirty yards away.

But all that was at first off-go. In time the Tongan or Samoan chief was avid for a gun. Though it often rusted into uselessness, it was indubitably an honorific thing to own. In orienting to firearms the native had to learn over and over again that damp powder was useless; that a dirty or overloaded musket would kill the aimer sooner than his enemy; that powder too close to fire was dangerous. Fijian effectiveness with firearms long suffered from a notion that size of charge should vary with size of human target. Sometimes the Fijian took the terrifying noise as the principal feature, firing at random when leaping out of ambush and then going to work with a club at close quarters. He saw nothing wrong with cutting down the stock of a musket for convenience and aiming it one-handed as a

[1]For what this was and how handled, cf. footnote, p. 211.
[2]Always on the Samoan's lips, this means "after the custom of Samoa." *Papalagi* is the white man's world.

sort of gigantic horse pistol, with no chance whatever of accuracy. But in time he learned. With proper training he made
a fair to good marksman in the recent war, say his officers. King
Tembinok of Abemama (Gilberts) never went out without
a repeating Winchester; the first time a subject stepped out of
line, the king dropped a bullet at his feet in fatherly admoni-
tion; the second time the offender got four shots, one over
each shoulder, one past each ankle; the third time he was
nailed cleanly in the back, no matter how fast he ran or how
frantically he dodged.

As soon as equipment was available, Tahitians as well as
Hawaiians slaughtered each other by this method. Cakobau of
Fiji would trade only for lead, powder, muskets, cannon—and
liquor. He distributed 5,000 muskets among his people and
always had at least 600 kegs of powder on hand. The Maori, always most adaptable of Polynesians, saw with unholy readi-
ness that this way of killing at a distance beat stones and spears
hollow. On acquiring guns ambitious chiefs from the north
end of the North Island swept southward, settling old scores
with traditional enemies armed only with clubs and spears, and
then went on into megalomanic raiding and conquest that
turned the island into a horror of treachery, burned pas,[3] massacred populations, and cannibal feastings. Hongi, one of the
grimmer of these adventurers, acquired his superior fire-power,
along with a steel helmet that once saved his ruthless life in
battle, in consequence of a trip to England. The modern of-
fensive, not the mediaeval defensive, weapon made him as
much the scourge of the North Island as Attila was of Europe.
The Maori also altered his style of fortification to match the
new tactics. His ditched and palisaded pa, with a tortuous entrance and calculated fields of fire, had already been greatly admired by Europeans; when, in the mid-century, white soldiers
came up against the fresh improvements he had made à propos
of guns, even artillery would not guarantee success. Officers
swore that no European engineer could have done as well with
the materials available.

[3] The pa was the fortified Maori village.

Gunpowder was a social solvent. For reasons indicated before, the Island chief was relatively safe in prewhite battle. But the musket picked him off from afar without identifying the marksman and, in small engagements involving firearms, he could not stay out of range if he accompanied the war party at all. So, as chiefs fell right and left, *mana* suffered and the common man with a gun grew in stature. Battles grew bloodier, since weapons were more dangerous;[4] in early Fiji Lockerby saw 200 killed on a side, fifty in the first ten minutes. Comfortable old feuds that had served for generations as periodic social adrenalin turned into occasions for extermination or wholesale massacre that upset everything. Some say that hearing of Napoleon put monopolistic conquest into the heads of such Island Alexanders as Kamehameha, Hongi, Maafu; perhaps so, but Kamehameha's ambitions somewhat preceded Napoleon's imperialism, and no such spur was necessary for an Island chief only slightly more able and prestige-obsessed than his rivals.[5]

Gunpowder also made geographical accident crucial for ambitious chiefs. People living near havens preferred by whites got the most guns first and, other things being equal, conquered their neighbors. Often they had white man's help in the fighting, for it conveniently advanced friendly relations if the ship's company helped their new brothers against tribes in the next bay—as Porter did on Nukahiva. Deserters found fighting the best way to keep in the good graces of their patron chiefs. The process has already been seen in Tahiti, where the Pomares won hegemony over the paramount Teva merely by happening to control Matavai Bay, where guns and renegades were plentiful earliest. This too was bad for *mana*; the triumph of the *parvenu* always unsettles things.

[4]Some doubt this; cf. E. Aubert de la Rüe, *Les Nouvelles Hébrides*, 181.
[5]The musket not only made kingdoms and emptied districts, it stimulated alienation of land in New Zealand. A musket-happy Maori tribe would conquer and occupy the territory of a musket-weak enemy, then quickly sell the newly acquired land to whites before the defeated could rally and acquire enough fire-power to retaliate. And guns were the eagerly sought price of land in early Samoa.

The equally eager native acceptance of tobacco was not important, however much it annoyed missionaries.[6] But alcohol was immediately to become another savagely powerful social solvent. Dignity, responsibility, intelligent reaction to white pressure went glimmering whenever the chiefs could lay hands on rum or squareface. As in the case of Liholiho, violations of *tabu* under the influence often helped to break down the old ways. Under white instruction Polynesians learned to make mash of *ti*-root[7] or sugar cane and developed crude but efficient stills; one type consisted of a hollowed stone for retort capped with the shaped butt of a tree and using a bamboo tube as worm. The first run was reserved for chiefs; even the weaker second was potent enough. But distilling is tricky and not essential to getting hog-drunk. The Islander was soon making "beer" or "swipes"—meaning any fermented liquid not too nauseous to swallow—out of mashes of banana, or the pineapple and orange that the white man brought. To this day the secretive bush conceals layouts of kegs for making orange beer in season, each brew signallizing a great if clandestine social occasion reputedly winding up in something orgiastic.

Doughty drinkers as some chiefs like Kalakaua were, the Islander in general has a weak head and uses alcohol strictly to arrive at a sloppy or dirty drunk. For results, read Stevenson's account of the murderous chaos on Makin (Gilberts) when the *tabu* against natives buying *peranti* and *din* was relaxed.[8] Only a die-hard anarchist would protest against the restrictions that seek to deny alcohol to Islanders today. It is class

[6] Islanders quickly learned to grow tobacco and still do—a marvelously strong leaf, seared and rolled into stumpy cigarettes with pandanus or banana leaf. In Melanesia stick tobacco early became a key currency. In order to deal with native communities not yet accustomed to money, the armed forces in the recent war pre-empted the world's entire supply of this type of tobacco—formidable black stuff that two U.S. firms alone can make to native taste.

[7] Ti (Hawaiian term) has a broad, ribbony leaf that was the material of the dancer's skirt, and a very sugary, fleshy root.

[8] *In the South Seas,* 275 *et seq.*

discrimination right enough;[9] but· the protestant need only visit Tahiti, where natives have the same right of purchase as whites, to see that for once equalitarian principle must be abandoned. The Tahitian squanders far too much of his meager cash-income on red wine and beer. His drinking-bouts, involving all ages over puberty and both sexes, have all the air of a witches' Sabbath patronized by juvenile delinquents.

Obviously the Islander would have been much better off if he had had alcohol in his prewhite background or, from the other point of view, if he possessed hereditary resistance to its effects. But that is condition contrary to fact and, though that sodden nightmare of Stevenson's on Makin was no credit to the Gilbertese, king or commoner, pious horror is pointless. One can merely assume that the Islander is unlikely to be temperate about anything but work. The New Caledonian, who raises a little coffee for market, often drinks so many cups at a sitting out of sheer inability to leave off that he ruins his heart with accumulations of caffein.

As for foods the native, always prestige-minded, at once came to a still persisting belief that the diet of the first whites he saw represented their highest gastronomy. Early exploring crews ate salt horse, ship's biscuit and dried peas because, with contemporary preserving techniques, such things alone kept well on long voyages. Though no white sailor, or landsman either, would eat such fare if he could get better, to this day ship's biscuit and kegs of salt beef are highly valued features

[9]This comes out most clearly in semiautonomous Tonga. There white residents are unlimited in purchases subject to the discretion of government, which can crack down if amounts bought indicate supplies are being diverted to natives. Only 150 permits to buy alcoholic drinks are issued to natives. Native cabinet ministers' permits are unlimited, subject to the same conditions as if they were whites. Nobles of the landlord class are allowed four to eight bottles of spirits a month, or equivalents in wine or beer; heads of government departments up to four bottles ditto; native ordinary citizens one bottle. One bottle of spirits is equivalent to two of wine or twelve of beer. It is easily seen that, when the various upper categories are taken care of, relatively few permits remain for ordinary citizens, and which ones get them is strictly a matter of governmental favor. Theoretically the mass of Tongans do not drink at all.

of Island feasts; and *pisupo* (pea-soup) is the honorific Samoan word for any and all preserved meats, of which, for all their dullness, Islanders are inordinately fond. (A veteran trader in the Cooks tells me that the Islander was reluctant to change from salt beef in kegs to the more easily handled canned beef until a clever processor put out a *Missionary* brand with a picture label of a fat and beaming parson on the can.) With all the scaly wealth of the Pacific available—and practically every edible Pacific fish I have ever tried is delicious—natives much prefer low grades of canned salmon whenever they can afford them.

Now consider how unpredictably shifts in ways of doing produce strange consequences. The use of canned meat strewed the Rarotongan village with empty meat cans that catch and hold rain water; such tiny accumulations are favored breeding places of the mosquito that infects people with filariasis; hence because a manufacturer had a clever merchandising idea, the Rarotongans are physically handicapped by unduly high incidence of a debilitating and disabling disease. During the last generation the Japanese imported thousands of Okinawan laborers into the Marianas, Palaus and Bismarcks. For their eating, a giant species of Asiatic snail, of which they are fond, was brought in; with Japanese defeat the "Okies" were moved out, but the snail remains, increasing rapidly enough to be a serious menace to vegetation on Rota, Guam, New Ireland.[10]

Too much white man's sweet stuff and demineralized foods are supposed to have ruined Islanders' teeth. The point will have to wait until dentists definitely determine just what does cause gingivitis and dental caries, but there is no denying that most Islanders have worse teeth than those in their ancestors' skulls.[11] Their extreme adoptions of white man's foods are

[10]The example is still good, even though, according to recent information, the giant snail on New Ireland has discovered an effective natural enemy, not yet identified, that is beginning to check its spread.

[11]For a detailed study, commended in a foreword by Hooten the anthropologist, see Weston A. Price, *Nutrition and Physical Degeneration.* A dentist in Fiji tells me, however, that he can detect little difference in incidence of tooth troubles between natives living on predominantly white-style diets and on diets very close to prewhite standards.

certainly bad for them in general. Fijian sugar-greediness has already been mentioned. The modern Maori lives on boiled-to-death meat, white bread, potatoes, and tea with too much sugar; he is bored by such "protective" foods as vegetables and dairy products. If white flour became unavailable he would probably, like the natives of the Tokelaus during a war shortage, refuse to use the more wholesome brown flour. His cousins out in the more northern Islands would probably like the Maori diet; but fortunately for most of them few can afford it, so taro, shellfish, breadfruit, yams and fruits still give them many of the nutriments that made their ancestors notably healthy. Fish also are a great help, where the art of fishing survives in full swing. But in too many islands, such as Tonga and the Marianas, the old traditions of fishing are dead or dying, and it is white men, not natives, who must plan to encourage revival for the native's own dietetic good.

Under white influences houses underwent technical revolution in most islands—whether for the better depends on circumstances. The New Caledonian is certainly much better off in the house that the French government advises—a plastered, thatched shack with doors and windows—than in his prewhite, smoke-choked beehive hovel. But the Tahitian is certainly worse off in a board shack that, for fear of ghosts, he closes tightly every night with a lamp burning inside. Corrugated iron is the roofing of choice in the modern islands. It is hot, ugly, and a nasty hazard when high winds rip off sheets of it and whirl them through the air with a velocity that will cut a man or a tree in two, but it is waterproof and easily laid. Even in conservative Tonga, which maintains traditional house shapes, iron often replaces thatch. So may concrete flooring replace traditional platforms of pebbles or gravel, a change encouraged by white doctors. But here Island social values interfere, for if the chief has a concrete floor in his *fale*,[12] few of his social inferiors have the cheek to aspire to such an improvement for themselves.

[12]Samoan for *house*, equivalent to Hawaiian *hale*, Maori *whare*, and so round the circle of Polynesian cognates.

Inside the house white man's furniture and doodads are popular, though use is sometimes another matter. The chief may well leave his brass bed for show, and sleep like his ancestors, on a mat on the floor. He has chairs to offer whites and for swank, but he himself probably sits cross-legged on a mat. Pillow slips are usually embroidered in pious cross-stitch mottoes, fruit of missionary endeavor to give native women wholesome recreation. The broken clock, the gaudy ash tray, are omnipresent. The Islander loves photographs and has all his closer relatives stuck up on the wall. On British islands the King and Queen, or Princess Elizabeth, cut out of illustrated papers, are there too; on French islands General de Gaulle is likely. In American jurisdiction the pin-up girl, usually of the more naked variety, is practically standard equipment in the teacher's little office in schoolhouses on Babelthuap (Palaus). On the data available, the teacher has assumed that pin-ups are the conventional ornament of American homes. In general, the white items that get genuine use in the native house are the hand powered sewing machine, the kerosene lamp and the photograph. The pandanus mats on the floor are still the handsomest movables in the place.

A survey of a Tongan village in 1938, when copra prices were low and purchases presumably closest to practical need, ranged imported items in the following order of demand: canned meat at the top, then flour, sugar, tobacco, piece goods, soap,[13] kerosene, fishline, fishhooks, canned fish, shirts, bush knives. The last item alone needs explanation. The long, heavy bush knife, of various shapes but always cognate to the Latin-American's machete, is to the Islander what the ax was to the American pioneer and it is handled with equal dexterity. In both cases admiring humorists have declared that the owner even puts a special edge on the thing and shaves with it for Sunday. In some parts of Micronesia the steel adz, sometimes made of a plane bit, has this rôle; the native carries it hooked

[13]The soap is probably made of coconut oil and may well be merely the Islander's own product come back to him. This list is from Ernest and Pearl Beaglehole, *Pangai*, 64.

round his neck with the keen edge disquietingly close to the jugular vein.

Whites' insistence on sanitation forced the privy on the South Seas with dubious results. The most impressive specimen is the jigsawed red-and-white little temple of ease, looking like a well-cared-for El station, in the palace grounds on Tongatabu. The least impressive is the flimsy screen of palm fronds round a shallow hole in the ground. Few Island governments have educated the native effectively in the theory of the thing; for most, out-of-sight-out-of-mind is the guiding principle. The telephone booth over water, approached by a catwalk from the beach, is supposed to stand beyond low-tide mark so the waves can do a good job. In practice, even in American Samoa where privies are in good shape, the catwalk is usually too short and it is quite evident why Polynesians prefer to bathe in fresh water when possible. The booth itself is often of so airy a construction or so tumble-down that privacy is a mere gesture. Here and there white neglect permits the inhabitants to revert to the old system of making the beach the latrine or, worse, to take to the adjoining bush. As a gloomy doctor described one situation, the latrine system consists of "a variation of the conventional pit-latrine without the pit."

The native has done much better with such white technical innovations as wheels, draft animals and fore-and-aft rig. On Rarotonga tough little ponies trot along with miniature wagons, descendants of the missionary buggy; sometimes the wheels are salvaged auto wheels with pneumatic tires, hence the curious spectacle of a native pumping up a flat on a horse-drawn vehicle. Though the Rarotongan hardly pampers his ponies, he does treat them more humanely than many Islanders.

Every island group handles the draft animal differently. The Samoan eschews wheels for packsaddles, the Tongan has a cart with two huge wheels, the Guamanian a cross between a cart and a sulky, hauled by a tiny bullock or carabao imported from the Philippines. By and large the automobile has been beyond the Islander's economic reach. He adores the thing however, and if he acquires a lump sum of cash will spend much of it on exultant joy-riding in taxis. Planes are even more honorific; the New Zealand service between Aitutaki and Rarotonga (Cooks) is always choked up with natives going visiting at a price they cannot conceivably afford.

On the water too "acculturation" has been ready and fertile. The Samoan longboat, up to fifty feet long with the matching sharp bow and stern of the white's beautiful whaleboat, rowed by up to a dozen men on a side, using a sail forward when the wind is favorable, is an inspiring craft, particularly when the rowers get to singing. On trips along steep-to, windward coasts they prefer to skirt points as close as possible; white passengers tend to shudder when a hulking Pacific swell shoulders the boat sky-high and then drops her to rise again just as the first smashes itself in eighty-foot spray on a fifty-foot black cliff about two oar's lengths to port. Nothing was ever prettier than the fore-and-aft rigged sailing canoes of Raiatea (Societies), marvelous syntheses of white man's sail plans and native hulls and outriggers. I am not seaman enough to know whether these white innovations of oars and fore-and-aft rig are improvements on prewhite deep-sea canoes with paddles and lateen or crab claw sails. It does not necessarily follow that they are, for prestige plays a part here too. The Palau man, for instance, resists suggestions that, for present lack of power launches, he should build cutters without auxiliaries for badly needed inter-island communication. He feels that, though wind is free and petroleum fuels scarce and expensive, to revert to wind power alone would be a comedown. Nowhere, of course, have any white innovations completely extinguished the smaller outrigger canoes used for lagoon fishing and informal ferrying; though sawn planks sometimes go into them, you can still find plenty dubbed out of the solid log, as if Captain Cook had never come calling.

Unquestionably the native often knows a good thing when he sees it. Witness the throngs of bicycles on Tahiti and Rarotonga; the coconut shredders made of bits of auto spring with one end flattened and serrated; goggles for underwater fishing constructed out of accurately fitted bits of window glass and hand-carved wooden frames laboriously shaped to a tight seal; the slingshot fishing spear of Tonga powered by a length of old inner tube; the biscuit- or kerosene-tin used as drum for ceremonial dancing. But how well the native adapted to white man's clothes is a matter for dispute.

Some doctors think that his prewhite seminudity was not altogether good for him, allowing too much ultraviolet and undue scope for the mosquitoes that carry malaria in Melanesia and filariasis almost everywhere. Yet a man in shirt and trousers constantly in and out of water while boating and fishing, exposed to heavy rain without much notion of changing to dry clothes and often without dry clothes to change to, but bullied into the belief that going trouserless is sinful and prestige-damaging, is not observing good hygiene for the respiratory tract. A common-sense minority of our grandfathers were convinced that clothing the native had much to do with his tragic susceptibility to tuberculosis and pneumonia. I suspect, however, that this factor has been exaggerated for its antimissionary content. Native's lack of immunity to those diseases was probably so marked that they would have died in droves of about the same size if they had remained stark as Adam.

In any case shorts or trousers, shirts, frocks for women, are the rule in the modern Islands. Shoes are neglected, except for dressing up, when torture does not matter; what torture it could be is indicated in the fact that the booted feet of Fijian soldiers in the recent war gradually shrank from, say size 14½, to 12½. Barefootedness provides another mixed case. The Islander's callused, hoof-thick sole, shoeless from infancy, goes scatheless on the coral reef that would cut our soft feet to ribbons; but bare feet and hookworm, that insidiously enervating complaint so widespread in the Islands, go automatically together.

As in every other department, degree of adaptation varies from group to group in clothes also. The tourist is delighted to see that Samoan, Tongan and Fijian, though usually shirted, eschew trousers for a wrap-around, ankle-length skirt—*lavalava* in Samoa, *sulu* in Fiji. This cool but hampering garment was imposed on the native by the missionary for lack of adequate supply of breeches. Nevertheless it is now an integral part of native life, like church on Sunday, and Apia and Suva look askance at the man who abandons it for bifurcation. A dark blue *lavalava* with a white stripe at bottom was the uniform of the Samoan *Mau* movement;[14] Tamasese, most active of the three principal chiefs of Samoa, still wears it in memory of those turbulent times and it has recently reappeared in token of present Samoan unrest. Often made with pockets nowadays, it is part of the dress uniform of Fijian soldier and policeman and the Samoan *fitafita* (native Marine auxiliary) in American Samoa. Any one of those outfits on parade makes it very clear that, though it may be a skirt scalloped at the bottom, this missionary's idea looks manly, soldierly, and dignified, on men as upstanding as these.[15]

In some islands the sartorial needle also stuck on the mission-inspired Mother Hubbard for women. The Loyalty Island lady makes hers with the standard square yoke and long sleeves out of the brightest red, pink, or flowered stuff she can lay hands on, shirring and embroidering and adding lace frills here and there. In a Noumea store I have seen a mother-and-daughter ensemble of Mother Hubbards for sale—to *les indigènes*, *madame* hastily explained, for the Noumea Frenchwoman would not sympathize with the young Honolulu matron's notion that it is amusing to wear the *holoku* at parties. A *popinée* from the Loyalties, her large dark feet at one end of a Nile-green Mother Hubbard, her staring dark face at the other, with a wreath of pink flowers round her bleached hair, is a striking object, though hardly what the missionary had in mind a hundred years ago. Her Fijian cousin is so firmly attached to

[14] Cf. p. 399 *et seq.*

[15] I have suspected that the stride-shortening effect of the *lavalava* had something to do with the somewhat duck-footed gait of Samoan and Fijian. I am told, however, that at least part of the background of this gait is, again, prestige: chiefs, traditionally portly, had to walk so to balance their corporations.

the *sulu* as token of respectability that she wears it even under white-style dresses as if her slip were showing five or six inches.

*   *   *

A dispersal of natives, small in scale but significant in results, began as soon as whites arrived. The earliest Spaniards took sample Solomon Islanders back to Peru where they died, some as converted Christians, or so their preceptors said. Bougainville and Furneaux appeared in their respective home ports with sample Tahitians, who were patronizingly lionized; Furneaux' Omai got back to the Islands with a mass of ill-assorted souvenirs of which he was quickly relieved by his numerous peers and superiors. Sometimes the whites took natives home to acquaint them with white notions as training to be go-betweens with their people: hence those Polynesians in the Cornwall mission school. The effect was usually picturesque. Boston was most intrigued by the spectacle of a stalwart Hawaiian coming ashore in his ceremonial red feather cape as guest of an early sea captain.

But it was working for white men that spread the Islander farthest. Maori, Rotumans and Hawaiians were frequently signed on as replacement hands for whalers and occasionally rose to be harpooners, who ranked as secondary officers. Of fifteen hands who deserted the "Lagoda" whaler to try their luck in locked-and-barred Japan in the 'thirties—thereby landing in a Japanese prison and occasioning the first visit of the U.S. Navy to the place—ten were Kanakas. Hawaiians took jobs with northwest fur traders; the Owhyhee River in California still commemorates a far-from-home Hawaiian who died on its banks as a member of a trapping party in 1819. There was a little colony of his compatriots at San Pedro in Dana's time. Early whites found Marquesans in the Bonins, Maori in New Caledonia, brought in as auxiliaries to white enterprise.

The Polynesian in particular, though deeply attached to his birthplace, likes travel, for prestige attaches to the man who can come home telling of faraway lands. As white ships gave opportunity, he not only signed on as seaman, but used them for passenger purposes, bringing wife, children, pigs, and dogs on board and paying in cash secured from the trader. Sometimes it was merely a visit to relatives on another island in the same group, sometimes it was temporary emigration, which might become permanent if the place settled in was comfortable. He usually chose the white settlement for residence; it was safer than the back country where he had no relatives and no rights. Blackbirded Melanesians[16] sometimes escaped from their overseers and "went bush," thoroughly mistrusted by local natives, but eventually working into local patterns of living by way of women. In recent years Samoans, Fijians, and Cook Islanders, men and girls too, have gone to New Zealand to take industrial jobs; as they return and tell of the wonders of Auckland, the movement gains momentum. One of the smartest merchant crews I have ever seen was the Gilbertese complement of a small motor vessel that operates largely in Fijian interisland trade and seldom takes her men anywhere near their home atolls on the Line.

Thus each sizable Island port—in the Islands sizable means two or more trading stores—has a relatively rootless quota of outlanders gradually mingling with the actual natives. Stevedoring, deckhanding, odd-jobbing keep them going. Suva, the South Seas capital with the most cosmopolitan style, is a miniature cross section of the whole Pacific; the last census of non-Fijian Islanders (in the patrilineal sense) showed 260 part-white Samoans, 527 assorted Polynesians, 1,696 Rotumans, 676 Micronesians, 942 Melanesians;[17] most of them, it is to be assumed, in the big town. There is little enough sense of solidarity among the cousin peoples of the Islands; but, if such a thing ever develops, these expatriates will have a good deal to do with it.

White educational schemes, however, will have more. The famous medical school in Suva which trains "native medical practitioners" for islands under guardianship of the British Empire, draws together bright native boys from Fiji, the New

[16]Cf. p. 360 et seq.
[17]Public Relations Office Press Release, Suva, 27 March, 1947.

Hebrides, the Solomons, the Gilberts, Tonga, Samoa and the Cooks. They live and study and play cricket and football together with surprisingly little squabbling,[18] all things considered. To some extent they must learn to get along with and respect the sometimes marked cultural differences among themselves, and begin to discover that most island groups have more common than peculiar problems. Current schemes similarly to train agricultural and educational native specialists in central schools will operate toward the same end. A sense of native integrity in general can hardly fail to be born. Girls are similarly influenced in nursing schools. The whole thing, of course, is reminiscent of the early missionary training of native pastors and teachers in such centralized and far-reaching schools as that at Malua (Western Samoa). In all such cases the trainee exposed to a center of white influence takes innumerable, if intangible, influences back to his family and village.

These intangibles are marvelously important. Music is the most obvious. The missionary hymn, the white man's guitar and its Island-developed cousin, the *ukulele*, revolutionize native music in a fashion most marked in Hawaii, but unmistakable everywhere. For generations a secondary influence direct from Hawaii to the rest of the Islands has added to the effect.

The style of the native leader of a native chorus is almost comically an imitation of the missionary choirleader. The singing itself is usually tremendous. Imagine something that sounds like a blend of *Lord Jeffrey Amherst, Bury Me Not on*

[18]The story of the "native medical practitioner" has been too well covered elsewhere, notably by the late Dr. S. M. Lambert, to be rehearsed here. The reader should be reminded, however, that these boys are not trained as fully qualified physicians. The idea is to enable them to handle simpler problems in public health, sanitation and elaborate first aid; they can give hypodermics, apply standard dressings, perform simple operations, prescribe less tricky drugs, but rely for the farther reaches of medicine on the government doctors in the local hospital. Though no such development is ever perfect, this "N.M.P." system is the single best thing that whites have done for the Islands. The quality of the graduates has been high and their work indispensable.

the Lone Prairie, La Cucaracha and *Shall We Gather at the River?* sung by brown-skinned angels. Their harmony and timing would guarantee a Fijian chorus a very profitable tour of the States.

Though seldom original, the air may be altered into unrecognizability. That is often just as well since, if identified, it can be startlingly anomalous. On Majuro (Marshalls) the current young folks' favorite, in English of which they understand little, is *Polly-wolly-doodle-alla-day.* I have heard a chorus of Samoan school children do a remarkable rendering of *Take Me Out to the Ballgame* complete with business. Every new governing power, every shift of history, leaves a moraine of adapted alien tunes behind it. Babelthuap (Palaus) writes its own words to the airs of *Die Lorelei and Stille Nacht* inherited from quondam German overlords. Since the recent war, the *Marine Hymn* is all over the Pacific. Radio, phonograph and movie have given the Islander a great taste for hillbilly numbers which, of course, have great affinities with his own acquired style.

Tin Pan Alley contributes constantly: Fiji is mad about *You Are My Sunshine,* and fuddled Tahitians sing in anachronistic succession *Show Me the Way to Go Home, Pistol-Packin' Mama,* and that radio commercial about bananas in the refrigerator. Or it may be an Island-composed song, to a white-style waltz tune, about how American women, though desirable, are expensive, whereas you can have a Tahitian girl any time for nothing. The sharpest of anomalies appears, however, when a certain highly westernized Polynesian chief, with gestures and leers straight out of the era of F. Scott Fitzgerald, gives tongue to *I Can't Give You Anything but Love, Baby.* For all the vulgarity occasionally involved, however, the white world probably did well by the Islander in giving him the diatonic scale and multi-stringed instruments with sound boxes. Up forward on dark, still nights at sea the native deckhands huddle sprawlingly together and, as the guitar plunk-plunks, they boom and wail and carol their own adaptations of white man's music with an organic enjoyment that keeps them at it most of the night. So sociable an addiction to the harmless cannot help being healthy.

Movies, on the other hand, are largely poison. They are almost the only means by which the native normally learns about the white man's world; which should be enough said. Worse, the native's tastes in movies keeps him away from the occasional commercial picture that might tell him something valid. He likes westerns first, then gangster stories, then musical pictures, so to him the States are full of violence, gunplay, and mile-wide ballrooms cluttered with beautiful girls wearing much less than any Island girl would dare be caught abroad in. What the trade calls "dramatic" films actively annoy him. Heaven knows a Hollywood picture about deep emotion is usually silly enough, but the native would lump both *Of Human Bondage* and *The Diary of a Chambermaid* as painful bores. Let hero and heroine encounter a complication that keeps them sorrowfully apart, let them even spend more than a few minutes getting acquainted before the pre-bedroom clinch, and the native audience howls protests from its inexpensive seats. There is probably more here than mere difference in ways of doing. This frenzy over the mere sight of a galloping horse, this angry impatience with any suggestion that emotion implies complicated controls, indicate that the Islander has dangerously few of the emotional habits needed for making headway in his part-white world. It sounds too much like the half-witted farmhand who, when asked in Forman's survey what he preferred in movies, answered succinctly, "Shootin' and kissin'."

Lack of curiosity is also troubling. The Samoan might be interested in *Moana*, because it concerns his own people; but he would probably have been put to sleep by the same producer's *Nanook*, which merely tried to show in the same quiet vein how another kind of people lives.[19]

[19]I did not have the good fortune to see a South Seas audience up against a Hollywood South Seas picture. Theatre owners tell me, however, that they take pretty kindly to the Dorothy Lamour kind of travesty of their own environment which, if true, argues a complete lack of critical sense even on topics with which they are intimately acquainted.

Island dancing has been affected less than Island music. Though some missions still frown, white-style round dancing seeps through the Islands out of the port towns by way of part-whites, and is socially honorific. GIs imported jitterbugging, which probably has a lively future. Nobody knows exactly what prewhite dances were like, not even the natives. But what re-mains—particularly in islands with self-conscious cults of keep-ing the old ways alive, such as Hawaii, New Zealand and Samoa —probably retains more resemblance than the sentimental antiquarian would like to admit. The erotic aspect in indige-nous dancing is now liveliest; I suspect that it was always strong. The less decorous type of Hawaiian *hula* has spread through-out the Islands and grafted itself on local tendencies toward the lewdly active pelvis. By now Tahitian dancing is strictly cooch, bumps, grinds, and all, with, as Robert Gibbings gently understates it, "rather obvious implications."[20] Many people see elegant aesthetic connotations in the best of these "lewd motions which characterize the . . . Society Isles" as Cook's surgeon wrote a hundred and fifty years earlier.[21] There is no disputing about subjective impressions; personally I find little in the modern Island erotic dance but smirking parody of that human activity of which a great Frenchwoman remarked: "The sensation is delightful but the position grotesque."

Ensemble dances have a political function, since they please and flatter white dignitaries on ceremonial occasions; and all kinds of native dances have an economic function in paid en-tertainment for tourists, as in Rotorua, center of commercial-ized Maori doings, and Honolulu. Beyond that is a consider-able area where dancing genuinely contributes to cultural cohesion among natives. At least one L.M.S. mission school teaches its girls decorous native dancing. Maori school children are often trained in their ancestors' dances. Maori troops in the recent war took with them the old tongue-protruding, roaring *hakas* for traditional use in working up an all-out fight-ing mood before attacking Germans in Italy. However much

[20]*Sweet Thames*, 220.
[21]Ellis, Voyage, II, 170.

Island dancing has changed, however artificial some of its survivals, at least it does survive with a role to play in native life.

Native games are another matter, pretty well replaced by western rivals and with an altered function. In prewhite times, it appears, athletic skill and strength short of war were primarily a means of individual showing off, as the leader of a boys' gang likes to show that he can throw a stone farther than his subordinates. Secondarily, sports were often part of the celebration of festivals as much patriotic—if such a word makes sense here—as religious. Generally speaking, competition stayed within the community. Under white influence the modern native is well on toward making competitive sports an example of James' "moral equivalent of war." Rugby, soccer, cricket, are means for increasing the mana of the community at the expense of other communities, precisely what war had been before.

In some islands under British influence, intervillage competition, with whole populations playing on a side for weeks at a time, grew so feverish that practically no work was done and cricket had to be legally restricted to certain days. A New Zealand educator of my acquaintance posted in a Polynesian island was morally horrified to see his school team come off the field from a lost Rugby match with their eyes streaming tears; he had been only partially prepared for the atmosphere of the occasion by the rooting of the spectators, which consisted of exhortations to their side to dismember and castrate the opposition. In large centers like Suva British influence toward a tempered sportsmanship is strong enough to keep mayhem under control; but if allowed to develop untrammeled, Island versions of western team sports would make an Irish hurling match look like pat-a-cake.

The Islander's athletic prowess is impressive even under wraps. In the Palaus and Marshalls, taught baseball by the Japanese, every child of six, girls often included, has a peg like Ray Schalk's; hard or soft ball, the average Micronesian youngster is more of a ballplayer than the average modern American boy. Maori and Fijian play excellent cricket, say those who should know, and even better Rugby—the opener, faster English game. Fiji plays it barefoot. A blocky Fijian youth can drop kick a heavy, hard football fifty yards apparently off his bare toes, and trot off without the sign of a limp. And cricket is as epidemic as the law allows in Western Samoa. Every village has its concrete cricket pitch. The bat is likely to be a most unorthodox bludgeon, the field cluttered with vegetable obstacles, and the costume a wrap-around skirt, but the fervor and dexterity of the proceedings are plain, even to a spectator to whom cricket is a murky mystery.

Speech is the most conspicuous intangible. Prewhite native languages have gamely absorbed hundreds of new concepts ranging from hammer and nails to the Christian idea of grace. The white man's word might be merely modified to suit native taste: as in *ehipe* (ship), *pisupo* (aforesaid), *kovana* (governor), *afikasi* (half-caste), *tupara* (two-barreled gun). Vowels are tucked in between consonants as lubricant, so a sermon in Fijian is full of the name Jesu Kerisito; a nativized half-Samoan has scrawled down his name on the Stevenson tomb on Mount Vaea as Livigisitone. The Tongan names of the months are a fine lesson in this dilution of English: Sanuali, Fepuali, Ma'asi, 'Epeleli, Me, Sune, Sulai, 'Aokosi, Sepitema, 'Okatopa, Novema, Tisema. Sometimes a new word is born of misunderstanding, as in the famous case of *bullamacow* for beef, derived from the white man's answer to inquisitive questions when the first bull and cow were set ashore; or through extending an existing concept, as when the horse was labeled with a word meaning *pig-that-runs*, for pigs were the Islands' largest quadrupeds.

Such accretions were richening, but, as native ways lost prestige, the old languages degenerated, nicely accurate terms and subtleties of syntax sliding into disuse. A young Samoan talking-chief tells me that it is more and more difficult to find proper tutoring in the ancient upper-class language which is the vehicle of his career. Experts consider the vernacular of Tahiti only a shadow of its former glory. The missions' lame translations of Scripture into native tongues do more than anything else to keep traditional idioms reasonably expressive, for—and this is an educational scandal—by and large the native Bible is the Islander's only written literature. With all the will in the world, few early missionaries had the scholarly background or the intimate knowledge of the native tongue to do a job of much quality. I know a native educator who, when setting faulty native texts for students to correct, grinningly chooses them from the local translation of the Book of Mormon.

In spite of basic differences in structure and underlying habits of mind, the native often learned English readily— enough to get by with on shipboard, at the trader's, and with white officials. Japanese quickly became the Micronesian's *lingua franca*. German never took on, partly because English was already well established in the German sphere. But the Tahitian's French, though limited, is considered of fair quality.[22]

Polynesia did not develop genuine pidgins, possibly because it was easy for a native of Tarafu to learn the closely cognate languages of equally Polynesian Samoa, New Zealand or Easter Island. The Hawaiian's dialect, for instance, locally called pidgin, is only ungrammatical English foreshortened and larded with native and Asiatic words, about like Deep South negro talk. In Melanesia, however, where even close neighbors cannot understand one another's splintered-up languages, a *lingua franca* was needed and a real pidgin developed. It applies a Melanesian language structure to a largely English vocabulary, producing a totally new tongue that is said to require much mastering. Idioms are as rigid as bridge conventions, and the wrong improvisation from basic symbols means blank misunderstanding. Analyzing the vocabulary, Churchill classed as "forecastle English" words like *calaboose* (jail),

---

[22]In New Caledonia, particularly among Asiatic imported laborers, there appears a rudimentary French pidgin. It indicates the future by "content" and an infinitive, the past by "fini" and an infinitive, and completely disregards inflection and grammar in dozens of other ways. Thus "I shall go" is "moi content aller"; "you ate" is "toi fini manger" and so forth.

savvy, squareface (gin); and as Australian such terms as black-fellow (native), hump (carry), gammon (lie) and the ever-present bloody. German and Frenchman must learn this strange tongue to do business in many parts of Melanesia. The Germans tried to concoct a parallel pidgin using German words, but it came to nothing: raus (get out) is the only sur-vivor.

Beach-la-mar (sometimes Sandalwood English) is the spe-cific name of this pidgin, in reference to its association with the old trepang trade. Every "colorful" writer on Melanesia gives his reader some of its famous agglutinations: box-you-fight-him-cry (piano), schooner-belong-bush (wagon) and pushem-he-come-pullem-he-go-all-same-brother-belong-ax (saw). I have not yet seen in print the following identification of an eclipse of the moon: kerosene-lamp-belong-Jesus-Christ-him-bugger-up-finish-altogether. This illustrates two things: English words cannot be assumed to mean what they do in Oxford: die is to ail; only die-finish is to succumb. Sore-leg is pain; headache must be specified as sore-leg-along-head. And the vocabulary is often lurid: the planter's wife instructing a Melanesian houseboy to take out the ashes must employ a phrase that would curl Mrs. Grundy's back-hair. For beach-la-mar sprang of contact between native and sandalwooder, trepang fisher, blackbirder. Necessarily it carries echoes of the exhibitionistic foulness of speech of the forecastle modified by the cynicism of the blackleg.

After one grins at the grotesqueries, this ruffianly, inhumane stuff leaves a bad taste in the mouth. Beach-la-mar has no politenesses beyond marster for the white man, savors much of brutal contempt from white to native—as in pickaninny or monkey for child. Pondering it recreates the initial scenes: a sunny beach within the surfy wall of reef; the ship's boat stern on in the wet sand for a quick getaway, a boatkeeper in the stern sheets with a loaded rifle; the straggly, watchful group of dirty, bearded whites, some with cocked revolvers, others handling the red cloth, beads, and shaving-mirrors; the half-awed, half-surly cannibals, one encumbered by a tied-up black pig, trying to understand what the whites want, while simultaneously pondering the practicality of massacring them on the spot. They have women along, which probably means peace, but their eyes flick suspiciously under their heavy brows and farther back stand limberly naked men with bows, spears and slings, just in case. The whites know the arrows are pointed with septic human bone, the natives know the whites are savagely contemptuous opportunists. Everybody is sweaty, uneasy, squint-eyed in the blaze of sun, ready to run or snarl at an instant's notice. The whites use many gestures, but adorn them with talk—rough, jocosely obscene baby-talk for savages:

"You black fellow, what name this beach?" So *what-name* becomes the *beach-la-mar* symbol of inquiry. "Boy, you belong bush?" So *man-belong-beach* and *man-belong-bush* come to designate shore or hill populations. "This fellow stout man—good labor?" So *this-fellow* is the *beach-la-mar* demonstrative, as in *this-fellow-boat* or *this-fellow-Mary* (this woman).

Considering this unpleasant jabber to be full, accurate, and eloquent English, the Melanesian is often proud of being able to talk it; it implies a prestige-swelling acquaintance with white ways. But his pronunciation can confuse the outsider. Here is a nostalgic song from a Catholic mission songbook transliterated into French phonetics that give a better notion than English orthography of what it sounds like:

"Ples bilong mi i namberwan,
"Place belong me he number one,

Mi laikim im tasol.
Me like him, that's all.

Mi tink long papa, mama tu,
Me think along father, mother too,

Mi krai long haus blong ol.
Me cry along house belong all.

Mi wok long ples i longwe tru,
Me work along place he long way true,

Mi stap no gud tasol.
Me stop no good, that's all.

Ples bilong me i namberwan,
Place belong me he number one,

Mi laikim im tasol.
Me like him, that's all.

Ol wantok, brader, susa tu,
All one talk brothers, sisters too,

Long taim i wetim mi.
Long time they wait for me.

Ol salim plenty tok i kam,
All send plenty talk he come,

Ol tink mi lus long si.	All think me lost along sea.
Nau mi kirap, mi go long ples,	Now me get up, me go along place,
Mi no ken lusim mor.	Me no can lose him more.
Ples bilong mi i namberwan,	Place belong me he number one,
Mi laikim im tasol."	Me like him, that's all."

—Herbert Krieger, *Island Peoples of the Western Pacific,* 49.

*   *   *

Mr. Turner, you do not mean to say that you think these Eromangans are men? Question put to the Rev. Mr. Turner by a sandalwooder. (George Turner, *Nineteen Years in Polynesia,* 442.)

The flavor of *beach-la-mar* is good preparation for what happened to natives as whites tried to use them to make money out of the Islands. Efficient production of likely commodities —coconut oil or copra, trepang, pearl shell, sugar, cotton— required prolonged labor from cheap, docile humans. Whites early assumed that the presence on the scene of thousands of natives could provide the necessary labor supply. It took a long time, details of the experiments being very nasty indeed, to prove this a mistake.

The nastiness originated in the less admirable characteristics of both exploiting whites and suspicious natives. Whites can be taken first:

They made the fundamental error of all recent slavers in considering the native subhuman. A soldier of Mendaña's set the tone three centuries ago. When ordered to fire to alarm the encroaching Marquesans, he took careful aim and killed a native; reproached, he said that a marksman's pride did not permit him to waste lead. He was spiritual brother of the American skipper at Easter Island a hundred years ago who shot natives on the beach strictly for sport. Sometimes the white brute's contempt was tinged with distaste for what he considered brutishness in the native. Thus Lockerby, after failing to prevent by either protest or bribery the strangling of a dead man's wife in Fiji, bombarded the offending village, burned its huts, and cut down its coco palms as deterrent. But a more characteristic picture was of the skipper of the early trading vessel on which Mrs. Wallis' husband was mate. Failing to bully a Fijian chief into making a disadvantageous bargain, this captain held him on board at the point of a gun to persuade him to change his mind. The chief tried to follow his retainers, who had jumped overboard to swim ashore, and was shot in the water. At the captain's orders the crew opened fire on the swimming retainers too; when they dived too skilfully for the marksmen, a boat's crew was ordered to pursue them. Mr. Wallis persuaded the captain that this was impractical. But he was not yet finished. As the ship went out through the break in the reef, he ordered muskets fired into a passing canoe without even knowing whether its crew belonged to the offending chief.

Those are the patterns. The sandalwooder unable to establish working relations with natives on likely islands might kidnap a a chief and hold him for ransom in sandalwood. On whatever commercial errand, the whites thought little of robbing, killing or torturing the subhuman native, even when it served no useful purpose. As revenge for hostility, they might put ashore natives or foremast hands infected with measles or smallpox to create epidemics. Yet even shock from such fiendishness should not blind the reader to the native's acceptance of such terms. The Melanesian from Tanna enlisted enthusiastically in boat's crews to help bully and kidnap his fellow-New Hebrideans on other islands. Rotuman, Maori, Hawaiian, had few scruples about brutalizing the people of strange places. And the foregoing already contains the incident in which Cakobau suggested making cannon-targets of his own people.

Nor was the native a passive victim. From the beginning he captured ships and massacred their crews whenever he could manage it, sometimes in retaliation for brutality, at other times for sheer love of plunder. A boat's crew from the "Brigand" were lured into the bush by leering promises of women on Mare (Loyalties), then knocked on the head for what they had on their persons. When the captain of the "Sisters" beat a Mare chief, he was boarded next day by a swarm of natives who massacred every man; their carelessness exploded the ship's powder, and killed numbers of them, so they vowed—and took vengeance on—the next whites to appear. After a friendly trading session with the natives of one of the Carolines, Captain Morrell of the "Antarctic" was astounded to see fifty canoes each containing twenty men in war-paint push off from the beach with his ship as their unmistakable objective. When, to avoid trouble, he took to the offing, the canoes stubbornly followed him for four miles.[23] The captain of the "Star" insulted a chief on the Isle of Pines. Next day, as previously arranged, thirty natives came meekly on board to sharpen their axes before cutting sandalwood for the ship. When the last ax was razor-sharp, the axmen turned on the crew, split every man's head open, looted the ship and burned her to the water's edge. The white man's notion of proper retaliation might be to drive the noncombatants of an offending village into a cave and build a fire at the mouth to cook or suffocate them all. Now distill the essence of these mutual savageries and forecast what would happen when, in such an atmosphere, white men tried to make willing or forcible laborer-exiles of the Islanders.

A New London sealing skipper apparently has the honor of first trying to enslave the Pacific native. Operating out of Mas Afuera (consort island of Selkirk's Juan Fernandez off the Chilean coast) in 1805, he needed labor to grow green stuff and cut firewood at a supply depot he planned there. So he put in at Easter Island and, after some bloody fighting, kidnapped twelve men and ten women. Considering the situation secure

---

[23]Morrell was a better type than many of his competitors in early pickings among the Islands. He comments: "No doubt this system of treachery, which prevails or did so once prevail, on every inhabited island in the Pacific Ocean, is a part of their education. They sin without the law, and should be judged without the law . . . I could not find it in my heart to throw cold lead and iron among them." (*Narrative of Four Voyages*, 393 et seq.) But he took a bloody mass-revenge on another island where he lost men in a surprise attack.

when he was out of sight of land, he took off his victims' bonds. Immediately they dived overboard. A boat was sent after them, but they dived under it and scattered. The last seen of the poor devils they were still hopelessly, compulsively, swimming toward the quarter of the horizon where their home island lay.

From the same quarter came more tragedy in the mid-century, when Peru was selling the world nitrates from the Chincha Islands. Chinese to mine the stuff in the smashing sun and eddying dust proved turbulent and demanding, so the Peruvians turned to the Islands and began busily to depopulate them. The slow murder of it was so notorious that, thirty years later, Micronesians seeking passage on a trading vessel were terrified to hear that she was to touch an atoll in the Marshalls named Piru. Of over 200 labor—this noun means not the unified body of workers but items in a human herd of cattle—taken from Nukulaelae in the Ellices by Peruvian slavers in 1867, only two survived to reach home again. The slavers occasionally found help in Christianity. On one island they made a huge haul because a psalm-singing beachcomber persuaded native pastors and communicants that men and women signing to go to Peru would learn all about God and bring home much money to build new churches with. A tale like that makes one wish he believed in hell. Along with this beachcomber should fry the captain of the Peruvian ship returning used-up labor to the Islands who found smallpox among his cargo, made for Rapa, south of Tahiti, and dumped sick and well there, creating ashore an epidemic that practically exterminated the Polynesians of that already hard-hit island.

On the other side of the Pacific opposite numbers of these gentry "recruiting labor" for plantations in Queensland, Fiji, Samoa and the New Hebrides, were presently notorious under the name of "blackbirders." The underlying principle is still lively: that, though few Islanders work well on their own islands, Melanesians earn their salt if taken clear away from home, which effectively removes the homesick temptation to quit after a few weeks and return to village life among mutually supporting relatives. Thus the dockwalloping of Noumea today is done not by the indigenous New Caledonian but by his cousins from the Loyalties.[24]

To lend some color of honesty to his activities and to secure the legal position of the eventual employer, the blackbirder usually went through the formality of having the "recruit" sign a written agreement, disregarding the fact that he could neither read nor write any language. Such a paper called for three, five, or seven years of labor in return for maintenance on the job, a certain sum payable in trade goods at the end of the contract, and free transportation home. In the employer's island re-calcitrance was treated as a criminal, not a civil, offense and punished by flogging, imprisonment or fines to be worked out in additional time served.

For years there was little or no public supervision of such contracts or their enforcement, and the inevitable occurred. Fines extended contracts to double the original agreement; by fraud time-expired labor was cajoled into re-signing; disease and homesickness killed the "recruits" off, payments were scamped or neglected. Repatriation often consisted of landing a time-expired recruit on any handy shore where, a thousand to one, he would be killed and eaten by the local tribes. Veterans of the trade told humorous tales of dropping over-board returnees too ill to be worth re-signing, and watching for the flash of hostile tomahawks that greeted them when they managed to swim to the beach.

Even when all was conducted honestly, and the recruit came home with a trade musket and a wooden box full of sticks of tobacco and red cloth, with a bell on its lock, vaingloriously wearing a red shirt and jean trousers, his chief and his relatives would promptly strip him of everything in compensation for his long absence from his village duties. For his years in

[24]Half a dozen New Caledonian Frenchmen told me that the Loyalty man is imported because, being part Polynesian, he works better than the Melanesian. Repeating that to planters in Polynesian islands produces raucous laughter. Actually, of course, the Germans had to import Melanesians to work in Polynesian Samoa, and the only going plantation on Polynesian Tahiti today is worked by imported Indo-Chinese.

Queensland, Samoa or Fiji he would have nothing to show but a corrupting smattering of white man's ways, a fluent knowledge of beach-la-mar and sometimes a lasting bent toward homosexuality.

In the early years of this traffic it was manifestly impossible for the native to understand to what he was agreeing or to conceive of daily, regular labor on a supervised job. So fraud and force were implicit in it all. The schooners and brigs, often disguised as bêche-de-mer or sandalwood traders, that scoured the New Hebrides, the Solomons, the Santa Cruz group for labor were known in beach-la-mar by the significant term snatch-snatch. Their captains were renegade Americans, Australians, Frenchmen, Germans; their home ports Sydney, Noumea, Apia; their crews white, Polynesian or Melanesian scum. The best that can be said of any is that some were worse than others. Payment went by head of labor landed—the 1865 rate varied between £4/10 and £6/10 per head.

The methods were grim lessons in how cunning and brutal men can be. Influenced by local talk about relative working conditions, a native might be willing to sign for Queensland but not for Fiji. Very well, tell him Queensland and take him to Fiji regardless. Once landed, there was precious little he could do about it. Or the fact that the last blackbirder had kidnapped six women to amuse his crew might make the whole village reluctant—so entice a canoeload of natives alongside with a show of trade goods, then drop a cannon ball to bilge their canoe and lasso or stun them as they flounder in the water. Those breaking free might be recaptured by a boathook through the cheek.

With their purpose so well known, it seems a wonder that blackbirders ever filled their quotas. But they had numerous tricks. The favor of the local chief might be secured by generous presents of trade goods—in his eyes not outright bribery, but compensation in advance for loss of the services of men to be recruited—and the chief's orders to such and such men to sign on were not easily ignored. Where dried human heads were highly esteemed, blackbirders used them as presents;[25] some manufactured their own fresh supply by random kidnapping and murdering. The wish of an individual to sign often came from maladjustment: the misfit might want to get away from it all. It is grimly significant that emigrating as an indentured laborer became a popular substitute for suicide in Dobu. Or the chief might hand the blackbirder the troublemakers whom he wanted to slough off. Besides, there was prestige in going overseas whence white men came with wonderful things. And recruiting was the only practical way to acquire a gun, which, as gunpowder bulked larger in Melanesian feuds, became almost the price of survival in some islands.

Spearheading the system were tactical experts called "recruiters," paid well for special skill in trickery and cajolery. They went in for impressively gaudy costumes, sleight-of-hand and ventriloquism to impress wavering chiefs with the mana of the recruiter. Sometimes, exploiting native faith in the friendliness of missionaries, they dressed up as parsons in black coats and top hats and tricked out the ships to resemble mission vessels. As soon as a dozen likely natives had crowded below to see the bishop, who was said to be ill in his berth but eager to meet them, hatches were clapped on and the bishop's visitors next saw the light of day off the coast of Viti Levu. When the missionary "Dayspring" was wrecked in the New Hebrides, a French blackbirding outfit went to elaborate trouble to salvage and refit her, considering that her familiar, innocent silhouette would be a great tactical asset. But the Lord slept not: the new crew got drunk, let her drag anchor in a squall, and irretrievably bilged her on a reef before she could begin her new career of treachery.

When both force and deception were indispensable, it stands to reason that there was often trouble on board. Blackbirders went armed like pirates. Tales of mutiny among the "labor" pile up in a bloody pyramid like Tamerlane's. One case can

[25]Before blackbirding this human-head trade was quite a thing, particularly in New Zealand, as traders found that European curio-fanciers would pay high for a well-tattooed and dried Maori specimen.

typify the whole. The "Carl" of Sydney was in grave danger when her human cargo belowside was discovered to be ripping up the bunks and sharpening the strips into wooden spears to fight its way out with. The hatch was opened and the crew, led by an American named Murray who sang *Marching Through Georgia* in sadistic exultation as he loaded and fired, pumped lead into its screaming, writhing depths. In the morning over fifty labor were found dead, twenty-four seriously wounded, only five unscathed. Higgledy-piggledy the dead and wounded were trundled overboard for the sharks and the red-soaked hold was hurriedly scraped and whitewashed; a most opportune measure, for the ship was presently overhauled by HMS "Rosario" cruising to check up on blackbirders. Finding nothing amiss, the commander of the boarding party let her go. It took elaborate investigation and trial, with Murray turning Queen's evidence, to get the story into the record. Such scenes were not the rule, for it was the blackbirder's business to land as much labor as possible alive, but they were always potential. Wholesale death struck again and again, and not always by violence. On the French blackbirder "Moorea" 280 labor jumped overboard to swim ashore; only thirty made it.

The first protest against the trade came from missionaries in the areas worked. Christian mercy demanded it. Besides, the repatriated recruit, usually addicted to smoking, cursing and other worldly white habits, was a moral blight on a missionized village. When missions forbade converts to sign on, blackbirders expressed bitter antimission feelings in violence and sabotage. As seagoing roughnecks and traders swapped yarns over their squareface, they not only roared with laughter over the cleverness of the recruiter's latest unscrupulous dodge, they also took great relish in incidents cooked up to make natives think missionaries were treacherously conniving at blackbirding.

With mission and blackbirder sworn enemies, as they would have been in any case, war resulted. The blackbirder's weapons were economic. Plantations had to have labor and their own-

ers often commanded great influence in Sydney. For all the
native's reputation for laziness, Melanesian labor paid like
houses. In Queensland a Melanesian plantation "boy" cost the
planter only £25 a year, including the expense of recruiting and
repatriation; whereas a white laborer, only two-thirds as handy
at cane cutting, cost two and a half times as much. Planters
washed their hands of responsibility for blackbirding methods,
confining themselves to protestations—not too well substantiated—that, in the "labor-lines," they themselves treated their
"boys" with firm but loving care. Court testimony from most
natives was not admissible as evidence. Thus, with the principal recruiting areas beyond the official shadow of the British
flag, it was very difficult to bring even the most brutal blackbirder to book in Australian courts.

But missions had influential friends too—in London. The
iniquities of the labor trade and the impossibility of controlling
it unless Fiji were British was a strong mission-inspired argument for annexation. A special squadron of light, fast men-of-
war based on Sydney was assigned to put the fear of God into
blackbirders in waters where his Majesty's writs did not yet
run. Such harassing—plus occasional strokes of luck in secur-
ing convicting evidence—had a healthy if minor effect. In time
regulation of contracts was stiffened, and all blackbirding vessels had to carry government inspectors to see that bargains
were fairly struck. The French followed suit lackadaisically.
But it can hardly be said that such administrative and legal
measures ever cleaned up the problem. The gentry concerned
were congenitally slippery and cynical. When, for instance, to
reduce homosexuality in labor lines, government required
wives to be shipped along with married natives signing on, the
schooner captains merely kidnapped women at random to be
landed as so many head of wives.

Though grosser abuses had disappeared, the system of indentured imported labor was still very much alive when
World War II struck the Pacific. It was the backbone of
copra in New Guinea, the Solomons and the New Hebrides,
and of mining in New Caledonia. Its defenders maintained

stoutly that plantation work improved the native's health, educated him in white ways, and raised his standards of living by increasing his wants. The position is not all nonsense, however biased the proponent; the high ratio of natives re-signing contracts of their own free will bears that out. Attackers contend that it unsettled the native emotionally and socially and contributed seriously to depopulation of the village from which he was absent during his most vigorous years. You can still hear both points of view in the Pacific. Soon, however, the whole question will be academic. Indentured service—meaning low wages and criminal penalties for recalcitrance—has recently been abolished in both the Australian and the French spheres of responsibility. Fiji abolished it after World War I. Recruiting is dead or dying, to be replaced by some as yet inchoate form of wage bargaining. The planter is shriekingly indignant, the reformer gloating. It is not yet clear whether the more elaborate phases of the copra industry in the Islands can survive the change.

In any case blackbirding proper has long been an anachronism. The substitute measures that Fiji took seventy years ago makes less sensational reading. But they typify the alternative in the white man's effort to get work done in the Pacific. In the long run they may have had even more serious consequences than all the killing accomplished by sandalwooders and blackbirders together. For blackbirded labor either died or was sent home. The imported Asiatic usually settled down to elbow the native off his own island.

*   *   *

The annexation of Fiji was still uncertain in 1871 when it was suggested that the inhabitants of British India, already serving as indentured labor in such places as the West Indies, would solve Fiji's labor problem and obviate the need for blackbirding. The treaty of annexation was hardly signed when the first shipload of Indians, fruit of stately negotiation between Lord Salisbury and the viceregal government of India,

appeared in Fiji. These slender, brown, poker-faced people
were leaving nose-to-the-grindstone poverty in their own over-
crowded land to apply their incredible industriousness to the
promising soil of Melanesia. Their carefully supervised contracts provided the usual free repatriation; but, if they chose
to stay after expiration, they were to enjoy the same political
standing as anybody else in Fiji. Few returned. Even under
indenture, life was better here. Besides, many had lost caste
by leaving home and could not return without great trouble
and expense for ritual rehabilitation. By now the Indian,
tenant-farming for the monopolistic Colonial Sugar Refining
Company or running a small business, outnumbers the Fijian
and is the colony's nearest insoluble problem.

Other Asiatics preceded the Indian into the isles of the
blest. Planters rushing into cotton and sugar in the Marquesas
and Societies during the American Civil War imported
Chinese plantation labor. Smoothfacedly keeping their own
counsel while they sweated in newly-cleared fields, the Chinese
knew precisely what they wanted and presently had it. As their
terms expired, they left the plantation—just as they did later
in Hawaii—to set up in business. Baker, storekeeper, sole
processor of vanilla, money-lender, the Chinese now controls
practically the whole economic life of the French islands in the
South Central Pacific. He liked Polynesian girls and has left
his hereditary mark on myriads of Chinese-Polynesian half-
bloods, though he seldom acknowledges paternity or marries
a brown girl. Here is a marked difference, due to heaven knows
what local variations, between the Chinese in Tahiti and those
in Hawaii. The difference in consequences is equally marked.
The Hawaiian Chinese has been usually well liked, eager to
mingle, and often acknowledged a valuable citizen, whereas
the Tahitian Chinese is even more harshly feared and hated
than the Indian in Fiji and, apparently from both unpopularity
and inclination, keeps aloofly to himself. What to do about
him—for hated or not, destructive or not, he is indispensable
in the French islands—appears absolutely insoluble. The one

saving grace is that there are only a few thousands of him and the natives[26] are increasing in the same proportion.

The French involved themselves in even stranger difficulties by using Asiatic indentured labor in New Caledonia. There the noble volcanic hills, covered on the dry side with a mor-. bidly stunted cousin of eucalyptus, are so full of useful metals that, as an Australian expert is said to have told a London banker: "My lord, if you was to take all the —— mineral out of those —— mountains, the —— mountains would fall to pieces."[27] To mine these ores the New Caledonian native was considered useless, of course. During early development French convicts were utilized as miners.[28] But when the con-. vict colony was abolished that supply vanished, though the ores were still there and much money had been invested. So France turned to her teeming colonies in southeast Asia whence indentured Annamese and Tonkinese, conical hats, sarongs, and all, were flooded into the mines, supplemented later by Javanese. Just as rugged and self-sufficient as Chinese or Indian, fairly docile though given to sudden hysterical violence, these "Chinois," as they are locally labeled, kept the clumsy, obsolescent economy of the island going until World War II.

Then things happened, all wrong from the local point of view. The Chinois' contracts ran out during the war; but on

[26]Natives in reference to Tahiti and the Marquesas by no means implies pure Polynesian descent. Those who should know best say that practically every ostensible Tahitian has some degree of white or Asiatic admixture.

[27]Wilfred Burchett, Pacific Treasure Island, 51.

[28]The New Caledonian convict colony was preceded by abortive efforts in the same direction in Tahiti and the Marquesas. In the background were humanitarian as well as punitive motives. The convicts were mostly second-raters who, it was hoped, would make something of themselves after serving their time. There was a separate colony for radicals sentenced to deportation after the Paris Commune. France was hoping to repeat the British success with Australia, but was violently denounced by the Australians for having the audacity to dump jailbirds on their doorsteps—a reaction that needs no exclamation point. A great many of the present locally established French in New Caledonia are probably descendants of convicts, but the matter is not openly discussed.

the tenable grounds that with the Japanese holding Indo-China and Java, repatriation was impossible, they were held, with indentures compulsorily extended, to carry on with their assignment of doing all the civilian manual labor. Two years ago, with commendably liberal intentions, France abolished indentures and threw them all on a free labor-market. They are now earning far more than enough to compensate for the local inflationary rise in living costs. The French, whom they thoroughly mistrust, tell them that these days Indo-China and Java are poverty-stricken and revolution-torn and they will be much better off staying on the job in New Caledonia, which is probably true. But the Chinois insist on the letter of the bond, and cling determinedly to the French obligation to repatriate them. They have stayed far longer than they originally agreed to, have sizable hoards of American dollars mostly disreputably earned, are chronically homesick and they want to go home, no matter what the suspect French may say. Recently seven of them actually paid the high airplane fare home via Sydney in token of their neck-or-nothing impatience.

Though still temporizing, sooner or later out of mere shame the French will have to find shipping and repatriate them. The world will then be presented with the extraordinary spectacle, unparalleled so far as I am aware, of a country full of things that the world needs, well-established as an economic entity, only a few days' sail from cities of a million people, running down like an unwound clock. Nobody to pick over nickel ore or screen chrome-bearing sand or repair buildings or work on roads or clean the streets of Noumea, so far as they ever are cleaned—nobody to do any of the sweaty, persevering things that keep communities operating. Tardily the French are trying to mechanize their mining, but they will still need numerous hands, and hands are precisely what they will not have available. The New Caledonian white man is either a discouraged broussard—a small planter trying to make ends meet with coffee trees or cattle—or a white-collar type, usually in the government bureaucracy, to whom manual labor is unthinkable. A fantastic situation, but it palpably exists in New Caledonia today. For a final touch, nobody has any concrete ideas as what to do about it in anticipation of the final catastrophe. The nearest thing to practicality is a hope that, as emotions cool after the war, New Caledonia can import Japanese or Korean labor on some controlled basis similar to indenture.

At best that is a mere evasion of the problem. This localized and superlative quandary is a convenient *reductio ad absurdum* of the whole Island system of imported labor. As an imaginative advisor might have foretold, it is evidently fruitless to look for healthy economic activity in people without a live personal or cultural stake in the country where they work. New Caledonia postponed the evil day first with convicts, then with Asiatics, but now here it is again, because the world's conscience will no longer sanction the punitive elements of the indenture system. No matter how New Caledonia makes out with her creeping nightmare, her absurd example re-emphasizes the necessity for welding Tahiti's Chinese and Fiji's Indians much more closely into the human, as well as the economic, local structure. Otherwise they will remain as they are now, corrosive irritants, inducing malignant social growths.

Hawaii accomplished much toward assimilation of her successive waves of imported labor. But it was done callously at the expense of the native. Strongly as Hawaiian genes are represented in the mixed inhabitant of Hawaii, old Hawaiian ways are pretty close to extinction and, as the reader already knows, the process of acculturation was greedy, venal and shattering. The groundwork for this ethnic tragedy—granting that the ending may be fruitful—was laid by selfishness and accident generations ago. The world's conscience as now sensitized would probably not tolerate the same harsh solution of the problems of Tahiti and Fiji.

With luck, to stir Fijian and Indian together, Hawaiian-style, into a catch-as-catch-can, bewildered, resentful mass might eventually produce a vigorous Fijian-Indian at the expense of Fijian culture as such. But thus to doom the most likable people in the South Seas is not a pretty idea; nor would the Fijian think so. If it were tried many an Indian would probably die a violent death and many an Indian shack go up in smoke. Nor does the Indian in Fiji show much desire to mingle. He usually disdains marriage with the Fijian, relies too much on the new Indian nationalism for emotional ballast, and spends most of his political energy shoving toward social and economic gain, directly at the Fijian's expense. During World War II he made unhappily sure of being detested by staging large-scale strikes in the sugar fields. As yet only a very limited stratum of Indian young people try to consider themselves people of Fiji, rather than Indians justifiably sulking under exploitation in a foreign land.

Much of this is to be expected of an underprivileged minority with easily distinguishable racial characteristics and ways stemming from an ancient and complicated civilization. But some of it is special, imported from India and deliberately kept alive by local leaders. Those sugar strikes, I am told by those who should know, came not so much from despair or disloyalty as from the Indian politician-leader's opportunism. The worst of it is that, though acting and treated like a minority, the Indians of Fiji are now a majority.

Fijians, on the other hand, came out of the recent war with increased strategic capital. Their chiefs wisely insisted that every able-bodied man among them join up; and the miraculous output-per-man-hour of Fijian labor battalions on Suva docks was excelled only by the terrific fighting record of Fijian combat troops on Bougainville. The contrast with the Indian— whose lackadaisical gestures toward going into uniform were marred by his making conditions about segregated units—was glaring. The white man's government on Fiji had always been more sympathetic with the outgoing, courteous Fijian than with the Indian's ostensible combination of cringing and contempt. Since the war the Fijian Indian has hardly a friend in the local world.

To exacerbate this cleavage, the British have painted themselves into a corner with conflicting commitments, much as they did in Palestine. Certainly these commitments can be readily interpreted as conflicting, which is quite as bad. Lord Salisbury's pledge of equal footing for Indians remaining in Fiji was explicit. But the Fijian and most responsible whites in Fiji have an ineradicable impression that the Deed of Cession, which established British sovereignty in Fiji, pledged Britain to favor native interests—a pledge that has been fairly well honored. As querulous Indians point out, the Deed actually contains no such clause; but their antagonists retain a conviction that it is somehow there implicitly, like Lord Peter's interpretation of the Gospel in A Tale of a Tub, or else that, at the time of signing, Sir Hercules Robinson said something to some chiefs that amounted to commitment, nobody is sure just what.

None of it is evidence; but the net intent—to guarantee the Fijian a paramount stake in his own country—is hard to quarrel with. But the Indians, whose numbers are growing very fast, already hanker after the large land-reserves set aside for Fijian use in traditional "slash-and-burn" sustenance-gardening. Pointing hysterically to Lord Salisbury and asserting with justification that the Indian makes more efficient use of land than any native, these clamorous interlopers call for opening up native reserves to all comers, a competition in which the Indian would win in a walk. The Fijian and his white ally point indignantly at the Deed of Cession, though carefully refraining from reading it, and hint ominously that encroachment by Indians on Fijian land, legal or illegal, will mean violently one-sided trouble. The newborn tendency among Indians to renounce militancy and exclusiveness can hardly grow to useful proportions in time to prevent some sort of explosion. A lovely place, Fiji, but uneasy.

Samoa is the lucky place—in this respect, at least. To work confiscated German copra- and cocoa-plantations after 1914, New Zealand maintained the German system of importing indentured Chinese. Since German development had not proceeded too far, their numbers have never been ominously high and quick repatriation kept them from biting deeply into local business. Thus, when the world's sense of native interests sharpened, Western Samoa could ship most of her indentured Chinese home after the war emergency without tearing the local economy apart.[29]

In the Pacific, however, as elsewhere, the solution of one problem invariably uncovers another waiting in the wings. Now that copra and cocoa prices are high, the Samoan Crown Estates—German plantations acquired as reparations by New Zealand in 1919—are paying well; current schemes for developing new export products, such as dried bananas, look very promising. But with most of the Chinese gone, who is to weed and prune? Government management is trying to get along by hiring Samoan labor. Some elements among the natives would greatly like to see the estates turned over to the Samoans. Both ideas bring up the old question: Can and will natives on their own islands work hard enough, in a sense recognizable to whites?

This notion of daily labor on cash exports is probably the most far-reaching innovation that whites brought to the Pacific. For their own varying reasons, missionary, trader, planter, government, all came to dislike the native's wealth-sharing and sought to teach him white-style industry and the thrift and acquisitiveness that go with it. Was the effort altogether a failure? On the answer to that hinges much of the future of the Islands.

*   *   *

On this point realistic extremes sound ironical. Said a high French official:

"Our planter sits on his veranda and says: 'Look at that lazy Kanaka—he won't let me hire him to work my crops.' "

An Englishman managing large plantations on an island that affords little but native labor said that he despaired of

[29]Samoan leaders, who are quite as given to race prejudice as anybody else, would like to see all Chinese sent home. Actually, under proper precautions to see that they do not go into retail trade, those with permanent relations with Samoan women and children by them are now permitted to stay, provided the children are legally classed and reared as Samoans.

ever training the native to steady employment. His records showed the average native employee working only nine and a half days a year. But, he said, once this unsteadiness was accepted, an answer was possible.

"Natives all want a certain amount of cash each year to take care of church contributions and purchases at the store. They will work until those wants are satisfied. I take on all comers as they appear and train them—these are simple jobs and hard to forget. When a certain native reappears next year to work a week or ten days, he doesn't need retraining. By now practically everybody of working age within five miles knows this work well enough. Say I need fifty men a day. I don't care what fifty, and the chances are that about that many are looking for work at the time. If they all work ten days a year, a revolving force of 1,500 does me nicely, and I have come reasonably close to developing just that."

That solution would drive an American personnel director mad, but then his type does not belong in the South Seas. In parallel, the government of Fiji deliberately spreads dockside jobs as widely as possible among Fijian longshoremen, hoping thus to keep them close to village relationships and taro patch, instead of allowing them to become proletarianized, dependent on wages alone under town conditions.

There in Fiji the question of whether natives will work under appropriate circumstances is easily answered, at least superficially. The Fijian labor battalions settled that. In the miniature shipyard in Suva now building eighty-foot ketches for inter-Island trade most of the shipwrights are earnest, deft Fijians adzing timbers for a subtly-curved hull much as their ancestors did when the splendid Fijian deep-set canoes brought admiring purchasers from Tonga. Since shipbuilding is a high-prestige trade among Fijians, absenteeism is low, efficiency high.

But gold mining has no prestige; until whites came the Fijian knew nothing of gold. For years, nevertheless, by agreement with Fijian sugar interests, the sizable gold mines above Tavua on the main island of Fiji have used only Fijian labor below the high-skill level. Nobody pretends that, though decreasing, labor turnover is not hamperingly high, or that Canadian hard-rock men could not get out more troy ounces per hour. Some maintain that the Fijian working in the gold mines loses his better personal qualities. But the arrangement does make a liar of the South Sea old-timer's axiom that arduous, steady jobs and natives are incompatible. The secret here seems to be managerial imagination in giving the native employee and his family a community life satisfactory in native terms, built, with modifications, on the chief's responsibility and on organized recreation.

In New Zealand the recent war taught many a manager of a freezing works or canning factory that, with tact and knowledge of Maori ways, he can use a high proportion of Maori on his pay roll. In Micronesia postwar shortages of personnel forced the U.S. Navy to train Marshall Islanders for jobs requiring both skill and responsibility. When I last saw Majuro, a skeleton force of whites was merely supervising Marshallese in the operation and maintenance of practically every mechanical device on the island, from jeeps to meteorological equipment. In local terms, the pay on these jobs is good, but that is not the main point—working for the Navy is honorific; Uncle Sam is a great chief.

So, if his habits of mind are allowed for, the native can be worth having on the job. One of his handicaps comes from not yet having the hang of money. True, he has made great progress with that institution since the days when the Tahitians, though accepting Chile dollars in trade, valued them according to beauty, and would swap two worn dollars for one new one. But the idea of a steady stream of regularly-earned purchasing power to balance future purchasable needs is still alien. In the Islands money is seldom a repository of value, but a means solely of exchange and the Islander acts as if, like the Israelites' manna or the Townsendites' pension-payments, his money will vanish if not soon spent. If he tried to save, for that matter, his relatives would probably relieve him of his hoard in a short while. His earnings from pearl diving or vanilla growing, which come all in a lump, usually mean a binge in the style of a lumberjack after the spring break-up— buying presents, riding in taxis, making feasts until all is expended. The steady, thrifty man committed to another-day- another-dollar would still be an unpopular anomaly in most Island communities. So the native is steadiest and most productive when working under arrangements involving issues other than individual gain—in semifeudal isolation, as on a mission- run co-operative farm or Hawaiian cattle ranch, or else on a job that carries traditional prestige.

It is hard to be patient with those who maintain that native "laziness" comes of genetic disability. Unproved "heredity" is always the last resort of stubborn prejudice. This notion of in- born incapacity is even worse in connection with native in- telligence and educability. Time and again better-than-average teachers of Pacific natives have told me that, though their pupils learn glibly by rote and do well up to a certain point, everything beyond that ravels away—it just isn't in them, some- thing racially lacking . . . On the other hand I know per- sonally native leaders with high university degrees whose ability to accumulate, digest, marshal, act on information, and manip- ulate complicated ideas is, flatly, as high as anybody's any- where. To mention two eminent names, the personalities, intellectual habits and dexterity in cerebration of Sir Apirana Ngata, Maori, and Ratu Sir Lala Sukuna, Fijian, are unquali- fiedly superlative. Even if complete trust can be placed in the newer intelligence tests designed to get away from specific cultural conditioning, they have not yet been used on Islanders on a large enough scale and in skilled enough hands to make any verdict on the Islander's fundamental intelligence scientifi- cally respectable.

Thus the they-just-haven't-the-capacity theory looks very dubious. No layman can go farther here than querulously to say that it is high time psychologists really settled this question of "racial incapacity" and promulgated their findings impressively for the general public.

The fact of apparent native lack of capacity past a certain

point is, however, unquestionable. For explanation consider the theory of a conscientious white teacher with whom I discussed the matter. He thought it a matter of language affecting a child's formative years. Even in their richer prewhite forms Island tongues had practically no abstract terms, gave scope for few general concepts, as missionaries early discovered. Yet much of the thinking in white-style education involves abstraction, requires high skill in manipulation of word tools ending in -ity and -ness. The native child, reared in a language poor in abstractions, is too clumsy with them to go either as fast or as far as the white child of no greater potential intelligence. As a rule, besides, the only book available in the native tongue is the Bible. To learn anything beyond Scripture the native must first learn English or French, which imposes the second handicap of an alien, and seldom thoroughly assimilated, language. The wonder is that there are any Ngatas and Sukunas to demonstrate that, given unusual ability and ample opportunity, the native can show himself his instructors' peer. Or so my man said.

Significantly the apparent capacity and intellectual responsibility of natives grades down from the peak without a gap. One meets samples of each successive grade on every hand. The native leader-chief making excellent use of university education but not quite with the utter ease and incisiveness of the brilliant men mentioned above. The cream of the Native Medical Practitioners who, with scanty and partial training, carry the elements of western medicine to so many islands. The completely self-educated chief in New Caledonia who, doing his own thinking, made more sense for us about civil rights and self-government for natives than most of his white guardians. The platitudinous leader-chief, ambitious victim of reading too many white men's truisms, whose jumpy half-bakedness does not altogether mar considerable capacity. The shrewd and, in his own tongue, incisive witch-doctor who scornfully doubles as deacon in the church and, for relish on the side, dabbles in native intrigue against white government. All those were people whom no competent educator would dare discount as congenitally ineducable beyond that "certain point." Down at the other end of the scale, of course, is the soddenly stupid native who, intellectually speaking, hardly wiggles when poked with a stick. But western civilization produces those too, with less excuse.

This must be the intelligent way to round it up: The Islands are populated by people probably, if not yet demonstrably, as intelligent *in posse* as anybody else. They have not yet thoroughly absorbed western economic ways, but it is clear that they display no heritable inability to work in western style. They have been highly selective, often imaginative, in taking over white gadgets. It is extremely important to keep all that in mind, because every year there will be more and more of those adaptable and potentially able people.

That—the population problem—is what makes every one of the Islands' problems a very hot potato.

*   *   *

Few outsiders are prepared to hear that Island populations are growing rapidly. So many books have described the tragedy of the doomed native, watching with melancholy dignity the gradual extinction of his noble race; so many writers have quoted the sad old Tahitian proverb about how palm and coral may go on growing, but man will cease. The fact is, however, that within the last generation or two, the drooping curve of population on practically all South Sea Islands first leveled off and then turned vivaciously upward. The Marquesans, proverbially worst off, recently joined the list of growing rather than of dying peoples, along with the natives of the Gambiers, where it took a long, long time to recover from Père Laval's pious ministrations.

Thus the accusation that whites doomed the Islanders to extinction by bringing alien diseases and vices has been disproved. Though the charge may never have been morally justified, it nevertheless gnawed at the western conscience. One commendable result was white effort to check the damage by use of western medicine so far as funds and native misunderstanding permitted. Whatever one may think of missionaries, traders, officials and anthropologists, nobody can deny an unimpeachable right to "interfere with the natives" to the man with a hypodermic syringe and a supply of neo-arsphenamin. But perhaps he is the worst threat of all.

That is one of a dozen aspects of the fascinating subject of population trends in the Islands—the more fascinating because nobody is at all sure just what went on or goes on now.

When the white man burst in on him, the native was not disease-free, as idyllists would like to believe. In Polynesia and Micronesia he probably suffered from hookworm, the intestinal parasite associated with bare feet and poor disposal of excreta; yaws, ulcerous cousin of syphilis so closely related that it baffles microscopes and serological tests, the disease apparently differing only in clinical aspects and in being acquired by way of flies, not sin; filariasis, the mosquito-borne infestation of the blood and lymph that culminates in the obscene, puffed incapacitation of elephantiasis; boils, ulcers, numerous and marvelously varied fungous diseases of the skin. Most of Melanesia had all those, plus malaria. In the opinion of some doctors, even the shorter Polynesian list helps considerably to explain the native's "laziness"; a man with yaws, hookworm, and filariasis is not likely to develop prolonged habits of sustained energy or the institutions that go with them. But the pertinent point about these Island diseases is that, except for some forms of malaria, they are not usually quick killers. Many of the white man's were, and none improved the Islander's viability.

Since he had none of our hereditarily transmitted partial immunities, not only smallpox and cholera, but measles, mumps, even chicken-pox, killed him by thousands. Every island remembers times when some such "childhood disease" laid low perhaps one native in five. The classic example appeared when H.M.S. "Dido" brought Cakobau's sons back to Fiji from school in 1875; one of them came down with measles acquired abroad and 30,000 Fijians died in the epidemic that resulted. Influenza did its share. Any disease developing a high fever usually moved the victim to go to cool off in stream or sea and die of consequent pneumonia. Tuberculosis made itself universally at home. As sailors patronized local girls, gonorrhea —and syphilis where it was not checked by endemic yaws, which apparently acts as a prophylaxis—ran rife.[30] Gonorrhea, which often renders women incapable of childbearing, probably had most to do directly with decline in birth rates. But tuberculosis notoriously strikes women at the most fertile ages, and lightning epidemics of traditional plagues and "childhood diseases" slaughtered breeders along with everybody else. The late Dr. S. M. Lambert thought that these diseases alone could account for the successive decimations that occurred wherever the white man trod.

Native efforts to account for the coincidence of visitors and mysterious death could be ingenious. Clinging to their supernatural theory of medicine, the Tikopia believed that the blowing of the whistle of the annual mission ship produced the subsequent disease ashore. Fortune's friends on Dobu developed an Edison-like god named Tauwau whom they credited with having invented all the new things brought by white men, diseases as well as canned beef and galvanized iron. White men too, some intelligent or learned or both, maintain that, in the sway-backed curve of Island populations, there is more than meets the eye of the epidemiologist alone.

So far as I am aware, Stevenson stated it best.[31] The Islander, he wrote, dies off primarily for lack of joie de vivre due to the decay of so much that once made life rewarding. Prestige is flawed, dancing frowned on, and "the most healthful, if not the most humane, of all field sports—'hedge-warfare,'" for-

---

[30]Leprosy also appeared, though it is not absolutely certain that it was not already present in endemic form in some islands. Lepers are effectively isolated on most islands, and the disease is not a serious problem except on New Caledonia. There, however, the white population are quite panicky about it, apparently with considerable justification.
[31]Roberts (Population Problems of the Pacific, 64–5) credits an Australian medical officer in Fiji with the first articulate statement of this theory in 1874.

bidden;[32] his whole pattern of life comes apart. Always able to die from such emotional causes as fear of sorcery, he might well have died of this other emotional cause, degenerative boredom. This certainly anticipates angles in which medicine is now very greatly interested. The modern medical enthusiast would speak of the psychosomatics of resistance to infection and of human fecundity.

Moreover, some sober ethnologists take this seriously. Says Malinowski:

> "Now once you make life unattractive to a man, whether savage or civilized, you cut the taproot of his vitality. The rapid dying out of native races is, I am deeply convinced, due more to wanton interference with their pleasures and normal occupations, . . . than to any other cause."—*Argonauts of the Western Pacific*, 465–6.

Pitt-Rivers elaborates this with an admirable ingenuity. Epidemics, he says, cannot exterminate, do not even permanently check, the growth of population; if they did, Europe would never have recovered so resiliently from the Black Death. The crucial factor is not widespread death of adults but general loss of fecundity due to inadequate adaptation of a society to new values. Actually, too little is yet known about the emotional factors involved in conception for this to be any more than fertile surmise.[33] But Island birth rates usually did slack off to an extent that can hardly be explained even by prevalence of gonorrhea. It is most difficult to laugh off altogether the notion that Island populations declined because white intrusion was socially too shattering.

That is important because we ought to know why, after apparently heading for extinction, these peoples arrived on the upgrade. The epidemiologist attributes it to gradual develop-

[32]*In the South Seas*, 49–51.
[33]Which does not mean there is nothing in it. For instance, it is observable but still inscrutable fact that a wife unwillingly barren for years often finds herself pregnant a short while after she has given up, and adopted a child; and that a previously childless couple who take a long vacation often succeed in impregnating the wife.

ment of immunity to white men's diseases, and to measures taken by missionaries and white governments against mortality among mothers and infants. Infant mortality among Island peoples was always colossal, of course, even without intentional infanticide, and most islands with growing populations show gratifying and significant decreases in this respect. The same tendency to rise can appear, however, in islands with scanty or bad medical services, such as Tahiti, as well as in those with relatively good services, such as American Samoa. And the presumption that so few generations could effect such substantial immunities is suspicious. Measles is still a dreaded scourge in the Islands, for instance; some U.S. Navy doctors considered it a public health crime to allow Navy officers to bring their families to Micronesia—white children mean great risk of sweeping epidemics fresh from Stateside. Tuberculosis is still shockingly prevalent in islands where the population is blithely skyrocketing. If one cannot discount psychosomatics on the downbeat, one cannot do it on the upbeat. It could be argued that the eclectic adjustment to white ways of which most Island peoples showed themselves eventually capable created an emotional climate stable enough for viability to resume. Yap, one of the few spots where population is still declining, is distinguished among Micronesian islands for reluctance to adjust.

The courageous Pitt-Rivers goes farther: Genetic strains now breeding in the Islands, he says, including many known and many probably existent but unidentified white, negro and Asiatic elements, make present Islanders hereditarily different from the peoples whom early discoverers found. (The modern Guamanian, whom he does not mention, would be the extreme case in point.) Hence they do not suffer to the former extent from emotional and immunological disabilities.

Action need not wait on the validation of these speculations. Obviously anything that can be done to develop Islanders' immunities to disease and to prevent epidemics should be done; so much for epidemiologist and immunologist. So should anything that makes Island life better integrated and more rewarding; so much for Stevenson, Malinowski and Pitt-Rivers. The western world, committed to the desirability of growing populations and of public preventive medicine, can make no other decision. But a white doctor told me that, heresy though it was, he considered gonorrhea a good thing for the Islands— it helped keep the birth rate down. He had begun to wonder what would happen when local resources became too slim for the snowballing populations. Consider, for instance, that the population of American Samoa, where arable land is sharply limited, has tripled since the States took over in 1900.

In most Islands this matter can still be taken up too late, say thirty years from now. In a few, notably the Gilberts, it is immediate. Britain has already had to ship hundreds of over-fertile Gilbertese to the empty Line Islands, where they can live much the same life on the same kind of land; more such swarmings are now planned. Such demographical phlebotomy is a good makeshift, but some day the High Commissioner of the Western Pacific will run out of spare islands and, as transplanted populations teem in turn, the problem will be larger than ever. The nominally self-governing kingdom of Tonga is also close to grave trouble. There, thanks to the Rev. Shirley Baker's tactful formalizing of Tongan feudal land use, each boy on reaching sixteen is granted a life tenure on eight and a quarter acres to grow food on. On Ha'apai, in central Tonga, the size of these allotments has already had to be drastically cut. True, the average Tongan makes anything but intensive use of his holdings; but long-standing specific expectation puts an edge on a situation that might otherwise be more easily glossed over. The Tongan government is already planning to shift population, Gilberts-style, to practically uninhabited islands, such as Tofua and Kao.[34] The population of Guam is booming so ominously that Uncle Sam may allow fertile Tinian to remain almost as empty as war left it for eventual swarming from farther south. This also is temporizing; but anything more than temporizing may not be practical.

[34]This situation tightened a little in 1947 when ruinous volcanic action made it necessary to move the 1,300 Tongans of Niuafoou (Tin Can Island) to Tongatabu for eventual moving to Eua, which had been previously counted on for general overflow.

In the old days, though high infant mortality supplemented catch-as-catch-can infanticide, overpopulation still often appeared. War and enforced emigration were the remedies. No modern government, whether sovereign, protector or United Nations trustee, can countenance such measures. Birth control comes to mind. The Gilbertese, aware that whites have such techniques, are secretly asking their British protectors for means and instruction; the Guamanians, though devoutly and almost unanimously Catholic, sometimes find their priests able to look the other way on the subject—both instances are great credits to Micronesian intelligence. But official provision of birth control supplies and instruction would certainly wring anguished screams from Catholic missions and, I have reason to suspect, from Protestant missions too—after all, other things being equal, births among the flock mean additional church members. Nor do Islanders' erotic habits, general self-control and sense of cause and effect fit with efficient birth control. The Tikopians might be good prospects; in view of their theories on procreation, the Trobrianders would not.[35] Five generations of education and social retraining might make the Islander a promising disciple of Margaret Sanger; one or two generations are hardly enough, yet that is all the time available. If effective birth control is the only way the Islands can avoid degenerative overpopulation, they are in a very bad way indeed.

More intensive food growing is sometimes advanced as a solution. This is longer-range temporizing. There are limits even to Japanese genius in that line. Most high islands in the South Seas no doubt could support triple their present numbers, but only through almost diametric changes in the natives' social and work habits. Handsomely as taro patch and coconut grove provide for local needs, it is nevertheless somewhat by the grace of God, who is kind in the Islands, and not too notably by continuous toil or long-range forethought.[36] The Cook

[35]Cf. pp. 278; 295.
[36]It could easily be maintained that the native was not always so sloppy a farmer. His agricultural techniques have probably gone the same way as the refinements of his language, in consequence of loss of prestige for the chief and kahuna who formerly bossed food-raising. But we are dealing here not with what he was but what he is.

Islander, for instance, values oranges for beer making and is well aware that orange trees need pruning and replanting; he once had the use of myriads of vigorous wild orange trees in the bush; but now, from sheer neglect, the trees are so high, thorny and discouraged that oranges are a relative rarity for the native who lacks a government-fostered plantation. So again it is a grave question whether re-education can revolutionize native agriculture quickly enough to forestall the damaging effects of overcrowding.

The native's need for cash also enters in. By and large he himself must pay, through taxes or contributions to missions, for the teachers, agricultural experts, nurses, engineers and doctors whom he needs in much greater numbers than he has ever had yet. No guardian nation will seriously subsidize such a staff for generations. So, if she is to learn how to pull herself up by her own bootstraps, Tarafu must foot the bill by growing—and finding markets for—more copra, vanilla, shell, cocoa and so forth on land that might otherwise produce sustenance-crops. At the same time growing population will demand more and more land for taro, yams and kumaras. The circle is frankly vicious and the means that might enable the Islands to feed a concentrated population are those inhibited by the very needs set up by population growth.

It looks distressingly as if western medicine and western notions of the sacredness of human life might prove the most destructive of all the things that white men brought.

* * *

The preceding text goes disproportionately often to the New Zealand Maori for examples of energy or enterprise. That is no accident. Sir Peter Buck (Te Rangi Hiroa), part Maori and proud of it, says it is unfair to compare other Islanders with his people, whom centuries of colder climate and greater need for adaptability so toughened and sharpened. Be that as it may, the Maori certainly distinguished themselves for ingenuity, malleability and backbone both before and after whites arrived. Rowdy and smelly as they were, they had

enough imagination and initiative to deal almost on even terms
with the interloper.

This was conspicuous in economics, where the Islander was
usually worst baffled. Within a generation of sizable white intrusion, the Maori of the North Island had the hang of money
as exchange and of farming for cash markets. Organized by
their chiefs, numerous tribes raised huge quantities of potatoes,
pork and wheat for sale to settlers and ships and to Australia.
These large-scale industrial farms were based, not on private
capital, but on communal holdings and cultivation, income
dripping down in traditional fashion from supervising chief to
obedient understrapper. In 1849 the village of Rangiowhia
turned out £11,000 worth of produce. In 1853 Maori enterprise
supplied half of New Zealand's exports. Horses and carts and
ploughs were secured, as obviously more efficient than the dig-
ging-stick and the human back. The chief often set up per-
pendicular industry, building a flour mill to process the
community's wheat, buying a schooner to take the flour to the
Bay of Islands for sale. You hear of elaborate, Island-style village discussions of the advantages of over- and under-shot
water wheels. A former henchman of the redoubtable Hongi
turned Christian dairy farmer near Kaihope and sold eighty
pounds of butter a week to ships. With relish the missionaries
told how, not many years before, this prosperous and peaceful
dairyman had killed an enemy chief, taken his wife and children prisoner, eaten the children in front of the widow, and
then married her in final token of complete revenge.

The Maori were not squeamish in adapting to white economy. They raised and sold women as well as pork and flour.
The head of a Maori family bringing his daughters out for
prostitution to whalers was a searingly familiar sight to the missionaries wringing their hands across the Bay of Islands, which
quickly became the superlative stew-grogshop-general store of
the South Pacific. Payment in advance was usually demanded;
cash preferred, tobacco accepted. An Australian reporter estimated that Bay of Islands chiefs thus drew £11,000 a year from
an annual 4,500 visitors. Practically every woman in the neigh-

borhood developed syphilis, for the Maori lacked yaws as prophylaxis. There were heights that native enterprise did not reach. The pimp who customarily loaded both girls and hogs into the same boat for sale and the proprietor of the Bay's best known clip-joint were both whites. But, for beginners, these Polynesians did very well indeed. True, Papeete (Tahiti) and Lahaina (Hawaii) were similarly active; but, as daughter-sellers, the Maori compared to Hawaiian or Tahitian as a small storekeeper to a street-hawker.

This prostitution industry gradually petered out. But the produce industry remained vigorous; the Maori appeared well on the way to becoming a prosperous collectivized peasantry. A body blow at this development was struck by a calamitous fall in world prices in the middle 'fifties. But even before that it had been apparent that so promising a future for quondam savages was illusory. Land-hungry whites were flocking in and, in spite of formal guarantees that native rights would be protected, which were taken seriously by conscientious people like "Good Governor Grey," the colonial government was more often than not hand in glove with the land-seekers. Law and cajolery were used, both most alarming to the dispossessed.

Under these circumstances, many an Island people—Hawaiians and Cook Islanders were exceptions—tried to fight. Several times the French found the Tahitian or Marquesan dangerous to track down in the bush, and expensive to dislodge from fortifications of his own contriving. Tongans, Samoans, Ponapeans (Carolines) have warming memories of occasions when they came out victors over professional white fighting men. In the 'seventies the New Caledonians' virtuosity with trade tomahawks on long handles at close quarters came near evicting the French. But these were all minor flare-ups compared to what happened when the Maori decided it was time to dance the *haka*, send the women and children into the *pa*, and go have it out with the *pakeha*.[37]

Though whites acquired legal title to most of New Zealand for a monetary song, they involuntarily made it up in blood

[37] *Pakeha* is the outsider, usually confined to whites, like *haole*.

and sterling; the intruding Briton needed 20,000 troops, artillery and armored steamers, to finish the job. If the Maori had had a higher sense of ethnic unity—for some redoubtable Maori tribes remained loyal to Queen Victoria, whom they had accepted by treaty—Britain might have found it too expensive altogether. In the end, thanks to such "friendlies," to persistence and organization, the Maori was done down and shattered. But he earned from his enemy a solid approbation that, though decreasingly, has been a great asset to him in adjusting to the white man's world. Said the London *Times* in the midst of the fighting:

> "[The Maori] can live in the mountains or the bush like a wolf; but he meets his pursuers with all the resources of military art. He manufactures excellent rifles out of old ships' muskets, and makes percussion caps out of soldiers' buttons. . . . Our soldiers actually respect them for their extraordinary talents and eminent valour."—Quoted in Sutherland, *The Maori People Today*, 26.

It was a kind of war most familiar to Americans. The Maori not only had superficial resemblances to the American Indian —he wore feathers in his hair for ceremony, adopted the white man's blanket as a garment, took hair from dead enemies—but he fought in the style of Pontiac, master of raid and quick evasion, but willing stoutly to defend a fortified post when cornered. The North Island, scene of the fighting, was often heavily forested and tentative settlement had been sporadic, so all the familiar elements appeared: sudden descents on pioneering settlements in the night; personal warnings from the friendly savage just before he made himself scarce; men slaughtered, noncombatants taken captive; the cabin left burning and the distant neighbors rallying for pursuit on horseback with guns; the irregular militia of settlers, often capable at the Maori's own game but ill-disciplined and at odds with regular troops; plodding, harassed regular regiments exhausting themselves in cutting roads for artillery and wagon trains long before they ever glimpsed a Maori as target for a volley; professional officers slowly learning this kind of fighting at unavoidable expense in their own and their men's lives. Massacre, ambush, road, camp, blockhouse, over and over again. The historical markers up the Waikato read very much the same as those on New York Seventeen along General Sullivan's route when he was harrying the Iroquois. Braddock's Defeat, the Horseshoe Bend, Cherry Valley, could be transplanted into this story without much change in idiom—except the British ability to concede virtues to their slippery and plucky enemy.

Much of the fighting was embittered by religious fanaticism. The alliance between missionary and state in New Zealand had been obvious since missionaries had midwifed the Treaty of Waitangi, in which representative Maori chiefs accepted nominal British sovereignty. Maori pseudo-Christian cults had a Mohammedan-like flavor of belligerency or, for the American analogy, a dash of the Shawnee Prophet. Hauhau cultists were promised miraculous immunity from *pakeha* bullets, and used a British officer's dried head as a spiritualistic medium—for ventriloquism was by no means a blackbirder's monopoly. The warlike "King" movement had religious aspects. But fieriest and grimmest of these was the Hauhau-connected Te Kooti, who made a religion of *utu* and wiped out plenty of whites in the process.

In a wholesale arrest during the Maori wars this inconspicuous young Maori was picked up in the neighborhood of Poverty Bay, where Captain Cook had first landed. Though he had probably never done any fighting, he was exiled, with scores of others, to the bleak, fogbound Chatham Islands. There, after understandable brooding, he organized his fellow exiles, cut out a government schooner, and landed back in New Zealand breathing a heady mixture of ancient revenge[38] and a new religion founded on the eye-for-an-eye Old Testament. At the first opportunity, he massacred those who had testified against him. Te Kooti was his own Messiah, his martyrdom woven into ritual as Christ's Passion is woven into the mass—they called

[38]On the voyage his followers were particularly impressed by the celerity with which the weather became favorable after Te Kooti had drowned his uncle as a sacrifice.

his cult "Ringatu" (upraised hand) after a ritual gesture borrowed from Hauhauism. The Church of England, predominant in missions in this area, was embarrassed to find that this prophet of blood and fire had once been a pupil in her schools and claimed her as mother church.

For months and years the whites tried to run Te Kooti down; but he infected his followers with his own wildcat-like stealth and savagery. His near-miraculous escapes sound like Robert Bruce crossed with Osceola. He never was captured, and survived to receive a pardon. Ringatu used old Maori music in its ritual and, like many another Maori cult, made much of faith healing. So, though its red-handed founder has long been dead, it is still strong and quite respectable on the East Coast. A tolerant government accords its ministers the right to solemnize marriage, and its congregations occasionally celebrate joint festivals with Maori Anglicans.

After lingering, mangling defeat the Maori were worse off than ever. As penalty for rebellion, government confiscated and sold large areas of their land; tardy compensation for these seizures was completed only a few years ago. Discouragement grew, numbers fell off, white observers predicted for the Maori the fate of the dodo and the Tasmanian. Round the turn of the century, however, a few young Maori, urged on by Sir James Carroll, a brilliant half-Maori statesman who had ably represented *pakeha* constituents in the New Zealand parliament, rallied their people in another effort to make sense in the white man's world. Their talents in politics and propaganda commanded great respect, as witness the handles to their names: Sir Maui Pomare, who looked like an old-style Philadelphia banker; Sir Apirana Ngata, who looks like a Spanish grandee; Sir Peter Buck, who, though half-*pakeha*, looks most of all like a portrait of an old-time Maori chief.

Cleverly making use of white-style education, they put as much canniness as zeal into a movement to use the remains of the old Maori community spirit as structure of, and fuel for, a new adjustment. Carroll's maxim had been: "Hang on to your Maorihood!" and the Young Maori hung on to it, while struggling with dedicated determination. Contrary to Scripture, a woman also was found to stand with these men-in-tenthousand. By imagination and doggedness Princess Te Puea, of a family of high-ranking chiefs, turned the poverty-stricken Maori remnants round the town of Ngauruawahia into a co-operative center for reviving old Maori building, dancing, carving, and living. Her work was merely one aspect of a general effort to restore badly needed cultural integration; the whole was aided by growing willingness among whites to value old Maori things and to wish these plucky aborigines the very best. The New Zealand nativophile, gaspingly making a picturesque pet of the Maori, convinced that all their faults sprang from white man's faults and all their virtues are gloriously their own, is just as silly as his opposite number in Hawaii. But the Maori is less amenable to patronizing than the Hawaiian. The atmosphere in which he is now struggling is still the most constructively friendly enjoyed by any Island people.

The Young Maori have seen great results from their work within their own lifetimes. Ngata still survives as father confessor of his people, Buck as an internationally known ethnologist heading the Bishop Museum in Honolulu. Ngata's schemes for encouraging Maori to use their remaining lands with white-style efficiency while retaining Maori-style collective motivation are too complicated to go into here, but were successful, and started trends that are still moving. Maori population has turned the corner and is now growing far faster than the *pakeha* population.[39] The vigor and ability of these people, who were doomed to hopeless pauperism not long ago, was apparent in the recent war, when the Maori Battalion, with a majority of Maori officers, became world-famous in Greece, North Africa and Italy. I have heard minor objections to this outfit's liaison work, but none to its fighting powers.

So rousing a resurgence is highly gratifying to anybody who wishes Island peoples well. The Maori are of practically the

[39]This contrast is still striking after being qualified by the statement that, in New Zealand, most quarter-bloods retain the political status and social background of the Maori.

same stock as the droopy Tahitian and Cook Islander. That finally disposes of notions about Polynesian "racial indolence." They stand a sporting chance of not only making their own lands count for their support, but even of working themselves usefully and without too much interim damage into white-style industries and professions. This bright cast over their future they owe mostly to themselves, directly or indirectly. A confirmed optimist might hope that their present circumstances foreshadow what might happen to the Fijian, Palauman or Samoan some generations hence.

But it would be a sentimental error, common in New Zealand and not good for the Maori, to consider them out of the woods. The *pakeha* likes to tell himself and anybody else willing to listen, that New Zealanders feel no anti-Maori prejudice. I could get no intelligent Maori to agree. True, in this respect the New Zealander behaves much better than an Englishman or American probably would, which is a great credit to him. But prejudice is still there, cropping up in discriminations in some employments, in hotel accommodations, among children, where strains are always most articulate.[40] Too many *pakeha* insist that the Maori are dirty, shiftless, lazy, unreliable, often in the teeth of sporadic local evidence that it is not necessarily true, never with any air of regretful clinical description, usually with great zest. Too many *pakeha*-Maori marriages involve the more shiftless type of whites from whom offspring get little help in adjustment. It will still take generations for Hore and Heke to get on the same footing with Smith and Jones that Smith and Jones enjoy with Brown and Robinson.

Recent political accident has heightened prejudice. The Maori have long sent four members to the New Zealand parliament; from these specially balloted for "Maori seats" came much of the dynamic statesmanship of Pomare, Ngata, Buck, & Co. Until recently Maori members were usually conservatives. That changed with the accession to power of Labor after

[40]Doubters should consult Ernest & Pearl Beaglehole, *Some Modern Maoris*, passim, particularly the generous *peccavi* of Sir Peter Buck in his preface, p. xiv.

the depression of the early 'thirties. The 1946 election in New Zealand was a narrow squeak for Labor; when the smoke of recounts cleared, the government had a margin of only four votes—the precise number of Maori members, all Labor. Imagine the shock if the Democrats had retained control of Congress in 1946 by a margin of only four seats held by American Indians, representing among them the entire Indian community.

Opposition could hardly have been expected not to deplore this shift of the balance of power into aboriginal hands. Week after week the cry grew shriller. The Maori were deserting old responsible leaders and turning to shallow young demagogues, a plaint made plausible by the regrettable defeat of Sir Apirana Ngata. They had voted Labor solely because, under New Zealand's social security, mothers get ten shillings maintenance per week per child—everybody knew that the Maori were just breeding children and living on accumulated allowances. (This will not hold water at all; vital statistics for the pertinent period need qualifying, but they show clearly that the white birth rate has grown three times faster than the Maori birth rate since 1935.[41]) They had been corrupted by handouts of public work jobs, sold a mess of pottage for their birthrights, but what could you expect of feckless people just up from savagery? And so forth. The cry will probably reach hysterical proportions if the Labor leaders among the Maori, who have poor reputations for judgment, try openly to exploit this strategic situation.

Besides, Labor foolishly lent color to the accusation of political cynicism in dealing with the Maori by tying up with the newest Maori pseudo-Christian cult—a heavily faith healing, politically active, and extremely popular affair called Ratana after its recently deceased prophet. Few well-informed New Zealanders on either side of the fence care to deny that Labor and Ratana are thick as thieves in an alliance that was important at the polls in 1946. Suppose the Republicans had tied

[41]The conservative New Zealand Herald of Auckland had the journalistic honesty to investigate this child-allowance situation. It reported that it seemed to be all cry and very little wool.

up with Father Divine to clinch winning back the negro vote
from the Democrats.

Ratana smells no better for its tendency during the first part
of World War II to court Japanese help in restoring the Maori
to his place in the land. It came to little—just some amateurish
signaling and treasonable scowling up in the district of North
Auckland—but it left a bad taste in the nation's mouth. Ratana
cannot erase the Maori Battalion from the national consciousness, but it helps to embitter Nationalists commenting on the
Maori-Labor-Ratana axis with more gift of gab than discretion. And the last thing the Maori needs, as he faces his trying
future, is bitter detractors or political exploiters.

The latter hazard is great because, able as some of his past
leaders have been, the Maori occasionally accept help without
too close an investigation of the helper's motives. The left wing
of the New Zealand Labor Party, strong in the Auckland
Trades Council, fades off, as in other countries, into fellow-
traveling and so into Communism. Auckland has long been
plagued by a smoldering quarrel between city planners and a
Maori colony whose unquestionably squalid settlement lies
right on the city's handsome water front. Inheriting the
quarrel, the Labor government has been in the delicate position of having to persuade a conspicuous lot of underprivileged
Maori to move out when they don't want to. When the matter
came to a head recently, with the government making efforts
at eviction and Te Puea, the grand old lady, summoned down
from Ngauruawahia to defy the lightning for her people, the
Auckland Trades Council sent union members by hundreds to
help. Maori and workers together, they built a fence studded
with tongue-protruding Maori images and a fine Maori carved
gateway, to defy due process of law. Fence and Maori are still
there; no matter what the government's next move, Communist influence is in a better position to use the Maori as a
lever inside Labor and a tool of general disruption. If the relation strengthens—and the Communists will tend it lovingly—
here is another heavy stick for the conservative to beat the
Maori with.

Over twenty years ago Te Rangi Hiroa (Sir Peter Buck) told the *pakeha* that he for one was reconciled, from the human point of view, to seeing the Maori gradually merge with the white man's world:

> "Many people express the opinion that it is a pity that the old Maori . . . dances are being lost. In the same breath they say that the Maori must work his land and live like Europeans. The two are incompatible . . . dances were the amusements of a people living together and spending their evenings in a communal meetinghouse. The Maori is adapting himself to changed circumstances, to a changed environment . . . It is a pity from the point of view of sentiment, but sentiment alone will not provide for man's material welfare."—*The Passing of the Maori*, 368.

But this healthy realism does not purge the word "adapt" of ambiguity. The Maori's current problem—like that of his cousins in other advanced Islands—is whether consciously to hold on to Maori speech, dances, and communal institutions, adapting only to the degree forced on him while he works out new eclectic techniques of living, or to let the white world flood in on him in a spirit of better-get-it-over-with in hopes that somehow his emotional head will stay above water. Both are "adaptation." One slows down the inevitable to minimize trauma, one speeds it up and hopes to take trauma in stride.

The first has great attractions. But for an outsider to tell the Maori what to do would be a shrieking impertinence. The people who, coming out of balmy Polynesia, conquered the raw and chilly Long White Cloud and learned to make it support them without help from imported resources—a thing no sizable white colony ever did yet—can probably solve this problem eventually. Provided, however, that the *pakeha* helps intelligently with schools and health education and that sentimentalist, opportunist, backbiter and fellow traveler keep their hands off.

The Maori are not the only Islanders honored with Communist attention. The Auckland Trades Council is also nursemaiding the Cook Islands Progressive Association—an organization started by Cook Islanders working in New Zealand, that now has thousands of members in the small Islands far to the northeast which began New Zealand's abortive colonial empire. Droopy administration since World War I has given the Cooks much to complain about. World War II so disrupted the flow of local fruit to Auckland that, under New Zealand's continuing price controls, tomatoes are the only local crop prospering. So nobody, either local trader or native villager or rootless off-Island water-front worker on Rarotonga, loves the government. The leader of the Association is an able man of a family of chiefs from Aitutaki; but he leans heavily for counsel and moral support on white leftists, and has learned to deny vigorously that there is any need to look his gift horse in the mouth. The moral here, however, is not that a worried man may seek any port in a storm; rather, that New Zealand made a large mistake a generation ago when permitting the Cooks to become precariously tied to a small-time, distant market for perishables.

The Tahiti water front, recently unionized in a weird fashion, feels Communist tentacles stretching out from French Red-dominated unions; so does the Noumea water front, where Loyalty Island wharfies under tutelage of local whites consider themselves Communists. Even the native New Caledonian feels the ferment in his villages far from the big town. It is dubious how well he understands the principles of surplus value; the principal tenet of Marxism as preached to him is that he owes it to himself not to work for the white exploiter, a notion to which he is temperamentally inclined anyway. Local missionaries try to counteract such propaganda, but are badly handicapped by their great loss of mana during the war. These French padres and parsons, mostly of Vichyite leanings, indiscreetly advised their native charges to sit out the war and welcome the Japanese when they arrived. The reader already knows enough of Island psychology to understand the loss of missionary prestige when not only did the Japanese fail to arrive, but New Caledonia was flooded with hundreds of thousands of American troops and billions of dollars' worth of equipment and food.

Unionization, of a definitely nonconservative type, has also become well intrenched in Hawaii. Conservative organization is being encouraged by government in Fiji in hopes that it will help stabilize the native worker. But all that is of outside origin. The greatest clinical interest lies in the occasional attempt among natives to organize for economic purposes along white lines. Forty years ago the Germans in Samoa discovered to their great annoyance that a local boy, who had worked in San Francisco offices, was organizing a Samoa-for-the-Samoans copra-co-operative right under their noses. He was planning retail trading stores in the villages to compete with established houses, and purchase of a ship to market Samoan copra without middlemen. He evidently had good political connections with important chiefs, for presently the chiefs' council, to whom the Germans allowed some parliamentary functions, voted to tax every Samoan a small sum per head to finance the venture. There was also suspicion of undercover connections with anti-government businessmen on Apia beach. Anybody who ever heard of Dr. Solf would know that the project was speedily suppressed and that it had much to do with the cessation of German efforts to give Samoans even a shadow of political responsibility. It probably was an unsound business proposition; the notion of financing it by taxation without full government auspices was obviously nonsense. But there it was —a half-baked but real, potentially corrupt but alive, Samoan move toward spontaneous adaptation of white economic organization.

Then there was Apolosi, a disreputable but imaginative Fijian carpenter, who put his whole archipelago in a ferment thirty years ago by adding economic enterprise to his nativist cult. Anti-Indian and antiwhite, a self-proclaimed Messiah, a great man for the ladies, he collected funds for co-operative schemes to emancipate the Fijian forever from economic dependence on white institutions. His persistence was amazing. Banished to Rotuma for seven years, he returned to take up right where he had left off; banished again in 1930 for ten years, he returned at the end of the sentence to pick right up again; he did not survive his third sentence of exile.

*   *   *

When white men have so much trouble handling their own newer ideas, such as unionism, self-determination and Communism, the Islander naturally gets them all twisted up in application. That is plainest in Samoa just now. Unions have not appeared yet, Communism, even in the dilute Island version, is only a spot on the horizon. But the idea of Samoa-for-the-Samoans, lively there ever since Steinberger's time, has since been stimulated by Wilsonian self-determination and the United Nations' recent inclusion of training for independence or self-government as an objective of trusteeships. Always sentiment for Samoan autonomy has been tangled up with local institutions and impulses that are ideological traps for the outsider trying to make out how to calm Samoa's fractiousness.[42]

It is clear at the moment what Western Samoa, which includes the bulk of land and people and the dominant prestige of the group, is alleged to want. In 1946, when New Zealand told the Samoan chiefs that she had asked the United Nations to convert the old League of Nations mandate into a trusteeship, they demurred vigorously. The decease of the mandate, they said in effect, was good; but, from their point of view, why install King Stork in the guise of a trusteeship? They recalled that in 1900, when the Samoan group was divided between the States and Germany, they had not been consulted; nor in 1919 when the mandate was set up. What they now wanted was self-government under a protectorate exercised by a stronger power. And while these matters were under discussion, they also very strongly desired reunion of American with Western Samoa. There was much sentiment for the States as protector but, as discussion progressed, it appeared they were amenable to New

[42]Anybody desiring a sporting chance to understand current doings in Samoa should first read the 486 closely printed pages of Felix M. Keesing, *Modern Samoa*, and then Stevenson, *A Footnote to History*.

Zealand in that role. A petition embodying these demands, on
which the highest chiefs collaborated with better educated
part-whites from "the beach," was duly forwarded by New Zealand to the United Nations. By mid-1947 a U.N. commission
was on the ground to look into the affair and recommend.

Actually none of it is as clear as that sounds. The obscurities
lie in determining what it means to say that Western Samoa
wants a thing, whether Samoans know the meaning of what
they say they want, who speaks for them, and why. Though the
fact does not necessarily label these expressed aspirations in-
valid, it is nevertheless true that none of those questions is
answerable in terms familiar to western democracies. In the
past, New Zealanders have not understood that too well—
which calls for a bit of history:

In the late 'twenties their Samoan mandate came all ablaze
with the "Mau" movement—an attempted revolution involving the exile of several prominent non-Samoans and the public
killing by police of Tamasese, one of the three highest Samoan
chiefs and forebear of the present most articulate spokesman
for Samoan autonomy. "Opinion" is the nearest translation of
"Mau"—the same word identified the Lauati rebellion which
Dr. Solf suppressed by a show of force and exile for its leaders.
The Mau of the 'twenties had some savor of its predecessor. It
was in considerable measure an effort to discredit white rule
in order to secure greater participation in government for
prominent Samoans. Its native leaders were annoyed by the
government's efforts to encourage individualization of communal land-tenure and to suppress the ceremonial mass visiting and exchange of fine mats that express Samoan prestige.
Many of such leaders were "outs"—important chiefs but not
as prominent as others in advisory councils and paid government posts. To some degree they represented the resentment
of the "talking-chiefs"—the executive officers, so to speak, of
the titular chiefs, who, in the old days, had often been the powers behind the throne but who, under both Germans and New
Zealanders, had been slighted in favor of titular chiefs. The
non-Samoan leaders were prosperous local traders from "the

beach"—O. F. Nelson, their part-Samoan principal, was legally and socially "European"[43]—on whose toes government measures had trodden. The last straw was a government project to benefit the cash-needy native by by-passing local traders and marketing copra direct in Europe with the government as agent, as the U.S. Navy had long done in American Samoa. The result has been, until very recently (see footnote) an alli- ance between a "nativist" movement and "the beach"—ele- ments that are traditionally antagonists but which, due to so large a proportion of mixed bloods in business in Apia and to mutual agreement that the New Zealand government was a nuisance, are not illogical collaborators in Samoa.

This sounds like overemphasis on *cui bono*, a tempting error. It is possible for instance, though unsound, to attribute the American Revolution solely to the merchant irked by Brit- ish trading regulations, the local politician yearning for more scope than the colonial assembly afforded, and the under- privileged hating direct taxation. Though tenable as far as it goes, that diagnosis would leave out such intangibles as gen- eral dislike for leading strings pulled from 3,000 miles away, and a dimly realized sense of strength grown to a point where independence was an emotional necessity. The latter factors were probably what made the Revolution succeed. The Mau doubtless contained some such dynamic intangibles. But they

[43]In Western Samoa society is divided into two classes, Samoans and "Europeans." Samoans are either full-blooded natives exercising all the social and legal rights appertaining to the traditional communal set-up and subject to protective restrictions to correspond, or part-Samoans who are born of extra-legal unions or have elected to assume Samoan status, an option for which legal provision is made. "Europeans" are all resident whites, all other outlanders of whatever shade, plus a con- siderable number of part-Samoans who have elected "European" status, which is legally possible under certain conditions. It is significant that the trend is all toward electing "European" status whenever possible; there is not only prestige-value in it, it also brings greater latitude in both social and economic life. It is the avowed purpose of the recent Samoan autonomy movement to eliminate the "European" category. When that became clear, "the beach" experienced a startled change of heart, and hastily backed water in its ardent support of the Samoan chiefs.

were all in peculiarly Samoan terms, and might have reflected
not so much an organic need for increased political responsibility for Samoans, as the inevitable reaction of a proud and
intrigue-minded people to outside supervision, whether or not
they possessed the social coherence and strength to engineer
their ambitions.

Samoans in general, unlike some other Island peoples, do
resent foreign leading strings. The mandate government was—
and was supposed to be—arbitrary. The Administrator in charge
as the Mau began to boil was an able up-from-the-ranks New
Zealand general named Richardson who, though he did Samoa
much good with new roads and sanitation, probably lacked the
right temperament for the job. But it does not follow that the
Mau was based on identifiable public opinion as you and I think
of it, corresponding to that behind Sam Adams' mass meetings and Washington's armies. The American colonist had had
long, slowly cumulative experience in making himself felt on
public questions deliberated in majority-voting assemblies. He
was already adept in republican government and insisted that
his Constitution include a firm Bill of Rights on which American equalitarian freedoms have developed. In sharp contrast
the average Samoan lives under the chiefs of his village—the
matai, presumably the ablest members of family groups—about
as a member of a political machine lives under precinct and
district captains. If leaders insist on something too outrageously unpopular, there is trouble. But by and large there
can be no such thing as up-from-the-grassroots sentiment; it
is all down from the top of the tree, suggested by traditional
authority and accepted because sponsored by men of acknowledgedly superior mana. Significantly the Mau saw no
neighbor-against-neighbor splits between adherents and opponents, such as occurred in the American Revolution and
Civil War, in evidence of individual political judgments.
Whole kinship groups abstained from or plumped for the
Mau, delivered en bloc by their chiefs as precinct leaders deliver the votes—or, for an analogue in the South Seas, as the

Family used to deliver the vote of their Hawaiian villeins on Niihau.[44]

For the Samoan is not yet democratically minded. In view of his traditional institutions, there is no reason why he should be. Nevertheless "the beach"-backers of the Mau cleverly represented it to New Zealand, the best lever for loosening up the mandate, as a conventional case of a tyrannized people rising against despotism and craving a greater degree of self-government along democratic lines. The average New Zealander, knowing nothing of Samoan ways and assuming that all other people were much like himself, swallowed this whole and was all the more shocked when shooting started in Apia. To outsiders it looked very black: a mandate power, delegated by the world to care for a tiny, defenseless country, shooting down its leader for demonstrating for greater freedom.

The Mau's militancy had made shooting likely. At its height it was a come-outer government in itself. Its capital was a village on the outskirts of Apia, its headquarters a converted bandstand still standing on the village green carrying the slogan "Samoa mo Samoa" which is close to "Samoa for the Samoans." It had its own laws, courts, taxes and police, in imitation of the government it hoped to undermine. But its principal weapon was a complementary boycott withdrawing its adherents from government courts, laws and schools, substituting its own. What portion have we in David? To your tents, O Israel!

Much of its career was astutely steered. Samoan subtlety in politics was supplemented by the white-style jugglings of businessmen-allies. But one detail—which probably cannot be credited to the junta on "the beach"—was startlingly significant of its unconstructively sulky ingredient. The Samoan village, instructed to wash its hands of white government because it was all *papalagi* doings, let sanitation as well as taxes go by the board. Privies were let fall apart, hospitals emptied, birth and

[44] I am told that, where there were exceptions to this, it was a matter of an eminent *matai* being told off to stay loyal as a hedge in case the Mau failed. This is difficult to substantiate.

death registrations, which would have been just as useful for an autonomous as a dependent Samoa, were neglected; so were government-sponsored campaigns against coconut beetles, which were ruining the trees on which Samoa depends for cash and emergency food. This was not disorganization—the chiefs kept the Mau villages well disciplined—but deliberate scornful neglect. There are wide gaps between the western world and Samoa when the Samoan can still think of hookworm prevention as a queer white notion on the same level as preferring thin women to plump. It is correct to deduce that there are equally wide gaps between us and Samoans on such matters as civil freedoms and equality before the law.

The Mau continued as a brake on government and a focus of intransigent nativism until, in 1935, New Zealand's shift to a Labor government gave the Mau's adherents what is said to have been a welcome pretext for abandoning a game of which they had begun to tire. To call the Mau Fascist would be as absurd as to call Polynesian economics Communist. But it had some resemblances to Fascism. In spite of liberal catch-words glued on by "the beach," it was a back-to-the-good-old-days movement, a take-advantage-of-governmental-tolerance movement, a South Seas version of using disciplined solidarity among the mass to divert power into the hands of people disappointed by the government's failure to consider their group-interests paramount. Whatever generalized loyalty to Samoa the Mau manifested, it can be regarded as to some degree another instance in which patriotism can be a destructive tool in clever hands. But the Mau also unquestionably meant a great deal. It reflected, as did Kalakaua, Ratana, Apolosi, the native's uneasiness under white control and his blind, sometimes self-damaging, urge to show that in his own way, he could manage his own affairs.

When the United Nations mission of inquiry arrived last year, they were met by a demonstration of Samoans displaying banners carrying a phrase from Campbell-Bannerman of which High-Chief Tamasese is very fond: "Good government is no substitute for self-government." It has a resounding ring. But the trick lies in the fact that, to western hearers, "self-government" sounds necessarily progressive, democratic, liberal, equalitarian. All it actually means, of course, is concentration of power within, instead of without, certain boundaries. Switzerland is self-governing; but so was Turkey under Abdul the Damned and the Kingdom of Italy under Mussolini. And it by no means follows that Samoan self-government, "good" or not, would be at all progressive or equalitarian.

In token articulate Samoans, like some other Islanders, point to Tonga as example of what they want. This sole surviving Island monarchy is a British protectorate, the British consul representing the High Commissioner of the Western Pacific in control of Tongan finance and foreign affairs, and exerting a by no means negligible advisory check over everything else. Helped by two dozen or so white key employees, Tongans themselves run internal government much as a municipality runs a city under state charter—and, to carry on a tempting analogy, pretty sloppily too. This is not "good" government, but to a considerable extent it is self-government, and Tongans are loyally proud of their self-bailing status, unique in the Pacific.

Few would care to mar their illusion of virtual independence in their sleepy, gossipy islands. But the results of grafting Tongan political personalism and upper-class ambition on western ideas of government as imported by missionaries, are worth study. The sedition clauses in the Tongan code would startle most English-speaking lawyers. The civil rights clause in the constitution is as tricky as the one already quoted from the Hawaiian constitution of 1894. The legislature consists of appointed members of the Queen's cabinet, who are all very high chiefs, and an elected handful of "nobles," also all high chiefs, and commoners. Until a British-inspired change to secret ballot so recent that it has yet to be used, the voter had to sign his ballot in elections for the lower house, which were infrequently contested. And the land-and-taxation system, based on the old Tongan feudal system, is well designed to keep power and revenue in the chiefs' hands.

As previously noted, each male Tongan receives a land allotment on reaching the age of sixteen—from the Crown, if he lives on Crown lands, from the local "noble," if he lives on the appanage of one of the forty landlord-nobles whose holdings aggregate an amount larger than the Crown's. As quitrent he pays an annual eight-shilling tax, which the Crown passes on to the landlord, less a handling commission. No wonder George Tubou I liked that system when Shirley Baker set it up; no wonder it was applauded by the chiefs who had backed him in conquering all Tonga. Difficulties in rent-collection occur; but, to the extent that the thing works, it makes the income of the hereditary aristocracy the first charge on national income; and it substitutes cash, good for imported white-prestige goods, for former feudal gift-dues in kind.

From the average Tongan's point of view, there is probably little wrong with these arrangements, for that is the way Tonga does things. Chiefs heading government departments show dignity and slow ability. Nobles maintain much of their traditional responsibility for their people. The present Queen, emotional focus of the whole system, is probably the most universally respected figure in the Island world; the Crown Prince is unmistakably an earnest and well-educated gentleman. The point here, however, is that there is good reason for its looking so very attractive to the Samoan chiefs who asked the United Nations for autonomy for Samoa, Tonga-style. The set-up they would develop might not resemble Tonga's in all respects—it is impossible that it should. But it very probably would work out to the same principle—that the primary object of self-government is the entrenchment of an aristocracy. It is no accident that Samoan spokesmen put so much emphasis on automobiles, houses, salaries, and uniforms for the high chiefs who may become executive coadjutors in governing Samoa.

The more thoughtful Tongan chiefs, who know Samoa well, doubt that Samoa could make any kind of autonomy work. Forty years before he died George Tubou I had the whole Tongan group solidly conquered and tamped down. Thus his kingdom was centripetal and had an organic tradition of aristo-

cratic centralization to keep it together under sloppy administration. The Samoans, chronically centrifugal in politics, never
got past the utterly temporary ascendancy of one "royal"
family-head and adherents over all the others. The three current holders of "royal" names in Samoa are of approximately
equal prestige; their rivalries are further complicated by the
chronic restlessness of the talking-chief group. Under a protectorate, Samoa would have the stability of a small, cabal-
ridden Central American republic, for political jockeying
within the framework of his traditions is the Samoan's national
sport.

"The beach" would try to steer the machine of government
and try to keep the peace among evanescent factions. But there
is no reason to believe that it would succeed any better than
the Steinberger government did seventy years ago, and for the
same reason—that it would have to tie up with one of the three
"kings" to get anything done, which would immediately af-
front the other two. Such tenuous jugglings are a poor equivalent for the solid, dignified, respected figure of the Tongan
Queen Salote.

All the Samoan has to go on is a by no means ill-founded
mistrust of white men and whatever they suggest, a passion for
things fa'aSamoa which is admirable, but discourages distinction between potentially healthy and hampering details of his
heritage, and a complete misunderstanding of the place of his
islands in the world in general. White V.I.P.s are often impressed by the Samoans' speeches about how honored Samoa
is to have such great people visit their faraway, insignificant
islands. That is merely the Polynesian rhetoric of self-apology.
Actually the speaker and all his native hearers consider that a
western nation would be honored by responsibility for Samoa's
safety and solvency combined with a pledge to keep hands off
her internal squabblings and inefficiency. In return the courteous white guest must refer to Samoa's glorious past; but it
would be embarrassing to ask him for a bill of particulars.

As the end of World War II opened up possibilities, the
present Administrator of Western Samoa embarked on pro-

grams of road building and use of a revived department of agriculture as a pilot plant to determine how best to train Samoans
for administrative work. That was well intended by probably
the best headman that New Zealand ever sent to Samoa; but,
as the petition to the U.N. showed, it was not at all enough.
The general stir-up resulting from the war, high local prosperity
due to fantastic postwar prices for copra and cocoa, New Zealand's loss of mana consequent on a look at American power
in action, combined to produce an atmosphere in which detailed improvements and slow experiment could not satisfy.
In consequence of a long and conscientious study, the U.N.
mission decided that it had to choose between giving a dangerous degree of power to Samoans and the practical certainty of
violent trouble if the degree of such concession were not
marked. So its recommendations—which New Zealand has
already promulgated as policy in substance—include genuine
legislative power for a legislature with a majority of Samoan
members (the former legislative council was merely advisory
and had a majority of government officials); participation by
the three "kings" in a Council of State advising the Administrator; and earmarking of revenues from the New Zealand-
managed Crown Estates for development of medical, educational and economic facilities for Samoa.[45]

The principle—that no less would prevent another Mau
—was unimpeachable. Whether the institutional consequences
are workable within Samoa is just as much of a question as
whether the net concessions are sufficiently dramatic to make
Samoans feel that their demonstrations have borne face-saving
fruit. Friends of the Samoans—and there is much justification
for feeling warmly toward these stately, nervous people—
would be highly gratified if a Samoan legislature with genuine

---

[45]The Samoans have periodically asked return to them of these lands,
which New Zealand took over from German owners as reparations after
World War I. They claimed, with some justice, that the original sales
had been fraudulent. This compromise is more of an apparent than a
real change, since New Zealand's grants in aid to Samoa over the past
generation have probably totaled more than the total profits from the
Estates, which have made money only during recent years.

powers proved able frequently to vote constructive measures. They would be even better gratified by indications that the Samoan leaders understand the advisability of making haste slowly in the direction of native administration for natives. But it is impossible to avoid the suspicion that the three "kings"— at least, the two of them that count—think of these issues as instruments in the never-ceasing business of mana-building. It is unhappily likely that the next couple of years will see further goings-on in these pride- and faction-ridden islands. Too many Samoans blossomed out in the old Mau lavalava—dark blue with a white stripe—the moment the U.N. mission landed; and well-intended remarks from members of the mission about the high desirability of self-government for Samoa as soon as possible were too widely taken as a pledge of everything Samoans had demanded.

The worst of it is that New Zealand's prestige, never high in Samoa, may have received its deathblow from the U.N.'s visit. Remember you are in the South Pacific, where these matters carry special weight. It is unjust to blame the U.N. Under the circumstances inquiry on the spot was unavoidable, and the calibre of the mission does credit to all concerned. Nevertheless, Samoa protested against an action of New Zealand's and lo, numerous representatives of a supranational world organization came winging to their whistle, listened gravely to everything they wished to say and, though not endorsing everything asked for, insisted that the U.N. was the solicitous father of the Samoan people.

The point was quickly exploited: a program submitted to the mission by Tamasese suggested blandly that any uses of the veto power residing in the New Zealand government should be subject to appeal to the United Nations. Again in hopes that the deduction is unsound, I consider it rather likely that the U.N. will hear a great deal more directly from the Samoans in the next few years. The mission appears to have explained at length that the U.N. had every faith in New Zealand as trustee, and that all relations between Samoa and the world would channel through that worthy and benevolent guardian.

But the Samoans—or their better informed leaders—know very well indeed that New Zealand is a very small duck on the international pond. To change the zoological metaphor, the cat has been shown the way to the dairy. And the Samoans are a difficult people to convince against their desires. After all these years of ups and downs in the copra market, the average Samoan still religiously believes that government can do what it likes to copra prices. He may be equally difficult to convince that by virtue of the trusteeship, the mana of New Zealand is equivalent to that of all the great powers banded together in the U.N.

The U.N. mission certainly exercised good judgment in politely neglecting the project of union between American and Western Samoa. It is hard to blame the individual Samoan for resenting having to pay cash for a special permit to visit his relatives on the other side of the imaginary line between Upolu and Tutuila. But the future of the scheme is not bright. The higher chiefs of Tutuila look askance at it, partly because it would put them back directly under the superior mana of the three "kings," partly because the shrewder ones understand that the U.S. Navy—or whatever American government agency eventually takes charge—will have more to spend and more posts to fill, particularly in the prestige-rich Marine auxiliary corps that the Navy maintains, than would fall to Tutuila's share if government were consolidated at Apia. Number Two reason is in terms familiar to westerners, but Number One has values that would hardly operate so strongly among us.

The project will probably founder anyway on the issue of what power would be in charge if union were effected. There is no sane reason why the States should take over the most persistent headache in the Pacific—responsibility for Western Samoa. If Navy control of facilities at Pago Pago were assured, the States might conceivably hand over American Samoa to New Zealand. But the details of such an arrangement would make an international lawyer see spots before his eyes. A national military force would then be the localized dictator of an area in an environment controlled by another alien nation, not as sovereign but as deputy of a supranational organization. It would be more logical for New Zealand, using the security features possible in U.N. trusteeships, to take over the Pago Pago base under agreement permitting the States full use on demand. But that would outrage the U.S. Navy, which has never been noted for the more latitudinarian type of logic and, unless the Royal New Zealand Navy has more to spend than it ever has had yet, would cause economic revolution on Tutuila. A solution cannot even be envisaged. The conclusion must be that the union of the two Samoas is going to wait a long time.

Supposing union were conceivable, Western Samoans would probably prefer Uncle Sam as trustee, as noted before. This stems from World War II, with roots going back to Steinberger's impressive second appearance at Apia unloading a mouth-watering cargo of white man's guns, uniforms, and band instruments as good will gifts to Samoa from Washington. The presence on Upolu during the war of thousands of U.S. marines bringing great engineering works, dollars, and good things was both breath-taking and invidious. You can still hear sung a war-born song about how Samoa saw plenty of American men and big guns when she was in danger, but where, oh where, were New Zealand's men and big guns? New Zealand actually did more than her proportionate share in the war in the Near East, Africa, and Italy, as well as in the Pacific. But little of that was visible in Samoa which, like most Pacific islands, is utterly parochial in information on, and judgments of, world affairs. This inchoate yearning for American guardianship has little to do with sober weighing of issues, however. It springs almost altogether from the Islander's traditional, and not exactly cynical, conviction that wealth and power are earmarks of the good and great, that high mana is manifested in liberal distribution of good things and carries automatic right to leadership.

The Islander's gods may be dead, but in many disconcerting ways his mind and emotions often run in the channels that the old gods would understand.

VI

OLD LEGENDS NEVER DIE

1

Hurry, Hurry, Hurry. . .

> . . . geography made easy and poetry realized in
> the everyday.
> —Extract from advance publicity for
> *A Bird of Paradise*

THE THIRD-FLOOR TENANT ON NEW YORK'S EAST SIXTY-
Fifth Street complained to the landlord that she was constantly
meeting outlandish-looking foreigners on the stairs; and that
she could no longer endure the monotonous, half-jingly, half-
wailing music that went on and on, the same tune over and
over and over, most of the night and every night. So the land
lord investigated the fourth-floor tenant, a young actress named
Laurette Taylor living with her mother. This was the year
1911. Unwittingly he was involved in a bit of American cultural history.

The outlandish callers proved to be Hawaiian musicians
imported from the Islands by the late Oliver Morosco jr., a
conspicuous theatrical producer. They were playing the same
tune so often because their leader, a chunky Polynesian who
took his assignment seriously, was trying quickly to teach Miss
Taylor the *hula* with appropriate musical accompaniment. She
had to balance walnut shells full of water on the backs of her
hands to keep her gestures true and, back flat against the wall,
wriggle her lower half without moving her upper half and
vice versa. It was all preparation for *A Bird of Paradise*, a
play by Richard Walton Tully which Morosco planned to

open in New York that coming season, Miss Taylor heading the cast in her first leading role.

The historical point in these goings-on is that *The Bird*, as show business was to call it, ineradicably imbedded the Hawaii-*cum*-South-Seas tradition in the mass-mind of America. The late Miss Taylor's sinuous *hula*—she once did me the honor to run through a few of its liquid manual gestures—plus her great beauty and charm, plus the throbbing, whining music of a sort new to most customers, added visibility and three dimensions to inchoate public notions of the world of palms, islands and voluptuousness.

Movies had not yet developed to the point where they could exploit this background as a favored *cliché*, and there was much difference between even an illustrated book—such as the lush *The Blue Lagoon* of 1910—and this flesh-and-blood presentation, of the way things were on a "South Sea Island." Nor had Hawaii yet initiated high powered publicity using such props. But after *The Bird* had trouped the country for a couple of years, for Omaha and Memphis the revolving haunch, the grass skirt, and the flower necklace had become as proverbial symbols of carnality as the name of Paris, France, in conjunction with a perfume or lewd picture. The undulating attractiveness not only of Miss Taylor, but also of Miss Lenore Ulric, whom this show also started on her way to fame, eventually obliged some thousands of women, some young, some not so young, some with Polynesian blood, some merely swarthy, to wear grass skirts on platforms while the barker intoned:

"Just the way they shake 'em in the Islands, friends. Only a dime, ten cents, the tenth potuvadollah, to see the genuwine Hywoyan hula danced without the aid of human feet. Hurry, hurry, hurry . . ."

Tin Pan Alley pricked up its battered ears as it never had at *Aloha Oe*, and within a few years the front porches of fraternity houses resounded with the hoarse whacking of the ukulele and jouncingly rhythmic accounts of how she gave me langwidge lessons on that beach at Wokkykee. When young Joe Cook went on stage carrying a ukulele everybody in the audience knew its connotations and, when he announced that he would now explain why he would not imitate four Hawaiians—which he then did for twenty minutes of the best monologue ever presented in vaudeville—the reference went solidly home to every customer who had been suffering under a nation-wide plague of Hawaiian acts. In at least one case *The Bird* seems to have inspired a youngster to go right out to Hawaii on his last cent. At twenty-one Don Blanding saw Lenore Ulric's sultry road-show Luana in Kansas City with that result. His description of the performance sets the tone:

> "A girl danced. With hands and arms undulant as restless waves, her body supple as a swaying vine, her bare feet moving with caressing lightness, she danced against an exotic background of trailing, tangled *lianas* and tall, sky-rocketing palm trees."—*Hula Moons*, 12–13.

Yet, though it spawned innumerable carnival- and cabaret-acts, *The Bird* itself was no carnival show. It was not even a musical, dances and musical numbers being incidental. (An anachronistic effort to make a musical of it—they called it *Luana*—was an abject failure in 1930.) It was rather a picturesque drama, culminating in the disgrace of the hero as a cad, and the suicide of the Kanaka heroine.

In terms of the period, its quality was not too low. The New York notices were better than average. But curiously, in view of its eventual importance, it was actually no great hit on Broadway, lasting only 112 performances, most of them in the tiny Maxine Elliott's Theatre. It drew nothing like as much money as such triumphs of the same season as *Kismet* and *Officer 666*. Nor does Mark Sullivan list it in *Our Times* as a memorable show of the period. Actually it was road companies that made it a theatrical property of great value and sank the *hula* so deeply into American folklore. The sticks liked it, all the more for the kind of ballyhoo that went ahead of the company—remember this kind of talk was new then:

> ". . . the play of a woman's soul . . . beautiful, intensely atmospheric . . . Hawaii with its shores girdled by lazy waves

in languorous moonlight, Hawaii with its intermittent volcanoes muttering menaces and blazing signals, Hawaii with
its laughing, dancing maidens crowned and garlanded with
brilliant flowers, maidens casting eyes of witchery on white
strangers . . ."

The author of *The Bird*, previously successful with an exotic
drama called *Omar the Tentmaker*, had visited Hawaii twice
and could make great play with appropriate atmospheric detail,
as such publicity promised. And he had plenty of plot: Luana,
the heroine, is a lost direct descendant of the Kamehameha
dynasty whom a brutal sugar planter tries to use as political
lever against Queen Liliuokalani. Luana's charms, and a taste
for *kava*, depicted as a soul-sapping beverage of great potency,
seduce a high-minded young white visitor into marriage,
chronic tropical languor, and eventual degeneracy. In the sub-
plot a gin-swilling, Omar-quoting beachcomber clears himself
of an embezzler's past by recalling his scientific training and
isolating the germ of leprosy. Said Tully's original scenario for
the play:

"Hope and salvation are working out for the dissolute beachcomber who climbs from degradation to the highest honor
among men through his having kept himself racially pure and
his mating with the clear-eyed intelligent girl of his own kind."

In the last act Luana is being prayed-to-death by a *kahuna*
and implored by her people on the Big Island to come back and
save them from a lava flow. She obliges the *kahuna* and ap-
peases Pele by jumping into Kilauea crater as a finale. This
heroine's role was gay, touching, sympathetic, glamorous,
tragic, and well-paced. No wonder Miss Taylor worked so
hard to persuade Morosco and Tully that she could and must
play it. Tully had wanted a genuine Kanaka girl from the
Islands, perhaps as a result of seeing what Luana had been like
when played by Miss Bessie Barriscale in a tryout of the piece
by Morosco's coast stock company.

Tully and Morosco liked stage effects. They not only had a

spectacular final curtain in the red glow of the volcano, but also a first act thunderstorm and subsequent rainbow that were very favorably commented upon. The script even called for electric fans to waft the smell of wet kelp out over the audience in the opening seaside scene, but it is dubious whether the actual production ever went to such lengths of verisimilitude.

Lepers—a point on which Honolulu was sensitive round the turn of the century—praying-to-death, volcanoes, *kava*, sugar planters, beachcombers, are only the beginning of the list of "color"-items that Tully skilfully worked in. The first act set showed a black sand beach backed by both a cave and a grass hut, and dragged in more missionaries, grass skirts, *holokus*, fish nets, underground ovens, prewhite idols, *poi* bowls, canoe paddles, royal feather cloaks, *kahilis* and smatterings of Hawaiian than a less ingenious dramatist would have dared to shake a stick at. It must have looked like a sheriff's sale in an ethnological museum. The ukulele was conspicuous, and the troupe of genuine Islanders who had so exhausted Miss Taylor gave their Island songs several times. All of it constituted a good money's worth for the customers; but there can have been no mistaking the fact that it was romantic sexiness that put it over.

Tully suffered colossal trouble from his success. An amateur dramatist named Grace A. Fendler slapped a suit on him and Morosco in 1912, charging plagiarism of her play *In Hawaii*, a scenario of which she had sent Morosco in his San Francisco office in early 1910. This was to be one of the most prolonged and famous plagiarism cases of all time. In 1924 the Supreme Court of New York State finally awarded the plaintiff $780,000, which gives a rough idea of how well the show did on the opera house circuit. The Appellate Division unanimously upheld the finding. Unanimity apparently choked off all possibility of further appeal; but four years later Charles H. Tuttle, still an eminent member of the New York bar, found the requisite loophole, and the New York State Court of Appeals reversed the lower courts in a fashion that, in all fairness, exonerated Tully.[1]

This victory, nineteen years after the opening night, was much too late. From all accounts the effect on the late Mr. Tully of having such weighty doubts cast on his integrity were most unfortunately—and understandably—serious. The author of two such well-paying pieces as Omar and The Bird did little more as a dramatist. For a decade before the final decision, Hollywood had been using the background that Tully first exploited for highly successful movies. But The Bird itself did not see the screen to which it had contributed so much until 1932. No movie company wanted a script so tied up in litigation; besides, you could always cash in on the ready-made tradition by shifting the locale to Tahiti or Samoa and shooting it all on Catalina Island anyway.

So, in order to reach popularity, South Seas material had to be violently adapted to fit western ideas. The same feeling runs through the Island souvenir business, which herds naturally with show business—the hustler selling pennants and patriotic ash-trays always worked right next to the barker for the hula troupe. The standard hula skirt as worn in sideshows and sold to tourists in Hawaii is made of rattan imported from the East Indies sewn on cloth woven in some such place as Biddeford, Maine; or consider the hula skirt of cellophane strands.

I am told that Fijian troops on Bougainville during the recent war used to scrounge rope from the U.S. Marines, tease out the fibres, make skirts of the resulting fuzzy strings, and sell them back as genuine cannibal costumes. Fiji has always been specially enterprising in that direction. Seventy years ago making fake cannibal-forks for sale to outsiders had al-

---

[1]The crucial point was that Tully's original scenario, containing most of the ideas and material used in the completed script, could be proved to antedate any opportunity for him to have seen the Fendler scenario. This, used as ground for claiming that there was categorically no evidence of plagiarism whatever, enabled Tuttle to go back into court on a matter of law, not of fact, which was essential if further appeal were to be legally possible.

ready begun there. The Indian merchant resident in Fiji in the last war made literally millions out of supplying GIs with cat's-eye silver jewelry made Indian-style, phony war clubs such as no prewhite Fijian ever laid eyes on, and picture post cards of leering Fijian belles stripped to the waist, a costume that no local girl has worn in public for four generations. You could go on and on; I remember the postcards that they used to sell tourists in American Samoa, showing a bell-breasted Samoan girl in similar disarray with the caption: "Would you like to see Samoa?" . . . The strange part of it is that the Fijian souvenir trade is still very lively, even though all the GIs were evacuated three years ago. The astute Indian tied up with smart boys in uniform who are now sending him back wholesale orders for more of the same for sale to States souvenir stores. By now souvenirs rank fourth among Fijian exports, exceeded in money value only by sugar, gold and copra.

Tully, however, did not originate popular entertainment with a South Sea background. The first such effort was a successful spectacle ballet called *Otaheite*, produced in London during the furore over Captain Cook in the late eighteenth century. Mark Twain's humorous lecture on Hawaii was one of the most popular items in his early repertory. Then a French painter, Jules Tavernier, delivered himself of a large cyclorama of the Kilauea volcano which Lorrin A. Thurston, most kinetic of Hawaiian annexationists, took to the Chicago World's Fair in 1893 as a commercial speculation—presumably also to bring Hawaii to the attention of the mainland at a critical juncture. For sweetening he recruited a quartet of Hawaiian singers, one of whom, a *hapa-haole* named Ben Jones, was later in the cast of *The Bird*; another was Duke K. Kahanamoku, father of the famous swimmer. In spite of the great drawing power of the Fair, however, Kilauea lost money; it did not show a profit until it reached the relatively Hawaii-conscious West Coast at the San Francisco Midwinter Fair of 1894–5. Thurston finally sold its 420 running feet of canvas to a professional showman who wanted it for the Buffalo Exposition of 1901. Then it disappears from view. Volcanoes and rich, deep-chested Hawaiian singing were all verv well, but Hawaii without sex was not box office.

Another amateur showman from more southerly islands apparently did better at the same period by including more action and a further dash of sex. This was Harry J. Moors, Michigan-born entrepreneur in Samoa, whose trading stores and vessels, leases on guano islands, and dabblings in politics were major features of Apia beach up to World War I. A wandering actor named Mason Mitchell seems to have suggested to Moors that the public might want something Samoan, preferably dancing, at the Chicago Fair. For the soon-to-be-famous Midway Plaisance was to include a Congress of All Nations—meaning units of exotic peoples, Dutch, Japanese and so forth, living and performing against backgrounds like those at home. (Hence, of course, the exhibit called the Streets of Cairo, in which Little Egypt introduced the cooch-dance to America.) So Moors recruited a Samoan troupe of both sexes, scattering Wallis Islanders and Fijians among them, and took them to Chicago, along with tapa costumes, weapons, fire-sticks, canoes, kava bowls, ceremonial headdresses and a knockdown Samoan house.

The appearance of the troupe at Honolulu, where they gave a break-in performance at the Opera House, temporarily relieved the political tension, then at its height because Blount had hauled down the American flag. Set up on the Midway in Chicago, they dutifully performed kava ceremonies, war dances, and sitting sivas, partook in a polyglot regatta—but, according to surviving photographs, the girls were required to cover their bosoms and the dances were probably chosen from the more decorous part of the Samoan repertory. They seem to have offered Little Egypt no serious competition.[2] But they did well enough for Barnum & Bailey to sign part of the troupe for

[2]The participants in this trip are all dead now, so most of this is from documentary sources. Representative Sol Bloom, who was general manager of the '93 Midway, has given the writer every indication that, for reasons best known to himself, he does not care to discuss the Samoans' career at the Fair.

the next circus season and Moors, unlike Thurston, seems to
have made money. At least he was back again with a larger
troupe at the St. Louis World's Fair in 1904.

This time the selection of Islanders was even more diversi-
fied, emphasizing energetic dances, and the props were so
numerous and heavy that Moors chartered a whole ship to
transport the outfit to the Coast. San Francisco seems to have
been characteristically chilly when they arrived and the fifty
performers, including Moors' small daughter, waited on board
until the boss could get ashore and buy them warm clothes to
stave off pneumonia. Their routine at St. Louis included cooking in underground ovens, climbing prop coco palms, and
much dancing, kava making, and sale of Island curios made on
the spot. Since the traditional accompaniment to Island dancing is no more than monotonous drumming, Moors hired a
Mexican orchestra to lend romantic color to the show, an
anomaly that troubled nobody. The dancing of the Gilbert
Islanders went over best. But any of the numbers would produce a shower of silver from the holiday-minded audience.
Moors' daughter still remembers how the innocent Samoan
maidens in the troupe cautioned her not to encourage cheap
skates by stooping to pick up anything smaller than a quarter.

The press seems to have been nice to these ventures. The
flier that Moors circulated in 1905 quotes Julian Hawthorne,
writing son of the great novelist:

> "the most delightful and refreshing performance at the Fair
> . . . The young men are models of manly beauty, just like
> antique statues of Greek gods or fauns . . . the girls . . .
> as beautiful at all points as any young women I should care
> to see . . ."

The Century Magazine noted, with perhaps a shade of disappointment: "the best dancing in the Plaisance. It makes no
pretense to grossness, but is simply downright savage." Best
of all was the great reporter, Richard Harding Davis:

> "imagination easily transports [the customer] to the little coral
> reefs on which these people live, and in their daily life do all

they represent on the stage except to eat human flesh—they having abandoned cannibalism a quarter of a century ago and embraced Christianity under the teachings of French Catholic missionaries. So strong is their religion that they will not perform on Sunday and they are the only World's Fair company that keeps closed house on the Sabbath."

The "little coral reef" whence most of them came from is an island with mountains several thousand feet high extending thirty miles one way and fifteen the other. Catholicism was a minor influence among these Samoans, Tongans, Fijians, Ellice and Gilbert Islanders; in the South Seas strict Sabbatarianism is the earmark of Protestant, not Catholic; cannibalism has always been absent or unimportant in most of the islands represented in this troupe. But the great Dick Davis had evidently liked the show and written a rave-notice and it is hard to blame Moors for reprinting it, errors and all.

After St. Louis, he took his troupe on the road in a year and a half of barnstorming coast-to-coast, two-a-day. The performers had the time of their lives, particularly during the Fair when, provided they remained in costume, they had free entry to all the other Midway shows. The girls were so handy at making friends in St. Louis and elsewhere that Moors had to enforce strict rules against ogling acquaintances in the audience during a performance—which resulted in the cast's dancing with chins in the air and eyes way up in the flies.

Yet there is little evidence that Moors' South Sea Islanders were much more than just another feature at St. Louis, nothing like as memorable as the aborigines from the Philippines who included in their daily routine the cooking and eating of a real dog. The achievement of *The Bird* remains unflawed, for the American public failed to become South Sea-minded from Moors' moderately profitable commercial show of genuine South Seas material. It waited until the South Seas appeared in the guise of a beautiful Irish girl in brown make-up who had never been near the Islands. As a matter of fact, at the time of her recent death, Laurette Taylor had still never seen Hawaii.

When *The Bird* was produced, the stage was still the only medium for acted-out stories dependent on scenic and atmospheric background. But within a few years the rise of the spectacle-movie relieved the stage of that somewhat vulgarizing burden. From then on things like *Ben-Hur* were in an element that no longer cramped them down to treadmills and backdrops in high perspective. Hollywood took the hint when O'Brien's books showed how avidly the post-World War I public would take to South Sea romanticizing, and at least half a dozen feature films a year have exploited that background, better distributing and pacing the elements that so cluttered Tully's stage.

Gloria Swanson, Joan Crawford, Gilda Grey, Dolores del Rio, Jinx Falkenburg, Ann Corio and, of course, Dorothy Lamour, are only a few of the variegated ladies of the box office severally concerned. The gentlemen in the case are less important for a curious reason. The South Sea convention has always spotlighted the native or half-native heroine and her attendant bevy of brown nymphs much at the expense of the native male. From all the evidence the screen ever offered, men had about as much to do with Polynesia as with the classical kingdom of the Amazons; the emphasis went on the white interloper as lover of the beautiful native princess Puaki. Further to labor the absurdities of the run-of-mine South Seas scenario is too easy to be sport. Its *clichés* rapidly became as stale as a burlesque blackout or the plot of the machine-made Owen Davis tear-jerker. The essence of it has always been a background suggesting high temperatures against which a husky youth with a bare chest embraces a toothsome lady in a single garment apparently about to fall off.

A generation ago, however, there were well-executed efforts to get a touch of the genuine into celluloid Polynesia. Nobody who saw Flaherty's *Moana of the South Seas* can ever forget the swimming, sunlightish charm of its photography and continuity. *Moana*, of course, was shot in Samoa with an all-Samoan cast picked for beauty or impressiveness. The falsification implicit in its material at least had the virtue of warping genuine materials, and the faults were strictly those of omission in the good cause of pleasing the spectators. In dilute form many of the same virtues existed in Murnau's *Tabu*—genuine background on Bora Bora for many shots, genuine Polynesian or half-Polynesian performers, an idyllic effect worked out of data that were genuine as far as they went.[3]

But after that the dark. The only perceptible effect of *Tabu* on the world of entertainment was the importation of Reri, the half-Tahitian heroine thereof, to dance in the *Follies*. At the age of sixteen she found herself approaching New York on the Twentieth Century Limited with a press agent insisting that, even if it was ungodly cold outside, she should be decanted on the platform in front of the news photographers wearing a pareu—the garment that movie-fans call a sarong, which is a Malay, not a Polynesian, word. The great Ziegfeld's idea of what sort of music and support should go with her dancing is best exemplified by his insistence on teaming her with Harry Richman. But she went over quite well indeed in New York night clubs and later in Europe, where she learned Polish and German. Reri is back in Tahiti now, plumper than when Ziegfeld sent that imperious cable, but still full of charm. The slender youth who played opposite her in *Tabu* was over military age when World War II broke out, but managed to enlist anyway in the French Pacific Battalion and had an excellent combat record.

For some time after Pearl Harbor it looked as if one minor but welcome result of war would be the extinction of the South Seas movie. GIs on duty on idyllic Pacific isles reacted most unfavorably to movies about idyllic Pacific isles. Sometimes, they say, the loud-speaker was drowned out by the raucousness of the disapproval. Central Casting told me in 1945 that the number of real Polynesians filed as available for extra roles in Hollywood had dwindled to ten—eight Hawaiians

[3]Murnau's shooting trip to Bora Bora left a wide trail of superstitious gossip behind it. The story is that some of the locations picked were *tabu* ground, so bad luck dogged the steps of several members of the party. Murnau was killed in a motoring accident not long after . . . his house burned down . . . and so forth and so on.

and two Samoans; and that they had seen a "very definite decrease" in the demand for such types for such jobs. Sideshow experts say that rumba and samba have pretty well shaken the duller hula out of the field. But though all returns are not yet in, it already looks as if the tradition may revive. English harbingers of J. Arthur Rank's enterprises are, as I write, on Fiji seeking locations for a picture based on The Blue Lagoon, which was not a Fijian story at all, but never mind. A Hollywood outfit is shortly to go into production with an Hawaii item. It is usually women who determine what movie is attended. After all, the GIs' wives and girl friends never saw the Pacific, never felt aggrieved at the bulgy lack of glamor of the average South Seas girl.

Even the GIs may not be too trustworthy on that point. Dorothy Lamour is something to look at regardless, and genuine cow hands are notoriously fond of Hollywood horse operas.

2

Fayaway's Children

> I know not where those islands lift
> Their fronded palms in air . . .
> —John Greenleaf Whittier

A MAGAZINE PUBLISHER STOOD BESIDE ME AT THE RAIL twelve years ago as the liner "Mariposa" sailed from Pago Pago in American Samoa. His eye fell on Centipede Row, a line of cottages inhabited by married officers of the miniature U.S. Navy base:

"Six little bungalows," he said dreamily. "Six little bungalows at Pago Pago. Ah, if only Willie Maugham were here!"

The lie of the hills round the harbor made it clear that we were floating de luxe on the waters of a flooded volcanic crater. This was the spot where Colonel Steinberger began his two-faced and double-jointed career as unctuous and benevolent dictator of all Samoa. A few miles to the westward La Pérouse landed the first whites to visit Samoa, and lost eleven men when the Samoans proved violently nervous and covetous. The seagoing tug at the Navy pier was presently to depart for her periodic trip to Manua, where Dr. Margaret Mead found material for pregnant ponderings about fashionable child psychology. Yet, in the presence of all these varied segments of significant reality, a publisher was pining for Willie Maugham.[1]

[1] In a manner of speaking, Willie Maugham was there. The only transient accommodations at Pago—a two-story boarding-house which had

425

It is easy to see why. The South Seas have too long acted as flats, wings, backdrop, cyclorama and props for good, bad and indifferent fiction, exploited in the same fashion as rustlers, sheriffs, cayuses, stagecoaches and six-guns in horse opera. That has gone on so long that, in spite of recent war and death thereabouts, attempts to restore the area to validity in the eyes of the literate world may well be hopeless. This publisher saw no reason for contemplating Pago Pago in its own lovely, tangible, politics-jittery right. He wanted it diluted and conventionalized in a story using Outline No. Five. It occurred to me at the time that the plot values of *Rain* had been used many times before *Miss Thompson* was ever written; and that, like its heroine, the story could have been laid practically anywhere.

For that matter, the anatomical detail in Gauguin's paintings of Polynesians is often taken as artistic distortion by people accustomed to thinking of South Sea Island beauty in terms of Dorothy Lamour today or Dolores del Rio twenty years ago. Actually, of course, the painter's record of relative waistlessness, big feet, thick lip, is closer to anatomical accuracy than any Hollywood figure. Gauguin's error as a reporter—which, of course, he was not trying to be—lay in making his figures flat, passive, and stolid, lacking the grace and vigor of the living subject. The elements in his work usually considered to derive from a South Seas background—composition, coloring, emotional impact—are already conspicuous in paintings that he did in France and the West Indies before he ever saw Tahiti. That is, like Maugham, he merely developed against a

---

just been badly damaged by a storm—calls itself the Saddie (sic) Thompson Hotel. House and sign were still there when I last saw Pago in May, 1947. A Navy officer stationed there some years ago tells me that the management once changed the name to the Samoa House because a missionary had protested against publicly displaying the name of a prostitute, however fictional. The officer warned the landlady that if things were the same with hotels as with ships, name-changing would be bad luck. But missionary superstition prevailed over nautical—until, soon after the change, the aforesaid storm took off the roof and stove in one wall. At that point the name was hastily changed back again.

South Seas set of references the idiom in which he would have painted anywhere. Surely fact and fantasy have never been more marvelously misidentified.

Alec Waugh once wrote that it has long been impossible to write "otherwise than conventionally"[2]—that is, with second-hand materials and attitudes—about the South Seas. Limit the agenda to "creative" writing—for certain ethnological studies of Pacific islands contain good reading and salutary thinking—and it is a useful three-quarter truth. For the literary creator the area has the disadvantages that too pretty a model has for the painter. The channels of association through which the data reach the beholder are imperiously well-worn, too cluttered with stimulating but nonaesthetic connotations. The South Seas, in fact, are a geographical Hedy Lamarr, who would be ill-advised to get herself cast as Lady Macbeth or even Candida.

By now most people apply the South Seas set of stereotypes even in the teeth of geography. Americans discussing the area are usually sure that many Conrad stories are laid there, whereas Conrad pretty well confined himself to the East Indies. Many are equally sure that *White Cargo*, a play set in Africa, was a South Seas affair. For, if a background of heat, jungle, lovely coffee-colored half-breeds and white men succumbing to all three does not spell South Seas, it ought to.

Most such stereotypes, those of the American West for instance, at least started from a basis of reality. In its time the West really did display ready gunplay, rustling and so forth, as the South Seas exhibited beachcombers, square-face gin and cannibalism. But the fact of the matter is that the foundations of the South Seas legend, as distinct from the details, had no relation to reality at all. They began as arbitrary, intellectual assumptions forcibly fitted on the most attractive collection of islands and peoples known at the time. And, whereas the founders of horse opera were inglorious hacks, few major writers ever bothering with that background, the founders of South-seasism were kings and councillors of the intellectual earth.

[2]*Hot Countries,* 41.

Rousseau usually receives credit for paternity here, which might not hold up in court under an ideological blood test. Even the phrase "noble savage" was not his, but John Dryden's before him. Though it is true that Rousseau most impressively formulated "natural man," he admitted that such a creature might never have existed; he deduced "natural man" from human nature as useful sociological fiction, not as prediction in reverse. He came closest to Southseasism in his subsequent picture of the postnatural but preownership, premetal, precereal savage whom he did consider probably to exist untrammeled by possessiveness and division of labor. But even here, though Havelock Ellis claims that Rousseau was "a careful student of the narratives of explorers in his time,"[3] the material that he used had little to do with the South Seas. His ideas were set well before Wallis, Bougainville, and Cook brought back detailed data from the Pacific. Accounts from previous explorers of those parts had been scanty and, for these purposes, insignificant. Rousseau apparently relied much more heavily on accounts of the Hottentots of Africa and the Caribs of the Antilles than on Polynesians.

What material he used does not greatly signify, however. The gadfly of Geneva was not seeking scientific validity but was whittling sticks to beat the civilization-dog with. His deductions from Caribs and Hottentots amount to almost as airy a set of hypotheses as his acknowledged fictions about natural man. He assumed absolute communism, for instance, a thing that so far as ethnography can find never existed anywhere. He assumed absolute promiscuity between the sexes, which again never existed among any known people. And in general he assumed a flexibility of primitive behavior so attractive to civilized men of a certain emotional bent that, try as they may, scientists have not yet been able to lay its seductive ghost. In discussing it Malinowski hits out with a sort of despairing frenzy:

"The word savage, whatever association it might have had originally, connotes ideas of boundless liberty, of irregularity,

[3] Preface to Malinowski, The Sexual Life of Savages, viii.

of something extremely and extraordinarily quaint. In popular thinking, we imagine that the natives live on the bosom of Nature, more or less as they can and like, . . . Modern science, on the contrary, shows . . . natives subjected to a strict code of behavior and good manners, to which in comparison the life at the Court of Versailles or Escurial was free and easy."—*Argonauts of the Western Pacific*, 10

It is important to comprehend the glaringly a *priori* character of Rousseau's teachings about primitive peoples, because otherwise it is difficult to believe that other of his contemporaries could so insist on seeing in the South Seas things that were not there and never had been. That is, the direct responsibility for the world's consistently warped picture of that end of creation is not Rousseau's. But he did give final polishing to the lens through which the Islands would look like Paradise.

The specific attribution of untrammeled noble savagery to prewhite Polynesia was characteristically the work of Frenchmen, who have a great way of inventing fertile ideas for other people to take seriously, while neglecting them themselves. For every Frenchman who has written a silly book about the South Seas or gone down there seeking spiritual solace from innocent brown children of nature, there have been a dozen Englishmen or Americans.

More precisely, the first observed case of typical Southseasitis occurred in an intellectual surgeon-naturalist who sailed with Bougainville. True to his national heritage, this M. Commerson couched his account of the tangible Golden Age in Tahiti largely in terms of *l'amour*. Since it was an important moment when the first pen scrawled off the first glorification of the South Seas, implying a pitying lesson for western man, that poor, hampered, frustrated changeling, lengthy quotation is justified:

"Born under the most beautiful of skies, fed by the fruits of an earth that is fertile without cultivation, ruled by fathers of families rather than by kings, they know no other God than love; to him all their days were consecrated, the whole island is his temple, all the women are his idols and all the men are

his adorers. And what women! Rivals of the Georgians for beauty, unveiled sisters of the Graces! Neither shame nor prudery manifest their tyranny here; the lightest of gauzes drift about them according to the whim of the winds or their own desires. The act of begetting one's kind is an act of religion; the preliminaries are encouraged by the prayers and songs of all the people assembled together, and the consummation is hailed with universal applause; every stranger is admitted to these happy rites. It is even one of hospitality's duties to invite strangers to take part, so the good Tahitian may enjoy himself incessantly either by way of his own pleasures or in observing those of others. No stern censor will fail to see in all this a breakdown of morals, a horrible prostitution, the boldest cynicism; but is this not the natural state of man, born essentially good, free of all prejudice, following without remorse the tender impulses of a consistently pure instinct, because he has not yet degenerated into reason? . . . This is no horde of stupid and crude savages; among these people everything bears the mark of the most perfect intelligence. . . . With what industry have they treated iron, a metal very valuable to them, which they convert only into useful tools, a metal so vile when we make of it the tools of despair and death! With what horror they rejected knives and scissors which we offered them, because they apparently guessed the use that could be made of such things! . . . We admired the simplicity of their customs, . . . their comradeliness among themselves, their horror at the shedding of human blood. . . . Their distaste for wines and liquors was insurmountable. . . ."
—In full in Corney, *Tahiti*, 462–4.

This projection of the preconceived noble savage on pre-white Tahitians—a convenient group of nonwestern people whom the witness had found charming—has one deviation into fact: the statement that Tahitians were not stupid and crude savages. Otherwise the thing could be used as horrible example of how not to do reporting. For a bill of particulars: some staples of Tahitian diet required more or less labor. Tahiti was ruled by chiefs of clans and sub-clans not heads of families in any western sense. Some Tahitian girls were undoubtedly attractive, but neither all nor many can have been such houris as all this. They had their own pruderies, stripping stark only under the frenzy of prolonged dancing or for religious observances. The arrangement of their clothes, by no means haphazard, was one arbitrary way of showing respect to their betters. They did not reject knives as potentially lethal; they grabbed for them, and for axes too, when the Spaniards' "Aguila" made Tahiti a few years later; they may have rejected scissors because they did not know what they were for. They had no horror of shedding human blood. Human sacrifice was integral in their magico-religious ceremonies; their mourning rites included slashing themselves with shark's teeth until the blood poured. Their aversion to alcohol broke down so soon that it can hardly be said to have existed beyond the novice's natural alarm at the burn of strong waters in the mouth.

But great men had said that admirable "savages" must be communistic, humane and without prudery, so M. Commerson told his eyes what to see and his brain what to remember. In ghosting the highest chieftainess of the Teva, Henry Adams recorded—or perhaps put in her mouth—a dry summary of the matter:

> ". . . at that moment Europe, and especially France, happened to be looking for some bright example of what man had been, or might be, and the philosophers seized on Tahiti to prove that, if man would only rid himself of restraints, he would be happy . . . the real code of Tahitian society would have upset the theories of a state of nature as thoroughly as the guillotine did."—*Memoirs of Arii Tamai*, 53, 56.

When a man who had been on the spot, as Commerson had, could so falsify and misinterpret, it is not surprising that great men who never saw the South Seas, or any other preliterate life, perpetrated the same fraud in their studies in Paris. For there was greater authority and even lower accuracy to come. On reaching home Bougainville published an account of his voyage. The great M. Diderot, chief of the Encyclopedists, read it and was moved to write the *Supplément au Voyage de Bougainville*, a decorously lustrous piece of prose of the special quality that only certain Frenchmen writing their beloved mother tongue can attain. But, for all its literary merits, it is hard to agree with Havelock Ellis that the *Supplément* "brought forward various correct facts . . . but misleadingly . . . ignorant of the social framework to which they belonged."[4] Heaven knows the thing is misleading; only the facts as well are not even remotely correct. This is probably the most extraordinary piece of misrepresentation that an intelligent man ever attempted. Though rhapsodic enough about Tahiti, Bougainville cannot be held responsible; neither can the cultivated sentimentalists, such as Hawkesworth and Georg Forster, who injected so much sugar water into accounts of Cook's first two voyages. Most of the facts alleged or customs referred to in the *Supplément* cannot be found in any voyager's book, cannot be found anywhere but in M. Diderot's tendentious imagination. They are witty fabrication in the interests of a preconceived idea.

The bulk of it is the apostrophe of an aged Tahitian chief to Bougainville, adjuring him not to infect a natural paradise with western corruptions. Then follows a long dialogue, great fun in places, between another chief and the French chaplain, who is finally cajoled, with much groaning of spirit, into sleeping with the chief's three daughters in succession. Among Ellis' "correct facts" consider that the old chief, Ulysses-like, defies his callers to bend his great bow and four French sailors cannot manage it, whereas the Tahitian bow was actually a toy. Still, a savage ought to have a superstrong bow and, since he lived under natural conditions on natural diet, should be far stronger than civilized man. The same chief tells Bougainville: "We follow the pure instinct of Nature, we are happy . . . We know only one ailment, that to which men and animals alike are doomed—old age"; whereas filariasis, yaws, probably hookworm, and certainly a multiplicity of skin diseases were prevalent. The second chief assures the chaplain that Tahitian fathers sleep with daughters, mothers with sons, sisters with brothers; whereas Tahiti had strong incest-*tabus*, some ex-

[4]Preface to Malinowski, *The Sexual Life of Savages*, viii.

ceeding ours. Still authority maintained that the uncorrupted
savage, not being possessive-minded, could develop no in-
hibitions against absolute promiscuity. Diderot was bent on
using these people to point any moral—medical, economic or
erotic—that he chose, and produced what Chinard calls "the
supreme expression . . . of the naturistic philosophy of the
eighteenth century."[5]

The trick was familiar in that period and is not unknown in
our day. Contemporary *savants* used the Chinese, the Middle
Easterner, or the American Indian as mouthpieces, distorted
according to whatever doctrine was being preached. There
were fabricated disturbing letters home from Europe by
mandarins and pashas. But the unwary reader, and the fiction
spinners who succeeded the *savants*, too often took this amusing rhetorical device at face value. Thus the European merchant skipper of some education first putting in at Canton
was indignant when the Chinese, whom he had learned to
consider a nation of genial and cultivated philosophers of the
highest principles, swindled him out of his own and his owner's
eyeteeth and took bribes with the aplomb of a headwaiter.

So it was that the South Seas made their bow in the world
of letters blatantly under false pretenses. The growth of the
legend was slow at first. Lord Byron gave it its next considerable lift. He had never been within 10,000 miles of the South
Seas either, but his family had. "Foul Weather Jack" Byron,
an ancestor, made one of the earlier and less stimulating English voyages to the Pacific.[6] Speculating like many others on
the fate of the mutineers of the "Bounty"—this was long before their colony on Pitcairn's Island was found—he translated the terms of *Paul et Virginie* into what he conceived to
be a South Seas idiom, inspired by reading William Mariner's
account of his captivity on Tonga, and delivered himself of
The Island. It is irresistibly reminiscent of the pictures in the

[5]*Diderot, Supplément au Voyage de Bougainville*, 42.
[6]It was another member of this family, the poet's successor in the title,
who commanded H.M.S. "Blonde" on her voyage to take the dead
Liholiho and his wife back to Hawaii with royal honors.

old *Life* of Paris, Hollywood, and the Bluegrass, "by one who has never been there." But it can also stand as type of the South Seas scenario, as it set a love affair in anomalous western terms against a backdrop out of the *National Geographic*.

The Island is not brilliant Byron. Few admire it, though many have quoted it. Nor did it start a snowballing fashion. The time still doted on the Oriental as type of the exotically romantic. Young Mr. Bedwin Sands was at his zenith, and, though people sometimes read detailed fact about the South Seas in Cook, Bougainville and Mariner, they did not yet see that, for juicy escapism, no Circassian slave could hold a candle to a brown, bare-bosomed island girl. Nevertheless a few poets of mark eventually followed Byron's lead in occasionally celebrating this background with which they lacked personal acquaintance. The passage in *Locksley Hall* about South Sea "Summer isles of Eden" where "the passions cramped no longer shall have scope and breathing space" was no less effective for being so intemperately scorned by the poet in succeeding couplets.[7]

The unworthy thought occurs that the writing gentry were waiting until there was regular steamer service to Paradise. The coincidence of such schedules with their appearance on the scene is at least striking. But that would not be fair. Stevenson, Charles Warren Stoddard, and Jack London used irregular and hazardous transport in the South Seas, and so did their predecessor, the man who first cracked the dam of artistic indifference to this background.

Before he set up as a writer, as everybody knows, Herman Melville was foremast hand on a whaler, probably the riskiest and least comfortable way to travel the South Pacific since the days, a thousand years ago, when the Polynesians were migrating in their huge double canoes. Distaste for the forecastle led him to skip ship at Nukahiva (Marquesas) like many a sailor

---

[7]Much later Tennyson returned to the area, piously this time, in a turgid ode to Kapiolani, the Hawaiian chieftainess who defied the volcano goddess. It is the least successful of his otherwise respectable experiments in adapting classical prosody to English.

This Was the Islander

Accurate knowledge of the prewhite Islander is not too plentiful. But we know his life was elaborately ceremonious. This (from Cook's Voyages) purports to show a human sacrifice.

Early white voyagers greatly admired the skill and daring of Polynesian and Micronesian seamen, whose craft were often large and fast. The New Zealand Maori war canoe (from Cook's Voyages) might be made from a single immense log and run 100 feet overall.

Because timber was always scarce in the Tuamotu, the ingenious Island shipwright made this sea-going vessel of bits of plank carefully shaped to match and sewn together with cocoanut fiber.

Island architecture, styles of which varied from group to group, was often handsome if impermanent. This is a modern version of traditional Samoan construction. Elaborate lashings of cocoanut fiber made nails unnecessary.

Even at the present day the presentation of a roast hog to the guest of honor in Samoa is both ceremonious and traditional.

Typical of the most picturesque "high" volcanic islands. It probably looked much the same as this to its first discoverer.

Barring the dog tags and shorts, the Melanesians of Goodenough Island, off New Guinea, look much as their ancestors probably did and are conducting their harvest in much the same way. Their people have less racial admixture than many Islanders.

This Russell Islander uses whatever comes his way—the cross from the Catholic mission, the flat fifty of Luckies from the U.S. Marines, the thwart in his dugout by indirect courtesy of the Shell Oil Company. The bleached hair is one of his own traditions.

Bathing in Samoa was probably always like this . . . . .

Nor have these ceremonial houses changed much.

Tattersall, Ap

Hawaii

The view from the Nuuanu Pali on Oahu in Hawaii is the South Seas at its most accessible best and a terrific tourist-magnet. King Kamehameha the Great consolidated his hold on the Hawaiian group by driving his last effectual enemies over the sheer cliff overhanging this plain.

It may look like Arizona at round up time, but this is Lanai in Hawaii. Cattle-raising is important in local economy. Hawaiians are enthusiastic and brilliant horsemen. The local cow hand, known as a *paniolo* (for *Español*), borrowed most of his traditions and methods from Mexico.

This husky, smiling pineapple field hand typifies the mixed but predominantly Asiatic labor that does Hawaii's heavy work.

Though Hawaii has much in common with the rest of the South Seas, she uses advanced western agricultural methods much more extensively. This mechanized pineapple harvesting is typical of postwar Hawaii. On the Big Island sugar cane is often flumed direct to the mill like timber in mountain-lumbering.

Missionaries

Dr. Judd

The Gordons

Dr. Coan

Bishop Patteson

Dr. Hiram Bingham

Bishop Patteson died with his boots on when Melanesians smashed his skull in retaliation for a blackbirding raid. The Presbyterian Gordons were slaughtered in the New Hebrides for more obscure reasons. Three other specimens of missionary here depicted worked in Hawaii, which was safer, though often ruggedly uncomfortable for whites. Boss of the lot was the Rev. Hiram Bingham—"King Hiram."

In 1917 war sentiment finally persuaded Liliuokalani, last queen of Hawaii, to appear on the same platform with Sanford B. Dole, president of the republican government that ousted her. It took extreme old age and a quarter century to get them to shake hands. The third figure is Henri Berger, founder of the Royal Hawaiian Band, who did much to develop "Hawaiian" popular music.

Here, in Cornwall, Conn., lies Henry Obookiah, martyred by New England climate and diseases while training to become an aide to the first mission to ·Hawaii. His epitaph: "In/Memory of /Henry Obookiah/a native of/ OWHYHEE/His arrival in this country gave rise/to the Foreign mission school,/of which he was a worthy member./He was once an Idolater, and was/designed for a Pagan Priest; but by/the grace of God and by the prayers/and instructions of pious friends,/he became a christian./He was eminent for piety and/missionary Zeal. When almost prepared/to return to his native Isle, to preach /the Gospel, God took him to himself. In his last/sickness he wept and prayed for Owhyhee,/ but was submissive. He died without fear/with a heavenly smile on his/countenance and glory in his soul/Feb. 17, 1818./aged 26."

Interlopers

Samoan longboats gathered at Apia for a great festival. These handsome craft, usually communally owned, are attenuated versions of the graceful and seaworthy whaleboat of the white man. The umbrellas and fashions of attire date this between 1910 and 1920, in the German days.

Though badly broken up now, the wreck of the German warship "Adler" is still the great sight of the harbor of Apia. This picture was taken shortly after she was heaved up on the reef by the hurricane of 1889 which also wrecked two other German and three American men-of-war. The sole Britisher got clear. Imperialistic jealousies had made all three forces unwilling to put to sea when the storm began to blow.

Governor Wilhelm Solf is still a legend in the Islands. From 1900 to 1913 this massive, shrewd German administered Western Samoa toughly but, for the most part, ably and justly.

Their Gods Are Dead

White man's goods and ways have spread and spread through the Islands.
Here a missionary-taught Marshall Islander, now a teacher himself, instructs
his small son.

Catholicism in the Islands is most strongly entrenched in the Marianas. Here is an outdoor Mass on Saipan.

Western sports, a milder substitute for intercommunity war, are played barefoot with all the vigor of Donnybrook Fair. The Islanders' skill in baseball, rugby, or cricket is extremely high.

This daughter of a Samoan chief would have worn no more than this in prewhite times. Now, except in negligee at home, she would also wear something topside. Her *lavalava* (wrap-a-round skirt) is of western-woven cloth secured from a trader. The girl below, caught in somewhat the same pose, is a modern Guamanian, but she shows in both her clothes and face the true Philippine influence that has been strong in Guam for two centuries. The original Chamorro of Guam was practically exterminated by the weapons and diseases of the early Spaniard.

The Bishop Museum

On Majuro (Marshalls) the old dances are occasionally dusted off, though perhaps not in highly authentic forms. This is a modern performance of a club-dance by visitors from another atoll. (Below) U.S. Navy oil drums clutter a Majuro beach near a spectacularly beautiful outrigger sailing-canoe of native build.

Theodore Boyd

These present-day shots show Tahitian girls all dressed up for a big occasion. Trading-schooners and private yachts moored at the quay in Papeete, Tahiti.

Theodore Boyd

Marshall Islands girls in European-inspired frocks do an old-time dance at a festival in the schoolhouse of Laura Island, Majuro atoll. Straiter-laced native church-members refused to attend this get-together.

Guamanian girls being trained as telephone operators for the island's post-war development as a permanent naval and air base. Their brothers often work for the U.S. Navy as skilled mechanics or laborers. Some enlist.

Development of "native medical practitioners" is one of the most useful and successful of white man's innovations in the Islands. Here two young Fijians, specially picked for intelligence and adaptability, study in their dormitory in Suva, Fiji, seat of the medical school that serves all the Islands under British control. The cross-stitched pillow slip is supplied by mother or sister as souvenir of home. Cross-stitching was part of mission efforts to keep native women piously busy.

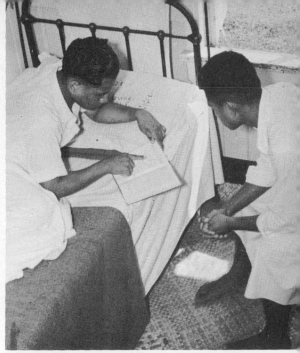

The Marianas, scene of this picture, were controlled by Japan under a League of Nations mandate between World Wars I and II. The place looks like a Hooverville because of war damage, not because the Japanese were negligent administrators. In some places and in some ways their record was pretty fair. Many of the children shown here are Korean or Okinawan, whose parents were brought in by Japan for cheap labor.

New gods for old.

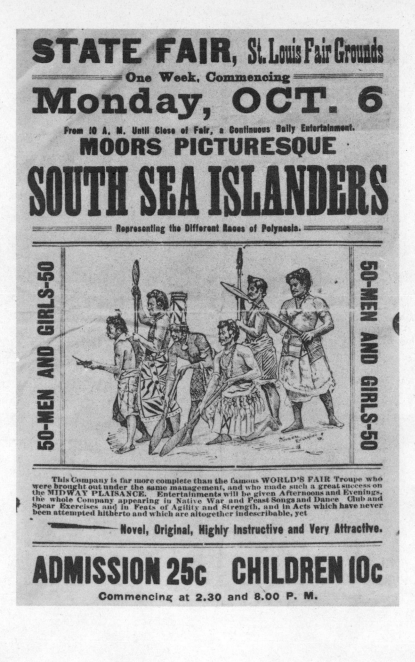

The South Seas legend is most easily illustrated by movies. It consists of sex, bare skin, idyllic settings, shoals of girls, few men except the male lead, and is strung on a plot as foolish as it is stereotyped. *Tabu* (1931) at lower left at least had a native cast and was shot largely on Bora Bora. The lighter tint of the dancer's breasts shows that this stripped-down costume was not

habitual. *The Idol Dancer* (1920) at upper left shows Richard Barthelmess as the victim of rum and Island sirens. The stills on the right are familiar from the recent *The Hurricane*. Casts and quality of photography change— Hollywood's South Seas do not.

This Goodenough Island Melanesian girl wears that crucial ingredient of the South Seas legend—the grass skirt. It was certainly made on the island, but the material could have been Manila hawser acquired from the U.S. Navy. The common Hawaiian grass skirt is made of rattan imported from the East Indies.

Brother's Keeper

The course of the flag, if not always of empire, has taken its way very far westward indeed. Whether either white or native wishes it, Uncle Sam is in the Islands to stay. This shot of a Marshall Islands school shows one of the better things that whites brought.

The cream of South Seas aristocratic leadership poses at the centenary of the Kingdom of Tonga: Ratu Apakuki Nanovo, Fiji; Malieatoa, Samoa; Mrs. Malietoa, Samoa; Ratu Sir Lala Sukuna, Fiji; Mrs. Tamasese, Samoa; Queen Salote, Tonga; Captain Vilai, Tonga; Lady Maraia Sukuna, Fiji; Tamasese, Samoa; Ratu Isireli Tawake, Fiji; Ratu George Tuisawau, Fiji. Ratu Sukuna, Oxford graduate, fought in the Foreign Legion in World War I and heads the department of native affairs in Fiji. Tamasese is leader of present Samoan efforts toward autonomy. Queen Salote (Charlotte) of Tonga is universally acknowledged as the great lady of the Islands. (On the left) Today's top Fijians —Ratu Sukuna and Ratu Edward Cakobau—consult as Fijian troops embark to fight alongside the Americans on Bougainville. Ratu Edward is descended from "King" Cakobau who ceded Fiji to Britain. Fijian troops made terrific records in both combat and stevedoring.

Fruits of a white idea previously illustrated—a Fijian Native Medical Practitioner on the job. Though not fully qualified doctors, these men are well trained in elementary diagnosis, minor surgery, and public health. Their work is usually excellent.

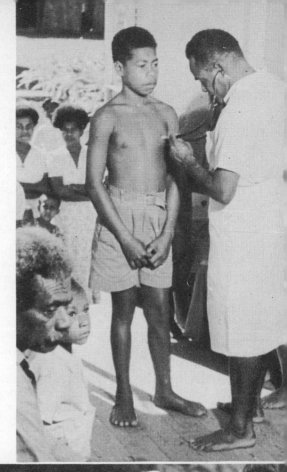

The forced mixture of Island populations illustrated in Noumea, New Caledonia. The dark stevedore at far left is an importee from the Loyalty Islands. All the other ostensible natives were imported from Asia as contract labor. They would like awfully to go home but can't.

Never forget the wide variety of human beings usually lumped as "South Sea Islanders." Above, a cheerful Melanesian family group in the Solomons. Below, with their teacher, seven girl graduates of Agana High School on Guam who plan to take teacher-training.

before and since. But none of his predecessors in desertion had had literary talent. Melville was a romantic, an egocentric, a rhetorician, probably a psychoneurotic. The consequences of exposing such a temperament to Marquesan scenery and ways of doing set the pattern for all his successors in creative inter-pretation of the South Seas. Diderot was the John the Baptist of Southseasism; Melville was its Apostle Paul.

He was more fortunate than Byron. Plenty of people have admired *Typee, Omoo* and *Mardi*. Critics treat them as seri-ous literary monuments, scholars devote whole books to exe-gesis of the data presented. The important thing about them for our purpose is that, in *Typee,* Melville created Fayaway, durable prototype of the South Seas enchantress, a young person with numerous offspring: Pierre Loti's Rarahu, Robert Keable's Numerous Treasure, and the thronging heroines of Nordhoff and Hall. Fayaway's effect on the aesthetic world is well illustrated by a water color that John La Farge did from imagination of the incident when, standing in a canoe, she takes off her *pareu* and lets it belly out for sail with herself as naked, living mast. He painted her with the attenuated figure of an Ingres model and a face of somewhat pre-Raphael-ite cast. The blue cloth swirling ahead of her is the identical piece of flowing studio drapery that appears in every third academic painting of the nineteenth century. She looks not at all like a Marquesan, but is a synthesis of beauties as under-stood in the salons of 1880. She has about as much relation to a live Polynesian as a Minoan design derived from marine life has to the actual gluey, squirming, squshy animal that acted as unwitting inspiration.

Yet La Farge did his author no violence. Melville's recorded Fayaway is a whimsical and cryptically voluptuous abstraction, no matter how tangible she may have proved during his stay among the Taipi. The book is good reading but dismally un-convincing, the more so for Melville's trick, conspicuous in everything but *Moby Dick,* of sounding implausible and pumped up. It should have been Richard Henry Dana, the other seagoing Yankee of literary parts at the time, who skipped ship and clambered down into that cannibal valley. There would have been much less condescending cuteness about the savages and much more pithy life in the observations.

Even Fayaway only cracked the dam. It was a generation before Stoddard took his talent for lush verse to Hawaii and southwards, and Loti gathered the background for the Gallic stereotype of the doomed Tahitian mistress, half child, quarter prostitute, and all charm. If you like Loti, *Le Mariage de Loti* is first-class Loti. If not, you will like it still less for having gone up to "Loti's Pool" above Papeete to see the author's monument—a bust of a male hairdresser in a Shubert road company costume, simpering archly at a flower held delicately in the left hand. Stoddard, outgoing friend of Stevenson, has not too much claim to quality, though he is still worth reading for his unintentional parody of Melville. When closer than usual to the master's skirts, he has moments; but principally it was Melville's appalling roguishness that stuck. Even the best moments are inadequate distraction from Charley Stoddard cutting the funny dog in purplish prose.[8]

By his time mailboats were running and the mass movement could begin. Before World War II choked it off, the roster of pilgrims had included Ella Wheeler Wilcox, V. Blasco Ibañez, Phillips Lord and Henry Adams. The last was invaluable. Adams' investigative editing of the recollections of the Tahitian Teva is probably the most intelligent anatomy of a pre-white Polynesian society.

Other intelligent men appeared earlier. Charles Darwin and T. H. Huxley left sane and well-written records of their experiences as scientists attached to Royal Navy surveys in the Pacific. But numbers do not imply quality in South Sea pilgrims of the pen. Most books on the area contain a sentence like this: "The Islands have long been the haunt and inspira-

[8]I was startled recently to be told on excellent authority that Stoddard's *The Island of Tranquil Delights*, one of his South Sea effusions, was a symptomatic favorite among intellectual homosexuals in New York a generation ago. It had never occurred to my innocence, but there is a great deal of emphasis on lovably pretty Polynesian boys in Stoddard. I do not mean to imply anything about the man's personal life.

tion of writers, poets and artists, like Gauguin, R. L. S., Rupert Brooke and Pierre Loti." One might add Melville, Jack London, Maugham . . . but that exhausts names of reasonable calibre. Stevenson invited Kipling and Henry James to visit Samoa, but neither ever arrived. It is a pity about Kipling. The world would have been richer for some better-than-average South Sea stories. James' nearest approach was to translate Daudet's *Port-Tarascon*, which sends Tartarin to spiritual destruction in the Marquis de Rays' swindle colony. Alexandre Dumas once ghosted a French whaler-surgeon's memoirs of early days among the Maori. Otherwise literary bibliography of the South Seas fills up with names meaningless to the general reader of today: Louis Becke, Thomas Alexander Brown (author, as Rolf Boldrewood, of *Robbery Under Arms*, Australia's national adventure yarn), Beatrice Grimshaw. And the general quality of the writer who goes bleating to the South Seas in search of "color" is well indicated in this self-description by one of them:

". . . painter, poet, vagabond, lusty lover of the physical, and withal a tireless aviator among the high, luminous clouds of idealism."—Blanding, *Hula Moons*.

Novelists native to the South Seas are rare. There is part-Maori Ngaio Marsh, one of whose better-quality detective stories depicts an impressive Maori physician; and Armine von Tempski, whose *Hula* gives the reader the vertiginous impression that Daphne du Maurier is rewriting *Rebecca of Sunnybrook Farm* under the guidance of Victor Hugo against an Hawaiian background. For some reason most novels about Hawaii came from women. Ruth Eleanor McKee's *The Lord's Anointed* about the early missionary period is the best so far. But the best women's work concerned with this area is fantasy: Sylvia Townsend Warner's *Mr. Fortune's Maggot* will be kindly remembered, and Rose Macaulay's *Orphan Island* is certainly one of the most entertaining places left in the twentieth century.

The occasional prewar poet who managed to get from

Carmel or Provincetown or Bloomsbury to Tahiti was usually even more obscure on returning than when he sailed; Rupert Brooke is a notable exception. The field of painting is even skimpier. Gauguin stands alone as an artist secure of major reputation who used the South Seas as material.

But none of this means that, low as the average calibre of South Seas-bound creators was, much good reading has not been produced against that backdrop. The world would be poorer without *The Moon and Sixpence*, and some of Maugham's South Sea short stories appear in anthologies with flattering frequency. As a rule Jack London's South Sea shorts are excellent London, particularly *The House of Mapuhi* and *The Whale's Tooth*. The man grew morbidly obsessed with the presence of leprosy in Hawaii, but then at the time that was true of the whole *haole* population of the Islands; and if the overloading of these tales with inevitable-white-man business annoys you, as well it may, you have only to conclude that reading Jack London is not for you.

Lloyd Osbourne, who was far better acquainted with the Islands than most writers and studied his trade under Stevenson's stepfatherly eye, actually succeeded in humor laid in the South Seas. His yarns of Island impostors, particularly *Old Dibbs*, may not be important, but they are good fun and a great relief from the general tradition that this background is sacred to the sentimentally solemn seven days a week. But the paying vein was not tapped until, in 1910, H. de Vere Stacpoole published *The Blue Lagoon*. This established for all time the idiom and atmosphere of the popular South Seas romance. Read it now with the author's name excised and you would swear it came from Nordhoff and Hall. For all I know neither of those capable collaborators ever saw the book, but the identification is still unmistakable by indirect channels; three out of four detective-story writers lean unabashedly on precedents set by Sherlock Holmes, and would so lean even if they had never read about him.

Only one writer ever importantly challenged the assumption made above that this sort of material is too rich for the blood of the creative process. You can forgive Charley Stoddard much when you remember that it was principally he who inspired Stevenson with the urge to go voyaging on the schooners that slipped out of the Golden Gate westward bound for the islands of the blest.

Unduly praised in his own time, Stevenson has yet to emerge from a cloud of subsequent revulsion. When he does emerge, the newly inquisitive reader exploring other aspects of the author of *Treasure Island, A Child's Garden of Verses* and *Dr. Jekyll* has pleasant surprises in prospect, in the South Seas vein and elsewhere. *The Beach of Falesá* is not only a fine composition of genuine Island values, it is one of the best novelettes in English; for all its artificial manner, *The Isle of Voices* is an ingeniously instructive blend of prewhite superstition with western economics. And *The Ebb-Tide*, though technically no success, anticipates many of the things that were to be Conrad's stock in trade. Huish the cockney, with his rat's courage and slimy emotions, would have ornamented *Victory*; Herrick, the high-minded beachcomber, could have been Lord Jim's long-lost uncle. (This neglects the issue of how much Lloyd Osbourne had to do with the merits of his collaborations with his stepfather—it may have been a good deal.) Conrad is again anticipated in the culminating narrative of *The Wrecker*. Few tales of fateful violence ever improved on the sickening moment when the impromptu murderers empty a revolver into the forecastle to silence the whimpering of the wounded and then, grimly and methodically, must shoot other survivors out of the rigging with shaking hands aiming fouled weapons.

The hurricane chapter in *A Footnote to History* is so brilliant a piece of reconstruction that every writer treating Samoa since has borrowed from it, sometimes with acknowledgment. And the literary world suffered a loss when Stevenson decided to drop the series of newspaper articles that make up the fragmentary *In the South Seas*. The Marquesan landfall "touching a virginity of sense"; the dark, liquid hush of an atoll by night, heightened by the near-by surf; Tembinok of Abemama pacing toward you in the glare of sun on sand, wearing a woman's dress and dark glasses, and carrying a Winchester to keep his subjects wholesomely in hand; no receptive reader can forget those things. The undue proportion of mottoes and quotations from Stevenson in this book is unconscious corroboration of the quality of his recording of the South Seas. Often and often he has set forth a detail or a pithy generality in terms that defy paraphrase. In fact this would be the best single book to give anybody who had never heard of the South Seas. Its contentions are sometimes mistaken, its attitude toward Island cultures somewhat romanticized; but it achieves an immediacy of effect and truth of spirit that are often glumly lacking in the work of more professional researchers.

The typical South Seas book, of course, shows neither careful statement of fact nor quality of treatment. In all soberness, more thousands of words of swill have been written per square mile of dry land about the Islands than about any other geographical entity, not even excepting the United States of America or the Union of Socialist Soviet Republics. Here the late Frederick O'Brien leaps to mind, which is unjust. Inaccurate, windy, and affected as his three best-sellers were, many competitors have excelled him in all those departments. It would be appallingly easy to name a dozen far worse. In preparation for a job like this one reads them all, so far as the weary flesh and uneasy stomach permit.

The only gauge of relative popularity lies in incidence of copies in secondhand bookstores, which I have much frequented in the last several years looking for specific items as well as for previously unheard of works with "Paradise" in their titles, for it is two to one such a title concerns the South Seas. On the evidence of the fifty-cent trays and the dollar shelves, the most popular South Seas items in the last three generations have been O'Brien aforesaid, Nordhoff & Hall and, for no conceivable reason, a book called A Voyage in the "Sunbeam": Our Home on the Ocean for Eleven Months published in 1884 by the wife of an English shipping expert named Brassey who took his family along on a yachting-cruise that included much of the Pacific. It is not the choice one would

OLD LEGENDS NEVER DIE

have preferred. The dry sense of the old voyages, the doughty good humor of the formidable ladies like Isabella Bird and Miss Gordon-Cumming who explored the Islands in the mid-century and wrote of them so tidily well, the expert impressionism of Stevenson, get a relative snubbing. I cannot account at all for the merely mild popularity of Miss Gordon-Cumming's works in their time. The title of one, *A Lady's Cruise in a French Man-of-War* should have guaranteed reader-interest, at least until it became clear that there was a Catholic missionary bishop along for chaperone.

In granting awards for silliness in this field, the referee must deal with some eminent names. Keyserling contemplated the Hawaiians whom he encountered on Waikiki Beach in the 'twenties and saw counterparts of the ancient Greeks of Homeric epic. Rupert Brooke visited the Samoans shortly after the snarling Lauati rebellion and saw "the loveliest people in the world, moving and dancing like gods and goddesses, very quietly and mysteriously, and utterly content."[9] This is more than poetic insight, it is hallucination. But for special flavor, people who like literary grotesques—who are fond of, say, *The Sweet Singer of Michigan*—should know a work written within this generation by a romantic who took the wife and kiddies to Tahiti to lead a wild life of nature, there encountered a smoldering poet with a frigid wife who insisted on wearing stockings—and presumably a girdle to hold them up—and wrote all about it, often to the following magnificent effect:

> The immediate future was portentous with heart-beating mystery made sweet with daring hope. Time stood still . . . Where would we spend the remaining hours of the night? Where would we sleep? [The poet] and his goddess were standing with their arms round each other. As I gazed into the poet's deep eyes I knew that the question, if not the *modus operandi*, was for him at least solved. We found ourselves strolling up a dim strip of road bordered by the ghostly palms, singing softly to guitars, arms round supple waists, cheek

[9]Edward Marsh, *Rupert Brooke*, 114–15.

against cheek—always the intoxicating fragrance from the
tiare wreaths. . . . [The writer's wife] possessed that marvelous faculty of converting herself, under the spell of the occasion, into a thousand different types at will. As she had in
former days been the coy school-girl, the seductive debutante,
the charming hostess, the haloed young mother, the efficient
housewife, when romance took a new breath—so was she a
South Sea sweetheart to me now . . . [The poet] and Terai
walked ahead . . . Then I, with the girl who was all things to
me clasped close . . . Surely this was love in the Golden Age,
complete, fearing nothing, exacting nothing, giving all. Could
we whose skin was white—bleached in the prison of a preposterous civilization—forget, even if but for a moment, that
we had made the Fall? Was this hovering close to sin?

Yes, very probably.

A minor but irritating literary fraud frequently practiced by
South Sea writers is their insistence on exotic nomenclature.
Many Island tongues, particularly Polynesian, are liquid and
sonorous enough to have roused admiration from experts like
Brooke and Stevenson, and Polynesian names sound marvelously picturesque in the original. The guileless reader, admiring the elegant name of Pomare attached to the postwhite
ruling dynasty of Tahiti, might feel different about it if he
knew that, if it means anything, Pomare signifies "cough in
the dark." For Polynesia had no such notions as ours about
suitable meaning-content in names. The Polynesian was named
after casual events at birth, however grotesque, after incidents
in his personal history; here are some samples out of the
genealogies in Teuira Henry's redaction of the Rev. Mr. Ors-
mond's account of ancient Tahiti. First the mellifluous Tahitian, then the literal meaning:

Pehupehu	debris
Faiau-po'a	fill cavity
Va'a-pau	swamped canoe
Opaipai	drifting sidewise
Te-ari'i-manava-'ure	sovereign with red intestines
'Opu-hara	violated stomach
Hotutu	flatulence

The romantic's shyness of translation is familiar elsewhere; otherwise so many parents would not name daughters Marie instead of Mary or Jeanne instead of Jane. To the Baedeker-toting tourist Trouville would not sound so enticing if it were called Holetown. The Polynesianophile occasionally translates, usually for a condescendingly jolly effect, to point up the childish hilarity of the natives, as when O'Brien wrote down his servant as Exploding Eggs, the meaning of his native name. But he was not consistent about it and, for all the reader knows, the gurgling, many-vowelled name of a South Sea heroine may mean rotten-fish-in-the-sunshine.

In the whole field of literary Southseasism, which is tautology, there is more than meets the eye. Americans are seldom aware, for instance, that in subscribing to this cult, they may be borrowing anomalous attitudes from their cousins who developed them in less favorable climates. Part of western man's obsession with this area may well spring from the mere contrast between the weather of Tahiti and of northern Europe. Significantly, neither Spaniard nor Italian has contributed much to the literature of the Islands, though many of both nations were among early arrivals. Rather, Englishmen, Frenchmen, and, to some extent Germans, identified the Islands with Paradise. For there is plenty of sunshine in Spain and Italy, whereas farther north the inhabitants go whole seasons with a minimum of sunshine, yet without the drama of heavy snows. So for centuries the meteorological miracle of a land where one is not always slightly shivering without a fire, even in summer, where something more than forest will grow spontaneously, where fruits develop without coddling, has always appealed inordinately to the European mind. There is something pathetic about this value which our transatlantic cousins set on reaching a sunny place to cook the lifelong chill out of their bones, about the thrill they get out of seeing a large item of vegetation and realizing that it is no seasonally deciduous oak or elm, skeleton half the year, but a palm! a vegetable that by definition will not put up with climates unfit for sustaining human life.

Americans might never have developed such ideas spontaneously, without reading about palm-and-pine in European-
produced books. Anybody who has ever fried in a New York
or Boston or St. Louis summer has little excuse for gratefully
wide-eyed wonder about mere sun and warmth. Suppose the
South Seas had waited to be discovered by a man from coastal
Georgia, reared on canned pineapple and plentiful oranges,
among other delicacies common in American life. He might
well not have come back spouting poetry, since sun is no
novelty to him and teeming vegetation is largely a pest where
he comes from, with palms represented by that most depressing
of ecological phenomena, palmetto-scrub.

Nevertheless the Island climate is often delightful and, while
concessions are in order, it should be admitted that the South
Seas are as good a locus for Paradise as the world offers. Nor, it
appears, were literary journeymen wrong, though perhaps ill-
advised, in taking that background as grist for their mills, as
an invitation to exotic, violent, sentimental, escapist incident.
The truth is that the best of all South Sea stories is a very
famous, lurid, and sentimental melodrama. It starts with institutionalized brutality, dips into psychopathology, goes
heavily into sex, fights a war, proceeds with exploration and
colonizing in a Crusoeish vein, declines into lethal violence,
and finishes on a strong, harmonious chord of simple piety. It
sounds as if author and publisher had cynically set out to throw
in all possible traditional elements for all tastes, and particularly insisted on action and more action in every line of the
narrative.

The author was God Almighty, the story that of the
"Bounty" and her crew. Apparently He realized that He had
created the perfect setting for fiction and, fearful lest it be too
much for mere men to handle, determined to write the perfect
South Sea yarn Himself. Men have picked at rewriting it ever
since, distorting it, leaving out crucial bits, making William
Bligh more of a villain and Fletcher Christian more of a hero
than the Lord's infallible taste had allowed, overplaying the
idyll and underplaying the vermin of Tahiti. But even in

redaction, mangled and foreshortened, it is a thundering fine tale at whatever point one picks it up. In the original, including the open-boat voyage and the wreck of the vengeful "Pandora," performed by unconscious actors with the trade-wind in their faces and actual bristling beards on their cheeks, it was such a bundle of related tales of action as would have served the Greeks for another Homeric cycle. Some write better and some write worse, but, when He puts His mind to it, the dear God who loveth us writes best of all.

VII

BROTHER'S KEEPER

> Cultures, nations, communities and tribes are
> stable and socially healthy according to the degree
> of integration they exhibit.
> —Pitt-Rivers, *The Clash of Cultures*, 216

Samoa IS BY NO MEANS THE ONLY PLACE WHERE World
War II left with the native a conviction, sometimes convenient, sometimes internationally embarrassing, that Uncle Sam
is a cross between Paul Bunyan and Santa Claus. For instance
the decision to put an air-and-naval base on Bora Bora, loveliest of the Societies, with the best anchorage in the group,
meant overnight construction of a large air-strip and a road
system such as the French would never have built in the next
five centuries. Bulldozers fascinate most people, the Bora
Boran by no means least, since he had never before seen such
a roaring, hulking devil of a machine. Huge planes sat down
on the fresh coral strip, jeeps scuttled along the new roads,
great ships anchored sleekly in the lagoon that Murnau used
as a paradisiacal background for *Tabu*.

Shiploads of clothes, food, Coca-Cola and cigarettes flooded
ashore, and every night there were movies, free movies, come
one, come all—a detail still salient in local memory. At once
invidious contrasts with French performance developed in
native talk and filtered over to Tahiti, seat of government.
Native habits of mind made it inevitable that Bora Borans
and Tahitians should express a lively desire to be cared for by

448

opulent, formidable, spendthrift Uncle Sam rather than by indigent, weak, penurious France. The Bora Borans highly embarrassed the U.S. Navy by asking the skipper to fix it up; the Tahitians embarrassed the U.S. consul even more by a demonstration for American suzerainty in front of his house.

In one form or another the same thing occurred in the Tokelaus, the New Hebrides, New Caledonia. The Wallis Islanders on their obscure islets south of the Ellices, staged an actual postwar revolt against the French with such warm pro-U.S. Navy motivation that the skeleton Navy force remaining there was withdrawn in frantic haste. Two years after the Japanese surrender, an abortive rising of the natives on Santa Aña in the Solomons seems to have been the eventual consequence of Communist propaganda spread by Australian troops during the war; but the misled natives had been told by their leaders that America, now a Communist country greatly in sympathy with them, would send warships to help, and that their appearance on the horizon would be the signal to rise. The scheme went off prematurely when the warships that did appear proved to be an Australian submarine and a British destroyer sent to look into rumors of local disaffection.

The beach of Tongatabu still tells you openmouthed of that apocalyptic day when the ocean off Nukualofa suddenly sprouted battleships, carriers, cruisers, transports, and planes and, in what seemed like a few hours, the whole island was stiff with men, supplies and machines. Every prewar white man's government was made to look puny and miserly, qualities unforgiveable in native terms.

On Babelthuap (Palaus) less than a year after the Japanese surrender, I sat in a palm-shaded schoolhouse behind a table ornamented with a Japanese vase, relic of the late defeated. The jetty at which we had landed had been built by Spaniards during their tenure. The pupils, all standing very straight in very clean clothes, sang us songs to German airs. But to open and close they sang, in nervous but comprehensible English:

"My country, 'tis of thee . . . Land of the Pilgrims' pride . . ."

Their solemn young teacher had not only been working like mad to revive his school after the dislocations of war, he had taught his pupils the most American song he could get wind of. It was cordially meant, even though the words were gibberish to the pupils and they had not the haziest idea who the Pilgrims were. Nobody acquainted with the situation in the American trusteeship area in Micronesia doubts that Uncle Sam is welcome thereabouts. A sociologist trying to explain in the Palaus that the States would probably want natives to develop toward self-government was met by the alarmed question:

"Does that mean the Americans will go away and leave us?"

But this attitude is also observant and hardheaded. The same investigator asked an articulate native what were the differences among Germans, Japanese and Americans. His witness pointed to the key island of the group:

"Germans built their town in the middle of that island. Japanese built theirs on that end. Now Americans are building theirs on the other end. That is the difference."

A year after the war it looked as if the States would insist on retaining control of bases all over the Pacific. American interests are conspicuous in the common strategic necessities of the English-speaking world, and the States can best afford to keep up installations south as well as north of the Line. But antipodean suspicion was great and strongly expressed, and Congress was toying with economy. So the flag was hauled down on all those places and many others, and Uncle Sam retired to north latitudes—American Samoa and Canton Island are the only exceptions. Australia, New Zealand or Britain may keep the top category of bases more or less in running order against eventualities. But where local strategic implications are too insignificant or local populations too small or too sluggish, the process of disintegration is already well under way. Vines bearing fruits like sick cucumbers creep out over the landing-strip. Weeds shoot up from the gritty coral surface. In a few months the distant effect is as if somebody had sprayed the white coral with pale-green paint. In a few years the very site of the strip will be unidentifiable. The peaked canvas roofs of the huts develop holes and the huts themselves slump, almost as you look at them. Close observation would enable an engineer to draw up a schedule of what element rots or rusts first, which corner collapses next. The torn olive-drab undershirt still lies in the corner where it was thrown, and when a heavy blow upsets the basketball backstops, there is nobody there to set them up again.

Now that American trusteeship over the former Japanese mandate Islands has been approved by the United Nations, it is time to reassess the reasons for Uncle Sam's being all over the northern half of the Pacific, particularly Micronesia, and what, now that he is permanently there, he should do about the natives. The pertinent data are already actually or im-plicitly in hand. This is like the point in an Ellery Queen detective story where the authors say Now, who did it? Most of the following applies, in one degree or another, to the essential problems of Britain, France, Australia and New Zealand in the South Seas.

Why the States are there and insist on staying is already clear: strategy. The Japanese made it dangerously plain that, in a world of long range war, the western security of the Amer-ican continent depends on Americans being in control of Micronesia, plus the Aleutians and Alaska. These considera-tions involve not only Russia as potential antagonist; in a few generations China may be well along in the centralization and industrialization of her immense resources. In long range plan-ning strategists are not tactful people. To sane persons trans-Pacific or trans-Arctic war with atomic weapons would be superlatively horrible. But if it should come to pass, the States will be better off if they monopolize potential take-off points in the North Pacific and off the coast of Asia.

The simplest way to make sure that nobody else uses a potential base is to use or guard it yourself. Yet strategy de-mands only a few of the hundreds of sizable islands in Micro-nesia. Backed by Hawaii, naval and air bases on Saipan and

Guam (Marianas), Peleliu (Palaus), Eniwetok, Kwajalein and Majuro (Marshalls), perhaps Ponape (Carolines), with listening posts on a dozen others, would safeguard the whole area. Tactical changes resulting from directed missiles may shorten that list. From the strictly military point of view, Uncle Sam need bother with no other Islands except for routine patrol to make sure that no potential enemy moves in.

Thus to turn such nonessential islands as Babelthuap, Rota, Kusaie and Jaluit loose to paddle their own canoes as they did before whites came, is a tempting idea. It would feel honest at long last. The Islanders never asked to be taken over; we moved in on them, not vice versa. Nobody warned their migrating ancestors hundreds of years ago that the scraps of land they were settling would experience the most destructive war in history. It should be possible for us to say to the people of non-strategic Islands:

"Sorry you've been shaken up so roughly. You offer nothing that we can't get more cheaply, securely or conveniently elsewhere. It will be expensive and troublesome to look after you; besides, our consciences forbid interfering with you any longer than necessary. Goodbye, good luck, and don't forget what we've tried to teach you about digging latrines and—look who's talking—loving your neighbor as yourself. You may occasionally see a plane overhead or a warship on the horizon but that will just be us making sure nobody troubles you again."

Thus put out of bounds, the Islanders could theoretically recreate the old self-sufficient ways. Gradually *kukui*-nuts or coconut oil in shell lamps would replace kerosene, the sewing machines rust into uselessness, clothing revert to the grass skirt, such old arts as weaving and deep-sea fishing revive. Church bell and Bible might well remain, but Christianity would gradually evolve into something only faintly recognizable; possibly a faint flavor of sin might still cling for centuries round premarital goings-on.

France could afford thus to turn loose all her Pacific islands but New Caledonia, Britain all but Fiji, Australia all but New Guinea, New Zealand all. But this is impossible for reasons of great variety—medical, technical, economic, ethical. A hundred and seventy years ago Captain Cook saw it plainly on Tahiti:

". . . it would have been far better for these poor people never to have known our superiority in the accommodations and arts that make life comfortable than, after once knowing it, to be again left and abandoned to their original incapacity of improvement. Indeed they cannot be restored to that happy mediocrity in which they lived before we discovered them, if the intercourse between us should be discontinued . . . it has become, in a manner, incumbent on the Europeans to visit them once in three or four years, in order to supply them with the conveniences which we have introduced among them, and have given them a predilection for . . . by the time that the iron tools, of which they are now possessed, are worn out, they will almost have lost the knowledge of their own. A stone hatchet is at present as rare a thing among them as an iron one was eight years ago; and a chisel of bone, or stone, is not to be seen."—*Three Voyages*, II, 211.

Those considerations apply most strikingly to places like Guam and Tutuila, where U.S. Navy pay rolls, booming population, and reliance on imported foods have tied local living most hazardously to the continued presence of Uncle Sam. They are all too real on most of the Micronesian islands. Readjustment to self-sufficiency would take a hundred years of abject poverty and shattering disintegration. Withdrawal of western technicians and supplies would let yaws, filariasis and gonorrhea run wild, as they did on islands where the by-passed Japanese garrisons fell into shortage-harassed confusion. Tempting as it is to say, when dealing with the occasional native leader who demands premature autonomy for his people: "Very well, you take over, we're leaving," the consequences would so distress men of good will that the notion becomes intolerable. Having intruded without justification, the white man is now ethically committed to the consequences of meddling.

So we are saddled with strategic and nonstrategic Islands alike. If new weapons so alter world strategy that the North

Pacific becomes pointless, some such international authority as the United Nations might take over. In any case western guardianship is inevitable, in our hands as long as we choose to keep it there.

The trusteeship that the United Nations granted us—by request—allows the trustee to close off any islands or parts of islands in which security demands secrecy, of which issue the trustee is sole judge. That could be used cynically. For decency, however, the States as trustee will have to observe—and permit inspection[1] of—the general principles of the trusteeship, which stipulates training the natives for self-government or independence, and protecting them. Neither "self-government" nor "protection" is defined; both need pondering.

A protector needs to know from what his ward needs protection. In the case of Islanders, from drink, yes; from drugs, yes; from internal violence, yes; from disease, yes; but what then? Do you protect his culture from stagnation or from Coca-Cola?

The reader has met this problem before. If he keeps his eye on the Pacific Islands he will never lose sight of it again. Congressional committees, ethnologists, hard-shell liberals and indignant romantics will still be disputing over it a hundred years from now. The extremes are Hawaii, Tahiti and Rennell Island, two previously described; but summary is useful here.

The dispossessed Hawaiian native is merging into a rapidly-hybridizing population descended largely from labor imported for an intensive agriculture tied abjectly to mainland economy. The former cultures of the component peoples—Polynesian, Asiatic, European—are rapidly giving way to the culture of democratic procedures, rapid transport, wages and movies. That is, Hawaii solved the native problem by extinguishing, though not absolutely exterminating, the native. The process was shattering, brutal, absent-minded, inexcusable; but is pretty well over now and the end product, however painfully manu-

---

[1] This right of inspection is one angle in which the United Nations' arrangements differ from those of the old League of Nations mandates. The trusteeship includes all of Micronesia except Guam and the Gilberts.

factured, is healthy and has a recognizable future. It is a more intelligible future than that of the Western Samoan, where hybridizing was artificially checked when it had produced only a dislocated class of peevish half-castes with just enough economic power to enable them to be a maximum of nuisance to both natives and the government.

Still, there are worse examples than Western Samoa. The same flood of western ways burst over Tahiti. Whether due to lack of intrinsic resources or to lack of French enterprise, Tahiti did not develop an economy high powered enough to raise standards of living and smother the native under masses of imported coolies. Though heavily hybridized, the native is still far more of a Tahitian than anything else, combining the worse features of his own with those of white cultures. Modern Tahiti is best defined as Tobacco Road with palms.

The native is plagued by syphilis, tuberculosis, and probably other diseases for which he has not been thoroughly checked. The remains of Polynesian communalized tradition keep him, in white terms, promiscuous and shiftless. He hates the several thousand Chinese relics of sugar and cotton schemes, who bleed him unmercifully and refuse effectively to mingle with him. He dully mistrusts his French guardians, whose attempts to align him with the west by giving him full French civil rights resulted only in making it legally impossible for special regulations to protect him. His missionaries regard him as congenitally incapable of self-control or any other virtue but a supine friendliness. His numbers are growing rapidly, but he has no future, and escapes from that dismal fact only through cheap red wine or through vague hopes that "independence"—or maybe the Americans—might improve matters. The first of the Isles of Paradise certainly got the messiest of it.

Such disintegration makes Rennell sound very good indeed. This is one of the half-dozen bits of land off Melanesia inhabited by strayed Polynesians who, because whites have bothered them relatively little, still retain many of their old ways. Trader and missionary had touched them only slightly when the British determined to throw a literal *cordon sanitaire* round them, keep away all except an absolute minimum of inspection and medical help, and so prevent the epidemics that swept these places every time a ship sent a boat ashore. Until some sentimentalist or wider realist alters this policy, there the Rennellese will stay peacefully vegetating, allowed only an absolute minimum of white man's goods. Nobody will think about them but the High Commissioner of the Western Pacific, the ethnologist pining to study them but sadly aware of the reasons for refusing him permission, and the militant missionary from the lunatic fringe who demands the privilege of landing to save souls even if it kills bodies. The difficulty is that the native, not impressed by epidemiology but well impressed by white man's ways, aware that there is a more complicated world outside, resents being put away in cotton wool.

This reaction to protection is understandable. The presence of Americans and American things in Western Samoa during the war is said eventually to have stimulated some natives to cling more firmly than ever to fa'aSamoa. But even the self-centered Samoan would be justified in bitter protest—though probably for the wrong reasons—if New Zealand evacuated the few hundred whites on his islands and installed such a *cordon sanitaire*.

In general the western world's moral obligation in the Islands is to effect a salutary compromise between insulation and flooding. The white man's crime in the Pacific and elsewhere was not that he brought new things, but that he brought them in indigestible masses. Assimilation of western ways must be positive but gradual, like immunizing a man to a poison by cunningly graduated and spaced dosage. Medicine, education, agricultural reform, economics that encourages self-sufficiency but leaves scope for gradually increasing a stable income from exports—all these must be co-ordinated under a central planner with the cunning and wisdom of a benevolent serpent.

Differences among Islands make over-all formulae absurd. The Palau man may need slowing down in his eagerness after our ideas, the Yap man, only a few hundred miles away, may have to be persuaded out of his present insistence that whatever he does and always did is right. From any reasonable point of view the assignment is impossible, even if the planner-administrator in charge has completely arbitrary powers and the good manners not to use them openly. But impossible or not, it has to be done. And it has to be done with the administrator aware, as an intelligent man must be, that his every success brings nearer the insoluble problem of overpopulation.

Nor is it likely that he will have the powers indicated to the degree advisable. The United Nations have plumped for "self-government." Colony as well as trusteeship Islands have already experimented in that direction for generations, in an unmistakable trend toward greater participation by natives in determining policy and procedure. The previously described examples of Samoa and Tonga are most pertinent. The issue of what kind of self-government immediately becomes acute.

Local traditions in these islands spell chieftain-personalism which, as we saw long ago, is undemocratic. The white guardian is inclined to install democracy in its full panoply of majority elections, secret ballot, guaranteed personal liberties, equality before the law, trial by jury, and so forth. The American sets value on such machinery because it is indissolubly connected with the growth of the democratic habit of mind. He naturally regards such things as probably good for anybody anywhere. Besides, it would look very queer for the States to insist on democratic procedures at home while permitting Islanders, for whose welfare they are responsible, the nonequalitarian, arbitrary features of the old local system. Having moved in on these bright and able brown people in our own selfish interests, we should be denying them rights on which we count ourselves—a policy that would be most difficult to justify on Capitol Hill.

Nevertheless government by chieftain-personalism works among those accustomed to it. A high ranking Navy officer governing a large chunk of Micronesia recently told me:

"The natives run their own show so well that I feel justified only in supervising health and interisland relations. I have every respect for their political know-how."

From some such feelings there has developed what is technically known as "indirect government"; the guardian power acts as top advisor and controller of policy, but leaves local administration as much as possible to natives working within their own institutions. The British have made the widest use of this idea, often with considerable success, as in Fiji and the Gilberts. But there are hazards. The chief backed by white power may become something that looks too much like a racketeer in white eyes; government may have to upset the traditional mechanism of chief selection if the man selected proves un-co-operative; interloping whites may use government to exploit the natives. But intelligent and impartial administration can juggle such matters effectively, if the interests of the natives remain the prime objective of everything done. John Collier has described the process well:

> ". . . a method and ideal of developing a native society from within, through cautious, specific, and preferably inconspicuous redirections of aim and engraftments of technology."— *Indians at Work*, Jan.–Feb., 1944, 2.

Such modified Rennellism, encouraging the native to work out his own adjustment while protecting him from too great masses of new things to digest or undue pressure from exploitation-minded whites, is intellectually quite defensible, even though it does not directly encourage democracy. For in this case it may not be ethically sound to do unto others as you would have others do unto you. No judicious angel ever determined, as God's referee, that the western equalitarian-liberal-democratic-bill-of-rights scheme of things is superior to all others everywhere. It may be so for all that, but the thing is not demonstrable, it can merely be felt; the Yap man feels the same way about his fantastically stratified society. It takes something approaching the fanaticism of Jesuit or Communist to justify forcing western traditions on Yap, however good the forcer's intentions. Besides, massive grafting entails grave risk. The shock to the local social system may wither the old order without leaving enough social vitality to develop the new. Forced democracy did well in Hawaii, but in Tahiti it resulted in a social and political degeneration pitiful to see.

The worst of the western world's assignment is that the men in charge must play God without being qualified for the role. Western parents have always had that difficulty, without solving it yet. *In loco parentis* in the Pacific our deputies must decide which western ways will assimilate without too much shock, and fend off all other factors, often in the teeth of native desire for them. The American's motives in Micronesia will be disinterested enough, for economically the Islands are liabilities.[2] But if Uncle Sam finds anybody capable of really resolving the implied difficulties and carrying out measures to correspond, he had better make him President over 140,000,000 people who need such genius quite as badly as a mere 80,000 appealing brown strangers thousands of miles away.

Modified Rennellism was the policy of the U.S. Navy in its prewar guardianship over Guam and American Samoa. "Why the hell should we teach them to like soda pop?" an admiral-governor once asked me; I can still think of no good reason. Particularly in Samoa, Navy desire for a quiet life and Navy officers' liking for the Samoans combined to develop a regime for which trained observers often had kind, if qualified, words. Outsiders with new projects for stores or plantations were sternly kept out; adequate cash income for natives came from odd jobs for the Navy, and from copra and souvenir handicrafts manufactured under Navy encouragement and marketed through the Navy as agent. Local government operated through chiefs and villages and an advisory council of perfunctorily elected chiefs. Being modified by an incurious spirit of leave-well-enough-alone, this benevolent dictatorship

[2]The United States Commercial Company, the R.F.C. subsidiary that has handled economic readjustment in the Islands for the U.S. Navy, recently reported immense deposits of bauxite, which the Japanese are known to have worked, in the Palaus. But even if the stuff proves economically practical under present methods of extraction, it is a much longer haul from Babelthuap to San Francisco than from Dutch Guiana to New Orleans; and the States are full of low-grade aluminum ores that may become technologically workable any day.

somewhat distorted, but did not destroy, prewhite traditions. It seems to have been quite possible for Navy four-stripers who took a personal fancy to the Samoans to be reasonably harmless governors of American Samoa without ever learning very much about what actually went on behind the façade of neat villages and kava-ceremonies.

Education was in English of a sort, and no more effective than most Island collaborations of government and mission schools. But the Navy also co-operated willingly when private benevolence offered to set up a special school to train boys of high rank in advanced subjects, while bolstering their knowledge of Samoan language and traditions. Navy medical service, using personnel and resources such as few other Island governments can afford, has done on Samoa what looks like the best job in the Pacific. There were obvious flaws: Navy personnel on the miniature base begot too many half-white babies, officers assigned to government had no special training, the normal tour of duty was only eighteen months—which meant that by the time a man had the hang of handling Samoans, he was relieved by a raw novice.[3] But this was certainly the best government that these eastern islands had had since La Pérouse discovered them. It was very good indeed for a job lot of men trained, not to govern, but to fight ships and manipulate red tape.

And small thanks the Navy got for it. True, that was partly its own stubbornness. Under Navy pressure, Congress for forty years neglected to define the legal status of Samoa and the Samoans, which kept the Navy in charge on the temporary basis set up in 1900. But it also led to sporadic American protests against irregular dictatorship in Samoa. In the 'twenties the Navy's Samoans tried to cook up a Mau in association with their cousins across the strait. They produced no such impres-

[3]A retired Navy officer of my acquaintance who served in prewar Samoan government objects to this. He says that a longer tour in so unstimulating an environment—which Pago Pago certainly is—would have encouraged routine droopiness. Within the last year, however, the Navy has pretty well committed itself to much longer tours of duty.

sive results, for American Samoa is a political backwater in
Samoan terms, but caused enough unrest to whistle up a Congressional investigation. It reported a favorable opinion of the
net results of Navy dictatorship, but after listening to numerous Samoan witnesses, plumped for giving Samoans American
citizenship and civilian, not uniformed, government.

The Navy got action on that delayed right up to Pearl
Harbor. It is still a mystery why these admirals and four-
stripers insist on the extra trouble of governing when it would
be so practical to put barbed wire round the Navy reservation
at Pago and let civilians from Washington worry about the
copra crop and the impaired dignity of Chief Lavalava. During
the recent war, however, the Department of the Interior began
to yearn for the job of managing Pacific islands, and made the
Navy target of a great deal of bureaucratic Billingsgate. Harold
L. Ickes, carrying the ball for this cause after his resignation,
did his best in speeches and newspaper columns to make Samoa
and Guam under Navy care sound like New Orleans in Ben
Butler's time. After a lightning trip through the Islands under
the auspices of the Interior last year, Congressman Poulson of
California told the Los Angeles *Daily News* that Navy proceedings out there "would put Tito and Stalin to shame." Such
hysterical misrepresentation naturally stirred up an interdepartmental bitterness that badly slowed up and confused the
genuine issues in the problem of what to do with the American-controlled Islands as permanent wards of Uncle Sam.

The Navy's one comfort might be that, if they had thrown
American Samoa open to planters and traders and forced
democratic procedures down the Samoans' flattered but un-
ready throats, they would have been berated with equal bitterness by nativophiles. In this game you can't win. Now under
the influence of zealous outsiders, American Samoan chiefs are
asking for a legislature with real lawmaking powers.

Guam also became a thorn in the flesh, though more intelligibly. The highly hybridized Guamanian was a quick-smiling,
alert, already markedly westernized person very proud of his
picturesque old capital city of Agaña, which was about the size

and general quality of Nicaragua's Managua. He was abandoning Spanish and taking fluently to English, sticking to a devout if somewhat puritanical Catholicism, accepting American trained, instead of his former Spanish trained, priests, and was healthily unable to see why he should study the Constitution of the United States in school without getting any of its benefits. Local mercantile business was largely in local, if monopolistic, hands. Guamanian boys saw prestige in enlisting as messmen in the Navy, even if it hurt a little that they could not enlist as regular sailors. Guamanian craftsmen and laborers took Navy jobs and did well at them, even though it was annoying to be paid less than white civilians for the same work. And—most significant sign of westernization—Guamanians were thrifty and foresighted, saving respectable sums in the Navy-run Bank of Guam.

When Japan struck, Guam was brilliant. Collaboration with the conquerors was close to *nil*. Guamanians took to the bush and so ably harassed the Japs that, by the time American forces reappeared in 1944, the south end of the island was about as much in Guamanian as Japanese control. The first seen of the inhabitants was a dugout canoe paddling madly out to meet the invading fleet far at sea, its crew beseeching the Navy not to shell southern Guam because there were so few Japs left in places worth shelling. Farther up the island however, Agaña, metropolitan pride of their hearts, and Agat, second in size, were blown into such powdery rubble by the American attack that a year later you had to look hard to find where they had been. Without grumbling the Guamanians moved into temporary villages built native-style, trusted Uncle Sam to put their island back together when he could get around to it, and went hard to work for the American forces as laborers and craftsmen. Their index of loyalty to the flag under which they had lived for little more than forty years was, in other words, as high as that of any Americans.

Now, according to his leaders, the Guamanian wants American citizenship and a large hand in governing himself. He does not make the Ickes sort of mistake by slandering the Navy who benevolently despotized him so long. By and large, a level-headed and intelligent Guamanian lady leader told me, there were more good governors than bad ones. The Guamanian appreciated the Navy's letting down the bars on enlistments during the war and its promised efforts to make the Guam Congress, the elected advisory council, count in local affairs. The first postwar election for the Congress saw hot contests, women voting for the first time, and a general impression among observers that Guam had a good start on learning democratic processes. Significantly the Guamanian has long resented the terms "American" and "Chamorro," insisting on "Statesider" and "Guamanian." He often can feel like an American, Heaven knows he has shown he can sometimes act like an American—and there is no good reason why he should not be made one formally, as legislation now current in Congress contemplates. It feels right to anybody who, as I have done, has sat on the porch of a Guamanian's house on Sunday afternoon drinking lemonade with the old folks while inside in the parlor the daughter of the family is playing and singing Hit Parade tunes on the piano with two callow gobs from Ottumwa, Iowa. These identifications are merely relative, of course; Guam is not Iowa and never will be; but it stands a very good chance indeed of acting sufficiently like Iowa in politics and social organization.

The example of Guam is dangerous, however. American Congressmen and their constituents, editorial writers who never saw the place, thinking of Pacific islands in the lump, may want to fit Guam, Samoa, and some lost Micronesian atoll like Kapingamarangi on the same last. Obviously it cannot be done, and to try will do a great deal of unnecessary damage. The other danger is that Islanders other than Guamanians, observing the new status probably to be accorded Guam and picking up catchwords from well-meaning Americans, will demand privileges and rights for which they are not yet prepared. Both Western and American Samoans are already doing something like that.

Nevertheless Guam, as a rapidly westernizing enclave of

democratic procedures and values, will probably play a crucial role in the American-controlled parts of the Pacific. It is to be the developing center of education for natives picked from all over the trusteeship and Samoa. The brightest youngsters are to go there for training in teaching, government, medicine, nursing, agriculture, mechanics, then back into the islands again to carry out what they have learned under occasional inspection. This will happen whether Navy, Interior or—as Congressional Delegate Farrington sensibly suggests—a third new agency directly under the President, is in charge. The westernizing culture of Guam may cling to the student just enough to affect the people of his own island to an assimilable and stimulating, but not shattering, degree. Though he is certain to take back with him destructive as well as constructive feelings and ideas, the net differential might well be good and digestible. Provided, of course—and these pessimistic qualifications must be made—his instructors are imaginative and intelligent gentlemen and the top level planning is of superlative quality.

Americans have some admirable, some most inconvenient qualities for Island government. In contact with natives for a reasonable time, our countrymen usually like them and try to do right by them. But flexibility of mind toward unexpected native quirks is not our strong point. Even a well-briefed American put in charge of a Micronesian island with orders to modify the old system as little as is consistent with health—to protect it, in fact, as the likeliest long range bridge to something else—will have to fight his equalitarian instincts day and night. Well-meaningness is no insurance against getting off on the wrong foot through inevitable ignorance of Island ways. One naval government officer has a dismaying list of instances: Being annoyed when the native doesn't laugh at one's joke, whereas it is impolite thereabouts to laugh in presence of a superior; impatience with the family of a murderer who, following local ideas of bloodguilt, demand to be executed too; resentment of lack of thanks for presents, and so forth.

I have seen an incoming Naval governor instruct native chiefs who were to make him welcoming speeches to cut their remarks down to three minutes apiece, as he himself intended to do. He was a nice fellow and probably able, but he did not know that in this particular island to stipulate short speeches was about as rude as to tell an old style Quaker meeting to stop all this nonsense of just sitting there and not saying anything. And race prejudice is understandably hard for many Americans to eliminate from their emotional habits, no matter how emancipated they may consider themselves. Still, that is no special reproach in the Pacific, for few Polynesians are tolerant of non-Polynesians. The Samoan, for instance, calls the Fijian, his superior in numerous details, by a Samoan word meaning "black thing"; the Palau man distrusts the Guamanian as a commercial-minded city slicker, and many a Maori is irritated if Cook Islanders are referred to as his close relatives.

For a while, too, Americans in charge of Micronesian islands will be handicapped by the belief that they cannot help doing better than their Japanese or German predecessors. Actually in certain respects they will do well to match them. Both spent money and energy wisely in education and health. Though both arbitrarily imposed alien law and ran the islands primarily in German or Japanese economic interests, both had the realistic intelligence to confine interference to specific purposes, using forced labor to build roads and ports but paying for it, developing outlets for Island products that, for special economic reasons, the States can never match. Americans taking over in the wake of Japan on former mandate islands had the impression that on the whole the natives had not been ill treated until, toward the close of the fighting, brutality and hysterical violence broke out among the starved and rock-happy Japanese. The most lurid instances of massacre and savagery toward natives occurred in islands that the Japanese took over from enemy powers, such as the Gilberts and Ocean Island (Nauru).

The Japanese in particular were set on making the Pacific count as far as they could reach. Their reach was long, their hands prehensile. By 1940 they were working New Caledonian iron ore, as the French had never done. They so monopolized retail trade in Tonga that local whites talk nostalgically of long-vanished bargains in Japanese stores; they fished and charted every reef in the Western Pacific, turned the timber, phosphates and bauxite of the Palaus to account, and made a Pearl Harbor of the group's central islands. They ran efficient sugar and sweet potato plantations on Tinian and Saipan (Marianas). From a less nationalistic point of view, much of such activity was destructive. But at least the Japanese were taking the islands seriously, with impressive procedures and equipment which the native observed with his dark, gentle, and sometimes thoughtful, eyes. It would be very healthy for American officials in the postwar Pacific occasionally to hear natives mention with a sigh the good old days when the Japanese were in charge.

Though the native usually reverted to his prewar ways more quickly and with less perceptible damage than anybody expected, to discuss his current situation means constant references to the recent war in his back yard. In cases where he did some fighting, the consequences are unmistakable. The Fijian or Maori officer who led his men as efficiently as his white brother-officers is in very little danger of accepting misguided assurances from white men that he is a fine fellow but needs leading strings as badly as ever. The *anciens combattants* from Free France's Pacific Battalion, which did very well in North Africa, are now back in Tahiti and New Caledonia with vague but unquestionably dynamic impulses to improve their standing in the white man's world. Tahitian veterans recently distinguished themselves by so vigorous a mass protest against a government official's using badly needed foreign exchange to return to France via the States, that the whole trip was put off until it could be made on one of the catch-as-catch-can French ships that occasionally trickle in. Here and there, advancing on an unhappily irregular front, the Islander, whether veteran or not, keeps demonstrating that he can play white men's games, each instance re-enforcing his impulses toward autonomy and equal standing.

So far Americans have not distinguished themselves in their

new responsibilities. The rebuilding of Agaña, most obvious symbol of good intentions, had hardly begun a year after hostilities closed. Restoration of cash purchases outside Guam and Samoa was slowed up by uncertainty as to who was to be permanently in charge, by the Navy's lack of shipping and personnel—fruit of American insistence on rapid demobilization —and by such legalisms as high duties on Marshall Islands handicrafts because the Marshalls were still technically enemy territory. The excuses are not all unacceptable but the results have not looked good to the Islander, who knows nothing of interdepartmental feuds in Washington and the needs of Congressmen with constituents to please. We must accept having made a bad, sloppy start on a job that already had obstacles enough.

Even if we do the job brilliantly from now on, the end product will not be very inspiring. It will consist at best of a series of somewhat healthier, somewhat better run Tongas, sleepy, not worth first-class communications, hampering to potentially intelligent natives yet to be born, intensely parochial, haunted by the impending dangers of overpopulation. But it will feel better to the western intruder, because it will absolve him of his present liability to guilt feelings consequent on the you-made-us-what-we-are-today complex now so evident in native thinking.

At least the States are joining in international efforts to cooperate in making sense out of the Islands. But an astute Frenchman told me that the one thing he learned at the 1947 Canberra conference on South Pacific problems was that widely effective measures are impossible in the Islands so long as responsible nations maintain separate policies. Others consider that the vast differences in relative development between, say, the New Hebrides and Tonga, make fusions of policy as among co-operating nations difficult if not impossible. Both are right. Such phenomena as the Canberra conference are mere uneasy gestures in a direction that nobody yet feels willing properly to explore—toward an international guardianship, acting in its own behalf without deputization, over all islands and parts of islands not actually required for national military reservations.

The advantages are patent. Such an agency in full charge, with a central executive and secretariat, would know just as much about the Marquesas as about the Solomons and would no longer, as international conferences must, have to behave like the blind men discussing the elephant. It could vary prescriptions to suit ailments out of an accumulating fund of clinical data and experience, and rotate trained personnel to arrive at a maximum of stimulus with a minimum of waste motion. As a world colonial service, it could serve in some small measure as the sort of integrating factor that the Northwest Territory was for the nascent United States. And, for a minor beauty, it would finally dispel the native's chronic suspicion, persisted in in the teeth of economic facts, that white governments insist on staying because they are making a good thing out of the Islands.[4] So long as the United Nations deputizes trusteeships to individual powers, so long will the native, unable to grasp the larger issues involved, assume that he is somehow being exploited for others' benefit.

Whether the United Nations or the nations subscribing to the Canberra conference or any other international organization can attain sufficient prestige and solidity to assume any such responsibility is something nobody knows. If such a thing should occur, benefits for the Islands will be only a microscopic fraction of the good results for a troubled world in general. But it would be an extremely good thing for the puzzled brown people in question. And—since this sort of book is supposed to end on a constructive note—there is the goal, if you think the Islands' problems are at all soluble.

[4]This was soberly insisted on in the case of Western Samoa by Quentin Pope in despatches sent to the Chicago *Tribune* from Apia in 1946; it appeared that, through the Crown Estates, New Zealand was grinding the faces of the Samoans to balance the Dominion budget. Actually New Zealand grants-in-aid to Samoa over the years have probably amounted to much more than all government profits from the Estates; and revenues from the Estates are now to be formally earmarked for improvement of roads, schools and medical services in Samoa.

VIII

THE MEN FROM MARS

I have often wished that I could be introduced
for a moment within a heathen's soul and see how
he thinks and feels. I have no doubt that I should
be greatly surprised.

—The Rev. Sheldon Dibble
History of the Sandwich Islands, 230

If you don't like the human race, why don't you
go back where you came from?

—Robert Cruise McManus

IN A POSTWAR REVIEW OF A WORK ON JAPANESE CUL-
ture, Mr. Francis Hackett had testily suggested that it was high
time somebody anthropologized anthropologists. Such a project is not to be "entered into lightly or inadvisedly," for it can
be properly carried out only by a nonanthropologist who, by
definition, is not professionally qualified for the job. Here goes
nothing:

As governments and publics develop consciences about western man's treatment of nonwestern peoples—a trend which
reached decent proportions only recently—they have come to
rely ever more strongly on the ethnological branch of anthropology to train specialists to handle such peoples. The
British Colonial Office, the Australian administrations in
Melanesia, the U.S. Bureau of Indian Affairs, are now committed to briefings in that field for at least some of their officials. In commendable if tardy imitation, the U.S. Navy
inaugurated in 1945 short courses in ethnology and related
subjects for young officers destined for Island government.
Better-established Christian missions encourage such studies
among their recruits.

Such civilian, military or religious custodians of native interests do not turn into scientists in consequence. But at worst

470

they are stimulatingly exposed to more catholic and relatively more scientific points of view than they might develop on their own, and at best they get detailed information on the idiosyncrasies of the areas where they are to work. Brass'hats, parsons, and politicians who decide thus to seek help from science, may not know too intimately just what ethnology can and cannot impart. But they are justified in their confidence that the ethnologist knows more than the layman about the terms in which native problems must be dealt with.

Thus to enlist the expert should absolve western societies of further responsibility, as it would if, finding a sick man in the road, you rushed him to the nearest hospital for expert care. But the case is not so simple. As yet ethnology is largely a descriptive science, more like meteorology than biology, and nothing like as accurate as either. To set the ethnologist, or the layman with a dash of such background, to determining as well as suggesting and lubricating "native policy" would be about like setting the meteorologist to arranging the weather. For though many of these professional attitudes and findings are indispensable to the responsible layman, they can be exceedingly treacherous unless corrected, as Mr. Hackett suggested, by the same Martian objectivity that this science tries to apply to cultures. Much of the following comment on ethnology may seem—and will be—acid. But keep in mind throughout that, for all its adolescent antics, the gist of this science is the last, best hope of civilization.

I first encountered one of the fundamental attitudes of ethnology in an old book for children. Selections from Mrs. Barbauld's *Evenings at Home* were in many school readers in your grandfather's time; you may remember *Eyes and No Eyes*. My favorite, however, was *Travelers' Wonders*. Captain Compass is home from a long voyage. His children gather round his knee and beg him to tell them of the strange peoples he has seen in his wanderings. Archly he describes a curious race whom he once encountered:

". . . clad partly in the skins of beasts made soft and smooth
by a particular art, but chiefly in garments made from the out-

ward covering of a middle-sized quadruped, which they were
so cruel as to strip off his back while he was yet alive . . .
Some of them ate fish that had been hung up in the smoke
until they were quite dry and hard; and along with it . . .
they ate a sort of coarse black cake made of powdered seeds.
The richer had a whiter kind of cake, which they were fond
of daubing over with a greasy matter that was the product of
a large animal among them. This grease they used, too, in
almost all their dishes and, when fresh, it really was not un-
palatable . . . Another great article of food was the curd of
milk, pressed into a hard mass and salted. This had so rank
a smell that persons of weak stomachs often could not bear
to come near it . . . The people were tolerably gentle and
civilized, and possessed many of the arts of life . . . The most
singular material was a fine glossy stuff, used chiefly by the
richer classes which, as I was credibly informed, is manufactured out of the webs of caterpillars—a most wonderful
circumstance . . . The language of this nation seems very
harsh and unintelligible to a foreigner, yet they converse
among one another with great ease and quickness."

Presently little Betsy caught on, and the good captain and his
bright-eyed brood had a merry laugh indeed at the way he had
cajoled them into looking objectively at their own culture. It
was merely a much wordier way of arriving at Will Cuppy's
point: "The Giraffe, or Camelopard, is rather fantastic, but
who isn't?" Once you get the way of it the trick is easy, as preceding comment on the Islands has shown. You squirm at
Polynesians eating fish alive? But what about oysters? The Hawaiian and the Ellice Islander were equally shocked to see the
missionary eat hen's eggs, which they thought of as embryos
surrounded by all the sloppy and unsightly nutriments needed
for their obscene growth; from their point of view it was like
eating the foetus of a pig boiled in its own membranous sac.

This is the *you're another* aspect of ethnology. Its shock
value is high and salutary, the intellectual sport involved is enjoyable, and it can induce a gratifying sense of superiority to
one's own culture. It also has scientific uses, for objectivity is
supposed to be the essence of science. The student of technical

and social man is as imperatively pledged to objectivity as the biologist, and must analyze his own ways and things with the same cool inquisitiveness that is easier to apply to Eskimo ways. He must be able to maintain on occasion that economic insecurity among us may be as crippling as the prewhite Hawaiian's cringing before his chief; that the western demon housewife's obsession with soap and water makes as little sense as the Dobuan's hypersuspiciousness; and that burial of all monetary gold in the United States at Fort Knox is as absurd as the cumbersome stone money discs of Yap. All that is useful to the scientist, while it intrigues the undergraduate fascinated by Anthropology I.

But the logical consequence is embarrassingly clear. If Fort Knox and Yap are equally absurd, if human devices to safeguard and hypothecate arbitrary repositories of value are all essentially similar—which is easily maintained—it follows that neither can be called absurd unless the whole human race is. And if that is true, the ethnologist is also absurd for taking so much trouble to learn about the human race. Thus the grease that Captain Compass' strange people smeared on their seedcake is merely the gastronomical opposite number of putrescent human flesh in Fiji; and with the indifference of a learned hangman, ethnology is tempted to culminate, as Linton points out, on the nihilistic statement: "Some do and some don't."

Such nihilism is not intellectually cozy. Even so cold an anatomist of society as Sumner could not square it with his emotional drives. Human beings have a compulsive tendency to turn tendentious. Being human, ethnologists often degenerate into using you're-another à la Rousseau for a stick to beat their own culture with, as Tacitus used the primitive Germans as implicit occasion to scold the Romans. Being impatient with western individualism, say, they sound unbecomingly pleased with the ancient Inca for showing that a complicated economy can work without the spur of insecurity. Or disliking the moral latitudinarianism preached in some quarters round the turn of the century, they develop the a priori notion that customs in flux are a morbid symptom in a society. Or, preferring greater freedom between the sexes, they become acutely admiring about an alleged lack of erotic strains in prewhite Polynesia.

Such impulses are not becoming in detached scientists whose hypotheses should follow where data lead. They recall the partisan lawyer searching casebooks for whatever bolsters his argument. As if he held a brief for the "savage" preliterate, the ethnologist quivers a little too much in maintaining that, to one who thoroughly understands it, the culture of the Aleut Indian appears as rewarding and full as any other. Only the uninformed outsider sees lacks and paradoxes; actually all details fit into an intricate and beautiful pattern of satisfactions which becomes steadily clearer the more thoroughly one investigates it. This must be true, since the thing works. The syllogism is: *Major premise:* any society that works is valid; *minor premise:* this society works—if it did not, it would not have survived to be studied; *conclusion:* therefore the Aleut culture is—or was—valid on the same footing as that of any known western culture.

This elaborate statement that "whatever is, is"—a point made more amusingly in *The Vicar of Wakefield*—leads into some strange places. Said "an American member" of a Pacific educational conference some ten years ago:

"No culture is good or bad except in terms of the people who follow it and believe in it. Religion, morals, social and economic philosophies, are functions of a given culture. They have no validity in themselves, but only as they are part of the culture . . . There are no good or bad people, no good deeds or bad deeds, except in terms of the morals defined within this or that cultural system."—Quoted in Felix M. Keesing, *Education in Pacific Countries,* 39.

It is an irresistible temptation to challenge the speaker to come down from that high mountain whence he is observing all the kingdoms of this world, and apply that in detail to the morals of existing cultures in lynch-minded southern states; or to the emotional trend that culminated in Belsen prison-camp.

Fortunately this nihilism, which nobody can bring himself to apply universally, is not necessary. The transition to something more intelligible is well exemplified in Herskovits, who says first:

"There is no generic difference between primitive societies and literate ones but that the world over, specialized local developments have come into being as a result of the unique historical vagaries that mark the past of each of them . . ."

only to confess with lame honesty a few pages later:

"that there may be said to be little difference in the total of human contentment from one type of society to another, primitive or literate, is an assertion . . . not susceptible of scientific proof."—Herskovits, *The Economics of Primitive Peoples,* 4, 22.

Two things need saying here: No scientist has any business with a word like "vagaries"; and though every science rests on indemonstrable assumptions, this one is particularly dangerous, because the first quote suggests relative measurement of qualitative values—a flagrant and crippling paradox.

The ethnologist's refuge is rashly to admit qualitative values, using Captain Compass merely as blunt instrument for pounding up the material, and try to do something with the mash. For though John Dewey, a sack of coal and a cobra all boil down to protons and neutrons or whatever, it is patently lunatic to maintain that therefore differences among them lack significance. When Einstein jots down a formula on paper with pencil, he has done more than merely to alter the physical relations of certain quantities of cellulose and graphite. However timidly, ethnologists are accomplishing this shift.

It will get them into further trouble, of course. The new axiom—that adequately informed intelligence can assess qualitative values in human institutions—is just as shaky as the old one. But it will feel better and, if pertinent data from sister-sciences are well and truly absorbed, may lead to something very useful. Unless this shift is taking place, there is no meaning in ethnologists' frequent recommendations that the western world help "primitives" absorb into their cultures a salutary selection of western ways. For, if some-do-and-some-don't is the only approach, who can determine which ways are salutary in any given context?

Perhaps due to this and other causes, ethnologists have long shown intellectual jumpiness. Confident sciences seldom apologize for existing. They pursue further knowledge without soul-searching, and only if challenged bother to explain that their by-products are often useful. But the ethnologist is always explaining, even in works published primarily for his peers, why he considers his work valuable. Says Malinowski, prophet of functionalism:

> "In grasping the essential outlook of others, with the reverence and real understanding due even to savages, we cannot but help widening our own. We cannot possibly reach the final Socratic wisdom of knowing ourselves if we never leave the narrow confinement of the customs, beliefs, and prejudices, into which every man is born . . . The Science of Man in its most refined and deepest version should lead us to . . . tolerance and generosity, based on the understanding of other men's point of view."—Argonauts of the Western Pacific, 517-18.

Says Lowie, destroyer of theories about pseudobiological growth of cultures:

> "The knowledge of primitive society has an educational value that should recommend its study even to those who are not primarily interested in the processes of cultural history. All of us are born into a set of traditional institutions and social conventions that are accepted not only as natural, but as the one conceivable response to social needs . . . Against this purblind provincialism there is no better antidote than the systematic study of alien civilizations . . . We see our received set of opinions and customs as merely one of an indefinite number of possible variants; and we are emboldened to hew them into shape in accordance with novel aspirations."—Primitive Society, 13.

It sounds rather too much like Kingsley's recommending the collecting of shells and seaweed as leading to healthy walks in the fresh air and instilling a proper sense of the greatness of

God. Both these great men have here shown they take popular causes to heart; but the quality of the cause does not disguise the impertinence of the context. Asking ethnology to foster Socratic wisdom or to stir people to shape the world nearer to the heart's desire is a trifle out of drawing. Surely if this branch of knowledge is not worth pursuing for its own sake, to the same degree as chemistry or paleontology, it is not worth pursuing for philosophical training or for building Jerusalem in England's green and lovely land. Few paleontologists find it necessary to assert that the study of fossils leads to spiritual humility in the student.

Then "reverence . . . due even to savages." (A man of integrity owes reverence to few things, perhaps to some special individuals, but certainly not to mankind in any sort of mass, civilized or savage.) This merely overstates something which is the ethnologist's greatest handicap and indispensable tool. In the last two generations the closet compiler of strange facts about strange people has been supplanted by the field investigator. No modern student of ethnology has the freedom of his profession until he has lived in and studied a given culture or subculture—an indubitable improvement. In order to learn what he needs to know, the student must be *en rapport* with his subjects. Otherwise they may tell him nothing or, even worse, feed him polite or scornful lies, as when the Tongans palmed off on an early student obscene words for the higher numerals in their language. He must feel good will and liking for his potential informants on Tawney's principle:

"A society, like an individual, reveals the secrets of its inner life only to those who bring to its study not merely scientific curiosity and a mastery of technique, but respect and affection . . ."—Preface to Raymond Firth, *Primitive Economics of the New Zealand Maori*, xiii.

Conscious hypocrisy will be of little use over the long periods necessary. The position is like that of the psychiatrist who cannot properly probe his patient's emotions without a warm personal relationship, or of the salesman who must like his customers to keep their business.

In such situations the operator often comes to feel what he has assumed, or perhaps must be abnormally able to like people whether they are likable or not. Consider the implications in cases of inescapably nasty people. Suppose Nazi Germany had walled itself off for a generation instead of trying to expand and, when isolation and internal propaganda working on fresh generations had produced a consistent and intensely Nazi culture, an ethnologist had been allowed to enter and study it. Unless he could manage to like the successors of Hitler, Goebbels and von Schirach, he would have failed in his assignment. Yet a report on the place from somebody who liked Nazis would lack aspects essential to its significance to the non-Nazi world. There is no help for this, nor has it always done serious damage; ethnologists often possess high intellectual courage and intelligence. But keep it in mind when hearing that the islanders of Tarafu, for all their cannibalism, status-anxieties, ghost-fears, bad dreams, great reluctance to bathe, taste for homosexuality, institutionalized torture of animals and light-fingeredness are nevertheless just as fine a people as any in the world.

Damage to objectivity would be more ominous, of course, if it had ever had a sporting chance to begin with. Actually, however, Lowie's antidote for provincialism is largely chimera. No man can hope effectively to free himself from the web of conditioning spun round or into him ever since he was born. That would require such violent emotional acrobatics that the personality would shatter, making him an inconceivable psychopathic brother to "the Squidgicum Squees 'at swallers theirselves." So—to put his trouble as soberly as possible—the ethnologist must arrive at subjective sympathy with his material while simultaneously maintaining an extracultural objectivity that is obviously impossible this side of sanity. The proverbial man from Mars, the only possible candidate for the job, is not available; Montaigne, the only human being I ever heard of who might have managed it, is dead these hundreds of years. We must put up with the fact that our best guide in dealing with nonwestern man is, at most, a conscientious and learned fellow being who must perform the impossible in order to function. Under such conditions the poor devil is dismally likely to make more mistakes than sense in any given practical context.

At least recent ethnology renounces the temptation to regard primitive peoples as primarily laboratory material, like so many lovable Rhesus monkeys, which is encouraging.[1] Highly idiosyncratic cultures, preliterate, isolated from more complicated cultures, are as important in ethnology as sterile agar in bacteriology. Two centuries ago Africa, Siberia, the Pacific and both Americas still teemed with such virgin material, detailed study of which would have told more than could ever be learned again about the whats and whys of humanity. But at the time there was no such thing as a science of ethnology, and barely the germ of its impersonal inquisitiveness about human doings. By the time the science developed most of its proper material was irretrievably ruined. The ethnologist felt as Sherlock Holmes would if thousands of people had milled over the site of the crime for days before he was called in. No wonder he often cursed explorer and missionary, though to do so was unscientific—after all, to regard the weird habits of a pack of cannibals as inviolate scientific data was no part of the culture of the time.

When it was born, the science had to spend millions of hours and dollars collating voyages and missionary journals with the remains of native cultures in efforts to piece back together the way things had worked in Tasmania in 1700 or Raiatea in 1750. This intellectual agony, with results acknowledgedly imperfect, emphasized the necessity for protecting relatively untouched material still surviving. There actually were prewar efforts to get certain such areas in the practically unexplored New Guinea mountains set aside as preserves, in which ethnologists could operate without the risk of gold seekers, traders, or missionaries taking the bloom off the primitive rose, already so rare a flower. Nice problems in ethics arose: Would conse-

[1] For examples, see Fortune, *Sorceress of Dobu*, 290-3; Tadao Yanaihara, *Pacific Islands*, 258.

quent social benefits be high enough to warrant this experiment in preserving people as if they were bison in Yellowstone Park? It could not conceivably harm the natives—in fact, it would fence them away from diseases; it could not conceivably redound to anybody's economic advantage, a cheering rarity among colonial policies. But it would also mean governmental connivance at institutionalized rape, man-eating, and head-hunting. In the end the idea of insulating preliterates was turned over to literary seekers after the picturesque.

But the scientific trouble about man-preserving is not that it may be immoral, rather that it leads to intellectual sins. It encourages the ethnologist to regard cultures as existing *in vacuo*, the same error underlying the doctrine of equal validity of all cultural traits everywhere. A millennium ago such a *cordon sanitaire* would have stifled intercourse between Fiji and Tonga, which made Fiji one of the most interesting cultural areas in the Pacific. For cultures are always in ceaseless change everywhere, at a greater or less rate depending, not only on degree of contact with alien cultures, but also on momentum of the dominant emotional trends within them.

The fact is that ethnologists often seem to yearn toward the relatively static. Perhaps that is because they have learned most from isolated and slowly changing societies, finding them easier to analyze than those where gross and rapid change produces inconsistent data in confusingly merging strata. There is an unmistakable flavor of gratification as well as of scientific interest in descriptions of things on Tarafu that still go on much as they did when Magellan was still a boy: how old men teach interminable genealogies to the brighter youths; how inherited social position permeates every action, each man, woman, or child knowing exactly where he stands—that is, where his grandfather did before him; how today's carver works in the same patterns as those on the timeworn stones of the temple platform. And complementary indignation is felt when the monograph records that the rhythm of the old dances is now beaten out on a biscuit tin instead of a drum.

The same investigator who so relishes the Maori's pride of

ancestry is likely to be very unhappy about the genealogical obsessions of the Daughters of the American Revolution. Rigidity of status delights him in Samoa and disgusts him in Boston. Nor can he plead in excuse that such rigidity has high social value in Samoa, but is inconsistent with dominant American patterns of equalitarianism. Sound as the point may be, the scientist should describe and analyze without passion. He may be allowed personal tastes in neckties, music, and cheese, but not in cultures or subcultures or cultural traits. To him the Tahitian Arioi and the D.A.R. should rank equally as examples of pathological overdevelopment of special attitudes that, in earlier and less exaggerated phases, may have had social value compensating for their destructive tendencies.

Since they would not so rank with many ethnologists—the evidence lies as much in tone as in content—the innocent layman must walk warily lest he absorb the witness' enthusiasm as well as his data. Nor can he fail to suspect that too many people of ability take up ethnology at least partly because its subject matter assures troubled souls that human society need not impose on human beings the western obligation frequently to make up one's own mind about what one proves and should do next. Dynamic, rapid, complicating change, which our elders chose to call progress, has now gone on so long in the Roman-mediaeval-European-cum-North-American world that it can almost be considered a major cultural trait in itself. Living with and by that tradition is by no means a task for which all men born in western cultures are well suited. But the best lens through which to study the significance of the contrasts between our relatively dynamic and Tarafu's relatively static cultures is probably not the man who hankers, whether consciously or not, after the beautifully patterned, imagination-stifling wonders of the beehive.

Ethnology has long been turning to the equally interesting if more demanding study of rapid "acculturation" as the native selects from and assimilates white ways. But vestiges of the zoo theory of native policy survive in laymen with a smattering of the former attitude, whether educated administrators or publi-

cists back home at the source of power. An extreme case was
the New Zealand member of parliament who suggested to a
Maori leader that the nation buy the Marquesas from France
and transplant the Maori thither to cultivate their beautiful
old ways without further risk of contamination. Such lags between more recent ethnological thought and the notions of
amateurs whose premises are a generation behind the times has
done damage in the past and will do more in future.

For instance, the ethnology on which Veblen based much of
his work was already dying when he used it; but he was unaware
of that, so his assumption of a primitive communism as basic
in social evolution still infects admiring readers. Wells' dram-
atization of the primitive-horde-headed-by-tough-old-man theory of societal development has firmly fixed it in the minds
of millions of readers, though the theory gets more dubious
every year. Marxist determinism based on economic motivation
as the root of all human behavior has been blown sky-high by
recent ethnological findings, which indicate very strongly that
emotions, particularly those of hunger for prestige and fear of
the supernatural, are dominant in many patterns of behavior;
yet millions of Marxists go right on talking, and worse, acting,
as if nothing of the sort had occurred. "He's dead," sings Gracie
Fields, "but he won't lie down." Long-exploded theories of
race, such as those about the fair, creative Aryan as dynamically
crucial in the development of western society, are still among
the most dangerous human obsessions, though in our fathers'
time the Aryan was banished from science as never having existed. Firth, a magnificently levelheaded ethnologist, has a fine
passage on this opportunity for error:

"A certain intellectual rapport has always existed between the
anthropologist and the social reformer, to be attributed perhaps to that strain of idealism which leads the student of
human affairs to see in both the past and the future state of
man gleams of a brighter and purer light than that which is
visible through the dingy atmosphere of present conditions.
The anthropological paradise has more than once been located
in the simplicity of primitive culture. Here, then, is the augury

of hope for the fashioner of a new Utopia, for what man has once experienced that he can taste again. Hence it is not difficult to understand the partiality of the apostle of social reform for some types of anthropological data which may serve as illustration for his theories."—*Primitive Economics of the New Zealand Maori*, 351-2.

The catch, of course, is that even if the "apostle of social reform" were always up to date, fundamental ethnological findings are subject to change without notice. So the world runs—and, under the circumstances, cannot refuse to run—double risk in using the ethnologist as a consultant: He is not only disqualified by being human and not a man from Mars, but on occasion he is also duty bound to abandon his whole theory of navigation and suggest returning to port for a fresh start on a different course when the ship has long been under way. Just now, for instance, his basic position is that, under their varicolored skins, the cultural potentialities of all peoples are alike and that even diametric differences in behavior mean no more than Herskovits' "unique historical vagaries." Taking ethnology's word for it, the intelligent world is proceeding on that basis; besides, it is a cordially equalitarian, self-respecting idea welcome to the liberal mind. But tomorrow some rival and better demonstrated theory may intrude, showing perhaps that temperaments and potentialities are in some degree heritable as, for their own nasty reasons, unpleasant and ignorant hatemongers always said they were. If that should happen—and I should be very sorry to see it—the intelligent world will have ruefully to contemplate irretrievable damage done by good intentions operating under false assumptions.

Yet ethnology has already made durable contributions to human thinking about such matters. As would be expected they are mostly negative: such as the aforesaid destruction of ideas about master races and of postulates stemming from Greek myth about communistic Golden Ages. It was also a great service to clear away previous attempts to classify cultures in an ascending scale of "savagery, barbarism and civilization." Greatest of all, however, has been the overthrow of the notion that "human nature" is a standard phenomenon.[2] The economist is not the only seer who can be fairly accused, à la Tawney, of regarding "the institutions and habits of thought of [his] own age and civilization as in some peculiar sense natural to man . . . and [who] dismisses as contrary to human nature the suggestion that such conduct might be other than it is."[3] Psychiatrist, sociologist, missionary, both the brotherhood-of-man radical and the I-got-mine conservative, make the factual error of considering one or another facet of the cultures they know as basic in human beings, much to the comfort of their own theories and the promulgation of emotional nonsense. Actually the most superficial acquaintance with the variations of human behavior and social organization turned up by ethnology shows human nature to be as startlingly versatile as animate nature in general. Social antics that would shatter a western-style society are indispensable to this or that isolated people.

[2]One such piece of constructive destruction is now so far behind us that few have ever heard of it: the theory widespread among the religious a century ago that such preliterate cultures as missionaries found in the South Seas were *degenerations* from western enlightenment. The basis was the cosmogony and history of the Old Testament. In their own time the conclusions were not as ludicrous as they sound to us. The Rev. Daniel Smith, contemplating Maori culture in the raw, thus turned the tables on the Rousseauistic romantic: "How misapplied are the epithets natural and artificial when employed as they often are to characterize the savage and civilized state! . . . the former in truth . . . is by far the more artificial; and much of civilization consists in the abolition of the numerous devices by which it has falsified and perverted the natural dispositions of the human heart and understanding." (*The New-Zealanders*, 135–6.) These "natural dispositions" are presumably those codified in the Decalogue and born of the natural orderliness and goodness of the human heart. The Rev. Sheldon Dibble, similarly viewing the Hawaiians, reminds his reader that these, like all other humans, are descended from Noah, who knew Jehovah, therefore: "There was a time, of course, when the ancestors of the Hawaiian nation were acquainted with the true God, and the service which he requires . . . Left to their own minds and depraved lusts, the descent is quick and easy down to the region of thick darkness and low degradation which we regard as heathenism." (*History of the Sandwich Islands*, 11.)

[3]Preface to Raymond Firth, *Primitive Economics of the New Zealand Maori*, xv.

Yet this does not mean that there is no such thing as human nature; rather that the observer must shift from description to analysis of function. In dozens of departments of life, it appears, all cultures exhibit specific arrangements to meet standard needs. All secure food, play, procreate, observe modesties in excretion, develop property rights, train the young in skills, and divide work arbitrarily between the sexes. It is only the *how* of these things that varies so fantastically. This notion that all peoples do things in the same fields of endeavour but no two do them alike was long, long in coming, but all the more valued for the delay. For it leaves scope for the ethnologist with the engineering mind, trying to balance the emotional value of an act against its relative efficiency in meeting a standard need.

So far, however, being subject to cultural lags like anybody else, many ethnologists have trouble admitting that a culture may have to survive *in spite of* the noxious character of some of its traits. The tendency is still to insist that because a society does so-and-so, to do so must somehow be salutary on balance. The point is dubious to say the least of it. It is certainly not arrived at scientifically, is rather a vestigial remnant of the view piously expressed by Keate six generations ago:

". . . a speculative reader . . . in the dispersed families of the world traces the hand of Providence guiding all things with unerring wisdom. He marks it balancing with equal scale its blessings to the children of men; and considers human nature, however unadorned when dignified by virtuous simplicity, as one of the noblest objects of contemplation."—*Account of the Pelew Islands*, 63.

A set of *tabus*, for instance, is apparently essential to satisfactory social "interaction," as Chapple & Coon call it. Human life, like sonnet-writing, is enriched by arbitrary restriction. But within limits, any *tabus* will do for that end if taken seriously; whereas ill-advised selection can make for appalling waste of energy and resources. Whatever Moses' motives, the Jewish *tabu* on pork, which is highly nutritious and easily and thriftily produced, is a case in point. The Hindu *tabu* on beef, according to most observations, has been responsible for grotesque and damaging consequences on health and nutrition. Many a culture has installed something even sillier and survived—but only because it had enough margin of health or wealth to keep the restriction from being fatal.

Tabus are emotional as well as social phenomena, of course. Once ethnology admits emotional values, it invades the province of the psychiatrist. Once it tries to find out how the Polynesian got to Easter Island, it invades that of the historian. The ethnologist has always run to other scientists for technical detail: to the mineralogist for the structural significance of various stones wrought into weapons here or there; to the ichthyologist for whether it is superstition or fact that certain fish are seasonally toxic; and so forth. It has long been obvious that all sciences dealing directly with man—psychology, medicine, history, sociology, economics, education, law, for a starter—should coalesce into a Science of Man proper. But academic prudery, a sentiment as strange as the Moslem lady's anxiety about her veil, still kept ethnology from viewing the Puritan migrations as a subject fit for study, while the psychiatrist neglected to deal with the curious behavior of the Indian *shaman*.

The need for ignoring the compartmentation of the sciences was well expressed for me by a scientifically trained South Seas educator who complained bitterly that under current methods available ethnographical material about the people with whom he was dealing was, necessarily, so superficial: "They've got to dig deeper," he said. "They've got to develop real information about personality trends and emotional conflicts before I can feel I know what I'm doing." For an example, no ethnologist or administrator in the Pacific actually knows how to plan economic futures until he knows whether the age-old accusation that the Islander is incurably lazy is mere slander, the pervasive result of cultural conditioning, a congenital defect perhaps with an endocrinological aspect, or partly, at least, the consequence of widespread infestation with yaws, hookworm and filariasis. For such investigation, correlating a socio-economic objective with medical and ethnological and psychiatric issues, the new Science of Man is indispensable. As of now no human being can honestly say he knows the answer to the above question.

The fact that such a Science of Man is not only conceivable but already developing goes far to overthrow the original premise of current ethnology that there is no generic difference between preliterate and western cultures. The distinction, which is probably qualitative, comes out in a remark of a clever lady: "It is very significant that the Trobriand Islanders never developed any ethnologists." Tawney wished he could have a Maori's study of western culture as good as Firth's study of the Maori; but no Maori could even have begun the job unless infected with a peculiarly western point of view by exposure to western man. For, whether or not we actually succeed in getting outside our culture in order to study it, we have at least developed an ambition to do so and, once the possibility is granted, techniques and attitudes for doing it. I know of no evidence that preliterate man shows any such ambition. True, as the casuistic ethnologist may assert, most of the time the behavior of most western human beings has little to distinguish it from the nonobjective, unreflective custom-following of the preliterate. But the layman cannot help thinking it enormously significant that it is not all western men all the time.[4] Nor is there much justification for the ethnologist's regarding the scientific attitude as merely a major cultural trait of some western societies intellectually and emotionally parallel to, say, the pervasive gift exchange principle. For western objectivity about our own doings puts a different face on the universe, morally altering the relations between man and his environment in a fashion unknown to preliterate man and to many a literate as well.

The Micronesian navigator, formulating his knowledge of the significance of star positions, found it emotionally necessary to clothe his formulae in magical mumbo-jumbo and to

---

[4]Cf. Pitt-Rivers, *The Clash of Culture*, 159–60, in a passage that is unhappily too turgid and long to quote.

confide such knowledge to a specially elect class of initiates sworn to secrecy. So, perhaps, did the mediaeval alchemist; but we are out of that stage now. It is disquietingly true that, as Boas pointed out, "primitive society . . . does not favor individual freedom of thought"[5]—a generality hardly worth making if a generic difference had not been felt between the world of *tabu* without formal law and the world that at least wrote, however imperfectly it observes, bills of rights. Or take it this way: For generations the western world has bitterly blamed western man for the crime of not understanding the savage. It seems never to occur to anybody that, other things being equal, it would be equally fair to blame the savage for not understanding western man. Since that would obviously be absurd, the two sets of cultures are unmistakably on different levels, a statement that can be made without specifying higher and lower. Western man has something which neither the preliterate nor any of his ancestors possesses or ever did possess, something that imposes the privilege and complicating duty of intellectual integrity, self-criticism, and generalized disinterestedness. If there is such a thing as the white man's burden, this is it.

But it need not be obsession as well as burden. And the suspicion will not down that much current ethnology-inspired solicitude for the natives of Tarafu reflects what psychiatry calls guilt-feelings—meaning a conviction of moral onus out of all proportion to the ostensible cause. Nobody asks the remnants of the Iroquois to feel guilty about what their ancestors did to the Delaware. Nobody suggests that the Maori are branded with ineradicable shame for their brutalizing of the peaceful Moriori. It is a fine state of affairs when western culture is thus put on the defensive, when the ethnologically-minded use as weapons against it its own glories of scientific objectivity, humanitarianism, efforts to respect the ways of others and catholicity of point of view. And far too often the native, who is no fool, makes dismaying use of the results as the matrix of emotional blackmail. I cannot get out of my head

[5]*Encyclopaedia of Social Sciences*, "Anthropology," I, 97.

a conversation between a white man I know and a shrewd Polynesian chief, in which the chief spoke about like this:

"You whites are queer people. You take a great deal of trouble to preserve my people and worry a great deal about making up to us what you did to us when you first came. When my people first came here and found other people occupying land they wanted, they simply killed them all and didn't worry about it."

It will probably be a long while before the Science of Man, with ethnology as its core, rids itself of such symptoms of intellectual adolescence. In the meantime the world must practice patience, however little it can be afforded. After all this field of investigation is only a few generations old, and in net effect the ethnologist's influence has already reduced the incidence and severity of trauma as varying cultures draw more closely together.

Besides, frail a reed as the Science of Man is at the moment, it is also indispensable. In looking to it for help, the world is in the same position as the inveterate gambler who, told scornfully that he was patronizing a crooked faro game, said that he knew it was crooked but it was the only game in town.

GUIDE TO PRONUNCIATION

Place-name spellings used herein follow those of the National Geographic Society's map *Pacific Ocean and the Bay of Bengal*, September, 1943. They may not altogether correspond to those on other maps available to the reader, since transliteration from South Seas languages into European orthography has always meant anomalies.

Pronunciation of South Seas words and proper names is generally indicated by a semistandardized spelling invented by missionaries. Vowels are: A equals "ah." E equals "ay" as in hay. I equals "ee" as in bee. O is a cross between "oh" and "awe." U is "ooh" as in coo. Each vowel marks a distinct syllable. The exceptions are two diphthongs: AI equals "eye" (actually a slurring of ah-ee); AU equals "ow" as in cow. Consonants are only the nearest European approximations, inaccurate but comprehensible if conventionally pronounced. Thus Hawaii is pronounced not Hywoyah, as in Tin Pan Alley, but Hah-wye-ee; Raiatea is Rye-ah-tay-ah. Practically accentless is the rule.

Fijian spelling is complicated by mission efforts to use the Roman alphabet for unfamiliar sounds. Here B equals MB; C equals TH; D equals ND; G equals NG; Q equals NGG. Thus Cakobau is pronounced Thah-kom-bow; Beqa is Mbeng-ga; Mago is Mang-o. Sometimes this style of spelling gives way to a style nearer European phonetics.

Traces of similar principles appear in Tonga and Samoa. In Samoa *malaga* (journey) is pronounced mah-lahng-ah; *papalagi* (generally alien) is pah-pah-lang-ee. New Yorkers who say Long Guy-land must watch their step here—it is not mah-lahng-gah. The Fijian Q is intended to indicate this second (doubled) type of NG.

An apostrophe indicates a dropped consonant still respected by a slight catch as the vowels slide by.

490

SOURCES CONSULTED

The appended list of books and periodical references will immediately show any scholar that this is not a work of professional scholarship. Its purpose is not to contribute to the bibliography of the South Seas, but to indicate the scope and character of the reading behind the foregoing book and to serve the convenience of any general reader who may wish to go farther into this field than I have been able to take him.

Anybody who may choose to read everything here appended need not sigh for lack of further grist for his mill: there are thousands more books on the South Seas still virgin. But that would be as indiscriminate as, for purposes of sampling, my own reading necessarily was. I have marked with an asterisk items that, whether he is vitally interested in the area or not, are well worth anybody's while.

* Adams, Henry (ed.). *Memoirs of Arii Tamai e Marama of Eimeo*, Teriirere of Tooari Teriinui of Tahiti Tauraatuu i Amo, Paris: Privately printed, 1901.

Adams, Romanzo; T. M. Livesay; I. H. Van Winkle. *The Peoples of Hawaii;* a statistical study by . . . of the University of Hawaii, Honolulu: Institute of Pacific Relations, 1925.

Alexander, James M. M‘ ʿon *Life in Hawaii* (Memoir of Rev. William P. Alexander), Oakland, Calif.: Pacific Press Publishing Co., 1888.

Alexander, W. D. *A Brief History of the Hawaiian People*, published by order of the Board of Education of the Hawaiian Islands, New York: American Book Co., 1891.
———. *Politics and Intrigues in Kalakaua's Reign*. (Typescript in Archives of Hawaii.)

All About Hawaii. Standard Tourist Guide: What to See and How to See It in the Island Territory, Honolulu: Honolulu *Star-Bulletin*, 1928.

Allen, Percy S. *Stewart's Handbook of the Pacific Islands;* a reliable guide to all the inhabited islands of the Pacific Ocean for Traders, Tourists and Settlers, Sydney: McCarron Stewart & Co., 1923.

Amherst of Hackney, Lord, and Basil Thomson (eds.). *The Discovery of the Solomon Islands, by Alvaro de Mendaña in 1568*, London: The Hakluyt Society, 1901.

Ancient Hawaiian Culture; a series of lectures delivered at the Kamehameha Schools by Handy, Emory, Bryan, Buck, Wise and others. N.P. N.D.

Anderson, Charles Roberts. *Melville in the South Seas*, New York: Columbia University Press, 1939.

Anderson, Mary E. *Scenes in the Hawaiian Islands and California*, Boston: American Tract Society, 1865.

Anderson, Rufus. *The Hawaiian Islands;* their progress and condition under missionary labors, Boston: Gould and Lincoln, 1864.

Andrews, C. F. *India and the Pacific*, London: G. Allen & Unwin, 1937.

Andrews, Loring. *Isles of Eden;* a South-Sea Idyll—with Music, New York: Ray Long & Richard R. Smith, 1932.

Anson, Lord. *A Voyage Round the World in the Years 1740-4.* Everyman Edition, London: J. M. Dent & Sons, Ltd., 1911.

Answers to Questions proposed by His Excellency R. C. Wyllie, His Hawaiian Majesty's Minister of Foreign Relations, Honolulu: 1843.

Armitage, George: *see* Bob Davis.

Armstrong, E. S. *The History of the Melanesian Mission*, London: Isbister & Co., 1900.

Armstrong, William N. *Around the World with a King*, New York: F. A. Stokes & Co., 1904.

Ash Slivers, Sr., Lumberman (pseud.). *The Land of the O-O*, Cleveland: The Cleveland Printing & Publishing Co., 1892.

Atkinson, Alatan T. *Sketch of Recent Events*, Honolulu: A. M. Hewett, 1887.

Babbage, S. Barton. *Hauhauism*, Dunedin: A. H. & A. W. Reed, 1937.

Baker, Beatrice Shirley. *Memoirs of the Rev. Dr. Shirley Waldemar Baker, D.M., LL.D.*, Dunedin: 1927.

Balfour, Graham. *The Life of Robert Louis Stevenson*, New York: Charles Scribner's Sons, 1901.

Bancroft, Frederick. *The Life of William H. Seward*, New York: Harper & Bros., 1900.

Bancroft, Hubert Howe. *The New Pacific*, Third Revised Edition, New York: The Bancroft Co., 1915.
———. *The Book of the Fair*, Chicago: The Bancroft Co., 1893.

Barber, Joseph, Jr. *Hawaii: Restless Rampart*, Indianapolis: The Bobbs-Merrill Co., 1941.

Barlow, P. W. *Kaipara*, London: Sampson Low, Marston, Searle & Rivington, 1889.

Barrow, Sir John. *The Mutiny and Piratical Seizure of H. M. S. Bounty*, Oxford University Press, 1914.

Barrows, Edward M. *The Great Commodore*, Indianapolis: The Bobbs-Merrill Co., 1935.

(Bates, George Washington). *Sandwich Island Notes,* by a Haole, New York: Harper & Bros., 1854.

(Baucke, William). *"Where the White Man Treads,"* by W. B., Te Kuiti, Auckland: Wilson & Horton, Ltd., 1928.

Beaglehole, Ernest. *Islands of Danger,* Wellington: Progressive Publishing Society, 1944.

———. *Some Modern Hawaiians,* Honolulu: University of Hawaii Research Publications, XIX, 1937.

———. *Pangai, Village in Tonga,* Memoirs of the Polynesian Society, Wellington: Ernest & Pearl, 1946.

———. *Some Modern Maoris,* New Zealand Council for Educational Research, Wellington: Ernest & Pearl, 1946.

Beaglehole, J. C. *The Exploration of the Pacific,* London: A. C. Black, Ltd., 1934.

Beatty, Jerome. *Americans All Over,* New York: Day McClelland Co., 1940.

Becke, Louis. *Wild Life in Southern Seas,* London: T. Fisher Unwin, 1897.

Beechey, Captain F. W. *Narrative of a Voyage to the Pacific Ocean and Beering's Strait,* Philadelphia: Carey & Lea, 1832.

Belcher, Edward. *Narrative of a Voyage Round the World,* London: Henry Colburn, 1843.

Benoît, Pierre. *Océanie française,* Paris: Editions Alpina, 1933.

Berge, Victor and Henry Wysham Lanier. *Pearl Diver,* London: William Heinemann Ltd., 1930.

Berkowitz, Captain Joseph: *see* Jean Laville.

Besant, Walter. *Captain Cook,* London: The Macmillan Co., 1894.

Best, Elsdon. *The Maori,* Memoirs of the Polynesian Society, Vol. V, Wellington: H. H. Tombs, 1924.

Bingham, Hiram. *A Residence of Twenty-One Years in the Sandwich Islands; or the Civil, Religious and Political History of those Islands,* Hartford: Hezekiah Huntington, 1848.

Bird, Isabella L. *Six Months Among the Palm Groves, Coral Reefs and Volcanoes of the Sandwich Islands,* Second Edition, London: John Murray, 1876.

Bishop, Sereno Edwards. *Reminiscences of Old Hawaii,* The Advertiser Historical Series No. 1, Honolulu: Hawaiian Gazette Co., Ltd., 1916.

Blackman, William Fremont. *The Making of Hawaii,* New York: The Macmillan Co., 1906.

Blanc, Mgr. *Les Iles Wallis,* Paris: Perrin et Cia., 1914.

Blanding, Don. *Hula Moons,* New York: Dodd, Mead & Co., 1930.

Blasco, Ibañez Vincente. A *Novelist's Tour of the World*, New York: E. P. Dutton & Co., 1926.

Bliss, William R. *Paradise in the Pacific*, New York: Sheldon & Co., 1873.

Bloxam, Andrew. *Diary of . . . Naturalist of the "Blonde" on Her Trip from England to the Hawaiian Islands*, 1824-25, Honolulu: Bernice P. Bishop Museum Special Publication X, 1925.

Boddam-Whetham, J. S. *Pearls of the Pacific*, London: Hurst & Blackett, 1876.

Bougainville, Louis Antoine de. *Voyage autour du monde*, Seconde édition, augmentée, Paris: Saillaut et Nyon, 1772.

Bradley, Harold Whitman. *The American Frontier in Hawaii*: The Pioneers, 1789-1843, Stanford University: Stanford University Press, 1942.

Braisby, A. L. (ed.). A *Documentary Record and History of the Lauati Rebellion* (O Le Mau Lauati) in Western Samoa—1909. Compiled from original Native Office documents . . . (Typescript in Administrator's office, Apia.)

Brassy, Mrs. A *Voyage in the "Sunbeam,"* New York: John B. Alden, 1884.

Brooke, Rupert. *Letters from America*, New York: Charles Scribner's Sons, 1916.

Brookes, Jean Ingram. *International Rivalry in the Pacific Islands*, Berkeley: University of California Press, 1941.

Brown, George. *Pioneer Missionary and Explorer*. An Autobiography, London: Hodder & Stoughton, 1908.

Brown, J. MacMillan. *Peoples and Problems of the Pacific*, London: T. F. Unwin, 1927.

Browne, G. Waldo and Nathan Haskell Dole. *The New America and the Far East*, I, Hawaii, Introduction by the Honorable Henry Cabot Lodge, Boston: Marshall Jones Co., 1907.

Buck, Peter H. (Te Rangi Hiroa). *An Introduction to Polynesian Anthropology*, Honolulu: Bernice P. Bishop Museum Bulletin CXXCVII, 1945.

———. *The Passing of the Maori*, Wellington: Transactions and Proceedings of the New Zealand Institute LV, 1924.

*———. *Vikings of the Sunrise*, New York: Frederick A. Stokes Co., 2d printing, 1938.

Burchett, Wilfred G. *Pacific Treasure Island: New Caledonia*, Melbourne: F. W. Cheshire Pty., Ltd., 1941.

Burrows, Edwin G. *Hawaiian Americans*, New Haven: Yale University Press, 1947.

Buxton, Patrick A. *Researches in Polynesia and Melanesia. Human Diseases and Welfare*, London: 1928.

Bywater, Hector C. *The Great Pacific War*, with an Introduction by Hanson W. Baldwin, Boston: Houghton Mifflin Co., 1942.

———. *Sea-Power in the Pacific*, Boston: Houghton Mifflin Co., 1921.

Caillot, A. C. Eugène. *Histoire de la Polynesie Orientale*, Paris: Ernest Leroux, 1910.

(Calderon, George). *Tahiti*, by Tihoti, London: Grant Richards, Ltd., 1921.

Callahan, James Merton. *American Relations in the Pacific and the Far East*, Baltimore: Johns Hopkins Press, 1901.

Calnon, William Lee. *Seeing the South Sea Islands*, New York: Frederick H. Hitchcock, 1926.

Cameron, Charlotte. *Two Years in Southern Seas*, Boston: Small, Maynard & Co., N.D.

Cameron, John. *John Cameron's Odyssey*, New York: The Macmillan Co., 1928.

Carpenter, Edmund James. *America in Hawaii*, Boston: Small, Maynard & Co., 1899.

Carter, Charles L. *The Hawaiian Question*, Honolulu: Star Publishing Co., 1893.

Carter, Mrs. H. A. P. *Kaahumanu*, Honolulu: 1893.

Castle, William R., Jr. *Hawaii, Past and Present*, New York: Dodd, Mead & Co., 1913.

Chalmers, James. *Pioneering in New Guinea*, London: Religious Tract Society, 1887.

Chaney, George Leonard. *"Aloha,"* Boston: Roberts Bros., 18··.

Chantepleure, Guy (pseud.). *Escales océaniennes*, Paris: Calmann-Levy, 1935.

Chapple, Major W. A. *Fiji*, its problems and resources, Wellington: Whitcombe & Tombs, Ltd., 1921.

Cheesman, Evelyn. *Islands Near the Sun*, London: H. F. & G. Witherby, 1927.

Cheever, Rev. Henry T. *The Island World of the Pacific*, New York: Harper & Bros., 1851.

———. *Life in the Sandwich Islands*, or the Heart of the Pacific as it was and is, New York: A. S. Barnes & Co., 1851.

———. *The Whale and His Captors*, New York: Harper & Bros., 1850.

Chinard, Gilbert (ed.). *Diderot, Supplément au Voyage de Bougainville*, Paris: E. Droz, 1935.

Christian, F. W. *The Caroline Islands*, London: Methuen & Co., 1899.

Churchill, Llewella Pierce. *Samoa 'Uma*, New York: Forest & Stream Publishing Co., 1902.

Churchill, William. *Beach-la-Mar*, Washington: Carnegie Institution of Washington, 1911.

Churchward, William B. *My Consulate in Samoa*, London: Richard Bentley & Son, 1887.

Clark, Sydney A. *Hawaii with Sydney A. Clark*, New York: Prentice-Hall, Inc., 1939.

Clark, Thomas Blake. *Hawaii; the 49th State*, New York: Garden City Press, 1947.

———. *Paradise Limited*, New York: Modern Age Books, 1941.

———. *Remember Pearl Harbor*, New York: Modern Age Books, 1942.

Clemens, Samuel L. (Mark Twain, pseud.). *Following the Equator*, New York: Harper & Bros., 1899.

———. *Letters from the Sandwich Islands*, Edited by G. Ezra Dane, Stanford University: Stanford University Press, 1938.

———. *Roughing It*, New York: Harper & Bros., 1899.

Cleveland, H. W. S. (ed.). *Voyages of a Merchant Navigator of the days that are past*, New York: Harper & Bros., 1886.

Clyde, Paul H. *Japan's Pacific Mandate*, New York: The Macmillan Co., 1935.

Coan, Titus. *Life in Hawaii*, New York: Anson D. F. Randolph & Co., 1882.

Codrington, R. H. *The Melanesians*, Oxford: Oxford Press, 1891.

Collection of Voyages Round the World, Lord Byron, Capt. Wallis, Capt. Carteret, Lord Mulgrave, Lord Anson . . . London: A. Millar, W. Law & R. Cater, 1790.

Collinson, Clifford W. *Life and Laughter 'Midst the Cannibals*, New York: E. P. Dutton & Co., 1927.

Colum, Padraic. *At the Gateways of the Day*, Published for the Hawaiian Legend Folklore Commission, New Haven: Yale University Press, 1924.

———. *The Bright Islands*, Published for the Hawaiian Legend and Folklore Commission, New Haven: Yale University Press, 1925.

Condliffe, J. B. (ed.). *Problems of the Pacific*; Second Conference of the Institute of Pacific Relations, Honolulu, 1927, Chicago: University of Chicago Press, 1928.

Cook, James. *The Voyages of Captain . . . Round the World*, London, N. D.

Cooper, H. Stonehewer. *The Islands of the Pacific*; A new and revised edition of "Coral Lands" for circulation in Australia, London: 1888.

Cooper, Harold. *Among Those Present*, Prepared for the Colonial Office by the Central Office of Information, London: 1946.

Coppinger, R. W. *Cruise of the 'Alert,'* London: W. Swan Sonnenschein & Co., 1883.

Corney, Bolton Glanville (ed.). *The Quest and Occupation of Tahiti,* London: The Hakluyt Society, 1913.

Corney, Peter. *Voyages in the Northern Pacific,* Honolulu: Thomas G. Thrum, 1896.

Coulter, John Wesley. *Fiji, Little India of the Pacific,* Chicago: University of Chicago Press, 1942.

Cravath, Paul D. *Letters Home from the South Sea Islands, China and Japan,* Privately printed, 1934.

Crawford, David Livingston. *Paradox in Hawaii,* Boston: Stratford Press, 1933.

Crawford, M. Leola. *Seven Weeks in Hawaii,* San Francisco: John J. Newbegin, 1917.

Crocker, Aimée Templeton. *And I'd Do It Again,* New York: Coward-McCann, 1936.

Cuzent, Gilbert. *Isles de la Société,* Tahiti: N. P., 1860.

* Dana, Richard Henry, Jr. *Two Years Before the Mast,* New York: F. M. Lupton Publishing Co., N. D.

Daniel, Hawthorne. *Islands of the Pacific,* New York: G. P. Putnam's Sons, 1943.

* Darwin, Charles. *The Voyage of the Beagle,* Everyman's Library, London: J. M. Dent & Sons, Ltd., 1906.

David, Mrs. Edgeworth. *Funafuti,* London: John Murray, 1899.

Davies, Theo. H. *The Kingdom of Hawaii,* Southport: Robert Johnson & Co., Ltd., 1891.

Davis, Bob and George Armitage. *Hawaii, U. S. A.,* New York: Frederick A. Stokes & Co., 1941.

Davis, W. M. *Les Côtes et les Récifs Coralliens de la Nouvelle-Calédonie.* Paris: 1926.

Deane, W. *Fijian Society,* London: Macmillan & Co., Ltd., 1921.

De Bisschop, Eric. *Kaimiloa,* Paris: Librairie Plon, 1939.

Decker, John Alvin. *Labor Problems in the Pacific Mandates,* New York: Institute of Pacific Relations, International Research Service, 1940.

Delano, Amasa. *Narrative of Voyages and Travel,* Boston: Privately printed, 1815.

De la Vergne, George H. *Hawaiian Sketches,* San Francisco: 1898.

Dennett, Tyler, *Americans in Eastern Asia,* New York: The Macmillan Co., 1922.

De Ricci, J. H. *Fiji*, London: E. Stanford, 1875.

Derrick, R. A. *A History of Fiji*, School Edition; I, Suva: 1946.

Deschanel, Paul. *La politique française en Océanie*, Paris: 1884.

———. *Les interêts français dans l'Océan Pacifique*, Paris: Berger Levrault et Cie, 1898.

Diapea, William. *Cannibal Jack*, New York: G. P. Putnam's Sons, 1928.

Dibble, Sheldon. *A History of the Sandwich Islands*, Honolulu: T. G. Thrum, 1909.

* Diderot, Denis. *Supplément au voyage de Bougainville*, Paris: Editions de la Nouvelle Revue Française, 1921.

Dole, Nathan Haskell: *see* G. Waldo Browne.

Dole, Sanford B. *Memoirs of the Hawaiian Revolution*, Honolulu: Advertiser Publishing Co., Ltd., 1936.

Dorsenne, Jean. *Polynésie*, Paris: Editions Emile-Paul Frères, 1929.

Dulles, Foster Rhea. *America in the Pacific*, Boston: Houghton Mifflin Co., 1932.

———. *Lowered Boats:* A Chronicle of American Whaling, New York: Harcourt, Brace & Co., 1933.

Dumas, Alexandre: *see* Dr. Felix Maynard.

Dumont-d'Urville, J. S. C. *Voyage de la corvette L'Astrolabe* 1826-29, Paris: J. Tastu, 1830-5.

Dunbabin, Thomas. *Slavers of the South Seas*, Sydney: Angus & Robertson, 1935.

Du Puy, William Atherton. *Hawaii and Its Race Problem*, Washington: Government Printing Office, 1932.

Edwards, E. J. *Malua Theological College Centenary*, 1844-1944. (Typescript in my possession.)

Elder, John Rawson (ed.). *Marsden's Lieutenants*, Dunedin: Reed, 1934.

Ellis, Sir Albert. *Midpacific Outposts*, Auckland: Brown and Stewart, 1946.

Ellis, William. *An Authentic Narrative of a Voyage performed by Captain Cook and Captain Clerke*, London: G. Robinson, 1783.

———. *A Narrative of a Tour Through Hawaii*; The Advertiser Historical Series No. 2, Honolulu: Hawaiian Gazette, Ltd., 1917.

———. *Polynesian Researches*, London: Fisher, Son, & Jackson, 1831.

Emerson, Nathaniel B. *Unwritten Literature of Hawaii*, Washington: Government Printing Office, 1909.

Emerson, Oliver Pomeroy. *Pioneer Days in Hawaii*, New York: Doubleday, Doran & Co., 1928.

Emory, Kenneth. *The Island of Lanai,* Bernice P. Bishop Museum Bulletin XII, Honolulu: 1924.

Endicott, William. *Wrecked Among Cannibals in Fiji;* with notes by Lawrence Waters Jenkins, Salem, Mass.: Marine Research Society, 1923.

Entrecasteaux, Bruni d'. *Voyage de . . . envoyé à la récherche de la Pérouse,* Publié par ordre de sa majesté l'empereur roi, imprimerie impériale, Paris: 1808.

Eskridge, Robert Lee. *Manga Reva,* Indianapolis: Bobbs-Merrill Co., 1931.

Establissements Français de l'Océanie. Papeete: Journal officiel, *Messager de Tahiti,* 1947.

Falk, Edwin A. *From Perry to Pearl Harbor,* New York: Doubleday, Doran & Co., 1943.

Fanning, Captain Edmund. *Voyages and Discoveries in the South Seas, 1792-1832,* Salem, Mass.: Marine Research Society, 1924.

Faris, John T. *The Paradise of the Pacific,* New York: Doubleday, Doran & Co., 1929.

Fergusson, Erna. *Our Hawaii,* New York: Alfred A. Knopf, 1942.

Ferri-Pisani. *Les Tourmentés du Pacifique,* Paris: Les Editions de France, 1936.

Field, Isobel (Strong). *This Life I've Loved,* New York: Longmans, Green & Co., 1937.

Fiji, Legislative Council of. *Nationalization of the Sugar Industry,* Deed of Cession. Session of 1946 (February), Fiji Legislative Journal.

Firth, Raymond W. *Primitive Economics of the New Zealand Maori,* London: G. Routledge & Sons, Ltd., 1929.

———. *Primitive Polynesian Economy,* London: George Routledge & Sons, Ltd., 1939.

———. We, the Tikopia; With a preface by Bronislaw Malinowski, London: George Allen and Unwin, 1936.

Fleischmann, Julius. *Footsteps in the Sea,* New York: G. P. Putnam's Sons, 1935.

Fletcher, Charles Brunsdon. *Stevenson's Germany,* London: Heinemann, 1920.

(Fletcher, Robert James). *Isles of Illusion,* edited by Bohun Lynch, Boston: Small, Maynard & Co., 1923.

Forbes-Lindsay, C. H. *America's Insular Possessions,* Philadelphia: John C. Winston Co., 1906.

Forster, Georg. *A Voyage Round the World in His Majesty's Sloop Resolution,* London: B. White, 1777.

Fortune, R. F. *Sorcerers of Dobu,* New York: E. P. Dutton & Co., Inc., 1932.

Foster, Harry L. A Vagabond in Fiji, New York: Dodd, Mead & Co., 1927.

Frear, Mary Dillingham. Lowell and Abigail, New Haven: Privately printed, 1934.

Freeman, John. Herman Melville, English Men of Letters Series, New York: The Macmillan Co., 1926.

Frisbie, Robert Dean. The Island of Desire, New York: Doubleday, Doran & Co., 1944.

————. My Tahiti, Boston: Atlantic Monthly Press Book: Little, Brown & Co., 1937.

Froude, James Anthony. Oceana, London: Longmans, Green & Co., 1886.

Furness, William Henry, 3d. The Island of Stone Money, Philadelphia and London: J. B. Lippincott & Co., 1910.

Garnier, Jules. Océanie, Paris: H. Plon, 1875.

Gauguin, Paul. Noa, Noa, New York: Nicholas L. Brown, 1920.

Gerbault, Alain. A la poursuite du soleil, Paris: Grasset, 1929.

————. Iles de beauté, Paris: Gallimard, 1939.

————. Sur la route de retour, Paris: Grasset, 1929.

Gerrould, Katharine Fullerton. Hawaii: Scenes and Impressions, New York: Charles Scribner's Sons, 1916.

Gessler, Clifford F. Hawaii—Isles of Enchantment, New York: D. Appleton-Century Co., 1937.

————. The Leaning Wind, New York: D. Appleton-Century Co., 1943.

————. Road My Body Goes, New York: Reynal & Hitchcock, 1937.

————. Tropic Landfall, New York: Doubleday, Doran & Co., 1942.

Gibbings, Robert. Blue Angels and Whales: New York, E. P. Dutton & Co., 1946.

Gibson, Walter Murray, The Prison of Weltevreden, New York: J. C. Riker, 1855.

————. Report, American Geographical and Statistical Society, New York: 1853.

————. Sanitary Instructions for Hawaiians, Honolulu: J. H. Black, 1880.

Gill, William Wyatt. From Darkness to Light in Polynesia, London: Religious Tract Society, 1894.

Goodrich, Joseph King. The Coming Hawaii, The World Today Series, Chicago: A. C. McClurg & Co., 1914.

Gordon-Cumming, C. F. At Home in Fiji, New York: A. C. Armstrong & Son, 1882.

———. *Fire-Fountains*, London: William Blackwood & Son, 1883.

———. *A Lady's Cruise in a French Man-of-War*, London and Edinburgh: William Blackwood & Son, 1882.

Greenbie, Sydney. *The Pacific Triangle*, New York: The Century Co., 1921.

Grey, Sir George. *Polynesian Mythology*, London: George Routledge & Sons, Ltd., 1906.

Grey, J. R. and B. B. *South Sea Settlers*, London: Arrowsmith, 1927.

Grimshaw, Beatrice. *From Fiji to the Cannibal Islands*, London: Thomas Nelson & Sons, Ltd., N. D.

———. *Isles of Adventure*, Boston: Houghton Mifflin Co., 1931.

Griswold, A. Whitney. *The Far Eastern Policy of the United States*, New York: Harcourt, Brace & Co., 1938.

Guild, Caroline. *Rainbow in Tahiti*, Garden City: Doubleday & Company, 1948.

Gulick, Addison. *Evolutionist and Missionary John Thomas Gulick*, Chicago: University of Chicago Press, 1932.

Gulick, Rev., and Mrs. Orramel Hinckley. *The Pilgrims of Hawaii*, New York: Fleming H. Revell Co., 1918.

Guppy, H. B. *The Solomon Islands and Their Natives*, London: Swan Sonnenschein, Lowrey & Co., 1867.

Hagen, A. *Voyage aux Nouvelles-Hébrides et aux Iles Salomons* (unidentified tear-sheets from French magazine, dated June 3, 10, 17, 1893. No. 4612 Bibliothèque Bernheim, Noumea.)

Hall, James Norman. *Mid-Pacific*, Boston: Houghton Mifflin Co., 1928.

Hamon, Renée. *Aux Iles de Lumiere*, Présentation de Renée Hamon par Colette, Paris: Ernest Flammarion, 1940.

Harnoncourt, René d': *see* Ralph Linton.

* Harrison, Tom. *Savage Civilization*, New York: Alfred A. Knopf, 1937.

Hawthorne, Nathaniel. *Our Old Home*, Boston: Ticknor and Fields, 1863.

Helton, E. C. N. *Pidgin English*, Wewak., N.D.

Henderson, G. C. *The Discoverers of the Fiji Islands*, London: John Murray, 1933.

Henry, Teuira. *Ancient Tahiti*, Bernice P. Bishop Museum Bulletin No. XLVII, Honolulu: 1928.

Hibben, Paxton. *The Peerless Leader; William Jennings Bryan*, New York: Farrar and Rinehart, Inc., 1929.

Hobbs, Jean. *Hawaii, a Pageant of the Soil*, Stanford University: Stanford University Press, 1935.

Hogbin, H. Ian. *Law and Order in Polynesia;* with an introduction by B. Malinowski, New York: Harcourt, Brace & Co., 1934.

Holman, Lucia Ruggles. *Journal of* . . . Bernice P. Bishop Museum; Special Publication XVII, Honolulu: 1931.

Hood, T. H. *Notes of a Cruise in H. M. S. Fawn,* Edinburgh: Edmonston & Douglas, 1863.

Hopkins, Ernest M. (chairman), Maurice J. Tobin and Knowles A. Ryerson. *Report on the Civil Governments of Guam and Samoa* (Full text, press release by US Navy Department May 11, 1947).

Hopkins, Manley. *Hawaii,* with a preface by the Bishop of Oxford. Second Edition, New York: D. Appleton & Co., 1869.

Horne, John. *A Year in Fiji,* London: E. Stanford, 1881.

Horne, William Kenneth: *see* Tonga.

Humphrey, Seth K. *Loafing Through the Pacific,* New York: Doubleday, Page & Co., 1927.

Huxley, Julian (ed.). *T. H. Huxley's Diary of the Voyage of H. M. S. 'Rattlesnake,'* New York: Doubleday, Doran & Co., 1936.

Ibañez y Garcia, Luis de. *Historia de las Islas Marianas, Carolinas y Palaos,* Granada: Imp. y Lib. de Paulino V. Sabatel, 1886.

Jackson, William C. *You'll Dance in Tahiti,* New York: G. P. Putnam's Sons, 1938.

Jarves, James Jackson. *History of the Hawaiian Islands,* Third Edition, Honolulu: Charles Edwin Hitchcock, 1847.

————. *Scenes and Scenery in the Sandwich Islands,* Boston: James Munroe & Co., 1843.

Jewett, Frances Gulick. *Luther Halsey Gulick,* Boston: Congregational Sunday School & Publishing Society, 1895.

Johnson, Captain and Mrs. Irving. *Westward Bound in the Schooner Yankee,* New York: W. W. Norton & Co., Inc., 1936.

Johnson, Osa. *Bride in the Solomons,* Boston: Houghton Mifflin Co., 1944.

Johnstone, S. M. *Samuel Marsden,* Sydney: Angus & Robertson, Ltd., 1932.

Judd, Laura Fish. *Honolulu,* New York: Anson D. F. Randolph & Co., 1880.

Keable, Robert. *Tahiti: Isle of Dreams,* London: Hutchinson & Co., 1923.

Keate, George. *Account of the Pelew Islands,* Journals and Communications of Captain Henry Wilson and some of his officers, Boston: Manning & Loving, 1796.

Keesing, Felix M. *Education in Pacific Countries,* Shanghai: Kelly & Walsh, Ltd., 1937.

————. *Modern Samoa*, London: G. Allen & Unwin, Ltd., 1934.

————. *Native Peoples of the Pacific World*, New York: The Macmillan Co., 1945.

*————. *The South Seas in the Modern World*, New York: Institute of Pacific Relations, International Research Service, John Day Co., 1941.

Keim, Jeannette. *Forty Years of German-American Political Relations*, Philadelphia: W. J. Dornan, 1919.

Kemp, Jonathan (ed.). *Diderot, Interpreter of Nature*, London: Lawrence & Wishart, 1937.

Keyserling, Count Hermann Alexander. *The Travel Diary of a Philosopher*, New York: Harcourt, Brace & Co., 1925.

Kingsley, Dr.: *see* Lord Pembroke.

Kotzebue, Otto von. *A New Voyage Round the World*, in 1823-26, London: Henry Colburn & Richard Bentley, 1830.

————. *A Voyage of Discovery into the South Sea and Beering's Straits*, London: Longman, Hurst, Rees, Orme & Brown, 1821.

Krieger, Herbert W. *Island Peoples of the Western Pacific*, Smithsonian Institution War Background Studies XVI. Washington: Smithsonian Institution, 1943.

Krout, Mary H. *Hawaii and a Revolution*, New York: Dodd, Mead & Co., 1898.

Kuykendall, Ralph S. *The Hawaiian Kingdom*, Honolulu: University of Hawaii, 1938.

————. *A History of Hawaii*, New York: The Macmillan Co., 1926.

La Farge, John. *Reminiscences of the South Seas*, New York: Doubleday, Page & Co., N.D.

La Pérouse, Jean-François de. *Voyage de* . . . Preface de Claude Ferrère. Paris: La Renaissance du Livre, 1930.

Larsen, Nils P., M.D. *Medical Art in Ancient Hawaii* (In 53d Annual Report of Hawaiian Historical Society), Honolulu: 1946.

Lambert, S. M. *A Yankee Doctor in Paradise*, Boston: Little, Brown & Co., 1941.

Lanier, Henry W.: *see* Victor Berge.

Laville, Jean and Captain Joseph Berkowitz. *Pacific Island Legends*, Noumea: Librarie Ed. Pentecost, 1944.

Lawrence, Mary Stebbins. *Stories of the Volcano Goddess*, Honolulu: Crossroads Book Shop, Ltd., 1912.

Ledyard, John. *A Journal of Captain Cook's Last Voyage to the Pacific Ocean*, Hartford: Nathaniel Patten, 1783.

Lee, Ida. *Captain Bligh's Second Voyage to the South Sea*, London: Longmans, Green & Co., 1920.

Leenhardt, Maurice. *Gens de la Grande Terre*, Paris: 1937.

Lemire, Charles. *La Colonisation Française en Nouvelle-Calédonie et Dépendances*, Paris: Challamel Aîné, 1878.

Leverhulme, William Hulme Lever, 2d Viscount, (ed.). *Viscount Leverhulme*, London: George Allen & Unwin, 1927.

Liliuokalani, Queen. *Hawaii's Story*, Boston: Lothrop, Lee & Shepherd Co., 1898.

Linton, Ralph and Paul S. Wingert in collaboration with René d'Harnoncourt. *Arts of the South Seas*, New York: 1946.

Lipscomb, Charles J. *Tiki*, New York: Dial Press, 1935.

Littler, Robert M. C. *The Governance of Hawaii*, Stanford University: Stanford University Press, 1929.

Lockerby, William. *The Journal of . . .* Edited by Sir Everard im Thurn and Leonard C. Wharton, London: The Hakluyt Society, 1925.

Lodge, Henry Cabot: *see* Theodore Roosevelt.

London, Charmian. *Our Hawaii*, New York: The Macmillan Co., 1922.

London, Jack. *The Cruise of the 'Snark,'* New York: The Macmillan Co., 1911.

Lovett, Richard. *The History of the London Missionary Society*, London: Henry Frowde, 1899.

————. *James Chalmers*: His Autobiography and Letters, New York: Fleming H. Revell Co., N. D.

Lubbock, Basil. *Bully Hayes*, Boston: Charles G. Lauriat Co., 1931.

Lucas-Dubreton, J. *L'Eden du Pacifique*, Paris: Librairie Gallimard, 1929.

Lucatt, Edward. *Rovings in the Pacific from 1837 to 1849*, London: Longman, Brown, Green & Longman, 1851.

Luke, Sir Harry. *Britain and the South Seas*, London: Longmans, Green & Co., 1945.

————. *The British Pacific Islands*, Oxford Pamphlets on World Affairs VI, London: Oxford University Press, 1943.

————. *From a South Seas Diary*, 1938-1942, London: Nicholson & Watson, 1945.

Lyman, Chester S. *Around the Horn to the Sandwich Islands and California*, Edited by Frederick J. Teggert, New Haven: Yale University Press, 1925.

Lyman, Henry M. *Hawaiian Yesterdays*, Chicago: A. C. McClurg Co., 1906.

Macdonald, Alexander W. *Revolt in Paradise*, New York: Stephen Daye, 1944.

Mackaness, George. A Book of the 'Bounty' and selections from Bligh's writings, Everyman's Library, London: J. M. Dent & Sons, Ltd., 1938.

———. The Life of Vice-Admiral William Bligh, New York: Farrar & Rinehart, 1936.

Mackellar, C. D. Scented Isles and Coral Gardens, New York: E. P. Dutton & Co., 1912.

MacQuarrie, Hector. Tahiti Days, New York: George H. Doran Co., 1920.

Mahan, Alfred Thayer. The Interest of America in Sea Power, Present and Future, Boston: Little, Brown & Co., 1911.

———. Retrospect and Prospect, Boston: Little, Brown & Co., 1902.

Malinowski, Bronislaw. Argonauts of the Western Pacific, London: George Routledge & Sons, Ltd., 1922.

*———. The Sexual Life of Savages, New York: Reader's League of America, N. D.

Malo, David. Hawaiian Antiquities (Moolelo Hawaii), Honolulu: Hawaiian Gazette Co., Ltd., 1903.

Mariner, William. An Account of the Natives of the Tonga Islands, by John Martin, M.D., London: Privately printed, 1817.

Markham, Albert Hastings. The Cruise of the "Rosario," London: Sampson Low, Marston, Low & Searle, 1873.

Markham, Sir Clements (ed.). The Voyages of Pedro Fernandez de Quiros, London: The Hakluyt Society, 1904.

Marsh, Edward. Rupert Brooke: A Memoir, London: Sidgwick & Jackson, 1918.

Marshall, W. P. Afloat in the Pacific, Zanesville, O.: Sullivan & Barrow, 1876.

Martin, John: see William Mariner.

Martin, Lady. Our Maoris, London: The Society for Promoting Christian Knowledge, 1888.

Martyr, Weston. The Wandering Years, Edinburgh: 1943.

Masterman, Sylvia. The Origins of International Rivalry in Samoa, London: G. Allen & Unwin, 1934.

Matches, Margaret. Savage Paradise, New York: The Century Co., 1931.

Mather, Helen. One Summer in Hawaii, New York: Cassell Publishing Co., 1891.

McElroy, Robert. Grover Cleveland, the Man and the Statesman, New York: Harper & Bros., 1923.

McGuire, Paul. Westward the Course! New York: William Morrow & Co., 1942.

McSpadden, J. Walker. *Beautiful Hawaii*, New York: Thomas Y. Crowell, 1939.

* Mead, Margaret. *From the South Seas* (Comprises *Coming of Age in Samoa, Growing Up in New Guinea,* and *Sex and Temperament*), New York: William Morrow & Co., 1939.

Mears, Eliot G. *Pacific Ocean Handbook,* Stanford University: James L. Deekin, 1944.

Melville, Herman. *Omoo,* Everyman's Library, London: J. M. Dent & Sons, Ltd., 1907.

————. *Typee,* Everyman's Library, London: J. M. Dent & Sons, Ltd., 1907.

Melville, Lewis (Benjamin Lewis Saul). *The South Sea Bubble,* London: D. O'Connor, 1921.

Merrill, Elmer D. *Plant Life of the Pacific World,* New York: The Macmillan Co., 1945.

* Millis. Walter. *The Martial Spirit,* Boston: Houghton Mifflin Co., 1931.

Missionary Voyage to the Southern Pacific Ocean 1796-8, in the ship "Duff," London: T. Chapman, 1799.

Moerenhout, J. A. *Voyage aux îles du grand océan,* Paris: Arthur Bertrand Librairie, 1837.

Moors, H. J. *With Stevenson in Samoa,* Boston: Small, Maynard & Co., 1910.

* Morison, Eliot Samuel. *The Maritime History of Massachusetts,* 1783-1860, Boston: Houghton Mifflin Co., 1921.

* Morrell, Captain Benjamin, Jr. *A Narrative of Four Voyages,* New York: J. & J. Harper, 1832.

Morris, Charles. *Our Island Empire,* Philadelphia: J. B. Lippincott Co., 1899.

Moss, Frederick J. *Through Islands and Atolls of the Great South Sea,* London: S. Low, Marston, Searle & Rivington, 1889.

Mullett, Charles F. *The British Empire,* New York: Henry Holt & Co., 1938.

Mumford, Lewis. *Herman Melville,* New York: Harcourt, Brace & Co., 1929.

Murray, The Rev. A. W. *Forty Years' Mission Work in Polynesia and New Guinea,* New York: Robert Carter & Bros., 1876.

Musick, John R. *Hawaii, our New Possessions,* New York: Funk & Wagnalls, 1897 *(sic)*.

Muzzey, David Saville. *James G. Blaine,* New York: Dodd, Mead & Co., 1934.

Mytinger, Caroline. *Headhunting in the Solomon Islands,* New York: The Macmillan Co., 1942.

Narrative of Five Youths from the Sandwich Islands, New York: J. Seymour, 1816.

Nevins, Allan. *Grover Cleveland,* New York: Dodd, Mead & Co., 1932.

Newell, F. H. *Hawaii,* Washington: Government Printing Office, 1909.

Nordhoff, Charles. *Northern California, Oregon and the Sandwich Islands,* New York: Harper & Bros., 1874.

———. and James Norman Hall. *Faery Lands of the South Seas,* New York: Harper and Bros., 1921.

O'Brien, Frederick. *Atolls of the Sun,* New York: Century Co., 1922.

———. *Mystic Isles of the South Seas,* New York: Century Co., 1921.

———. *White Shadows in the South Seas,* New York: Century Co., 1919.

Old New Zealand, by a Pakeha Maori, Auckland: Whitcombe & Tombs, Ltd., 1930.

Oleson, W. B.: *see* John L. Stevens.

Osborn, Fairfield (ed.). *The Pacific World,* New York: W. W. Norton, 1944.

Overell, Lilian. *A Woman's Impressions of German New Guinea,* New York: Dodd, Mead & Co., 1923.

Page, Jesse. *Among the Maoris,* New York: Fleming H. Revell Co., 1894.

Paine, Ralph D. *The Ships and Sailors of Old Salem,* New York: Outing Publishing Co., 1909.

Palmer, Albert W. *The Human Side of Hawaii,* Boston: Pilgrim Press, 1924.

Palmer, George. *Kidnapping in the South Seas,* Edinburgh: Edmonston & Douglas, 1871.

Palmer, Julius A., Jr. *Memories of Hawaii,* Boston: Lee & Shepard, 1894.

Paton, Frank H. L. *Lomai of Lenakel,* New York: Fleming H. Revell Co., 1903.

Paton, John G. *John G. Paton;* An Autobiography edited by his brother, New York: Fleming H. Revell Co., 1898.

Paton, M. Whitecross (Mrs. John G. Paton). *Letters and Sketches from the New Hebrides,* London: Hodder & Stoughton, 1896.

Patouillet, Jules. *Trois ans en Nouvelle Calédonie.* Paris: 1873.

Paullin, Charles Oscar. *Diplomatic Negotiations of American Naval Officers,* Baltimore: Johns Hopkins Press, 1912.

Peck, George W. *Melbourne and the Chincha Islands,* New York: Charles Scribner, 1854.

(Pembroke, Earl of, and Dr. Kingsley). *South Sea Bubbles,* by the Earl and the Doctor, New York: D. Appleton & Co., 1872.

Perkins, Edward T. *Na Motu;* or Reef-rovings in the South Seas, New York: Pudney & Russell, 1854.

Perry, Matthew Calbraith. *Narrative of the Expedition of an American Squadron to the China Seas and Japan*, New York: D. Appleton & Co., 1856.

Pinchot, Gifford. *To the South Seas*, Philadelphia: John C. Winston Co., 1930.

Pitt-Rivers, George Henry Lane-Fox. *The Clash of Cultures and the Conflict of Races*, London: George Routledge & Sons, Ltd., 1927.

Porter, Captain David. *Journal of a Cruize Made to the Pacific Ocean*, Philadelphia: Bradford & Inskeep, 1815.

Porteus, Stanley D. *Calabashes and Kings*, Palo Alto, Calif.: Pacific Books, 1945.

Powdermaker, Hortense. *Life in Lesu*, New York: W. W. Norton & Co., 1938.

Powell, S. W. *A South Sea Diary*, Harmondsworth: 1945.

Pratt, Helen Gay. *Hawaii, Off-Shore Territory*, New York: Charles Scribner's Sons, 1944.

Price, Weston A. *Nutrition and Physical Degeneration*, New York: Paul B. Hoeber, 1939.

Price, Willard. *Japan's Islands of Mystery*, New York: John Day Co., 1944.

———. *Pacific Adventure*, New York: Reynal & Hitchcock, 1936.

Priday, H. E. L. *Cannibal Island*, Wellington: A. H. & A. W. Reed, 1944.

Pritchard, W. T. *Polynesian Reminiscences*, or Life in the South Pacific Islands, Preface by Dr. Seemann, London: Chapman & Hall, 1866.

Puleston, Captain W. D. *Mahan*, New Haven: Yale University Press, 1939.

Raabe, Captain H. E. *Cannibal Nights*, New York: Albert & Charles Boni, 1931.

Ramsden, Eric. *Marsden and the Missions*; with an Introduction by Peter H. Buck (Te Rangi Hiroa), Sydney: Argus & Robertson, Ltd., N. D.

Rawson, Geoffrey. *Bligh of the 'Bounty,'* London: Philip Allan & Co., Ltd., 1932.

Reed, Stephen Winsor. *The Making of Modern New Guinea*, Philadelphia: American Philosophical Society, Institute of Pacific Relations, 1943.

Rees, William Lee and Lily. *The Life and Times of Sir George Grey, K. C. B.*, Auckland: 1892.

Reeves, Edward. *Brown Men and Women*, London: Swan Sonnenschein & Co., Ltd., 1898.

Reeves, William Pember. *New Zealand* (Ao Tea Roa) (The Long White Cloud), Third Edition, Boston: Houghton Mifflin Co., 1925.

Restarick, Rt. Rev. Henry Bond. *Hawaii, 1778-1920, from the Viewpoint of a Bishop*, Honolulu: Paradise of the Pacific, 1924.

Reynolds, J. N. *Voyage of the United States Frigate "Potomac,"* New York: Harper & Bros., 1835.

Riesenberg, Felix. *The Pacific Ocean,* New York: Whittlesey House, 1940.

Rivière, Henri. *Souvenirs de la Nouvelle Calédonie,* Paris: C. Lévy, 1881.

Roberts, Stephen H. *Population Problems of the Pacific,* London: G. Routledge & Son, Ltd., 1927.

Robertson, H. A. *Erromango, the Martyr Isle,* London: Hodder & Stoughton, 1902.

Robson, R. W. (ed.). *The Pacific Islands Year Book.* 1945. Sydney: 1945.

———— and Judy Tudor (eds.). *Where the Trade-Winds Blow,* Sydney: Pacific Publications Pty., Ltd., 1946.

Rochas, Victor de. *La Nouvelle Calédonie et ses habitants,* Paris: 1862.

Rogers, Stanley. *The Pacific,* New York: Thomas Y. Crowell Co., N. D.

Rogers, Woodes. *A Cruising Voyage Round the World;* with Introduction and Notes by G. E. Manwaring, The Seafarer's Library, London: Cassell & Co., Ltd., 1928.

Romilly, Hugh Hastings. *The Western Pacific and New Guinea,* London: John Murray, 1886.

Roosevelt, Nicholas. *The Restless Pacific,* New York: Charles Scribner's Sons, 1928.

Roosevelt, Theodore and Henry Cabot Lodge. *Selections from the Correspondence of Theodore Roosevelt and Henry Cabot Lodge,* 1884-1918, New York: Charles Scribner's Sons, 1925.

Roosevelt, Theodore, Jr. *Colonial Policies of the United States,* New York: Doubleday, Doran & Co., 1937.

Rowe, N. A. *Samoa Under the Sailing Gods;* introduction by Lloyd Osbourne, New York: G. P. Putman's, 1930.

Rudy, John Farney. *And the Poor Travel Too,* Nashville: Baird-Ward Printing Co., 1941.

Ruë, E. Aubert de la. *Les Nouvelles Hébrides,* Montreal: Editions de l'Arbre, 1945.

Russell, The Right Rev. M. *Polynesia,* New York: Harper Bros., 1943.

Russier, Henri. *La partage de l'Océanie,* Paris: Vuibert et Nouy, 1905.

Ryden, George Herbert. *The Foreign Policy of the United States in Relation to Samoa,* New Haven: Yale University Press, 1933.

Ryerson, Knowles A.: see Ernest N. Hopkins.

Safford, William Edwin. *The Useful Plants of the Island of Guam* (extracted by Seaman first class J. E. Coulson. Typescript.) (Washington: Government Printing Office, 1905.)

Saffroni-Middleton, A. *South Sea Foam*, New York: George H. Doran Co., 1920.

St. Johnston, Lieut.-Col. T. R. *The Islanders of the Pacific; or The Children of the Sun*, London: T. Fisher Unwin, Ltd., 1921.

Saul, Benjamin Lewis; *see* Lewis Melville.

Sauvin, G. *Un Royaume polynésien*, Paris: E. Plon, Nourret & Cie., 1893.

(Sauvy, Elizabeth). *Mademoiselle Against the World*, by Titäyna, New York: Horace Liveright, 1931.

Sayer, Edgar Sheappard. *Pidgin English*, Toronto: Privately printed, 1944.

Schenck, Earl. *Come Unto These Yellow Sands*, Indianapolis: Bobbs-Merrill Co., N.D.

Scholefield, Guy H. *New Zealand in Evolution*, New York: Charles Scribner's Sons, 1909. *The Pacific, Its Past and Future*, London: John Murray, 1919.

Schriftgiesser, Karl. *The Gentleman from Massachusetts*: Henry Cabot Lodge, Boston: Little, Brown & Co., 1944.

Seddon, R. J. *The Right Hon. . . .'s Visit to Tonga, Fiji, Savage Island and the Cook Islands*, Wellington: John Mackay, Government Printer, 1900.

Seeman, Berthold C. *Viti*, Cambridge: 1863.

Seligmann, C. G. *The Melanesians of British New Guinea*, Cambridge: University Press, 1910.

Shand, Alexander. *The Moriori People of the Chatham Islands*, Wellington: 1911.

Shapiro, Harry I. *The Heritage of the Bounty; Six Generations*, New York: Simon & Schuster, 1936.

The Shepherd Saint of Lanai, Honolulu: 1882.

Shepherd, C. Y. *The Sugar Industry of Fiji*, London: 1945.

Shurcliff, Sidney Nichols. *Jungle Islands*, Field Museum of Natural History, Chicago, New York: G. P. Putnam's Sons, 1930.

Simpson, Sir George. *Narrative of a Journey Round the World*, London: H. Colburn, 1847.

Sloan, Donald. *The Shadow-Catcher*, New York: Doubleday, Doran, 1940.

Smith, The Rev. Daniel. *The New-Zealanders*, New York: Carlton & Lanahan, N. D.

Smith, S. Percy. *Maori Wars of the Nineteenth Century*, Christchurch: Whitcombe and Tombs, Ltd., 1910.

Smythe, Mrs. *Ten Months in the Fiji Islands;* with an introduction and appendix by Colonel W. J. Smythe, London: John Henry & James Parker, 1864.

Sprout, Harold and Margaret. *The Rise of American Naval Power,* Princeton, N. J.: Princeton University Press, 1939.

Spry, W. J. J. *The Cruise of Her Majesty's Ship "Challenger",* New York: Harper and Bros., 1877.

Spykman, Nicholas John. *America's Strategy in World Politics,* New York: Harcourt, Brace & Co., 1942.

Stair, John B. *Old Samoa;* with an introduction from the Bishop of Ballarat, London: Religious Tract Society, 1897.

Stanwood, Edward. *James Gillespie Blaine,* Boston: Houghton Mifflin & Co., 1905.

Stephens, F. B. *Report on Education in the Colony of Fiji,* Council Paper No. 18.

Stevens, John L., and W. B. Oleson. *Picturesque Hawaii,* Honolulu: Edgewood Publishing Co., 1904.

Stevens, Sylvester K. *American Expansion in Hawaii,* 1842-1898, Harrisburg, Penna.: Archives Publishing Co. of Pennsylvania, 1945.

Stevenson, Mrs. M. I. *From Saranac to the Marquesas and Beyond,* New York: Charles Scribner's Sons, 1903.

* Stevenson, Robert Louis. *In the South Seas,* New York: Biographical Edition, XXII, Charles Scribner's Sons, 1940.

————. *Letters,* New York: South Seas Edition, III, IV, Charles Scribner's Sons, 1925.

————. *Vailima Papers,* New York: South Seas Edition XXVI, Charles Scribner's Sons, 1925.

Stevenson, Mrs. Robert Louis. *The Cruise of the "Janet Nichol" Among the South Sea Islands,* New York: Charles Scribner's Sons, 1914.

Stewart, C. S. *A Private Journal of a Voyage to the Pacific Ocean,* New York: John P. Haven, 1828.

Stewart, George R. *Names on the Land,* New York: Random House, 1945.

Stock, Ralph. *The Chequered Cruise,* New York: Dodd, Mead & Co., 1916.

Stoddard, Charles Warren. *Summer Cruising in the South Seas,* London: Chatts & Windus, 1905.

Stone, William S. *Tahiti Landfall,* New York: W. Morrow & Co., 1947.

Stout, Sir Robert and J. Logan Stout. *New Zealand,* Cambridge: The University Press, 1911.

Strong, Josiah. *Expansion Under World Conditions*, New York: Baker & Taylor Co., 1900.

———. *Our Country*, Revised Edition, New York: Baker & Taylor Co., 1891.

Sullivan, Josephine. *A History of C. Brewer & Company Limited*, the Hawaiian Islands, 1826-1926, Honolulu: Privately printed for C. Brewer & Co., 1926.

Sumner, William Graham. *The Conquest of the United States by Spain*; Lecture before the Phi Beta Kappa Society of Yale University, Boston: Dana, Estes & Co., 1899.

Sutherland, I. L. G. (ed.). *The Maori People Today*, London: Oxford Press, 1940.

Tahiti and Its Missionaries. Nelson's British Library No. IX, London: Thomas Nelson, N. D.

Taylor, Albert Pierce. *Under Hawaiian Skies*, Honolulu: Advertising Publishing Co., Ltd., 1922.

Te Rangi Hiroa: *see* Peter H. Buck.

Thomas, Lowell. *Count Luckner, The Sea-Devil*, New York: Doubleday, Page & Co.,1927.

Thompson, Laura. *Fijian Frontier*, San Francisco: American Council, Institute of Pacific Relations, 1940.

———. *Guam and Its People*; Studies of the Pacific No. 8, New York: Institute of Pacific Relations, 1941.

Thompson, Warren S. *Danger Spots in World Population*, New York: A. A. Knopf, 1929.

* Thomson, Basil. *The Diversions of a Prime Minister*, Edinburgh, & London: W. Blackwoods Sons, 1894.

———. *The Fijians*, London: William Heinemann, 1908.

———. *Voyage of H.M.S. "Pandora"* (ed.); The narratives of Captain Edward Edwards, R.N., the commander, and George Hamilton, the surgeon, London: 1915. (*See also* Lord Amherst of Hackney.)

Thurston, Lorrin A. *Writings of* . . . Honolulu: Advertising Publishing Co., 1936.

Thurston, Mrs. Lucy G. *Life and Times of* . . . Ann Arbor, Mich.: S. C. Andrews, 1882.

Tobin, Maurice J.: *see* Ernest M. Hopkins.

Todd, Mabel Loomis. *Corona and Coronet*, Boston: Houghton Mifflin & Co., 1898.

Tonga, A Revised Edition of the Laws of . . . by William Kenneth Horne, Chief Justice of Tonga, Nukualofa, Tonga: C. S. Summers, 1929.

Tongan Mission Affairs, Resumé of Inquiry in re . . . October, 1879, Mr. A. P. Maudslay, H. B. M. Vice Consul v. Rev. S. W. Baker, Auckland: 1879.

Tripp, Bartlett. *My Trip to Samoa*, Cedar Rapids, Iowa: The Torch Press, 1911.

Trollope, Anthony. *New South Wales and Queensland*, London: Chapman & Hall, 1874.

Turner, George. *Nineteen Years in Polynesia*, London: John Snow, 1861.

Twain, Mark: *see* Samuel L. Clemens.

Twombly, Alexander S. *Hawaii and Its People*, Boston: Silver Burdett & Co., 1899.

United Nations. *Report to the Trusteeship Council by the United Nations Mission to Western Samoa;* T/46 September 25, 1947. *The Population of Western Samoa*. Reports on the population of Trust Territories, Number 1. January 17, 1948.

United States House of Representatives (44th Congress, Executive Document No. 161). *Message from the President of the United States transmitting a report from the Secretary of State and accompanying documents;* 75-7, Washington: Government Printing Office. (79th Congress, First Session). *Statehood for Hawaii:* Hearings before the Subcommittee of the Committee on the Territories . . . Washington: Government Printing Office, 1946. *Study of Pacific Bases:* A report by the subcommittee on Pacific bases of the House Committee on Naval Affairs . . . Washington: Government Printing Office, 1945. (79th Congress, Second Session).

United States Senate (43d Congress, First Session Exec. Document No. 45). *Message from the President of the United States: a communication from the Secretary of State and the report by which it is accompanied from Samoa or the Navigators Islands;* 1873-4, Washington: Government Printing Office. (71st Congress, Third Session, Senate Document 249, serial number 9346). *The American Samoan Commission Report,* Washington: Government Printing Office, 1931. (75th Congress, Third Session Exec. Document No. 97). *Public Documents Relating to Samoa,* Washington: Government Printing Office, 1938. (75th Congress, Third Session, Document No. 151). *Statehood for Hawaii:* Letter from the chairman of the Joint Committee on Hawaii . . . 1938.

Usher, Leonard G. (ed.). *Fiji:* Handbook of the Colony. Special Wartime Issue, Suva: 1943.

Vancouver, George. *A Voyage of Discovery to the North Pacific Ocean and Round the World,* London: John Stockdale, 1801.

Vandercook, John. *Dark Islands,* New York: Harper & Bros., 1937.

———. *King Cane,* New York: Harper & Bros., 1939.

Van Loon, Hendrick Wilhem. *The Story of the Pacific,* New York: Harcourt, Brace & Co., 1940.

von Tempski, Armine. *Born in Paradise,* New York: Duell, Sloan & Pierce, 1940.

Voyage of H. M. S. 'Blonde' to the Sandwich Islands, London: John Murray, 1826.

Wakeman, Captain Edgar. *The Log of an Ancient Mariner;* edited by his daughter, San Francisco: A. L. Bancroft, 1878.

Wallis, Mary D. *Life in Feejee,* Boston: William Heath, 1851.

Waterhouse, Rev. Joseph. *The King and People of Fiji,* London: 1865.

Watson, Robert Mackenzie. *History of Samoa,* Wellington: Whitcombe and Tombs, Ltd., 1918.

Waugh, Alec. *Hot Countries,* New York: Farrar & Rinehart, N.D.

Weaver, Raymond. *Herman Melville, Mariner and Mystic,* New York: George H. Doran Co., 1921.

Weckler, J. E. Jr. *Polynesians: Explorers of the Pacific.* Smithsonian Institution War Background Studies VI, Washington: Smithsonian Institution,1943.

* Weinberg, A. K. *Manifest Destiny,* Baltimore: Johns Hopkins Press, 1935.

Weller, George. *Bases Overseas,* New York: Harcourt, Brace & Co., 1944.

Westbrook, G. E. L. *Gods Who Die,* New York: The Macmillan Co., 1935.

Westervelt, W. D. *Hawaiian Legends of Ghosts and Ghost-Gods,* Boston: Ellis Press, 1916.

————. *Hawaiian Legends of Volcanoes,* Boston: Ellis Press, 1916.

————. *Legends of Old Honolulu,* Boston: Ellis Press, 1915.

Wheeler, Daniel. *Extracts from the Letters and Journals of* . . . Philadelphia: J. Rakestraw, 1840.

Whiting, Lillian. *Kate Field,* Boston: Little, Brown & Co., 1899.

Whitney, Caspar. *Hawaiian America,* New York: Harper & Bros., 1899.

Wilcox, Ella Wheeler. *Sailing Sunny Seas,* Chicago: W. B. Conkey Co., 1909.

Wilkes, Charles. *Narrative of the United States Exploring Expedition,* London: Ingram, Cooke & Co., 1852.

* Williams, John. A *Narrative of Missionary Enterprise in the South Sea Islands,* New York: D. Appleton & Co., 1837.

Williams, Thomas. *Fiji and the Fijians,* London: T. Woolmer, N.D.

Wingert, Paul S.: *see* Ralph Linton.

Withington, Antoinette. *Hawaiian Tapestry,* New York: Harper & Bros., 1937.

Wood, A. H. *History and Geography of Tonga,* Auckland: 1945.

Wood, C. F. A *Yachting Cruise in the South Seas,* London: Henry S. King & Co., 1875.

Wood, F. L. W. *This New Zealand,* Hamilton: Paul's Book Arcade, 1946.

Wycherley, George. *Buccaneers of the Pacific*, Indianapolis: Bobbs-Merrill Co., 1928.

Yanaihara, Tadao. *Pacific Islands under Japanese Mandate*, London & New York: Oxford University Press, 1940.

Yonge, Charlotte Mary. *Life of John Coleridge Patteson*, London: The Macmillan Co., 1875.

Young, Gerald (ed.). *The Voyage of the Wanderer*, London: The Macmillan Co., 1883.

Young, Lucian. *The Real Hawaii* (A Revised and Enlarged Edition of "The Boston at Honolulu"), New York: Doubleday-McClure Co., 1899.

Yzendoorn, Father Reginald. *History of the Catholic Mission in the Hawaiian Islands*, Honolulu: Honolulu *Star Bulletin*, 1927.

Zimmerman, John Lee. *Green Land of the Maoris*, New York: 1946.

PERIODICAL REFERENCES

Beaglehole, Ernest. "Psychic States in a Tongan Village." *Proceedings of the Sixth Pacific Science Congress*, Volume IV.

Clark (Thomas) Blake. "The Japanese in Hawaii." *New Republic*, Sept. 14, 1942.

———. "One World on an Island." '47, July, 1947.

Cogniat, Raymond. "The Fiery Life of Paul Gauguin." In catalogue of loan exhibition of Gauguin at the Wildenstein Gallery, New York, 1946.

Collier, John. "They are America, Too." *Mademoiselle*, May, 1947.

Coulter, John Wesley. "Impact of the War on South Sea Islands." *The Geographical Review*, July, 1946.

de Camp, L. Sprague. "Lost Continents." *Natural History*, May, 1946.

Embree, John F. "Military Government in Saipan and Tinian." *Applied Anthropology*, Winter, 1946.

Fiske, John. "Manifest Destiny." *Harper's New Monthly Magazine*, March, 1885.

Flaherty, David. "Serpents in Eden." *Asia*, October, 1925.

Flaherty, Frances Hubbard. "Setting Up House and Shop in Samoa." *Asia*, August, 1925.

———. "Behind the Scenes with Our Samoan Stars." *Asia*, September, 1925.

Furnas, J. C. "Utopia, Limited." *The Saturday Evening Post*, August 13, 1936.

———. "The Isle of Keep-Out." *Coronet*, January, 1937.

———. "Will Hawaii Become a State?" *The Saturday Evening Post*, April 6, 1946.

————. "Uncle Sam Moves Out." *The Saturday Evening Post*, June 14, 1947.

————. "Beautiful Responsibilities," *Holiday*, March, 1948.

"Hawaii: Sugar-Coated Fort." *Fortune*, August, 1940.

Hawthorn, Harry. "Indentured Labor in New Guinea." *Far Eastern Survey*, March 13, 1946.

Hubbard, John. "America's Pacific Empire." '47, May, 1947.

Keesing, Felix M. "Administration in Pacific Islands." *Far Eastern Survey*, March 26, 1947.

Lardner, John. "Those of the First Generation." *New Yorker*, March 31, 1945.

Lee, Clarke. "Hawaii—49th State?" *Cosmopolitan*, May, 1946.

Mead, Margaret. "Talk-Boy." *Asia*, March, 1933.

Palmer, Albert W. "Hawaii Revisited." Honolulu *Star Bulletin*, August 22, 24, 25, 1946.

Parsons, James. "Coffee and Settlement in New Caledonia." *The Geographical Review*, January, 1945.

Porter, Edward G. "The Ship Columbia and the Discovery of Oregon." *New England Magazine*, June, 1892.

Rossiter, William S. "The First American Imperialist." *North American Review*, Vol. 182.

Schurz, Carl. "Manifest Destiny." *Harper's New Monthly Magazine*, October, 1892.

Spoehr, Alexander. "The Marshall Islands and Transpacific Aviation." *The Geographical Review*, July, 1946.

Start, Edwin A. "General Armstrong and the Hampton Institute." *New England Magazine*, June, 1892.

Strong, Austin. "His Oceanic Majesty's Goldfish." *Atlantic Monthly*, May, 1944.

Symes, Lillian. "The Other Side of Paradise." *Harper's Magazine*, December, 1932.

Taylor, Frank J. "Hawaii." *Holiday*, April, 1948.

Taylor, Robert Lewis. "The Nicest Fellows You Ever Met." *New Yorker*, December 16, 1944.

Thompson, Laura. "Guam: Study in Military Government." *Far Eastern Survey*, August 9, 1944.

————. "Crisis on Guam." *Far Eastern Quarterly*, November, 1946.

Trumbull, Robert. "A Swing Around Our Pacific Empire." *New York Times Magazine*, May 19, 1946.

Useem, John C. "Americans as Governors of Natives in the Pacific." *Journal of Social Issues*, August, 1946.

――――. "The Changing Structure of a Micronesian Society." *American Anthropologist*, October-December, 1945.

――――. "Governing the Occupied Areas of the South Pacific: Wartime Lessons and Peacetime Proposals." *Applied Anthropology*, Summer, 1945.

――――. "Social Reconstruction in Micronesia." *Far Eastern Survey*, January 30, 1946.

Winne, Jane L. "Father of Hawaiian Music." *Paradise of the Pacific*, December, 1944.

Worden, William L. "Our Dubious New Empire." *Saturday Evening Post*, March 17, 1945.

LITERARY REFERENCES

Becke, Louis. *The Adventures of Louis Blake*, Philadelphia: J. B. Lippincott Co., N. D.

――――. *Edward Barry* (South Sea Pearler), London: T. Fisher Unwin, 1900.

――――. *Pacific Tales*, New York: New Amsterdam Book Co., N.D.

Benoît, Pierre. *Erromango*, Paris: Albin Michel, 1929.

Blanding, Don. *Stowaways in Paradise*, Two Boy Adventurers in Hawaii, New York: Dodd, Mead & Co., 1943.

Boldrewood, Rolf: *see* Thomas Alexander Brown.

Brooke, Rupert. *Collected Poems*, introduction by George Woodberry and biographical note by Margaret Lavington. New York: Dodd, Mead & Co., 1941.

(Brown, Thomas Alexander) pseud. Rolf Boldrewood. A *Modern Buccaneer*, London: Harper & Bros., 1891.

Byron, Lord. *Poetical Works*, British Poets' Series, Boston: Little, Brown & Co., 1861.

Daudet, Alphonse. *Port Tarascon*; the Last Adventures of the Illustrious *Tartarin*, translated by Henry James, New York: Harper & Bros., 1891.

Dawson, Edward Walter. *The Isles of the Sea*: being an Entertaining Account of a Voyage to the Pacific and Indian Oceans and embracing full and authentic accounts of the islands of Polynesia, Micronesia and Melanesia . . . , Hartford, Conn.: Betts & Co., 1886.

Field, Isobel (Strong). *The Girl From Home*; a Story of Honolulu. New York: McClure, Phillips & Co., 1905.

(Ford, Corey) pseud. Dr. Walter E. Traprock. *The Cruise of the Kawa*. Wanderings in the South Sea, New York: G. P. Putnam's Sons, 1921.

Frisbie, Robert Dean. *Amaru;* a Romance of the South Seas, New York: Doubleday, Doran & Co., 1945.

Goudge, Elizabeth. *Green Dolphin Street,* New York: Coward-McCann, 1944.

Grimshaw, Beatrice. *Vaiti of the Islands,* New York: A. Wessels Co., 1908.

Hall, James Norman. *Lost Island,* Boston: Little, Brown & Co., 1944.

Henty, G. A. *Maori and Settler;* a Story of the New Zealand War, New York: Hurst & Co., N.D.

Jarves, James J[ackson]. *Kiana;* a Tradition of Hawaii, Boston, 1858.

Kassel, Al. *I went Native in Tahiti,* New York: Richard R. Smith, 1939.

Keable, Robert. *Numerous Treasure;* a Romantic Novel, New York: G. P. Putnam's Sons, 1925.

Kyne, Peter B. *Never the Twain Shall Meet,* New York: Cosmopolitan Book Corp., 1923.

London, Jack. *Adventure,* New York: Review of Reviews, 1917.

————. *The House of Pride* and other tales of Hawaii, New York: The Macmillan Co., 1914.

————. *The Faith of Men* and other stories, New York: Leslie-Judge Co., 1925.

————. *South Sea Tales,* New York: Regent Press, 1911.

Loti, Pierre pseud. Julien Viaud. *Le Mariage de Loti,* Paris: Calman-Levy, 1881.

Marsh, Ngaio. *Vintage Murder,* New York: Sheridan House, 1940.

Maugham, W. Somerset. *The Moon and Sixpence,* New York: 1941.

————. *The Trembling of a Leaf,* New York: 1921.

McKee, Ruth Eleanor. *The Lord's Anointed,* New York: Doubleday, Doran & Co., 1935.

————. *After a Hundred Years,* New York: Doubleday, Doran & Co., 1935.

Newell, C. M. *Kalani of Oahu,* Boston: Privately printed, 1881.

Nordhoff, Charles. *The Pearl Lagoon,* Boston: Atlantic Monthly Press, 1924.

—and James Norman Hall.

————. *The Dark River,* Boston: Little, Brown & Co., 1938.

————. *The High Barbaree,* London: 1946.

————. *The Hurricane,* New York: Blue Ribbon Books, 1935.

————. *Men Against the Sea,* Boston: Little, Brown & Co., 1934.

————. *Mutiny on the Bounty,* Boston: Little, Brown & Co., 1932.

————. *No More Gas,* New York: Little, Brown & Co., 1940.

Osbourne, Lloyd. *Wild Justice;* Stories of the South Seas, New York: D. Appleton & Co., 1906.

Rose, Stanley H. *The Tattooed Crown,* New York: House of Field, 1941.

Schenck, Earl. *Lean With the Wind,* New York: Whittlesey House, 1945.

Sexton, Ethel. *Count Me Among the Living,* New York: Harper & Bros., 1946.

Stacpoole, H. deVere. *The Blue Lagoon,* London: T. Fisher Unwin, 1910.

Stevenson, Robert Louis. *Island Nights' Entertainments.* London: T. Nelson & Sons, Ltd., N. D.—and Lloyd Osborne.

————. *The Ebb-Tide,* New York: XXIV South Seas Edition, Charles Scribner's Sons, 1925.

————. *The Wrecker,* New York: XXIV South Seas Edition, Charles Scribner's Sons, 1925.

Thomson, Basil. *The Indiscretions of Lady Asenath,* London: Innes, 1898.

Thwaites, Frederick J. *Whispers in Tahiti,* Sydney: 1940.

Viaud, Julien: *see* Pierre Loti.

von Tempski, Armine. *Dust;* a novel of Hawaii, New York: Frederick A. Stokes Co., 1928.

————. *Fire;* a novel of Hawaii, New York: Frederick A. Stokes Co., 1929.

————. *Hula,* New York: Frederick A. Stokes Co., 1927.

Wright, S. Fowler. *The Island of Captain Sparrow,* Harmondsworth: 1945.

Index

H